DATE DUE

AP25'00			
MY16'00			

DEMCO 38-296

Wilderness by Design

Landscape Architecture and
the National Park Service

Ethan Carr

University of Nebraska Press
Lincoln and London

© 1998 by the University of Nebraska Press
s reserved
ctured in the United States of America

on Books printing: 1999
cent printing indicated by the last digit below:
9 8 7 6 5 4 3 2 1

Library of Congress Cataloging-in-Publication Data

Carr, Ethan, 1958–
Wilderness by design : landscape architecture and the National
Park Service / Ethan Carr.
p.   cm.
Includes bibliographical references (p.   ) and index.
ISBN 0-8032-1491-X (cl: alk. paper)
ISBN 0-8032-6383-X (pa: alk. paper)
1. United States. National Park Service—History.   2. Landscape
architecture—United States—History.   3. National parks and
reserves—United States—Design—History.   I. Title.
SB482.A4C37   1998
712'.5'0973—dc21   97-22127
                                                             CIP

Contents

Acknowledgements and Archival Sources

The National Park Service funded and supervised this study as a National Historic Landmark Theme Study of National Park Service landscape architecture. The historic districts described in this text have also been designated by the Secretary of the Interior as National Historic Landmarks. Katherine H. Stevenson, the associate director in charge of the National Center for Cultural Resources Stewardship and Partnership Programs, oversaw the project. Chief historical architect Randall J. Biallas and manager of the park cultural landscape program Robert R. Page supervised the study and, through their good work, made it possible. The National Park Foundation, in particular, Todd McCreight, provided the opportunity to publish this study in a manner that would make it readily available to those interested in the history of the development of the national park system. As a National Historic Landmark Theme Study, all work was also submitted to the National Park Service chief historian, Dwight T. Pitcaithley. An advisory committee also reviewed the project as it progressed. I am indebted to the members of this group: Cathy A. Gilbert (NPS), Laura Soullière Harrison (NPS), Linda Flint McClelland (NPS), Barry Mackintosh (NPS), Prof. Robert Z. Melnick (University of Oregon), Prof. Elizabeth K. Meyer (University of Virginia), Paul Schullery (NPS), Richard West Sellars (NPS), and William C. Tweed (NPS). I would especially like to thank Charles E. Peterson for sharing his personal papers and recollections, and for encouraging this project.

Many park planners, managers, historians, and archivists in both state and national parks generously assisted in the research for this study. At Grand Canyon National Park, Doug Brown provided expertise and insights on the history of the south rim. At Glacier National Park, Bob Dunkley and Dennis Holden shared their profound knowledge of Going-to-the-Sun Road. At Mount Rainier National Park, Stephanie Toothman and Craig Strong assisted in what otherwise would have been an impossibly complex investigation. I owe a special debt to national park superintendents Robert Arnberger (Grand Canyon), David A. Mihalic (Glacier), and William J. Briggle (Mount Rainier) for supporting the National Historic Landmark districts proposed for their parks.

In Texas, James Wright Steely shared his work on Bastrop and other parks in that state; in Wyoming, Jeff Hauff and Jim Snyder familiarized me with Lake Guernsey State Park; in Minnesota, I greatly benefitted from working with Rolf Anderson and Susan Roth on the history of St. Croix State Park; in California, Carol Roland and Ronnie James provided much needed assistance in researching Mendocino Woodlands; and in Georgia, Billy Townsend and my colleague Lucy Ann Lawliss shared their great knowledge of Pine Mountain State Park.

The bibliography of works cited in this study includes published and unpublished records of the National Park Service, especially the bureau's *Annual Reports* and *Proceedings* of official conferences. These government publications (as well as other reports and minutes) are available at the Department of the Interior Library in the Main Interior Building, Washington, DC. Other reports and archives relating to the National Park Service are available at the National Park Service History Collection, Harpers Ferry Center, Harpers Ferry, West Virginia. I am grateful to David Nathanson and Thomas DuRant for guiding me through both the textual and photographic records available at Harpers Ferry.

The majority of the archival records of the National Park Service are conserved as Record Group 79 at the National Archives in College Park, Maryland. An inventory of this record group, compiled by Edward E. Hill, is a tremendous help in navigating through the correspondence, plans, reports, and other records of National Park Service directors and other officials. The inventory is reprinted in Barry Mackintosh's publication, *National Park Service Administrative History: A Guide* (Washington, DC: National Park Service, 1991), which itself is an important tool for national park research.

Most national parks also maintain park archives that conserve unique textual and photographic records. Documents and photographs for this study were made available at the Yosemite National Park Research Library, the Yellowstone National Park Archives, the Grand Canyon National Park Museum, and the Glacier National Park Archives. Perhaps the most important archive for a national park design history is the Technical Information Center of the National Park Service Denver Service Center. This active map file conserves thousands of Park Service construction drawings from 1917 to the present. I am grateful to Edie Ramey and Jolene Lindsay for their assistance with these records. Many state park departments and state archives also contain records of the New Deal-era park developments, since most state park drawings and records, even when they represented the work of the National Park Service, reverted to the states. The Center for Research Librarians in Chicago conserves the most complete collection of Civilian Conservation Corps camp newspapers, which are an invaluable record of camp daily life and activities.

The considerable task of sorting through hundreds of photographs and many boxes of archival records was greatly facilitated by the help of a talented assistant, Susan A. Begley, to whom I am indebted. Candace Clifford designed and laid out this publication. All photographs, unless otherwise credited, are by the author.

Wilderness by Design

National Parks and Landscape Architecture

In the years between the end of World War I and the American entry into World War II, the National Park Service modernized and developed the national park system extensively. Park Service landscape architects and engineers designed scenic roads, campgrounds, administrative "villages," and myriad other park facilities in what proved to be the most intensive period of such human alterations in the history of the parks. It was during this era that the "developed areas" in national parks (and in many state and local parks as well) acquired the consistent appearance, character, and level of convenience that most visitors have since come to associate, almost unconsciously, with their experience of park scenery, wildlife, and wilderness.

Park design, or landscape architecture, has figured in the history of national parks since the 19th century. This may seem a paradox since many people intuitively reject the importance of human design in an environment valued primarily for its pristine, natural condition. The natural wonders of national parks obviously brook no comparison to any works of landscape art; but the significance of landscape architecture in such a setting lies in how and where these natural features are appreciated, not in the creation of alternative attractions. Designed landscapes guide the experience of many park visitors and enhance their appreciation of the vast wilderness beyond. Roads and trails, for example, lead visitors to certain areas and through a considered sequence of views. Campgrounds, park villages, scenic overlooks, parking areas—all the designed portions of the park—shape the overall pattern of public activities and frame visual encounters with the awesome (and certainly "undesigned") scenery of the larger park landscape.

The importance of landscape architecture to the history of national parks, in other words, relates to the public's use and appreciation of the parks. For most visitors, even today, the emotional enjoyment achieved through the appreciation of landscape beauty is not an inevitable, accidental, or haphazard affair. The designed landscapes within the park choreograph visitors' movements and define the pace and sequence of much of their experience. The designed landscapes mediate between the individual and the vast terrain of the backcountry. Wilderness and designed landscape together generate the aesthetic appreciation of landscapes and emotional communion with the natural world which, at least historically, the word "park" implied.

This study examines these intermediary landscapes, particularly those designed by the National Park Service between the two world wars. During these years Park Service landscape architects and engineers located and designed park entrances, roads, campgrounds, park villages, trail systems, maintenance areas, and buildings not only in national parks, but (after 1933) in state and local parks as well. Today, different priorities affect national park management, and park development on the scale described in this study has mostly halted. Many parks have been completed, in the sense that the planned extent of roads, villages, and other facilities has been reached. But there are other reasons for a change in attitudes towards park development: in 1939 there were about fifteen million visits to the national park system; in 1991 there were over 250 million.[1] Although the Park Service has acquired many new properties since World War II, recreational opportunities in the system have not expanded at the exponential rate of demand. The impacts of overcrowding have eclipsed almost all other concerns for park management in many of the country's favorite parks.

Visitors admire the Grand Canyon from along the south rim in 1938. The low parapet wall along the rim, the paths lined with stone curbs, the "rustic" log bench, and transplanted native trees and shrubs at key points typified the design of "developed areas" in national parks in the 1920s and 1930s. Courtesy Grand Canyon National Park Museum.

In the early 20th century, however, when the federal government was only beginning serious efforts to manage the national parks and reservations that had been set aside since 1832, many argued that national parks suffered from a lack of public attention rather than a surfeit. Secretary of the Interior Walter L. Fisher called the first National Park Conference in 1911 based on his conviction that "the attendance in the parks [had] not increased as those most familiar with them believe it should have increased . . . particularly during the past five years."[2] Just over 200,000 visitors had visited the twelve existing national parks in 1911. Appropriations for all national parks between 1906 and 1913 totaled less than one million dollars.[3]

The lack of interest on the part of Congress, it was felt, could be directly attributed to the apparent indifference of the traveling public. Increased appropriations would come only with increased use of the parks; and increased appropriations were needed, ironically, because poorly planned visitor accommodations were already degrading scenery and polluting natural systems in several parks. The numbers of park visitors may have been low by today's standards, but with few facilities and little supervision, those few managed to do great damage. In Yellowstone, for example, poaching of game and vandalism of geologic features were commonplace until 1894 when the Lacey Act finally provided criminal penalties for the infraction of park regulations.[4] By that point, visitors had defaced the prominent geyser formations in the park and hunters had decimated the herds of elk and bison. Sewage from 19th-century hotels and tent camps in Yosemite Valley flowed directly into the Merced River, making that stream unfit for drinking or swimming by the turn of the century. In his tour of national parks in 1916, the geographer Robert B. Marshall (who was appointed "general superintendent" of national parks in 1915) was "consistently impressed with the total lack of any systematic sanitary arrangements." He observed that "there [was] not an adequate sanitary system in a single park."[5]

The Department of the Interior could offer little assistance to the parks that were its responsibility since it had little money, and no bureau (or even a consistent set of policies) for park management or improvement. Since 1886, the War Department had deployed the U.S. Cavalry to administer Yellowstone, and the troopers eventually ended the most egregious abuses there. After 1890 troops patrolled Yosemite, Sequoia, and General Grant national parks as well. Although these arrangements resulted in dual administrations and overlapping jurisdictions in the parks, they were unavoidable since no other means were available to keep order. "There was no effective national park policy" within the Department of the Interior, according to historian Donald C. Swain, "only a haphazard, day-to-day administrative arrangement."[6]

In contrast, the management of the nation's forest reserves epitomized Progressive efficiency in the early 20th century. Gifford Pinchot arrived at the Division of Forestry at the Department of Agriculture in 1898. Connected and ambitious, Pinchot was also professionally trained in the principles of scientific forestry. By redefining the role of the Division of Forestry, he eventually helped redirect government policy regarding the management and use of all public lands. In 1905, Congress transferred jurisdiction over sixty-two million acres of national forests from the Department of the Interior to Pinchot's growing forestry agency. Pinchot's rapid success in the scientific management of public forests through the issuance of leases and permits demonstrated how the federal government could efficiently manage what remained of the public domain in the early 20th century. Modern forestry and reclamation engineering promised perpetual yields of lumber, electrical power, and water to irrigate semi-arid Western lands. Theodore Roosevelt vastly expanded the national forest system between 1901 and 1909 and justified his executive actions through the assumption that forests could be managed for sustained, multiple uses only if they remained in public ownership.

The complete preservation of an area exclusively for its scenic qualities, however, was ridiculed by Pinchot and his scientific foresters. They felt that improved logging techniques and the regulation of grazing could prevent the degradation of landscape scenery (if necessary) while also allowing for controlled forms of commercial exploitation. Since it prevented planned multiple uses and scientific management, the total preservation of natural resources was as outdated and inefficient, in its way, as the opposite extremes of overuse and exploitation. By 1905, Pinchot pushed for legislation that would transfer jurisdiction over the national parks to the Department of Agriculture, where they would be managed together with the national forests. Representative John F. Lacey of Iowa prevented the legislation from passing in 1906 and again in 1907.[7] But even Roosevelt's secretary of the interior, Ethan Allen Hitchcock, supported the transfer of the parks from his department, as did James R. Garfield, who replaced Hitchcock in 1907.

A coalition of park advocates opposed this position, however, because they opposed logging, grazing, and dam construction in national parks. They contested the transfer of the parks to Pinchot's Forest Service and recommended instead the organization of a separate national parks bureau within the Department of the Interior. In order to offer a viable alternative for the management of national parks—an alternative that would justify the exclusion of extractive industries and dam construction—park advocates needed to justify other uses for these places. Tourism, they argued, would create economic activity, prevent Americans from spending their money abroad, and inspire patriotic sentiments among an increasingly diverse population.[8] Richard B. Watrous, as secretary of the American Civic Association, in 1911 described tourism as the only "dignified exploitation" for national parks.[9] Tourism would also mean profits for railroad companies and other concessioners, who in turn would put their considerable political influence to work on Capitol Hill in favor of maintaining the integrity of the parks. The increasing number of tourists drawn to national parks would be a quantifiable measure of success of this policy, and such public use would justify the exclusion of other forms of exploitation. After 1909, President Taft endorsed the idea of a separate bureau of national parks within the Department of the Interior, perhaps in part as a check on the influence of Roosevelt's chief forester, whose efforts were received with less enthusiasm by the new administration. In 1910, Taft's secretary of the interior, Richard A. Ballinger, also endorsed the creation of a bureau of parks as a first step towards increasing the number of park visitors.

But politicians such as Ballinger had only vague ideas regarding "comprehensive plans" for how the parks should be "opened up for the convenience and comfort of tourists and campers and for the careful preservation of natural features."[10] There were other park advocates, however, who had been professionally trained in such "park development." The profession of landscape architecture in the United States had grown rapidly in the 19th century largely due to the enthusiasm shown by hundreds of municipalities for acquiring and developing public parks. Adapting the principles and professional practice of 18th-century British "landscape gardeners," American landscape architects such as Frederick Law Olmsted planned the development of parks that would preserve, reveal, and often enhance the existing scenic characteristics of a place by regrading, planting, and otherwise "improving" as necessary to create calculated visual compositions. The construction of refined systems of roads and paths, as well as places to congregate and promenade, all were combined in a single work of landscape art: the public park.

In the early 20th century, as tourism—and therefore "park development"—was advocated as the alternative to logging, grazing, and dam construction in national parks, landscape architects were called upon to give formal articulation to that development. Mark Daniels, a landscape architect appointed "general superintendent and landscape gardener" of the national parks by Secretary of the Interior Franklin K. Lane in 1914, acknowledged that "land is not always land, but is sometimes coal, sometimes timber." He went on to say that, "It is also sometimes scenery, and as such merits the careful study and development that would be extended to other national resources."[11] Daniels began drawing up "comprehensive plan[s] for the road and trail development of all the national parks." Stephen T. Mather, who arrived at the Department of the Interior in January 1915 as an assistant to the secretary for park matters, later stated that "all of the improvements in the parks must be carefully harmonized with the landscape, and to this end, engineers trained in landscape architecture or fully appreciative of the necessity for maintaining the parks in their natural state must be employed."[12] In 1918, Mather hired landscape architect Charles P. Punchard, Jr., to continue the work Daniels had begun.

Many historians have remarked on the "dual" or "contradictory" mandate contained in the 1916 Act of Congress that finally authorized the establishment of the National Park Service within the Department of the Interior. The most often quoted portion of this legislation states that the purpose of national parks is "to conserve the scenery and the natural and historic objects and the wild life therein and to provide for the enjoyment of the same in such a manner and by such means as will leave them unimpaired for future generations." Frederick Law Olmsted, Jr., drafted this portion of the legislation. But to a landscape architect such as the younger Olmsted, steeped in the tradition of American park design, there was no inherent contradiction in preserving a place through its thoughtful development as a park. Without such development—without well-designed roads, marked trails, sanitary facilities, and permanent campgrounds—the damage caused by tourists compounded brutally, especially in a fragile environment. And Olmsted knew that bringing people into the parks and facilitating their appreciation of the flora, fauna, and scenic beauty to be found there was the surest means of building a public constituency for preserving such places in a relatively "unimpaired" state. Since the 1890s, a second generation of American landscape architects and park planners had expanded the idea of the municipal park and parkway system to a regional scale, creating park and forest reserves in the outer suburbs of many American cities. Park systems like the Metropolitan Park Commission reservations around Boston and the Cook County forest preserves around Chicago preserved scenic areas from encroaching development by acquiring and developing them as regional parks. Regional park development involved the construction of parkways and overlooks, trail systems, picnic and campgrounds, and other facilities for outdoor recreation and the convenient appreciation of regional scenery. Since regional reservations were typically much larger than their municipal antecedents, most of the parkland was not designed as much as managed.

To scenic preservationists of the era, among whom the younger Olmsted was an outstanding example, the limited development of scenic places as regional parks offered the best means available for preserving threatened areas of natural beauty. By the time Stephen Mather became the first director of the National Park Service in 1917, the term "park development" had come to imply certain aesthetic values, and even suggested specific landscape design features. Mather consulted landscape architects such as Frederick Law Olmsted, Jr., as experts who could provide not only professional design services, but expert validation as well, analogous (in a more artistic vein) to the scientific expertise provided by Pinchot's foresters. Landscape architects subsequently planned the physical development of national parks from the earliest days of the National Park Service.

The history of development in national parks of course had begun earlier, when the federal government first set aside a number of areas for the general purposes of public health and recreation. The necessary provision of hotel accommodations and livery services had originally been left to private concessioners (often subsidiaries of railroad companies) who built large, centralized hotels in obvious places such as next to the Old Faithful geyser or on the rim of the Grand Canyon. But in the early 20th century, the social and geographic range of domestic tourism broadened rapidly. Many workers enjoyed the two-day weekend and the two-week vacation for the first time, and former luxuries—including the automobile—were becoming affordable. The American countryside opened to middle class tourists as never before. The increasingly mobile public, looking for destinations on Sunday outings or for summer vacation accommodations, swarmed into what had been relatively remote scenic areas a generation earlier. Visiting national parks by car became popular as soon as it was feasible to do so.

By 1917 (the year the Park Service began operations) acting director Horace M. Albright reported "an astonishing increase in the number of cars in the national parks" during the previous four summers. "Motor fees" already constituted a considerable source of revenue, and park superintendents had abandoned all restrictions on the use of automobiles.[13] The development plans subsequently drawn up by Park Service landscape architects expressed and exploited the social and technological opportunities of the early 20th century. In the 19th century a visitor to Yellowstone typically arrived by train, saw the park from a hired conveyance, and stayed in a centrally located hotel. But a typical automotive tourist drove to the park, camped out, and controlled his or her own itinerary for seeing the sights. As the annual number of national park visitors climbed during the 1920s from thousands to millions, the increase was taken up almost entirely by people arriving in cars. These tourists needed campgrounds, parking lots, decentralized conveniences, and park drives with frequent scenic overlooks, modernized alignments, and increased lane widths. Without these improvements, multitudes of auto campers would easily mar or destroy the landscape beauty they came to admire.

Going-to-the-Sun Road, Glacier National Park. This view, facing west on the approach to Logan Pass, has changed little since this portion of the road was completed in the late 1920s. The first of a series of collaborations between Park Service landscape architects and Bureau of Public Roads engineers, the design of the road preserved the park's scenery as much as possible, while providing an unforgettable experience for park visitors.

By the mid-1920s, Park Service landscape architects such as Daniel R. Hull and Thomas C. Vint, working with other architects and engineers, had initiated a characteristic and original style of national park development that responded to the practical necessity for modernizing park facilities, while remaining firmly rooted in the theory and practice of American landscape park design. The subsequent construction of park roads, bridges, trails, buildings, and entire park villages retained the "rustic" inspiration considered appropriate for a wilderness park setting. All of this work was conceived within "comprehensive plans," which by 1931 were called "master plans." These documents, which consisted of many sheets of planning and design drawings as well as textual supplements, made clear that the extent of development in each park should have definite limits, planned in advance. Park superintendents, landscape architects, and engineers collaborated to produce plans that zoned parks for various uses, from "developed areas" that provided basic services for thousands of visitors a day, to remote "research areas" that maintained wilderness conditions and restricted all public access. The master plans delineated roads, fire roads, and trails, which together made up a hierarchy of complementary circulation systems. Sewers, utility lines, and maintenance areas were also necessarily expanded, but landscape architects and engineers located and designed them to minimize their visual and environmental impact. Unified planning for an entire park assured that the needs of visitors would be met in the most efficient and therefore the least damaging way.

Stephen Mather helped convene the first National Conference on State Parks in 1921, and he believed that encouraging state and local park development was an important part of achieving a truly national park system. The greatest opportunities in assisting local park development arrived later, however, as a result of the economic disaster of the early 1930s. When Franklin Delano Roosevelt launched his New Deal programs in the spring of 1933, the Park Service was in a unique position to provide the technical services and field supervision that "emergency conservation work" desperately needed. Scores of formerly unemployed, professional landscape architects came to work in new positions with the Park Service, where they designed state, county, and metropolitan parks. They also continued to plan for the national park system, which grew in both its size and its variety. The greatest expansion resulted from the Executive Order reorganization of 1933, in which Roosevelt shifted responsibility for dozens of historic sites, battlefields, and national monuments from other agencies to the Park Service. These additions constituted a formidable range of Park Service properties in the East for the first time, and they extended the idea of what a national park could be.

Many important initiatives of the New Deal involved Park Service landscape architects and planners. The design and construction activities they supervised in national and state parks represented a wide mandate of national planning for public recreation. The 1936 Park, Parkway and Recreational-Area Study Act allowed the Park Service to plan for the future recreational uses of public lands generally, not just of national parks. New kinds of parks, like the recreational demonstration area, the national recreation area, and the national seashore were planned in the 1930s, often on land acquired in connection with other activities, such as soil conservation or dam construction. Since all of these different types of park and recreation landscapes were to be considered as parts of a connected park system, a national parkway plan was begun. The Blue Ridge and Natchez Trace parkways are the best known results of what was originally conceived as a system of parkway corridors linking national parks, seashores, and recreation areas with other scenic and historic areas across the country.

Part One of this study provides an overview of the history of the landscape park in the United States up until the early 1920s. Part Two presents a series of landscapes designed by National Park Service landscape architects and engineers for national and state parks during a twenty-year period of intensive design and construction activity after

1920. The designed landscapes presented in Part Two represent the full range of the design and construction activity undertaken during these busy years. They are examples of outstanding historical significance and possess exceptional physical integrity. On the basis of the information presented in this study, these landscapes are being nominated as National Historic Landmarks for their significance in the history of American landscape architecture.[14] The planning and design efforts represented by these landmarks continue to shape the experiences of millions of visitors to national and state parks throughout the United States. Subsequent maintenance and reconstruction in many cases have not significantly altered the experience of landscape scenery that park planners hoped and planned for over sixty years ago.

Despite the continued use and importance of these designed landscapes, they have only recently begun to command the attention of park managers and historic preservationists as potentially significant historic resources. As noted above, landscape architecture does not immediately come to mind when considering national parks; national parks are, after all, great wilderness preserves, valued primarily for their primeval qualities. The roads, trails, overlooks, and other carefully planned and designed works of landscape architecture that convey us through and mediate our experience with those larger landscapes are often taken for granted—quite understandably—in the presence of the awesome drama of a Grand Canyon or Mount Rainier. The history of the parks as natural resource and biological reserves similarly has overshadowed the history of their physical development. Park development, in fact, has often been represented as a necessary evil in otherwise Edenic settings. This unfortunate characterization obscures what Frederick Law Olmsted, Jr., knew so well: that it is the cultural value invested in natural places through their physical development as parks that best assures the preservation of those places in a relatively natural state. The designed landscapes in national and state parks, as works of art, directly express the value society invests in preserving and appreciating natural areas. Few other arts, with the exception of landscape painting, more fully explore this leitmotif of American culture. Neither pure wilderness nor mere artifact, the national park is the purest manifestation of the peculiarly American genius which sought to reconcile a people obsessed with progress with the unmatched price paid for that advance: the near total loss of the North American wilderness.

"The Power of Scenery": Picturesque Theory and Landscape Design in American Parks

In the course of the 19th century, a broad coalition of interests in the United States successfully advocated the acquisition and development of thousands of public parks in American cities, suburbs, and wilderness regions. Various levels of government participated in American park making. Following the declaration of New York's Central Park as a "public place" for "public use" in 1853, hundreds of municipalities developed peripheral tracts of land into pastoral scenery and picturesque woodlands.[1] In 1864, the federal government created a park when Congress granted Yosemite Valley to the state of California, provided that the state government would manage the scenic wonder "for public use, resort, and recreation . . . inalienable for all time." In 1872, Congress went further and withdrew two million acres of Wyoming Territory from settlement and established Yellowstone National Park, a "public park or pleasuring-ground for the benefit and enjoyment of the people," under the jurisdiction of the secretary of the interior.[2] By 1890, the American public park embraced a wide range of policies, purposes, and geographies across the continent.

It is harder for us today, perhaps, to understand the commonalities between Central Park and Yosemite Valley. Issues of urban park systems seem distant from those of wilderness preservation. In the 19th century, however, both parks expressed the cultural value placed on scenic landscape beauty. Since the 1820s, tourism, painting, and literature had converged in the United States in a common fascination for the description and celebration of American landscape scenes, from the Hudson River eventually to the Far West. Americans sought to buttress an insecure sense of national accomplishment by identifying the young Republic with its unparalleled landscape features, as several historians have shown.[3] But the pervasive desire to see and appreciate scenery did not spring from cultural nationalism alone. The interpretation of geographic features into landscape scenes—which the historian Christopher Hussey describes as "picturesque vision"—implied a broad cultural basis and aesthetic tradition for understanding places as pictures, and seeing land as landscape.

This cultural tradition of "seeing nature with the painter's eye" determined attitudes towards the appreciation and the preservation of natural beauty on both sides of the Atlantic. In his 1927 book, *The Picturesque*, Hussey points out that in Great Britain between 1730 and 1830 "the relation of all the arts to one another through the pictorial appreciation of nature was so close that poetry, painting, gardening, architecture, and the art of travel may be said to have been fused into the single 'art of landscape.'" He goes on to observe that once tourists had learned to "connect scenery and painting in their minds, the picturesque became the nineteenth century's mode of vision."[4] Aspects of picturesque culture—above all picturesque travel—exhibited a broad and intense appeal among Americans. The American farmer may not have been a builder of landscape parks in the manner of English gentry, but by the 1820s residents of growing American cities had become avid tourists seeking out picturesque scenery. England had its serene parks and storied forests; but American mountains and river valleys had inherent potential for picturesque interpretation that offered a domestic source of satisfaction. In Great Britain, picturesque guidebooks by the Reverend William Gilpin and others had popularized the Lake District and other scenic areas since the 1780s. By the 1820s such books began to appear for the Hudson River Valley and the White Mountains.[5] Sublime (or awesome) scenery, epitomized by Niagara Falls, held a particularly powerful hold on the American imagination.[6] Sightseeing has had a wide appeal in the United States since that time, and the pleasure of such travel has resided in the appreciation of regional landscape beauty. The popularity of American tourism, however, expressed deeply rooted cultural tendencies of European origin, as well as distinctly native responses to indigenous scenery. From the pastoral scenes of the Connecticut River Valley to the sublime spectacle of Niagara, British picturesque aesthetics underlay the American tourist's awakening to landscape beauty.

William Gilpin, in his 1792 essay "On Picturesque Travel," described the "high delight" produced "by the scenes of nature." Yet sometimes, he observed, the same effect could be produced by "artificial objects," by which he meant works of art, especially landscape drawing and painting.[7] In addition to a taste for recreational travel, 19th-century Americans demonstrated their appetite for composed rural imagery through a passion for visual representations of American landscapes. This was especially the case in growing cities where such scenery, receding from immediate view in reality, flourished in art galleries and on engravers' plates. In 1825, an English immigrant named Thomas Cole (1801-1848) traveled up the Hudson River from New York and subsequently revealed in sketches and oil paintings the marvelous propensity of Hudson River scenery for picturesque interpretation. The positive reaction to Cole's paintings among New York cultural figures, such as William Cullen Bryant, was immediate and decisive. The Hudson River Valley, they averred, was scenic; in other words it readily provided the visual elements of impressive landscape pictures.[8] Nowhere in the United States at the time was such a large city more closely juxtaposed with such fine scenery. The accessibility of the Hudson River Valley shaped the first great school of American landscape art and firmly established the Hudson River and the Catskill Mountains as destinations on an early "grand tour" of American scenic places.

By mid-century, landscape painting enjoyed a popularity never equalled before or since in the United States, and New Yorkers by the thousands swarmed up the Hudson on steam launches that transformed the river valley into vast, moving panoramas of palisades and highland scenery. The literary arts experienced a contemporary enthusiasm for native scenery. William Cullen Bryant, a poet as well as an influential New York newspaper editor, created a sensation in 1817 when he published his Romantic paean to American scenery, "Thanatopsis." Both as a poet and as an indefatigable tourist, Bryant exhibited the influence of Wordsworth and other Romantic poets. Washington Irving's dramatic success in the 1820s derived, in part, from the local settings of some of his tales in *The Sketch Book* (1820). Although most of these stories were set abroad, the most popular fabricated a folklore for the small towns of the lower Hudson River Valley. James Fenimore Cooper relieved his

Asher B. Durand, Kindred Spirits *(Oil on canvas; 1849; 46 x 36; Collection of The New York Public Library, Astor, Lenox and Tilden Foundations). A principal figure of the Hudson River School, Durand depicted his mentor Thomas Cole admiring Catskill Mountain scenery with the poet William Cullen Bryant. Cole had died the year before.*

turgid narratives with extensive, detailed descriptions of (mostly imaginary) American landscapes. Cooper's descriptions were distanced, like Irving's, by their historical setting, or by an equally effective device for his mostly Eastern audience, a Western locale. Artistic expressions of many genres found the American landscape in the 1820s and exploited its visual, narrative, and poetic potential.

But in addition to distinguishing an American identity from its European forebears, the enthusiasm for discerning native landscape beauty also demonstrated the continuing influence of European cultural traditions. The degree to which American painters and writers envisioned native landscapes through the distancing lens of pictorial composition revealed the extent to which "picturesque vision" continued to be a principal mode of perception on both sides of the Atlantic in the 19th century.

That some form of the landscape park—and therefore landscape design—would soon appear in the United States, in retrospect, seems inevitable. Along with poetry, literature, and painting, the art of landscape design had defined picturesque culture of the 18th and early 19th centuries in Great Britain. British farmers and landlords, growing rich through land enclosures and agricultural modernizations, patronized a change in the traditional planning and design of their parks and gardens in the mid-18th century. As park "improvers" such as Lancelot ("Capability") Brown (1716-1783) began to offer professional design and construction services, the technology and aesthetics of the modern landscape park emerged in the English countryside.

The gardens of earlier, 17th-century English estates had been characterized by massive terraces and elaborate knot gardens that surrounded the house and extended its architectonic spaces. Such villas often were sited in, or adjacent to, ancient hunting parks: wooded enclosures set aside (perhaps centuries earlier) primarily to reserve hunting rights for a particular land owner. Gradually the wooded park came to be valued more as the setting for house and garden than as the scene of ritualistic hunts. By the mid-18th century, an increased interest in the design and management of parkland eclipsed the more conservative enthusiasm for architectonic gardens, and many terrace gardens were simply removed. The landscape park that replaced those gardens, however, differed from the medieval hunting park that had preceded it. The landscape park exalted a modern appreciation of picturesque views and aesthetics, not a medieval preoccupation with hunting rights and rituals. Lancelot Brown, for example, who was preeminent among a new group of professional landscape designers, transfigured ancient parks by regrading topography into rolling meadows, by impounding streams and ponds into large lakes, and by planting thousands of trees in scattered groves that framed and directed views. If rectilinear avenues of sometimes ancient trees were felled, entire new forests were planted in isolated clumps and winding belts of beech, oak, and elm. Meandering lakes extended through the recast park landscape with an air of placid mystery. Expansive lawns swept to the walls of the house and obliterated the knot gardens and parterres of an earlier era. Grazing stock was kept away from the house by sunken fences (the "ha-ha") that reinforced the impression that the house was set directly in the park landscape. Such scenes followed visual rules of composition derived (at least indirectly) from landscape painting, descriptive poetry, and of course the existing visual character of British pastureland and woodlots.[9]

A shift in landscape technology accompanied this new aesthetic in landscape design. The Renaissance garden had relied on architectural construction (such as terraces) to articulate outdoor space. Brown relied on landscape engineering: the regrading of existing topography into smooth, continuous slopes; the manipulation of natural drainage patterns to create lakes and drain swamps; the management of forests for sustained yields; and improved road alignment and construction. This was the technology of agricultural modernization that would have been familiar to the landlords and farmers who were often Brown's clients. Brown eschewed retaining walls, terraces, and most other forms of architectural construction including steps and fences. As landscape art, Brown's picturesque design adhered zealously to the elements of the landscape itself—trees, rolling topography, and sheets of water—which were composed without even the implied presence of geometric organization in plan. The suppression of architectural elements in the landscape park (or their planned inclusion as specific elements of a larger picturesque composition) characterized modern landscape park design from its inception.

The compositional rules of picturesque landscape aesthetics, combined with the technologies of land improvement, resulted in a powerful and flexible tool for altering landscapes for modern social and economic purposes. At times, landscape park development established prototypes for modern land planning. At Milton Abbey in Dorset, for example, Brown designed a new village in 1763 to rehouse the villagers displaced by the park he was building for his client. The new village was carefully laid out and employed a unified, vernacular cottage architecture in all the buildings. The total visual effect of the village was calculated as a component of the park landscape scenery. The British landscape park also preserved certain areas from the more direct economic exploitation of modernized agriculture and extractive industries, and so amounted to an early form of regional planning. Although there were important economic considerations in the management of parkland (grazing and timber, for example, could have considerable value), there was a conspicuous contrast between a landscape park devoted to the visual effects of sweeping expanses and hidden boundaries, and the ever more dominant, modernized landscape of hedgerows, rectangular fields, turnpikes, and canals.[10]

But the parks designed by Brown and others certainly did not attempt to preserve the disappearing medieval landscapes of open fields and common lands; in fact, park construction often required even greater amalgamations of land titles and therefore further dislocations of people. Reconfiguring ancient farms, medieval fish ponds, open fields, and villages into picturesque scenery required further conversion of tilled land to pasture and other major alterations in the appearance and functions of land. The landscape park did preserve, however, certain (often "scenic") areas from the more direct forms of exploitation occurring around them. But like any act of preservation, the park required an alteration of the essential qualities of what it preserved. The park preserved the landscape as landscape art, through both the Claudian lens of picturesque aesthetics and through the more substantial effects of Brown's landscape engineering. Both physically and conceptually, the park interpreted a place as a view; it transmuted land into landscape. Such alchemy became an essential and prototypical means of landscape preservation in a modernizing world.

British picturesque landscape design, described as "landscape gardening" in the 1790s by Brown's self-styled successor, Humphry Repton (1752-1818), established the basis of the future profession of landscape architecture in the United States.[11] The design features and technology of the picturesque landscape park would remain at the core of that American professional practice well into the 20th century. But if British picturesque culture was nurtured on the cultivated estates of Whig landlords, American picturesque sensibility derived from a growing urban culture on the Atlantic seaboard. Divorced from the countryside, it never developed a tradition of private park design as had its more bucolic British counterpart. In addition, the American picturesque was a product of the 19th century, and distinctly 19th-century realities, such as urbanization and mass transportation, profoundly changed the professional practice of landscape design on both sides of the Atlantic. In Great Britain, for example, the end of the Napoleonic Wars brought economic upheavals that eventually made many large landholdings less lucrative. Estates diminished in size, and professional landscape gardeners followed the trend, diversifying into the design of suburban residences and urban public parks. These 19th-century adaptations of 18th-century British landscape design techniques also served as the basis of early efforts to establish a landscape design profession in the United States.

The most important American figure in this transition was Andrew Jackson Downing (1815-1852), the son of a Hudson River Valley nurseryman, who became the most prominent American horticulturist and advocate of "rural improvement" of his day. Downing modeled his career on that of John Claudius Loudon (1783-1843), a Scottish landscape gardener, who made a career in the 1830s primarily in the sale of books and magazines to middle class home owners in Great Britain who, unable perhaps to hire professional consultants, nevertheless desired to improve their modest grounds. In the 1840s, Downing's own horticultural magazines and architectural pattern books exerted a similar influence on middle class tastes in this country. His residential garden designs, influenced by Loudon's "gardenesque," accommodated smaller lot sizes and emphasized the display of specimen plants.

Downing died in a steamboat explosion on the Hudson in 1852, and so did not live to finish the implementation of his one great public landscape commission, the 1851 design of the Mall in Washington, DC. His influence on the public landscape was felt, nevertheless, through his published encouragement of the creation of public parks and rural cemeteries in and around American cities. Rural cemeteries had provided the earliest opportunities in the United States for the development of public (or at least semi-public) landscapes designed in the picturesque mode. The first of these, Mount Auburn Cemetery (1831) outside Boston, combined a modern, suburban cemetery with a public garden for the display of botanical collections and specimens.[12] Other suburban cemeteries followed, and combined the gardenesque display of botanical collections with the speculative development of what were, in effect, subdivisions for the dead. Cemeteries such as Laurel Hill in Philadelphia (1836) and Brooklyn's Green-Wood (1838) took advantage of scenic locations near large cities, and immediately became popular resorts for day-tripping urbanites who were having difficulty finding destinations with open spaces and scenic views.

Cemeteries, however, could not fully accommodate these tourists. The platting of cemeteries maximized the number of grave sites for financial reasons and could provide only a limited number of meadows for picnicking or other activities. Restrictions on visitation and activities were almost immediately necessary to preserve proper decorum and to make sure the cemeteries could continue to function as dignified burial grounds.[13] The Sunday crowds at Mount Auburn and Green-Wood, nevertheless, demonstrated a huge middle class appetite for the kinds of public urban spaces the European bourgeoisie had enjoyed for years.

American cities, however, had no former royal hunting parks (like the royal parks of London) to open to the public. Frustrated by the lack of such topographical vestiges, American park advocates urged municipal corporations to acquire and develop public spaces on a much greater scale than had been necessary for European cities. But neither Downing's literary output nor the example of the rural cemetery directly precipitated a widespread movement to acquire certain places and develop them as public parks. That movement began with the opening of Central Park in New York in 1858.

New York, like other cities in the United States, grew with awesome rapidity in the 1830s and 1840s. The residential neighborhoods of old New York were transformed into commercial and industrial districts near the downtown waterfronts. The relatively well-to-do fled north, up the narrow island of Manhattan, to establish new and (they hoped) healthier and quieter residential neighborhoods uptown. The steady exodus proceeded, however, along the predictable framework of the Commissioners' Plan. This 1811 city plan designated a simple grid of streets that divided almost all of Manhattan into some two thousand rectangular blocks. The shortcomings of this survey soon became clear, as mile after mile of streets and row houses covered the last available open spaces in or near the city. A consortium of individuals and groups soon advocated a modification of the city plan. Their motivations varied, but many found a common theme by the 1840s: the creation of a large public park as a massive intervention in the 1811 grid.

Many groups felt a large park would benefit the city. Park advocates like Bryant and Downing believed that the appreciation of landscape scenery—the experience of the picturesque tourist—could figure in the daily patterns of the modern city and improve the quality of life of thousands of people. Some of the most influential park advocates owned property uptown, property that would increase in value if an uptown park became an important amenity. Others saw the general healthful benefits that could be achieved by preserving a large area of woods and meadows within the city; they believed that unhealthy "miasmas" would be dispersed by such a green space, and that experiencing rural scenery and quiet could have a positive effect on nervous disorders and other afflictions that seemed to be on the rise.[14] Most proponents of the idea knew that a park would exert an influence on the type and character of development around it. In London, expensive residential areas (with stable property values) had been established around the royal parks in that city, such as Hyde Park. Again and again, park advocates like Bryant compared New York, now the largest city in North America, to London, the largest city in Europe. London already had over two thousand acres of public parks that provided for public recreation, enhanced public health, and instilled civic pride. New York, which by 1850 reached north to 42nd Street, had less than one hundred acres of public spaces, and no park over ten acres. In the mayoral campaign of 1850, both parties made the creation of a large uptown park part of their platforms.[15]

Today it may seem remarkable or naive that a city park could be seen as a response to the new and profound problems presented by the 19th-century metropolis. But Central Park did not merely provide a quiet refuge or a place to recreate; the park transformed the city plan of New York. The country as a whole faced an increasingly industrial, urban, and ethnically diverse future, and Central Park offered a new diagram for American cities that might make that urban future more healthful and feasible. In place of the ubiquitous, rectangular grid of streets that characterized the expansion of cities before 1858, the new diagram featured a large public park strategically laid out in advance of urban growth, a park which then became surrounded by the grid of streets as the city continued to grow around it. This new diagram reduced the overall density of the city and provided other practical benefits over a city plan that was no more than an undifferentiated grid. Above all, in the context of a developing American civic culture, the new park embodied a successful republican commitment to the public well-being. Public parks—highly visible public art forms as well as desirable amenities—had been bequeathed to European cities as remnants of aristocratic privilege; but Central Park became what Calvert Vaux described in 1865 as "the big art work of the Republic."[16]

It was the specific, physical design of Central Park that would determine whether the many, sometimes conflicting, goals of the emerging American park movement could be realized. In the fall of 1857, the Central Park commissioners announced a design competition, and in the program statement they specified an array of outdoor spaces and facilities that indicated some of the activities foreseen for the park.[17] A forty-acre parade ground was to be included, as well as three playgrounds of up to ten acres each. Sites were also to be indicated for an exhibition hall, a flower garden, a large fountain, a prospect tower, and a skating pond. Frederick Law Olmsted (1822-1903), a thirty-five-year-old journalist and sometime gentleman farmer, had recently been hired to supervise the initial clearing of the park site. He was reluctant to enter the design competition, but a young English architect, Calvert Vaux (1824-1895), the former partner of Andrew Jackson Downing, convinced him to form a partnership. Together they produced a plan called simply "Greensward," which won first prize the following spring.

Many of the landscape gardeners and architects who submitted entries in the Central Park competition conceived their plans to some degree around the required program elements. Most of the plans are known today only by their textual descriptions, but "Greensward" seems to have differed from most of them in one essential aspect: the functional program elements were subordinated to an overall aesthetic conception of landscape art. The greenswards (or smooth, spacious meadows) of the plan, for example, doubled as the required playgrounds and parade ground. The park's serpentine lakes also served as the skating ponds. The "Greensward" plan called for the exhibition hall to be housed in an existing arsenal building (already within the park site) in order to minimize further architectural intrusion. In composing the Central Park landscape, Olmsted and Vaux did not rely on architectonic interpretations of the required program elements, and they suggested very few new buildings. They relied instead on the artistic tradition of British landscape gardening. The park itself, as Olmsted and Vaux later put it, was to be "a single work of art . . . framed upon a single, noble motive, to which the design of all its parts, in some more or less subtle way, shall be confluent and helpful."[18] The landscape composition, in other words, would serve the intended program; but formally it was arranged according to a unified set of aesthetic principles (those of picturesque landscape park design) that made it a great work of art as well.

It is important to discuss Central Park as a work of art, because although it would only cover 840 acres of decidedly urban terrain, it provided a prototypical example of how the landscape park, a formal type of landscape design first developed one hundred years earlier in the English countryside, could be adapted to varied American purposes in the 19th century. European botanical gardens and public parks of the 1830s and 1840s had prefigured events in New York, but only to a limited degree. The London royal parks, some of which had been redeveloped in the "modern style" and opened to the public since 1800, and Joseph Paxton's Birkenhead Park (1843), which Olmsted visited in 1850, provided the most significant precedents of picturesque landscapes in urban settings. But the context and size of Central Park made the American version an unprecedented experiment. Working in what would soon be the middle of a heterogeneous city of two million, the designers relied on the purist tenets of Reptonian design, and skillfully employed the engineering technology and formal devices of the landscape park. The carriage drive, for example, formed a scenic, winding loop around the perimeter of the park. A heavy belt plantation concealed the boundaries of the park and diverted attention to the composed views of the park's interior. Other trees and shrubs formed clumps and belts to frame and screen these views. Smooth, rolling meadows obviously figured prominently in a plan named "Greensward." The park lakes were the result of impounding water in serpentine sheets through low lying areas. The most architectonic features in the plan, the Mall and connecting water terrace, were described in the accompanying description as occupying "the same position of relative importance . . . that a mansion should occupy in a park prepared for private occupation."

The most important formal feature of the design was the Mall, a straight walk flanked by rows of elms extending from the main entrance of the park to the shore of the lake proposed near the center of the site. A single formal avenue among the otherwise curvilinear paths and drives of the park, this "promenade" recalled Rotten Row in Hyde Park or the Broad Walk of Regents Park. A formal avenue might have seemed out of place in a landscape park (Olmsted and Vaux acknowledged as much), but in urban parks such avenues had proven useful in organizing and orienting large crowds. The angle of the Mall, so independent from the geometry of Manhattan's grid plan, was derived from a response to the site's topography: the rows of trees were planted on a line drawn from the park entrance to "Vista Rock," one of the largest of the schist outcrops that characterized the area. This orientation of the Mall also allowed for the largest possible open meadows to the west where the terrain was best suited to this purpose—again the landscape design responded to the intrinsic capabilities of the site. While congregated along the Mall, visitors were drawn north to the secluded center of the park, where they were presented with a view across a narrow neck of water of the most intricate and personal area in the design, the Ramble. Like the "close walk" of an 18th-century park, the Ramble featured a diversity of trees and shrubs (including exotics) that were planted for the visual variety of their habits, textures, and colors. The Ramble offered intimate paths and more picturesque (or rugged) landscape scenery, which complemented the smooth expanses and pastoral scenes of the greenswards.[19]

The park expressed the theory as well as the form of landscape park design of an earlier era. A response to Pope's "genius of the place" predicated every aspect of the plan.[20] The terrain, vegetation, and pre-existing character of the site determined the intended functions of various individual areas, the layout of paths and drives, and the aesthetic treatment of each part of the park. Olmsted and Vaux's desperate attempts to prevent memorials, institutions, and other architectural intrusions into the park landscape also echoed the concerns of landscape park designers of the previous century, who had eschewed architectural construction in favor of landscape engineering. If Brown is supposed to have said, "One does not go up and down steps in Nature" (indicating his preference for smoothly graded contours in favor of retaining walls or terraces), Olmsted and Vaux repeatedly asserted equally purist intentions for maintaining the integrity of their landscape park: "We feel that the interest of the visitor . . . should concentrate on features of natural, in preference to artificial, beauty. . . . Architectural structures should be confessedly subservient to the main idea. . . . The idea of the park itself should always be uppermost in the mind of the beholder."

These quotations, from the written description that accompanied the "Greensward" plan, are usually interpreted as indicating an American assertion of the moral and spiritual superiority of "nature" over the degrading influences of the industrial metropolis; but if these sentiments did reflect an Emersonian pantheism, the physical landscape they describe embodied orthodox—at the time even atavistic—principles of landscape park design. The physical appearance of the park, in the end, was more the product of a British design tradition than of domestic nature philosophy.

There were important differences, nevertheless, between the design of an 18th-century private park and a 19th-century public park. Olmsted and Vaux were aware that, unlike a landscape park in a rural setting, Central Park would receive millions of visitors annually. The designers still hoped to provide individual visitors a calming, personal experience of pastoral meadows and picturesque woodlands. This individual appreciation of landscape beauty, however, might be compromised by a second, equally important function of the park: to assemble the diverse population of the city in healthful and beautiful surroundings, thereby promoting a sense of democratic community.[21] Olmsted and Vaux described these two complementary, yet potentially conflicting, purposes in public landscape park design while they were designing their next major commission, Prospect Park in Brooklyn. "*A sense of enlarged freedom* is to all, at all times, the most certain and the most valuable gratification offered by a park," they stressed, and "scenery offering the most agreeable contrast to the town" produced this sense. But the second purpose, the "opportunity for people to come together for the single purpose of enjoyment, unembarrassed by the limitations with which they are surrounded at home," might be at odds with the first, since "scenery which would afford the most marked contrast with the town, would be of a kind characterized in nature by the absence, or at least the marked subordination of human influences." And since in a park, "men must come together, and must be seen coming together, in carriages, on horseback, and on foot," the "opposing requirements" of the landscape park would need to be "harmonized."

Olmsted and Vaux felt they knew how this could be achieved. Although "success in realizing either [purpose] must be limited . . . by a careful adjustment of parts, and by accommodating the means necessary to the effecting of one purpose to those necessary to the effecting of the other, both may be accomplished in a degree which experience shows satisfactory." Landscape design, specifically picturesque design, could produce this synthesis of the "rural character required in a park," with the "assemblage and movement of great crowds," as long as "the driving room, riding room, walking room, skating, sailing and playing room" were "not only liberally designed," but "studied and adapted to the natural circumstances of the site with the greatest care."[22]

At Central Park, therefore, the lion's share of the construction budget was spent on elaborate systems of carriage drives, pedestrian paths, and bridle trails, not new buildings. A remarkable variety of bridges, tunnels, and underpasses eliminated all grade crossings, so that traffic could flow freely, reducing concern and care for visitors. By making movement through the park as effortless and carefree as possible, the designers allowed for thousands of individual visitors to appreciate landscape scenery personally, by minimizing interference from other

"Rustic" landscape development in the 1860s (from Cook, A Description of Central Park, *1869). The wooded and more remote north end of Central Park, which Olmsted and Vaux felt should be "interfered with" as little as possible, was the first American park project of its type: a scenic area set aside and minimally developed with paths, drives, and "rustic" facilities to enable the public to appreciate examples of regional landscape beauty.*

RUSTIC BRIDGE AND CASCADE IN RAVINE.

visitors. Through the skill employed in its design, the park assembled a great public congregation and yet also allowed individuals to experience rural scenery with an appropriate sense of isolation. The overlaid and interlocking systems of pedestrian, equestrian, and vehicular circulation choreographed visitors' movements and allowed the multitude to experience the effects of pastoral scenery, both as individuals and as a group, remarkably, in the middle of the largest city in North America. Central Park also created an important precedent because it assumed, through each visitor's experience, a picturesque mode of perception: the perception of the viewer in motion, seeking out the raw landscape materials with which he or she might compose mental pictures. The experience of scenery—especially the cinemagraphic experience achieved on a winding park drive—motivated the park's design.

In this sense, landscapes like Central and Prospect parks offered condensed, accessible examples of scenic beauty that not only imparted healthful benefits (through the subconscious influence of experiencing scenic beauty), but that also instructed urbanites in the appreciation of other scenic places they might encounter elsewhere. Central Park and other municipal landscape parks therefore advocated picturesque tourism and scenic landscape preservation generally, as did contemporary landscape painting and Romantic poetry.

It was the 1858 plan of Central Park, and the creative implementation of the design by a dedicated group of engineers, administrators, and laborers over the next dozen years, that made it possible for Central Park to meet many of the ambitious expectations held for it. The overall success of Central Park, however, has been debated for many years. Already in 1863 the architect Richard Morris Hunt challenged the notion that a landscape park—a landscape of pastoral scenes and rural associations—could possibly exist within a city of millions. He proposed monumental entrances and other architectural features that would make Central Park "more of a garden and less of a park," a change he deemed inevitable once the city had completely surrounded the site.[23] Although Hunt's entrances were never built, historian David Schuyler has concluded that the addition of cultural institutions and architectural monuments in the late 19th century irreversibly transformed many "naturalistic" urban parks, and that a "neoclassical civic form supplanted the mid-nineteenth-century vision of a naturalistic urban landscape" by the end of the century.[24]

There is no question, however, that in the decades following the Civil War the example of Central Park inspired other municipalities and state legislatures to authorize park commissions to condemn and develop land for the general purposes of public health and recreation. Professional landscape designers (called "landscape architects" in the United States after Olmsted and Vaux coined the term in the 1860s) were often hired by such commissions as consultants, and the profession of landscape architecture grew as a result. Largely because of the influence of Olmsted and Vaux, many landscape architects of the period espoused the theories and techniques of picturesque landscape design, as expressed at the end of the 18th century by aesthetic theorists such as Uvedale Price and by practitioners such as Humphry Repton.[25] The art of picturesque landscape design arrived somewhat belatedly on American shores; but thanks to the enthusiasm generated by the park movement, the landscape park quickly assumed major proportions in the history of 19th-century American art. Philadelphia and Baltimore sponsored designs for Fairmount Park and Druid Hill Park in 1859 and 1860 respectively. Olmsted and Vaux produced the design for Prospect Park, Brooklyn, perhaps their greatest artistic collaboration, beginning in 1865. By the 1890s, hundreds of American towns and cities had acquired and developed landscape parks.

The popularity of public parks among municipal governments had many sources. Certainly the provision of such public amenities was much appreciated, especially among the middle classes. But because of the effect parks could have on adjacent property, their acquisition and development also functioned as a form of city planning. In London, John Nash had adapted the landscape park to the purposes of speculative residential development at Regents Park as early as 1812. It was in American cities, however, that the application of picturesque landscape design as a form of city planning would be pursued most effectively. Olmsted had carefully demonstrated in the Central Park *Annual Reports* that tax assessments on the land adjacent to the park (much of which had gone up three to ten times in value since the park was built) had quickly more than paid for the cost of acquiring and developing the site. "If the park is regarded in a pecuniary point of view only," the park commissioners asserted in 1860, "it is the most profitable enterprise ever undertaken by the city."[26]

In neighboring Brooklyn, design innovations extended this effect. In their 1868 report to the Brooklyn park commissioners, Olmsted and Vaux elaborated their plan for "parkways" connecting Prospect Park with residential districts being developed to the south and east. These corridor parks were intended to provide some of the benefits of larger parks, "furnishing ample public walks, with room for seats, and with borders of turf in which trees may grow of the most stately character."[27] Parkways had other effects, however, of considerable interest beyond their amenity. Since the 1820s, improved forms of transportation had been extending the effective range people could commute to work, resulting in a natural separation of uses between the industrial inner cities and new residential neighborhoods developing rapidly around them. Zoning-type restrictions on the uses of private property, however, were difficult to legally impose. But since park commissions were empowered to issue regulations regarding public access and use of parkland, access to the carriage drive of a parkway could be legally restricted to non-commercial traffic, and physically limited to certain points of entry. In the prototypical parkway Olmsted and Vaux envisioned for Brooklyn, a limited-access, non-commercial center lane provided an expressway for private carriages, unimpeded by slower local and commercial traffic. Later parkways would simply ban commercial traffic altogether and guarantee a relatively swift commute for private vehicles. Since the parkway provided efficient access to the lots adjacent to it, those lots could greatly increase in value; but this was only true if they were used for residential or institutional purposes, since commercial traffic was banned and could not exploit the convenience of the roadway. The parkway landscape therefore could create a corridor of residential properties with relatively high and stable values—a "parkway district"—that could stabilize otherwise mercurial patterns of land use, and influence property values and land uses in surrounding neighborhoods as well.[28]

The parkway was only one of the new landscape types being designed as park and parkway systems were developed by a growing number of American landscape architects, including Olmsted and Vaux, H. W. S. Cleveland, Jacob Weidenman, Howard Daniels, and others. Historians such as Albert Fein and more recently David Schuyler have demonstrated how municipal officials and their design consultants used landscape architecture as a basis for planning the new, mostly residential areas that mushroomed around cities from Boston to San Francisco in the second half of the 19th century. Park and parkway design was complemented by the platting of picturesque subdivisions that represented an ideal form residential development might take in residential wards.[29] Olmsted and Vaux, whose partnership ended in the early 1870s, provided integrated park and parkway plans for Buffalo (1868) and Chicago (1871) that included the design of squares, playgrounds, and a system of parkways in addition to larger, landscape parks. Park planning rapidly became city planning; but the physical design of landscape parks and parkways (as well as various squares, playgrounds, and smaller parks) remained at the heart of this planning practice well into the 20th century. Although often described merely as Romantic reactions to 19th-century urbanization, municipal parks served as instruments in the appropriation and physical transformation of land. Park development quickly became an enabling device and integral part of American urbanization, not a protest against it.

During the same period, the federal government also involved itself in park making, of course on a much larger scale. While advocates of environmental reform joined with real estate speculators to plan urban growth around cities, an analogous amalgamation of public and private interests proposed state and national parks in more remote scenic areas. In the years following the Civil War, these larger parks came to define a vision of republican nationhood, much as municipal parks embodied American civic ideals. And just as municipal park development became an integral part of the process of subdividing and developing land on the edges of cities, setting aside scenic reservations also became part of the process of subdividing and distributing larger tracts of land in Western states and territories.

From its formal origins in the 18th century, the landscape park presupposed both a means of "improving" and enclosing land, as well as a means of preserving it through its interpretation into picturesque scenery (which is itself a form of conceptual and at least limited physical development). This meaning of preservation—preservation through picturesque interpretation—would have particular significance in North America. Even at Central Park, a landscape routinely described as completely man-made, significant characteristics of the pre-industrial geography of Manhattan Island were preserved through the development of the site as a park. "There will come a time," the park's designers observed, "when New York will be built up . . . and when the picturesquely-varied, rocky formations of the Island will have been converted into formations for rows of monotonous, straight streets, and piles of erect buildings. There will be no suggestion left of its present varied surface, with the single exception of the few acres contained in the Park. . . . It therefore seems desirable to interfere with its easy, undulating outlines, and picturesque, rocky scenery as little as possible, and, on the other hand, to endeavor . . . to increase and judiciously develop these . . . characteristic sources of landscape effects."[30]

American landscape architects not only enhanced the scenery in the areas designated as parks, they also preserved existing features and exploited their ready-made potential as civic ornaments. Landscape architects designing park systems in Midwestern cities, for example, often were in a position to preserve major landscape features that had not yet been altered. H. W. S. Cleveland, who had worked for Olmsted and Vaux in the 1860s on Prospect Park, moved to Chicago in 1869 to apply "landscape architecture to the wants of the West." The park and parkway system he designed for Minneapolis in the 1880s preserved a ring of lakes around that city, as well as major natural features such as Minnehaha Falls. Lakes, waterfalls, and the bluffs over the Mississippi were "judiciously developed," in Cleveland's plans, by adding paths and overlooks, controlling water levels, and by connecting new parks with non-commercial parkways. From the rolling meadows of West Roxbury to the lakes and ravines of Seattle, the preservation of natural features and attentiveness to pre-existing landscape character defined the peculiarly American version of the 19th-century landscape park.[31] In their 1917 textbook on landscape architecture, Henry V. Hubbard and Theodora Kimball described a "Modern American Landscape Style" in the design of parks and certain large estates. That style, they explained, descended directly from the "English landscape school," but in American parks, "the designers sought with much more appreciation the preservation and interpretation of natural character."[32]

Many historians of national parks, on the other hand, have suggested separate origins and inventors for an American "national park idea."[33] But scenic preservation on the state or national scale was not entirely independent from the precedent and influence of the landscape park as it was being advocated within the contemporary municipal park movement. In New York, for example, the interest in scenic preservation among municipal park advocates naturally extended to Niagara Falls. In California, a number of public figures from the East, such as Horace Greeley and Thomas Starr King, had become aware of the spectacular scenic qualities of Yosemite Valley through their own activities as tourists. Artists such as the photographer Carleton Watkins and the painter Albert Bierstadt visited the valley in the early 1860s, and the images they produced enjoyed wide popularity and commercial success in a national art market hungry for composed images of American landscapes. In 1863 Frederick Law Olmsted arrived in California to take the position of manager of the Mariposa mining estate, which was felicitously headquartered at Bear Valley only a day's ride from Yosemite. In 1864 he camped for several weeks in Yosemite Valley with his family. There he was overwhelmed by the scenery, noting that it combined the "beautiful" scenery of open parkland on the valley floor, with the awesome, "sublime" effects of the surrounding granite precipices. The "union of the deepest sublimity with the deepest beauty of nature," wrote Olmsted, continuing to express himself in terms drawn from late 18th-century aesthetic theory, "constitutes the Yo Semite the greatest glory of nature."[34]

Writing of the "power of scenery to affect men," Olmsted's appreciation of landscape beauty remained consistent whether it was applied to the "landscape effects" he sought to enhance in Central Park just several years earlier, or to the less contrived magnificence of Yosemite. The framework of American picturesque culture allowed him (and apparently others) to conceive of Yosemite Valley as a landscape park: land that could be set aside and managed specifically for the preservation and appreciation of scenic qualities conducive to interpretation according to certain aesthetic rules.[35]

In February 1864, in fact, Israel Ward Raymond, a representative of the Central American Steamship Transit Company of New York, had written to Senator John Conness of California urging that both the Valley and the nearby Mariposa Grove of giant sequoias be granted to California "for public use, resort, and recreation" (in other words requesting that it be retained in the public domain as a public park). Conness put the legislation forward in Congress where it was passed with little debate that year.[36] The motives of Raymond and Conness must be inferred; but clearly the Central American Steamship Company stood to profit from any increased tourist travel to California, and especially to Yosemite Valley. Olmsted's presence nearby, bringing to mind his recent achievement at Central Park, may also have contributed to the suggestion that Yosemite Valley could become a park, in this case simply by keeping it in public ownership. And as a park, Yosemite might galvanize and enhance the public's image of California as a state, the way the New York park had for that city. In any case, the Yosemite Park Grant of 1864 demonstrated a convergence of influential interests, involving advocates of scenic preservation and those of a powerful private corporation that could move land grant legislation quickly and quietly on Capitol Hill when it so desired.[37]

It is doubtful that Olmsted helped initiate the Yosemite legislation, but once it passed, California Governor Frederick F. Low named him chairman of the commission created to manage the park and make proposals for its development. Governor Low clearly perceived that Olmsted's experience with Central Park was applicable to the management of the new California park, despite the very different situation of Yosemite Valley.[38] Charged with the extraordinary task of proposing how the area should be developed as a public park, Olmsted produced a remarkable plan for what he called in 1865 "the noblest park or pleasure ground in the world."[39]

Olmsted first turned to famous artists who had rendered Yosemite on canvas and film and asked them for their opinions on how to correct "conditions affecting the scenery of the Yo Semite unfavourably," as well as for advice regarding what could be done to "enhance the enjoyment now afforded by the scenery."[40] The report, which was presented to the commissioners assembled in the valley in August 1865, consisted of a survey of the area and a verbal description of its proposed treatment. He began by comparing the federal grant of the Yosemite in 1864 to other great works of civic art that had also continued through the dark war years, notably the Capitol dome and Central Park.[41] He noted there were "two classes of consideration" behind the Yosemite legislation, the "first and less important" being "obvious pecuniary advantage." Switzerland had exploited its scenery into a national industry, and once Yosemite was more "accessible," Olmsted felt it would "prove an attraction of a similar character and a similar source of wealth to the whole community, not only of California but of the United States." But the more important consideration for Olmsted (who was writing the report when the news of Appomattox reached California) was "of a political duty of grave importance . . . the grounds of which rest on the same eternal base, of equity and benevolence with all other duties of a republican government."

Noting that it was "the main duty of government" to protect and provide the means for the "pursuit of happiness," Olmsted observed that "it is a scientific fact that the occasional contemplation of natural scenes of an impressive character, particularly if this contemplation occurs in connection with relief from ordinary cares, change of air and change of habits, is favorable to the health and vigor of men . . . beyond any other conditions that can be offered them." Other forms of government made the pleasures of such outdoor recreation available only to the privileged few; republican government had the responsibility of making sure the "enjoyment of the choicest natural scenes in the country and the means of recreation associated with them" be "laid open to the use of the body of the people." Because of the natural desire among the wealthy to monopolize such places, however, "all places favorable in scenery to the recreation of the mind and body will be closed" unless "means are taken by government to withhold them from the grasp of individuals." Once the importance of accessibility to places such as Yosemite was understood as vital to "public happiness," it was clear that "the establishment by government of great public grounds for the free enjoyment of the people" was "justified and enforced as a political duty."

Olmsted went on in his report to establish priorities for managing Yosemite as a landscape park. Since the reason Yosemite was "treated differently from other parts of the public domain . . . consists wholly in its natural scenery," the "first point to be kept in mind" was "the preservation and maintenance as exactly as is possible of the natural scenery." This involved "the restriction . . . within the narrowest limits consistent with the necessary accommodation of visitors, of all artificial constructions and the prevention of all constructions markedly inharmonious with the scenery." This proscription of "inharmonious" building that might "detract from the dignity of the scenery" could have been taken directly from Olmsted's entries in the Central Park *Annual Reports* of the late 1850s.[42] The origins of such a landscape management philosophy—a philosophy completely oriented to the appreciation of landscape scenery—can be found even earlier, in the landscape parks of Great Britain, which had placed the appreciation of composed landscape scenes above other concerns in their management and design.

The physical development Olmsted proposed for Yosemite derived from the same tradition of landscape park design and management. His design proposals revealed his understanding that "if proper facilities are offered . . . in a century the whole number of visitors [to the valley] will be counted by millions." He did not find this deplorable in itself; in fact the lion's share of his proposed budget would be used to complete a road from the valley to the steamboat docks at Stockton, greatly reducing the cost of visiting Yosemite and opening the experience to greater numbers of people. But Olmsted was concerned that "an injury to the scenery so slight that it may be unheeded by any visitor now, will be one of deplorable magnitude" when multiplied by millions. Therefore he also suggested the construction of a one-way carriage loop (up one side of the valley and down the other) "which shall enable visitors to make a complete circuit . . . reaching all the finer points of view." This was a classic park carriage drive, in other words, "with suitable resting spots and turnouts . . . at frequent intervals." Such a drive would reduce the "necessity for artificial construction within the narrowest possible limits." It would minimize the impact of visitors by concentrating their activities through the thoughtful development of the valley with features (such as a carriage drive) drawn from landscape park design.

Other features of Olmsted's Yosemite plan indicate how the landscape park model could further be adapted to provide the amenities of a regional park in a wilderness setting. The circuit drive would be complemented by a system of pedestrian paths leading to "points of view accessible only by foot." Five cabins near "convenient camping places" would be occupied by tenants charged with maintaining "one comfortable room as a free resting place for visitors, and the proper private accommodations for women," as well as supplying "simple necessities for camping parties." This formula for the careful, minimal development of Yosemite Valley was based on the formal and theoretical precedents of the landscape park, a genre Olmsted had already exploited with great success to accommodate large numbers of tourists seeking picturesque scenery in a public setting. In his 1865 plan for Yosemite, Olmsted identified and articulated the tremendous

Thomas Moran, The Grand Canyon of the Yellowstone *(Oil on canvas; 1872; 84 x 144 1/4; National Museum of American Art, Smithsonian Institution, Lent by U.S. Department of the Interior). As a member of F. V. Hayden's 1871 expedition to the Yellowstone, Moran produced sketches and paintings that helped convince Congress of the unique and awesome character of the region. This depiction of the view from Artist Point, which hung for many years in the Capitol, was unveiled two months after the Yellowstone National Park legislation was signed by Ulysses S. Grant on March 1, 1872.*

potential of the landscape park concept—and of the formal elements of its physical articulation—for preserving areas of natural scenic beauty in the United States.

After its propitious beginning as a state park, however, Yosemite Valley suffered. After Olmsted returned to New York later in 1865, the remaining members of the park commission immediately suppressed the development plan. The valley floor was subsequently logged (John Muir was employed there as a mill hand after he arrived on the scene in 1868) and the lumber was used to build precisely the types of hotels Olmsted wished to avoid. Because the road to Stockton was not completed, supplies could not be brought in economically; delicate meadows full of wildflowers therefore were plowed, cultivated, and fenced to provide food and fodder for guests and their stock.[43] Yosemite was on its way to becoming a resort development within a state park.

There is no reason to believe that Yosemite Valley would have fared better if the federal government had retained ownership. Eight years later, Congress again acted to create a public park on a frontier of settlement, this time in Montana and Wyoming territories. Reports of a "wonderland" of thermal features and waterfalls around the headwaters of the Yellowstone River had interested Jay Cooke, the New York financier acting at the time for the Northern Pacific Railroad. Cooke was interested because the planned route of the Northern Pacific's transcontinental line passed through Livingston, Montana, to the north of the region; the construction of a branch line would generate substantial profits if the Yellowstone country became a tourist destination.[44] Several expeditions were organized to explore the Yellowstone Plateau, the most important of which was led by the geologist Ferdinand V. Hayden in 1871. Hayden's five hundred-page report to Congress, illustrated with dozens of paintings and photographs, became the basis for a surprisingly brief legislative campaign to withdraw a huge rectangle of public land from settlement and create Yellowstone National Park. According to historian Aubrey L. Haines, the impulse for this remarkable legislation almost certainly originated with representatives of the Northern Pacific. Upon his return from Yellowstone, Hayden received a letter from A. B. Nettleton (one of Jay Cooke's operatives) repeating a suggestion that "Congress pass a bill reserving the Great Geyser Basin as a public park forever." Such a bill was promptly introduced and was enthusiastically supported by Hayden and others, who had their own, perhaps more altruistic reasons for wanting to see the area preserved from private resort development. Within only three months (and again after little debate) Congress approved "an act to set apart a certain tract of land lying near the headwaters of the Yellowstone River as a public park," early in 1872.[45]

The Yellowstone Park act was explicitly modeled on the Yosemite Grant legislation; the new park remained under the jurisdiction of the secretary of the interior, however, since there was no state government to receive a land grant. Yellowstone therefore became the first national park. The motivations for such legislation again must be inferred. But clearly if the area were withdrawn from settlement and instead developed (at government expense) with carriage drives and other facilities to make it accessible and convenient, the Northern Pacific would be provided with a free and lucrative tourist attraction along its line. The legislation included little indication of how to develop the property, although the secretary of the interior was directed to "publish such rules and regulations as he deems necessary," and to "grant leases for building purposes for terms not to exceed ten years" to provide accommodations. The revenue from leases was intended to help pay for "roads and bridle-paths" as well as the prevention of poaching and vandalism.[46]

The federal government, in fact, showed very little interest in Yellowstone until 1883, the year the Northern Pacific (reorganized after a bankruptcy) finally completed its line across Montana, complete with a forty-mile branch line to the northern edge of the national park. That year, Congress finally appropriated funds for park management and authorized the Army Corps of Engineers to plan and supervise road construction. Early civilian administration of the park had been notoriously corrupt and inefficient, and in 1886 the day-to-day administration of the park was placed under military control as well. Without the legal and financial means to properly police the park, however, not even the U.S. Cavalry could stop the abuses at Yellowstone. The military superintendents in charge of the park after 1886 continued to report serious problems with tourists vandalizing geothermal features and carelessly causing forest fires. Herds of elk and bison had been poached ruthlessly since the 1870s, but authorities could do little more than expel hunters from the park. Significant progress was finally made in 1894, when Representative John F. Lacey of Iowa succeeded in passing legislation that provided criminal penalties and the authority to prosecute infractions to back up the efforts of the patrolling soldiers.[47]

Over the thirty-five years the park was under military supervision, the Army Corps of Engineers planned and constructed a system of roads and bridges in Yellowstone. Lieutenant Daniel C. Kingman of the Army Corps arrived in 1883 and in four years succeeded in building sixteen miles of the first good roads in the park. Kingman began a tradition of road construction that met aesthetic standards considered appropriate for a national park. In 1891 another Army Corps engineer, Hiram M. Chittenden, arrived in the park and furthered the road building work with characteristic efficiency and integrity.[48] By 1906, with the help of adequate Congressional appropriations, Chittenden completed and improved most of the park's road system: a "general circuit or belt line connecting all the important centers of interest," which he also called the "Grand Loop Road of the Park."[49] The Grand Loop formed the basis of the 150-mile figure-eight loop drive still in use today. By 1905, over one hundred miles of roads were kept sprinkled with water to reduce dust, and Chittenden was experimenting with oil treatments in limited areas.[50]

Like Kingman, Chittenden expressed an awareness of the aesthetic value of the park landscape, which he did not want to mar with inappropriate construction. In this, he expanded on the theory and practice of earlier park designers, such as Frederick Law Olmsted. "As a general policy, the extension of the [road] system should be restricted to actual necessities," said Chittenden, echoing Olmsted's concerns at Yosemite; "the Park should be preserved in its natural state to the fullest degree possible." For Chittenden as well, the visual experience of picturesque tourism guided park development. "The primary considerations" in roadway alignment for Chittenden, after "good gradients and safe locations," were to "carry the roads where they would best develop the scenery."[51] Kingman and Chittenden understood that in the setting of "the national park" (Yellowstone), engineering should take into account the aesthetic impacts of construction and should facilitate the appreciation of scenery; engineering should become what would later be described by the National Park Service as "landscape engineering."

Engineering of this type was not a new discipline in 1899. The specifications and guidelines for Yellowstone roads described by Kingman and Chittenden show a technical awareness of the park drives and parkways being built from Boston to Seattle by the 1890s. Well-aligned roads that followed the suggestions of the land contours, grading of earth that blended the edges of construction into surrounding topography, and improved roadway surfaces all characterized the design of non-commercial park roads and parkways in the late 19th century. The desire to preserve park landscapes while developing them for public use had been fully expressed by a number of American park designers, including Olmsted, Vaux, and Cleveland. Chittenden embraced municipal park engineering and design theory in his effort to design roads for "the national park." He advised that "the structures" of such roads (bridges, drainage structures, guardwalls, etc.) "should be built, as far as possible, of rustic design, and all other work should be carried out with due reference to the purpose of the roads as public highways in the world's greatest of natural parks." The aesthetic of the landscape park also informed his suggested treatment of roadsides. "Dead and decaying timber should be cleared away from the roads to a distance of one hundred feet," he advised, "the trees thinned out, and grass and shrubbery introduced to beautify the roadside and induce game to show themselves."[52]

The formal diagram of Yellowstone's development at this time, although greatly increased in scale, also comprised an analogy with municipal landscape park design. A vastly extended park drive, the Grand Loop, completed a circuit around Yellowstone Park and reached the major points of scenic interest. At Yellowstone, as at smaller landscape parks, resort-type businesses and amusements (and architectural construction in general) were excluded when possible in order to avoid what Kingman described in 1887 as "Coney Island" park development.[53] That Brooklyn beach resort was also the favorite negative example of municipal park advocates, who witnessed with trepidation the growing popularity of amusement parks in the 1880s. Perhaps the best indication of Chittenden's aesthetic sense in park development was his design for a bridge over the Yellowstone River at a point just above the Upper Falls. The main reason for a bridge at this critical location in the heart of the park was to reach Artist Point, on the east rim of the Grand Canyon of the Yellowstone, where one of the best views in the park (the view Thomas Moran painted in 1872) was available. Chittenden delayed building the bridge, realizing that the "remarkable scenic attractions of the rapids made any ordinary structure seem out of place." In 1903 he chose "a single arch of slender profile," for which, ". . . the exact form was a matter of careful study in order to get the lines that would appeal to the eye as meeting the artistic requirements." The result was a single, continuous arched span (known as the Chittenden Bridge until its demolition in 1962) that bore a somewhat striking resemblance to Bow Bridge in Central Park. The lines of that Central Park span, similarly located at a central and critical moment in that municipal park landscape, apparently embodied the "artistic requirements" Chittenden hoped to fulfill.[54]

The entire Yellowstone project, in fact, relates diagrammatically to other examples of 19th-century landscape park development in the United States. Just as Central Park was set aside as a scenic reservation in the otherwise relentless grid of streets and avenues on the urban frontier of northern Manhattan, Yellowstone was reserved out of another comprehensive, rectangular grid—on a much vaster scale—the federal land ordinance. The 1785 federal land ordinance that led to a national survey of range and section lines, like the 1811 city plan for New York, provided a comprehensive rectangular survey as the basis for the subdivision of land for various commercial purposes. In both cases, the landscape park appeared as a reservation from the commercial

Wilderness by Design

transformation of land, and at the same time as part of the inexorable progress of modernity.

Whether undertaken by government at the national, state, or local level, the American public park did not merely express a Romantic rejection of the city or a Transcendental reverence for nature. Governments created public parks—whether they were mostly designed or mostly left in their existing condition—in order to appropriate land on the edges of cities and on the frontiers of settlement for certain purposes. Parks became ubiquitous in part because they served speculative commercial interests of the most powerful sort in the 19th century: real estate and railroads.

But by transmuting places into views and land into landscapes, 19th-century American parks also emblemized the higher hopes of modern progress. From Manhattan Island to Yosemite Valley, the idea and the formal design components of the landscape park proved adaptable to the needs of both cities and the nation to demonstrate the vitality and virtue of republican government. Parks embodied optimistic themes in the larger and otherwise less idealistic project of exploiting North American land and resources, because certain assumptions about the value of preserving landscapes underlay their creation. The shared, public experience of appreciating landscape beauty implied a shared impulse to preserve such beauty; and in the context of the 19th-century landscape park, the preservation of unimpaired scenery could be identified with civic virtue, public health, and considerable commercial profits.

By 1900, however, the large landscape park no longer claimed the central position in municipal reform that it had in the mid-19th century. Urban reformers of the Progressive era moved beyond the manipulation and preservation of landscape scenery in their crusades to make cities more efficient and healthful. Landscape parks and parkways had been planned primarily for the expanding edges of cities, and inevitably they most strongly affected those who lived in more expensive suburban wards or who could afford to own private vehicles. But industrialization and immigration had created ever larger slums in older, already densely developed neighborhoods where the creation of large parks had never been an option. Many public health advocates, journalists, religious leaders, and others interested in improving conditions in the city as a whole began turning away from the "large park" and advocating the "small park," or playground, instead.

Since the 1840s, the need for open space for public recreation had been an important justification for municipal parks. Three "playgrounds" were required program elements in the 1857 Central Park competition, and most 19th-century landscape parks accommodated baseball, tennis, and other sports, at least to a limited degree. As cities grew larger, however, the need to provide public spaces for various types of recreation intensified. Increased demands on available open spaces resulted in pressure to open landscape parks to different uses, and to create new parks specifically planned for sports and other group activities. In 1892 Frederick Law Olmsted and his stepson John Charles

Olmsted designed Charlesbank in Boston, an early example of a ten-acre park that featured a running track, sand boxes, and outdoor gymnasia, as well as sitting areas and a waterfront promenade.[55] The most influential innovators and advocates for new playgrounds, however, were not landscape architects or park commissions; playgrounds often first appeared as outdoor kindergartens operated on the grounds of "settlement houses," social service centers staffed by volunteers, which were being established in the tenement districts of many American cities. The residents of Jane Addams's Hull-House, for example, established the first playground in Chicago in 1893, and a similar facility opened the same year at Lillian Wald's Henry Street Settlement in New York.[56]

Various groups and individuals concerned with the environmental and social conditions in American cities seized on playgrounds and organized recreation as the means to improve the physical situation and reform the daily activities of children growing up in the city. In 1897 a municipal Committee on Small Parks was formed in New York with the journalist and reformer Jacob Riis as secretary. In his report that year, Riis stated, "In the original plan for the city of New York, the children seem to have been forgotten," referring to the failure to provide neighborhood playgrounds in the relentless grid of streets. Riis also claimed, echoing the sentiments of many playground advocates, that "since the city . . . secured the larger parks," there had been "a strange oversight of the necessity of providing . . . for the children the opportunity to use these grounds freely for games and recreative sports."[57] Landscape parks and parkways on the urban periphery had done little for children in poorer neighborhoods. Such parks were either too distant or too restricted in the activities they allowed. Small park advocates felt that landscape parks should be opened for all kinds of activities—especially for children—and that more parks should be provided for the older parts of the city.

Riis's 1897 report used police and health department statistics to recommend acquiring a system of "small parks" located in the areas with the highest statistical incidence of crime, death, and disease. Since small parks could be developed on vacant lots of just a few acres, they were feasible in densely populated wards where they were needed the most. Statistical data and the requirements of organized recreation, not the perceived benefits of appreciating scenery, determined the locations and character of the small parks suggested in the committee's report. Landscape architectural theory and practice figured very little in the early advocacy of small parks and playgrounds.

In 1898 a settlement worker named Charles B. Stover, with the help of Riis, Wald, and others, organized the Outdoor Recreation League in New York. The league operated a public playground covering several acres on the Lower East Side, and demonstrated outdoor gymnasia, team sports, and various other activities supervised by professional play leaders. The league goaded municipal government into taking responsibility for a system of such public playgrounds in 1903.[58] A watershed was reached in New York when Stover was appointed a New

York park commissioner in 1910. He immediately created a Department of Recreation within the city's Parks Department and established dozens of new playgrounds. He also opened the lawns of Central Park to a much wider variety of activities and organized sports, such as school pageants and field days. Many felt that the park's delicate greenswards and understory shrubs would be destroyed by large crowds of school children and ball players.[59] Samuel Parsons, Jr., the landscape architect for Central Park at the time, had been Calvert Vaux's protégé and represented a last link to the generation that had created the park. After clashing with Stover over his landscape management policies, Parsons was fired in 1911.[60]

In Chicago, the South Park Commission, which had previously built large parks and connecting parkways, developed the most admired playground system in the United States after the Illinois Legislature authorized one million dollars for new small parks in 1903. The playgrounds, which were not to cover more than ten acres, were devoted to organized sports and other activities for both children and adults. J. C. Olmsted and Frederick Law Olmsted, Jr., provided a set of plans for the Chicago small parks, which became influential prototypes for other landscape architects, who were now expected to design both small and large parks for municipal park commissions. Chicago's older landscape parks, Washington and Jackson parks, featured tennis courts, ball fields, and golf courses when they reopened after the 1893 World's Columbian Exposition. By 1905, park systems in thirty-five cities included municipally owned playgrounds; few American municipal parks of any size would ever again be managed strictly as scenery.[61] Joseph Lee, a playground advocate and one of the founders of the National Recreation Association in 1906, wrote in an article titled "Play as Landscape" that "'Keep Off the Grass' signs have been abolished in all civilized park systems. . . . Parks that are made of so delicate a constitution that they are destroyed or seriously injured by children's play are too delicate for this world."[62]

The advocacy for playgrounds and public recreation did not grow out of the application of picturesque aesthetics and landscape engineering that had shaped the park movement in the 19th century. Progressive era "small park" design responded to social science, not landscape scenery. Large parks and parkways continued to be planned in American cities, but a shift in aesthetic sensibilities indicated a change in attitude towards the large municipal park. At the same time that these larger parks were opened for more intensive recreational uses, many also became the sites for new museums, conservatories, and architectural memorials. New and imposing public institutions made portions of these parks settings for grand buildings and monuments rather than scenes of landscape beauty composed and preserved for their own sake. Olmsted had proscribed such architectural additions and entrances to his municipal parks (and in his plan for Yosemite Valley) because they detracted from the integrity and the effect of the landscape scenery itself, which he hoped would remain the principal attraction in large public parks. But from Richard Morris Hunt's massive expansion of the Metropolitan Museum of Art

(1902) in Central Park, to the Museum of Science and Industry (1891) in Jackson Park in Chicago, to the De Young Museum (1917) in Golden Gate Park in San Francisco, imposing institutions dominated scenes that were once planned to provide an alternative to architectural monumentalism.[63]

The preference for Renaissance and Baroque architectural styles extended to the organization of groups of buildings, and therefore to the design of new civic spaces. As many American cities espoused Beaux-Arts-influenced designs for their proliferating public institutions, Baroque architectural planning, not picturesque landscape design, now typically defined the ideal city plan. If the landscape park had embodied the ideals of mid-19th-century American urbanism, the emblematic space of Progressive municipal reform was the "civic center," a great plaza surrounded by an imposing group of museums, courthouses, municipal offices, and other new public buildings. Such centers often were planned as the heart of "city beautiful" plans for municipal improvement, which often included proposed boulevards that, like the boulevards of Paris, cut through the existing blocks of buildings and created diagonal express routes. Schemes for wide, straight boulevards meeting in *étoiles* and *pattes d'oies* represented a tradition of urban design sympathetic with André le Nôtre's gardens at Versailles and the Paris of Napoleon III, not British landscape parks.[64]

Landscape park and parkway planning did continue in the early 20th century, however, sometimes as part of now more comprehensive city plans. The architect Daniel H. Burnham, for example, included waterfront parkways and suburban forest reservations in his monumental Plan of Chicago, published in 1909. But the aesthetics of civic improvement had shifted away from picturesque composition and the appreciation of rural landscape beauty. The most captivating imagery in city plans such as Burnham's depicted, not regional scenery, but wide, radiating avenues, lined with uniform architectural facades and terminated by the imposing, usually neoclassical elevations of new civic institutions.

Municipal park design of the period also reflected the shift in civic aesthetics. In Kansas City, the landscape architect George E. Kessler designed a municipal park system in the 1890s and early 1900s without including a large landscape park at all. His Kansas City plans featured small, decentralized parks and playgrounds, sunken gardens, pergolas, and terraces, all linked together along a grid of widened, non-commercial streets, which he called boulevards. In certain ways, Kessler relied heavily on key principles established by earlier park and parkway systems. The financing for the project, for example, depended on the oldest principle of park planning: the anticipated increase in the value of property adjacent to new parks and boulevards.[65] The boulevards in Kansas City also recalled the rectilinear parkways Olmsted and Vaux had designed for Brooklyn and Buffalo in the 1870s. But European gardens and boulevards, not Reptonian park design, were the aesthetic inspirations of Kessler's system. Terrace promenades and sunken gardens, not greenswards and rambles, were the principal public spaces. The centerpiece of the Kansas City system, a wide residential boulevard called the Paseo, featured gardens and pergolas along its length and was terminated by a Parade devoted to ball fields and playgrounds. Rather than setting a large, landscape park as an intervention in the grid of Kansas City's streets, Kessler adopted the existing grid and widened certain streets into orthogonal boulevards that structured a decentralized system of playgrounds and small parks. This more comprehensive idea of civic improvement sought to reform the physical attributes of the city streets themselves, not just to preserve an area of landscape beauty from their encroachment. Park and parkway systems such as Buffalo's had suggested this approach; but Kessler adopted a different aesthetic sensibility—one based on architectonic garden styles—to accomplish a more comprehensive urban design that presented the redesigned street as the principal public space, adorned with street furniture, improved pavements, lighting, and other amenities of the European boulevard.

The shift away from picturesque aesthetics in the design of municipal public spaces so evident in Kansas City illustrates a general trend that had been underway for some time in residential landscape design. This trend had been foreshadowed, predictably, by trends in American landscape painting. In the opulent decades following the Civil War, the popularity of the Native School of landscape painting that had characterized American picturesque culture fifty years earlier gave way to an enthusiasm for European artistic influences. Although they continued to make the American landscape the subject of much of their work, painters such as George Inness and Homer Martin also grounded their art in an appreciation of contemporary French and other European landscape painting. The fortunes made during the Gilded Age built art museums, and collectors returned from Europe laden with pictures. The influence of the landscape paintings of the Barbizon school, and later the Impressionists, increased as artists and their patrons turned away from simpler, Claudian compositions of native scenery in favor of more sophisticated landscape imagery.[66]

American architecture also reinforced its European associations in the late 19th century. Following the example of Richard Morris Hunt, American architects in the 1880s embraced the academic influence of the École des Beaux Arts. Hunt, while reviving Renaissance and Baroque architectural styles for private mansions and public institutions, had become the favorite architect of a new class of wealthy patrons. American architects became more disciplined and consistent in their historical borrowings, reflecting the increased rigor of their academic training and the professionalization of their practice. Residential garden design necessarily followed the trend; Renaissance architecture, for example, demanded axial site plans, parterres, and elaborate fountains and statuary. Even Frederick Law Olmsted, beginning in 1888, provided an appropriately architectonic landscape design for Biltmore, a massive French chateau designed by Hunt for George W. Vanderbilt in the Great Smoky Mountains of North Carolina. The revival of historical styles in residential garden design could have been considered overdue in the

United States by the 1880s. In Great Britain by that time, Victorian landscape gardeners such as Sir Charles Barry and William Andrews Nesfield had made eclectic revivals of architectonic garden styles commonplace. But American landscape architecture, in part because of Olmsted's influence, had remained dedicated to an essentially picturesque practice, often applied in the public or semipublic realms of park, campus, subdivision, and cemetery design. By the end of the century, however, residential commissions for wealthy clients grew more numerous, stimulating rapid growth in the profession. As the number of landscape architects grew and diversified, they depended on an academic familiarity with Italian and French garden history to be in demand with estate owners.

The artist and architect Charles A. Platt personified some of the changes affecting the practice of landscape architecture. Trained as an etcher and painter in New York and Paris, Platt traveled to Italy in the spring of 1892 with his brother, William, who was an apprentice with Olmsted at the time. The trip reflected the growing interest in Renaissance Italian civilization among the upper classes generally (which the Platts represented) and especially among leading cultural figures, from Bernard Berenson to Edith Wharton. Charles Platt's stated intention for the trip was to draw his brother away from Olmsted's influence and educate him in the "purely architectural side" of the "great gardens of Europe." Platt produced a series of photographs and sketches of Italian villas, which were published in an extremely popular book, *Italian Gardens*, in 1894.[67] At that point, Charles Platt began a successful career as a garden designer and architect himself, producing reduced variations of Italian villas for wealthy clients on the East Coast and in the Midwest. Platt, a self-taught architect, certainly had never apprenticed with Olmsted and probably had little interest in the writings of Price and Repton; yet he rapidly became the leading figure in "country place" landscape design in the 1890s.[68]

Under these circumstances, the profession of landscape architecture reinvented itself at the turn of the century. The increased demand for residential landscape designs and the revival of historical styles demanded a professionalized practice and an academic approach to landscape architectural education. In 1899 the American Society of Landscape Architects formed in the offices of Samuel Parsons, Jr., in New York. Among the founding members were former Olmsted apprentices, such as J. C. Olmsted, Frederick Law Olmsted, Jr., and Warren H. Manning, as well as others who like Parsons and Downing Vaux (Calvert Vaux's son) had strong connections to 19th-century landscape architectural practice. Other members, however, revealed a growing diversity in the group. Beatrix Jones Farrand, the only woman present, was from New York and had established her practice—as Ellen Biddle Shipman and other women now did—in residential design. The niece of Edith Wharton, Farrand had few cultural or professional allegiances to Fairsted (as Olmsted's Brookline office was known), which remained exclusively male. Another original member of the society, Ossian Cole Simonds, was a Midwesterner who had relied on an education in civil engineering and professional experience in architectural offices for his education as a landscape architect.[69]

The next year, Harvard University began the first academic program in landscape architecture under the direction of Frederick Law Olmsted, Jr. Olmsted's appointment at the age of twenty-nine reaffirmed the importance of the Olmsted office in the profession; but thereafter Harvard (soon joined by the universities of Massachusetts and Kansas in 1903, Cornell in 1904, and Michigan in 1907) eclipsed Fairsted as a center of landscape architectural training.[70] University degree programs inevitably emphasized an academic interest in historical prototypes and architectural training, as opposed to the more personal course of instruction in picturesque theory and Reptonian practice that the elder Olmsted had devised for his apprentices.[71]

In addition to these economic and institutional forces affecting landscape architecture and the design of parks at the turn of the century, developing transportation technologies continued to exert a critical influence on American park planning. In the early 19th century, omnibuses, railroads, and steam power had decentralized cities, which in turn had made the creation of parks in new, residential wards both feasible and desirable. But the revolution in transportation technology had only begun to shape the park movement. By the 1890s, electric traction increased the range and efficiency of commuter rail services and allowed subways to be built. Economical and durable street surfaces, such as asphalt, adapted formerly multipurpose streets into specialized conduits for vehicular traffic. With improved transportation, cities assumed ever greater diameters of metropolitan influence that soon exceeded even the expanded municipal boundaries that had been created through annexations of neighboring towns and villages. At the same time, such political expansion of municipal boundaries virtually ceased in older, more established urban areas. Once suburban villages had (or anticipated) basic services such as waterlines, sewers, and schools, they no longer favored incorporation into their larger neighbors. As a result, many older American cities, especially in the Northeast and Midwest, today retain municipal boundaries set in the late 19th and early 20th centuries.[72] As urban expansion continued to accelerate in the 20th century, metropolitan areas usually no longer coincided with a single political entity. Park systems limited by municipal jurisdictions, then, could no longer affect events occurring on the peripheries of metropolitan growth, where new park development typically had occurred in the past. Municipal park commissions—which had never been comprehensive planning agencies in the current sense—now typically concentrated on the maintenance of existing park systems and on the organization of recreational programs.

Park planning had been a municipal phenomenon in the 19th century; it reached the zenith of its influence during the most intense period of expanding municipal boundaries in the second half of the century. If the park movement were to continue to influence the subdivision and development of American landscapes in the 20th century, it would need new (and multiple) political sponsors and legislative mandates. It would also need new goals in some cases. Preserving public health, for example, could not be put forward as convincingly in the 20th century as a reason to develop parks. The belief that large public parks could improve public health depended on 19th-century miasmatic disease etiology, which held that gasses and odors rising from poorly drained, polluted areas spread disease. Large stands of trees were assumed to dissipate miasmas and encourage the flow of fresh, sanitized air. Because park development often involved improving drainage and eliminating sources of pollution in a given area, it reduced the perceived threat of disease. By the end of the century, however, germ theory was accepted, and advances in public sanitation had made urban epidemics less lethal. Although parks would continue to be associated with environmental health and improvement, they would no longer be considered major factors in the prevention of communicable disease.

Advances in public health, as well as transportation technology, meant that a fundamental reorientation of the park movement would need to take place if large, landscape parks were to continue to be set aside on the edges of American urbanization. Some of the premises of that reorientation appeared in the late 19th century. If the prevention of disease became a less effective argument in favor of parks, scenic preservation—the preservation of certain areas as parks based on their scenic qualities—increased in importance. The increased interest in scenic preservation was another function of improved transportation in the decades following the Civil War. From trolleys to transcontinental railroads, more affordable transportation encouraged tourism both near and far from home. As tourism expanded socially and geographically, the urge to preserve threatened scenery broadened as well. The creation of municipal parks had also helped establish a constituency for scenic preservation. Whether appreciating the engineered scenes of landscape parks close to home or the less contrived beauty of more remote scenic areas, the visual grammar and aesthetic language needed to interpret places as pictures, and land as landscape, remained constant for park visitor and regional tourist alike.

In William Cullen Bryant's massive 1874 catalog, *Picturesque America*, full-page engravings depict the variety of picturesque scenery available in the United States: municipal parks in cities such as Baltimore and Buffalo; regional scenic areas around cities from New York to San Francisco; classic tourist destinations from the White Mountains to Niagara Falls; and the more recently appreciated western scenery at Yosemite Valley and Yellowstone National Park.[73] The majority of the engravings selected in 1874 to be part of *Picturesque America*, in fact, depict places that either were, or have subsequently become, municipal, county, state, or national parks (or recreation areas within national and state forests). All of these places were more easily visited by tourists as metropolitan and national rail systems coalesced. Railroad executives like Jay Cooke had been quick to appreciate that as the numbers of domestic tourists swelled, the profits they generated could be significant;

but as a broader range of people engaged in tourism, scenic preservation became more of a popular cause.

Niagara Falls, the icon of American tourism, appropriately became the site of the first great victory for a popular coalition of scenic park advocates. Niagara, located on one of the most important transportation corridors of the 19th century, was already frequented by tourists in the 1820s. Many observers lamented the profusion of vendors, inns, and "catch-penny amusements" that had followed the tourists and settled permanently on both the Canadian and American sides of the falls. In his description of Niagara in *Picturesque America*, Bryant remarked that the falls resembled "a superb diamond set in lead."[74] Although many regretted Niagara's descent into a commercialized attraction, specific remedies remained elusive. The municipal park movement, however, offered the kind of legal and conceptual precedents needed to preserve Niagara. Olmsted, who had seen the potential for preserving Yosemite Valley as a landscape park in 1864, by 1869 advocated that the New York State Legislature condemn and acquire the property on the American side of the falls and appoint a park commission to administer it.[75]

Working with the surveyor James T. Gardner in 1879, Olmsted produced an initial plan for the restoration of the scenery above the falls, calling for the demolition of offending structures and the restoration of the shoreline to resemble its condition previous to industrial and commercial development. The necessary legislation, however, stalled in the state capital; in order for the Niagara campaign to succeed, public opinion would need to be enlisted. In 1880, Olmsted and Charles Eliot Norton, the Harvard art historian and a long time friend, launched what would from that time become the most effective tool of scenic preservation: the media campaign. They encouraged fellow advocates to write articles on the falls, and they raised funds to subsidize those efforts. They pressed editors to publish articles and letters in magazines and newspapers and to add their own editorial voices in favor of the legislation. In 1883, the New York State Legislature responded to public opinion—not to a request by a railroad or other special interest—and created a commission empowered to acquire the land around the falls and to manage it as a scenic reservation. In 1887, Olmsted and Vaux presented a report to the Niagara commissioners further elaborating how park development could be employed to preserve the scenic value of the falls by eliminating structures and re-establishing indigenous communities of trees and shrubs along the shoreline. Partially restored to its earlier condition, after 1885 Niagara was open to the public as the Niagara State Reservation.[76]

In 1883, as the campaign to preserve Niagara was moving to a successful completion, Frederick Law Olmsted relocated to Brookline, Massachusetts, and became increasingly committed to the design of a major park system for the city of Boston. Between 1879 and 1900, Boston acquired over two thousand acres of parks, much of the land in suburban areas that, like West Roxbury, had been recently annexed.[77]

Olmsted became the principal consultant for the design of these parks in 1878, and beginning in 1883 he conducted business from his home at 99 Warren Street, which he named Fairsted.[78] Olmsted was now in his sixties, and in 1884 his stepson John Charles, who had been working with the firm since 1875, was made a full partner in the business. Other young assistants and apprentices joined the firm in the 1880s and 1890s, including Henry Sargent Codman, Charles Eliot, Warren H. Manning, and Frederick Law Olmsted, Jr.[79]

If Fairsted served unofficially during this period as the first American school of landscape architecture, the city of Boston was its laboratory. The Fairsted apprentices worked on projects such as the Back Bay Fens, the Arnold Arboretum, and Franklin Park, all completed or well advanced in the 1880s, as well as the Muddy River Improvement, Jamaica Pond, and Marine Park, which were being planned.[80] This work also allowed Olmsted to work with architects, especially Henry Hobson Richardson, and later the firm of Shepley, Rutan and Coolidge, who were amenable to his suggestions for the character and materials he preferred for park bridges, shelters, and other structures. Earlier in his career, Olmsted had acquiesced to the more colorful and playful Gothic revival of Calvert Vaux in the design of cast iron and carved limestone details for park structures. Richardson, best remembered for his Romanesque revival churches and Shingle Style homes, provided more sympathetic structures, such as his Boylston Street Bridge design for the Back Bay Fens (ca. 1880), which suggested a rough masonry of native fieldstone. In other commissions, such as the Ames Monument (1879) and the Ames Gate Lodge (1880), Richardson employed massive scale and rough masonry finishes to evoke geological formations in architectural design. The increasingly professional and diverse group at the Fairsted office also produced many of the plans for bridges and structures themselves. Boulder masonry, log furniture, and other construction details featuring native stone and rough lumber were widely used in the Boston park system in the 1880s and 1890s. Shelters and benches often featured oversized proportions and rusticated finishes.[81]

Architectural construction of this type had always been employed in the more wooded areas of municipal parks, such as the Ramble and the north end of Central Park, where it recalled mountain resort architecture from the Adirondacks to the Alps; but various forms of stylized "rustic" construction gained increasing currency as an appropriate architectural style for large parks generally in the late 19th century. As smaller parks and playgrounds in Boston (such as the contemporary Charlesbank) were devoted to recreation and institutional uses, larger parks, like Franklin Park and the Riverway, retained their association with picturesque scenic values. The massive proportions and rough materials of Shingle Style architecture and the boulder bridges and log furniture designed by the Fairsted office in the 1880s reinforced the association of these larger parks with the experience and appreciation of relatively rural scenic beauty.[82] Smaller parks and playgrounds, in contrast, featured outdoor gymnasia, neoclassical bathhouses, fountains, and pergolas, all organized in axial site plans. The distinction between the large park and the small park—and the appropriate physical development of each—increased as playground and recreation advocates redirected the policies of many municipal park commissions. The "rustic" site furniture and construction details associated with the more wooded and remote portions of earlier landscape parks increasingly identified the value of large parks as a whole, because the larger, often wooded portions of these parks were the principal visual assets that distinguished them from the playgrounds and small parks in the inner city.

The design precedents set by the Olmsted firm in Boston in the 1880s influenced the character of the landscape development subsequently proposed for large, regional parks beyond Boston's municipal boundaries (and soon outside other large cities as well). One of Olmsted's most important apprentices at Fairsted, Charles Eliot, planned the first "metropolitan" system of "reservations" in the early 1890s. Eliot's concept of a regional system of scenic reservations for the suburbs around Boston proceeded directly out of his participation in the design of the municipal park system in the 1880s. We know a considerable amount about his apprenticeship at Fairsted at that time because his father, Harvard University president Charles W. Eliot, described it in detail in the biography he wrote after his son died, at the age of thirty-seven, in 1897.[83]

Charles Eliot began a two-year apprenticeship in Olmsted's office in 1883. His father reports that he "was taught to distrust specimen planting," and that "parks" (large parks, in other words) should not feature "trimmed trees, flowers in pots, clipped grass, and variegated flower or foliage beds." Such artifice "savored of the city, or at least of the suburb," whereas "undulating meadows fringed with trees, quiet, far-stretching pastoral scenery, and groves which preserved the underbrush and the rough surface of the natural forest" typified the rural qualities preferred for the landscape park. And of course "artificial features," such as "paths, roads, resting-places and restaurants," were "not the objects of any landscape undertaking, but its necessary impediments." President Eliot went on to state that his son's teacher, Olmsted, "regarded park-land in its actual condition as a fine piece of rural scenery, to be religiously preserved so far as the use and enjoyment of the place by the public would permit, as a scene of quiet character, graceful and picturesque by turns, in which only such changes and additions should be permitted as would bring out still further the prevailing character of the place . . . in furtherance of nature."[84]

Charles Eliot imbibed these orthodox principles of picturesque aesthetics and Reptonian park design as Olmsted's student.[85] After his apprenticeship and a European tour, Eliot went into practice on his own in Boston in 1887. Olmsted had reminded him that he had "a professional duty" to "write for the public," since he was able to serve "the cause," in this regard, "better than any English writing man."[86] Eliot began writing on his converging interests in landscape design and scenic preservation. He found a ready publisher in Charles Sprague Sargent, the director of the Arnold Arboretum and founder of *Garden and Forest*, a magazine which between 1888 and 1897 demonstrated its publisher's combined interests in landscape architecture, horticulture, scenic preservation, and scientific forest management. Sargent himself was an important advocate for the creation and management of forest reserves and national parks, as well as the co-designer of the Arnold Arboretum and a pioneering figure in American horticulture.[87] His magazine advocated scenic preservation and scientific forestry in both the Boston area and the Far West. In 1888, Eliot wrote a letter to the editor of *Garden and Forest* on the subject of the "Waverley Oaks," a picturesque grove of ancient trees near Boston that was endangered by expanding residential development. Noting that "a crowded population thirsts, occasionally at least, for the sight of something very different from the public garden, square, or ball-field," Eliot remarked that "the railroads and new electric street railways . . . carry many thousands every pleasant Sunday through the suburbs to the real country . . . for the sake of the refreshment . . . the country brings to them." But the areas around Boston possessing "uncommon beauty and more than usual refreshing power" were largely in private hands and "in daily danger of utter destruction."

The ancient grove of oaks in Waverley was one such area; but there were many others to be added to the list, and almost all of them were outside the municipal boundaries of Boston. In his letter, Eliot suggested "the finest bits of natural scenery near Boston" might be saved "to delight many future generations" if an incorporated association made up of citizens of the towns around Boston were empowered by the State Legislature to hold various parcels of land, free of taxes, for the use of the public.[88] Working with Sargent, as well as George C. Mann, the president of the Appalachian Mountain Club, and Sylvester Baxter, a journalist from Malden, Eliot organized an effective public relations campaign, reminiscent of the efforts to create the state reservation at Niagara; but in this case the campaign sought to preserve not a single outstanding natural feature, but a system of scenic places representing the characteristic landscapes of the region. In 1891, they succeeded in having legislation passed to create the "Trustees of Public Reservations," a group of citizens empowered to hold "real estate such as it may deem worthy of preservation for the enjoyment of the public."[89] The Trustees, who appointed Eliot as secretary, depended on gifts and bequests to create parks; but they also began assembling the surveys and recommendations that would result in the creation of a Metropolitan Park Commission one year later, when the State Legislature authorized a park commission to suggest a system of scenic reservations for the suburbs around Boston.

In 1893, this unique park commission, with Eliot as landscape architect and Baxter as secretary, was given the powers to condemn land and "acquire, maintain, and make available . . . open spaces for exercise and recreation" in thirty-seven separate Massachusetts municipalities.[90] Over the next several years, Eliot oversaw the acquisition of over nine thousand acres of large, scenic parks and connecting parkways in the suburbs within a ten-mile radius of Boston, including shores and islands of the inner Massachusetts Bay, beaches, estuaries, forests, and characteristic geological formations of scenic interest.[91] Eliot demonstrated that scenic preservation could be a basis for regional planning in the 20th century, based on the precedent of municipal park and parkway planning in the 19th century. Since improved transportation allowed park visitors to reach suburban woods, waterfalls, and geologic features with close to the same level of convenience that they had once visited municipal landscape parks, the scenic reservation could become an enlarged landscape park in an expanded park and parkway system. The goal of Eliot's scenic reservations was, as it once had been for the municipal landscape park, to provide what he called in his 1893 plan for the Metropolitan Park Commission, the "space for air, for light, for exercise, for rest, and for the enjoyment of the peaceful beauty of nature which, because it is the opposite of the noisy ugliness of towns, is so wonderfully refreshing to the tired souls of townspeople."[92]

Eliot's call for scenic preservation around Boston echoed the rhetoric Olmsted had composed for the municipal park movement almost fifty years earlier.[93] The ideal had not changed but the geographic setting of the landscape park had moved out to where such park development had always made the most sense: the periphery of the urban sphere of influence. The ultimate justification for such parks remained the same as well; Eliot emphasized the healthful benefits available to the individual, and to society as a whole, through the free, public opportunity for the aesthetic appreciation of landscape beauty.

Many city, county, and state governments, emulating the metropolitan Boston work, created regional historic and scenic reservations in the 1890s and the first decade of the 20th century. In 1895, Andrew Haswell Green, the former comptroller of Central Park, founded the American Scenic and Historic Preservation Society, a group authorized by the New York State Legislature and dedicated to the "preservation of natural scenery from disfigurement, for the creation of public parks for the health comfort and recreation of the people, and for the beautification of cities and villages."[94] Green hoped the society would "provide the machinery for performing the same work for New York State that 'The Trustees of Public Reservations' provides for the Commonwealth of Massachusetts."[95] The society was active in the campaign to preserve the Palisades, a prominent escarpment of volcanic rock along the Hudson River opposite New York City. Local businessmen had discovered that the basaltic formation of the Palisades crushed into excellent gravel, which was in demand to satisfy the huge local demand for asphalt and concrete. The scenic cliffs were rapidly excavated and blasted in the 1890s, in full view of thousands watching from across the river. In 1900, legislation was passed in the state legislatures of New Jersey and New York creating an Interstate Park Commission empowered to condemn and develop parkland in the two states to preserve the cliffs.[96] The American Scenic and Historic Preservation Society subsequently participated in the creation of a series of scenic parks across New York State, including Watkins Glen (1906), Letchworth Gorge (1907), and the extension of the Palisades Interstate Park up the Hudson to Bear Mountain (1910).[97]

In Minnesota, the action of the Minneapolis park commissioners in preserving Minnehaha Falls in 1885 served as a precedent for the preservation of Lake Itasca as a state park (1891), and at the Dalles of the St. Croix River (1895), an area of scenic rapids that had been a tourist destination since the mid-19th century. The Dalles became part of another Interstate Park five years later when Wisconsin created a complementary park on the other side of the river.[98] In California, the Sempirvirens Club was organized in 1900, and after a concerted public relations campaign succeeded in having the California Legislature pass a 1901 bill authorizing a California Redwood Park Commission. Over the next ten years, the commission acquired thousands of acres of old growth coast redwoods, including the California Redwood State Park in 1902. In 1918, another private group in California, the Save-the-Redwoods League, was organized and successfully lobbied for more coast redwood reservations to the north.[99] One of the those most active in the Save-the-Redwoods League was Stephen Tyng Mather, a native Californian who in 1917 had become the first director of the new National Park Service.

Before the end of World War I, state governments in Ohio, Idaho, Illinois, Pennsylvania, Connecticut, Indiana, Iowa, New Jersey, and North Carolina all empowered park commissions to acquire and manage parks in areas determined to have outstanding historical interest or scenic value.[100] County governments became active in creating scenic reservations beginning in 1895, when Essex County in northern New Jersey created a system of parks that included scenic reservations in the hills around Newark, as well as smaller parks and playgrounds in the city.[101] In Chicago, a Special Park Commission was organized in 1899 to suggest an outline for a Cook County park system based on Eliot's metropolitan park system. In 1904, the landscape architect for the commission, Jens Jensen, proposed a system of scenic reservations around Chicago based on the scenic, geological, and ecological characteristics of the area.[102] Although not immediately implemented, the plan was reiterated by Burnham in his 1909 city plan, and many of the reservations were eventually set aside after the Illinois Legislature passed a 1913 bill authorizing the creation of county "forest preserve districts" that functioned essentially as county park commissions.[103] In the West, municipal governments were sometimes able to create regional park systems. The Denver Mountain Park system, begun in 1912, extended the Denver municipal park and parkway system with a series of scenic reservations that were acquired outside municipal boundaries.[104] Such mountain parks, with connecting scenic drives, became characteristic of regional park development undertaken by many western municipalities in the early 20th century.

In almost all of these cases, the physical development of regional scenic reservations—whether in the suburbs of a metropolis or in relatively remote scenic areas—followed certain tendencies. The geometric gardens, axial site plans, and architectural embellishments that had become common in city parks usually found no place in scenic reservations. Playgrounds, outdoor gymnasia, and other recreational development, although not completely banished, were kept subordinate to avoid interfering with the visitors' appreciation of landscape scenery. The 20th-century scenic reservation, like the 19th-century municipal landscape park, featured curvilinear drives and paths that conformed to topography and offered constantly shifting views in a considered sequence. In the Boston metropolitan parks and other regional parks, views were carefully considered in the placement of roads, buildings, and other facilities, and response to indigenous landscape character and features determined the particulars of site planning. And since the appreciation of landscape scenery remained the primary purpose of these parks, all construction—whether of a simple guard rail or of a large hotel—was designed to remain a consonant, subdued element in perceived landscape compositions.

Charles Eliot recognized, however, that larger scenic reservations demanded a new balance of landscape development, forest management, and preservation of natural systems. If the 19th-century municipal park had required extensive landscape engineering to produce desired picturesque effects, the 20th-century scenic reservation often eliminated the need for heavy manipulation of topography and hydrology, since the reservation (to a greater degree than the municipal park) could be selected according to its existing scenic qualities. But the formal features and engineering techniques developed earlier in municipal landscape park design were adapted as needed in the more limited development of scenic reservations.

In 1897, Eliot described some of the management priorities for the Boston metropolitan reservations in a report to the Metropolitan Park Commissioners. It was "quite unlikely," he wrote, "that there will ever be any need of artificially modifying . . . [the reservations] to any considerable degree. Such paths or roads as will be needed to make the scenery accessible will be mere slender threads of graded surface winding over and among the huge natural forms of the ground."[105] He went on to discuss other traditional aspects of landscape park engineering as they applied to the development of his metropolitan reservations. Although "the waters of the reservations . . . may be artificially ponded here and there," major hydrological engineering would be unnecessary, since the natural flow of seasonal streams was preferable, and would not affect "more than the local scenery of the hollows or ravines in which they flow." The element of traditional park design for which Eliot perceived the greatest need was the control of "the vegetation which clothes the surface everywhere." Whereas "much of the most striking scenery of the world," he noted, "is almost or quite devoid of verdure . . . here in New England, we cannot get rid of verdure, even if we would."[106] Eliot advocated selected cutting of forests based on the aesthetic desirability of the resulting views. Having determined that "vegetation in the reservations is an exceedingly important component part of the scenery," he concluded that the character of that vegetation resulted from "continuous interference with natural processes by men, fire, and browsing animals." It followed that "the notion that it would be wrong and even sacrilegious to suggest that this vegetation ought to be controlled and modified must be mistaken." Eliot believed that "to *preserve* existing beauty, grass-lands must continue to be mowed or pastured annually, trees must be removed from shrubberies, competing trees must be kept away from veteran oaks and chestnuts, and so on. . . . To prepare for *increasing* the interest and beauty of the scenery, work must be directed to removing screens of foliage, to opening vistas through 'notches,' to substituting low ground-cover for high woods in many places, and to other like operations." He provided watercolor sketches to illustrate his points.[107]

In scenic reservations in other parts of the country the specific remedies may have been different, but landscape architects and park officials managing those parks shared Eliot's concern for the visual experience of regional landscape scenery. If scenic views were lost or impaired through the growth of vegetation, the public would miss an important aspect of its experience of the place. Keeping vistas open from roads, paths, and overlooks therefore figured in management plans. Landscape management otherwise was kept as inconspicuous as possible, and physical development exhibited a character considered appropriate to the character of what were often wooded, relatively secluded landscapes. In terms of construction details, this meant that the Boston metropolitan reservations continued the use of native stone masonry and wood construction that had been started in Boston municipal parks, such as Franklin Park.[108] Comfort stations, shelters and other buildings considered necessary for day-trippers and weekend tourists were not allowed to overwhelm the primary purpose of the scenic reservations, which was to provide the free and public opportunity for the appreciation of large-scale landscape beauty. Other regional parks and regional park systems showed the same inclinations. In parks developed in the years before World War I, such as Bear Mountain, New York, and Lake Itasca, Minnesota, tourist lodges were built of peeled logs and boulders, and scenic drives employed stone guardwalls and heavy wooden signs.[109] The Bear Mountain Inn was described at the time as "a rugged heap of boulders and huge chestnut logs assembled by the hand of man, and yet following lines of such natural proportions as to resemble the eternal hills themselves."[110] Curvilinear roads and trails, decentralized services for camping, hiking, and other activities, and minimal alterations to the existing landscape all characterized the development of regional scenic reservations in the early 20th century.

Landscape architects such as Charles Eliot provided the formal and conceptual basis for 20th-century landscape park development by adapting their training in 19th-century municipal landscape park work to the scale and context of regional parks. The continuity between municipal and regional park design was particularly evident in the 1890s, when civic improvement, scenic preservation, horticulture, and forestry were among interests shared by landscape architects, civic groups, and other park advocates.

In the spring of 1897, shortly after Eliot's premature death, a group of professionals led by J. C. Olmsted and Warren Manning began efforts to organize landscape architects nationally, eventually leading to the establishment of the American Society of Landscape Architects two years later. The first group they organized, however, the American Park and Outdoor Art Association, was intended to bring together a much broader coalition than an ordinary professional society. Made up of landscape architects, park commissioners, village improvement societies, women's groups, and various other individuals interested in parks and civic improvement, the American Park and Outdoor Art Association held its first meeting in Louisville to "promote the conservation of natural scenery, the acquirement and improvement of land for public parks and reservations, and the advancement of all outdoor art having to do with the designing and fitting of grounds for public and private use and enjoyment."[111]

J. C. Olmsted, the principal spokesman for his profession since his stepfather's retirement two years earlier, gave the keynote address for the group on "The True Purpose of a Large Public Park."[112] His description of the true purpose of large municipal parks matched Eliot's ideals for metropolitan reservations, emphasizing the common goals shared by the scenic preservationists and landscape architects present at the conference. The purpose of large parks, he asserted, was "to provide for the dwellers in cities convenient opportunity to enjoy beautiful natural scenery." "Large parks" should "contain a complete natural landscape, where the boundaries will not be obtrusive, where one may stroll over hill and dale, across meadows and through woods always amid natural surroundings for hours and hours . . . where many thousands of visitors may be enjoying the scenery at the same time without crowding each other . . . [where] the roar of street traffic is less noticeable than the rustle of leaves."[113]

His ideas for how the large, municipal park should be developed also reiterated Eliot's prescriptions for the management of regional parks. The preservation of "beautiful natural scenery" was justified by "public use and enjoyment"; but public use demanded the construction of roads and paths, as well as overlooks, shelters, and provisions for other activities. Grading for this construction "should be so shaped and finished as to appear natural or at least as closely in harmony with natural surfaces as study and care can make it." Olmsted criticized those municipal parks in which, he felt, through the "lack of appreciation of the true purpose of a large public park," the grading of earth was "made as regular and unnatural as possible, so that what might have been done in harmony with the natural scenery antagonizes it and greatly lessens its value for its true purpose." In the same vein, "water surfaces" in parks should appear "natural in their outline," an effect again dependent on working with the "plans and directions of a trained artist" to produce "natural effects in park grading." And since "the verdure of a large park is what the eye rests upon almost everywhere," the management of vegetation again demanded special consideration. An interesting woodland understory, for example, would be preferable to thinning the trees and establishing turf; shrubs and trees "indigenous to the region" were more likely to produce "a nearly natural landscape" than were gardenesque displays of ornamental and exotic plants.

In general, Olmsted felt that "if gardeners studied natural scenery more, they would almost surely discover many opportunities in parks for the application of what they could observe in the country." Echoing his stepfather's concerns for the management of parks devoted primarily to the appreciation of scenic beauty, he emphasized that "conspicuous artificial objects unnecessary for the convenient use of the park should be excluded . . . there is no more important matter, after a large park has been acquired and its natural scenery perfected, than that of protecting it from serious injury by the introduction of buildings and other artificial objects." The justification for excluding what J. C. Olmsted called "Coney Island" amusements from these landscapes, and for the other rigorous aesthetic guidelines he summarized for his colleagues in 1897, was "preserving a large park in its simple, natural beauty, as a priceless heritage for future generations."

The principles of picturesque landscape design described by J. C. Olmsted had served the American park movement since the 1860s, when his stepfather and Calvert Vaux had harmonized two potentially opposing goals: preserving the "sense of enlarged freedom" that beautiful scenery could impart to the individual, while also providing the "opportunity for people to come together" and create an enlarged sense of community. The 19th-century park movement also provided legal and administrative precedents for how scenic areas outside cities could be acquired and administered as public places. The maturing profession of landscape architecture, represented by a second generation of practitioners, provided the technical and aesthetic discipline that suggested how to develop such places for public use—in other words how to make them into parks.

If the imposition of monuments and institutions had altered the carefully composed landscape sequences in Central Park or Golden Gate Park, picturesque aesthetics and Reptonian principles continued to guide development at new state parks like Lake Itasca or California Redwoods. If organized recreation had made inroads on 19th-century urban greenswards and "Keep Off the Grass" signs were taken down, the preservation of natural features, plants, and animals would assume increased urgency in the larger reservations, farther from the city. If improved transportation technology had made the municipal landscape park obsolete by making what Eliot called "the real country" more accessible to city dwellers, the same technology made scenic reservations viable by bringing day-trippers to the countryside, creating a constituency for regional parks not unlike that which had existed earlier for municipal landscape parks. As the municipal landscape park perhaps became, in the words of Richard Morris Hunt, "less of a park and more of a garden," a new generation of park advocates employed the aesthetic ideals of pastoral calm and picturesque beauty—ideals that had been embodied in scores of municipal parks—to identify and appreciate areas of natural beauty in still rural counties around cities like Boston and Denver, as well as in more remote scenic areas in states like New York, Minnesota, and California.

The American landscape park was born in the city but moved to the country. The public's use of such regional parks in some ways represented an extension of their use of older municipal parks. The American industrial economy matured in the early 20th century, and American workers began to enjoy increased leisure time and a higher standard of living. The urban middle class grew into a proportionately larger segment of society.[114] Many Americans, leaving behind the restrictions of farm life, achieved new levels of material comfort and personal freedom by finding work and living in cities. Measured in leisure time and disposable income, affluence increased; measured in the widespread popularity of certain games and recreational activities, interest in recreation intensified.

Organized sports and recreation of all types attracted both participants and spectators after the Civil War, and their appeal steadily grew in the 1880s and 1890s. But no form of recreation ultimately proved more popular to Americans than discretionary travel—tourism—and related activities. By the 1890s, Saturday half holidays and two-week annual vacations encouraged weekend outings and summer vacations not just for the wealthy (who had always traveled) but for laborers and salaried workers. Ever more numerous urban populations bypassed municipal parks and scoured the countryside looking for appropriate destinations for Sunday outings. Getting "back to nature" with enthusiasm, these vacationers engaged in a variety of outdoor activities, such as walking, riding, mountain climbing, fishing, hunting, camping, and boating.[115]

In the years preceding World War I, regional landscape parks such as Bear Mountain, New York, drew large crowds of the mostly urban, middle class visitors who had always been the core constituents for municipal landscape parks.[116] When early-20th-century tourists arrived at county or state reservations, they expected to find parks that encompassed the natural scenery they had come to admire, that had roads and trails to make the scenery accessible, and that often featured lodges, campgrounds, and facilities for various outdoor activities. Some of these activities, such as boating and horseback riding, were directly analogous to what visitors had done in municipal parks in the 19th century. In other cases, activities changed, reflecting a more egalitarian and vigorous approach to outdoor recreation. The promenade, for example, was replaced by the more vigorous hike or climb. Sports like lawn tennis and croquet rarely made the transition to the larger park, while swimming greatly increased in popularity.[117] The more remote destinations of regional parks meant that, in some cases, overnight lodging or camping were necessities; in other cases, camping was just another form of recreation. Above all, the upper-class rituals of the

Sunday carriage parade were soon replaced by what became the more middle class preoccupation with motorized vehicles. The intermingled activities of picturesque tourism and outdoor recreation reached new heights at this time, in no small part fueled by recreational uses of new automobiles. The advocacy for regional and state parks was led by people who, more and more, arrived in the countryside in motor vehicles and who made those vehicles an integral part of their recreational activities and sightseeing.

The availability of relatively inexpensive and mechanically reliable automobiles facilitated this move "back to nature" in ways that carriages, electric rail, and bicycles could not. The automobile remained somewhat of a luxury before 1910; but in 1908 Henry Ford introduced his Model T, and within five years he had increased production efficiency and lowered retail prices to unprecedented degrees. In 1916 Ford sold over 760,000 of the vehicles, a huge number that nevertheless accounted only for half the automobiles sold in the United States that year. By 1920, over eight million automobiles were registered in the United States, or one for every thirteen people.[118] Although many of these vehicles were used for commercial purposes, many more simply made life more convenient and bearable for people who had previously been isolated, whether that isolation was rural or urban; just as the amenities of town life beckoned to those on remote farms, country scenery drew tourists out from crowded cities.

Independent of rail lines, schedules, and tour operators, automobiles enhanced all forms of outdoor recreation, since they offered access to the most scenic places to hike, picnic, or camp. Auto tourism and camping, at first adventurous hobbies for the well-to-do, soon were a more affordable (and for many a more enjoyable) means of touring the countryside than traveling by train and staying in hotels had ever been.[119] And of course driving an automobile enabled and extended what had always been the principal mode of experiencing regional landscape beauty: the view from the road.

As leisure time became a reality for a much broader segment of American society, the availability of automobiles transformed patterns of recreational activities. And in the national parks, the influence of automotive technology pervaded almost every aspect of how parks were developed, managed, and used. Automobiles—and the crowds of tourists they conveyed—made the national park system as we know it possible. The model of the 20th-century landscape park, and the success of scenic preservation in the early 20th century in general, depended on the ever-broadening appeal of outdoor recreation and regional tourism. Affordable and reliable motor vehicles made those opportunities possible for more people than ever before, and allowed the national park to assume a central role in the culture of popular recreation.

"Conserve the Scenery":
The National Park as 20th-Century Landscape Park

Chapter 2

National parks flourished, often despite considerable opposition, amid the rapid social and technological changes of the Progressive era. Progressive enthusiasms for scenic preservation and outdoor recreation precipitated an unsurpassed era of federal legislation establishing scenic reservations out of federal lands in the West.

Before 1890, Yellowstone was still "the national park," as unique institutionally as it was geologically. Over the next twenty-five years, Congress passed legislation establishing many of the famous western parks: Yosemite, Sequoia, and General Grant in 1890; Mount Rainier and Crater Lake in 1899 and 1902; Glacier and Rocky Mountain in 1910 and 1915. In addition, Congress passed an act for "the preservation of American antiquities" in 1906, which allowed the president to proclaim "national monuments" on public land that contained "objects of historic or scientific interest."[1] Passed the same year that Congress created Mesa Verde National Park, the Antiquities Act led to the preservation of numerous other archeological sites, as well as a number of geological wonders such as Devils Tower, Wyoming, that were declared national monuments. Presidents since Theodore Roosevelt have also used this executive power to withdraw large areas quickly, reserving them from private claims while a less decisive Congress was coaxed into passing the necessary legislation to create a national park.[2] Roosevelt declared Lassen Peak and Grand Canyon national monuments, for example, in 1907 and 1908; President Taft declared Mount Olympus and Zion Canyon national monuments in 1909. Congress then created Lassen National Park in 1916 and Grand Canyon and Zion Canyon national parks in 1919; it finally established Olympic National Park in 1938.[3]

The legislative campaigns to create this array of federal scenic reservations differed from park advocacies at state and local levels in several respects. Since national parks were proposed in areas still in the public domain, for example, the drive for a national park often became mired in congressional politics. Proposed national parks might contain lands that were potentially valuable for grazing, reservoir sites, or logging; park bills that restricted an identifiable commercial opportunity of any type were likely to antagonize local senators and representatives.[4] The contemporary Progressive conservation movement, which sought to reform government management of natural resources in the public domain, also challenged the national park as an outdated and inefficient method of managing public land. And potential tourists for new national parks, unlike visitors to regional scenic reservations, lived much farther from the parks themselves. The national parks created during this period were all in the West, but in 1890 over ninety percent of the American population remained in the East and Midwest. San Francisco had grown into the country's eighth largest city with 297,000 people, but among other western cities only Denver exceeded 100,000 residents.[5] The smaller populations of western urban centers and the vast amounts of open space in the West meant that national parks would obviously serve different interests and constituencies than, for example, Eliot and Baxter brought together in the suburbs of Boston in the 1890s.

Despite these differing contexts, however, national park campaigns at the turn of the century shared values and tactics with the rest of the American park movement. If municipal park development had been encouraged by the clear relationship between parks and enhanced real estate values, national park legislation drew political support from another proven economic reality: tourism yielded great profits to those who transported and accommodated tourists. Tourism offered a lucrative form of development for arid or mountainous lands, which, not conducive to agriculture and regular settlement, might not otherwise experience a rise in value or generate paying traffic for rail lines. Just as real estate interests lent their political weight to municipal park advocates, railroad companies, who stood the most to gain from western tourism, wielded decisive political power on Capitol Hill in favor of national park legislation. But popular scenic preservation campaigns on the model of the Niagara effort also increased in their relative importance during the Progressive era. This confluence between the interests of powerful capitalists and the aspirations of Progressive idealists characterized scenic preservation efforts on the national scale in the decades before World War I.

In California, for example, a remarkable sequence of events led to the passage of legislation that authorized three national parks in the Sierra Nevada. By the 1880s Sierran mountain meadows provided pasture for huge herds of sheep, while sequoia groves and pine forests attracted growing logging operations. A local journalist, George W. Stewart, began to advocate a park or scenic reservation in the High Sierra to protect alpine meadows and giant sequoias. His campaign gained momentum when farmers in the San Joaquin Valley became convinced that overgrazing and deforestation in the southern Sierra threatened the seasonal waterflow of streams that irrigated their land.[6] Apparently Stewart also succeeded in attracting the attention of the Southern Pacific Railroad. Water for irrigation increased land values and made agricultural and commercial development possible over large areas. Preserving watersheds therefore protected many of the railroad's economic interests. Stewart had pursued some kind of state or federal legislation to protect the high Sierran peaks since 1880; but not until Representative William Vandever of Los Angeles introduced a bill based on Stewart's recommendations in 1890 did Congress consider the proposal seriously. At that point, both houses passed the bill with little or no debate. In fact, Congress also passed a second bill (introduced by Vandever later in 1890) which had, again, originally been urged by a group interested in scenic preservation in the Sierra Nevada. In this case John Muir, the nature writer, and Robert Underwood Johnson, the editor of *Century* magazine, had orchestrated a campaign to create an extended Yosemite National Park around the state park at Yosemite Valley. Getting such legislation through Congress at all presented challenges enough. When this second bill came before the House of Representatives for a vote, however, Vandever had it replaced at the last moment with substitute legislation that delineated a Yosemite National Park five times the size originally envisioned. In addition, the substitute bill tripled the size of Sequoia National Park (which had just been created) and established a third park, General Grant National Park, to preserve a giant sequoia grove just north of Sequoia. This remarkable and mysterious legislation subsequently moved through Congress quickly, again with almost no debate, despite the fact that it withdrew hundreds of square miles of public land from private claims or development.

In a recent history of Sequoia and Kings Canyon National Parks, historians Lary M. Dilsaver and William C. Tweed conclude that although the "origins and motivations" of the Sequoia-Yosemite legislation of 1890 remain mysterious, Representative Vandever (whose district was not anywhere near the proposed parks) was probably acting as an agent of the Southern Pacific Railroad, which wanted to protect the watersheds vital to its interests. "Presumably the motivation was nothing less than corporate greed," they observe, "an irony seldom appreciated by modern students of the Sierran national parks."[7] On the other hand, without the activities of individuals like Stewart, Johnson, and Muir, the railroad might not have ever become involved in backing park legislation in the first place.

Individuals and groups advocating outdoor recreation and scenic preservation were active in other parts of the West as well. Since 1886, a Portland judge, William Gladstone Steel, had campaigned for the creation of a Crater Lake National Park in Oregon, to preserve the unique and spectacular lake that had begun to draw tourists to the southern Cascades.[8] In another example in the Pacific Northwest, several groups, including the National Geographic Society, the Sierra Club, and the Appalachian Mountain Club, launched a concerted effort in 1893 to create a national park at Mount Rainier, in Washington. This volcanic peak, visible from the growing Puget Sound communities of Seattle and Tacoma, had received initial protection that year when it had been made part of a national forest reserve. Logging and grazing were difficult to control, however, and since the 1880s, Muir and others had felt that park legislation would be the most effective way of preserving meadows and forests at lower elevations around the mountain itself.[9] In the Rocky Mountains, spectacular scenery was also attracting tourists, and therefore the interest of scenic preservationists. George Bird Grinnell, a sportsman and journalist from New York, first saw the lakes and glaciers of the northern Rockies in the 1885, when he explored the St. Mary Lake region. He later reported his experiences in his magazine, *Field and Stream*. Over the next twenty-five years, in addition to publishing and his other work in the fields of conservation and ethnography, Grinnell urged the creation of Glacier National Park.

In many areas of the country, magazine publishers, nature writers, sportsmen, and mountain climbers gradually developed into organized interest groups with the common goal of preserving wilderness, mountain scenery, game habitats, and other areas of natural beauty. In 1892, Muir organized a group of Californians interested in outdoor recreation and scenic preservation and established the Sierra Club in San Francisco, in order to "explore, enjoy, and render accessible the mountain regions of the Pacific Coast . . . [and] to enlist the support and cooperation of the people and the government in preserving the forests and other natural features of the Sierra Nevada Mountains."[10] In 1894, George Stewart organized another mountaineering club, the Mazamas, which publicized the recreational opportunities of the Cascades and lobbied for the creation of national parks in the Northwest. Eastern groups, such as the Appalachian Mountain Club, the Boone and Crockett Club, and the American Scenic and Historic Preservation Society often expressed interest in western scenic preservation, since many of their members traveled in the West while vacationing. All of these groups cultivated a constituency of scenic park advocates by organizing park visitors and representing their interests. By publicizing and encouraging outdoor recreation in its many forms—from simply appreciating scenery to actually ascending its highest peaks—park advocates widened the appeal of scenic preservation.

Events in the 1890s, however, complicated the situation for national park legislation, and the success of Yosemite and Sequoia national parks was not easily repeated in the Rockies or the Cascades. The Sierran park bill of 1890 had successfully confused the goals of scientific forestry with those of scenic preservation. Since the 1870s, scientific forestry and scenic preservation had often been part of the same cause: to prevent the wasteful despoliation of the remaining natural resources in the United States. The founding members of the American Forestry Association established in 1875, for example, included landscape architects and scenic preservationists as well as professional foresters.[11]

No one better illustrates this combination of interests than Charles Sprague Sargent. A scientist as well as a landscape designer, in 1879 Sargent began a government survey of the condition of American forests that was the first comprehensive study of its type. In the 1880s, he collaborated with Frederick Law Olmsted in the design of the Arnold Arboretum, while encouraging Charles Eliot to pursue the creation of a metropolitan park system. After seeing the northern Rockies in 1882, he became an effective supporter, with George Bird Grinnell, of Glacier National Park legislation.[12] In 1884, Sargent headed the New York State commission investigating the condition of the newly created Adirondack Forest Preserve, of which he had earlier been a prominent advocate. He subsequently helped draft the 1885 New York State legislation dictating that the unprecedented forest preserve should "be forever kept as wild forest lands." At that time, apparently, "forever wild" did not necessarily preclude logging operations, which continued in the Adirondacks. Even the 1892 legislation creating the Adirondack Park, which included the forest reserve lands, continued this policy, stating that the park was to be "forever preserved . . . for the free use of all the people for their health and pleasure, and as forest lands necessary to the preservation of the headwaters of the chief rivers of the State, and a future timber supply."[13] It was not until the New York State constitutional convention of 1894 that the Adirondack Park Commission received the authority to exclude logging and other commercial activities from the park. And it was not until the 1890s that, for Sargent and others, the interests of scenic preservation and outdoor recreation were clearly becoming separate from those of scientific forestry and water conservation for irrigation and electrical power.

A turning point came in 1891, when Congress passed the Forest Reserve Act authorizing the president to declare "public reservations" on "any public land bearing forests." By 1909, four presidents had declared 150 million acres of forest reserves—an area greater than Colorado and Wyoming combined—out of the remaining public lands in the West.[14] The locations and boundaries for many of these early forest reserves had been suggested by contemporary proposals for national parks. The borders of the Yellowstone Timber Land Reserve proclaimed by Benjamin Harrison in 1891, for example, coincided with proposed extensions to Yellowstone that had unsuccessfully been sought by General Philip Sheridan, Grinnell, Sargent, and other park advocates since the early 1880s. The status of the new Yellowstone forest reserve was at first ambiguous. The U.S. Cavalry in charge of Yellowstone simply extended its jurisdiction to include the forest reserve on the southern and eastern boundaries of the park, suggesting that the park had been expanded; but future attempts to legally add the reserve territory to the park failed.[15] In 1893, Harrison proclaimed the four million-acre Sierra Forest Reserve between and around Yosemite and Sequoia national parks, including the Kings Canyon region that Muir had earlier advocated for national park status.[16] The Cascade and Pacific forest reserves, also declared in 1893, included the territories of the proposed Crater Lake and Mount Rainier national parks. Steel and other Northwest park advocates had seen their park legislation defeated in Congress repeatedly in the 1880s; the forest reserves—which covered a far vaster area of the high country of the Cascades—had been accomplished with relative ease by executive proclamation.[17]

The new forest reserves typically embraced far greater areas than park advocates had dared to suggest, and a benign ambiguity persisted regarding the exact distinction between forest reserves and national parks in the early 1890s. The scenic qualities of proposed reserves, for example, were considered in their selection and demarcation. In 1891, Secretary of the Interior John W. Noble felt that the reserves could be "of great interest to our people because of their natural beauty, or remarkable features," as well as their economic value.[18] The 1893 declaration of the Grand Canyon Forest Reserve, which consisted mostly of the canyon itself, clearly did not rely on forest conservation as its only justification. And the forest reserves, like the national parks, remained under the jurisdiction of the Department of the Interior; the Division of Forestry, which had been created in the Department of Agriculture in 1881, remained an advisory body. Since no explicit policies yet existed for the management of the reserves, Secretary Noble and his immediate successors at the Department of the Interior attempted to strictly limit logging, grazing, and other commercial activities.[19] Although such anti-trespass policies were politically and logistically impossible to enforce, the official policy continued to blur the distinction between national park status and that of the forest reserves.

In 1897, however, Congress clarified matters by legislating some of its goals for the selection and management of forest reserves. The effect was to officially open the reserves to authorized timber sales, grazing, and other forms of development. These activities were to be regulated by the secretary of the interior. In 1898, Gifford Pinchot arrived at the Division of Forestry and revitalized that office, providing technical assistance to private logging companies as well as official advice to the Department of the Interior on forest reserve policies. Pinchot's influence grew steadily, as did the Division of Forestry, especially once Theodore Roosevelt became president in 1901. By 1902, Pinchot and his division effectively wrote the policies and procedures for forest reserve management.[20] The secretary of the interior subsequently granted permits and collected fees for increased commercial uses of the reserves according to principles that promised sustained yields of lumber, grass, electricity, and water.

Pinchot enlisted the political support of western politicians, stockmen, and irrigationists, who favored policies that defined the forest reserves in terms of multiple economic use—even if such use involved fees and permits—rather than as inviolate game preserves or vast parks. The policy of multiple use relied on the fact that, if properly regulated, logging and grazing could continue in the forests without threatening the flow of water for irrigation; water conservation therefore was an essential counterpoint to Pinchot's forest management. In 1902, Congress passed the Newlands Reclamation Act, and the Reclamation Service (later the Bureau of Reclamation), headed by Frederick H. Newell, began to plan, permit, and subsidize major irrigation and hydroelectric projects on public lands.[21] Working closely with Newell and Pinchot, Roosevelt developed the policies of planned exploitation of water and land resources that defined the Progressive conservation movement and strengthened the political appeal of Progressive government. In 1905, Pinchot, with Roosevelt's support, succeeded in transferring responsibility for the forest reserves from the Department of the Interior to the Division of Forestry in the Department of Agriculture. At the same time, the forest bureau was expanded and renamed the United States Forest Service; in 1907, the forest reserves were renamed national forests.

By 1908, what was now known as the conservation movement—a term that implied the coordinated exploitation of various natural resources—

had become a powerful political force, endorsed at a White House conference of state governors organized that year by Pinchot. Scenic preservation, however, had been virtually excluded from the Progressive agenda of natural resource conservation. National parks, both existing and proposed, depended on aesthetic justifications for the preservation of scenery; but efficiency, not aesthetics, determined the conservation policies set by the Roosevelt administrations. Just as the contemporary Progressive playground movement challenged the management of municipal parks as scenic landscapes, Progressive conservation dismissed scenic preservation as a basis for federal land policies. Scientific forestry and reclamation engineering offered instead the promise of sustainable commercial utilization of public lands and resources.[22]

The situation was a serious one for national park advocates. The Forest Service had explicitly made scenic preservation a secondary concern in the management of national forests, and now most proposed national parks would have to be carved out of the territory of this powerful new government bureau. At the same time, the park movement lost potential allies, such as irrigationists, whose watersheds were now protected through applied forestry, and who also benefited from dam construction and other projects that were inconsistent with the preservation of scenery. The national park legislation that did succeed after 1891 often had amendments attached that either allowed for future development of natural resources or contained some other compromise to gain the support of a politically useful ally. The Mount Rainier park campaign succeeded in 1899, for example, but only after a clause had been added allowing the Northern Pacific Railroad to exchange its patented land within the proposed park boundaries for much more valuable timber land at lower altitudes. This sop to the Northern Pacific purchased necessary support in Congress; but even so, another clause allowed continued mineral claims and mining in the new park.[23] After years of lobbying by William Steel and his allies, in 1902 Congress finally passed a Crater Lake bill; but again only after tight boundaries had been drawn around the lake excluding potentially valuable timber and grazing land in the surrounding forest reserve. And mining was to be allowed in Crater Lake National Park, as well.[24] Glacier National Park legislation passed in 1910; in this case, Louis W. Hill, president of the Great Northern Railroad, exerted his considerable influence. The Great Northern ran along the southern edge of the proposed park, and Hill had soon built lodges and chalets in the park to serve the visitors who arrived on his trains. Even so, the Glacier legislation failed to provide much more protection of natural resources than it would have received as a national forest; the bill allowed for the development of hydroelectric dams, railroads, limited logging, and even leases for summer homes.[25] The comprehensive successes of 19th-century national park legislation would not be repeated easily in the 20th century.

Despite these flaws and setbacks, by 1915 national park advocates had successfully lobbied for legislation and executive proclamations that had established a legacy of scenic reservations in the West. Also during this period, assorted entrepreneurs and railroad companies supervised the construction of a remarkable series of hotels, observation platforms, photography studios, and other buildings in the national parks and monuments. Because these concessioners sought to attract affluent tourists, they often invested considerable sums to create buildings that embodied the romance of touring the West, and in particular of touring the national parks. The Northern Pacific hired architect Robert Reamer to design the Old Faithful Inn in Yellowstone (1903), which was sited just a few hundred yards from the geyser itself. Built of huge peeled logs and featuring a seven-story atrium with gnarled wood balustrades and enormous stone fireplaces, the inn recalled eastern resort architecture of the Adirondack and Blue Ridge mountains. Reamer thoroughly exceeded such precedents, however, in both the scale and ambition of the Old Faithful Inn. If the Yellowstone landscape reinforced the monumentality of the building, the exaggerated architecture managed in return to provide an artistic complement to the geothermal wonderland of the geyser basin.

The peeled log construction, boulder masonry, rough finishes and textures, massive proportions, and pseudo-pioneer construction techniques of the inn also helped establish what would thereafter be perceived as an appropriate style for buildings, furniture, and other construction in many national park settings. In 1905, the Atchison, Topeka, and Santa Fe Railway hired Charles Whittlesey to design El Tovar, an enormous wood and stone hotel perched on the very edge of the south rim of the Grand Canyon. Described by architectural historian Laura Soullière Harrison as a "combination of the Swiss chalet and the Norway villa," the hotel was named for an early Spanish explorer to the region and featured interior decoration inspired by Hopi crafts.[26] This stylistic pastiche somehow worked and created, again, a characteristic image of rustic luxury that managed to complement, as well as benefit from, its extraordinary location. In Glacier National Park, Louis W. Hill began investing heavily in his system of hotels and backcountry chalets as soon as the park legislation was signed in 1910. Inspired by Swiss resort architecture, these stone and timber buildings evoked what were, for Hill, the appropriate precedents of exclusive Alpine resorts.[27]

The situation in Glacier, however, illustrated both the strengths and weaknesses of early national park development planned and financed by concessioners. Hill gave Glacier needed publicity (as other railroad executives did for other parks), a tactic that served to publicize his company as well as the park. He even adopted a mountain goat as the Great Northern's corporate symbol. He probably also used his influence to secure relatively generous federal appropriations for the construction of some roads and saddle trails in the park. Other proposed roads, trails, and sanitary facilities, however, awaited more substantial funding. The civilian ranger force also remained inadequate for patrolling the park. And without a road over the continental divide, the park was effectively cut in half for administrative purposes; not even a telephone line connected the east and west entrances.[28] Owners of private property and summer houses in the park—including two Montana senators who owned property on Lake McDonald—exerted a potentially unhealthy influence over park management. And hydroelectric development, logging, and extensions of railroad lines into the park all continued to threaten the preservation of the park landscape, since they had not been precluded legislatively. Even at Yellowstone, proposals for utilitarian development threatened constantly. Beginning in the 1880s, bills that would have allowed dam or railroad construction in Yellowstone were repeatedly put forward in Congress, where they were only defeated thanks to the dedication of certain individuals, such as Representative John F. Lacey of Iowa and Senator George G. Vest of Missouri.[29]

In 1901, Congress, caught up in the enthusiasm for western land reclamation, passed an act authorizing the secretary of the interior to grant right-of-ways through national parks for utility lines and irrigation projects.[30] Secretary Hitchcock approved hydroelectric development for the Middle Fork Canyon of Sequoia National Park in 1902. In the absence of what were considered compelling arguments to disallow such activity in what was then a little-visited portion of the park, the construction of roads, flumes, and dams began in 1905. The preservation of Sequoia was threatened in other ways as well. The Giant Forest, according to a later description by a park superintendent, "was given over to camping, and in every direction there were pit toilets, cess pits, and a criss-cross of water lines under the Big Trees." As auto tourists made their way into the park, they camped where they liked; there was no organized system of sewage and refuse disposal, a situation that became more unacceptable as the number of park visitors began to climb.[31] In Yosemite Valley, tourist operations had begun in the 1850s. Under the control of a usually accommodating state park commission between 1864 and 1906, numerous hotel operators and turnpike companies had developed the valley into a particularly chaotic resort.[32]

At Yosemite, as well as Sequoia and Yellowstone, the U.S. Cavalry continued to patrol in order to prevent illegal grazing, logging, and poaching. But in the 20th century, the threats of poaching and trespass were overshadowed in all these parks by the potential damage caused by increasing tourism, uncontrolled foot and vehicle traffic, and large hydroelectric and irrigation schemes that threatened major alterations to park landscapes. To continue to be useful, the army would need to shift from patrolling the backcountry to policing and guiding visitors, a change military leaders were not likely to approve. Increasing crowds of tourists, however, were the new reality of 20th-century outdoor recreation, and "back to nature" enthusiasts brought civilization with them. By 1915, almost forty thousand people visited Yosemite Valley, over five times the number that came in 1904. During the same period, the total number of visitors to Yellowstone rose from under fourteen thousand annually to over fifty thousand. In Sequoia the increase was from about one thousand in 1906 to about five thousand in 1915; Glacier had about four thousand visitors the year after it opened and over fourteen thousand four years later. By 1915, the total number of visitors to parks and monuments had risen to 335,000—a tenfold increase from 1906—and restrictions regarding automobiles on park roads were being abandoned. In 1920, the total visitor count reached one million.[33]

As these human populations increased, the national parks faced many of the same challenges that the urbanizing nation faced. The parks themselves were, in effect, urbanizing. The situation could not be adequately administered simply by granting leases for luxury hotel construction. Park concessioners interested primarily in operating parks as resorts could not assume capital costs that would dwarf their potential profits. Fine hotels were built during this period, but basic improvements to the parks were not. Sewers, water lines, roads, trails, and campgrounds were needed in order to assure public safety (if not convenience) and to prevent the degradation of landscape scenery and the destruction of significant features.

In addition, hydroelectric developers, irrigationists, and stockmen felt that dam construction and grazing underway in national forests should not necessarily stop at national park boundaries. The Forest Service supported this position, and so did Theodore Roosevelt's secretaries of the interior. Secretary Hitchcock, who earlier had approved hydroelectric dam construction in Sequoia, in 1907 reasoned that "the problems for the maintenance and the development of the parks are practically the same . . . [as those] in the national forests," denying a significant distinction between national forest and national park designations.[34]

The ambiguities between national forest and national park status evident in much of the original park legislation, together with this administrative attitude at the Department of the Interior, threatened to annul the entire federal effort to manage national scenic reservations. From his arrival at the Department of Agriculture in 1898, Gifford Pinchot hoped to transfer the national parks (as well as the forest reserves) to his forestry division, where the parks could be managed according to policies that would not proscribe limited logging, grazing, or dam construction. After 1901, Roosevelt endorsed the transfer of the parks from Interior to Agriculture, where he assumed they would at least benefit from more consistent and active management. Secretary of the Interior Hitchcock fully supported the transfer, as did James R. Garfield, appointed by Roosevelt to replace Hitchcock in 1907.

There were institutional as well as political reasons for their support of the transfer. By the late 19th century, the secretary of the interior disbursed Civil War pensions, granted patents, conducted the Geological Survey, managed the Bureau of Indian Affairs, and oversaw the transactions of the General Land Office, among myriad other activities. Even by the standards of the day, the department suffered from corrupting influences and administrative inefficiencies.[35] The lawyers and political appointees at Interior contrasted with the motivated, professionally trained foresters that Pinchot attracted to his Forest Service. Pinchot's successful transfer of the forest reserves in 1905 had been a major bureaucratic coup, one he hoped to repeat with the national parks, which, after all, were usually contiguous with the forests and often completely surrounded by them. Pinchot offered strong reasons for placing parks and forests under a single jurisdiction, and the Department of the Interior could not refute them. There were no competent foresters or land managers in the General Land Office, for example, while the Forest Service had acquired a reputation for efficient probity and scientific expertise.

But in the case of the 1905 forest reserves transfer, Pinchot's promises to open the reserves to limited grazing, logging, and dam construction had generated political support from western congressional delegations. The much smaller national parks offered fewer commercial rewards and so were of less interest in this regard. The parks were also more likely to be defended by ardent "nature lovers," who may have agreed with Pinchot's policies for national forests, but who emphatically contested the extention of those policies into Yosemite and Yellowstone. Representative Lacey, for example, a committed scenic preservationist, happened to be the chairman of the House Public Lands Committee, where he thwarted efforts to transfer jurisdiction over the parks in 1906 and again in 1907. Lacey had also counterattacked as early as 1900 by introducing legislation to create a new national parks bureau, which would have effaced Pinchot's main argument for the transfer by creating a corps of professional park managers within the Department of the Interior. Other legislators introduced bills to create a bureau of parks in 1902 and 1905; but they all failed, in large part due to Congressional opposition encouraged by Pinchot.[36]

Within government, those in favor of rigorous scenic preservation and exclusively recreational uses for national parks did not make much progress until after Theodore Roosevelt left office in 1909. Although the national parks at least remained under the jurisdiction of the Department of the Interior, the parks still had little central administrative support or funding. No bureau—or even a full time staff person—looked after park affairs in Washington.[37] Many in the federal government doubted the feasibility of scenic preservation that excluded commercial uses, with Pinchot himself expressing the greatest skepticism over such "sentimental nonsense."

Scenic preservationists outside of government, however, had not abandoned their goals. After the American Park and Outdoor Art Association was founded in 1897, the group had attracted new members and broadened its agenda. The association became even less of a professional society, with park superintendents and landscape architects outnumbered by representatives of village improvement societies, women's federations, and members of the public at large who expressed interest in "civic improvement," generally, as well as in scenic preservation and landscape design.[38] In 1904, the association merged with another group, the League of Civic Improvement Associations, which had been founded in 1900 and was headed by an energetic printer from Harrisburg, Pennsylvania, named J. Horace McFarland. McFarland then presided over the combined group, renamed the American Civic Association.[39] In pamphlets, speeches, and conventions,

McFarland and the American Civic Association advocated a full range of urban environmental reforms, including smoke abatement, sewage treatment, restrictions on outdoor advertising, planting of street trees, and the creation of "playgrounds for the children and parks for grown-ups."[40] During this period McFarland participated on Harrisburg's municipal park commission, which (with landscape architect Warren Manning as a consultant) implemented environmental reforms and completed an impressive park system. His interest in municipal parks and civic improvement extended naturally to state and national parks.[41]

As the membership and influence of the American Civic Association grew, McFarland became a national spokesman for scenic preservation causes. Niagara Falls was under assault in the early 20th century by hydroelectric proposals that threatened to diminish the flow of the cataract. For over twenty years, McFarland worked to preserve the falls and acquire more parkland around the state reservation.[42] Perhaps because he was less threatening than figures such as John Muir and Robert Underwood Johnson, in 1908 Gifford Pinchot allowed McFarland to attend his White House governors' conference on conservation.[43] If he anticipated that McFarland would represent the national park cause ineffectually, however, Pinchot erred. Speaking in terms of economic value that his audience could appreciate, McFarland urged them "to consider the essential value of one of America's greatest resources—her unmatched natural scenery." He gave the governors a memorable and impassioned summary of why national parks should be managed as parks, not national forests: "The love of country that lights and keeps glowing the holy fire of patriotism. . . is excited primarily by the beauty of the country . . . . The national parks, all too few in number and extent, ought to remain absolutely inviolate. . . . The scenic value of all the national domain yet remaining should be jealously guarded." He also proclaimed, in defiance of the opinion of his host, that the "Hetch-Hetchy Valley of the Yosemite region belongs to all of America and not to San Francisco alone."[44]

The controversy surrounding the Hetch-Hetchy Valley in Yosemite National Park had become the most divisive scenic preservation issue of the day and was the reason why Pinchot did not invite Muir, Johnson, and other former allies to his governors' conference. In 1905, the City of San Francisco had requested permission (based again on the provisions of the 1901 Right-of-Way Act) to dam the Tuolumne River in Yosemite in order to make a municipal reservoir out of the Hetch-Hetchy Valley. Pinchot, near the height of his influence, approved of the plan and advised Roosevelt accordingly. Park advocates, led by Muir, considered the Hetch-Hetchy a scenic rival to Yosemite itself and immediately tried to persuade Roosevelt and Secretary Hitchcock not to follow Pinchot's advice in the matter. Sentiment in favor of improving municipal water supplies for San Francisco was strong, however, especially after much of the city burned in 1906. The same month Pinchot convened his triumphant conservation conference in 1908, Secretary of the Interior Garfield granted permission to dam the Hetch-Hetchy.[45]

The situation changed dramatically for Yosemite, however, and for all the national parks, in 1909 when William H. Taft succeeded Roosevelt in the White House and appointed Richard A. Ballinger as secretary of the interior. Ballinger, a westerner and former commissioner of the General Land Office, did not continue the close cooperation with the Forest Service that his predecessors had found expedient. The new secretary immediately infuriated Pinchot by allowing valuable hydroelectric sites (that Garfield and Pinchot had retained in public ownership) to once again become available to private hydroelectric power interests. Ballinger soon found himself on the defensive, however, when charges of improprieties involving Alaskan coal lands were leveled against him by a clerk who had worked under him in the General Land Office. The charges were almost certainly false; but Pinchot encouraged them and spread the story in the press in order to destroy his rival. Taft, who had no intention of allowing Pinchot the same level of influence he enjoyed under Roosevelt, backed Ballinger and forced the Chief Forester's resignation for insubordination in 1910.[46] In the meantime, Ballinger, perhaps as part of a calculated attempt to gain support in his public relations battle with Pinchot, revoked permission to dam the Hetch-Hetchy, a move hailed by scenic preservationists, who bitterly resented Pinchot's failure to side with them on the issue. The battle resumed, however, and only ended in 1913 when Congress passed legislation directly authorizing the construction of the dam. Without the permanent, organized influence that a national park bureau could have exerted within the government, private groups such as the American Civic Association and individuals such as Muir and Johnson would find it difficult to frustrate lobbying efforts that could be sustained for years on the part of established commercial and industrial interests.

But the battle of the Hetch-Hetchy proved a Pyrrhic victory for Pinchot. While Ballinger failed to prevent the waterworks construction, he did redirect the institutional attitude of the Department of the Interior towards its national parks. Ballinger adopted the rhetoric of McFarland and other scenic preservationists who claimed that the commercial value of landscape scenery could be economically exploited, without destroying it for posterity, by developing better facilities for tourists.[47] "It has been broadly estimated that one hundred million dollars has been spent in some years abroad by American tourists," Ballinger reported in 1910, noting that "only a fraction" of that amount was spent by domestic tourists visiting national parks.[48] To remedy this, he suggested that all parks be brought under civilian administration, and that Congress create a "bureau of national parks and resorts . . . with a suitable force of superintendents, supervising engineers, and landscape architects, inspectors, park guards, and other employees." Noting that the Army Corps of Engineers had done important work in Yellowstone and Mount Rainier, Ballinger nevertheless felt that "the Interior Department should have supervision over the construction and maintenance of park roads . . . according to [a] general plan of development" for each park. This process was hindered, he confessed, by a lack of "well-defined policies and plans for their general development and improvement." He went on to claim that if national parks were to be fulfilled as "national institutions, a definite policy for their maintenance, supervision, and improvement should be established, which would enable them to be opened up for the convenience and comfort of tourists and campers and for the careful preservation of natural features. Complete and comprehensive plans for roads, trails, telegraph and telephone lines, sewer and water systems, hotel accommodations, transportation, and other conveniences should be made for each of the national parks before any large amount of money is expended."[49]

Ballinger's motivations for these policies were encouraged by the prospect of embarrassing Pinchot and scoring a public relations victory; perhaps they also reflected general policy in the Taft administration to reduce the Forest Service's influence in public land management. In any case, Ballinger, hardly known as a scenic preservationist himself, summoned J. Horace McFarland to Washington in 1910 to begin drafting legislation for a national park bureau.

McFarland recognized that such legislation would create what would become the country's largest and most important park commission, charged with developing some of the most scenic places in the world as a system of public parks. He therefore turned for assistance to Frederick Law Olmsted, Jr., who at age forty was emerging as the leader of the profession of landscape architecture.[50] The younger Olmsted, growing up around the landscape architects at Fairsted, had entered the profession at an early age. Since 1898, he had been a full partner, with his older half-brother J. C. Olmsted, in the firm Olmsted Brothers, which replaced Olmsted, Olmsted & Eliot after Charles Eliot's death. That year the younger Olmsted had also replaced Eliot as landscape architect for Boston's Metropolitan Park Commission. In 1900, at the age of twenty-nine, he headed the new academic program in landscape architecture at Harvard, the first degree program offered in the field. In 1901 he became a member of the Senate Park Commission, and was a co-author of the 1902 McMillan Plan for the Capital, the first comprehensive city plan of its type in the United States. One of the founders of the profession of city planning, in 1917 Olmsted was named the first president of the American City Planning Institute. He contributed to dozens of park and subdivision designs throughout his career, including some of the most important projects of the day, such as Biltmore (1895) in North Carolina and Forest Hills Gardens (1911) in New York.[51]

Olmsted was particularly interested in scenic preservation, a field in which he made some of his greatest professional contributions. He had met McFarland during his efforts to prevent hydroelectric development at Niagara and Yosemite, preservation campaigns in which they had both played important parts. The Hetch-Hetchy controversy, in particular, helped define Olmsted's thinking on national park policies. During the Hetch-Hetchy debate, Gifford Pinchot had flatly rejected the role of park planning and design on the national level.[52] Olmsted, however, better understood the continuity between municipal, state, and national park planning. In 1906, he and fellow landscape architect John Nolen pubished their description of a formal typology of "public open spaces," encompassing a range of types from the smallest neighborhood playground to "great outlying reservations."[53] He brought this comprehensive understanding of the American park movement to his analysis of the Hetch-Hetchy dispute.

Proponents of the Hetch-Hetchy dam insisted that, far from being a scenic liability, the reservoir would be a pleasant addition to the park and would even enhance the scenery of the valley. This was no idle sophistry; since the mid-19th century, American landscape parks had often included reservoirs for municipal water supplies, and those lakes had indeed contributed to the composed scenes of municipal park landscapes. Clean water, even more than verdant meadows, embodied the ideal of public health. In dozens of cities the greenswards and groves of municipal parks, combined with large lakes that served as reservoirs, resulted in compelling visualizations of healthful beauty and utility.[54] One of the younger Olmsted's first professional writings, published by the American Park and Outdoor Art Association in 1899, detailed "The Relation of Reservoirs to Parks." In this paper he encouraged close cooperation between park designers and municipal engineers, since almost "all reservoirs . . . have an element of landscape effect; namely, that of an expanse of clear, sparkling water." He went on to observe that "this same element forms the chief feature of many landscapes in public parks, where it is created at large cost, and is clearly a thing of great value. . . . Where a reservoir occurs in a public park, as frequently happens, it might be made to add largely to the value of the park instead of striking a discordant note." He then provided diagrams and examples, including Middlesex Fells and Fresh Pond parks (both near Boston), in which Olmsted Brothers had artfully integrated major reservoirs into park landscapes.[55]

It was the Hetch-Hetchy proposal to add a reservoir to Yosemite that forced Olmsted to distinguish what might be appropriate in a regional park, such as Middlesex Fells, from what was appropriate in a national park. And the imagery and rhetoric of public health in the 19th-century park would, again, be replaced by 20th-century aesthetic and economic arguments in favor of scenic preservation. Olmsted opposed the Hetch-Hetchy reservoir forcefully, and he felt compelled to explain his resistance to what he might otherwise have considered a "thing of great value." In 1913, as the controversy neared its end, the *Boston Evening Transcript* published Olmsted's summary of the entire affair.[56] The principal point to be considered, in his opinion, was "the effect of the proposal upon the value of the Yosemite National Park." At issue was the legitimacy of the assertions of the San Francisco municipal engineers that reservoir construction would not inhibit the appreciation of landscape scenery. Olmsted quoted the engineers' position: "Granting the desirability of keeping certain areas free . . . of population for the purpose of drawing public water-supplies from them, and the purpose of keeping certain areas free of population for the purpose of using them for parks . . . there seems to be no reason why these two classes of areas should be kept separate. . . . There is every reason why the two uses should be combined." Olmsted recognized this logic. "I have urged this principle again and again," he admitted, "and have not done a little in helping to put it into practice. . . . Not infrequently, land acquired and policed primarily for park purposes may serve incidentally . . . [as] sites for reservoirs, with no impairment of their park value or even with an actual increase in park value." But at Yosemite there was another principle involved, one that demanded that "aesthetic value" should not be compromised by "utilitarian value." "Some things . . . are of a value wholly or primarily for their beauty, and if they have any direct utilitarian value it is utterly secondary and incidental," Olmsted explained. "If we can afford it, we direct our efforts toward conserving and making available its primary value, its beauty."

Olmsted reinforced his position in the terms that had justified public parks since the 1850s, updated with a Progressive emphasis on value and efficiency: "Certain kinds of valuably refreshing scenery are so incompatible with the ordinary economic uses of land . . . [that they] must be given over specifically to that purpose. . . . Until it is deliberately concluded that the value of the landscape beauty is no longer the prime justification for the maintenance of the park, the only safe rule is to permit no other avoidable use . . . which in any degree impairs the value of the park for that purpose." The advocates of the dam, in other words, "must bear the burden of proving that the new use [would] not impair the scenery." Olmsted quoted his father's 1865 analysis and descriptions of the beauty of Yosemite, and then specifically refuted the municipal engineers' claims that the reservoir would not damage "the landscape qualities which, in all the world, are peculiar to Yosemite scenery . . . and which in the next few centuries will, I believe, become of incalculably larger value to humanity."[57]

Again and again, Olmsted defended "this commodity called Yosemite scenery" as a sound investment that would accrue "value" in the 20th century as beautiful scenery became increasingly scarce. He also summarized a basic preservationist philosophy for the new century. "The lesson of history in this respect is unmistakable," he concluded, "a thing which many people have held to be of great and peculiar beauty and which cannot be replaced, even if the predominant men of the day fail to appreciate its beauty . . . ought not to be destroyed or radically altered." Other figures in scenic preservation, such as John Muir, may have been superior polemicists; but probably no one in the early 20th century was better qualified than Frederick Law Olmsted, Jr., to prepare legislation and policies that would establish a national park system and a national park commission to manage it.

In the meantime, Taft replaced the embattled Secretary Ballinger in 1911. The new secretary of the interior, Walter L. Fisher, continued Ballinger's national park initiative, however, and that September he convened a national park conference at Yellowstone. The conference assembled park concessioners, superintendents, railroad executives, and Interior officials for the first time to specifically discuss national park management. Many of those present took up the "See America First" slogan and urged that American tourists be encouraged to consider visiting California or the Rockies before making the typical tour to European destinations. Even Canada seemed to be besting the United States in the competition for tourist dollars. Louis W. Hill, for example, who was just beginning his development of Glacier, spoke immediately after Secretary Fisher's opening address at the conference. "Thousands of Americans go to Canada every year for things they might just as well get in the United States," Hill complained, "we all want to go ahead and do a great deal more in the way of advertising . . . [which] will change the current of travel from Europe and Canada to this country. . . . We are going ahead with this in view in our 'See America First' campaign."[58]

Secretary Fisher noted that American national parks had "grown up like Topsy . . . with no one particularly concerned with them." Most of the participants in the conference agreed that publicity was a good first step in correcting the situation. In the words of one Northern Pacific executive, "the principal purpose of this meeting is to consider in what manner the number of visitors to the various parks can be increased." The railroad companies had advertised the parks for years, but Fisher reported that the Department of the Interior now supplied press releases and other information to newspapers as well.[59] A national park bureau could institutionalize this kind of effort, and could also effectively request increased appropriations from Congress for park improvements— roads, trails, and sewers, for example—that concessioners wanted to improve their resorts.

A new park bureau was therefore advocated by most of those who spoke at the conference, but J. Horace McFarland in particular was called upon to address that specific concern. Introduced by Fisher as "one of the persons in the United States who is most deeply concerned with the development and use of our national parks," McFarland announced that "it seems to me that it is now time that the national parks shall cease to be incidentally handled and come to such handling as will make them as definite on the map of the United States as are the parks in any large city." His goal to create a national park bureau modeled on the precedents of municipal and county park commissions was clear: "Parks are successful when they are the primary object of attention on the part of some one person. . . . A park commissioner is the usual means."

The concessioners, railroad executives, and park superintendents assembled at Yellowstone apparently did not feel, as Gifford Pinchot did, that McFarland's experience with "Eastern municipal parks" and "civic improvements" disqualified him from appreciating the exigencies of national park administration. On the contrary, the development and administration of scores of municipal and county park systems presented successful models for accommodating tourists in settings calculated to enhance their appreciation of landscape scenery.[60]

From 1910 on, McFarland and the American Civic Association mobilized to create a national park bureau. Immediately after the Yellowstone conference, McFarland convened his group's 1911 annual meeting (held that year in Washington) and dedicated the entire program to presenting the "needs for a federal Bureau of National Parks."[61] Among the speakers endorsing the creation of such a bureau was President Taft, who noted that the national parks, after being set aside, had simply been stored in "the 'lumber room' of the Government . . . the Interior Department." "If we are going to have National parks," Taft affirmed, "we ought to make them available to the people, and we ought to build the roads . . . in order that those parks may become what they are intended to be when Congress creates them. . . . And we cannot do that, we cannot carry them on effectively, unless we have a bureau which is itself distinctly charged with the responsibility for their management and for their building up."[62]

In McFarland's own address at the Washington conference, he offered a brief history of "the American park idea." Like Olmsted and Nolen, McFarland recognized the continuity between playgrounds, municipal parks, parkways, and "the nation's larger playgrounds": state and national parks. All these parks promoted the general goals of public health, enhanced welfare, and improved productivity. "Everything that the limited scope of a city park can do as quick aid to the citizen," McFarland explained, national parks "are ready to do more thoroughly, on a greater scale." He emphasized the difference between national parks and national forests: "The primary function of the national forest is to supply lumber. The primary purpose of the national park is to maintain in healthful efficiency the lives of the people who must use that lumber. The forests are the nation's reserve wood-lots. The parks are the nation's reserve for the maintenance of individual patriotism and federal solidarity."[63]

With Pinchot now out of the government and Taft's address to the American Civic Association transferred as a special message to Congress, the campaign led by McFarland and Olmsted to define policies for the management of national parks began to achieve results. Fisher convened a second national park conference at Yosemite in 1912 in which the proposed creation of a "national park service" again met unanimous approval.[64] In addition to many of the same railroad executives and park superintendents that attended the first conference, a phalanx of California "automobile people" also appeared and made their views known. Ex-senator Frank Flint, for example, a member of the Automobile Club of Southern California (which with 4,500 members claimed to be "the largest automobile club in the world") expressed great dissatisfaction with the restrictions on automobile use in the Sierran parks. The condition of roads and the admission of automobiles into the parks were principal subjects discussed at the Yosemite conference, with few voices raised against admitting auto tourists and improving roads and facilities for them. Even William E. Colby, speaking for the Sierra Club, noted that although his group was "blamed for keeping the automobile men out," he hoped that "they will be allowed in when the time comes, because we think the automobile adds a great zest to travel and we are primarily interested in the increase of travel to these parks." The head ranger at Sequoia, Walter Fry, made a comment that typified the tone of the conference: "The American people, in my opinion, have outgrown the stagecoach habit, and the automobile is a factor that will have to be recognized. . . . I should strongly advise that its admission be encouraged."[65] Improving park roads and tourist accommodations, admitting automobiles into more parks (and making it safer to do so), and creating a national park service all surfaced at the 1912 Yosemite conference as interrelated, desirable goals for improving park management.

The election of Woodrow Wilson that November only bettered the chances for reform in national park administration. In 1913, Wilson appointed Franklin K. Lane, a Californian and former San Francisco city attorney, as secretary of the interior. On the one hand, the appointment sealed the fate of the Hetch-Hetchy Valley; Lane felt the dam was necessary for the continued prosperity of his home city. On the other, Lane brought with him informed concern for the national parks and an active agenda for their improvement. While park service legislation stalled in Congress, Lane took what administrative steps he could in the meantime. Faced with limited resources for park planning, he improvised and sought out cooperative agencies. He sent out a chemical engineer from the Geological Survey to inspect sanitary conditions in the parks, which were confirmed to be execrable. At Yosemite, for example, the park's superintendent recommended that "stables should be moved downstream from areas devoted to residential and camping purposes," and that outhouses in the valley, "a constant menace and a source of danger," should be replaced by toilets and sewers. At Yellowstone as well, the "question of sanitation and stream pollution" was a serious one, that the superintendent of that park felt "must be met by some general plan in the near future."[66]

Roads in most parks also remained inadequate to the increased demands put upon them. Although Lane felt that the roads in some parks "were not in such a condition to permit . . . their joint use by motor-driven vehicles and vehicles drawn by horses," he nevertheless liberalized policies, allowing automobiles into Yosemite and Sequoia on a limited basis, and recommending further improvements that would allow all park roads to be safely opened to combined traffic.[67] He also enlisted the Good Roads Office of the Department of Agriculture (later the Bureau of Public Roads) which paid "experienced highway engineers" to begin "comprehensive surveys for a system of roads and trails" in the parks. In 1914, the Forest Service also cooperated by assisting in fire suppression programs. Lane was also able to replace soldiers in Yosemite, Sequoia, and General Grant with civilian rangers in 1914.[68]

Through such innovations, Secretary Lane established the nucleus of a future parks agency, anticipating the legislation that would give him an entire new bureau. In 1913, Adolph C. Miller, a professor of economics from the University of California, was appointed assistant to the secretary in charge of the national parks. Professor Miller brought along a Berkeley law student, Horace M. Albright, as his assistant. In the spring of 1914, Professor Miller also engaged a San Francisco landscape architect, Mark Roy Daniels, to design "a comprehensive general plan for the development of the floor of the Yosemite Valley." Of specific concern were "the best locations for roads, trails, and bridges, so as to bring into view the full scenic beauty of the surroundings, the clearing and trimming of suitable areas of woods to provide attractive vistas, [and] the proper location and arrangement of a village in Yosemite Valley." Two months later, apparently enthusiastic about his work, Miller expanded the landscape architect's commission, and Daniels became "general superintendent and landscape engineer" of all the national parks.[69]

Professor Miller, however, was soon on loan to the Treasury Department, where he applied himself to the more appropriate task of drafting Wilson's Federal Reserve Board legislation. Daniels remained in San Francisco and continued his private practice while also performing his duties for the Department of the Interior. That summer, Daniels went to work visiting parks and drafting preliminary plans for their orderly development. He also designed the first uniforms for the civilian park rangers. Park superintendents, however, perhaps jealous of their authority, were displeased that Miller deducted the landscape architect's fees from already inadequate park appropriations. Miller also attempted to rename the superintendents "supervisors" (to avoid confusing them with his new "general superintendent") and ordered them to report to Daniels in San Francisco rather than directly to him in Washington. Such policies rankled superintendents accustomed to complete autonomy in their parks.[70]

In January 1915, Secretary Lane found a replacement for Adolph Miller, a Chicago businessman named Stephen Tyng Mather. Mather had already made a fortune in the borax industry, but at age forty-seven he had no interest in retirement. A committed mountaineer and scenic preservationist, he responded with characteristic enthusiasm to Lane's offer to come to Washington and oversee the administration of the parks. Although initially Mather anticipated a brief stint of public service to benefit the parks he loved, he went on to become the first director of the new National Park Service in 1917 and continued to serve energetically until crippled by a stroke in 1929. During that time he devoted his considerable energies (and occasionally his personal fortune) to assuring that the national park system met the highest standards of design, development, and management.

Upon beginning his new duties, Mather immediately scheduled a third national park conference, this time on the campus where he and Lane had known one another as students, the University of California at Berkeley. Mather used the event to size up the park superintendents, as well as his "general superintendent and landscape engineer," Mark Daniels, who remained based in San Francisco.[71] Daniels, who resigned his position with the Department of the Interior at the end of the year, perhaps had been forced into more of an administrative role than originally anticipated. A Berkeley graduate who had studied landscape architecture and city planning at Harvard in 1913, he had not been able to successfully centralize the administration of the parks. And his planning efforts, which preceded the establishment of the necessary organization to implement them, never materialized in more than token ways. He did manage to institute a centralized purchasing procedure for some of the parks and oversaw the organization of a civilian ranger force; but Daniels had been trained as a landscape architect, not as an administrator. In 1914 and 1915, Daniels also planned "park villages" for Glacier, Mount Rainier, Crater Lake, and especially for Yosemite, the park which from the beginning received most of his attention. Most of the specific features in these village plans were either never implemented or were incorporated into different plans provided later by other landscape architects.[72] Daniels seems to have encountered certain personal difficulties as well. Horace Albright, in his memoirs, adopts a condescending tone in his descriptions of Daniels, who "had no government experience whatever, and no expertise in the national parks."[73]

But Mark Daniels, the first landscape architect to be officially involved in managing the national park system, contributed to planning and design policies during a formative period. At the 1915 Berkeley conference, Daniels made the first coherent and comprehensive policy statement for the management of the national parks. He began at Berkeley by reciting the now familiar "economic justification" for the parks: "Economics and esthetics really go hand in hand . . . there are four to six hundred million dollars that go to Europe, being spent by American tourists for the purpose of seeing scenery." Daniels also warned that national parks, unlike state or county parks, "should only be created . . . in those areas where there are bits of scenery or natural phenomena which would attract people from different parts of the country," and should exemplify certain scenic standards that warranted federal involvement. He noted that all parks, "city or county, State or National," furnish the "mental as well as the physical stimulus to tired and exhausted workers"; but the educational role of national parks distinguished them from other parks that merely provided "recreational grounds." In national parks "the scenery or natural phenomena [were] of such a character to be largely educational," and the visitor could not experience such scenery "without feeling that his mental horizon [had] been broadened materially."

Daniels also made it clear that the "inevitableness of creating villages in the parks" demanded "village plans . . . so drawn that [they] suit the various conditions—not only the topographic features, but all the various physical conditions." Daniels knew from his experience at Yosemite that as the numbers of visitors grew by the thousands, their "community ceases to be a camp; it becomes a village. . . . It has municipal problems . . . [and] will demand some sort of a civic plan in order to properly take care of the people who visit." In his Yosemite plan, for example, "the building locations [were] carefully thought out," and the architectural character of every building was determined "in the light of a careful study of the best arrangement of the buildings and for picturesqueness."[74] Daniels called for design guidelines for a new Yosemite Village on the north side of the Merced River that would "do

A proposed park "village" for Yosemite Valley, as drawn by landscape architect Mark Daniels in 1914. The view is of a new lodge on the north side of the Merced, with a new "information bureau" sited in a wye intersection in the foreground. Daniels established basic principles for national park village planning: consistent architectural expression, careful site planning, and strong visual relationships with surrounding natural features. Courtesy Yosemite National Park Research Library.

Proposed Village, Yosemite National Park.
VIEW TOWARDS HOTEL, INFORMATION BUREAU IN THE FORK OF WAY   MARK DANIELS General Superintendent & Landscape Engineer of National Parks

away with unsightly buildings that now mar the scenery . . . and establish a village properly planned, comprising buildings of carefully studied architecture." Daniels was also aware of the need for planning that would encompass the entire park system: "It was evident during the first days of the life of this office that a comprehensive plan for the road and trail development of all the national parks was an essential."[75]

The early administration of what Mark Daniels and others referred to even in 1914 as the "park service" attempted to take full advantage of whatever expertise was available. Entomologists, foresters, hydrologists, and road engineers, for example, were borrowed on an ad hoc basis from the Department of Agriculture and the Geological Survey. Daniels expected park superintendents to share the particular expertise they had acquired through experience: Walter Fry (Sequoia) spoke at Berkeley, for example, as an expert on fighting forest fires; Gabriel Sovulewski (Yosemite) shared his experience in trail construction; and S. F. Ralston (Glacier) presented his knowledge of road construction. But Daniels, who was still continuing his private practice, was attempting to run this "park service" out of his office in the Monadnock Building in San Francisco. It never amounted to more than a worthy improvisation. "The title of general superintendent and landscape engineer . . . carries with it two distinct and separate classes of duties," he observed shortly before his departure, "it is not humanly possibly for one man . . . [to] perform the duties that each of these two titles require."[76]

That December Mather replaced Daniels with Robert B. Marshall, the chief geographer of the Geological Survey, who became "general superintendent" (but not "landscape engineer") of the national parks. During his long career, Marshall had surveyed Yosemite and General Grant national parks and had supervised the surveys for most of the other parks. No one could boast a greater familiarity with the varied geography represented by the fourteen existing parks in 1916.[77] Working out of Washington and well connected within the bureaucracies, Marshall (with four employees) concentrated on improving park administration and became the first full-time executive in Washington to be so charged. Without regular appropriations or the framework of a park bureau, however, Marshall was still mostly limited to pointing out what was wrong with the ways parks were being run. Insufficient and irregular funds for road and trail construction, for example, discouraged comprehensive planning and added to the costs of construction. The total lack of sanitary systems in the parks was particularly shocking. "I shudder at the probability of an epidemic of typhoid fever or some other common epidemic [in the parks]," he reported in 1916, "that could be directly charged to the lack of proper sanitation."[78] The numbers of visitors kept rising, however, because by 1916 Mather and Marshall had lifted all restrictions on allowing automobiles in the parks.

Although Marshall had expected to become the director of the new park service once it was created, Mather soon lost confidence in the geographer's "administrative abilities," as he had with the those of the landscape architect, Daniels. It was soon clear that Mather would not be satisfied unless he administered the national parks himself, as the head of the new parks bureau. Mather and Albright, in the meantime, continued to make the passage of national park service legislation—clearly a prerequisite to further progress—their first priority.

Mather coordinated what was by now a familiar device for scenic preservation activists: a massive media campaign. A born flack, Mather had begun his working life as a reporter at Charles Anderson Dana's New York *Sun*, and he later put his press connections to good use. He brought the journalist Robert Sterling Yard, who he knew from his days at the *Sun*, to Washington, where he made him a public information officer while paying Yard's salary (as well as a supplement to Albright) out of his own pocket. Mather commissioned several photographers to produce views of the parks and issued the most scenic as a popular booklet, "Glimpses of Our National Parks," with an enthusiastic text by Yard. He then convinced seventeen railroad companies to contribute forty-three thousand dollars towards the publication of a more elaborate *Portfolio of National Parks*, of which 275,000 were distributed to a carefully compiled list of legislators, civic leaders, and other potentially influential individuals.[79] Numerous civic groups, especially McFarland's American Civic Association and the General Federation of Women's Clubs, under the leadership of Mary Belle King Sherman, continued their enthusiastic support.[80]

Magazine editors aided the cause by publicizing the parks. George Horace Lorimer of the *Saturday Evening Post* and Gilbert Grosvenor of *National Geographic*, for example, published articles claiming that national parks encouraged patriotism, national productivity, and public health. The economic value of domestic tourism and the estimation of "scenery as an asset" were stressed as well.[81] In other publications, more suggestions for park policy were being made. In February 1916, the American Society of Landscape Architects devoted their annual conference to a discussion of national parks; the proceedings were then published in a special issue of the group's quarterly, *Landscape Architecture*. Richard B. Watrous, secretary of the American Civic Association, made the keynote address, noting that the new park service would "have a large work to do in the proper exploitation of the parks."[82] The landscape architects at the conference then passed resolutions on the national parks, and on the proposed park service. The resolutions, if not written by F. L. Olmsted, Jr., fully reflected his thinking. "The need has long been felt not only for more adequate protection," the text stated, "but also for rendering this landscape beauty more readily enjoyable through construction in the parks of certain necessary roads and buildings for the accommodation of visitors in a way to bring minimum of injury to these primeval landscapes." None of this work should proceed, the resolutions continued, without "comprehensive plans . . . [and] designs for construction" approved by "qualified expert advisors," in other words, by professional landscape architects.[83] Between about 1908 and 1916, a broad consensus had formed among many scenic preservationists (including landscape architects such as Olmsted) that tourism was the only "dignified exploitation" of national parks. Tourism, a relatively benign economic activity, would justify the exclusion of more destructive dams, logging, and grazing in the parks. And tourism—especially auto tourism—would encourage a broader, middle class constituency for the parks.

Olmsted's contribution to the 1916 conference elaborated on the all important distinction between national parks and national forests, which he felt hinged on a broad public appreciation of the beauty of landscape scenery. "National *Forests* are set apart for economic ends, and their use for recreation is a by-product. . . . National *Parks* are set apart primarily in order to preserve to the people for all time the opportunity of a peculiar kind of enjoyment and recreation . . . to be obtained only from the remarkable scenery which they contain."[84] In other words, the idea of the landscape park—a park set aside to preserve areas of scenic beauty and developed to enhance the appreciation of that beauty— could be extended from its 19th-century, metropolitan context to become the basis of management policies for western scenic reservations in the 20th century, but only if the parks were visited and appreciated by the "public." The national parks could then become a "national park system," a term which implied that "park development" would proceed in all the parks according to a consistent set of policies. National park advocates such as McFarland, Olmsted, and many others assumed park development would be the key to the successful administration of national parks in the 20th century. But all agreed, as well, that such development would prove disastrous for the parks if it were not implemented in ways consistent with the ultimate goal: the preservation of landscape scenery. The art of landscape architecture— specifically landscape park design—would therefore be the critical undertaking of the new park bureau if it were to successfully develop parks in ways that would assure the preservation of scenic qualities.

In August of 1916, the public relations and lobbying efforts of the park advocates paid off when President Wilson signed "an Act to establish a National Park Service."[85] Although the actual organization of the Park Service would await appropriations that were only forthcoming in 1917, the 1916 act expressed the mandate and philosophy of the new bureau in an elegant statement drafted by Olmsted. "The fundamental purpose" of the parks, as Olmsted phrased it, "is to conserve the scenery and the natural and historic objects and the wild life therein and to provide for the enjoyment of the same in such manner and by such means as will leave them unimpaired for the enjoyment of future generations."[86]

The foundation of this statement is the underlying premise that landscape preservation could be achieved through park development, a premise that had sustained the American park movement since the mid-19th century. This statement of policy reiterated and condensed the recommendations Olmsted's father had made, for example, in his 1865 Yosemite Valley report.[87] In dozens of municipal, metropolitan, and state park development plans since then, landscape architects such as the elder Olmsted, H. W. S. Cleveland, and Charles Eliot had demonstrated that beautiful scenery could be made "available," without destroying it for posterity, through development that drew on the formal vocabulary and planning traditions of landscape park design. Through the wording of the 1916 Park Service legislation, Frederick Law Olmsted, Jr., and his colleagues endeavored to continue this tradition on the federal level, by establishing management and design policies that would lead to the systematic development of national parks as landscape parks, and therefore to the preservation of these scenic places from other more destructive forms of exploitation.

Once the Park Service bill was passed, Mather called for a fifth national park conference, this one to be held in Washington, DC, where Congress now needed to be lobbied for appropriations. The conference met in the new National Museum in January 1917 and featured an exhibition of paintings of national parks by Thomas Moran and Albert Bierstadt, among others. The Washington conference, a less staid affair than earlier conferences had been, featured popular lectures on a wide variety of topics, as well as slide presentations and motion pictures in the evenings. At the previous national park conferences railroad executives and hotel operators strongly influenced the agenda of topics discussed, but a greater diversity of park promoters participated in the Washington conference. Colorful, long-time park advocates such as Enos Mills (the "John Muir of the Rockies") and William Steel of Crater Lake played a greater role in the proceedings. Women, in particular, were noticably more present. Mary Belle King Sherman spoke on the history of the "women's part in national parks development." Ada F. Chalmers, Marion Randall Parsons, and Anna Louise Strong made presentations on "family hiking," "living in the parks," and "using national parks" from the perspectives of women visiting and working in national parks. The second day of the conference was designated "Education Day," and a number of natural scientists and educators spoke of the importance of parks as outdoor laboratories and classrooms. On the fourth day of the conference, "motor travel to the parks" was the featured issue. Mather had inaugurated a new era of park management and policy concerns, an era which the Washington conferees greeted with enthusiasm. Among the many distinguished officials to attend the conference, Secretary Lane, Chief Forester Henry S. Graves, Senator Reed Smoot (Utah), representatives William Kent (California), Frederick H. Gillett (Massachusetts), and Scott Ferris (Oklahoma), all expressed unqualified approbation for Mather and his policies.[88]

Mather's behavior during the conference, however, struck some as despondent and erratic. Immediately after the conference, in fact, he suffered a nervous collapse during a dinner being given in his honor at the Cosmos Club. He was hospitalized for the next six months and was unable to resume his rigorous schedule for a year and a half.[89] In April 1917, with Mather in the hospital and the United States entering World War I, Congress funded the National Park Service. Secretary Lane named Mather director of the new bureau, with Horace Albright as his assistant, acting as director in his stead. The fact that Lane apparently had no qualms naming the hospitalized Mather as director of the new bureau was an indication of the nearly universal high regard Mather enjoyed among his peers. A charismatic and effective executive, Mather created a cadre of loyal park executives and superintendents that continued to direct Park Service policy long after his death in 1930.

Albright, at the age of twenty-seven, had already demonstrated himself to be an exceptional legal and administrative aide, and he now directed the Park Service from its establishment in 1917 through the spring of 1918. His first priority was responding to the demands of opportunistic stockmen who, wrapping themselves in the flag and exploiting wartime emotions, wanted national parks open for "emergency grazing."[90] But Albright did far more than defend the parks during this critical period. He organized personnel, secured the next year's appropriations, and avoided offending more senior colleagues, such as Robert Sterling Yard, who might have resented the amount of responsibility assumed by Mather's young assistant.[91] His 1917 annual report, the first such report of the National Park Service, amassed comprehensive information on the condition and needs of the parks. Albright summarized a history of the "National Park Idea," and he compiled visitor statistics, Congressional appropriations, and legislative histories going back as far as records allowed.[92] He reported that an "astonishing increase in the number of cars in the national parks" was underway, as well as "an astounding increase in . . . park-to-park travel," indicating that visitors were beginning to see more than one park at a time and were visiting the parks as a system—a trend made possible by the increasing use of automobiles. He recommended the creation of a "National Tourist Bureau" and further recognition of a "Park-to-Park Highway" route to encourage this popular discovery of the parks.

In his summary, Albright made a series of ambitious recommendations: the transfer of the Grand Canyon from the Forest Service to the Park Service, the enlargement of Sequoia to include the Kings Canyon and

Kern River regions as well as the summit of Mount Whitney, and the removal of remaining U.S. Army troops from Yellowstone and the addition of Jackson Hole and the Teton range to that park.[93] Albright actively pursued Mather's agenda, in other words, and even expanded on it. By the spring of 1918, Albright had also assembled a consensus among a broad range of park supporters and public officials for a statement of policy to direct the activities of the new Park Service. He drafted the letter late in 1917 and had it reviewed by the entire cast of park supporters in Washington before submitting it to Mather for approval.[94]

In May 1918, after Mather had returned to health and had officially assumed his role as director of the Park Service, the document was made official in the form of a letter addressed to Mather and signed by Secretary Lane. As a set of instructions setting out official policy, the letter summarized the principal ideas of Lane, Mather, Albright and other leading park advocates in Washington at the time; these policies, in turn, clearly reflected the influence of McFarland, Olmsted, and the scenic preservationists who had been active in the Hetch-Hetchy controversy and other debates since the turn of the century. The statement, for example, that "every activity of the Service is subordinate to the duties imposed upon it to faithfully preserve the parks for posterity" simply restated the position F. L. Olmsted, Jr., had glossed from his father's Yosemite report. Other lessons imparted by the younger Olmsted, Mark Daniels, and others had been absorbed by Albright and appeared in the 1918 policy letter: "In the construction of roads, trails, buildings, and other improvements, particular attention must be devoted always to the harmonizing of these improvements with the landscape. This is a most important item in our program of development and requires the employment of trained engineers who either possess a knowledge of landscape architecture or have a proper appreciation of the esthetic value of park lands. All improvements will be carried out in accordance with a preconceived plan developed with special reference to the preservation of the landscape, and comprehensive plans for future development of the national parks on an adequate scale will be prepared as funds are available for this purpose."[95] The 1918 letter, bearing Lane's signature, clarified and validated the intended central role of planned "park development" (landscape architecture in other words) in the early activities of the National Park Service.

Upon his return to work in 1918, Mather resumed a tireless and energetic pace promoting national parks and domestic tourism generally. The subsequent dramatic increase in numbers of visitors to national parks has often been described as proof of Mather's genius as a "salesman"; but Mather did not create the rising tide of interest in domestic tourism as much as he was lifted by it. A new public—a public that traveled the country in motor vehicles not trains—grew to prominence quickly in the years following World War I. From the beginning, the Park Service scrambled to keep up with the needs of this more numerous, more middle class group of patrons. But auto tourism did not begin or end with the national parks; wherever significant urban populations were within driving range of outstanding scenery, auto clubs and park promoters (often one in the same group) soon appeared. National park promotion sometimes coincided with nearby municipal and regional park campaigns as well.

In Denver, for example, under the autocratic benevolence of Mayor Robert W. Speer, the city park commission hired George Kessler, the designer of the Kansas City parks and boulevards, to design an ambitious municipal park and parkway system in 1907. But Mayor Speer's interest extended beyond municipal parks and parkways. In 1912 the city charter was altered to allow the municipality to acquire "mountain parks" and connecting right-of-ways in the scenic areas around Denver. Olmsted Brothers were then hired to plan a regional park system of scenic reservations within a fifty-mile radius of the city. In reports to the city in 1912 and 1913, F. L. Olmsted, Jr., described a system of large reservations that would preserve scenic landscapes in the foothills of the Front Range near Denver by acquiring them and making them accessible for tourism and recreation. Picnic areas, campgrounds, shelters, and hotel sites were designated, in addition to routes for new parkways and other road improvements that would make it possible for Denverites to visit the parks on day trips. Denver, by 1910 a city of over 200,000 people, recognized the economic and other benefits such a system could bring, and acquisition and development of the mountain park system began immediately.[96]

Recreational uses of automobiles around Denver also stimulated interest in Rocky Mountain scenery at higher elevations. Lodges and hotels began to proliferate in the Estes Park region after 1907, the year F. O. Stanley—best known as the co-inventor of the Stanley Steamer—began construction on a large resort hotel there. Stanley arranged for visitors to be brought up to his mountain hotel in eleven-passenger versions of his famous steam-powered vehicles, which negotiated the steep ascent from the railhead on the plains below.[97] The village of Estes Park grew into a major resort as both roads and automotive technology improved and made the spectacular peaks and serene "parks" (as the high meadows of the Rocky Mountains have been known since the early 19th century) more accessible. By 1911, prominent citizens in Estes Park had formed a Protective Association, which advocated the creation of a surrounding Rocky Mountain National Park to preserve the scenery from which they derived their incomes. Urged on by the volatile Enos Mills, one of the hotel owners in the village, the park advocates decried the Forest Service for allowing indiscriminate logging and grazing that destroyed the forests and wildflower meadows tourists came to see. Scenic preservationists such as Mills and J. Horace McFarland (who was easily recruited to the cause) were soon joined by the Denver Chamber of Commerce, local elected officials, the newly organized Colorado Mountain Club, and local auto clubs.

Tourism, again, was the unifying interest; by 1914 there were an estimated 56,000 visitors to the region and ten thousand automobiles climbed steep roads into the mountains every year.[98] Once accessible to an urban population, scenic landscapes, it was agreed, generated more economic activity in an "unimpaired" state than they could through agriculture and extractive industries that destroyed scenic qualities. Congress enacted legislation creating Rocky Mountain National Park in 1915, shortly after Stephen Mather arrived in Washington to begin his efforts on behalf of the parks. Mather must have been impressed by the success of the legislative campaign and by the role of the auto interests in promoting domestic tourism. At the dedication of Rocky Mountain National Park that summer, he encountered several groups of auto enthusiasts (in over three hundred cars) who were anxious to improve connecting routes to other parks. Mather immediately endorsed the "Park-to-Park Highway" campaign, to designate a 3,500-mile route connecting all the major western parks with improved roads. The Denver auto enthusiasts (who included the head of the Denver Chamber of Commerce, a future mayor, the local Packard dealer, and assorted other civic leaders) then set off for the five hundred-mile drive to Yellowstone, inaugurating the first leg of the proposed interpark system.[99]

The importance of early auto tourism to national park campaigns was being demonstrated in other regions of the country as well. In the Pacific Northwest, auto tourists, not train tourists, made up the significant portion of early park visitors at Mount Rainier National Park, as they did at Rocky Mountain. Like Denver, the Puget Sound cities of Tacoma and Seattle were growing quickly in the early 20th century, and these communities also had spectacular mountain scenery within a day's drive. Seattle had a progressive attitude about municipal park and parkway planning as well; beginning in 1903, J. C. Olmsted had designed a comprehensive municipal park system that exploited views of the Cascade and Olympic ranges and conformed to the rugged topography of that city. Interest in regional scenery followed as soon as improved automobiles and roads began to open new opportunities for tourism in the nearby Cascades. In Tacoma, the local "good roads" movement brought together boosters, businessmen, bicycle clubs, and automobile owners all of whom concentrated their efforts on improving the Mountain Highway from Tacoma to Mount Rainier. In 1899, the same year that Congress made the great volcanic peak a national park, the Washington Good Roads Association first came to order in Spokane. The Good Roads Association, along with other groups, soon lobbied for state and federal funds for improvements to the Mountain Highway.[100]

In 1912, a coalition of commercial clubs, chambers of commerce, and other civic groups formed the Seattle-Tacoma Rainier National Park Committee, which advocated the "development and exploitation of the great Park." The committee especially concerned itself with improving roads both to and in the park, and that December they hired a civil engineer, Samuel C. Lancaster, to go to Washington and lobby Congress for increased appropriations for park roads. Lancaster, a road engineer of national reputation, was familiar to many in the area as the engineer in charge of the construction of J. C. Olmsted's parkways in Seattle. As a former consultant to the Bureau of Public Roads in Washington, he was

The Columbia River Gorge, as seen from the Columbia River Highway. The road "form[s] the frame," according to the engineer Samuel C. Lancaster, "connecting humanity with the Divinely beautiful pictures which everywhere abound."

also well connected in the capital. In 1912, however, his efforts to lobby Congress for significant appropriations for development on Mount Rainier were probably premature.[101] Upon his return to the Northwest, Lancaster made his greatest contribution to the advance of auto tourism and scenic preservation. Lancaster was close friends with the president of the Washington Good Roads Association, Samuel Hill, and had designed a system of roads for Hill's estate. In 1913, Hill arranged for Lancaster to be hired as the consulting engineer for what would be the most significant highway project of its type in the West: the Columbia River Highway. Conceived in part as Portland's response to the development of the Mountain Highway to Mount Rainier National Park (which benefited Tacoma), the proposed Columbia River Highway passed through the fine scenery of the Columbia River Gorge and opened possibilities for tourism in Oregon's Mount Hood region as well.

Although the Columbia River Highway followed an established transportation corridor of great commercial significance, the fact that it was planned primarily as a "scenic highway" indicates the degree to which the economics of tourism in the West bolstered early movements to finance road improvement projects (as well as early park campaigns). "Talk about Switzerland," Samuel Hill liked to say when promoting the Columbia River road, "there are thirty Switzerlands in Oregon. . . . We will cash in, year after year, on our crop of scenic beauty, without depleting it in any way."[102] Completed to Lancaster's exacting standards in 1916, the highway was the first in the Northwest to be paved with asphalt. Lancaster designed sturdy concrete bridges and guardwalls in a consistent and characteristic idiom, and he provided scenic overlooks near the many waterfalls and vistas that lined the route. Lancaster made the highway a showcase of the most advanced engineering of the day, while at the same time, since the road was intended for the pleasure and convenience of tourists, the scenic qualities of the region were carefully considered and preserved in the alignment and construction of the highway. An accomplished publicist as well as an engineer, Lancaster later described this process: "When fixing the location of the Columbia River Highway, we tried to preserve the great natural beauty, and . . . to have the road form the frame connecting humanity with the Divinely beautiful pictures which everywhere abound."[103]

In other regions of the country as well, the creation of scenic highways and promotional route designations of various types became powerful tools for scenic preservation. Mather's Park-to-Park Highway was only the most obvious example of designated scenic or tourist routes that maximized the unfolding recreational opportunities that the combination of automobiles, improved roads, and developed scenic reservations offered. The huge increases in national park visitation recorded by Albright in his 1917 annual report consisted almost entirely of a massive influx of people in automobiles.[104]

The park advocates who cared most deeply about preserving scenic landscapes in the United States welcomed this trend, which allowed a broader range of Americans to appreciate landscape beauty and (hopefully) become advocates for its preservation. The automobile opened western tourism to a wider range of people because it was less expensive to drive and camp outdoors than it was to ride in a train and pay for hotels and livery services. Several historians have observed that auto tourism, and national park tourism in particular, remained almost exclusively a middle class pursuit, appealing mostly to particular segments of society.[105] American landscape parks, however, whether municipal, regional or national, have always been quintessentially middle class institutions, and therefore have embodied the civic ideals of particular groups. But automobiles allowed national parks to enjoy the same middle class patronage previously more characteristic of parks in or near cities, and therefore to become appreciated by the "public" in this specific sense of the word. Only then could formerly remote scenic reservations function as "public parks" in the sense that Olmsted and Vaux used that term in the 1860s: public landscapes in which large, at least somewhat diverse groups could congregate and become a community through their common appreciation of scenery. The reaction to landscape beauty, like any aesthetic experience, remained deeply personal; but in the context of the landscape park, an individual's reaction to scenery transcended Romantic isolation and engendered a sense of community (Olmsted's "communitiveness") based in shared aesthetic appreciation.

Such ideals of community had tantalized the generation that had been torn by civil war and frightened by the diversity of urban immigration.

Longings for social unity continued to fascinate the next generation of scenic preservationists and landscape architects. If Central Park had been, in Vaux's words, "the big art work of the Republic," the development of a national park system in the early 20th century sought to complete this project and, in Mark Daniels's duller rhetoric, "encourage patriotism." But in either case, the presence of large, at least somewhat diverse groups of people was not simply a necessary evil that enabled the preservation of scenic places; the public's communion through a common aesthetic appreciation of picturesque scenery infused landscape scenes with cultural significance and value. From the crowds that first wandered up to Central Park in 1858, to the crowds that were seeking out Yosemite Valley, Paradise Park, and the high peaks of the Front Range fifty years later, Americans sought to invest scenery—and the experience of appreciating scenery—with ideals of social and national unity, through the development of landscape parks.

It was the mass production of automobiles, above all, that allowed this expansion of the American park movement to take place. In the national parks, "sagebrushers," or auto campers, soon overwhelmed the carriage trade "dudes" who preferred the resort hotels.[106] In 1921, Mather observed that "the advent of the automobile with the opportunity for its use freely in all the parks in the past five years has been the open sesame for many thousands." He went on to observe that as early as 1919, "74 percent of the visitors of Yosemite National Park entered in their own machines."[107] These demographics indicated that the model of the national park as a minimally funded, semi-private resort had seen its day. Auto tourists, unlike earlier park visitors, were not paying customers; they were the "public." This implied that the costs of providing better roads, campgrounds, sanitary facilities, and other improvements would be met indirectly, through taxes of one form or another, as they were for public highways (another type of public landscape the federal government began to subsidize during this period). In both cases, private interests (as represented by countless chambers of commerce and other groups) desired such improvements and profited by them. Such groups could not, however, command the capital, engineering expertise, or legal authority that park and highway projects demanded. The development of municipal parks and parkways had been publicly planned and financed since the 1850s for precisely these reasons. As national parks also became "public" parks, in this sense, their development also required government planning and funding.

Stephen Mather poised the National Park Service to be the agent of this physical development, which from the beginning was predicated on the already "astonishing increase" of auto tourists. Crowds of people in automobiles, therefore, could hardly be considered merely by-products or necessary evils in national parks. The public was as vital to the success of national parks as was the scenery; without people there were no parks, only wild regions of the public domain, which, as such, were easily subject to other forms of ownership and exploitation. The picturesque alchemy that shifted wild lands into valued landscapes—still the principal mechanism of scenic preservation in the early 20th century—occurred through shared public experiences of landscape beauty. The expansion of this phenomenon on a national scale depended on large numbers of people being able to reach national parks affordably.

In 1920, Mather reported that "the great bulk of travel to our national parks [is] by automobile." That year he dedicated the nation's "greatest scenic drive," the "National Park-to-Park Highway." The route, which Mather had been publicizing for five years, connected all the western parks, describing a great loop from Denver down the Rockies, across to California via the Grand Canyon, up the Sierras to the Cascades, across to the northern Rockies at Glacier, and back to Denver. By 1921, the Park-to-Park Highway formed a six thousand-mile loop of designated state and county roads, about two thousand miles of which were paved. The total number of visitors to the national parks now surpassed one million annually.[108] Mather understood that a successful park system—whether a municipal system of parks and parkways or a national system of scenic reservations—depended on well-built connections between each of its components. From Boston's "Emerald Necklace," to Minneapolis's ring of parks and parkways, to Eliot's metropolitan parks, many successful park systems (at various scales) had taken the form of great circuits. By 1921, Mather had begun to shape a true national park system: a physically connected group of varied public reservations, all managed according to a consistent set of policies.

Mather, Albright, and others concerned with developing a national park system, however, now needed to secure Congressional appropriations adequate to achieve the ambitious project. Although park auto entrance fees immediately provided a considerable source of income to the new Park Service, the parks themselves could never directly generate enough income to offset the cost of their development and operation. Mather did cling to the assertion that national parks would "pay their own way" through auto fees and concession contracts, but they never came close to doing so.[109] Hotels and other facilities continued to be financed by concessioners, but the expense of road, trail, and utility construction demanded Congressional appropriations if these improvements were ever to be done efficiently and according to "comprehensive plans."

While Congress moved slowly to provide adequate appropriations for park development, Mather expanded the administrative and professional capabilities of the Park Service to undertake the work. In 1917, the Park Service, apart from the park superintendents and rangers in the field, consisted of only six Washington employees, including Mather, as director, and Albright, his assistant director.[110] In 1919, Albright transferred from Washington to become the superintendent of Yellowstone, and Mather named Arno B. Cammerer as his new assistant director. Cammerer was a career civil servant who had risen to assistant to the secretary of the national Commission of Fine Arts, where he had gotten to know Albright while working on some of the numerous park matters in which the commission was involved.[111]

It was Cammerer, while still with the Commission of Fine Arts in 1918, who had suggested to Mather and Albright that a landscape design division be created in the Park Service. Cammerer also suggested that they arrange for the transfer of a young landscape architect, Charles P. Punchard, Jr., from the District of Columbia Office of Public Buildings and Grounds to the Park Service.[112] Punchard had begun his career working for his uncle, the landscape architect William H. Punchard, in Massachusetts. He then attended the landscape program at Harvard beginning in 1909, and in 1911 he went into business with a partner, Frederick Evans, in Cleveland. In 1913 he was diagnosed with tuberculosis, however, and at the age of twenty-eight he relocated to Denver, where the mountain air made his condition more bearable.[113]

In 1917, Punchard moved back East to Washington to take the position of landscape architect with the Office of Public Buildings and Grounds. As the capital's landscape architect, Punchard had many contacts not only with Cammerer at the Commission of Fine Arts, but certainly also with F. L. Olmsted, Jr., who had planned the Washington park and parkway system (in his work for the McMillan Commission) and subsequently served as a founding member of the Commission of Fine Arts, which was established in part to oversee the execution of the Washington plan.[114] Punchard was not as recovered, however, as perhaps he had hoped. The transfer to the Park Service that Cammerer arranged in the summer of 1918 was done in large part because Punchard's physician had ordered him to get out of Washington; working with the Park Service meant that he would immediately be sent back West, where he hoped the drier climate would again ease his chronic lung condition.

In 1918 Mather expanded the Park Service organizational chart to include a "field engineering" division, in which Punchard was given the title "landscape engineer," while a civil engineer, George E. Goodwin, was named "chief engineer." The new engineering division was based in Portland, Oregon, where Goodwin concentrated exclusively on surveying, contracting, and building park roads and trails.[115] The landscape engineer, on the other hand, according to Mather, was a sort of more practical landscape architect: "A man trained in landscape architecture and yet possessed of the ability and willingness to take a very practical view of the problem to be solved." His activities included "planning the location and development of permanent camps," the design of "appropriate gate structures . . . harmonious with their surroundings," and the planning and review of plans for "buildings of all kinds, whether they are to be erected by the government or by the business interests catering to the needs of the public." "Forest improvement" and "vista thinning" were undertaken in several parks, "with excellent results." In all, however, "the guiding principle is that the natural conditions of the parks must be disturbed as little as possible consistent with necessary development in the public interest."[116]

That summer, an apparently reinvigorated Punchard inspected most of the parks, consulting and advising superintendents, providing some sketches and working drawings, and giving in some instances "detailed instructions on the ground," or field supervision of maintenance and construction activities. Punchard's training in picturesque aesthetics and the techniques of landscape park management guided his recommendations in 1918 and 1919. At Yosemite, where he spent his first winter with the Park Service, he recommended dredging Mirror Lake, which had already silted in considerably, and thinning the trees on the valley floor to "open up and develop very interesting open spaces and vistas." In both cases, the proposed actions were intended to assure that the classic views that painters and photographers had made famous since the 1860s remained unimpaired. At Yellowstone (which like Yosemite was being overrun by auto tourists) he devoted almost all his time to locating new campgrounds and to studies of the existing permanent camps "with a view to making . . . them more attractive."[117] Later, he recommended "industrial groups" for parks, or maintenance yards, in which garages, shops, and stables could be placed in a consolidated group, like the service area of an estate plan. He advocated standardized signs for all the parks, an important element of systematic park management; and he recommended that "the study of . . . the automobile camp should go on with renewed vigor. This form of visiting and enjoying the parks . . . has by no means reached the peak of its popularity."[118]

In the spring of 1920, Punchard described the work of the "landscape engineer" in an article directed to other members of his profession.[119] "He works in an advisory capacity to the superintendents," Punchard explained, and is "a small art commission in himself," since "all plans of the concessioners must be submitted to him for approval as to architecture and location before they can be constructed." In addition, "he is responsible for the design of all structures of the Service, the location of roads and other structures on the ground which will influence the appearance of the park . . . [including] ranger cabins, rest houses, checking stations, gateway structures, employee's cottages, [and] comfort stations." "Forest improvement and vista cutting," activities Charles Eliot had stressed in scenic reservation management, were necessary to keep important views from disappearing behind screens of vegetation. Other major activities included "the design of villages . . . [and] the design and location of the automobile camps."

One person obviously could not undertake all these activities comprehensively. Arno Cammerer later admitted that his friend, "because of the shortage of funds, and due to the amount of work before him," had been able to do little more than "hit the high spots."[120] But Punchard made a spirited and well-received essay into a new branch of landscape architectural practice between 1918 and 1920—a branch he was helping to invent. His tuberculosis, however, worsened, and in the fall of 1920 he died. That August, Mather had hired Daniel R. Hull as assistant landscape engineer; after Punchard's death Hull assumed the principal landscape engineer's position. A few months later a new assistant landscape engineer, Paul P. Kiessig, was hired.[121]

In many ways, however, the practice of landscape architecture was still premature at the Park Service since Congress resisted making regular and adequate appropriations for park development. While Punchard reviewed concessioner proposals and offered advice to superintendents, Mather, Cammerer, and Albright busily lobbied for funding to implement more ambitious proposals. By 1920, Mather expressed impatience with the inadequacies of "wartime appropriations in times of peace," especially since road improvements in parks were being delayed. In 1921, he continued to boost the "Great Circle Highway," or Park-to-Park Highway, working with the Park-to-Park Highway Association that his Denver allies had established. Park appropriations, however, lagged behind the increasing interest in parks already being shown by tourists. Good roads often ended at park entrances, a situation not considered conducive to building a loyal constituency of park visitors. In 1921 Mather compiled a chart comparing visitor statistics, appropriations, and the "absolute minimum" estimates for budgets that would provide "the essential needs of the respective parks," according to the park superintendents. The chart showed a widening gap between the projected needs of the parks and the budgets actually appropriated between 1916 and 1921.[122] Appropriations were going up, but not to the degree necessary for a comprehensive, system-wide park development program to accommodate increased numbers of tourists.

Besides neglecting to provide adequate appropriations for the number of visitors making use of the parks, however, Congress also threatened the integrity of the reservations in more direct ways. While plans for park development were being drawn up by Punchard and Hull, other plans were proposed that were not likely to leave national park scenery "unimpaired." In 1919, members of the Idaho congressional delegation approached Secretary Lane for permission to conduct preliminary surveys for major reservoir construction in the southwest corner of Yellowstone National Park. Their plans would have flooded thousands of acres of the park in order to irrigate the arid lands of the Snake River Plain to the west. Lane granted permission for a reconnaissance survey, perhaps relying on the knowledge that he had no authority to grant permits for private irrigation or power projects in national parks in any case. In 1920, however, western congressmen succeeded in altering the Federal Water Power Act (which created a Federal Power Commission that year) with provisions that opened all the national parks to hydroelectric and irrigation development.[123]

The result was what Mather described in 1920 as "a crisis in national conservation." In his *Annual Report*, Mather outlined not one, but five proposals for Yellowstone that would have flooded the Bechler and Falls River valleys, and converted Yellowstone, Shoshone, Heart, and Lewis lakes into reservoirs by damming their outlets and inundating them. Dam, road, and water tunnel construction would have been necessary over a large portion of the park. Even worse, "there is not a lake or a waterfall in any one of our national parks," Mather warned, that would not be open to similar development. Applications for dam construction in Yosemite, Sequoia, and Grand Canyon national parks (in addition to the five Yellowstone applications) immediately were put before the new Federal Power Commission. Thanks to Mather's efforts, however, President Wilson had arranged that no permits in national parks would be granted by the new power commission until Congress had the opportunity to exempt the parks from the provisions of the bill.[124] New legislation achieved this in 1921 by requiring that Congress specifically authorize any permits granted by the Federal Power Commission in national parks.[125] A first great test of the ability of the Park Service to protect the integrity of the parks had been met successfully.

The arrival of the Republicans of the Harding administration later that month, however, began a new and infamous era in the Department of the Interior.[126] Harding's secretary of the interior, Albert B. Fall, immediately indicated that he would be sympathetic to power development in national parks. The direct target was Bechler Canyon in Yellowstone, a magnificent wilderness of waterfalls, forests, and boggy meadows, which now seemed likely to suffer the same fate as the Hetch-Hetchy Valley. In 1921, however, Mather was ready to employ his network of political allies, press connections, and local park advocates to thwart what was soon known as the "Fall-Bechler Irrigation Plot." Thanks to intensive lobbying and campaigning to educate both Congress and the public on the value of "unimpaired scenery," Mather eventually turned back all of the many power and irrigation plans proposed for national parks over the next five years.[127]

Park advocates of every type were roused to defend Yellowstone; but perhaps one of the most affecting voices raised was that of the landscape architect, Charles Punchard. In an article published posthumously in 1921, he recorded alarm at the "bombshell that has landed in our midst, in the shape of an irrigation project." Exhausted after three seasons of efforts in the parks, dying of tuberculosis, and frustrated that he had not been able to do more to accommodate tourists and deter the threats of power and grazing interests, Punchard reminded his readers that they "should bear in mind . . . the newness of the whole [national park] movement and the difficulties under which the small personnel is now working."[128]

Mather had proved that he personally could provide the political skills and organization needed to stop Congress from despoiling national parks to satisfy local constituencies. The second great test the Park Service would face would be to provide landscape designs, engineering guidelines, and planning policies that would make it possible to bring the American public into these places in unprecedented numbers, without degrading either the parks themselves, or the experience for park visitors. In the long run, the fight to preserve national parks from power and grazing interests hinged on the outcome of the struggle to successfully develop them as landscape parks. Park administrators and landscape architects therefore were under considerable pressure to increase park appropriations and devise workable plans for national park development.

But as F. L. Olmsted, Jr., had discovered through his ruminations on the Hetch-Hetchy controversy, designs for landscape development in national parks could not simply be enlarged versions of plans for municipal parks. The Park Service would require a special variety of landscape park design and planning appropriate for far vaster areas, which were of great scientific, as well as aesthetic, importance. The model for this development would be that of the 20th-century landscape park: a large, scenic reservation that preserved existing landscape features "unimpaired" through the limited construction of scenic drives and other features of "park development." These designed elements—from trails and overlooks to entire "park villages"—would draw on a formal vocabulary of landscape park design that had been elaborated by two generations of American landscape architects. This design work would be buttressed by an even older tradition of picturesque aesthetics and design theory, which since the 18th century had guided physical development of certain scenic places in order to preserve their beauty and increase their accessibility. The response to the inspiration of the site ("the genius of the place"), the subordination of all architectural construction, the emphasis on winding drives and paths that revealed scenic vistas in considered sequences—these were the fundamental principles of picturesque landscape design, a tradition that may have been fading in the early 20th century, but still provided a foundation for the landscape architectural practice developed to meet the requirements of American national parks.

In this context, the landscape architects Daniel Hull and Thomas C. Vint (who replaced Paul Kiessig as Hull's assistant in 1922) undertook the tasks of "landscape engineers" at the point when the Park Service entered its most significant period of design and development. Throughout the course of the 1920s, Mather, Cammerer, and Albright consolidated political support for the Park Service, frustrated attempts to compromise the integrity of the parks, and secured significant appropriations for park development. During the same period, Park Service landscape architects were required to define the design idiom, the planning policies, and the administrative agreements that would consummate this political success. They needed to design landscapes that would forever fix an image of park development appropriate for national scenic reservations. Over the next twenty years, the period covered in the next portion of this study, Park Service landscape architects, engineers, and architects invented a unique idiom of landscape architecture (and architecture as well) that succeeded in many of these goals. For millions, Park Service landscape architecture of this period continues to epitomize what state and national park development should aspire to be.

The designed landscapes described in the second part of this study established a necessary middle ground: the mediation between the American automotive tourist and the vast reservoirs of natural resources and national imagination that are our state and national parks. These landmarks of landscape architecture are among the most important public park designs in the history of the American park movement; for when the National Park Service applied the practice of park development to the great wildernesses and relatively unspoiled scenery of North America, it realized the fullest potential of what parks could be. A landscape design history that had begun two hundred years earlier in Great Britain culminated in the preservation of scenic places on a continental scale, for the benefit of hundreds of millions of park visitors.

The Grand Canyon Village Historic District:

The "Fairsted School" and American Town Planning

PART TWO

Chapter 3

By 1920, the American park movement had been active for seventy-five years. Hundreds of municipalities and dozens of state and county governments had formed park commissions and developed park systems. The federal government had taken a newly active role in managing the national park system beginning with the authorization of the National Park Service in 1916. With Stephen Mather's return to health and active duty in the spring of 1918, the new bureau engaged in a period of intense and successful public relations and lobbying campaigns and, following the armistice that fall, automotive tourists took to the roads as never before. The seventeen national parks and twenty-two national monuments under the care of the National Park Service were poised to assume unprecedented significance in American life.

Landscape architecture, the profession Olmsted and Vaux named and legitimized in the 1860s, had matured with the American park movement. By 1920, enrollment in the American Society of Landscape Architecture was well over two hundred individuals, mostly located in the Northeast, Midwest, and California. The leadership of the organization reflected decades of experience in municipal, county, and state park design. Frederick Law Olmsted, Jr., presided over the group that year, for example, and Warren Manning, George Kessler, and O. C. Simonds served as officers.[1] Other prominent professionals, such as Henry Hubbard and Frank Waugh, had established careers primarily as educators in the university degree programs that, since 1900, had been established at sixteen institutions, from Texas Agricultural and Mechanical College, to Smith College.[2] By 1920, a new generation of university educated landscape architects had entered the field.

Among them were individuals such as Mark Daniels, Charles Punchard, Daniel Hull, and Thomas Vint who brought to the National Park Service the training and skills acquired at Harvard, Berkeley, and the University of Illinois. In addition to the contributions of these younger individuals, some of the most prominent landscape architects of the day offered the Park Service free consultation. Jens Jensen, for example, advised on planting plans for Hot Springs Reservation (now Hot Springs National Park), Arkansas in 1918; Olmsted advised on Lafayette (now Acadia) National Park in 1919; and both Olmsted and Harvard Professor James Sturgis Pray advised on developments at Yellowstone in 1921.[3] The Commission of Fine Arts in Washington, of which Olmsted was a founding member in 1910, also took an official interest in national park work (as it was entitled to do). In 1918, Olmsted was replaced as the landscape architect on the commission by James L. Greenleaf, who served until 1927, when he was replaced by landscape architect Ferruccio Vitale.[4]

Landscape architects like Greenleaf and Vitale, however, represented the residential, or "country place," branch of American landscape architecture. This practice put a premium on the ability of landscape architects to design gardens in a range of historical styles. After the turn of the century, estate designers were expected to have extensive knowledge of Italian Renaissance and French Baroque garden history, as well as thorough architectural training. New university programs in landscape architecture typically emphasized such academic training, preparing their students for careers in residential landscape design. Interest in picturesque theory and practice noticeably waned in the profession. Many among the younger generation of landscape architects probably would have agreed with Norman T. Newton, a 1920 graduate of the new landscape program at Cornell, who later wrote in his influential textbook, *Design on the Land*, that the "English Landscape Gardening School" was no more than "an unfortunate distortion of nature and a failure . . . to distinguish between the native glories of open landscape and the architectonic requirements of areas closely associated with human habitation."[5]

Newton's dismissal of picturesque design recalls critiques of the landscape park that were as old as the formal type itself. In the late 19th century, however, these controversies had been recast as a public debate regarding the relative virtues of "formal" versus "informal," or "natural style," garden design. This controversy began in Victorian England, where the widespread revival of historical and architectonic garden styles had precipitated a strong negative reaction. The landscape gardener William Robinson had published his descriptions of "the wild garden" already in 1870. In sometimes heated polemics, Robinson rejected terrace gardens and elaborate parterres and advocated less structured gardens, produced through the unorthodox use of native, hardy perennials (some that had previously been considered weeds) and the "naturalization" of exotic plants that would thrive in British climates and soils. Masses of bulbs and other hardy spring flowers planted in "natural groupings" could transform meadows and stream banks into "wild gardens" that bloomed year after year, with no need for reworking beds or propagating new plants. Native roses and anemones in "ditches, lanes, copses, and hedgerows" could produce floral displays far more beautiful than tender annuals bedded out in contrived geometries. Robinson's "wild garden" was actually many gardens, each defined by ecological associations and conditions: the woodland garden of shade tolerant ferns and trillium, the stream bank lined with wild roses and poplars, the meadow planted with daffodils and snow drops, the hedgerow of holly and briars planted with clematis and ivies.[6] Robinson laid the foundation for Gertrude Jekyll and other Edwardian gardeners who thoroughly repudiated the Victorian taste for hothouse annuals and geometric arrangements, and who established a golden age of flower gardening in Great Britain through the intensive study of the textures and colors of both native and exotic perennials.

In the United States, the relative merits of "formal" and "natural" garden styles were also debated, although slightly later and with less of the acrimony that infected the exchanges between Robinson and his critics. The American debate reflected different circumstances. On the one hand, the American "formal" garden in the 1890s expressed considerable sophistication and elegance. Gardens designed by Charles Platt, for example, hardly manifested the eclectic, ornamental excess that Robinson had condemned so forcefully in earlier Victorian gardens. On the other hand, picturesque landscape design—the original "natural" style—survived in American landscape architecture in ways that it had not in British landscape gardening. In the 1890s, landscape architects such as Charles Eliot, J. C. Olmsted, and Warren Manning had opportunities to plan and design park systems for municipal, county, and regional park commissions, and this park development, at least in the context of large scenic reservations, continued to be guided by picturesque theory. Centered around Fairsted and the apprentices who had trained there, this essentially Reptonian design practice still characterized the American profession of landscape architecture to a significant degree. Contemporary gardening in the United States perhaps never attained the level of art and craft that it did in Edwardian England; but through the development of public landscape parks, "natural" landscape design expanded in the United States in ways that the more limited geography and relatively dense populations of Great Britain had not allowed.

Perhaps as a result of these differences, many American gardeners and landscape architects seemed to feel that the two modes of design—"formal" and "natural"—represented parts of a whole, each with its appropriate application. In 1893, Mariana Griswold Van Rensselaer, the preeminent American garden writer of her day, wrote that although "naturalistic methods of gardening are the most interesting and important to Americans," such methods are not themselves devoid of "formal elements." Furthermore, "a consistently formal scheme of design is sometimes better for use than any other," under the appropriate circumstances. Each "artistic ideal" has its place, and "there is no real opposition between the two systems, widely apart though their extreme results may lie."[7] American garden writers and landscape architects, in fact, often called for a catholic embrace of "formal" and "natural" design skills in the early 20th century. In 1917, the landscape architect Frank A. Waugh claimed that "every well-trained landscape architect in America designs freely in either the formal or natural style."[8]

More partisan American advocates of "natural gardens" did appear after the turn of the century, especially in the Midwest and California; but while these advocates of "nature gardens" certainly admired William Robinson, they were at least as influenced by garden design and ecological science emanating from Germany and northern Europe. Jens Jensen, the guiding spirit of the American "natural garden," emigrated from Denmark in 1884. He later secured a job as a laborer in the Chicago West Parks District, where he rose quickly and assumed responsibility for park design and construction supervision.[9] After 1900, Jensen left his park work and became more active in residential design in the Chicago area. In his private work, Jensen repudiated the historicizing, architectonic estate designs of most of his Eastern counterparts. His clients responded to his suggestions that they create essentially park-like estates, designed in a "natural" style that emphasized curvilinear paths and drives, irregular sheets of water, secluded meadows ("clearings"), and massed planting of trees and shrubs.

By 1915, after collaborating with contemporary "prairie style" architects (including Frank Lloyd Wright and Henry Babson), Jensen was being identified as a "prairie style landscape architect." That year, Wilhelm Miller, a professor of landscape architecture at the University of Illinois, launched a publication called "The Prairie Spirit in Landscape Gardening," which was devoted to publicizing the work of landscape architects (principally Jensen and O. C. Simonds) who had developed "a new mode of designing and planting, which aims to fit the particular scenery, climate, soil, labor, and other conditions of the prairies."[10] Jensen claimed to be inspired by the Midwestern prairie landscape, and the layered, limestone masonry he designed around pools and stream banks recalled Midwestern river bluffs and natural rock outcrops. He also rigorously restricted his choice of plants to native Midwestern species. Native hawthorns and dogwoods with strongly horizontal habits, for example, created "symbols of the prairie" that recalled the "horizontal lie of land and sky" typical of the Midwest. Jensen, as quoted by Miller, aimed "to re-create the atmosphere of the prairie by restoring as high a proportion as possible of trees, shrubs, and flowers native to Illinois."[11]

The "prairie spirit," so defined, remained largely a horticultural phenomenon. But Jensen's desire to cultivate and preserve native plants also extended to a related impulse to preserve "native scenery." Like many Americans in the early 20th century, Jensen enjoyed weekend outings to local scenic areas, such as the Indiana Dunes on Lake Michigan. As noted earlier, he had been instrumental in planning the Chicago "forest preserve districts" that resulted in a metropolitan system of scenic reservations around the city in 1913. The same year, he founded a local outing and conservation club, Friends of Our Native Landscape. Among the original members was Stephen Mather, then still a private businessman in Chicago. Another member of the group was the botanist Henry C. Cowles of the University of Chicago, who helped develop the science of plant communities through his study of the flora of the Indiana Dunes. Professor Cowles later influenced Jensen's ideas on grouping plants by ecological association.[12]

Ecological science developed quickly in the early 20th century and affected both Jensen's landscape design and his scenic preservation efforts. The Danish botanist Eugenius Warming published the English translation of *The Oecology of Plants* in 1909, and over the next ten years ecology (still primarily a science of plant communities) was discussed and taught by botanists and biologists in many American universities.[13] Several other American landscape architects, including Frank Waugh and Elsa Rehmann, were soon writing on the implications of ecological science on "natural styles" of landscape design. Waugh, another Midwesterner, initiated the landscape architecture program at the Massachusetts State Agricultural College (now the University of Massachusetts) in 1902, and taught there for the next thirty-seven years.[14] In 1917, he published *The Natural Style in Landscape Gardening*, a book that influenced Jensen and many other "natural garden" designers. Waugh describes a "natural style," in which it is the "aim of the artist to discover and to follow the principles of composition followed by nature." This "structural form" is further distinguished by comparison to "the formal garden form, which is symmetrical, balanced, enclosed and determinate." The "informal," or "natural form," on the other hand, is "unsymmetrical, not obviously balanced, not apparently enclosed and not marked by visible boundaries."[15]

Although Waugh's inspiration seems to be related to traditions in American residential landscape design going back to A. J. Downing, he differentiates his "natural style" from earlier "naturalistic," or picturesque design, which he disparages. Whether his references are intended or not, however, he does reiterate certain premises of picturesque design theory. When he states that "the natural style of landscape gardening endeavors to present its pictures in forms typical of the natural landscape and made vital by the landscape spirit," Pope's "genius of the place" does not seem far away. Much of Waugh's landscape theory—not unlike much of Jensen's landscape design—consciously or unconsciously restates selected tenets of American landscape park design as the basis of a "natural style" of "landscape gardening" that responds to the "spirit of the native landscape" and "accentuates the characteristic natural forms" that "clarify and interpret the spirit of the place." The scientific appreciation of native plants and plant communities did not in itself imply new artistic forms for landscape design; and although Waugh urges a consultation with "the spirit of the place" as a source of formal inspiration, it is unclear to what extent this intention differs from what American picturesque landscape designers had undertaken to achieve since the 19th century.

What was new about Waugh's "natural style" was, again, its emphasis on the virtues of native plant species over exotics. For Waugh, excluding the "common lilac and the homely apple tree . . . simply because they are not native to America" would be excessive, and "not good democratic Americanism, either." Nevertheless, only native plants express "native spirit," and the "natural style in landscape gardening is largely dependent on the native landscape" as evoked through the cultivation of plants native to the region. Waugh distinguishes the "natural" style from the "naturalistic," in the end, primarily through an emphatic proscription of exotic plant species.[16]

It should be noted that Waugh credits the German garden designer Willy Lange as his inspiration for the application of "ecological principle" in the "natural style" of garden design.[17] As early as 1900, Lange, who was influenced by contemporary pioneers of ecological science in Germany, had called for the creation of "nature gardens" in Germany based on "biological aesthetics" and the "germanic spirit of race [that] remembered its age-old relation to forest nature with its sunny clearings." Although Lange at first was alone in calling for such gardens based on ecological science and horticultural nativism, in the early 1930s his ideas were adopted by National Socialist ideologues. Lange's garden philosophy, according to historians Gert Groening and Joachim Wolschke-Buhlman, became "a milestone on the path to the amalgamation of National Socialism." The "nature garden" and the elimination of non-native plants later became official landscape management policies of the Nazi government.[18] But neither Waugh nor Jensen ever directly associated their design theories with nativist or xenophobic political views. Their enthusiasm for native Midwestern plants complemented the regionalism of Prairie Style architects and, in both cases, the "prairie spirit" was rooted in an appreciation of regional scenic beauty and local ecology, not hateful ideology.

The rhetoric associated with American regional and "natural" styles of garden design influenced Park Service landscape architects during a critical period. In California, gardens designed to complement contemporary Arts and Crafts residences (by Bernard Maybeck and Greene and Greene, for example) would have been regional adaptations of the "natural style" familiar to Mark Daniels, Daniel Hull, and Thomas Vint, all of whom worked in California before joining the Park Service. In the mild climates and rich soils of the West Coast, however, the cultivation of exotic plants from all over the world was at the heart of regional landscape design, whether in the "natural" style or not. But by the 1920s, Park Service landscape architects often specified native species in planting plans, and a ban on the introduction of exotic plants in parks was made official in 1930.[19] But trends in contemporary garden design only affected national park development to a certain extent, simply because the role of horticulture was limited in park planning. The construction of scenic roads, trails, and planned villages, for example, involved design and construction efforts of a broad scope, and therefore necessarily drew on a range of theoretical and practical sources beyond those suggested by Jensen, Waugh, or Lange. Nevertheless, the "natural garden" provided a revealing metaphor of the national park in the early 20th century. And in some national park developed areas, Waugh's "natural style" provided an appropriate theoretical framework for planting design that specified native species grouped by ecological associations.

In 1917, the U.S. Forest Service hired Waugh as a consultant to advise on potential recreational developments in scenic areas of national forests. It is interesting to note that in this context, Waugh's subsequent advice to the Forest Service was not drawn from his own advice to home gardeners. It clearly echoed instead the recommendations Mark Daniels had made to the Department of the Interior several years earlier regarding the management of national parks. Waugh wrote in a 1918 Forest Service publication that "the art of handling forest lands is to serve best the purpose of the owner. That purpose is sometimes money income; sometimes it is the production of material for some particular kind of use; or it may be the embellishment of a pleasure park." Waugh also adopted the Park Service title "landscape engineer" in his work for the Forest Service (in private practice he preferred the title "landscape gardener"). He described priorities for the management of scenic areas in national forests that would have sounded familiar to Daniels or Punchard: first, to preserve the landscape (for Waugh, the "native landscape"); second, to "make it physically accessible to the largest number of persons"; and third, to "present its beauties in the most logical . . . and convincing manner." And like Mark Daniels, Waugh also emphasized the economic value of scenery. Waugh estimated that $7,500,000 was spent annually by tourists visiting national forests, and concluded that the "recreation use of National Forests has a very substantial value." Recreation should be considered, he advised, as a "major Forest utility" on a level with timber production, grazing, and watershed protection.[20] These arguments related only tangentially to Waugh's contemporary "natural style" of garden design; they derived directly from policies that Department of the Interior officials had advanced for national parks since at least 1914.

The Forest Service, apparently convinced that the recreational development of scenic areas deserved more attention, hired a full-time landscape architect, Arthur H. Carhart, in 1919. (Waugh also continued his consultancy on a sporadic basis throughout the 1920s and into the 1930s.) Carhart, a graduate of the new landscape program at Iowa State, correctly saw that the national forests presented a "new and unequalled opportunity for [recreational] development." In three years with the Forest Service, he produced a general plan for recreational development in the San Isabel National Forest, Colorado, as well as recreation studies for other heavily visited national forest areas.[21] But in 1921, shortly before he resigned from the Forest Service in frustration, Carhart reported that "not one cent of money has been appropriated by Congress which is for the purpose of recreational development in the National Forests."[22] Congress could not be persuaded that appropriations for recreational development were necessary at the Forest Service, perhaps since a whole new agency, the Park Service, had just been created for purposes that seemed to overlap.[23] After Carhart's departure, the Forest Service would not take on significant planning and design for outdoor recreation again until the 1930s. Even then, it would continue to allow the Park Service to lead the way in the design of recreational facilities for scenic areas in the public domain.

A number of other landscape architects and authors described variations on the theme of "natural style" landscape design at about this time. Most recognized a necessary continuity between 19th-century American landscape park design and any "natural style" proposed for the new century. In 1920, for example, the Chicago landscape architect O. C.

Simonds asked rhetorically, in reference to the old debate between the advantages of "formal" and "informal" landscape design styles, "Are we going to ignore the glorious progress of the 19th century . . . instead of striving to carry landscape-gardening to perfection along the natural lines on which it has made its greatest growth?"[24]

The most influential statement of the theory and practice of American landscape architecture to appear in the early 20th century, however, was *An Introduction to the Study of Landscape Design* by Henry V. Hubbard and Theodora Kimball.[25] Since neither Olmsted, Eliot, nor F. L. Olmsted, Jr., had attempted to summarize their professional practice in a single volume, Hubbard and Kimball's 1917 textbook became the standard for universities and, reprinted in 1929, it remained so for decades. In 1901, Hubbard was the first Harvard student to receive a university degree in landscape architecture. He apprenticed at Fairsted and then began teaching at the Harvard School of Landscape Architecture in 1906. A founding editor of *Landscape Architecture* magazine in 1910, he later became a partner at Olmsted Brothers.[26] Kimball, the librarian at the Harvard School of Landscape Architecture for many years, went on to write many books on landscape architecture and city planning. She also succeeded in making the School of Landscape Architecture library an invaluable repository for information and statistics on park design and planning.

Although their book contains little that could be considered new or original in 1917, *An Introduction to the Study of Landscape Design* was the most thorough summary of landscape architectural theory and practice that had yet been published in the United States. The authors provide a comprehensive account of the profession by assembling a range of historical and contemporary sources. The foundation of much of the professional practice they describe remains rooted, not surprisingly, in Reptonian tradition. In a discussion of "landscape effects," for example, they note that there are two categories of "emotional response in the observer" to landscapes: the "beautiful" and the "picturesque." Picturesque theory, particularly as expressed by Humphry Repton and later by Frederick Law Olmsted, reverberates through large portions of the book. Hubbard and Kimball's discussion of the critical influence of landscape painting in the composition of landscapes, for example, concludes that despite the close relationship of the two arts, inherent limitations exist when applying aesthetics derived from easel painting to the three-dimensional medium of landscapes. This argument simply restates Repton's famous comments on the subject first published in 1795.[27]

In other parts of the book Hubbard and Kimball draw on more contemporary sources. In describing a typology of "outdoor recreation areas," for example, they reproduce the formal types first outlined by F. L. Olmsted, Jr., and John Nolen in 1906. Hubbard and Kimball's version includes playgrounds, the "small park," the "country park," and the "reservation . . . of country land."[28] Of these types, the authors provide a detailed description of only one, the "country," or landscape park, which is described precisely as J. C. Olmsted had described the "large park" at the first meeting of the American Park and Outdoor Art Association in 1897. Hubbard and Kimball's description also draws heavily on the writings of Frederick Law Olmsted, not surprisingly, since Franklin Park in Boston is their primary example of a landscape park, and Hubbard had worked on the Boston parks while apprenticing at Fairsted.[29] In describing their final type of recreation area, the "reservation of outlying land," Hubbard and Kimball (again, not surprisingly) closely follow Charles Eliot's definition of areas that (in their words) "keep open a freer and less humanized kind of landscape beauty which otherwise, if it were preserved at all, would be in private hands and closed to the public." The authors also note that in such "preservation of natural scenery for public enjoyment" there is a legitimate role for the federal government. "In the case of natural wonders such as the Yosemite," they assert, reiterating F. L. Olmsted, Jr.'s reasons for opposing the Hetch-Hetchy dam, "it is fairly obvious that their landscape beauty is a function not to be destroyed by any other use." And of course, in the development of all large parks and scenic reservations, "the introduction of buildings into them . . . is undesirable except such structures as shall serve the legitimate purposes of the park." Necessary buildings should be made "harmonious with the landscape in form . . . [and] in texture and color." This is achieved through "irregular shape, perhaps a thatched roof . . . the gray green of its painted woodwork . . . [and] the texture and tone of its stonework, taken from a local quarry."[30]

These priorities for the management of large municipal parks and regional scenic reservations, as summarized by Hubbard and Kimball, can be described as the Fairsted School of landscape architecture. A traditional theory and practice of picturesque design had remained vital at Fairsted and had been applied in the design and planning of landscape parks and municipal park systems in the late 19th century; younger designers who had trained at Fairsted (or had some other connection to the office) expanded picturesque landscape design theory as the basis for planning regional parks and even a national park system in the early 20th century. Hubbard and Kimball's 1917 description of the design and management of "country parks" and "outlying reservations" conveys the basic theory of the Fairsted School at its zenith of influence.

It was also at this point that many of the Fairsted School landscape architects (including J. C. Olmsted, John Nolen, Warren Manning, Henry Hubbard, and F. L. Olmsted, Jr.) were extending their professional activities to include more subdivision design, regional and state park planning, and city planning. Just as landscape theory had bifurcated into models of "formal" and "natural" design, professional practice also diverged into camps: estate (or "country place") design, and the varied activities often described as some form of "planning."

Many of the goals of city planners in the early 20th century reformulated the intentions and objectives of earlier municipal park planning.

"Naturalistic" park development in the 1880s, as illustrated by Henry Hubbard and Theodora Kimball for An Introduction to the Study of Landscape Design *(1917). Henry Hubbard's photograph of steps in the "Wilderness" area of Franklin Park (Boston) captured the desired effect produced by employing locally quarried stone, rusticated finishes, and handworked masonry.*

Improved platting of land and control over the relative locations of industrial and residential areas, for example, had always been implied corollaries of 19th-century landscape architecture.. The design of subdivisions and campuses had made up a significant portion of the Olmsteds' work since the 1880s. For professionals trained in park planning and subdivision design, the new discipline of city planning represented logical extensions of existing methodologies. Just as landscape architects consulted natural systems and the "genius of the place" in landscape design, early planners performed statistical inventories and "city surveys" as a more "scientific" consultation of existing conditions. Traffic patterns, demographic trends, recreational needs, and public health concerns structured early 20th-century city plans much as existing topography, vegetation, and hydrology had shaped landscape park and parkway designs of the previous century. But city planning demanded legal expertise, statistical compilation and analysis, and other skills unfamiliar to traditional landscape designers; the practice was based in applied "science," as well as in what were considered the more "aesthetic" concerns of landscape architecture. Landscape architects taking on these roles increasingly identified themselves as city planners. Others entering the field were as likely to be trained in social science or law as in design or engineering.[31] A number of civic groups and municipal governments sponsored new city plans (some cities even created municipal planning commissions) that demonstrated the effectiveness of multidisciplinary city planning teams. From that point on, park commissions were less likely to be the principal planning entities for municipalities, and landscape architects were expected to collaborate with engineers, architects, lawyers, and others engaged in gathering statistical data and suggesting regulatory solutions to urban problems.

Many historians have pointed to the 1893 World's Columbian Exposition in Chicago as an influential example of professional collaboration. If the "city of dreams" could result from the coordinated design of parks, parkways, civic architecture, and public art, then certainly real cities might benefit from similar collaborative planning efforts. An early result of this influence was a new plan for the nation's capital, which as a federal district offered unique opportunities. The campaign to replan Washington began in 1894, and resulted in the creation of the Senate Park Commission (the "McMillan Commission") charged with "the development and improvement of the entire park system of the District of Columbia" in 1901. Daniel H. Burnham, the architectural impresario of the Chicago fair, and F. L. Olmsted, Jr., were the first appointees to the new commission. They were soon joined by architect Charles F. McKim and sculptor Augustus Saint-Gaudens. All had been key figures in planning the Chicago fair, except the younger Olmsted, who stood in for his retired father in that regard. Their recommendations led to the development of the Mall as a national civic center—the ultimate American "city beautiful"—lined by imposing, architecturally unified facades. Often overlooked, Olmsted's contributions to the plan also assured that the District of Columbia would subsequently develop one of the nation's finest system of parks and parkways.[32]

Other expositions—and other comprehensive city plans—soon followed. Plans for St. Louis (1907) and Chicago (1909), for example, employed multidisciplinary collaboration and featured extensive data and compiled statistics as the basis for recommended policies and improvements. Early planners such as Burnham, Olmsted, George Kessler, and John Nolen combined the use of city surveys and statistical information with the long established practice of park and parkway planning; the latter practice remained based in the assessment of the topography, visual character, and natural systems of regions likely to be engulfed by urban growth. In 1910, Olmsted, working with the architect Cass Gilbert, produced a plan for the City of New Haven that utilized extensive data on demographics, tax roles, and industrial trends. In 1911 he published surveys of Pittsburgh and Rochester that also assembled unprecedented statistical information for those cities.[33] Kessler, the designer of the Kansas City park and boulevard system, produced a "city plan" for Dallas in 1910 that included a "general plan" for railroad and other transportation systems, as well as the more expected proposals for new "parks and boulevards." Kessler's Dallas plan employed a comprehensive assessment of industrial needs, traffic patterns, and railroad consolidations in its recommendations.[34] In 1912, John Nolen, with the architect Randolph Coolidge, Jr., and the philanthropist Edward A. Filene, produced a visionary scheme for a regional planning authority for the Boston metropolitan area.[35]

Between 1907 and 1917, over one hundred American towns and cities established comprehensive city plans based on the systematic gathering and analysis of statistics and other information.[36] In 1909, James Sturgis Pray at the Harvard School of Landscape Architecture offered professional instruction in "City Planning," the first such courses in the country. The same year, the group that would become the National

Conference on City Planning first convened in Washington. In 1917, Olmsted and Flavel Shurtleff, a Boston lawyer specializing in planning issues, formed the American City Planning Institute (later the American Institute of Planners) as a professional organization affiliated with the National Conference. Of the original members of the new professional group, landscape architects were the single largest constituency, followed proportionally by engineers, lawyers, architects, realtors, and others, all of whom set out to establish an increasingly scientific and multidisciplinary planning profession.[37]

It was significant that at the same time Frederick Law Olmsted, Jr., was developing scientific techniques in city planning and organizing the new profession, he was also working with J. Horace McFarland in Washington to draft the legislation authorizing the National Park Service. The legislative drive to reform the management of national parks shared certain inspirations and motivations with the civic movement to reform the planning and management of cities. In the activities of key figures such as Olmsted and McFarland, the nexus was clear. Other figures lobbying for the new park bureau also saw it as a potential agency for implementing scientific, systematic planning. As early as 1910, Secretary Ballinger had called for "complete and comprehensive plans for roads, trails, telegraph and telephone lines, sewer and water systems, hotel accommodations, transportation, and other conveniences" to be drawn up for every park before substantial amounts of money were invested in them.[38] Four years later, the landscape architect Mark Daniels had reiterated the desire for "comprehensive plan[s] . . . for all the national parks."[39] It was Daniels as well who pointed out that once a community reached a population of thousands, as Yosemite Valley did by then on a regular basis, "it ceases to be a camp; it becomes a village." And what was more, "it has municipal problems . . . it must have a sanitary system, a water-supply system, a telephone system, an electric light system, and a system of patrolling." What was needed, according to Daniels, was "some sort of civic plan."[40]

Both Department of the Interior officials and the leaders of groups such as the American Civic Association expressed their concern for the future management of national parks in the contemporary language of professional planning. Estate design (and the "formal" style associated with it) clearly would not be the primary source of landscape architectural theory and technique applied in national park development. The emerging multidisciplinary approach of planners, however, included "scientific surveys" and techniques for planning coordinated "systems" of utilities, transportation, and housing. Faced with what was, in effect, the urbanization of certain portions of the national parks, "comprehensive plans" could assure that park development would be efficient and aesthetically consistent—and therefore less destructive to both natural systems and scenery. As the professional practice of landscape architecture became more divided, the landscape architects who called themselves planners were developing skills and techniques highly relevant to national park work.

The Fairsted School, then, had double significance in the formation of national park planning and design. First, as park and parkway planning expanded into city planning (as illustrated by the careers of F. L. Olmsted, Jr., and John Nolen) the scientific techniques and comprehensive approach of the planner would provide the framework for overall development schemes. Secondly, Fairsted landscape architects had created naturalistic design features and "rustic" architectural details that had become standard for municipal and regional landscape parks in the late 19th and early 20th centuries. Hubbard and Kimball describe such "naturalistic" park design features as appropriate for large parks and reservations, confirming generally accepted aesthetic assumptions of the period. This formal vocabulary reinforced and complemented the goals of the comprehensive plan, since "naturalistic" landscape design expressed the same underlying picturesque design theory. In addition, the "natural style" of landscape design described by Waugh and others at this time conveniently reinforced the perceived appropriateness of naturalistic construction in national park settings.

True comprehensive, or master plans, however, were not undertaken at the Park Service until more substantial and consistent funding made them both possible and necessary later in the 1920s. In the meantime, various problems associated with vastly increased populations of visitors demanded that some kind of plans be made to address the problems associated with increased visitation. In Yosemite Valley, the impact of visitors was particularly evident. By 1913, the acting military superintendent had called for a "plan for development" by "competent landscape, architectural, sanitary, and engineering specialists for the development of this park." Of particular concern were the dangerous sanitary conditions and the lack of basic utilities and accommodations for both visitors and the growing number of permanent residents in the valley.[41] Secretary Lane's appointment of Mark Daniels as "landscape engineer and general superintendent" of the national parks in 1914 in large part responded to the growing problems at Yosemite.[42] Lane had initially asked the San Francisco landscape architect that March to "prepare a comprehensive general plan for the development and improvement" of the valley "so as to bring into view the full scenic beauty of the surroundings." Daniels's plans included locations for roads, trails, and bridges, as well as suggestions for pruning and removing trees in some areas in order to maintain the scenic views that had become obscured since seasonal burns of the valley meadows had been suppressed.[43]

Daniels's most ambitious plans for the park, however, involved the "proper location and arrangement of a village in Yosemite Valley." Several alternative studies for such a park village were drawn up, and at least one was published as the "Plan of Yosemite Village."[44] The village plan (which was not implemented) featured a central lodge on the north side of the Merced River flanked by separate residential and service districts. Daniels's statement, quoted earlier, that the location and character of every building was determined "in the light of a careful study of the best arrangement of the buildings and for picturesqueness,"[45] is borne out by the placement of new buildings along gracefully curving roads that met in large wye intersections. Daniels apparently also proposed substantial excavation and impounding of the Merced River to create pools and lagoons along the edge of the new town. Lane was impressed enough with Daniels's work at Yosemite in 1914 to expand the scope of his appointment to include all the national parks.

Whether or not the village plan for Yosemite was advisable in all its features, its basic purpose was "to do away with unsightly buildings that now mar the scenery . . . and establish a village properly planned, comprising buildings of carefully studied architecture."[46] The "old village" at Yosemite was a disparate amalgamation of hotels, residences, and barns that had been deposited along the Merced over the previous fifty years of sporadic resort development. Whatever the aesthetic shortcomings of the old village, there were practical inadequacies involving sewage disposal, adequate drinking water, and traffic circulation.[47] These were problems not that different from those faced by towns and municipalities all over the country. But Daniels's response in the spring of 1914—a proposed new town plan—reflected the unique circumstances of working within the setting of a national park. In such a context, Daniels was free to advise the total demolition of the offending town and its replacement with a unified, comprehensively planned new town on the other side of the Merced River.

Park village planning of this type was as old as the landscape park itself; the controlled setting of the landscape park had always offered planners the opportunity to express ideal civic arrangements. In 18th-century British landscape parks, old villages were sometimes demolished to make way for a new lake or expansive greensward. The people so displaced might be rehoused in architecturally unified villages of arranged, pseudo-vernacular cottages, like the ones designed by Lancelot Brown for Milton Abbey in the 1760s. In the later context of American national parks, the device of a new "park village" continued to imply that groups of pseudo-vernacular buildings would be arranged and sited as visual elements of the larger landscape composition (in other words as parts of picturesque scenes) and therefore would not dominate or detract from the scenery that visitors came to appreciate.

In the early 20th century there were, of course, far more direct precedents for the design of such new towns than the park villages of Lancelot Brown. Landscape architect/planners such as F. L. Olmsted, Jr., and John Nolen had brought American "town planning" to a high degree of sophistication by the time Mark Daniels made his proposals for Yosemite. In 1911, working with the architect Grosvenor Atterbury, Olmsted had developed Forest Hills Gardens in New York for the Russell Sage Foundation. This "garden suburb" employed a consistent vocabulary of tree-lined streets, rusticated construction finishes, pitched tile roofs, and carefully articulated public spaces to create a unified visual effect and "village" atmosphere. Nolen, in particular, became the most prolific "town planner" of the era. An early graduate of the Harvard landscape program and initially a close associate of the younger Olmsted, Nolen opened an office in Cambridge in 1904. As municipalities began to search for planning consultants, Nolen received commissions for the design of new towns, such as Kingsport, Tennessee (1915), as well as for city plans for more established cities such as Little Rock (1913) and Bridgeport (1916). His firm was soon the most active planning office in the country.[48]

The distinction between "town planning" and "city planning" was an important one to Nolen. In one of the earliest of his many publications, he pointed out the very different requirements of providing services for "cities and towns planned in advance of settlement" (town planning) and for "existing cities replanned or remodeled to meet new requirements" (city planning).[49] But the term "town planning" was also an Anglicism ("city planning" being the more common term in the United States) and revealed the extent of the influence of British planners in this branch of American landscape architecture. The backers of projects like Forest Hills Gardens attempted to create American "garden cities" modeled on the new model towns and suburbs that had been developed in Britain since the turn of the century. The most influential of the new British town planners was Raymond Unwin, whose 1909 book *Town Planning in Practice* immediately became an important source for planners on both sides of the Atlantic.[50] Unwin in turn had been influenced by 19th-century German city planners (who had greatly impressed Nolen and Olmsted, as well) and Unwin reproduced city plans for Nuremburg, Rothenburg, and Cologne in his textbook. The primary examples Unwin used in 1909, however, were the "garden city" developments he and the architect Barry Parker had undertaken since 1904. Letchworth, the prototypical garden city designed by Unwin and Parker, employed a broken grid of streets that partially conformed to topography, a hierarchy of street types from "Broadway" to narrow cul-de-sacs, and a segregation of industrial and residential areas. Civic buildings were to be sited along a centrally located town square, and the residences of the new community typically were intended to be "workingman's cottages" and other housing types of Arts and Crafts inspiration. The architectural office of Unwin and Parker had already done much to popularize simple and affordable cottages that emphasized traditional construction materials and unpretentious craftsmanship. In the arrangement of such houses in cul-de-sacs, closes, and other alternatives to traditional grid schemes, the architects also incorporated generous setbacks, garden spaces, and communal open spaces in their town plans.

At first disseminated by example and through Unwin's textbook, British town planning along these lines increased in popularity in the United States partly as a result of World War I. At the outset of war, the British government recognized that a national dearth of decent housing for workers impeded vital defense production. Private capital, under the pressure of wartime prices, could not meet demand, and a major public housing effort began immediately in 1914. New towns for war workers were hastily laid out, many by Britain's foremost town planner,

Raymond Unwin. In 1917, the United States faced a similar, if less desperate, situation. Although the government did not react with alacrity, the Department of Commerce eventually organized the U.S. Housing Corporation to spend millions of dollars building housing near shipyards, munitions factories, and other centers of wartime industry. An unprecedented mobilization of American landscape architects, architects, and engineers provided plans for the new communities. Olmsted headed the Town Planning Division of the corporation, and Nolen, Hubbard, Kessler, Arthur A. Shurtleff, James Sturgis Pray, Charles Downing Lay, James S. Greenleaf, Albert D. Taylor, Ferrucio Vitale, and William H. Punchard (Charles Punchard's uncle) were among the many landscape architects who acted as town planners for the over sixty projects initiated.[51]

Perhaps because the effort was modeled on its British counterpart, principles of British (or "garden city") town planning were emphasized, and judging by the results, the experience proved a crash course in Unwin and Parker's techniques, as interpreted by Olmsted and others. John Nolen, for example, had employed radiating street grids, central town squares, and zoned land uses in the design of new towns before 1917, and he subsequently produced one of the finest subdivisions of the war effort in Camden, New Jersey. All of the landscape architects and architects working for the Housing Corporation received "standard" or "type" plans from Olmsted at the outset, as well as detailed "suggestions for town planners."[52] Olmsted's advice for the group summarized his town planning methods at a critical and opportune moment. Planning, he insisted, should be initiated through a consultation of topography and other natural features. Detailed topographic surveys were repeatedly emphasized as the sine qua non of town planning; other environmental factors were to be considered as well. "Whatever the present condition of the site," he advised, the town planner "must see what it offers as a developed site; how its exposure will suit its occupancy; whether the topography is such as to afford convenient . . . disposition of communication and subdivisions, [and] what natural features . . . may be retained or improved as recreational and breathing spaces." The practical components of the plan ("lay-out, grading, and planting") were "the best possible foundation for the good appearance which comes from the artist's touch. . . . The curving street that minimizes the cost of grading and gives picturesque interest to the buildings along it must be a convenient means of circulation and make for the most advantageous subdivision of the lots on which those buildings are set."[53]

For many landscape architects and planners, wartime experience would prove a strong influence on their subsequent professional practice. One of the American landscape architects drawn into World War I planning efforts was Daniel Ray Hull. A native of Kansas, Hull had studied at the University of Illinois under Charles Mulford Robinson, who had just joined the faculty there as professor of "civic design." Robinson, a journalist and municipal reformer from Rochester, New York, had become a leading proponent of "civic art" and town planning through numerous publications, beginning in 1901 with *The Improvement of Towns and Cities*. In 1913, Hull was one of four students who worked closely with Robinson on a city planning study (which was later published) that suggested planning strategies for the communities of Champaign and Urbana.[54] Hull then went on to receive his Master's degree in landscape architecture from Harvard in 1914. At that time Harvard professors Henry Hubbard and James Sturgis Pray would have been the principal influences on his education. After traveling in Europe, Hull began his professional career in California, where he planned the Montecito Country Estates subdivision in Santa Barbara with Francis T. Underhill.[55] He also worked for a San Francisco firm, Daniels, Osmont and Wilhelm, and his probable association with Mark Daniels at that point might explain how he later came to be chosen as Charles Punchard's assistant at the Park Service.[56]

From 1918 to 1919, Hull planned cantonments and hospital camps as an officer in the U.S. Army. Planning camps for the Army differed substantially from designing new subdivisions for civilian factory workers; but basic town planning procedures were applied systematically in this aspect of war planning as well, again in large part because of Olmsted's influence. Olmsted, with E. P. Goodrich and George B. Ford, had offered the services of American planners to the Cantonment Division of the U.S. Army immediately in 1917, and the landscape architect subsequently played a central role organizing wartime cantonment planning. George Kessler, Warren Manning, and James Sturgis Pray were among the civilian planners employed by the Cantonment Division.[57]

Hull's early experience qualified him as one of the growing number of landscape architects who specialized in town planning. His education in "civic art" and "city planning" at Illinois and Harvard would have been reinforced by his professional work in California and by his military experience as a cantonment planner. After leaving the Army, Hull went to work at the National Park Service in August 1920 as assistant to the ailing Charles Punchard. Since 1918, Punchard had picked up where Mark Daniels had left off, reviewing concessioners' plans, advising superintendents, and acting as a one-man art commission to assure that buildings and other proposed facilities were "harmonious with their surroundings" and "disturbed the natural conditions of the parks" as little as possible. Yosemite was a particular concern, and Punchard had continued work on a village plan for the valley while being stationed there for over seven months between 1918 and 1919.[58] He advised that the new village north of the Merced River, which had been "for many years . . . the subject of much discussion," be divided into commercial, industrial, and residential "zones."[59] That summer he oversaw the construction of the new rangers' club (1920) in the proposed village area. Designed by Charles K. Sumner with steeply pitched roofs pierced by dormers, the facility recalled (at a reduced scale) concessioner architecture at Yellowstone and Glacier.[60]

Punchard died that fall, and Daniel Hull found himself, at the age of thirty, the chief landscape architect of the Park Service. Director Mather, by that time, had secured some of his most important early victories in Washington, including the amendment to the Federal Water Power Act that exempted the parks from becoming the sites of new power and irrigation dams. The "principle of complete conservation," Mather reported in 1920, "has been upheld." In not unrelated developments, Mather also dedicated the new Park-to-Park Highway route that year, "a truly national highway system" which provided "well-built feeders to the entrances of the various parks and monuments" and encouraged the "tremendous increase in motor travel to the parks" that had been underway for years. Appropriations for the Park Service exceeded one million dollars for the first time in 1921, but an ambitious Mather estimated that well over twice that amount would be necessary to meet just the "essential needs" outlined by his superintendents.[61] Hull had arrived at a turning point in the administrative history of the Park Service. The crusades and campaigns of the past were giving way to secure annual appropriations and bureaucratic growth. Hull would soon have opportunities to see plans and designs realized in ways that Daniels and Punchard had not.

Hull's first step was to establish headquarters at Yosemite Valley, a logical center for his Park Service activities where he could also remain in touch with associates and clients in Santa Barbara and Los Angeles. In February he was joined by an assistant landscape architect, an old friend from University of Illinois days, Paul P. Kiessig. Kiessig traveled extensively that summer reporting on conditions in other parks.[62] Hull immediately made it known that he was not satisfied simply offering advice and reviewing concessioner proposals on an ad hoc basis. Immediate needs, however, demanded his attention: "The construction of parapets along dangerous roads, removal of poles and wires from conspicuous locations, improvement of springs to make them more attractive and at the same time more sanitary, screening objectional views by planting native materials," and other tasks occupied much of his and Kiessig's time. With only one assistant, Hull felt that "it has been difficult to give proper study to many of our most pressing landscape problems," such as planning "civic groups, or village plans" to centralize administrative and utility areas. Still, by 1922 Hull and Kiessig had begun "tentative general plans" for Yellowstone, Yosemite, Sequoia, Grand Canyon, and Mesa Verde.[63]

Although overwhelmed by the enormity of providing landscape plans for the entire national park system, Hull also pursued private work, in part to supplement the relatively meager salary the Park Service offered its early professional staff. In 1923, another friend of both Hull's and Kiessig's from undergraduate days, Gilbert Stanley Underwood, moved to Los Angeles and opened his own architectural office. Hoping to collaborate with Underwood booming Southern California, Hull relocated the landscape engineering branch of the Park Service to Los Angeles that year and began sharing Underwood's offices. There, he felt, "we have contact with the best architectural and engineering talent." Hull began working with Underwood on private projects and also prepared plans "for many park projects."[64] In what was a de facto partnership, he had brought Underwood to the attention of Mather as a suitable architect for the new post office and administration buildings for Yosemite, both of which had been funded that year. Underwood prepared plans for the buildings in 1923, and Mather submitted them to the Commission of Fine Arts in Washington for review.[65]

Mather, although he subsequently proved to be a great friend and patron to the architect, felt that Underwood's initial plans for the Yosemite buildings were overly elaborate. On the advice of the Commission of Fine Arts, Mather hired another Los Angeles architect, Myron Hunt, to design an administration building.[66] Myron Hunt represented a considerably safer choice for this early and significant Park Service commission. The most prominent architect in Southern California, he had not only designed the Rose Bowl (1922) and dozens of other major buildings, but also had planned several major campuses including Occidental (1910) and Pomona colleges (1913).[67] A facile designer, in his Yosemite work Hunt appropriately evoked contemporary California Arts and Crafts architecture and produced a rectangular administration building (1924) with a lower story veneered in rough granite and an upper story sheathed in dark shingles. The heavy, battered stone of the first level, as well as the peeled log trim of the upper floor, created a convincing impression of structural elements that seemed to have been drawn from the raw materials of the surrounding landscape. This illusion (the stone and peeled logs did not bear structural loads) became a defining attribute of early Park Service Rustic style architecture.[68]

Myron Hunt's abilities as a planner were employed at Yosemite as well. The annual meeting of park superintendents, held at Yosemite in 1922, had pushed the issue of planning future improvements for the valley to the forefront. "For years," Hull reported that year, "the building of [the new village] and the elimination of the present dilapidated shacks . . . has been considered essential both from the standpoint of practical operation and landscape effect."[69] Hunt and Hull collaborated on the village plan, which in 1923 finally set the shape of the new village on the north side of the Merced. The nature of Hunt and Hull's collaboration on the plan remains uncertain. Hull clearly credits Hunt with the plan, which was selected from among several alternatives by James Greenleaf and the other members of the Commission of Fine Arts. The plan, however, was entirely unlike Myron Hunt's orthogonal campus plans of the previous decade. Devoid of grand axes and monumentalism, the plan for Yosemite Village epitomized the priorities for park planning that had been articulated by Mark Daniels and others since 1914; the plan also embodied the principles of town planning that Olmsted had described for his World War I planners, and which had been inculcated in the young Hull through his education and professional experience.

A recent reconstruction of the 1923 village plan shows that the post office and administration buildings, with several studio buildings, a museum, and the ranger club, originally defined a central civic "plaza" that served as the arrival point and parking area for automobiles.[70] Separate residential areas featured winding, tree-lined streets, generous setbacks, and cul-de-sac access to rear garages. Single family and duplex cottages were preferred housing types; architectural detailing was generally of Arts and Crafts inspiration. Utility areas, organized orthogonally, were well segregated both visually and in terms of circulation from the public area around the plaza and from the private residential areas. Apparently Hunt, both in the design of the administration building and in the delineation of the town plan, acquiesced to what were considered appropriate formal idioms and planning strategies for a landscape park setting. Over the next eight years, over two dozen buildings were built in the new village, adding to the rangers' club and other buildings already constructed in the area. Most followed Hunt's lead, employing simple rectangular floor plans, granite veneer below, and dark wood siding above, to create a unified architectural presence for the village. During the same period, most of the structures of the old village (some of them dating to the earliest period of the valley's development) were razed.[71]

A 1926 view of the "new village plaza" in Yosemite Valley. Myron Hunt's 1924 administration building is on the left, and Herbert Maier's slightly later park museum is in the center. The Yosemite plaza, defined in part by the facades of these public buildings, also retained an openness that allowed views of the surrounding granite cliffs and Yosemite Falls. Courtesy Yosemite National Park Research Library.

Even while Yosemite received this attention, Hull was actively planning other national park villages. At Sequoia, where automotive tourists had also begun to swarm, Hull worked on a new village plan for the edge of the Giant Forest, where visitors would be less likely to compact root zones and damage the trunks of the great trees as they did when camping in the forest itself. A new administrative village was also planned on the park's western, Ash Mountain, entrance.[72] At Mesa Verde, a park village was being constructed in the early 1920s, beginning with the construction of a unique superintendent's residence in 1921. The buildings of the administrative core of the Mesa Verde village, designed primarily by superintendent Jesse Nussbaum and his wife Aileen, were constructed of sandstone blocks and had flat roofs supported by viga poles. The village again exemplified how a unified architectural ensemble could be conceived as a contextual element of the larger landscape scene. In this case, the ethnological study of "early modern Pueblo Indian" architecture provided an appropriate inspiration for a group of buildings that complemented and preserved the aesthetic qualities of the surrounding park scenery and archeological sites. Mather felt the architecture perfectly "fit in with the atmosphere of the park."[73]

The largest and most significant Park Service town plan being pursued in the early 1920s, however, was that for the south rim of the Grand Canyon. Park Service planning for the Grand Canyon began officially in 1919, when long anticipated federal legislation finally transformed the national monument into a national park, and so transferred jurisdiction from the Forest Service to the Park Service.[74] Interest in the region as a tourist destination, however, had developed in the 1880s when the Atlantic and Pacific Railroad first reached Flagstaff. Although numerous attempts to finance a spur line to the rim of the canyon failed, stage services were soon initiated. By 1892, three regularly scheduled stages were making the difficult sixty-mile journey to the very edge of the precipice, at a point christened Grandview. That year, the Santa Fe and Grand Canyon Railroad also began rail service to Anita, only twenty miles from the canyon. From that point a stage carried passengers to a hotel near the Bright Angel trailhead, nine miles west of Grandview. In 1901, the railroad extended its track all the way to this location on the rim, which had become the site of a growing settlement called simply Grand Canyon. Ever since, this area has been the principal point of arrival for visitors to the region.[75]

Proposed national park status for the Grand Canyon had always inspired influential support. No scenery in North America more obviously deserved such designation. Benjamin Harrison, while still an Indiana senator, had first proposed national park legislation in 1882. In 1893, he had the opportunity as president to declare the region a forest reserve, and he did so. Theodore Roosevelt, as well, had a personal determination to preserve the canyon from inappropriate development. In 1903 he visited the canyon, and in 1908 he enhanced its status as a public reservation by creating the 800,000-acre Grand Canyon National Monument.[76] In the meantime, the south rim railhead had grown into a small town. When Roosevelt visited in 1903, there was a post office, two voting precincts, a population of miners and, increasingly, of tourists. That year the Santa Fe Railway (through its subsidiary the Fred Harvey Company) began construction of its second hotel, the luxurious El Tovar. Several other tourist establishments continued to operate in the vicinity.[77]

Efforts to pass park legislation in Congress did not end with the declaration of national monument status; Secretary Ballinger advocated national park status for the region beginning in 1909. Park legislation met difficulties, however, because of complex local politics and conflicting interests among those who hoped to operate businesses on the south rim. Local entrepreneurs had used mineral claims (allowed even after the forest reserve designation) to assert sometimes dubious rights to develop tourist accommodations and guide services. For Fred Harvey and the Santa Fe Railway, national park status would be a welcome step not only to assure the more complete preservation of the area, but also to eliminate competitors, since as a national park concessioner the railroad could hope to be granted a limited monopoly. The Forest Service, for its part, would have welcomed national park status. In 1914, Chief Forester Henry S. Graves held several meetings with Mark Daniels, and he subsequently described "an informal cooperation arrangement" with Daniels that allowed the national monument to "be administered along national park lines as far as possible." But Graves felt there was little the Forest Service could do to improve the situation until the General Land Office cancelled the "fraudulent" mineral claims that had been placed with the sole intention, he felt, of controlling public access to key points along the south rim.[78]

The Forest Service exacerbated the situation in 1915, the year of the San Francisco World's Fair, when visitation to the canyon skyrocketed. As expected, thousands of California-bound tourists made side trips to national parks; but at the Grand Canyon, over 100,000 tourists arrived, a total greater than that for Yosemite and Yellowstone combined that year. In order to augment totally inadequate visitor services, the Forest Service had made an open invitation to local entrepreneurs to operate livery services. Enough cowboys and ranchers responded to the potential windfall that the scene on the south rim soon degenerated into what park historian Margaret Verkamp describes as "considerable unpleasantness." The noisy competition made support for creating a national park that much stronger.[79]

The Forest Service had attempted to plan the growth of the town of Grand Canyon, but with little expertise or funding for such work their efforts had foundered. In 1909, forest examiner (later forest supervisor) W. R. Matoon produced a detailed "Working Plan for Grand Canyon National Monument." In it he described some of the problems of the young town, including the critical lack of water, inadequate sanitation, and few roads or trails from which tourists might view the scenery from surrounding points on the rim. Matoon felt a scenic rim drive was particularly warranted. It was clear that some sort of conveyance along the rim would soon be built one way or another, and "all development along the rim," the forester urged, should be made "for the benefit of the public at large rather than in the interest of any individual or commercial enterprise." Matoon also recommended "thinning for scenic effect" along the rim, and the construction of seats and "rustic shelters" at the most popular points for viewing the canyon. Shelters consisting of "a roof, stained green, and resting on natural juniper posts," he suggested, would be "in good harmony with the surroundings."[80]

In his general desire for "rustic" design details that would "harmonize" with the landscape, Matoon simply expressed the widely prevailing sensibility for construction details appropriate in the setting of a landscape reservation. In a separate report the next year, however, he proposed a more ambitious scheme for the planned extension of the town of Grand Canyon; and here the forester demonstrated how useless "rustic" architectural inspiration could be when unaccompanied by correspondingly appropriate site planning techniques. Matoon's proposed "townsite plan" was no more than an even grid of four square blocks, subdivided into eight lots apiece. The new blocks were surveyed parallel to the train tracks just south of the point at which the rails ended.[81] The plan, like countless railroad towns laid out in the19th century, drew its geometry and orientation from its relationship to the railroad, not surrounding natural features. Far from a response to topography, the grid was laid out without the benefit even of a topographic survey.

In the meantime, the town of Grand Canyon had grown larger, with three hundred to four hundred permanent residents and a transient population that often exceeded that number. Over fifty temporary and permanent buildings (including a school) had been erected by 1914, most of them since railroad service began in 1901.[82] After 1915, the Forest Service reactivated its planning efforts for Grand Canyon, in part due to the negative publicity generated by the events of that year's travel season. In 1916, Matoon's successor as forest supervisor, Don P. Johnston, teamed up with a new forest examiner named Aldo Leopold to author a "Grand Canyon Uses Working Plan." They began their report by acknowledging that visitors to the canyon were subjected to "offensive sights and sounds . . . unsanitary conditions . . . [and] inconvenient facilities," to name just some of the municipality's problems. Noting that federal ownership and administration of the monument allowed for the legal enforcement of "regulations" over both permitees and, importantly, over those entrepreneurs operating by right of mineral claims, Johnston and Leopold urged a far-reaching plan of land-use "zones" to restrict specific land uses to specific parts of the town.[83] Johnston and Leopold implied (as did many city planners of the day) that land-use zoning could be a regulatory solution to the kinds of conditions plaguing the town of Grand Canyon. The "division of the ground into zones" and the "segregation of various classes of services," they insisted, could "reduce the offensiveness of material service as far as possible" and make it possible for visitors to avoid the sights and sounds of the mules, steam engines, trash, and offal that were the inevitable result of tourism to the canyon.

Municipal zoning plans and ordinances of this type, although widely discussed and occasionally employed in the United States by 1916, would only be fully validated by the Supreme Court in a series of decisions in the early 1920s. But Johnston and Leopold pointed out that the unusual situation of a city within a national monument made the implementation and enforcement of a zoning plan far more feasible than it would have been among private property owners at that time. Their revised 1917 plan described seven zones, each with prescribed land uses and regulations: the "Rim Zone," the "Accommodation Zone," the "Residence Zone," the "Commercial Zone," the "Seasonal Camp Zone," the "Public Camp Grounds," and the "Stables Zone." As refined as these categories were, the authors did not neglect to specify a range of variances and grandfather arrangements that allowed "inferior use of a superior zone," such as the intrusion of Verkamp's Curio Shop in what was otherwise the most restrictive area, the rim zone. The foresters also determined the relative aesthetic merits of structures that might be considered "objectionable" or not, depending on the standards that applied for each zone.[84] Although Johnston and Leopold did consider the location of future development for the town, they offered little insight on what physical form expansion might take. Included as an appendix to their 1917 revision were Mary E. J. Colter's plans for Fred Harvey's proposed cabin group at Indian Gardens; but this was no more than an endorsement of the concessioner's proposals on the part of the planners.[85] The Grand Canyon Working Plan mainly sought to eliminate existing nuisances and stabilize future land uses for specific areas. The residential zone, for example, (located in approximately the same area Matoon had suggested) precluded hotels, stables, and stores; the rim zone allowed only trails, "rustic shelters," and inconspicuous signs. Seasonal and temporary camping were assigned to specific areas, and each activity was limited to its proper location.

Johnston and Leopold's analysis would prove valuable for future park managers, and their 1917 plan revision did include a feature that Olmsted had called the first prerequisite of town planning: a detailed topographic survey. The planners did not, however, plat land for anticipated residential developments, nor did they delineate future streets or public spaces. In 1918, the Forest Service took the next step and engaged Frank Waugh to devise a more detailed plan for the expansion of the town. Waugh's plan for the "Village of Grand Canyon," which took Johnston and Leopold's land-use zones as a starting point, was published separately that year. In the residential zone south of the railhead, Waugh proposed to subdivide lots along new streets that curved to conform to the gentle slope of the site. A "civic center" was proposed directly in front of the new Fred Harvey garage (1914), between the railroad tracks and the proposed subdivision to the south. This center, Waugh suggested, could be a "grassy parklike . . . public square," around which he proposed siting new stores, a federal building, a community club, and a church. Near the main automotive entry to the town (still via Grandview Road from the east) and across the tracks from the Grand Canyon Depot (1910), the proposed plaza would have provided a prominent civic space and a central arrival and gathering point for the village.[86]

Frank Waugh was more experienced as an educator and a garden designer, however, and at this point his town plan descended into idiosyncrasy. Suggesting that the canyon landscape required "some sort of introduction," Waugh proposed "a broad straight walk . . . rising by rustic stone steps" from Grandview Road directly up to the canyon rim, at a point just east of Verkamp's Curio Store. Extending in an equally straight alignment in the opposite direction, the new avenue, named "Tusayan Mall," cut through the proposed residential district and terminated in a proposed "aviation field" located, remarkably, on the high ground in the middle of the residential subdivision. The proposed mall also bisected the property of the new school (1917) "in an objectionable manner," Waugh admitted; but Fred Harvey's compound to the west left little alternative for siting a dramatic "introduction" to the canyon near the center of town. Other unusual features of the plan included an "automobile outlook" on the rim, and "Tusayan Garden," a botanic garden also located on the rim. The botanic garden, of course, was to feature only native plants.[87]

Even as Waugh made these proposals, however, the shift to Park Service administration had been widely anticipated for some time. In 1916, Mather had gone so far as to include the Grand Canyon in his *National Park Portfolio*. Charles Punchard, in his capacity of Park Service landscape architect, visited the canyon in January 1919, a month before the park legislation had even been signed.[88] Although the Forest Service continued to administer the new park for several months (while the Park Service awaited an appropriation) Mather's chief engineer, George Goodwin, and the new acting superintendent, William H. Peters, immediately assessed conditions at the park. Goodwin and Peters advised that, as a first priority, the road to Hermit's Rest be improved and opened to automobiles. They predicted that private automobiles, a growing presence in the park already, were about to increase in number exponentially.[89] Annual park visitation had doubled since 1916 (to over 67,000 in 1919) and many of the new tourists were arriving in their own motor vehicles, making the arduous journey from Flagstaff to the town of Grand Canyon via Grandview. That year Mather reported that Grand Canyon National Park was in need of "broad development" in a number of areas, but the widening and resurfacing of scenic rim drives to the east and west of the town of Grand Canyon was "the most urgent work."[90]

After the construction of roads and trails, Mather described a second major category of concern as "administrative village betterments." He outlined a construction program, including new administrative buildings, residential quarters, campgrounds, utilitites, and other facilities, which amounted to nothing less than a project to build a small city.[91] That winter, Charles Punchard returned to the canyon and met with Peters to consider issues such as the siting of the new Park Service administration building. In considering new construction at Grand Canyon, Punchard asserted in a letter to Mather that "too great a variety in architecture . . . is going to make the place look like a jumble." He felt that it would be best to "adhere to the free rough [sic] which has been done by the rail road company in its small rest houses and curio stores, or else to the adobe architecture which is indigenous."[92] For his part, Mather had made it policy that no permanent buildings were to be erected in any park without the prior approval of the Park Service landscape engineer.[93] Inexperience, however, took its toll. Despite Goodwin's assistance estimating the cost of road improvements, Peters drastically overspent his first year's budget and bankrupted the park even before its official dedication, which had been delayed until April 1920. Mather was forced to personally plead with the Fred Harvey Company to assist with routine maintenance for the remainder of the fiscal year.[94]

Congress soon increased appropriations, however, and visitor numbers continued to climb. As Daniel Hull took charge of landscape engineering in the fall of 1920, Grand Canyon National Park, like Yosemite, was poised to undergo a major development program. Hull remained headquartered at Yosemite, but he visited Grand Canyon that winter. He sent Kiessig to the park at least twice, the second time for the entire summer of 1921 while the new administration building was being built.[95] The opportunity to design the Grand Canyon administration building (and other buildings at Grand Canyon) gave Hull a unique chance to affect the course of Park Service architectural style and planning procedures. He noted that the situation at Grand Canyon, where the park was being administered out of a few temporary shacks and the superintendent was housed in an old log cabin, presented an opportunity for a "practically new field in administrative development." And it is significant that his design of new administrative buildings in the early 1920s proceeded in tandem with the delineation of a new plan for Grand Canyon Village. In 1920, Hull and Kiessig undertook a "careful study of the landscape," which resulted in "the adoption of a layout for future development."[96] Using the 1917 topographic survey as a base, Hull sketched initial suggestions for the town plan and distributed them for review early in 1921.[97]

Hull's training as a landscape architect/town planner was evident in his sensitivity to existing natural features. Circulation at the site had already been determined to a large degree by topography: both the railroad approach (from the west) and the Grandview Road (from the east) followed the natural right-of-way of the Bright Angel drainage, a long swale parallel to the canyon, typically at an elevation about fifty feet below that of the south rim itself. Hull proposed a large "village square" (as Waugh had) at the point where the railroad and motor road came together below El Tovar in the usually dry bed of the drainage. The new administration building was sited on the north side of the proposed square, slightly elevated on the slope leading up to the rim. The elevated site made the administration building, which also served as a visitor center and contact station, a prominent feature for visitors arriving by train or car. Like most of Hull's proposals for Grand Canyon, however, it was well away from the rim itself, which remained unencumbered by botanic gardens or other "introductions."

The rest of the proposed administrative development of the new village was even farther from the rim, on the south side of the natural divide offered by the Bright Angel drainage. The land to the south of the drainage was, itself, naturally divided into two small hills, divided by a central, north-south swale perpendicular to the larger swale of the Bright Angel creek bed. Hull proposed a central road down this smaller swale, with residential subdivisions on either side.[98] The effect was to create two neighborhoods which were subsequently assigned to Fred Harvey staff (to the west) and Park Service personnel (to the east). Already evident, as well, was some indication that Hull intended each subdivision to have its own character. To the west, three parallel streets all curved to suit the slope and each connected to the perpendicular center road, forming a gently distorted grid. On the other side of the road, only one main entry to this considerably smaller development implied an extended cul-de-sac arrangement. A new Park Service utility area also on the east side (where it was convenient to the Park Service residences) was arranged orthogonally; the arrangement of utility buildings created central work yards that were well screened from the nearby residential area.

Hull also exploited the character of the existing vegetation. While the subdivisions were proposed on lightly wooded, well-drained slopes, almost no new construction was proposed for the lower ground along the Bright Angel drainage, preserving a fine stand of ponderosa and pinyon pines. These trees reinforced the division between the accommodation zone near the rim and the new residential and utility zones to the south. The older resort development (already long established on the rim of the canyon) was also accommodated in the new village plan. The hotels along the rim established their own land-use zone (as the Forest Service planners had observed) which was respected in the new village plans. The Fred Harvey utility area, which had been developed along the railroad right-of-way on the west side of the town, also created its own zone, in this case characterized by livery barns and mule corrals. These existing uses helped determine Hull's overall layout; the new Fred Harvey residential area, for example, was on the west side of the new village, in order to be more convenient to the existing Fred Harvey utility area.

The basic spatial organization and zoning implied in Hull's early sketch were suggested by topography, vegetation, existing development, and circulation needs in the village area. Hull's village plan, which was already taking shape in 1920, would become (with some important alterations) the essential blueprint for construction in the village over the next twenty years. The town planning methods he employed established a basic procedure for planning new "park villages" that protected the visual character of the surrounding scenery, and responded both to natural features and to the demands of maintaining and ameliorating earlier tourist developments.

This was not, however, Hull's only contribution to Grand Canyon Village at this time. While at Yosemite and elsewhere Hull often collaborated with architectural consultants in the design of new administrative facilities; beginning in 1920 he had the chance to design his own buildings at Grand Canyon. Hull's Grand Canyon administration building, which was serving visitors as well as park managers by the end of 1921, helped define what would later be described as Park Service Rustic architecture two years before Myron Hunt and Gilbert Stanley Underwood undertook their Yosemite commissions.[99] At the lower level of the two-story structure, Hull employed Kaibab limestone, heavily rusticated and laid in random courses. The upper level, sheathed in darkly stained board and batten, was dominated by the intersecting gables of the broad, wood-shingled roofs.[100] As was Myron Hunt two years later, Hull clearly was familiar with contemporary California Arts and Crafts architecture. He also had the example of earlier "rustic" park buildings built by concessioners. The buildings Mary E. J. Colter had designed for the Fred Harvey Company must have made a particularly strong impression; she had already completed Hopi House (1905), Hermit's Rest (1914), and the Lookout Studio (1914), which together had determined the fanciful character and high quality of the resort architecture along the rim itself.[101] The first administration building at Grand Canyon, however, remains today as clear evidence that Park Service Rustic architecture did not develop independently from park planning, but as a consistent formal articulation of the same principles that guided the overall landscape development effort that was underway at the Park Service.

The designers of landscape parks, really from the 18th century on, had vigorously reiterated that buildings were appropriate in the landscape park setting only to the degree that they contributed as visual elements in perceived landscape scenes. Perceptions of scenery therefore ultimately determined the appropriateness of any architectural additions to the landscape; and perceptions of scenery had been shaped through a long history of the artistic genres of landscape, not the history of architecture. Painting (and later photography), descriptive poetry (and later travel guides and other literature), and landscape design (in the United States, the design of large public parks in particular) had

Daniel Hull's 1921 Grand Canyon administration building, inspired by contemporary Arts and Crafts architecture, is among the first significant examples of Park Service Rustic style. The building was originally sited on what was then the central town plaza. The building now looks down on a busy intersection at the main entrance to Grand Canyon Village. The steps and a retaining wall in the foreground were built later by the Civilian Conservation Corps (CCC) to define the termination of the railroad tracks at this point.

established over many years sensibilities of what defined an appropriate architectural image in a landscape scene. Whether the cottage vernacular of Lancelot Brown's landscapes, the Shingle Style of Franklin Park, the Mesa Verde Pueblo style, or Park Service Rustic, "appropriate" park buildings shared an initial inception as visual elements of another, previsualized artistic composition—the landscape—which to some degree predetermined the desired visual character of new construction. Since the 18th century, park designers had attempted to evoke some variation of local vernacular construction technique and craftsmanship in the design of park buildings. In the same vein, the construction materials employed often were (or appeared to be) drawn from surrounding forests and quarries. Such construction conformed to expectations derived from artistic genres of landscape, and therefore resulted in buildings that did not conflict with the desired appreciation of places as pictures, and land as landscape. As Mather would say, such architecture "fit the atmosphere of the park."

Since at least the 1880s, some form of "rustic" architecture had been deemed appropriate in larger scenic reservations of all types, including national parks. Virtually everyone involved in early national park management, including Army engineers, railroad executives, and Forest Service supervisors, agreed that proposed architectural development should "blend" and "harmonize" with its surroundings. The physical characteristics of such architecture included dark wood siding, prominent wood-shingled roofs, heavily rusticated or boulder masonry, and peeled log walls, columns, and trusses; the success of Robert Reamer's Old Faithful Inn in 1903 had cemented this association in the popular imagination. What Daniel Hull brought to the Grand Canyon Village in 1921, however, was landscape architectural design that used such "rustic," or naturalistic, architectural construction as a logical extension and consistent expression of an overall strategy for park development. The precedent of municipal and regional landscape park design of the Fairsted School therefore provided the essential model. Since the days of the elder Olmsted and Charles Eliot, naturalistic design details had been applied in municipal and regional landscape parks not only in the design of individual buildings, but in coordinated schemes of park development that included roads, bridges, guardwalls, and drainage structures, as well as in shelters, comfort stations, and other buildings necessary for the convenience of park visitors.

Working within this tradition of landscape park development, Hull designed buildings at the Grand Canyon that were conceived as formal expressions of an overall landscape development plan. The construction details employed in his administration building, for example, were consistent with the materials and workmanship eventually employed in the needed roads, guardwalls, trails, signs, and other built features of Grand Canyon Village. In the setting of the 20th-century landscape park, "rustic" architecture did not imply the splendid, if isolated, presence of an Old Faithful Inn or an El Tovar. For Hull, architecture formed one element of a coordinated, understated landscape development scheme, governed above all by the "comprehensive plan" that assured all parts were expressions of a unified artistic purpose. Hull's Park Service Rustic architecture, unlike earlier park architecture sponsored by concessioners, emanated from the overall landscape plan; the scale, location, and character of individual buildings depended on their place as elements of that plan. Each structure, large or small, was calculated as a contribution to the larger work of art, the unified artistic expression that the elder Olmsted would have called the "single work of art . . . framed on a single, noble motive": the landscape park.

For Mather, Hull, and others who shared these cultural assumptions regarding the development of landscape reservations in the early 20th century, architecture considered suitable to form part of a landscape scene—architecture that Mather would have felt "harmonized" with the landscape—depended above all on the visual qualities of that landscape. The architecture itself might vary significantly from park to park. What made buildings appropriate for the landscape park setting did not depend on specific construction or materials as much as on stylistic consistency and contextuality. Hull's early Park Service Rustic buildings became the basis of architectural uniformity in Grand Canyon Village (and in other park villages) and therefore averted the potential "jumble" that had so alarmed Punchard. The Nussbaums' design for the Pueblo style superintendent's residence at Mesa Verde in 1921 served a similar purpose. The subsequent construction of the park village at Mesa Verde in the 1920s extended the use of the same architectural idiom, again creating a stylistically unified village, which because of its unity more easily contributed as an element in the perceived landscape scene. In each case, the unified visual impression of the village was calculated to correspond and contribute to a previsualized image of landscape scenery. National park architecture, whatever its visual characteristics, would be successful only if it contributed to the culturally determined aesthetic perception of landscape scenery considered appropriate to the specific region.

Seen in this light, Myron Hunt's 1924 administration building at Yosemite succeeded, as did his town plan for Yosemite Village that year, primarily because the architect wisely chose to meet the criteria for national park landscape development that Daniel Hull had already begun to establish at Grand Canyon Village. In both cases, the separation of different uses characterized the overall town plan. Utility areas, laid out orthogonally, were well separated but convenient to residential subdivisions. Visitors arrived at open "plazas," defined in part by the facades of the most important public buildings of the village, which together established a civic zone. The buildings themselves expressed a unified, pseudo-vernacular architectural ensemble. These procedures and priorities represented standard town planning practice of the day, as described by Unwin, F. L. Olmsted, Jr., and Nolen; and it was Hull's training and experience as a landscape architect/town planner that assured the consistent application of these procedures in the national park system.

Hull, assisted by Kiessig, designed numerous other buildings for Grand Canyon at this time, some of which were built. By May 1921, Hull's locations for the "cottages" for railroad employees had been determined, and the first bungalow in the Park Service residential area was completed in 1922.[102] A dormitory, community buildings, and other buildings were still on the drawing boards, however, when the entire planning effort at Grand Canyon was temporarily derailed in 1922. At that time, Mather was at the height of his disputes with Ralph H. Cameron, a well connected entrepreneur who was elected to the Senate in 1920. Cameron, who was the principal holder of opportunistic mineral claims on the south rim, used his position in Congress to promote his interests in Arizona—and to vilify Mather on Capitol Hill. Animosities raged for years, but Cameron's mineral claims on the south rim remained embedded.[103] Partly as a result, early in 1922 Mather suffered his second nervous breakdown since assuming his work for the Park Service. Horace Albright, while visiting the Grand Canyon that spring, discovered that the Fred Harvey Company had engaged a prominent Chicago architect, Pierce Anderson, to redesign the entire Grand Canyon Village plan around a proposed multi-million dollar hotel complex. Although the timing may have been suspect, the offer by the concessioner to invest millions of dollars in new visitor facilities was received warmly. Albright and Cammerer (acting for Mather) instructed Hull to suspend all planning efforts until Pierce Anderson had presented his plans; the famous architect's proposals were to take precedence.[104]

A new community building designed by Hull, a new store planned by the Babbitt Brothers, and several other projects were immediately "put on hold" until their final locations in the new plan could be determined. Hull continued, nevertheless, to consider his plans for the village. Cammerer, responding to some restlessness on Hull's part, wrote to him that summer telling him again to "stop all work on the Grand Canyon plans . . . with the idea of cooperating with the general development scheme . . . entrusted to Pierce Anderson."[105] By December, Hull still had not met with Anderson. In response to Hull's inquiries, the new superintendent at the Grand Canyon, Walter W. Crosby, confessed that he "knew nothing of Mr. Anderson's plans," nor could he "get any definite line on them." Anxious to spend the appropriated money for the new community building, Crosby took the unusual step of encouraging Hull to make his case directly to Mather (who by then had resumed his duties) in order to get access to Anderson's plans.[106] Mather, however, had not seen the plans himself; he was as distraught as Crosby at the necessity of delaying the Babbitt Brothers' store and other needed buildings. Cammerer wrote to Ford Harvey (president of the Fred Harvey Company) stating roundly that "we are shortly going to be up against it with the location of some new buildings at the Grand Canyon." They were waiting, he added, to know what Anderson's plans would look like.[107]

They continued to wait. But Pierce Anderson had fallen gravely ill soon after receiving the Fred Harvey commission. Although that January the plans already had been delayed "somewhat longer than we expected," according to Cammerer, it was not until the following October that he and Mather finally reviewed several alternative "general layouts" in Anderson's Chicago offices. Shortly after the meeting, however, Anderson returned to the hospital, critically ill. In the meantime, Mather explained apologetically to Hull that he "fully realized the perplexities you and Colonel Crosby have been in . . . [but] the fact is we have not yet got an approved plan."[108] Superintendent Crosby, for his part, was exasperated; virtually all permanent construction in the park had been stalled for eighteen months. The new community building was a particular sore point; but the superintendent had a long list of buildings, especially utility buildings and employee residences, which had been delayed.[109] In January 1924, after another visit to Chicago, Mather communicated to the new superintendent at Grand Canyon, J. Ross Eakin, that "on account of Pierce Anderson's illness, things are more or less at a standstill as regards the landscape plans at Grand Canyon."[110]

The standstill had continued long enough. Anderson's long illness may or may not have affected the Fred Harvey Company's plans, but at about the time the architect died in February 1924, the concessioner decided to delay the construction of a new hotel. That spring, Hull (who in the meantime had completed the village plan for Yosemite with Myron Hunt) drafted a new plan for the "community development" at Grand Canyon. The new plan essentially improved and elaborated the village scheme he had been developing all along. Hull signed the plan, dated June 1924, and Mather, Superintendent Eakin, and Ford Harvey subsequently approved it.[111] Mather attributed the plan to "Park Service landscape engineers, the Santa Fe System engineers, and Fred Harvey officials." Myron Hunt was also thanked for his "advice and assistance."[112]

The new plan did differ in several regards from Hull's earlier sketches. Most importantly, a new automotive approach from Williams allowed a main entrance from the south, rather than the east. This plan transformed Hull's earlier center road between the residential subdivisions, making it the new South Entrance Road. Because the entrance road followed a natural valley, the residential neighborhoods remained relatively undisturbed on either side of the through road. The new automotive entrance also brought visitors to the center of Grand Canyon Village, rather than to its east side. As early as 1922, Hull probably had already decided to relocate the town's principal civic space, the "plaza," to this central arrival point. This plaza, which was originally intended as a large open square, figures prominently in its new location in the center of the 1924 plan. The new Babbitt Brothers' store, the post office, and a second park administration building were all sited around the plaza (as was a proposed museum that was never built). Like the plaza in the 1923 Yosemite plan, the Grand Canyon plaza also terminated the automotive entrance into the village. In both cases, these plazas became prime parking locations, eventually detracting from their usefulness as gathering places. Overall, however, the redesigned entry and plaza combination vastly simplified and centralized the Grand Canyon Village plan.

Another major change from Hull's earlier plans involved the expansion of future hotel accommodations on the rim. Ford Harvey had made it clear that, sooner or later, his company would like to expand its operations significantly. Mather welcomed such cooperation from the concessioner, who was widely reputed to run the finest hotels in the Southwest. On the 1924 plan, Hull indicated that El Tovar would be expanded with a new western annex, and that the Bright Angel Camp would be completely rebuilt. Two sites east of El Tovar were also set aside: one for a "new first-class hotel for future consideration" and a second for a "proposed casino." Both presumably represented the remnants of Pierce Anderson's proposals for the Fred Harvey Company. Near the site of the existing Fred Harvey mule barns and utility buildings along the railroad tracks, Hull proposed a consolidated complex of power house, laundry, and public garage. The mule barns and other buildings were to be relocated to an area along the southern arm of the railroad wye at the western edge of the village.

Over the next decades, the approved 1924 plan guided the development of Grand Canyon Village, although numerous alterations were made. The new hotel and casino complex was never built, nor was the annex to El Tovar. The Fred Harvey mule barns remained in their original locations, and the new power house and laundry (1926) were built next to them.[113] Perhaps most significantly, the plaza was reduced in size, and apparently from an early date it was used for parking. The first administration building, located near the original site of the proposed "town square," ended up fronting on the busy intersection between Grandview Road, the access to El Tovar, and the new main route to the town center.

With the approved plan finally in place, however, construction in the village proceeded rapidly. Between 1924 and 1933, sixteen new bungalows, duplexes, and assorted garages were built in the Park Service residential subdivision. Several buildings were added to the nearby Park Service utility area, and a new park hospital (1930) was completed. During the same period, on the concessioner's side of town, the Santa Fe Railway completed over fifty new residences, garages, and other structures along the three parallel curving streets that Hull had designated.[114] This building campaign was directed primarily by Hull and, after 1922, by a new assistant landscape architect, Thomas C. Vint. When Hull left the Park Service in 1927, Vint continued as chief landscape architect. Also in 1927, Minor R. Tillotson replaced Eakin as superintendent, and for the next eleven years "Tilly" Tillotson oversaw and managed the most intensive period of development in the park's history.

The new residential areas at Grand Canyon Village continued to be built along distinctive lines. On the Park Service's side of town, the cul-de-sac arrangement allowed automobile access to the back (kitchen) sides of residences; the front doors therefore opened onto communal public space and connected to informal pedestrian routes leading to school and work. In the 1930s (under Vint's direction) these implied routes were paved in asphalt and lined with rounded pieces of limestone set as curbs. Pedestrian and automotive circulation remained separate in this arrangement, and the network of pedestrian paths became fully integrated into the pedestrian paths elsewhere in the village. The arrangement established a hierarchy of semi-public and public spaces and enabled a convenient pattern of daily pedestrian circulation for residents. This type of arrangement would later be called "the Radburn idea," after the New Jersey subdivision designed by architects Clarence S. Stein and Henry Wright in 1929; its application at Grand Canyon Village, however, appears to have been underway at least several years earlier.

The Santa Fe Railway (Fred Harvey) residences on the other side of the South Entrance Road demanded a different treatment. This larger subdivision had been designed as a grid of connected streets, and the standard cottage designed by the concessioner's architect was slightly larger and more elaborate than the simple Park Service bungalows. Generously set back, the front doors of the cottages faced the streets, lending the neighborhood an entirely different character. Access to garages set at the rear of building lots required long alleys, parallel to the streets, down the center of the blocks. This arrangement introduced yet another street type to the hierarchy of street sections being developed by Hull and Vint. Within the residential areas alone at Grand Canyon Village there were five distinct street types: pedestrian paths lined with front entrances; a narrow main street lined with back entrances and garages; a slightly wider main street lined with the fronts of houses; service alleys; and the South Entrance Road itself, which carried through traffic. On the Park Service side, houses were organized along a (modified) cul-de-sac; on the concessioner's side, all the alleys and streets connected in a grid. The new Park Service utility area, with its very wide, rectilinear streets, featured a sixth typical street section. This refinement in the hierarchy of street types typified the contemporary town plans of, for example, John Nolen. The sophistication of circulation patterns, the varied modes of residential entrances, and the emphasis on the development of public and semi-public outdoor spaces were all lessons of British "garden city" planners, disseminated in particular through Unwin's 1909 textbook. The studied response to topography, vegetation, and natural systems that made this kind of town planning so particularly appropriate in a national park setting had been promulgated by F. L. Olmsted, Jr., in his various capacities as the leading planning professional in the United States. Grand Canyon Village epitomized the most skillful town planning techniques of the day.

One of the most important features of any successful town plan of this type was the central civic space. The town square typically served as a hub of circulation, an arrival point, and the site of the community's most important public buildings. At Grand Canyon, the Babbit Brothers' store finally opened in 1926 on the southern edge of the plaza, where Hull had sited it in 1924. In 1929, Thomas Vint contributed one of the most important buildings in the entire village, a second administration building, also located on the new plaza (where it had been sited in the

Grand Canyon Village Historic District

This 1924 plan for the future expansion of Grand Canyon Village was signed by landscape architect Daniel Hull and approved by the park superintendent, the principal park concessioner, and Park Service Director Stephen Mather. The plan employed design features typical of American town planning in the 1920s: defined residential, civic, and industrial zones; careful response to existing topography, vegetation, and natural systems; and a refined hierarchy of street types from pedestrian paths to through roads. New residential subdivisions were delineated for park employees (to the east) and the concessioner's employees (to the west). The new village "plaza," with the park's most important new public buildings sited around it, was located at the center of the plan. Courtesy National Park Service Technical Information Center, Denver Service Center.

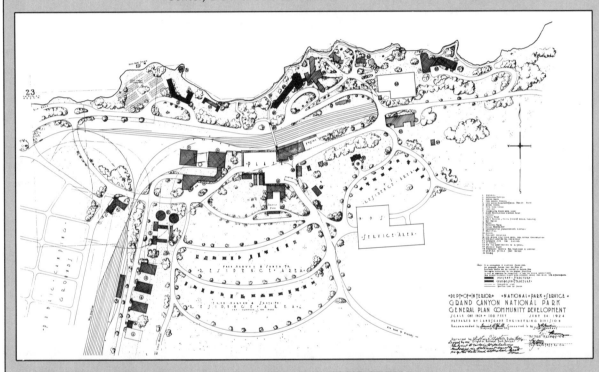

Bird's-eye view of Grand Canyon Village in 1935. A new school playing field is visible to the right, below the Park Service utility area, which at the time was serving as a CCC camp. The curvilinear streets of concessioner's subdivision are to the left of the playing field, and the Bright Angel Lodge and El Tovar are along the canyon rim. Photo by Spence Air Photos, courtesy of Grand Canyon National Park Museum.

The Lookout Studio (1914), designed by architect Mary E. J. Colter, is one of six buildings in the Grand Canyon Village historic district that have been designated individually as National Historic Landmarks for their significance in architectural history. Colter's Hopi House (1905) is also in the district. The masonry wall and path in the foreground were built in the 1930s.

A consistent masonry parapet wall follows along the edge of the Grand Canyon through much of the Grand Canyon Village historic district. The wall was completed by CCC recruits, who replaced the last remnants of various wooden fences and boardwalks that had characterized development along the canyon rim before 1919 (the year the area became a national park). Park Service landscape architects insisted on randomly laid masonry of native sandstones, hoping to create a visual effect that would recall the sedimentary bedding of the surrounding geology.

The railhead at Grand Canyon Village, with the luxurious hotel, El Tovar (1903), looming above on the canyon rim. The Grand Canyon Depot (1910) is barely visible behind the train. In the 1980s, steam rail service was restored from Williams, Arizona, to Grand Canyon Village, making Grand Canyon National Park once again the only national park with direct rail access to a central developed area.

The "plaza" at Grand Canyon Village, as it appeared in the early 1930s. Boulder curbs, the preservation of existing pines and junipers, and log wheel stops were all typical of parking lot site development supervised by Park Service landscape architects. Like other plazas in national park town plans, the Grand Canyon plaza was located at the main automotive entrance to the park, and was therefore soon crowded with parked automobiles. National Archives, Record Group 79.

Above left: Thomas Vint's second administration building, built on the plaza of Grand Canyon Village in 1929. One of the most successful of all Park Service Rustic buildings, the facade projected a powerful official presence over this important public space at the entrance to the village. The sandstone veneer and dark wood siding cover a concrete foundation and wood frame construction.

Above right: Civilian Conservation Corps enrollees removing pines to be replanted in Grand Canyon Village. "Landscape naturalization," which involved soil improvement and the transplanting of native trees and shrubs, was a major task of the CCC in Grand Canyon Village. Courtesy Grand Canyon National Park Museum.

1924 plan). Vint's two-story building, now considered one of the finest existing examples of Park Service Rustic style, again featured rusticated limestone and an upper level of dark wood siding surmounted by intersecting roofs covered in wood shingles. In this case the stone foundation extended up into the second story in massive rectangular piers reaching almost to the roofline. Peeled log columns set on the piers carry the roof beams and frame walls of dark wood siding pierced by windows.[115] As in many classic Park Service Rustic structures, neither the rough courses of stone nor the peeled logs serve their apparent structural purposes; the building does, however, project a powerful image representing the civic administration of the park. The presence of the second administration building dominated the Grand Canyon town plaza, and the peeled log trusses and rough stone or boulder masonry came to be completely identified with the scenic wonders of the Grand Canyon, and of national parks in general. For many park visitors, the decorative facades of the Park Service Rustic style also came to visually embody another aspect of the increasingly convenient national park system: the efficient and ethical management of national parks by a modern government bureau.

Other parts of Grand Canyon Village were developed before 1933 as well, including the Fred Harvey tourist cabin complex west of the railroad wye. After 1933, however, when the copious funds and abundant manpower of Franklin D. Roosevelt's New Deal suddenly were available to the Park Service, construction in the village received new impetus. By 1942, when the Civilian Conservation Corps and other New Deal programs effectively came to an end, over seventy new buildings had been built, including residences, utility buildings, tourist cabins, dormitories, a new school, a firehouse, and a new post office (the last located next to the Babbit Brothers' store on the town plaza). During the same period, the Fred Harvey Company redeveloped the Bright Angel Camp area and built the Bright Angel Lodge (1935), a motor lodge and cabin complex. Mary E. J. Colter, who designed the new lodge with Robert L. Nussbaum, had already done more than anyone to determine the character of commercial development along the rim. The Bright Angel Lodge was her last and most ambitious contribution to the development along the rim of the Grand Canyon. Less imposing and more decentralized than El Tovar, the new facility was geared to the more middle class clientele that typically arrived by automobile. The low, sprawling complex incorporated several historic cabins in the area, and as a whole it maintained a low profile along the canyon rim. The interiors, as in all Colter's buildings, featured fantastic stone fireplaces, Hopi rugs and other crafts, and handcrafted furniture and details.

The presence of up to four Civilian Conservation Corps (CCC) camps in Grand Canyon National Park between 1933 and 1941 was especially significant for the Grand Canyon Village itself, since large numbers of youths could be employed there in labor intensive tasks such as digging utility lines and sewers, paving roads and trails, and smoothing and regrading roadsides. Two CCC camps ultimately were located in Grand

Canyon Village itself: the first near the Park Service utility area and the second south of the residential area. The initial camp at Grand Canyon Village was made up almost entirely of Texas boys, who like other CCC recruits, were from families that had been receiving some sort of public relief.[116] The recruits, working under the supervision of "local experienced men" as well as the (now more numerous) Park Service landscape architects, built many of the most significant landscape structures in the village during the 1930s. The stone guardwall along the canyon, although portions of it dated back to 1905, eventually was completed and regularized along its length. It was complemented by the treatment of the rim trail, which like other heavily used footpaths in the village was paved in "oil bound macadam" to a width of five feet and lined on either side with pieces of limestone set as curbs. "Log seats" were set at advantageous points along the trail.[117] The last traces of wooden boardwalks and fences along the rim were removed during this period, and the flagstone esplanade in front of the Bright Angel Lodge was completed in 1939. Stone walkways, stairs, and retaining walls were built all around the village, including the wall around the mule corral at the head of the Bright Angel Trail. CCC recruits also completed numerous headwalls, culverts, and catch basin structures throughout the village.[118]

In general, the Park Service landscape architects and CCC foremen made a point of preserving existing vegetation, even relocating trenches for sewers and utility lines, for example, to minimize the damage to the roots of trees. In one of the most successful road projects in the village, the main road between the Fred Harvey garage and the town plaza (along the south edge of the railroad tracks) was replaced by two new roadways, which were separated by a straight, thirty-foot wide mall. This type of mall was a favorite device of Thomas Vint's; he used it at Yellowstone, Glacier, and other parks during the 1930s. In this case, the two roadways, each carrying one-way traffic, were laid out on either edge of the mature grove of pinyon and ponderosa pines that remained in the Bright Angel drainage. The effect fully exploited the beauty of the trees, and probably also preserved more of them than a single two-way road would have.

Perhaps most significantly for the appearance of the village, scores of CCC boys were employed in the difficult and time consuming tasks of improving soils and transplanting native trees and shrubs from surrounding areas. Few plans exist for landscape work of this type, and apparently much of it was directed in the field by the crew supervisors and by the Park Service landscape architects who oversaw all the work being done by CCC recruits.[119] The work is described in some detail, however, in reports submitted by CCC project superintendents to Superintendent Tillotson. Assistant and resident Park Service landscape architects also made regular and detailed reports to Vint, and both types of reports included photographs of construction progress and activities.[120] The work typically involved transplanting native plants in areas damaged by visitors or by new construction. This so-called "landscape naturalization" of disturbed areas attempted to recreate not so much the original conditions at an individual site, as a "beautified" condition featuring composed displays of native flora. At Grand Canyon, the planting designs emphasized the native plants of the pinyon-juniper belt that characterizes the 4,500- to 6,500-foot elevations in the park. Yuccas, fernbush, squawbush, and bush mint were all used effectively to establish shrub borders and woodland understories. Pinyon pines and junipers, some of them large enough to require hoists and trucks to move the boxed roots, also were transplanted in the village area wherever ornamental plantings were desired. Areas around new construction received special attention, a fact that contributed immeasurably to the successful "harmonization" of new buildings. Such planting never hid the architecture behind a screen of vegetation, however, but enhanced and augmented the effect of the facade elevation. Local trees and shrubs planted strategically at the corners of buildings or as foundation plantings contributed as much to the building's total effect as did the choice of building materials. In other heavily used areas, such as along the rim walk, small islands of junipers, yuccas, and fernbush were arranged as ornamental compositions that also contributed to the aesthetic appreciation of the park's flora.

Planting design and "landscape naturalization" of this sort clearly were influenced by the "natural gardens" described by Frank Waugh and others in the early 20th century. By the late 1920s, assistant Park Service landscape architects working under Vint had developed refined approaches to "naturalizing" disturbed areas by transplanting native trees and shrubs. In addition, by 1930 park scientists and interpreters such as Harold C. Bryant had put forward compelling environmental reasons for precluding the use of exotic species as ornamentals in national parks.[121] In any case, the use of nursery exotics in remote areas under harsh conditions would not have been cost effective (or even feasible) compared to making use of the hardened plant stock so readily available in nearby forests and meadows. The great success of assistant Park Service landscape architects, such as Ernest Davidson and Merel Sager, was in developing artistically compelling ornamental compositions while making use of local plants transplanted from nearby woods. Such planting design reinforced the general goals of landscape architectural development by strengthening spatial compositions or augmenting architectural facades; by using local plants grouped by correct ecological associations, work of this type also "naturalized" areas that had been disturbed by construction or overuse, fulfilling the mandate to minimize the impact of physical development.[122]

In planting design, certainly, Park Service landscape architects successfully drew on the contemporary theory and examples of "natural style" gardeners such as Jensen or Waugh in order to create strategies for ornamental planting design appropriate for national parks. The use of native plants in "natural" arrangements had also been established as an appropriate complement to Arts and Crafts domestic architecture in California and elsewhere, and so it was a logical strategy for site work around new Park Service Rustic construction. Such horticulturally intensive work, however, made up only one component of the landscape architectural planning and design underway on the rim of the Grand Canyon in the 1920s and 1930s.

By the time the United States entered World War II, Grand Canyon Village had been essentially completed. It remains, remarkably, largely unaltered. Today there are 302 buildings and structures in the Grand Canyon Village historic district, which was first included in the National Register of Historic Places in 1975. Of these, only forty-six were built after 1941 or have been modified enough to significantly alter their appearance.[123] There are numerous other examples of Park Service village planning of this era, including Yosemite Village, the Mesa Verde administrative district, Yellowstone's Mammoth Hot Springs and Fishing Bridge Museum areas, Longmire and Yakima Park villages at Mount Rainier, the Munson Valley and Rim Village areas of Crater Lake, the Giant Forest and Ash Mountain areas of Sequoia, and others. In some cases, such as Mammoth Hot Springs, Park Service planners merely reorganized circulation and visitor services in what was already an established administrative center. In others, such as Yakima Park (now called Sunrise), planners designed an entirely new developed area. The situation was usually somewhere in between, as it was at Grand Canyon. With the exception of Yosemite Village, however, none of these examples of park village planning compare to Grand Canyon Village in terms of size, historical significance, and artistic distinction.

Yosemite Village, because conditions there kindled the first attempts at national park village planning in 1914, can claim to be the first site at which visitor and administrative services were consolidated in a picturesque village landscape. But like many park villages in the national park system, Yosemite Village was extensively altered after World War II, diminishing its historical integrity. The rapid increase in visitor numbers that boded so well for the future of national parks in the early 1920s completely overwhelmed many visitor facilities by the 1950s. As postwar automotive tourism soared, many parks reverted to the overcrowded, potentially unsanitary situations that had inspired officials to undertake planned park development in the first place. Beginning in 1956, the Park Service began a major park redevelopment campaign, called "Mission 66," to accommodate far greater numbers of tourists in developed areas. One of the park villages most affected, in the end, was Yosemite. The construction of a new Degnan's concession building (1959) and a large Park Service visitor center (1967) began a transformation of the central village civic zone. In 1972, much of the village circulation system was "pedestrianized"; since then motor vehicles have been forced to either bypass the village center or park in nearby lots. The central plaza, no longer an arrival point, became part of an extended pedestrian mall, with new paths, lighting, and construction details dating to the early 1970s. The plaza itself was partially filled with raised, planted islands surrounded by seating walls.[124]

The "revegetation" of areas previously used for parking or other vehicular purposes led to the establishment of dense foliage in front of buildings and in open areas. This attempt to recreate oak woodland communities of native trees and shrubs may or may not have been successful ecologically. It is hard to imagine that a woodland ecosystem has been viably reestablished in an area which, even in 1914, was already a small city. What the reestablished vegetation definitely has done, however, is obscure the carefully crafted Park Service Rustic building facades behind screens of vegetation. This effect also diminishes the relationships of the buildings to one another, eroding the perception of the public spaces that the buildings once helped define. The central plaza, now largely "revegetated," is no longer perceptible as an important public space. Visitors no longer arrive at a well-defined public plaza at Yosemite Village, and that plaza is no longer imbued with the sense of civic responsibility that Park Service Rustic architecture once embodied. As Daniel Hull knew so well, outside the context of an appropriate site plan, "rustic" architecture loses a great deal of its expressive and symbolic power. No longer "harmonized" with the landscape, the original buildings at Yosemite Village are now simply buried behind it. Perhaps most sadly, the maturing vegetation planted in the early 1970s now obscures many of the views from the village of the cliffs and other geologic formations of the surrounding valley. This geographic detachment greatly contributes to the generic, placeless quality of the village today—an ironic fate for a settlement privileged by such an extraordinary location.

At Grand Canyon Village, however, postwar development averted major alterations to the original village area. Planners sited a new southern approach road to the rim at Yavapai Point, east of the historic village, where a new visitor center, campground, and shopping mall were subsequently developed. Hull's South Entrance Road no longer served as a main public entrance to the village, and therefore reverted back to Center Road (as it is known today). Motor vehicles again began arriving at Grand Canyon from the east, via what was once Grandview Road. This alteration to the overall circulation plan has reduced Hull's town plaza to a less significant location in the village. The new traffic pattern also further complicated the already busy intersection at what became (again) the main arrival point to the village: the area where the railroad tracks end, between the first administration building and the Fred Harvey Garage. Two new motels were also developed in the village, on the rim near the location that had been proposed in 1924 for the El Tovar annex. Assembled from modular, precast slabs of darkened concrete and massed with extremely low silhouettes, the Kachina (1968) and Thunderbird (1971) lodges are successfully understated presences on the rim.

Besides these changes, Grand Canyon Village remains little changed. Even rail service, suspended in the 1960s, was resumed in 1989, making Grand Canyon once again the only national park with direct rail access into a central area of the park. Under the special circumstances offered by its legal and physical context, the village became, and has remained, an idealized vision of how new towns can be developed in ways that enhance civic life, minimize environmental damage, and remain visually consistent with established conventions for the visual appreciation of land as landscape.

The Park Service policies for village planning that Hull established at Grand Canyon would remain largely unaltered through the 1920s and 1930s. Unity in architectural inspiration, for example, continued to be an essential feature of park village development, as it always had been. Park Service planners would also continue to devise village plans that separated uses, mainly between residential, civic, and utility areas. Another type of use, first suggested by Johnston and Leopold's "rim zone" and later reaffirmed by Hull, attempted to eliminate all development from the immediate vicinity of visually or environmentally sensitive areas, such as the rim of the Grand Canyon. A central civic space remained a feature of national park village plans of the era, as did the refined hierarchy of street types, such as those that Hull and Vint devised. New village streets typically conformed to topography, but in legible patterns that prevented overly circuitous circulation systems. Ornamental planting was intended to reaffirm the general goals of spatial organization and circulation and also to provide well-composed displays; but since plants were usually transplanted from somewhere nearby and grouped by appropriate ecological associations, ornamental plantations could also serve to "naturalize" areas that had been disturbed by construction or visitor traffic. And in general, the response to topography and the preservation of natural features that F. L. Olmsted, Jr., emphatically recommended to his World War I town planners continued to be hallmarks of all aspects of National Park Service planning.

The Grand Canyon Village historic district survives, like other great landscape parks in American history, to express the particular ideals of civic form originally articulated by the park's managers, advocates, and constituents. If New York's Central Park preserves the "new urban vision" put forward for 19th-century American cities, Grand Canyon Village embodies the highest standards of American "town planning" of the early 20th century. The precedents established at Grand Canyon for the development of national park villages were, at least for some, ideal prescriptions for urban development generally. In this sense, Daniel Hull advanced the role of national parks as 20th-century landscape parks; he initiated planning and development that would make the national park system a showcase of American planning ideals in the 20th century, just as municipal landscape parks had been in the 19th century.

The plan for Grand Canyon Village expounded the civic ideals of a generation of American planners and helped put National Park Service planning on the course it would follow at least until World War II. The challenges that face Grand Canyon Village today are those that face American cities in general. As Grand Canyon Village has grown, it has sprawled—not unlike many American cities—in ways that early planners could not have anticipated. Increased traffic congestion and historic preservation are concerns that demand far greater attention than they did earlier in the century. Millions of tourists now arrive annually from all over the world, making the Grand Canyon one of the most visited places on earth. With luck, Park Service planners will continue to create design solutions that illustrate the best of what landscape architectural planning can achieve under such circumstances: development that alleviates the pressure put on delicate environments, while assuring that an ever larger and more diverse public continues to be able to fully appreciate "unimpaired" scenery, both as individuals and as a community. The Grand Canyon Village historic district survives as evidence that this can be done.

The Going-to-the-Sun Road Historic District:
"Landscape Engineering" and Changing Roles of Park Service Professionals

Chapter 4

Park village planning at Grand Canyon and Yosemite proceeded successfully in the early 1920s, but in some ways the landscape architect Daniel Hull still conducted his professional practice more as a part-time consultant than as a full-time employee of the Park Service. Hull retained the right to pursue his private practice in California, for example, and he did so out of offices he shared with Gilbert Stanley Underwood in Los Angeles. His office letterhead advertised his services as a "Landscape Architect, Town Planner," and he often collaborated with Underwood on both private and Park Service commissions. Horace Albright later asserted that there was a common perception on the West Coast that Hull and Underwood were the partners of a private design firm.[1] Hull was a government employee, however, and the shared office where he worked with his assistant Thomas Vint nominally served as the "landscape engineering division" of the Park Service.

The precarious balance between private and public practice that Hull maintained between 1923 and 1927 mirrored the cooperative partnership that Stephen Mather engineered during this period between private concessioners and the Park Service. In a remarkable series of national park developments, notably in the Southwest, private concessioners hired Underwood as the architect for new lodges and cabins while Hull acted as the landscape architect and site planner. The two friends worked on the projects out of the same office as collaborators, a situation that facilitated the remarkable integration of architecture and site typical of their work. The unusual business arrangement, however, eventually put Hull in an ethically untenable position: if he really were Underwood's partner, contributing to and benefiting from their common success, then as the Park Service landscape engineer he was in the position of reviewing his own firm's proposals. In 1927, this evident impropriety helped end Hull's career with the Park Service.

There were many reasons why the canyonlands of the Southwest offered tremendous potential for new park development in the early 1920s. The scenery of southern Utah and northern Arizona was only just becoming more accessible and better known. Many felt Zion Canyon the scenic equal to Yosemite, and Bryce Canyon was reknowned for its colorful and fantastic geologic formations. The north rim of the Grand Canyon, more remote than the south rim, was at a higher elevation and therefore received more annual precipitation and was more thickly wooded. These sites remained undeveloped and largely unvisited, but they were

Stephen Mather (center, wearing cap) and Park Service officials in Yosemite National Park in 1926. Landscape architect Daniel Hull is second from the left; assistant director Horace Albright is second from the right. Chief naturalist Ansel Hall is on Mather's left, and the park's superintendent, Washington B. ("Dusty") Lewis, is on his right. Courtesy National Park Service Historic Photograph Collections, Harpers Ferry Center.

logical stops along the Park-to-Park Highway route, and Mather and Albright seized the chance to expand the young park system.

As usual, local civic boosters, politicians, and automobile clubs initiated the efforts to have federal park legislation introduced in Congress. In 1913, in response to requests from Utah's governor and the recently created state road commission, the Forest Service started construction on a road to the Grand Canyon's north rim from Jacob's Lake. That year Theodore Roosevelt again visited the Grand Canyon, but this time he went to the north rim, where he hunted cougar on the Kaibab Plateau. In 1916, Senator Reed Smoot of Utah, who became one of Mather's most important allies in Congress, succeeded in funding the construction of a federal road into Munkuntuweap National Monument, later renamed Zion. That year *The Salt Lake Tribune* sent an "auto pathfinding tour" from Salt Lake to the Grand Canyon's north rim. From there the pioneers blazed new automotive routes to Zion and Bryce canyons, Pipe Spring, and other potential "tourist meccas."[2] In 1917, one local booster, Douglas White, convinced Horace Albright to visit Zion Canyon; Albright was astounded, and from that point on strongly advocated national park status for the monument.

Another group with particular interest in southwestern scenery was the Union Pacific Railroad. Railroads had profited greatly by operating hotels and livery services in national parks, and they also benefited from the increased passenger traffic on trunk lines near national park destinations. The Union Pacific main line from Los Angeles to Salt Lake City passed through Lund, Utah, and railroad executives quickly realized that a short spur line to Cedar City would put Zion, Bryce, Cedar Breaks, and even the north rim within an easy motorcoach ride. For their part, Mather and Albright pressed for the necessary legislative steps to allow new parks along this scenic loop to be developed. President Wilson responded in 1918 and declared a vastly enlarged and renamed Zion National Monument. In 1919 Congress passed the legislation creating Zion National Park. In 1923, Warren G. Harding declared Bryce Canyon a national monument and personally visited it (as well as Zion) on his ill-fated tour of the West later that year. In 1924 Senator Smoot introduced park legislation for Bryce, and although the monument remained under Forest Service management until 1928 (while land transfer provisions were negotiated), Hull and Underwood planned its development as if it were already a national park.[3] The Grand Canyon, as noted, also made the long anticipated shift from monument to park in 1919, and plans for north rim development followed only slightly behind those for Grand Canyon Village.

In the early 1920s, however, Mather could not expect the federal government to invest in lodges, or even in more modest tourist accommodations. Hard won Congressional appropriations were applied to urgently needed roads, trails, administration buildings, and residences that were essential to the basic supervision and operation of the parks. But in 1923, the year the spur line to Cedar City opened, the Union Pacific railroad formed a subsidiary, the Utah Parks Company, which Mather immediately designated as the concessioner for Zion and the north rim of the Grand Canyon.[4] Having a railroad as a park concessioner necessitated significant construction near the points of interest. Visitors who arrived by train (and were then shuttled by bus) were not prepared to camp and required centralized accommodations. The Union Pacific architect, W. P. Wellman, therefore drew up plans for a large hotel in Zion Canyon. When Daniel Hull saw the plans for the hotel, however, he urged the Union Pacific to reconsider. Alarmed by the "star shaped layout" of the building, he wrote the railroad executives that "as a general principle in park planning we try to avoid a symmetrical development . . . which is apt to be contrary to the feeling we try to create in the parks."[5] Probably at Hull's suggestion, the Union Pacific then hired Gilbert Stanley Underwood to design the lodge, and later that year the Commission of Fine Arts approved that architect's plans for a hotel in Zion Canyon.

But Stephen Mather held high expectations for Zion, the newest park in the system, and he decided to reject Underwood's proposals in any case. "I felt the construction of a large hotel in the canyon was not the proper development," he explained curtly. Underwood obliged the director with a new scheme for "an ample central building with cottages for sleeping quarters nearby."[6] This decentralized scheme, which was built, replaced the single massive hotel with a smaller central building and a complement of small cottages, all unified by the landscape site plan. Underwood and Hull subsequently employed the same strategy at Bryce Canyon and the north rim of the Grand Canyon as well. By 1924, the Utah Parks Company was already conducting motorcoach loop tours to the Zion and Bryce lodges, although construction at both complexes continued through most of the decade.[7]

Underwood's most ambitious park lodges were built later in the 1920s on the north rim of the Grand Canyon and in Yosemite Valley. His

Grand Canyon Lodge (1928), also built for the Utah Parks Company, was located on Bright Angel Point across the canyon from Grand Canyon Village. In addition to the central lodge there are currently twenty-three deluxe and ninety-one standard cabins in the decentralized north rim complex. The lodge was rebuilt in 1937 following an earlier fire; but with almost all of its original cabins in good condition and the original site work still intact (if now eroded) the Grand Canyon Lodge retains a high degree of integrity. Underwood's Ahwahnee Hotel (1927) was built for another concessioner, a company that had been formed in 1925 to consolidate two fractious park entrepreneurs into a single manageable group. The Yosemite Park and Curry Company, like the Utah Parks Company, was then encouraged to hire Underwood, who worked with Hull on the site development plans for the Ahwahnee. Located in a secluded meadow in the far east end of Yosemite Valley, the six-story steel frame building was sheathed in textured concrete and stone veneer to simulate rough wood siding and massive stone piers. Luxurious, striking, and uniquely situated, the Ahwahnee culminated the tradition of massive, centralized national park lodges built by concessioners to cater to wealthy tourists.[8]

Although only two of the four remain in their original condition, Underwood's lodges built during the 1920s are among the most memorable buildings in the national park system. Their success must also be attributed to the landscape architect Daniel Hull, who collaborated on these and other projects with Underwood. The role of both Hull and his assistant Thomas Vint helps explain the stylistic unity that the Park Service was able to sustain and develop in the far-flung park system during this formative period. But if Underwood's lodges awed park visitors, he was not the consulting architect who most influenced the future of architectural design in national and state park development at this time. That architect was Herbert Maier, a relatively obscure Bay Area designer who began working on modest building projects for national parks in 1922. And the building type that more than any other would become the ideal expression of Park Service Rustic style was not the tourist lodge, or even the administration building, but the park museum.

Maier was a native San Franciscan who, like Vint and numerous other Park Service designers, had graduated from Berkeley and then, following service in World War I, worked for various California architectural firms.[9] In the early 1920s he began an association with Ansel F. Hall, who had been a key figure in the rapidly developing education programs fostered by the Park Service. Since the days of John Muir and Enos Mills, "nature guides" had added immeasurably to the experience of park scenery, flora, and fauna by providing tourists with enough information to add scientific and historical dimensions to their appreciation of places. Interpreting parks for visitors had been one of Mather's strongest enthusiasms, and in 1923 the director asked Ansel Hall, then the park naturalist at Yosemite, to oversee the development of interpretive programs in all the parks. Hall moved from Yosemite back to Berkeley, where the University of California provided offices and other support for his activities through its School of Forestry.[10]

Ansel Hall and Herbert Maier may well have known one another since college days; in any case Hall, who graduated from Berkeley with a degree in forestry in 1917, had asked the architect to provide illustrations for his *Handbook of Yosemite National Park* in 1921.[11] In 1922, he persuaded Maier to provide sketches (at no charge) for a proposed new museum building at Yosemite. The Yosemite museum had been a special cause for Hall; as a park ranger he had personally established the park's first museum in 1921 by converting an artist's studio in the old village. In his efforts to raise private funds for a new museum, Hall appealed to Chauncey J. Hamlin, a Buffalo philanthropist who in 1923 became the president of the American Association of Museums. Hamlin, who had been impressed by Hall's work during his visits to Yosemite, in turn secured funds for a new museum through the Laura Spelman Rockefeller Memorial. Hall was placed in charge of the Yosemite museum project, and he immediately hired Herbert Maier to design the new museum building, which was completed in 1925.[12]

Maier's Yosemite museum was one of the first buildings specifically dedicated to an educational function built in a national park.[13] The young architect moved cautiously, however, designing a simple rectangular building that Thomas Vint helped to site on the plaza of the new Yosemite Village. Rough granite boulders veneered the concrete of the lower level, and darkly stained shakes covered the second story; the building nicely complemented Myron Hunt's nearby administration building. Chauncey Hamlin must have been pleased, because at his request the Laura Spelman Rockefeller Memorial funded an expanded program of park museum construction, and in 1926 Herbert Maier moved to Washington, DC, to design and administer the construction of two more model museum projects for the American Association of Museums.[14]

Maier's next two museum buildings were as different from one another as they were from the Yosemite museum. On the south rim of the Grand Canyon, Maier designed the Yavapai Point observation station, which opened in 1928. Perhaps because the station was to be sited on the very edge of the rim (about two miles east of Grand Canyon Village) Maier again responded to the work of a great park architect who preceded him, in this case Mary E. J. Colter. Like Colter's Lookout Studio and Hermit's Rest also on the south rim, Maier's Yavapai museum was cloaked in native stone. Like Colter, Maier also referred to Native American building traditions in architectural details. Amorphous in plan, the building was set as low and as deep in the canyon rim as possible; heavy foundation plantings camouflaged what would otherwise have been a prominent location. Maier explained that the elevation was "designed to conform as nearly as possible to the vertical front of the cliff and the horizontal line of the rim."[15] The building frankly acknowledged the architectural standards Colter had set for "rim zone" development.

In the other museum he designed at this time, however, Maier initiated what would become his own contributions to national and state park architecture. His Bear Mountain museum, built for the Bear Mountain section of the Palisades Interstate Park, became what historian Ralph H. Lewis describes as "the prototype of trailside museums."[16] At Bear Mountain, apparently Maier felt free to devise a more original expression of a park museum. The individual structural elements of the building possessed exaggerated proportions, an effect that resulted from the use of massive boulders and logs in the construction of a relatively modest building. These massive elements recalled the use of oversize logs and boulders in "rustic" park structures, such as park entranceways and shelters, which since the late 19th century had been common features of many scenic reservations. As was the case in such landscape structures, Maier's boulders and logs were not veneers, but usually served their apparent structural function. This was in part because Maier's trailside museums were smaller, less complex structures than contemporary park lodges or administration buildings. The specific program of the park museum allowed it to evolve—structurally and thematically—more as an enlarged interpretive display than as a building. And like a trailside interpretive display, the Bear Mountain museum was sited as an element of a "nature trail" that was being developed at the same time; again the building was conceived as one part of an overall site development plan. Maier's architecture, and the displays of local geological and historical significance contained within, emphasized the role of the park museum as it was being defined by Maier and by park educators such as Ansel Hall: to encourage visitors "to consider the park itself as the museum."[17]

The potential for park museum architecture suggested at Bear Mountain came to fruition at Yellowstone. In 1928 the Laura Spelman Rockefeller Memorial again responded to the request of the American Association of Museums, this time to fund a series of museums in the country's largest national park. Initial plans for a centralized facility were soon abandoned in favor of a decentralized scheme of trailside museums (in this case roadside would be more accurate) designed by Maier and sited at strategic points along the Grand Loop road system. The first, at Old Faithful, was open already in 1928; three others followed, at Madison Junction (1929), the Norris Geyser Basin (1929), and Yellowstone Lake near the Fishing Bridge (1931).

The Yellowstone museums were, as architectural historian Laura Soullière Harrison points out, "unlike anything that came before" in park architecture.[18] At the Fishing Bridge museum, the boulder foundations were not only massive, but heavily battered in courses that seemed piled as much as laid. Massive log posts and beams were chosen for interesting grains, knots, and twists. Both stone and wood was selected for visual interest and left as little worked as possible. The Norris museum was divided by a high, central hall, open at either end and supported by massive log trusses above. The building itself framed the dramatic geyser basin that suddenly came into view as one entered the open, central hallway. All the museums featured large terraces and nearby amphitheaters that encouraged outdoor extensions of museum activities.[19] At Yellowstone, the park museum became a park museum system; the main trailside museums were to be supplemented by a series of smaller exhibit panels, called "nature shrines," that interpreted individual features at roadside overlooks.[20] Heavy projecting eaves and massive shakes typically completed these unique visions of park architecture that became programmatically, visually, and structurally, inseparable from the function of trailside park interpretation.

The scientific and cultural interest of national parks had of course been among the reasons for setting aside large, scenic reservations from the beginning, but the standards that lifted national parks over their municipal and regional counterparts had usually been described through pictures and in terms of aesthetic qualities. By the 1920s, however, in part because of the efforts of early Park Service interpreters and the American Association of Museums, the unique educational opportunities and scientific content of national parks were asserted more vigorously not only as reasons for park preservation, but also as criteria to guide future park planning and management. The museum system in Yellowstone to some extent reprogrammed the scenic Grand Loop with an itinerary of geological and biological education. This change in emphasis increasingly characterized 20th-century tourism in the parks. Over the next decade, Herbert Maier's Yellowstone museums would epitomize the ideal of "rustic" architecture for both national and state parks, and in part this architecture owed its success to its complete identification with the role of large parks as living classrooms and museums of natural and cultural history. If the facade of Vint's contemporary second administration building at Grand Canyon exalted the bureaucratic propriety and efficiency of the 1920s, Maier's variation of Park Service Rustic came to signify the educational role of national and state parks in the 1930s. Maier's park architecture, in this sense, could literally improve the view; it embodied the intellectual keys— scientific research and interpretation—that could open the experience of places to new dimensions of appreciation. Intellectually and visually, Maier's park museums added new meanings to landscape scenery in the 20th century just as surely as the carefully placed ruined temple or peasant cottage once did in landscape imagery of earlier eras.

Architects such as Underwood and Maier, however, still worked as consultants to the Park Service. Working for a concessioner and for a charitable group, their affiliation with the government bureaucracy was tenuous. Daniel Hull, although an employee, apparently envisioned his role with the bureau in essentially the same terms. These arrangements had resulted in significant success, but the expanding demands of Park Service operations required that the roles of some of its professionals be recast. Planning, architecture, and interpretation all increasingly converged as aspects of professional park management in the 1920s. The achievement of Park Service Rustic as an architectural style, for example, would have been impossible without the contributions of landscape architects, educators, and park superintendents. For this synthesis to occur, all of these professionals to some degree adapted their practices to specifically address national park concerns. The Park Service had begun to depend on the experience and expertise developed by a corps of career managers. As the bureau grew, it required a cadre of professionals to provide a range of technical services specially tailored to its own priorities and procedures. The time when consultants could lead planning and design efforts for the Park Service was ending.

Architectural design was a highly visible and symbolic aspect of Park Service planning and design efforts, but it was not the most vital to the successful preservation and development of the national park system. Neither was architecture the first professional discipline to be assimilated into the Park Service bureaucracy. By 1927, Stephen Mather had already reorganized Park Service landscape architects and civil engineers, bringing these professionals together under new management in a centralized "field headquarters" in San Francisco.

New demands on the Park Service planning and engineering staff had necessitated the reorganization. Funds for park road construction, in particular, increased dramatically beginning in 1925 and challenged the ability of the bureau to manage technically demanding projects. Mather had been calling for more and better park roads since his arrival in Washington. At least since 1915, when he attended the dedication ceremonies at Rocky Mountain National Park, he had recognized that "the great flow of tourist gold" that brought prosperity to western towns and cities followed the routes of improved highways.[21] That prosperity, in turn, created local constituencies in favor of national parks, which were identified (along with highways) as instruments of local progress. After 1916, when Congress passed both the National Park Service and the Federal-Aid to Highways legislation, the fate of the national park system was linked, for better or for worse, to the construction of a national system of federally financed, modern roads. The startling ascendancy of automotive highways as a means of domestic tourism after 1890 had elevated the national parks to a central position in American popular and leisure culture; the completion of an interstate system of improved roads would make the parks viable as a park system, just as municipal and regional parkways had connected smaller scenic reservations since the 19th century.

For Mather, road improvements "headed the list" of needed construction in every park except Yellowstone. The director regularly reiterated that "the road problem [was] one of the most important before the Service," since little had been done "to enable the motorists to have the greater use of these playgrounds which they demand and deserve." Mather wanted to assure that the "great out-of-doors movement" underway in America would first discover the national park system, and then demand its improvement and expansion.[22] Automobile clubs, good roads advocates, and local chambers of commerce all shared these goals for the eventual development of the national park system as an automotive tourist route, roughly along the lines of the Park-to-Park Highway that Mather had endorsed at Rocky Mountain in 1915.

The Park-to-Park Highway route, as published by Stephen Mather in the 1920 Park Service Annual Report. Mather, backed by countless chambers of commerce, good roads boosters, and park advocates, urged state and local governments to improve existing roads between the national parks to facilitate "interpark travel" by automobile. Connecting the parks, as well as managing them all according to consistent policies, were essential steps in transforming the federal scenic reservations into a modern park system. Glacier National Park, in Montana, was the most egregious gap in the interpark automotive route.

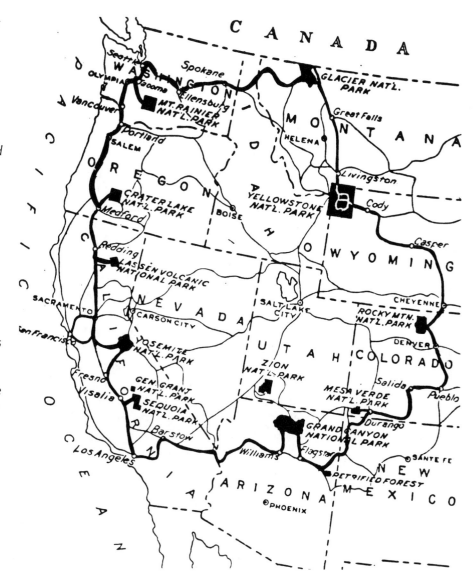

In 1921, the year after that route was officially designated, he further elaborated his vision for "interpark travel" to include a "truly national highway system . . . for the accommodation of the touring public within their borders," while testifying to Congress in favor of federal funding of an "interstate highway system." "Travel is based on the enjoyment of scenery," he asserted, not for the first time.[23] Connecting national parks with improved highways could yield huge returns through domestic vacation travel and spending. And once the national parks were perceived as co-agents of this economic impetus, Mather knew that the Park Service would be likely to receive the support necessary to accomplish its primary purpose: preserving extraordinary places from other forms of (non-park) development. In the early 1920s, private development—from huge reservoir schemes to minor scenic tramways and toll roads—threatened to destroy natural systems and scenery, or at least to limit public access. Power, grazing, and mining interests obviously had no mandate to preserve the existing conditions of scenic places, but they did have powerful political allies. To successfully compete (in other words to fulfill the Park Service's preservation mandate) Mather knew the national parks must be made accessible and convenient to the swelling ranks of automotive tourists who were ready to make the cause of national parks their own. The limited construction of roads, more than any other aspect of park development, would strengthen and validate the goal Mather described as the "complete conservation" of national park areas.

Approaches and connections to national parks, however, were faring far better than roads in the parks themselves in 1921. With the passage of the Federal-Aid to Highways Act in 1916, Congress had authorized seventy-five million dollars to be distributed to state highway authorities over a five-year period. The Department of Agriculture administered the money through its Office of Public Roads, which reorganized in 1918 as the Bureau of Public Roads. Since the 1890s, the Office of Public Roads had steadily reinforced its position as the authoritative source of unbiased highway engineering expertise. As the administrator of federal aid to state highway departments, the office enforced standards for individual construction projects and decided whether they qualified for federal funds.[24] The role of the bureau's highway engineers was not limited to technical guidance and review, however, since after 1916 they directly managed the construction of roads in national forests and on some other public lands. By a provision of the 1916 act (which essentially was extended in 1921) roads in national forests could be requested by state authorities and then planned and constructed with federal funds by the engineers of the Bureau of Public Roads. The first authorization for "forest roads and trails" was for one million dollars in 1917; by 1923 an average of $7,500,000 was being spent annually on roads in and through national forests, a rate of spending that continued through the decade after Congress extended federal aid through the Federal Highway Act of 1921.[25] No funds for national park roads had been included in the federal-aid legislation of 1916 or 1921.

The arguments in favor of government financing for national park road development, however, paralleled the reasoning of the contemporary "good roads" advocates who had lobbied successfully for federal aid to state highways. Park development, like road construction, could not proceed without the legal powers of governments to condemn and acquire land for public purposes (or in the case of the federal government, to designate reservations and right-of-ways out of the public domain). Other conditions justified public investment in both park improvements and highway improvements in the 1920s. Both efforts required long-term investments of capital that did not accrue value to a single property, owner, or investor. The benefits returned were part of the general economic stimulus and movement away from rural isolation usually described as "progress." The private resort, like the private turnpike, was hardly unknown; but in both cases, the need for public (if not federal) planning and investment had been well established since the heyday of municipal parks and parkways in the 19th century. Mather, however, missed the opportunity of participating directly in the federal road building spree that began in 1916. The sponsors of that legislation had worried that federal funds for non-commercial roads (in parks) would be impossible to justify. On its own, the Park Service now faced the difficult job of lobbying Congress to pass generous, phased appropriations specifically for national park roads.

But sporadic funding continued to undermine park road development plans. In 1919 and 1920, Congress failed to fund any road construction in the parks, a condition which reduced chief engineer George E. Goodwin's activities to "gathering of data and the preparation of plans . . . for future operations."[26] In 1921, an exasperated Mather wrote in an article describing the "ideals and policies" of his bureau, that "definite projects [had] been laid out by the Service in all the larger parks calling for road building, but up to the present time no substantial funds have been available to carry them out."[27] In the early 1920s, while Daniel Hull and his assistants planned the villages at Yosemite and Grand Canyon and designed numerous residences, administration buildings, and entrance stations for other parks, the larger appropriations necessary for improved road systems remained elusive.

Although regular appropriations in 1921 had allowed at least for the initiation of several important park road projects, in 1923 Mather still noted with irritation that "the most urgent need of the national parks at this time is for new roads . . . to measure up to the high standards of the roads being constructed to their boundaries by various states, either with or without Federal aid." He estimated that the sixty percent of park visitors who now arrived in parks by car did so "along excellent roads" through national forests, only to see them turn to narrow, rutted lanes at park boundaries. The Bureau of Public Roads assured that the new state highways, even when not paved, featured high crowns, functioning ditches, and reasonable grades. Mather was acutely aware that park roads suffered by comparison. He judged them inadequate, incomplete, and also dangerous considering the cavalcades of automobiles—over 270,000 in 1923—that rumbled up to park gates thanks to improved state highway systems. In his *Annual Report* that year, Mather suggested to Hubert Work (Albert Fall's replacement as secretary of the interior) that $7,500,000 phased over several years would be needed to put park road systems in "satisfactory and safe conditions." It was a small amount, he could not resist adding, compared to the "tremendous amount authorized and spent by the Federal Government"—and administered by the Department of Agriculture—on roads outside the parks.[28]

By 1923, however, Mather, Cammerer, and Albright finally had begun to convince even reluctant members of Congress that national parks, like state highways, warranted substantial investment of federal funds. In the meantime, planning and reconnaissance for park road construction had proceeded under chief engineer George Goodwin. Goodwin had graduated from the University of Maine in 1910 and had worked on railroads and government reclamation projects in the West before he went to work for the Army Corps of Engineers in 1913. He spent the next four years at Crater Lake National Park building the park road system. Mather and Albright had first met him at Crater Lake in 1915 and recognized that his experience in park road construction would be a valuable asset to the future parks bureau.[29] Goodwin, an experienced civil engineer at age forty-two, joined the Park Service during its first year of operations in 1917. He usually made his headquarters in Portland, where he could oversee road and trail planning in all the parks, but especially in Glacier and Mount Rainier. Most park superintendents made new road construction a top priority for their parks, since the few existing roads open to cars were in poor condition and sometimes crowded with frustrated motorists. During the next few years, Goodwin investigated and developed a list of the most desirable road projects, including the Carbon River Road in Mount Rainier, the Middle Fork Road (the Generals Highway) to the Giant Forest in Sequoia, and the Transmountain Highway (Going-to-the-Sun Road) across the continental divide in Glacier.

In 1921, limited funding allowed all three of these projects to get underway, an important fact since, as Mather noted, Congress had thereby committed itself (hopefully) to finishing what it had started.[30] But road construction presented difficulties enough in mountainous terrain, where contractors faced high labor and mobilization costs and short construction seasons. Inconsistent and inadequate appropriations exacerbated the problems and made essential multi-year contracts impossible to plan. Progress was slow, but by the end of 1922 contractors had completed about five miles of the Carbon River Road at Mount Rainier. Four miles of the Middle Fork Road were graded at Sequoia using park "force account" (temporary) labor. At Glacier, where the Transmountain Highway apparently was a priority, seventeen miles of road were under construction in two separate projects.[31]

Mather also altered his strategy for advancing his road budgets in 1922. That year he received approval from Secretary Work to submit a separate park road budget to Congress for over seven million dollars phased over three years. Mather was requesting, in other words, an additional annual construction budget nearly twice the size of the regular Park Service budget at that time. Seen another way, the amount was twice the total that had been spent on all national park roads since 1872. To justify the increase, the director attempted to draw a parallel between federal-aid highway legislation and a substantial park road appropriation, which would only put the park roads "on a par with the good roads now being constructed . . . through Federal aid."[32]

The strategy of presenting park road construction as a separate issue from regular park appropriations soon succeeded. While Mather continued to lobby through his Washington network, he asked Horace Albright to gather data on park roads and organize the legislative effort. With about 350 miles of park roads at Yellowstone under his care since 1919, Albright had far more experience with road maintenance and construction than any other superintendent. Albright had also continued in his capacity as "assistant director in the field," while Arno Cammerer had replaced him as assistant director in the Washington office. As

Mather's field assistant, Albright often guided congressmen and other VIPs through Yellowstone and other parks. During the summer of 1923, for example, he exploited a golden opportunity to influence members of the House Appropriations Committee on their tour of the Grand Canyon.[33] On visits to other parks, Albright had begun making special notes on road and trail conditions, together with park road budgets and estimated costs of construction. Road and trail construction became a professional interest for him; to record his observations while traveling he carried a small notebook, which also contained carefully organized summaries and projections of road budgets and complete lists of engineering personnel for each park.[34]

As Mather pushed park road legislation forward, he would rely on Albright's expert testimony to make the case on Capitol Hill. In February 1924, the House Committee on Public Lands held hearings on a bill authorizing $7,500,000 for national park road and trail construction phased over three years, an appropriation that would dwarf previous federal investments in national parks. Important congressional park promoters sat on the committee, including John E. Raker (California) and Nicholas J. Sinnott (Oregon). Over four days, the congressmen demanded detailed accounts and exact plans for all proposed construction. Mather made the opening statement, reiterating the necessity of modernizing park roads to automotive specifications. In 1917, less than 500,000 people had visited the park system and just over 50,000 motor vehicles paid motor fees to use park roads. Over the next seven years the number of visitors had mushroomed to almost 1,500,000 annually, and the annual number of vehicles approached 300,000. An ever increasing majority of park visitors now arrived in their own cars. The statistics only confirmed an observation obvious to Mather and anyone involved in national park management: the parks were being overrun by automotive tourists demanding better roads. During this same seven-year period, Mather continued, Congress had responded to public demands for improved state highways and national forest roads by disbursing $600,000,000 in federal aid. National forest roads, which like state highways charged no fee for public use, had accounted for $52,000,000 of the total. National parks, which collected over $385,000 in motorist fees in 1923 alone (and another $225,000 from concessioner fees) had been allocated only $180,000 for all road construction in the regular 1924 Park Service budget. With Albright and Cammerer at his sides chipping in with precise figures and informed views, Mather made a characteristically strong impression with the legislators.[35]

After this introduction, Albright began a careful exposition of a multi-year park road building program. Thorough and precise, his responses to searching questions revealed his long study of the subject. He not only knew the figures for the new and reconstructed roads being proposed, but generally seemed to recall anything else that was asked of him: the acreages of individual parks, the mileages of existing roads, the total amounts spent on roads in individual parks since they were created, the number and quality of automotive approaches to each park, each park's total numbers of visitors, and total revenues from motor fees and concessions. The representatives with parks in their districts had to be persuaded that those parks had received their fair share of the proposed funding, based on the objective criteria of compiled statistics. At times the questioning, especially from well-informed park advocates such as Raker, grew intense and specific. (When asked the population figures for individual Hawaiian Islands, Albright finally appeared stumped; but on the other hand he was thoroughly informed on the science of volcanology and the use of volcanic ash in road pavements at Hawaii Volcanoes National Park.) Methodical but not pedantic, Albright explained every decision and justified every amount, personifying the Park Service's reputation for efficiency and expertise in a good cause.

If the total amount requested seemed large compared to earlier park appropriations, Albright made it clear that there were no frivolous expenditures involved. Although only twelve miles of paved roads existed in the park system (out of a total 1,060 miles), the plans called for almost no new paved roads, except in Yosemite Valley where the concentrated volume of traffic made pavement a necessity. Pavements were the least of Albright's concerns. Park roads that had been built for horse-drawn vehicles would have to be realigned with gentler grades (preferably a six percent maximum) and wider curves. Only minimum widths of eighteen to twenty feet would make park roads safe for two-way automobile traffic. Surrounded by plans and maps (and photographs of scenic views), Albright suggested that an extensive park road system could be built with the requested appropriations, but only if expensive improved surfaces were left until later. "What we want to do with this fund is get our roads graded, with good curvature, wide enough to be safe, with parapets to protect travel in the extremely dangerous places," he explained, which would also "give a good base for the future paving if that should become necessary."[36] The proposed realignments, regrading, and crushed stone base courses would be necessary, he pointed out, regardless of what type of improved surface proved advisable in the end.

The hearings indicated a turning point in the attitude of Congress towards park appropriations. After remarking on Albright's "marvelous knowledge" of the parks and their needs, Chairman Sinnott and the committee favorably reported the bill to the House, where it was placed on the unanimous consent calendar and passed unanimously in March. The legislation fared as well in the Senate, where it passed with a unanimous vote the next month. Calvin Coolidge immediately signed the bill on April 9. The votes were a resounding endorsement of Mather and Albright's work, and perhaps a recognition of the place national parks had assumed in the nation's public life. As Mather put it, "This legislative record clearly reflected the will of the people in demanding that the roads in national parks be placed in good and safe condition for motor travel."[37]

The Park Service finally had the funds to undertake a major campaign of road construction, but Mather's reaction appears not to have been one of jubilation as much as anxiety. He knew that the damage to the parks could be catastrophic if road plans were ill conceived; no other aspect of park planning threatened greater impacts. But the traditions of landscape park design, again, offered sound guidance for national park plans. In the 1890s, Charles Eliot had advised that landscape park roads be "no more than slender threads of graded surface winding over and among the huge natural forms of the ground."[38] At Yellowstone, the U.S. Army engineers Daniel Kingman and Hiram Chittenden had established a tradition of national park road engineering that exemplified the highest technical standards of the day, while minimizing the total extent of construction. "The true policy of the government," Chittenden wrote in 1895, should be "to make the roads as limited in extent as will meet actual necessities, but to make such as are found necessary perfect examples of their class."[39] More recently, the Columbia River Highway had opened in 1916. The road demonstrated the economic potential of automotive tourist routes in the West, and also exemplified the highest standards for mountain highway engineering. Albright had photographs of the Columbia River Highway on display in the committee hearing room in 1924; in a sense, it was already part of the national park system, since Mather had designated it an approved side trip on the Park-to-Park Highway.

In 1924 Horace Albright was also engaged in an early experiment in park "roadside cleanup" at Yellowstone, which indicated his goals for the appearance of improved park roads. Albright had rejected proposals for extending the Grand Loop system at Yellowstone for the simple reason that he felt enough roads had been built and that the remaining regions of the park should remain "untouched wildness."[40] But since their first visit in 1915, both he and Mather had been very concerned with the appearance of the existing roads in the park. Utility poles, eroded slopes, and tree stumps lined park roadsides; dead wood and debris left over from road construction were still evident in some places. Certain stretches of road had failed to exploit scenic views or needed relocation for other reasons. In general, Albright wanted to present a neater and more finished roadside appearance, which he felt would detract less from the appreciation of scenic views from the road.[41]

Beginning in the fall of 1924, Albright personally supervised "roadside cleanup work," thanks to a donation made specifically for that purpose by John D. Rockefeller, Jr. After touring Yellowstone that summer, Rockefeller had become concerned with the visual quality of the Grand Loop roadsides. An accomplished amateur road builder, the millionaire was already deeply involved in the design and funding of carriage roads for Lafayette (later Acadia) National Park on the coast of Maine. Imbued in the aesthetic of park drives through his experience in carriage road development, Rockefeller agreed to finance the demonstration roadside improvement project for Yellowstone in order to make the roadsides smoother and neater—in a word, more parklike.[42] Albright closely supervised the work in the fall of 1924, and characteristically accounted for every aspect of its cost and efficiency. By that winter, the superintendent could report that the work exceeded all expectation, and that down and dead timber was removed from fifteen to one hundred feet from the ditch lines of the road, "depending upon the visibility of the roadsides from an automobile." Rockefeller responded to the "satisfactory and economical work" with expanded grants for the work at Yellowstone. "Roadside cleanup," including the regrading of eroded slopes, the relocation of utility poles, and the replanting of bare roadsides, quickly became part of the standard specifications for future road construction and maintenance projects throughout the park system.[43]

Albright and Rockefeller's desire to eliminate utility poles, tree stumps, and debris from the roadside belonged to the same set of general aesthetic assumptions regarding the development of scenic reservations as did the preference for "rustic" bridge, shelter, and overlook construction. Chittenden had described the same ideals in 1895 when he wrote that "dead and decaying timber" should be cleared from shoulders and replaced with "grass and shrubbery" to "beautify the roadside."[44] These general goals for roadside beautification echoed similar policies advocated by municipal reformers since the turn of the century, not only for park roads, but for roads and streets in general. Garden clubs, municipal reformers, and advocates of "civic art" had urged the removal of utility poles and other visual nuisances from roadsides as well as the planting of roadside trees and grass strips. Many "city beautiful" activists shared a broad interest in the appearance of streets and roads, including figures such as J. Horace McFarland who also campaigned for scenic preservation at the federal level. The aesthetic ideals they espoused, in turn, had originated in the visual character of 19th-century municipal parkway and estate roadway design.

But the situation and scale of national parks demanded that "landscape engineers" develop a new sense of park "roadside beautification" specific to the conditions and technical exigencies of national park work, just as architects had begun to establish "rustic" styles of architectural construction appropriate to the contexts of the federal reservations. Park Service landscape architects and road engineers needed to tailor their practices to specifically address their bureau's policies and requirements. Architects produced the Park Service Rustic style while working mostly as consultants, but "landscape engineering" of the type Mather hoped to employ in national parks would necessarily be cultivated within the government bureaucracy.

Since their creation in 1918, the "civil engineering" and "landscape engineering" divisions of the Park Service had not cooperated to a great degree. Located in Portland and Los Angeles in 1923, the geographic distance reinforced the still separate approaches of the road builder, George Goodwin, and the landscape architect/town planner, Daniel Hull. Mather encouraged his professional staff to collaborate, hoping to fuse aspects of civil engineering and landscape architecture in park design work. In 1921, when appropriations had allowed some road construction to get underway, the director optimistically reported that in the Carbon River and other early road projects, "excellent cooperation"

between the two field engineering divisions produced "location work
. . . eminently satisfactory in every way."[45] But it was too early to predict
success in this regard. By 1924, as huge increases in road appropriations
were anticipated, all Park Service procedures and personnel for
managing large construction projects were under comprehensive review
in Washington.

Mather's growing anxieties regarding park road construction manifested
themselves in the many reassurances he made to Congress and in his
annual reports. From the early 1920s on, he repeatedly stated that the
Park Service would not "gridiron the parks" with unnecessary or poorly
planned roads. "There is danger to our parks through injurious road
building," he avowed in 1922, "our purpose is to construct only such
roads as contribute solely toward accessibility of the major scenic areas
by motor without disturbing the solitude and quiet of other sections."[46]
He also began to describe the role of Park Service landscape architects
in "landscape preservation," noting that "the landscape division" had
been "confronted with greatly increased problems . . . due to the road
development program." Although Daniel Hull was perhaps preoccupied
with his collaborations with Gilbert Stanley Underwood, by 1925 the
landscape division could no longer afford to ignore park road
construction. They now had the difficult task, Mather reminded them,
"of fitting these road developments into the landscape with the least
marring of native beauty."[47]

If Mather insisted his landscape architects and engineers were
performing well, already in 1924 he was making serious inquiries
regarding the feasibility of having the Bureau of Public Roads directly
administer all road projects within national parks. The Forest Service
had worked with the federal road engineers since 1916, and in 1924
Mather asked Albright to examine the potential of an interbureau
agreement for the Park Service. Albright, who had returned to
Yellowstone after his victory on Capitol Hill that winter, quickly rejected
the idea. He reminded the director that the Bureau of Public Roads had
its own policies regarding standards for road construction. The highway
engineers would want to build roads with wider curves and gentler
grades than necessary or desirable for park roads; that meant the new
construction funds would not go as far as planned. Adherence to more
stringent specifications for curvatures and grades also could result in
massive cuts and fills, increased destruction of forests, and permanently
scarred roadsides. In general, the Bureau of Public Roads had no
"supervision in its road building from landscape engineers," Albright
pointed out, while the Park Service had experienced landscape
architects who could influence engineering plans to circumvent
unnecessary destruction of scenery.[48] For the time being, only by
keeping control of the road initiative within the Park Service could
Mather hope to avert potentially unsympathetic construction.

Albright went on to suggest, however, conditions under which an
agreement with the Bureau of Public Roads might be acceptable. The
Park Service would have to set the standards, specifications, budgets,

and priorities for each project. The landscape engineering division would have to review and approve all design work before contracts were let, and continue to supervise the contracts once construction began.[49] Mather continued to explore the possibilities for an interbureau agreement, and that fall he sent Arthur E. Demaray to the Forest Service offices to investigate whether officials there were satisfied with their cooperative agreement. Demaray reported that although the Forest Service retained control over smaller projects, and although the Bureau of Public Roads had proved receptive to revised construction specifications suited to forest conditions, generally the foresters felt they had been handicapped by "dual control" over forest road construction. He urged that the Park Service, above all, retain complete control over setting construction standards and practices for proposed road work.[50]

But as Mather continued his investigations and considerations regarding a potential working agreement with the Bureau of Public Roads, events overtook him. At Glacier National Park, work on the Transmountain Highway had continued since the first funds were made available in 1921. The new road appropriations made available in 1925 put the project, which continued to be a priority, on an accelerated schedule. Crucial choices regarding route selection and contract specifications could no longer wait. Over the next several years, the Glacier highway project tried the efficacy of Park Service "landscape engineering" and tested Mather's determination to make good his reassurances that park road development would not unduly mar landscape scenery. In the process, Mather, Albright, and their professional staff devised the basic procedure for what became an interbureau agreement with the Bureau of Public Roads.

The first suggestion for a transmountain automotive route through Glacier was made in 1910 by Robert B. Marshall, the chief geographer of the Geological Survey who five years later would briefly serve as "general superintendent" for national parks. Marshall visited Glacier just after Congress created the park and recommended that a north-south route be located that would begin at Belton (now West Glacier), follow the west side of Lake McDonald, and from the north end of the lake traverse the continental divide and connect with the Waterton Lakes near the Canadian border. This road bisecting the length of the park was only one part of Marshall's ambitious proposals in 1910; he recommended a total of 213 miles of "first-class road, with good permanent surface at an estimated cost of two million dollars." Other aspects of his plan called for trails, fire towers, and a telephone system.[51] Marshall gave no indication why he believed Congress might spend two million dollars on a road system for Glacier when the total amount appropriated for all expenses in all national parks that year was under seventy-five thousand dollars.[52] In 1911, the Department of the Interior sent another investigator, Edward A. Keyes, who proposed a less ambitious circuit drive around Lake McDonald. Nothing came of either scheme.

But once again, local park promoters, elected officials, and commercial clubs were actively seeking increased appropriations for their park. Leading citizens of the nearby communities of Whitefish, Kalispell, and Columbia Falls had been instrumental in the original legislative campaign to create the park, and with the achievement of that goal they now pressed for highway construction funds. In the summer of 1914, the secretary of the Kalispell Chamber of Commerce, P. N. Bernard, organized the Interstate Wonderland Trail Association, a good roads group boosting an improved highway from Duluth to Puget Sound. Representing communities from Minnesota to Washington, the route's promoters noted that this "national park transcontinental highway" would be one of the most "direct and beautiful" ways across the country, and that it would go through both Yellowstone and Glacier on its way to Mount Rainier. They also noted that, as of 1914, the route was "practically open to travel, except that portion through Glacier National Park." The association, which represented communities that together had spent hundreds of thousands of dollars improving roads locally, specifically sought $500,000 in federal funds to complete an east-west highway over Gunsight Pass in Glacier. "As the matter now stands," the boosters complained, "Glacier National Park is a barrier to interstate motor traffic." With no motor route through the mountains, the park's potential for diverting the tourist gold into their communities went unrealized.[53]

In a related effort that summer, the Montana State Highway Commission joined the Kalispell Chamber of Commerce and the Columbia Falls Commercial Club in memorializing Congress for "the construction of an east and west highway through Glacier National Park." Senator Henry L. Myers (Montana), who also happened to be chairman of the Committee on Public Lands, responded by pressuring Secretary Lane to "comply with the wish of the citizens of Montana" and find a way to fund road construction out of the Interior budget.[54] The following spring, the state legislature and governor of Montana issued a joint memorial urging the federal government to make an appropriation to start the construction of an east-west highway through Glacier that would "connect with highways which are now open for travel [on either side of the park] from the Great Lakes to the Pacific Coast."[55] Upon his arrival in Washington in January 1915, Mather was kept busy responding to memorials, resolutions, and endorsements from congressmen, local businessmen, and civic groups all urging some form of east-west automotive route through Glacier National Park.

Noticeably absent from the ranks of the good roads advocates was Louis W. Hill, president of the Great Northern Railroad, who up to that time had financed and controlled the development of the park as its sole concessioner. Glacier had been Louis Hill's park. He had helped sway Congress to create the reservation in 1910, and by the time he incorporated the Glacier Park Hotel Company as a subsidiary of the Great Northern five years later, he had spent at least $1,500,000 on a system of lodges, chalets, and connecting roads and trails. His largest investments had built the Glacier Park Hotel (outside the park near the

East Glacier rail station), the Many Glacier Hotel (within the park on its east side), and a series of backcountry chalets set along the park's growing system of saddle trails.[56] The hotels and chalets, of Alpine inspiration, today are among the finest buildings in the national park system. The hotel developments in Yellowstone (built by the rival Northern Pacific line) may have provided a precedent, but Hill avoided the melange of architectural styles employed in the larger park to the south. As a group, the surviving Glacier hotels and chalets are a unique example of a single theme carried through in the architectural development of an entire national park.[57]

But Hill's tourists arrived at Glacier on his railroad, and they relied on livery services to transport them via rough roads and horse trails to the elegant Glacier Park Hotel Company accommodations. He may not have considered motor roads a threat (he was an avid motorist himself), but neither had he made ambitious road construction a priority. The wagon roads he had built were on the east side of the park, connecting his major hotels. The most important of these was a one-lane dirt road that ran through the Blackfeet Indian Reservation east of the park, connecting the East Glacier rail station to St. Mary Lake and the Many Glacier Hotel. The few roads inside park boundaries were built out of park appropriations, although they too had been laid out by Great Northern engineers. By 1915 these included (on the east side of the park) the spur road to the Many Glacier Hotel and a second spur that followed the northern shore of St. Mary Lake for about half its length.[58] A transmountain route connecting the east and west sides of the park did not interest Hill for an obvious reason: his railroad already connected East Glacier with the western entrance to the park at West Glacier, via the Marias Pass on the southern boundary of the park. Automotive tourists arriving on the east side of the park, in fact, paid Hill up to fifteen dollars to haul their vehicles to West Glacier, where they could visit Lake McDonald and then perhaps continue cross country to the Pacific Northwest. The alternative was to drive south (over halfway back to Yellowstone) to cross the divide near Butte.

Further complicating the situation, in addition to local civic boosters and the president of the Great Northern Railroad, members of the Montana congressional delegation also had special interest in developments at Glacier. Senator Thomas J. Walsh, chairman of the Committee on Mines and Mining, enjoyed a private summer residence on Lake McDonald, as did Senator Burton K. Wheeler. Walsh also had personal connections to concessioners at Yellowstone. In 1916, when Mather reorganized Yellowstone concessions (removing some of Walsh's associates) Walsh attempted to remove Mather from the Department of the Interior. The two men became the bitterest of enemies; but Walsh still pushed for Glacier appropriations, at least those that served his general interests, including funds for improved roads.[59]

A number of different groups pressed for road construction in Glacier even before the creation of the Park Service. But at other parks as well, especially in the Sierras, tourists and automobile clubs clamored just as loudly for improved new roads that would open parks to them. In 1914, Secretary Lane had responded to the pressure by entering into a cooperative agreement with the Office of Public Roads (the predecessor to the Bureau of Public Roads) to prepare preliminary surveys and plans for park road projects. Over the next two years, Office of Public Roads engineer T. Warren Allen (named "chief of division of national park roads") investigated national park road projects in Glacier, Sequoia, and Yosemite national parks.

When Mather arrived at the Department of the Interior, he invited Allen to speak on his work at the Berkeley national park conference in the spring of 1915. Allen's performance at Berkeley helps explain Mather's subsequent misgivings about allowing the Bureau of Public Roads into national parks. Allen went out of his way to assure the park managers that "the problems encountered within the park areas are very similar though not altogether identical with those encountered in the [national] forests." In both cases, the construction of roads was necessary, first, "in order that these tracts may not be obstacles blocking the free movement of traffic between adjoining areas." He continued in this vein to suggest that park roads should not only be convenient through routes for commercial traffic, but should also provide access to "valuable salable mature timber." Although Allen eventually added that park roads should lead to "hotel and camping sites and features of beauty," he clearly did not appreciate the critical difference between national forests and national parks. This attitude had been commonplace within the Department of the Interior up until 1909, but at the national park conference of 1915 it amounted to heresy. The ongoing campaign to create a national parks bureau depended entirely on the recognition that national parks should be treated differently from national forests, and therefore should be managed by a new park bureau, not the Forest Service. Although Allen went on to describe how in the park setting the engineer should affect a special concern for "scenic or landscape effects produced," in his eagerness to reassure his audience that park road construction would present no technical difficulties for his bureau, he entirely missed the point. Technically, he told them, national park roads were no different than "the average country highway."[60]

Allen then went on to describe the proposals he had devised for Glacier in the summer of 1914. He had decided, surprisingly, that an east-west road was not a priority. He suggested instead that a north-south route from West Glacier to the Waterton Lakes (almost identical to Marshall's route) would become "the main artery for traffic into Glacier Park." He also revived the proposed circuit drive around Lake McDonald and suggested other roads; but he generally avoided proposals for the east side of the park, where apparently Louis Hill would continue to control planning decisions. Mather was using the Berkeley conference to assess the personnel available to him as he undertook his efforts at the Department of the Interior. He could not have been pleased with an engineer who referred to parks as "obstacles" and ignored the wishes of the civic boosters and automotive tourists whom Mather counted as his strongest allies.

Soon after the Berkeley conference, Mather decided to promote the Park-to-Park Highway campaign with all his enthusiasm. The Denver automotive cohorts he met at Rocky Mountain that summer had inspired the idea when a group of them clattered off on the five hundred-mile trip north to Yellowstone. The next portion of the route, from Yellowstone through Glacier to Mount Rainier, was already being promoted by the Interstate Wonderland Trail Association. Other groups all over the West, from the Southern California Automobile Association to the Washington Good Roads Association, promoted routes in and between national parks. The National Park-to-Park Highway Association, organized in Yellowstone in 1916, posted signs and lobbied for road improvements, especially between Yellowstone and Glacier. In 1917 the National Parks Highway Association, headquartered in Spokane, mapped and posted signs for the "National Park" route connecting Glacier to Mount Rainier; they then extended the route south to Crater Lake. Mather felt that the "park-to-park system," including the highways of the national parks themselves, would be "the greatest scenic highway in the world."[61] He continued to work with numerous park road boosters, who in 1918 assembled at Yellowstone to form the National Park Touring Association, a conglomeration of groups from twelve western states dedicated to promoting "a composite road system leading to and connecting all the national parks." In 1919, the National Park-to-Park Highway Association began holding annual conventions of park road groups. After the route was officially designated in 1920, thousands of maps and brochures of a six thousand-mile park-to-park system were printed with the assistance of the Park-to-Park Highway Association, the American Automobile Association, and the National Highways Association in Washington, DC.[62]

In 1918, Mather himself traveled much of the proposed park-to-park route in his chauffeured Packard. Although he reported that road improvements were "needed everywhere," by that time most of the national parks offered some access for tourists in cars.[63] Grand Canyon, Rocky Mountain, and Crater Lake had some automotive routes that made them legitimate (if not convenient) components of the park-to-park system. The Mountain Highway connected Tacoma and Mount Rainier, and the Government Road extended from the entrance of that park to Paradise Valley. At Yosemite, one of Mather's earliest acts of personal generosity to the park system was his gift of the Tioga Road, an old turnpike crossing the park from east to west, which he purchased from its private owners (he raised about half the funds from fellow enthusiasts) and donated to the park. Several California auto clubs then contributed to improve the road to make it usable for their machines.[64] The Yellowstone concessioners had resisted the automobile, and it was true that the Grand Loop may have needed modernizations; but by 1915 the largest national park offered 350 miles of roads to automotive tourists. In 1916 Mather lifted the few remaining restrictions on allowing cars in parks and began lowering the previously exorbitant motor fees. That year Mount Rainier, Yosemite, and Yellowstone all sold between three thousand and four thousand motor permits. The total number of permits issued rose from about 4,200 in 1914 to almost 54,000 in 1918; but the increase only hinted at what was to come.[65]

At Glacier, however, Louis Hill continued to exact tribute to transport vehicles over the continental divide. The park itself still had practically no roads, and without a transmountain connection it remained "the last unconstructed link" in the park-to-park system. There was no adequate site even for a Park Service headquarters area until Mather purchased some land himself and donated it to the park. Significantly the new headquarters was located on the west side of the park, near the West Glacier entrance, despite the fact that the vast majority of park visitors still arrived on the east side and stayed at Louis Hill's hotels. Mather had his own plans to develop Glacier, however, which implied a greater importance assigned to the west side of the park. And the Transmountain Highway comprised the essential first step not only in his plans for Glacier National Park, but for the entire park system.

Shortly after joining the Park Service in 1917, George Goodwin was assigned to Glacier to act as superintendent. While filling what had been an unexpected vacancy, the engineer had the opportunity that summer to perform reconnaissance surveys for road proposals. Although a north-south road through the park was still under consideration, Albright (acting as director while Mather remained hospitalized from his 1917 collapse) clarified his mentor's priorities: an east-west road would "join the highway systems of the two sides of the park" and would "form a very important link in the park-to-park highway system" by affording motorists "a crossing of the range without the difficulties and expense of shipping their cars."[66] The following year Goodwin was made "chief engineer" of the Park Service, responsible for planning and supervising road and trail projects. Although Congress appropriated no funds for construction, the engineer began preliminary surveys in a number of parks during his first year in his new position. "The most important project to be developed," he reported that year, was "a transmountain road connecting the east and west sides of Glacier National Park." Goodwin had spent that fall making preliminary surveys for the route, and that winter he developed quantities and estimates for construction.[67]

The terminal locations for Goodwin's 1918 survey had been fixed by initial park developments on both sides of the mountains. On the west side, a two-mile park road led from West Glacier to the foot of Lake McDonald, where a small resort community named Apgar had grown up since the 1890s. From that point, launches carried tourists to the Glacier Hotel (1914), a hotel and cabin complex run by an independent operator near the head of the lake.[68] The long, straight shore of the narrow glacial lake provided a logical and level route for the first portion of an east-west crossing of the park; the location of the hotel made it desirable for the planned route to follow the lake's eastern shore. Across the mountains on the east side of the park, the spur road that Louis Hill had begun along the north shore of St. Mary Lake provided a similarly convenient and straight route for approaching the Continental Divide from the east, roughly near the center of the park. By 1918 Mather had determined that the transmountain project would begin with the construction of a road along the east shore of Lake McDonald, and that the spur road along St. Mary Lake would be extended to the Going-to-the-Sun Chalets near the head of that lake.[69]

These routes, following the long, narrow lakes on either side of the park, offered straight and level access to the park interior along a roughly east-west line. The real question for Goodwin in 1918 was which pass over the Continental Divide should be selected to connect the roads on either side. In 1915, P. N. Bernard and the Kalispell Chamber of Commerce had invited the geologist and lecturer Lyman B. Sperry to suggest the most appropriate route over the divide. Sperry had proposed Gunsight Pass, a high pass near the Sperry Glacier due west from the head of Lake McDonald.[70] Bernard and the other early transmountain road boosters continued to advocate the Gunsight Pass option, which would have descended on the east side of the park along the St. Mary River to St. Mary Lake. George Goodwin, however, felt that Logan Pass offered practical advantages. A trail over Logan Pass had just been completed in 1918 providing the first real connection between the two sides of the park, and Goodwin had observed certain obvious benefits to the route. Logan Pass was the lowest pass with the most gradual approaches in the immediate area. Since the road would generally have southern and western exposure, it would be clear of snow earlier in the season. In 1915 the Office of Public Roads engineer, T. Warren Allen, had also advised that Logan Pass would eventually be the best location for an east-west connection in the park. The two engineers, with similar training and backgrounds, both emphasized practical justifications for the Logan Pass route.

In his 1918 preliminary survey, Goodwin located a route that proceeded from the head of Lake McDonald (near the Glacier Hotel) northwest along McDonald Creek at an average grade of one percent. At the confluence of McDonald and Logan creeks, the route turned west, up the Logan Creek Valley, and ascended about 2,600 feet to Logan Pass (elevation 6,646 feet). An average grade of six-and-a-third percent could be maintained on this ascent through the construction of "long loops and switchbacks . . . taking advantage of the various level places upon which to turn." The proposed route crossed Logan Creek seven times in the process.[71] Thomas Vint later asserted that the route would have required the construction of fifteen switchbacks in Logan Creek Valley.[72] Vint bemoaned the potential destruction of one of the most scenic valleys in the park, but for Goodwin, such "spectacular" engineering could be an attraction in itself. In his later textbook on "Mountain Highway Location," Goodwin observed that "it is oftentimes desired to have the location a spectacular one, and in some cases . . . the roads themselves become quite wonderful because of their being located so that they offer certain spectacular effects." Such effects included "benching of the road out of the side of a cliff," the "construction of half-tunnels . . . and the use of overhead loop crossings." Multiple switchbacks, as well, could be an attraction "in making ascents from the valleys to the tops of ridges" because looking down at certain points "several elevations of the road are often visible."[73] "Spectacular effects" that drew attention to road engineering rather than scenery, however, would prove incompatible with Mather's goals for the "preservation of landscape scenery." Landscape engineering demanded construction that would maintain an understated presence in park landscapes. And if Goodwin's persistent emphasis on the most pratical, cost-efficient engineering solutions answered the needs of the Park Service while the bureau was operating with extremely limited funds, once generous appropriations were available for road building, Mather and other officials would argue that the most important priority for park road engineering should be landscape preservation, not cost efficiency.

On the east side of the park, Goodwin's 1918 route descended the West Fork of Reynolds Creek through a shorter series of switchbacks at an average grade of six percent, emerging at the shore of St. Mary Lake near the Going-to-the-Sun Chalets. The entire road, about fifty miles from one park entrance to the other, was to be graded (but not paved) to a width of twenty feet. The maximum grade would be eight percent, and the minimum radius of curvature a tight fifty feet. "Rustic log bridges or culverts" of course were specified, and "brush" was to be cleared in a corridor up to fifty feet wide, depending on the topography. But like T. Warren Allen, Goodwin did not necessarily distinguish the requirements of a national park road from those of any mountain road traversing scenic regions. Goodwin claimed the transmountain route, a "first-class highway or automobile road," would "meet every requirement for park travel or commercial hauling"—requirements that he assumed were more or less identical.[74] Economic and practical considerations remained Goodwin's primary concerns, even if he acknowledged that the road when built would be "one of the most scenic, if not the most scenic, in America." He may have been aware of the scenic potential of the Transmountain Highway, but that awareness had not led him to significantly adapt or tailor his professional practice to meet the new and evolving needs of the Park Service.

Park appropriations over the next two years, however, remained at levels that precluded road construction. During that time, Goodwin served a second tour as Glacier's superintendent, in part because lack of funding forced the engineering office to temporarily suspend operations.[75] While stationed in the park he was able to supervise the construction of a new bridge over the Middle Fork of the Flathead River at West Glacier, but he did not make any other progress on the transmountain project. "Paradoxically as it may be," the engineer reported of his second superintendency of the park, "the one vital missing link that exists in the Park-to-Park Highway is this transmountain road, which will some time become the strong link of the chain."[76]

That May, Goodwin was recalled to Portland where he went back to work with a small staff in an office in the Couch Building. The 1921 budget for Glacier was almost doubled to $195,000, with $100,000 dedicated specifically to the construction of the Transmountain Highway. The money would be available beginning July 1, and

Goodwin immediately prepared grading contracts for the first portion of the road along Lake McDonald. Bids were scheduled to be opened that August. In the meantime clearing began on the Lake McDonald route using park force account labor.[77]

With construction underway in 1921, local concerns over the practicality of the route immediately surfaced. Good road boosters joined by other local interests now questioned the wisdom of building the much needed transmountain motor road within the national park at all. That April, J. M. Hyde published a scathing editorial in the *Cut Bank Pioneer Press* titled "That Fairy Highway Through Glacier National Park." Hyde, the Glacier County Commissioner, claimed that the entire project was a plot by the Great Northern Railroad to prevent a usable automotive route through the mountains from ever being completed. Louis Hill, according to the furious county commissioner, backed the entire scheme in order to retain his lucrative business shipping about eight thousand vehicles annually between East Glacier and West Glacier. The Park Service had been duped into undertaking a quixotic and expensive road through a pass that would be snowbound "ten or eleven months of the year." Hyde wanted a road built parallel to the Great Northern tracks over the lower, far more practical Marias Pass before any scenic road schemes were funded for the park.[78] A. J. Breitenstein, representing the "Yellowstone-Glacier Bee-Line" (one of the interpark highways being promoted since 1918) also wanted to know why the more practical Marias Pass had not been considered as a route for the Park-to-Park Highway. George Goodwin responded with a long (and at times fanciful) explanation of how the Logan Pass route would only be slightly longer, slightly more expensive, and snowbound only one or at most two extra months of the year.[79] Arguments based on the practicality of the Logan Pass route, however, were easily refuted since a road over the lower Marias Pass, although not the scenic route, obviously would be less expensive and easier to maintain.

Fortunately the new park superintendent, J. Ross Eakin, also joined the effort to ease local concerns regarding the value of the Logan Pass road project. Eakin more cogently argued that the two proposed roads (over the Logan and Marias passes) would serve "two distinct purposes." The Logan Pass route, if less convenient, would dramatically complete the Park-to-Park Highway, and it would therefore draw thousands of tourists into the communities surrounding Glacier. The "unspectacular" route would not do this, even if it would serve other useful purposes and would remain open for more of the year. Visiting the Kalispell Chamber of Commerce and other local groups, Eakin reminded businessmen and residents that the purpose of the Transmountain Highway was not just to move local traffic, but to attract tourists from all over the country. Besides, he reassured them, the Park Service would do whatever it could to encourage the Forest Service to build a federal-aid highway over Marias Pass as soon as possible (the proposed route lay almost entirely in the adjacent forest to the south, not in the park). That fall Eakin wrote to Mather assuring him that with the exception of some "non-influential residents" of East Glacier, he had "line[d] up the community solidly for our Transmountain road."[80]

Goodwin continued to oversee construction over the next three years as Congress appropriated $65,000 for the 1922 construction season and then $100,000 in both 1923 and 1924. At first work was limited almost entirely to the west side of the park. Contracts for the east side were postponed in 1922 in part because Goodwin wanted to push the west side road from the head of Lake McDonald north and west along McDonald Creek as far as possible. He feared that if the Marias Pass highway were begun (and built far more quickly over that easier route) then Congress would lose interest in the Logan Pass route—unless the road had already been advanced significantly towards the Continental Divide.[81] In 1922, the first seventeen miles of the road were being graded on the west side of the park, along the shore of Lake McDonald and up McDonald Creek. On the east side, grading on the St. Mary Lake portion of the road began the next year. With construction underway on both sides of the divide in 1923, Mather felt that construction would now "be pushed with more speed to completion," although he confessed that if work continued to be funded out of annual park appropriations alone, it would be "a long period of years before it [was] completed."[82]

But after the 1924 congressional hearings, work would not have to proceed on regular appropriations alone. The new funds were not available for the 1924 construction season, but that December Congress appropriated one million dollars for park road construction through a deficiency act. In March, the regular Interior appropriation included an additional $1,500,000 for road construction and carried the authority to obligate against future appropriations for up to another one million dollars. With millions of dollars now available for improving park roads, Mather faced the need of "suddenly expanding the civil engineering forces" of the Park Service. But the director made no such expansion. He claimed there was a scarcity of "competent road engineers with civil-service status" and blamed the problem on an inadequate pay scale; but clearly other concerns had begun to undermine the director's confidence in his bureau's engineering capabilities.[83]

In anticipation of the funds that would soon be available for the Transmountain Highway, Mather went to Glacier during the summer of 1924 to inspect Goodwin's proposed route over Logan Pass. Work on the Lake McDonald and St. Mary Lake portions of the road had progressed; it remained now to complete the final and most demanding sections of the project over the steep ridges of the Continental Divide. Final decisions regarding the location of the route over Logan Pass would have to be made immediately if contracts were to be let for the 1925 construction season. The Transmountain Highway promised to complete the entire Park-to-Park Highway, and it would make Glacier a legitimate component of the 20th-century national park system. Considering the awesome views from the approaches to Logan Pass, there were expectations that the Glacier road would be the most spectacular scenic drive in the country. But the potential for failure was just as great: if the road permanently scarred the scenic heart of Glacier National Park, or if the project were merely bungled through inept management, the reputation of Park Service professionalism would never recover. Finalizing the location of the route over Logan Pass presented the most important single road-building decision yet faced by Mather and the Park Service.

Daniel Hull, however, did not accompany the director on his visit. In general, the landscape architect had been content to leave the road engineering to George Goodwin. At Glacier during the early 1920s, Hull had been primarily concerned with laying out the West Glacier administrative village, and he made no direct mention of the Transmountain Highway in his annual reports. Although he inspected Glacier road construction in the fall of 1923, his brief memorandum to Mather on the subject failed to rise above vague reassurance and platitude. Hull favorably assessed the built portion of the road along Lake McDonald and McDonald Creek, advising the director that so far Goodwin had given "careful thought . . . to the matter of securing maximum value from the landscape point of view." He worried about the impact of construction around Logan Falls, however, and closed his report by postulating that "each park [road] project . . . should be considered with the primary thought of protecting [the] . . . landscape, and at the same time make it accessible to the public."[84] The next year Hull made what he called "a study of road conditions" at Glacier and suggested some "changes in future road programs with an idea of better landscape protection."[85] Hull's suggested changes in 1923 and 1924, however, mostly involved removing dead trees from near the road and protecting other trees with "guards placed around the trunks or by the construction of retaining walls" to avoid damaging them during blasting and grading operations. Hull was justifiably preoccupied during these years with his town plans for Yosemite and Grand Canyon, as well as the concessioner lodge developments at Zion and Bryce and his private practice in Los Angeles. Although he advised Goodwin on details and procedures to help minimize the impacts of road construction at Glacier, he apparently did not overly involve himself in more demanding engineering issues such as route location, roadway geometry, and construction standards.

But Mather needed greater assurance that "landscape protection" would be carried out not only in details, but in the more fundamental civil engineering decisions that now loomed large in plans for development at Glacier and almost all the other parks. With newly funded construction only months away, bromides about "the landscape point of view" did not soothe the director's anxieties regarding the high profile Glacier road project. That summer, while Mather arranged to inspect Goodwin's route over Logan Pass himself, Hull was satisfied to have his assistant, Thomas Vint, accompany the director. At the park, Mather spent a day riding over the divide inspecting the preliminary survey route with Goodwin, Vint, and the new superintendent at Glacier, Charles J. Kraebel. Dismounting just west of Logan Pass, the group took in the view of Logan Creek and the summits of the Livingston Range that marked the Continental Divide down the center of the park. Flanked on one side by the huge, almost vertical cliff called the Garden Wall, the green valley of Logan Creek provided the foreground of a stunning panorama of the Glacier high country. The vista captured the very heart of the park: a region containing dozens of lakes and glaciers and scores of jagged, alpine peaks. Then Thomas Vint began describing the effect that building fifteen switchbacks up the valley would have on the foreground of the awesome scene they were admiring. Vint felt that it would "look like miners had been in there" if they went ahead with Goodwin's plan. What they should do, he urged the director, was replace the series of switchbacks with a much longer (and more expensive) road that would be carved directly into the rock of the Garden Wall. The roadway would traverse along the steep face of the escarpment, gradually descending for ten miles, until it could drop down to the road along McDonald Creek in a single switchback. If this relatively straight roadway could be benched into the sedimentary rock of the Garden Wall all the way down the valley, the scene below would be preserved completely untouched. The solution was simple, elegant, and certainly more expensive and less practical since it called for a much longer road benched into solid rock for many miles. Mather remained silent. Vint persisted, and risked offending Goodwin further by stating, "This job is important enough for you to hire the best engineer and the best landscape architect in the country to look after; this is a big thing." According to Vint, Goodwin took up the challenge by responding, "Mr. Mather, there is nobody in the United States that knows as much about road building in the mountains as I do."[86]

Goodwin indeed knew a great deal about road building in the mountains; but he had not developed road engineering adapted to the Park Service's need to put scenic preservation above economic and even practical considerations. Goodwin insisted that some form of direct approach up the valley—simply because it was more direct—had to be featured in the final location survey for the transmountain route. Now almost fifty years old, Goodwin embodied confident technical authority and experience. Handsome and silver-haired, he also tended to pomposity in his correspondence and clearly held high opinions regarding his own abilities. Vint, on the other hand, was short and already slightly overweight, although he possessed tact and humor that his older colleague perhaps lacked. He was still in his twenties, and his professional experience had been limited to a few years with California design offices as a draftsman, and even "pick and shovel work, grading and planting" with nurseries and contractors in Los Angeles.[87] But Vint had also spent the last two years working for Hull as a Park Service landscape engineer at Yosemite and in Los Angeles. Vint was making his career as a Park Service professional, while Goodwin's attitudes had been shaped through earlier experience in federal dam construction and Army road engineering. Mather now faced a choice regarding the fate of the Logan Creek Valley and the Transmountain Highway; the choice also bore directly on the future roles of professionals within the Park Service.

Mather, always emotional regarding park issues, grew visibly angry. He gathered up his horse's reins and with hardly a word moved down the trail before his companions even had time to get mounted. Vint did not see the director again for two days. Neither Goodwin nor Vint realized it, but Mather was probably already deciding the course he would take not only on the Glacier project, but for the development of future park roads in general.[88]

Several days earlier at Jackson Hole, in fact, Mather had met a young Bureau of Public Roads engineer, Bill Austin, in one of the random and fortuitous encounters that characterized Mather's peripatetic management style. Austin, who possessed the unimpeachable qualification of being a brother Sigma Chi, showed the director some of the national forest road work he was supervising nearby. Mather was impressed by the high standards of construction the Bureau of Public Roads employed in their work. After his experience at Logan Pass, Mather sent his Packard back down to Jackson Hole to pick up Austin and bring him up to Glacier for a consultation with Vint. The director wanted to know from an objective engineering standpoint whether Vint's alternative to Goodwin's route had any merit.[89] This unorthodox and personal contact with Bill Austin (so typical of Mather) initiated the collaboration between the Park Service and the Bureau of Public Roads that would be formalized as an interbureau agreement two years later. The agreement has been renewed in various forms to the present day.

Austin and Vint spent several days going over the route and considering whether the Garden Wall option would be feasible. Consultations continued late into the night back at their hotel. Superintendent Kraebel then joined Austin and together they drove back to Yellowstone to consult with Horace Albright, who by now clearly had supplanted Goodwin as the Park Service's chief expert on road policies.[90] Soon afterwards, Mather and Albright officially contacted the Bureau of Public Roads in Washington in order to negotiate a preliminary interbureau agreement. The legendary bureau chief, Thomas H. MacDonald, instructed his deputy chief engineer for the western states, Laurence I. Hewes, to make the arrangements. Early in September, Frank A. Kittredge, a locating engineer in the road bureau's San Francisco office, received a telegram from Washington telling him to leave immediately for Portland to prepare to undertake preliminary and location surveys for a new route over Logan Pass. He arrived at Glacier and began organizing survey crews on September 11.[91]

If the entire affair seemed rushed, it was because location and preliminary survey work would need to be completed (or nearly so) that fall if construction contracts were to be let in the spring of 1925. Although Kittredge later wrote that "the reconnaissance [had been] completed, [and] the decision made as to the route" by the time he arrived at Glacier, he still was presented with an enormous challenge.[92] Road surveys at this time typically proceeded in three stages, each with a greater level of precision and descriptive information: the reconnaissance, preliminary, and location surveys. Kittredge had to complete the entire preliminary survey and much of the final location work over a twenty-one-mile route if quantities were to be accurately estimated for contract bidders that spring. Winter promised to close in on the high mountain passes within a matter of weeks; precipitous terrain and thick forests assured that survey work would have been difficult under the best of circumstances.

But Kittredge had strong qualifications for the job. Born in Minnesota, he had begun his career in his early twenties surveying for railroads in Alaska in 1905 "in country known only to prospectors," and later working as a highway engineer for the Washington and Oregon state highway departments. He received a graduate degree in civil engineering from the University of Washington in 1915. After serving in France, he worked for the Bureau of Public Roads doing reconnaissance and location surveys, often in extremely remote and inaccessible regions.[93] As Vint recalled, the locating engineer was "their man that they sent out on all the trouble jobs. . . . Kittredge could work like a dog."[94] He would need tenacity. The remoteness of the Logan Pass route required long, steep hikes from base camps up to job sites at the beginning of each shift. In order to keep a thirty-two-man survey crew in the field continuously, Kittredge employed up to 135 men at a time in three crews: "one coming, one working, and one going." The long daily climbs "over cliffs and through brush," as well as hazardous working conditions on steep slopes in rain and sleet, "proved too strenuous for many" according to the engineer. In addition to a high rate of turnover, Kittredge had to work with crews that had little or no experience in location surveys. But the additional trouble and expense were necessary to complete the work in time. The crews worked continuously between September 15 and November 10, when the snow became too deep (they had already been working in up to three feet) to allow further work.[95]

In that time, enough topographic information had been gathered for Kittredge to present three alternative schemes to Mather in February. He presented Goodwin's 1918 survey as the first alternative. He pointed out all the shortcomings of the original plan, emphasizing its practical drawbacks: the hairpin turns would be clogged with snow late into the season, the road would be impossible to widen or modernize and would become obsolete, and the switchbacks would require turns with fifty-foot radii and grades as high as eight percent. The series of sharp turns assured it would always be a "second-gear road . . . increasing the hazard and decreasing its efficiency." Kittredge also investigated a second route, at chief engineer Goodwin's request, which was a revision of the 1918 survey. This revised route still wound directly up Logan Creek Valley, but employed fewer switchbacks and wider turning radii. This alternative would have cost significantly more than the first; but Kittredge concluded that any objections to the original route applied (to a lesser degree) to this revision of it.

The third—and "strongly recommended"—alternative presented in Kittredge's February report described the Garden Wall option that Vint and Austin had initially reconnoitered the previous summer. Since this third alternative "met the requirements more than any other," it was the only one actually surveyed by Kittredge that fall. The surveyed route descended from Logan Pass at an even six percent grade for ten miles, following "the contour of the mountainside . . . for the entire distance from Logan Pass to a point below Granite Park." There, a single switchback with a one hundred-foot radius brought the route to the elevation of the McDonald Creek portion of the road, which Kittredge suggested extending farther west along the stream valley. The sharpest curves of the route were on one hundred-foot radii for open curves and two hundred-foot radii for blind curves. Tangents (straight sections) of at least forty feet intervened between curves. Kittredge felt that this route, unlike Goodwin's earlier survey, would "permit safe grades and curvature," would be "capable of future improvement," and would be kept free of snow for the longest possible season. Besides these respectably practical considerations, the engineer also allowed himself to add that the third alternative would "exhibit the grandeur of the park to the maximum." Realizing the additional expense involved in this recommended route, Kittredge offered several strategies for reducing costs, including estimates for alternative roadway widths between twenty-two and twenty-eight feet. "Width of road," he noted, "is of less importance than grade or alignment." The roadway could always be widened; the basic location of the road, however, could not be changed later without abandoning all work done to that point.[96]

If Kittredge was trying to convince Mather, Albright, and the rest of the Park Service that Bureau of Public Roads engineers were worthy collaborators, he could not have succeeded more brilliantly. Superintendent Kraebel, who witnessed the heroic survey work in 1924, wrote Mather before the work was even finished, gushing that he found it difficult "to speak in anything but terms of superlative praise" for Kittredge's work. Kraebel feared that Mather would hesitate to support the more expensive alternative that Kittredge now championed. Pointing out the advantages of the Garden Wall route, the superintendent wanted to assure him that "the new location is emphatically worth the increased cost, whatever it may be." Kraebel wanted the entire road budget for Glacier spent on the Transmountain Highway alone, in order to bid it out as a single, three-year contract that spring.[97]

Thomas Vint reviewed Kittredge's February 1925 report with almost as much enthusiasm. "It is a pleasure to have at hand such a complete and comprehensive report," he wrote in his official memorandum to Daniel Hull. Vint was particularly taken with Kittredge's technique for visualizing the effect of road construction. The road engineer had pasted black and white photos into a panoramic mosaic, and then inked the alignments of the three alternative proposals directly on the photographs. Goodwin's switchbacks appeared in contorted graffiti of red ink disfiguring Logan Creek Valley; the Garden Wall route, drawn in blue on the same photos, etched a placid line curving gently across the steep slope above. It was precisely the picture that Vint had drawn verbally for Mather several months earlier. "From my knowledge of the ground," Vint concurred, the third alternative was "the one we should recommend to the service as the one to be built." The photographic technique for showing the impacts of proposed road locations on scenic panoramas became a standard procedure for park projects.

Vint appreciated the fact that the longer, straighter Garden Wall route gave "less views (especially close views) of the road itself . . . . One might say it performs its work more silently."[98] In his approbation of Kittredge's work, Vint completed his rebuttal of Goodwin's idea of "spectacularity" in road engineering. In Kittredge, Vint had found a worthy ally who could validate "landscape preservation" not only as good policy, but as good engineering. Vint's only criticism of Kittredge's 1924 survey involved relocating a short section of the road away from the shore of St. Mary Lake near the Going-to-the-Sun Chalets. Perhaps a small point, Vint wanted to preserve that corner of the lake from the direct presence of the road; he also knew that panoramic views of the entire lake would result from relocating the road to higher ground away from the shoreline. Kittredge, who understood Vint's concerns and goals for road construction, also was able to see the advantages of the relocation. The Bureau of Public Roads perhaps passed a test as well: recognizing the right of the Park Service landscape engineers to request the change, the roads bureau agreed to alter the alignment in the final location survey. A new partnership had begun.

That April, Vint, Kraebel, Kittredge, and two other engineers from the Bureau of Public Roads, Thomas Purcell and J. A. Elliott, met in Spokane to determine the particulars of how the Transmountain Highway contracts would be drawn up and supervised. In the process, they laid out the ground rules for how the Park Service and the Bureau of Public Roads would cooperate on park road projects for the next twenty-five years. Their "Suggested Procedure for Co-operation" described the protocol to be followed.

First, the director of the Park Service initiated a given project by requesting the chief of the Bureau of Public Roads to send an engineer to investigate. The road engineer, the superintendent of the park in question, and the Park Service landscape engineer then investigated the project together and afterwards filed independent reports to Mather. The director then had the option of ending the project or requesting that the roads bureau perform a location survey. With a location survey in hand (as the Transmountain Highway survey now was) the road engineer and the landscape engineer, representing each bureau, prepared contract plans and specifications. The final product required both their signatures, and the signatures of the park superintendent and the director of the Park Service. Once signed, the contracts could be bid and let through the Park Service. During construction, a resident engineer from the Bureau of Public Roads filed monthly reports to his supervisor, who forwarded them to the park superintendent. Park Service landscape engineers and the park superintendent had the right to review construction work at any time. The park superintendent made the final acceptance of completed work.[99] These arrangements met all of the conditions set by Albright the year before. The agreement also produced advantages for both bureaus: the Bureau of Public Roads effectively increased its budget by becoming the manager of the now considerable appropriations for park road construction, and the Park Service would be able to ask Congress to put park roads "on a par" with federal-aid highways by funding them through the same general roads legislation that authorized Bureau of Public Roads expenditures.

The Transmountain Highway across Glacier continued to be the testing ground for the interbureau arrangement. From the west entrance of the park, the first twenty miles of the road had been completed up McDonald Creek past its confluence with Avalanche Creek. From that point, Kittredge had surveyed a route of about twelve miles along the Garden Wall to Logan Pass. Proceeding east from the pass, the route dropped down about eight miles to the road along St. Mary Lake. While meeting in Spokane, however, Kraebel, Kittredge, Vint, and the others had decided that it would be wise to concentrate available funds on finishing the west side of the road up to Logan Pass—and to build it to the highest standards possible—before committing funds to projects on both sides of the park. In early May, the Spokane group went back to Glacier and inspected the twelve-mile portion of the surveyed route (from McDonald Creek to Logan Pass) that they intended to put out to bid that month. With contract specifications drafted and other fine points addressed, advertisements were published on May 21 and bids were opened on June 10. The principal items of work included 480,000 cubic yards of general excavation, 16,000 cubic yards of tunnel excavation, 2,200 cubic yards of retaining wall and other masonry construction, 7,000 cubic yards of guardwall construction, and 14,500 cubic yards of surfacing. On May 20, Bureau of Public Roads engineer W. G. Peters arrived at the park with four assistants to oversee the project, which according to Peters was the largest single contract so far let by the Bureau of Public Roads. The bid was awarded to a Tacoma contractor on June 11.[100]

The start of construction on the western approach to Logan Pass implied more than a new location survey for a single project; if all park roads were to be governed by the same policies and considerations, the $7,500,000 appropriation won in 1924 would never go as far as Albright had described to Congress. He had estimated the Transmountain Highway, for example, as a five-year project costing something over $600,000; the contract let that June was for about $900,000, and it only covered construction of only one portion of the road. If the Transmountain Highway were a precedent for future park road projects, new construction standards and policies would require vast new appropriations to complete the road system originally envisioned. But Mather and Albright (who had always proved shrewd judges of the moods of Congress) sensed that, with an acceptable agreement established with the Bureau of Public Roads, greatly increased road appropriations would in fact be available.

The successful initiation of the Transmountain Highway project also implied numerous changes in the Park Service organizational structure. Chief engineer George Goodwin soon discovered that he had lost his place in the new order of things. Albright, Vint, and Kittredge all later recalled slightly different reasons for his dismissal, but clearly the proud engineer did not agree willingly to the abrogation of the authority he had exercised over park road construction since 1917. Since 1924 when Mather had begun making serious inquiries regarding a cooperative agreement with the Bureau of Public Roads, there had been a heated exchange of telegrams and letters between Goodwin and Mather regarding Goodwin's reluctance to acquiesce to such an arrangement. In 1925, Mather finally responded to an officious declaration from his chief engineer with a terse reply: "Resignation accepted." Goodwin's termination became effective the same day that the new road appropriations secured by Albright became available for expenditure, July 1, 1925.[101] Goodwin's former assistant became acting chief engineer, but the fate of the Portland engineering office had been sealed as well. That winter only three of the eleven engineers kept their jobs when the office was reorganized and moved to Yellowstone, presumably where Albright could oversee it.[102]

In the fall, Mather had convened the eighth national parks conference at Mesa Verde National Park. There could be no mistake regarding the main emphasis of the meeting since the the director had asked his superintendents to assemble in "auto caravans" and converge on Mesa Verde making use of the Park-to-Park Highway. The superintendent of Yosemite, Washington B. ("Dusty") Lewis, led one caravan from California while Albright assembled another at Yellowstone. The goal was for superintendents to see "a number of parks that they would not have seen if they had come by train," and to "familiarize themselves with the country surrounding the parks . . . and with highway conditions in general."[103] The caravan of superintendents, accompanied by their families and members of the press, made news. The editor of the *Stockton Record*, who drove three thousand miles with Lewis's group through California and the Southwest, pronounced the October conference "the most successful since the National Park Service was first inaugurated."[104] The guest of honor at the conference, L. I. Hewes of the Bureau of Public Roads, used the opportunity to further demonstrate the cooperative attitude that would be the necessary basis of a successful working arrangement with the Park Service. "We are learning something of your large vision," he assured the group, "brought about by our already permitted glimpses of how your people operate." He went on to confess that faced with a "rolling stock" of twenty million American automobiles in 1925, his bureau had been too busy to "give much thought to the beautifying of highways." But, he added, "We have come into contact with your men Mr. Hull and Mr. Vint, and we have learned that we have been a little dilatory. . . . The boys of the bureau that are doing this work in the parks are more worried lest they offend the landscape engineers than that they offend me." The bureau's engineers, he confirmed, were "being versed in all the laws of landscape engineering."[105]

Despite his patronizing tone, Hewes acknowledged that the cooperation between Park Service landscape architects and Bureau of Public Roads civil engineers had already begun to produce significant results. By the fall of 1925, Bureau of Public Roads engineers had taken over some park road projects, were performing preliminary surveys for others, and were preparing to enter into a formal interbureau agreement that would give the roads bureau full responsibility for all future park road construction. Albright described the Mesa Verde conference, during which "the preliminary program of cooperation was mapped out," as the beginning of the "cooperative arrangement" between the two bureaus.[106] In 1925, the roads bureau assumed responsibility for the reconstruction of the Nisqually Road and began location surveys for the West Side and Yakima Park roads at Mount Rainier. At Zion Canyon, surveys were begun for the spectacular Zion-Mt. Carmel Highway; at Sequoia the roads bureau began considering alternate routes for the continued construction of the Generals Highway, the first portion of which opened in 1926. The many successful developments initiated in 1925 led Mather to report "excellent progress on the road development program . . . under the cooperative arrangement" entered into with the Bureau of Public Roads.[107]

The Transmountain Highway in Glacier had set the precedent for how all of these projects and many others subsequently proceeded. The overall task of determining the location and character of park roads rested with the park superintendents, who consulted with the landscape engineers, Hull and Vint. The interbureau arrangement then allowed

Stephen Mather and L. I. Hewes shake hands after agreeing on the terms of a memorandum of agreement between the National Park Service and the Bureau of Public Roads regarding future cooperation in the design and construction of roads in national parks. The 1926 memorandum structured decades of cooperation between the two federal bureaus. National Archives, Record Group 79.

the Park Service to tap the expertise and organization of the Bureau of Public Roads for surveys, contract specifications, and construction supervision—without giving up control over deciding where, when, and how park roads would be built. The landscape engineers retained the right to review and alter location surveys and contract specifications to assure that construction met their standards for landscape preservation as well as the Bureau of Public Roads standards for sound and economical engineering. In January 1926, these arrangements were formalized through a "memorandum of agreement" between the National Park Service and the Bureau of Public Roads.[108] The contract specified the precise terms of the working arrangement that had evolved over the previous year at Glacier and elsewhere.

As the construction of the western portion of the Transmountain Highway proceeded over the next three years, the experience continued to guide the evolution of the interbureau arrangement. Certain items of the construction contract had been written specifically to avoid excessive damage to roadside trees and slopes during construction. The blasting item, for example, required that a series of smaller charges be used rather than a large, single blast that could scar trees over a wide area. Another contract item required excavated material to be cast over the side of the road only in certain areas, where roadsides and trees were less likely to be damaged. Both clauses apparently were flouted during the construction of the west side approach to Logan Pass, despite the ineffectual objections of resident engineer W. G. Peters. Only in 1927, when Kittredge left the Bureau of Public Roads to become the chief engineer of the Park Service, were objections to these practices presented effectively to Chief MacDonald of the Bureau of Public Roads. Future construction supervision, Kittredge made clear, needed to enforce provisions intended to protect surrounding landscape features, even at the cost of convenience and economy.[109] Work on the contract proceeded mostly to everyone's satisfaction, however, and by the end of the construction season of 1928, the road had been completed to Logan Pass. J. Ross Eakin, who had returned as Glacier superintendent in 1927, reported that "the first section of highway through spectacular mountain scenery [would] be open to travel next season."[110] The road on the east side of the pass still remained to be completed.

Long before the first tourist drove the spectacular route along the Garden Wall to Logan Pass, however, the implications of the transmountain road project continued to affect the policies and organizational structure of the Park Service. The cost of the road had been greatly increased both by Mather's commitment to "preserve the landscape" at any cost and by the higher construction standards of the Bureau of Public Roads. Following the signing of the interbureau agreement in 1926, Mather noted that "the highest road standards covering grade and alignment have been adopted for [all] national park roads," following the example of the Glacier road.[111] The appropriations authorized in 1924 obviously would no longer be sufficient; the Bureau of Public Roads engineers were in fact already gathering the preliminary data necessary to put forward new estimates for completing park road projects throughout the park system. In the fall of 1926, L. I. Hewes again addressed the national park conference, which was held in Washington, DC, that year. "There are going to be necessary about a thousand miles of road in the national parks," he announced, "as suggested by the superintendents and measured by the bureau." He had a "tentative figure," he added, for what it would cost.[112] This "second program" of road construction, finalized by the Park Service and the Bureau of Public Roads in 1926, estimated that fifty-one million dollars would be necessary to build and modernize park roads throughout the system. In 1927 Congress approved the new budget, beginning with five million dollars for the 1928 construction season, an amount which effectively doubled the annual rate of road appropriations beginning that year.[113] Now fully integrated into the general road building efforts overseen by the Bureau of Public Roads, national park road budgets began to claim their fair share of federal-aid subsidies.

Park Service policy regarding road planning and construction matured rapidly as budgets grew in the mid-1920s. The road construction program had been launched successfully; now Park Service officials needed to confirm the desired limits of development. As the funding (and quality) of individual road projects went up, Mather and Albright refined their policy for new road construction: each park really needed little more than one great road that made some portion of the park's main scenic attractions accessible to all. Such a road should exhibit the highest standards of construction and would reveal superlative scenery. The Transmountain Highway, which was christened "Going-to-the-Sun Highway" when finally dedicated in 1933 (it later was changed to "Going-to-the-Sun Road"), epitomized this ideal. The increased cost of the Glacier road had siphoned funds and attention away from other road projects in the park, and as a result the transmountain road had become the perfect example of an exceptional and expensive—and solitary— road for a given park. Although other roads had been planned for Glacier (and portions of them built) the extraordinary quality of Going-to-the-Sun Road reinforced the conclusion that no other major through roads were needed in the park. Earlier models for national park development had featured more extensive park drive systems, on the model of Yellowstone's Grand Loop. In the model suggested by Going-to-the-Sun Road at Glacier, however, one great automotive road would be enough; the rest of the park would remain accessible by trail or remain completely "undeveloped."

This important policy shift occurred over a period of years and carried with it an implied need to develop a far more sophisticated process for planning the type and extent of all development in each park. Albright already recognized this at the 1925 Mesa Verde conference. In preparation for the road construction program that would result from the planned interbureau agreement, he and Arno Cammerer suggested to the assembled superintendents that they adopt a planning "program" to help organize and prioritize their many park road proposals. Albright asked each superintendent to produce a park map showing "the areas not to be developed at all," and suggestions for road projects in those areas that were to be developed. Also at the Mesa Verde conference, Cammerer suggested that Daniel Hull's recently completed town plan for Grand Canyon Village (1924) could become the model for expanded "general development plans" that would include not only detailed plans for villages, but also general plans for roads, trails, utilities and other park development.[114] The prospect of an unprecedented amount of park development to be realized through the interbureau agreement with the Bureau of Public Roads forced Park Service administrators to begin implementing new procedures for planning. Policies that until then had been expressed mostly in terms of general goals would have to be refined. The example of Going-to-the-Sun Road suggested that a single road, if it were exceptional enough, could meet a park's total need for highway development, an idea of great significance for what would soon be known as park "master planning."

The experience of planning and building the first portions of Going-to-the-Sun Road had also forced Park Service officials to reconsider—and then reorganize—the engineering and planning functions of the bureau. In 1927 Frank Kittredge filled the chief engineer vacancy at the Park Service, but the Bureau of Public Roads had permanently assumed the responsibility for providing the surveys and construction supervision for park road construction. The role of Kittredge and other Park Service personnel therefore stressed planning and review, as well as cooperation with the engineers from the roads bureau. This situation, in turn, demanded a reassessment of the Park Service landscape engineering division. As matters stood, it was hard to imagine that Hull and Vint would be able to effectively plan and review fifty-one million dollars of park road construction. Observing the situation in 1926, L. I. Hewes commented, "I think it is manifest that the landscape personnel, two men, are going to be driven distracted if they try to cover one third of the United States in a few months."[115]

The situation was made more serious by Daniel Hull's limited professional commitment to the Park Service. In 1925, a busy year for him in his collaborations with Underwood and in his private work, he reported that he and Vint had given "a larger proportion of time than ever before . . . over to landscape protection in connection with the road construction program."[116] He might have added that clearly his assistant, Thomas Vint, had assumed a key role in this pressing area of concern, especially at Glacier. Hull himself had grown more flagrant in building his private practice while continuing to occupy what were technically Park Service offices. In 1926 Hull received a new, part-time appointment with the Park Service in order to spend more time on his private work. The landscape architect, talented and well liked, obviously worked hard to keep both his public and private practices afloat; if Vint were able to meet the Park Service responsibilities that Hull did not have the time or the inclination to assume, the situation might have continued indefinitely. But apparently his new appointment brought attention to an evident conflict of interest. Although Mather, Cammerer, and Albright seemed to feel they were getting the best of both worlds, other Department of the Interior officials were less inclined to overlook the situation. In September 1926, two Department of the Interior inspectors visited Hull's Los Angeles office. Noting that he shared offices with Underwood, they also quickly determined that Underwood paid Hull to collaborate with him on national park development plans (commissions that Hull had helped secure for Underwood). In his part-time capacity as the Park Service chief landscape engineer, Hull subsequently reviewed and approved plans that he had helped develop as a private landscape architect. The arrangement, the inspectors quickly concluded, was "wholly wrong and liable to subject the Department to just criticism." Their recommendation was that Hull "be immediately discontinued." Secretary Work concurred and ruled that Hull's "dual capacity" was untenable.[117] By October, Daniel Hull's career with the Park Service seemed to have come to an end.

Arno Cammerer, however, supported the landscape architect and successfully delayed any immediate action. The otherwise unassuming assistant director, perhaps because of his early experience with the Commission of Fine Arts, had enjoyed a special rapport with the landscape architects and architects who periodically presented their work to the Washington office. On receiving the inspectors' report, he quickly contacted Mather (who was in California at the time) writing that the news had "come out of a clear sky," although he had warned Hull that the part-time appointment (which raised the question of what Hull was doing with the rest of his time) might cause trouble. Secretary Work had already signed the report recommending Hull's dismissal, but Cammerer requested and received a grace period to try and find some way to retain the landscape architect, even if only temporarily.[118] Albright, however, was less convinced of Hull's indispensability. While in Berkeley that December, he discovered that Underwood and Hull shared offices not only in Los Angeles, but in San Francisco as well. "He is more tied up with Underwood than we think," he wrote back to Cammerer, "and it is common talk out here that they are partners." He urged that Hull be asked to resign immediately.[119]

But Hull lingered on as Cammerer found ways to maintain his part-time situation. In his defense of the landscape architect, Cammerer pointed out that Hull had the confidence of Frederick Law Olmsted, Jr., and James L. Greenleaf, the past and present landscape architects on the Commission of Fine Arts. John D. Rockefeller, Jr., also thought highly of Hull; and Cammerer pointed out that "in the ticklish Lafayette [Acadia] situation," at least, "we had better have Hull do all the preliminary work," since Rockefeller at the time had already spent $750,000 developing that park. But Cammerer had been somewhat crushed to learn from Albright the extent to which Hull had been surreptitiously building his partnership with Underwood. "Have it out with Hull" while in California, he advised Albright, "but don't get his resignation right away." Cammerer had secured another part-time appointment for the landscape architect (on the condition that his office be separated from Underwood's), but after letting the matter "carry along quietly" in order to allow Hull to finish certain jobs, "then he should go." Albright approved of Cammerer's position, since he thought Hull had "lost all his interest in the National Park Service."[120] By the summer of 1927, after continued problems getting Hull to meet his (greatly reduced) Park Service obligations, Cammerer recommended to Mather that Hull immediately be replaced by Thomas Vint. "I'm off Dan," the assistant director assured Mather, "no matter whether he comes across now or not . . . . He has had nothing but his own interests in his head for several years now, and I resent it for the Service and for you."[121] Vint officially became chief landscape engineer on August 1, 1927. His new assistant landscape architect, Ernest A. Davidson, was sent to Glacier where he inspected Going-to-the-Sun Road construction.[122]

Even if Hull had been able to find more time for his Park Service duties, like George Goodwin he had failed to adapt his practice to what had become the more specific requirements of the Park Service. The events at Glacier in the summer of 1924 had made it clear that George Goodwin had failed to grasp the potential for "landscape engineering," as road budgets grew and opened new possibilities of how park roads could be built. In retrospect, Daniel Hull's absence at Logan Pass also revealed his failure to fully appreciate the role of the landscape architect as "landscape engineer." Hull's practice of town planning needed to be expanded, as Albright and Cammerer suggested in 1925, to include all aspects of national park development, above all road and trail systems. Town planning, in other words, needed to be done in the context of competent regional planning—a conclusion that many landscape architects and town planners in the United States were reaching by the mid-1920s. But Hull remained committed to his more limited role as a subdivision and resort designer. This commitment was expressed in his ultimate concern for his private, not his public, practice.

Park Service officials apparently could tolerate Hull's ethically ambiguous situation in the 1920s; but Albright and Cammerer were incensed when Hull repeatedly refused to become the kind of professional they needed him to be. His recalcitrance, not his complex professional arrangements, finally ended his involvement with the Park Service. Years later, when the Depression had crippled the California economy, Hull again asked Albright for a position with the Park Service. Albright (who was capable of bearing a grudge) took the opportunity to explain to the landscape architect that the Park Service needed professionals who had adapted their practice to the bureau's needs. "I could not in justice to our organization appoint you to a position for which a man already in the Service had fitted himself," Albright wrote. "We have adopted the policy in the last few years of advancing our younger men to higher positions . . . as they demonstrate their ability." A professional corps of trained professionals within the bureau had proved more valuable to Albright than even talented and experienced consultants such as Daniel Hull.[123] Hull's contribution to Park Service landscape architecture had been great; but as a professional he never committed himself to establishing an atelier of Park Service "landscape engineers" specifically trained to design, plan, review, and supervise scenic road and trail construction, park village development, roadside improvement, and myriad other tasks peculiar to national park work. His former assistant Thomas Vint, however, had already begun to form just such a professional school. Over a forty-year career with the Park Service, Vint would do more than any other individual to establish the distinctive design and unique "master planning" procedures that characterized Park Service "landscape engineering" by the end of the decade.

In both civil engineering and landscape architecture, the design and construction of the transmountain route in Glacier—Going-to-the-Sun Road—had first indicated the need for reassessing the professional capacities of the Park Service. Up until 1924, vague commitments to avoid "gridironing" the parks with roads and to "harmonize" construction work with park scenery had not been seriously tested. Hull and his assistants had provided excellent town plans and architectural designs that met the immediate needs of park managers and visitors but limited appropriations had precluded more ambitious development plans that encompassed entire parks. The Glacier road, however, and the fifty-one million dollar "second program" of road construction that followed it, demanded that town planning be expanded into regional planning. At a more detailed level of landscape design, the decision of how to locate the final route up to Logan Pass demanded that Park Service landscape architects involve themselves directly in fundamental civil engineering decisions. It was the Glacier road project that first indicated that the Park Service would need to produce "landscape engineers" in fact as well as in name.

More than any park road project, Going-to-the-Sun Road embodied Stephen Mather's evolving hopes and policies for developing the national parks as a coordinated system. The transmountain road allowed Glacier to be developed and administered as a 20th-century landscape park: accessible to the growing legions of automotive tourists and thereby preserved from other forms of development. Louis Hill's role in the management of Glacier (and his essentially 19th-century vision of national park administration) steadily waned as the number of visitors to the park quickly grew. Crucial not only to the future development of Glacier, Going-to-the-Sun Road erased the single greatest deficiency in Mather's Park-to-Park Highway route, completing that early ideal of an "interstate highway system" that would bear a steady stream of "tourist gold" into western communities. Mather, however, suffered a stroke in November 1928; Albright, his long-anticipated successor, was sworn in as the second director of the National Park Service in January. That summer, Going-to-the-Sun Road opened to tourists between West Glacier and Logan Pass; but Mather remained in very serious condition. A second stroke killed him in January 1930, at the age of 63.

Construction on the east portion of Going-to-the-Sun Road continued for the next three years. During that time, many other high profile road projects were undertaken under the terms of the 1926 memorandum of agreement between the Park Service and the Bureau of Public Roads. Among them are some of the most scenic roads in the country, and the

Going-to-the-Sun Road Historic District

Above: *A photographer composes Rocky Mountain scenery from an overlook on a recently constructed portion of Going-to-the-Sun Road. Since the western half of the road (from West Glacier to Logan Pass) first opened in 1928, Going-to-the-Sun Road has been considered among the most scenic highways in the world. National Archives, Record Group 79.*

Below: *Opening ceremonies for Going-to-the-Sun Road, July 15, 1933. Over four thousand attended the formal opening of the transmountain road in Glacier National Park, which in 1933 finally was completed from West Glacier to East Glacier. Hundreds of CCC boys were in the crowd, having only recently arrived in the park following the creation of the CCC that March. National Archives, Record Group 79.*

Left: *Going-to-the-Sun Road as it appears along McDonald Creek. The Garden Wall section of the road is faintly visible as a light line traversing the massive escarpment directly ahead (about three thousand feet above) and slowly ascending from left to right towards Logan Pass.*

Below: *The East Side Tunnel, between Logan Pass and St. Mary Lake, completed in 1931. The tunnel is over four hundred feet long and bored through solid sedimentary rock. Tunnels on national park roads were used to minimize the amount of blasting and excavation necessary on steep slopes; the dramatic effect of a sharp constriction in the spatial sequence experienced by motorists, however, also figured in decisions regarding the locations of tunnels.*

The West Side Tunnel, completed in 1926. The tunnel features an opening, or adit, that provides a dramatic overlook from within the enclosed space. Where rockfalls threatened, the Park Service specified inconspicuous masonry portals of native stone at tunnel entrances, as seen here. The motor coach is one of a fleet of historic vehicles recently restored by the park concessioner.

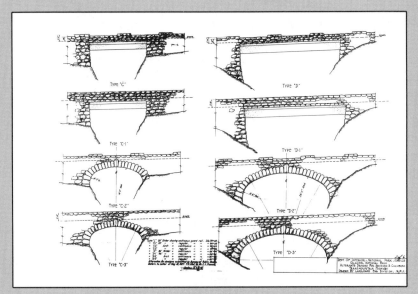

A typical design drawing by the Park Service landscape division in the mid-1920s, in this case suggesting appropriate bridge designs for Going-to-the-Sun Road. Park Service landscape architects submitted studies like these to Bureau of Public Roads engineers. The final approval of all park plans rested with Park Service officials. Courtesy National Park Service Technical Information Center, Denver Service Center.

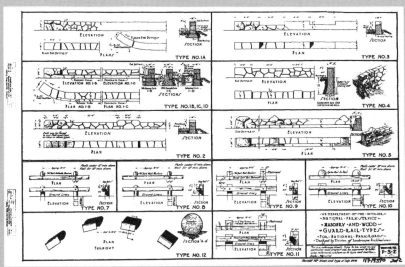

This standard detail sheet produced by the Park Service landscape division in 1928 represents one of the most important goals for the modernization of the national park system: standardization of construction system-wide. Courtesy National Park Service Technical Information Center, Denver Service Center.

finest examples of that blend of disciplines called "landscape engineering." The Generals Highway, in Sequoia, opened between the Ash Mountain headquarters area (laid out by Hull) and the Giant Forest in 1926. The extension of the road to General Grant National Park was completed in 1935, but only after another prolonged controversy over route location. Once again convenience was pitted against scenic preservation in road development plans; in this case Superintendent John R. White assured that the Generals Highway became not only one of the most scenic roads in the country, but also that the road plans for the park as a whole minimized intrusions on wilderness areas.[124] Construction began on the new Trail Ridge Road in Rocky Mountain National Park in the fall of 1929. Another transmountain route over the Continental Divide, the Trail Ridge Road replaced an earlier state road that was full of switchbacks and tight curves. As Kittredge had predicted might happen in such cases, the old road had to be completely abandoned. The new Trail Ridge Road, completed in 1933, ran for ten miles at above eleven thousand feet and remains one of the most spectacular scenic routes in the country. At Zion Canyon, the Zion-Mt. Carmel Highway opened in 1930. Located along an impossible route from the valley floor to Mt. Carmel Junction, the road employed switchbacks, extensive benching, and a tunnel over one mile long through solid sandstone. One of the greatest achievements of the Bureau of Public Roads, it is the most intensively engineered of all the national park roads.

One of the most remarkable of all the "second program" road projects built after 1926 was the new Wawona Road at Yosemite, built by the Bureau of Public Roads to replace the wagon road that had served as the southern entrance to the valley since the 1870s. The new road, which was begun in 1930, had been a subject of concern for the Yosemite National Park Board of Expert Advisors, an advisory board of the type first suggested by Frederick Law Olmsted, Jr., in 1911. Olmsted, in fact, was named the first chairman of the Yosemite board when it was formed in 1928. In that position he had been able to continue his father's work and exert timely and thoughtful influence, not only on the Wawona Road project, but on a range of important issues at Yosemite. The location of the new Wawona Road required a steep grade in order to drop into the valley near Inspiration Point, a location that featured one of the most famous views of Yosemite Valley. The road plans eventually called for a tunnel at that point, bored four-fifths of a mile through solid granite under Turtleback Dome. Olmsted advised taking the huge amount of loose rock blasted out for the tunnel and using it to create a "hand-laid rock embankment" to serve as a viewing terrace at the eastern portal of the tunnel. This would prevent the enormous amount of rubble from permanently scarring the slopes below; it would also create an overlook providing motorists with a breathtaking vista of the valley immediately as they exited the tunnel.[125]

Such a spatial sequence—from the constricted space of a tunnel to a suddenly awesome vista—was a landscape effect familiar to the younger Olmsted. His father had used a similar strategy at the entrance to the

Long Meadow of Prospect Park and at Franklin Park as well. When opened in 1933, the Wawona Tunnel and its overlook proved to be another strong collaboration of the Park Service and the Bureau of Public Roads, preserving scenery through technically advanced road construction. It also illustrated the continued influence of established landscape park theory and design in the development of 20th-century landscape parks—a continuity that the younger Olmsted had done so much to assure over the previous twenty years.

All of these national park roads are of great significance and have retained extraordinary physical integrity. This is due in part to their privileged locations: while many scenic roads outside parks were widened, straightened, and turned into interstate arteries after World War II, these national park roads remain excellent examples of some of the finest highway engineering of the period. None of these examples, however, played the pivotal role in the history of national park development that Going-to-the-Sun Road did.

But in 1929, the Glacier road project had been briefly delayed by the complex local politics that initially had encouraged its development. The proposal for a Marias Pass road, never forgotten, was boosted as part of the "Roosevelt Highway" and funded through federal aid in 1926. Completed in 1930, it provided the first automotive link between East Glacier and West Glacier, and so reduced the urgency of completing Going-to-the-Sun Road. There were other reasons, however, for the Park Service to delay the completion of its Logan Pass transmountain route. A new priority for Director Albright was the elimination of "inholdings," or private property within park boundaries. The completion of Going-to-the-Sun Road, he feared, would greatly increase the value of the private land within Glacier that he hoped to acquire for the park. Construction soon resumed, however, when it became apparent that property values were rising anyway.[126]

In 1930, the next resident Bureau of Public Roads engineer, A. V. Emery, completed a new location survey for the remaining section of the transmountain route on the east side of Logan Pass. Grading and construction began on the east side in 1931, and continued through the next season. The new road, finally connecting Logan Pass to the St. Mary spur road near the Going-to-the-Sun Chalets, was completed ahead of schedule in October 1932.[127] Early in the summer of 1933, Superintendent Eivind T. Scoyen (who had replaced Eakin in 1931) prepared for a major celebration. On July 15, more than four thousand people assembled at Logan Pass, including the governor of Montana, Senator Wheeler, and two hundred Blackfeet, Kootenai, and Selish Indians "in full tribal regalia," according to the press release.[128]

During the ceremony, a bronze plaque was dedicated to Mather at the summit of Logan Pass. A number of identical memorials had been commissioned by a group of the former director's friends and dedicated the year before in prominent locations in most of the parks. The Glacier plaque had been reserved for this moment, when the great transmountain road across Glacier National Park finally completed the vast scenic loop of the Park-to-Park Highway. It had been eight years since Kittredge re-surveyed the western approach to Logan Pass, and eleven years since the first congressional appropriations for road construction. The transmountain road that Albright and Goodwin had estimated at about $600,000 had cost over $2,500,000. But it was, according to a proud Superintendent Scoyen, "the most beautiful piece of mountain road in the world." And the policy the road had helped inspire was clear in the letter from Director Albright that Scoyen read at the 1933 dedication: "The major portion of Glacier Park will always be accessible only by trail . . . . Let there be no competition of other roads with the Going-to-the-Sun Highway. It should stand supreme and alone."[129]

Among the crowd that July afternoon were hundreds of CCC recruits who had just arrived that summer and were busily setting up no less than eight of their camps in the park. Their presence was a reminder that Going-to-the Sun Road had not really been completed. Even while construction had continued on the Logan Pass portions of the road, plans had been underway for major reconstruction projects. A series of new bridges, wider travel lanes, and improved surfacing were already envisioned, especially for the Lake McDonald and St. Mary Lake sections of the road that had been built before the Bureau of Public Roads had introduced its standards for width, curvature, and culvert design. After 1933, Franklin Roosevelt's New Deal, which the crowds of CCC boys cheerfully represented, would be the source of another one million dollars for the reconstruction of the Glacier road. By 1937, the entire road had been improved to Bureau of Public Roads standards and contracts were being prepared to cover the crushed stone base courses with asphalt pavement. The final section of pavement was finally poured in 1952.[130]

Today, Going-to-the-Sun Road historic district encompasses almost forty-nine miles of the road, from the foot of Lake McDonald to the Divide Creek on the eastern park boundary (the West Glacier to Apgar portion of the road has been altered and is not in the district). The historic district contains the original road, its bridges, tunnels, arches, culverts, retaining walls, and forty thousand feet of guardwalls, all built between 1922 and 1937. The West Side Tunnel (1926) was cut through 192 feet of rock; the East Side Tunnel (1931) is 408 feet long. The original alignment of the road, running along the Garden Wall on the west side and above St. Mary Lake on east side, remains true to the locations that Thomas Vint suggested, and which Frank Kittredge, W. G. Peters, and A. V. Emery finalized. The original twenty-two-foot width of the roadway has been maintained, except on the ten-mile traverse of the Garden Wall, which in places has always been narrower. In 1983 Going-to-the-Sun Road was included in the National Register of Historic Places; in 1985 it was made a National Historic Civil Engineering Landmark.[131]

Since World War II, Glacier National Park, like the rest of the park system, has been visited by ever greater numbers of motorists. The pressure to widen and modernize national park roads in some cases has been irresistible. Road modernizations, while certainly necessary in some cases, have permanently altered the initial (and for many people the only) experience of many park landscapes: the view from the road. Higher design speeds and greater traffic capacities alter the experience of driving through a national park, and that alteration implies a loss of integrity of the historic park design. Road widenings and other postwar reconstructions were done primarily to serve larger numbers of tourists, and in many cases to accommodate recreational vehicles with physical dimensions and turning radii unheard of for non-commercial vehicles before the war. This policy may have been called for during the Mission 66 period and beyond, but today many park managers argue against endlessly increasing the capacity of parks to serve larger numbers—and longer vehicles—than ever before.

This shift in policy hopefully has assured that the remarkable integrity of Going-to-the-Sun Road will be maintained. The road is of an age that demands maintenance and, for certain features, reconstruction if it is to continue to serve its historic role as the unique vehicular crossing of Glacier National Park. Fortunately the reconstruction of historic guardwalls and the resurfacing and stabilization of other parts of the historic road promise to be completed in coming years without altering the historic road alignment, and even without raising the historic guardwall height. If this is achieved, the restoration of Going-to-the-Sun Road should be among the finest historic landscape restorations of its type. Considering the number of extraordinary (and aging) scenic roads of this period in the national park system, the ongoing restoration and reconstruction of Going-to-the-Sun Road may continue to define Park Service policy and standards for road construction and management today, just as the transmountain project determined road planning policies and influenced Park Service organizational structures during its original construction.

The Mount Rainier National Park Historic District: Regional Planning and National Park Service "Master Planning"

Chapter 5

After Stephen Mather abruptly left George Goodwin and Thomas Vint at Logan Pass in the summer of 1924, he instigated a gradual upheaval of the professional structure of the Park Service over the next three years. The creation of the San Francisco field headquarters in 1927 brought together the new chief engineer, Frank Kittredge, and the new "chief landscape architect," Thomas Vint, at least on the organizational chart and in the same office building, if not in other respects. In Washington at about the same time, Arno Cammerer was raised to a new "associate director" level and four new assistant directorships provided legal, administrative, and other support. Horace Albright retained his old positions as assistant director (field) and superintendent of Yellowstone; but Mather now often thought of retiring, and he asked Albright to consider becoming director when he did. The administration of larger budgets and the continued explosive growth in park visitation justified and required bureaucratic growth; but as the Park Service matured, it retained the vitality and creativity that had made it a popular success story of the otherwise staid Harding and Coolidge administrations.

In what was now known as the "landscape architectural division" in San Francisco, Thomas Vint had the opportunity to hire a number of young designers to assist him with planning, design, and construction supervision for numerous park projects, including the ambitious "second program" of park road building already underway. Ernest A. Davidson had already joined him and helped supervise Going-to-the-Sun Road construction in the summer of 1926. With Davidson and other recruits, Vint had the opportunity to encourage the specific skills and sensibilities required for a professional corps of Park Service landscape architects. By the late 1920s, Vint had developed an atelier of designers with experience both in the parks and in the central design office. Soon the small group began drafting the comprehensive park development plans that Albright and Cammerer had suggested at the 1925 Mesa Verde conference. But the exact procedures and responsibilities for comprehensive planning within the Park Service had not yet been fully determined. Because of the importance of road construction at this time, for example, chief engineer Frank Kittredge (who shared a parallel position to Vint in the new organizational chart) initially served as the "senior officer" in charge of field headquarters operations. In San Francisco, Vint and Kittredge struggled to clarify their respective places in the planning process. By the end of the decade, however, Horace Albright had defined a procedure for "master planning" that would further reinforce the historic role of landscape architectural theory and practice in the development of the national park system.

No individual influenced Park Service planning process and design details in the late 1920s and 1930s more than Thomas Chalmers Vint. Born of Scotch-Irish immigrant parents in Utah in 1894, Vint grew up in Los Angeles where he attended Polytechnic High School. After graduating in 1914, he went to work as a draftsman for Lloyd Wright, Frank Lloyd Wright's son, who practiced landscape architecture in Los Angeles. Working in Wright's office during the years before World War I, Vint was immersed in a world of burgeoning nurseries and palatial gardens typical of the period in Southern California. After a year in that world, Vint decided on a career in landscape architecture and enrolled in the landscape program of the University of California at Berkeley. The next summer he returned to Lloyd Wright's office to work. During his second year at Berkeley, World War I interrupted his education; but while serving in France with the Air Corps, he nevertheless managed to receive a semester's worth of architectural training at the University of Lyon. He then returned to California and re-enrolled at Berkeley in the summer of 1919, graduating with a Bachelor of Science degree in landscape architecture the next winter.

After graduating, Vint went to work for a Los Angeles construction firm as a laborer, but soon found work as a draftsman with Mayberry & Jones, a Los Angeles architectural office. Within less than a year he went into business for himself as a "landscape contractor . . . grading and planting residence grounds." He also briefly took a position as the chief landscape designer for the famous Armstrong Nurseries in nearby Ontario. In the fall of 1922, however, after two years as a journeyman, Vint moved to Yosemite National Park to take the job of Park Service assistant landscape engineer. There his real apprenticeship began.[1]

At Yosemite, Vint drafted architectural and landscape plans and prepared specifications for Daniel Hull during the period that the Grand Canyon and Yosemite Village plans were being developed. Vint also supervised construction at Yosemite and in other parks. When Hull relocated to Underwood's offices in Los Angeles, Vint came along and continued to prepare plans and specifications for "general park development plans." During the Los Angeles years Vint shouldered increased responsibility for the Park Service. He loved to travel to park job sites (as he did to Glacier in 1924) and he did so with increasing frequency, since Hull was often less inclined to travel long distances from Los Angeles. Although Park Service work required a rigorous travel schedule, Hull's responsibilities to his private clients made it difficult for him to leave Southern California for extended periods.[2] When Hull's Park Service commitment officially became part-time in 1926, Vint was promoted from assistant to associate landscape engineer in recognition of the greater scope of his responsibilities.

Although he had proven to be an able apprentice and assistant over the previous four years, Vint came from a very different background than Daniel Hull. One can hardly imagine Hull, with his Harvard degree and professional connections, taking a first job as a construction laborer or starting his own business as a landscape contractor. Vint had never gone East for a graduate degree, nor had he established a professional practice in the accepted sense of the term. In the 1920s, a career as a public employee (rather than as a professional consultant) was a new kind of landscape architectural practice. Vint had not yet become a member of the American Society of Landscape Architects, for example, and when he did, his professional status appeared to require some explanation in order for him to be deemed eligible. Arno Cammerer initially recoiled at the idea of having Vint replace Hull as chief landscape architect. He insisted it was because Vint was "not as good as Hull on design"; but Cammerer later revealed that his first concern was that Vint would not develop key personal relationships with figures such as Ferruccio Vitale (James Greenleaf's successor on the Commission of Fine Arts) or John D. Rockefeller, Jr.[3]

Maintaining the good will and confidence of such individuals certainly remained an essential task for a chief landscape architect at the Park Service. But what Cammerer had failed to see, perhaps, was that the relationships that Hull (as a "consultant") cultivated with individuals such as Rockefeller or the executives from the Union Pacific Railroad (as "clients") would not figure as prominently in the activities of Park Service landscape architects in the future. Increased budget appropriations had changed the nature of park planning and design work. A new kind of landscape architectural practice was taking shape that demanded professional adaptations to new procedures and priorities. The experience with Hull suggested that this professional commitment to practice within the Park Service needed to be full-time; Hull's attempt to have it both ways had resulted in ethical improprieties and practical difficulties.

Horace Albright had confidence in Vint and remarked already in 1925 that the landscape architect "had gotten a wonderful hold on his work" and had "developed very fast." Albright was particularly pleased with the part Vint had played in the Going-to-the-Sun Road project. Vint also proved to be popular with the superintendents, an essential qualification that earlier assistant landscape architects had failed to meet.[4] Frederick Law Olmsted, Jr., who grew to know Thomas Vint well through their work together at Yosemite, strongly endorsed the landscape architect in 1930 when Vint finally applied to the American Society of Landscape Architects. Olmsted not only sponsored Vint as an individual, but also supported the professional practice that the landscape architect had developed as a full-time government employee. "His experience has probably been specialized in a manner distinctly different from . . . successful candidates for membership in this society," Olmsted wrote to the examining board, a fact which made it difficult for Vint to present the usual portfolio of residential gardens and commercial developments ordinarily required for admission. "But it is the very essence of most landscape architecture," Olmsted continued (perhaps remembering his own father's career), "that it involves . . . the arrangement and management of land on a large scale, often under difficult administrative

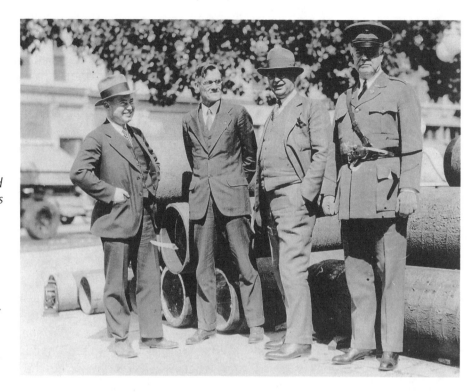

and personal conditions." Since Vint had proven his ability to shape such arrangements "toward worthy ends, with a good appreciation of appropriate landscape values and an intelligent grasp of appropriate and available means for attaining the ends in view . . . he seems to come clearly within the proper definition of a good landscape architect."[5]

Thomas Vint had not only replaced Daniel Hull, he had begun to indicate a new professional path for other landscape architects. But he could not create a new, specialized practice on his own. Now in his early thirties, Vint had the opportunity to expand his office as the landscape architectural division prepared to relocate to larger offices in San Francisco. There were specific qualities that he looked for in potential assistants, qualities that seemed to have little to do with previous education. The first indication of Vint's priorities had been his selection of Ernest Davidson, who had studied design at Washington State College in Pullman but had not graduated. When Vint hired him in 1926, Davidson was in his mid-thirties and had worked a variety of jobs. Remembered as a debonair and personable figure, Davidson had little or no experience as a landscape architect.[6] But Vint, a fine draftsman himself, appreciated Davidson's drawing ability; and during the winters in the San Francisco office Vint had time to train Davidson to become exactly the kind of landscape architect the Park Service needed. Vint's next addition to the office was John Wosky, an Iowa native who had been a draftsman in Underwood's Los Angeles office since 1924. In 1926, Wosky also began working with Vint; and again Vint took the opportunity to develop a designer with little design education into a specialized professional who could, for example, produce Park Service Rustic architectural designs, assess a Bureau of Public Roads location survey, and work with superintendents drafting development outlines. Only in 1928 did Vint hire a landscape architect who had an academic degree in landscape architecture; Merel S. Sager, who received his Master in Landscape Architecture degree from Harvard that year, had already been working for the Park Service as a seasonal ranger since 1922. Again Vint found a ready student willing to specialize in landscape design (and architectural design) specifically tailored to development in the parks.[7]

After 1927, Vint's expanding landscape office was located in the Underwood Building in San Francisco. An essential step to this continued growth was the creation of a civil service title and examination for Park Service landscape architects. Merel Sager helped Vint draft a job description and examination in 1928. (Perhaps not surprisingly, Sager became the first to pass the test, assuring himself a permanent position.) The job description made Vint's priorities for recruiting landscape architects clear: the work they would be expected to perform would be "of a different character than the general practice of the landscape profession." In what was a frank admission from a former chief designer of the Armstrong Nurseries, Vint confessed that he had "little use for men whose experience is limited to the planting of shrubbery and allied landscape work." There was "little planting done within the National Parks," he pointed out, and the work of his office "merge[d] into the field of architecture," since it involved primarily "the location and construction of communities, buildings, etc., within an existing landscape." The examination problems included the design of alternative facade elevations (using either stone, logs, or milled timber) and site plans for park residences and community buildings. The design of bridges also was stressed.[8] Vint needed to develop a multidisciplinary office to accomplish comprehensive park plans, and he soon hired A. Paul Brown, an architect who had also worked for Underwood, and Herbert Kreinkemp, who specialized in construction documents and specifications. Charles E. Peterson, an architect from the University of Minnesota, joined the office in 1929. Peterson had begun his involvement with national parks as a rodman surveying in Sequoia National Park in 1928. He joined Vint's staff after taking the new civil service examination for landscape architects that year.[9]

Vint's office expanded rapidly, drawing recently graduated landscape architects from the Berkeley landscape program and elsewhere, as well as engineers from various disciplines. But whatever discipline they had been trained in, they all adapted under Vint's tutelage to become part of a multidisciplinary park planning office. Within three years, as historian Linda Flint McClelland observes, "Vint had transformed the Landscape Division into a design office with increasing emphasis on general planning . . . involved to some degree in all phases of park development."[10] By the late 1920s, architect, site planner, regional planner, and civil engineer had come together to create a distinctive practice that can only be described, finally, as Park Service landscape architecture. "The work of the landscape division is that of a professional advisor to the service in matters pertaining to the field of landscape architecture," Vint reported in 1929, "its primary purpose is to obtain a logical, well-studied general development plan for each park, which includes a control of the location, type of architecture, planting, grading, etc., in connection with any construction project within the parks." The office's work fell into two categories: first, the general development, buildings, and other improvements initiated by the park superintendent or concessioners; and second, the work done through road appropriations administered by the Bureau of Public Roads. Most of Vint's designers spent the construction season in the field, working in a particular park or regional group of parks. New employees typically spent their first year in the San Francisco office with Vint, since their chief felt it took "at least a year to make national park men out of the best new men, as it is specialized work." A certain number of the staff worked in San Francisco all year preparing contract documents and specifications. There could be no replacement for adequate field supervision of construction work, however, and Vint emphasized this function. Often given brutal travel schedules, Vint's landscape architects were expected to be directly involved in park development plans from the initial discussions with park superintendents to the final inspection of a contractor's work. By 1929, Vint's atelier consisted of eight landscape architects, and he was still trying to fill vacant positions.[11]

Vint often suggested that the professional arrangements he devised for his landscape architectural division were "much like that in private work between the landscape architect and the client . . . the landscape architect must 'sell' his plan to those who are to live with it," namely the park's superintendent and staff. The Park Service had placed the responsibility of drawing up plans into the hands of its professionals, but the director and the park superintendents decided whether the plans would be implemented. Vint felt the situation served the Park Service well, since the bureau received "the professional services of a group who are familiar with the ground and the mode of operation of the area." But Vint's landscape architects were not his only students. His division "succeeded in making good landscape men out of our park superintendents and the project engineers of the Bureau of Public Roads," as well, he boasted in 1929. If Vint's designers had specialized their professional practice to suit the needs of parks, park administrators were also educated in the planning process over the years, and became what Vint described as ideal clients.[12]

Vint might have added that his office also did its planning and design work in an ideal context: the national parks. Earlier in the decade, Daniel Hull had implemented national park development through the formal device of the town plan; it remained for Thomas Vint and his office to expand that practice and articulate national park development through the larger instrument of the regional plan. Park villages were only one aspect of Vint's comprehensive planning framework. Park roads, for example, had already been dramatically introduced as an essential consideration for Park Service planners if they were to continue to preserve landscape scenery while encouraging increased public use and appreciation. Other aspects of park development demanded attention as well; utility lines, sewers, water treatment plants, forest management, and land-use zoning all were aspects of the "general development plans" that Vint now undertook to produce for each park and monument of the national park system.

The goal of producing rational, comprehensive plans that would coordinate and control all aspects of park development had been put forward at the Department of the Interior since 1911. Horace Albright and Arno Cammerer had called for comprehensive plans at the Mesa Verde conference in 1925, mostly because they realized that the desirable limits of park development needed to be established before the Bureau of Public Roads began the fifty-one million dollar "second program" of park road construction. But the desire for comprehensive plans for parks also reflected the contemporary ideology of many city and regional planners in the United States, who had concluded that planning at a local level had little chance of success if it were not part of a coordinated approach to regional development. American city planning of the 1920s above all stressed two, complementary tactics: zoned land-use restrictions and the comprehensive regional plan. The national park plans devised by Vint's landscape architectural division employed aspects of both procedures. In so doing, the planning process developed by Vint again demonstrated how national parks, as 20th-century landscape parks, continued to be settings for the expression of ideal civic arrangements.

The fascination with land-use zoning had a long history among American landscape architects. Before World War I, F. L. Olmsted, Jr., John Nolen, and others had traveled to German cities, such as Dusseldorf and Frankfort, which had planned their rapid expansion in the 19th century in ways that American cities could not. Olmsted noted that while in the 1870s his father was attempting to implement a plan for the northern wards of New York "with a conception of town planning at least a whole generation in advance of the public opinion of the day," the Prussian government already enforced "comprehensive city planning" in many German cities.[13] The ability of German and other European municipalities to control land use, building height, and architectural design through direct ownership of land and restrictions on individual property rights was not practicable in American cities. But by 1916, American planners such as Olmsted, Nolen, and Edward M. Bassett, a lawyer specializing in planning law, frequently wrote on the desirability of some form of land-use zoning.[14] Some early zoning ordinances had been established in New York and other cities before the war as well, but these were exceptional cases with relatively limited effect. As planning historians have noted, the real impetus to provide local governments with the legal means to control the uses of private land originated with private property owners themselves, mostly after World War I. Homeowners in suburban towns and villages, in particular, were anxious to protect the homogeneous neighborhoods of single-family houses that had been built around industrial cities since the Civil War. The value of suburban residential property could be ruinously affected by the incursion of a new industrial facility or multifamily dwelling in what had been a relatively exclusive neighborhood. Once middle class property owners identified the municipal zoning ordinance as the most effective means of stabilizing property values and protecting residential enclaves from unwanted development, land-use zoning quickly became the most widespread city planning phenomenon in the United States since the municipal park commission.[15]

The 1920s were the heyday of the zoning movement. In 1921, as many states were passing their own city planning laws to enable municipalities to enforce zoning regulations, Secretary of Commerce Herbert Hoover appointed a committee, chaired by Edward Bassett, to draft a standard city planning enabling act. The model legislation encouraged states to pass city planning laws necessary to enable municipalities to enforce local zoning ordinances. In the meantime, legal challenges to zoning culminated in a 1926 Supreme Court decision upholding the basic principle of local land-use restrictions. By 1927, when the Department of Commerce published its new standard city planning act, over five hundred cities all over the country had already created municipal zoning commissions; in the next two years the number rose to over 750, including all but a handful of American cities with populations over 100,000.[16]

Judges, planners, and the drafters of the new planning legislation all emphasized that zoning restrictions on the use of private property were only justified when they reflected general, preset goals for the development of a community. These goals were intended to be set down in advance in the form of a comprehensive plan. The 1927 standard enabling legislation described the comprehensive plan as a "master plan," a term that was in general use by the end of the decade.[17] Without such an objective and comprehensive plan, decisions regarding land-use restrictions represented an arbitrary infringement on property rights, and the zoning process could more easily be subverted to benefit particular interests. Much to the dismay of the planners who had advocated land-use zoning for the previous twenty years, however, "zoning without general planning" was widespread. The master plan of a community, intended to guide zoning decisions, often simply recorded them. Planners had envisioned city plans informed by objective statistics and devised to serve the general interests of the larger community; but zoning commissions often protected entrenched property interests and merely reinforced existing patterns of development. Since statistical surveys took time and were expensive, scientific data on land uses, demographic trends, and industrial patterns rarely were available to early zoning commissions. Far from an objective and absolute control on land-use zoning regulation, the master plan in the 1920s often represented the result of the zoning process rather than its starting point.[18]

Horace Albright revealed the underlying conceptual relationship of Park Service planning to the contemporary practice of land-use zoning in 1932, when he directed that the "general development plans" Vint and his planners had devised for the national parks be renamed "master plans."[19] But in comparison to their municipal counterparts, national park planners worked in an ideal context; Park Service officials exerted unchallenged control over land uses within park boundaries.[20] Planning techniques, such as land-use zoning, therefore assumed a purer form than they could when applied to private property by municipal zoning commissions. Implied land-use zones had already been evident in the park village plans drawn up by Mark Daniels for Yosemite Valley in 1914. In 1916, Aldo Leopold and Don Johnston had specifically remarked on the potential for land-use regulations in the context of a federally administered reservation, and Daniel Hull incorporated parts of their zoning plan for Grand Canyon Village in his 1924 plan. The residential, utility, and civic zones delineated by Hull for Grand Canyon and other park village plans roughly corresponded to typical municipal zoning classifications of the 1920s: residential, industrial, and civic. The practice of land-use zoning clearly was an aspect of contemporary professional planning that affected the formation of Park Service planning procedures in the early 1920s.

The more comprehensive "general development plans," or master plans, that Vint and his colleagues produced after 1927 further exploited the unique legal situation and symbolic potential of national parks. The primary impetus for the national park general development plan, as expressed by Albright in 1925, was to assure that the vast majority of every park would be free of automobiles and the intensive uses implied by such accessibility. The master plan of a national park therefore implied zoning the entire park for different levels of use, from the most intensively developed areas (road corridors) to entirely inaccessible portions of the backcountry where even trails were prohibited. If local zoning plans in hundreds of cities and towns in the United States had been devised primarily to preserve residential suburbs, the desire to preserve what began to be called "wilderness areas" or "research areas" motivated early general planning for national parks.

Indeed, both types of landscapes—suburb and wilderness—had long assumed iconic significance in middle class American life, and professional planners in the United States were working to preserve both during the 1920s. Just as municipal zoning plans protected the character of residential suburbs, regional planners sought to preserve rural landscapes and wilderness areas through the extension of land-use controls over far greater areas. The term "regional planning" described a number of related activities in the 1920s. City planners, for example, recognizing that metropolitan areas exceeded municipal boundaries, advocated unified, "regional plans" for entire metropolitan regions. A master plan for a region, like the municipal master plan, could graphically and statistically assemble pertinent data and objective information. Surveys of populations, industrial trends, and traffic patterns for an entire metropolitan area facilitated the coordinated planning of transportation systems, park systems, and land-use zoning over an area administered by many local governments. Regional planning therefore required the cooperation of sometimes dozens of municipal and county authorities. The regional plan of New York, which got underway in the early 1920s, took a decade to complete and covered a geographic area governed by scores of individual municipalities in three states. In 1922, Los Angeles County created a true regional planning commission that attempted to coordinate the rapid urbanization spreading over dozens of local political jurisdictions in Southern California. By the end of the decade, many other large cities had attempted to initiate regional planning schemes that would put local planning efforts into the context of a coordinated and efficient "regional plan."

The desire to implement plans for entire metropolitan regions reflected a broader search for more comprehensive forms of regional government in the 1920s. Many American cities, having grown to engulf regions, experienced traffic congestion, shortages of fresh water, inadequate facilities for sewage disposal, meager park systems, and myriad other deficiencies that could be attributed to poorly coordinated or unplanned metropolitan growth. But municipal governments in suburban areas usually resisted any inroads on local control of zoning and other planning decisions. If suburban homeowners had embraced local land-use restrictions, they just as vehemently defended local control over those restrictions, frustrating attempts by planners and officials to create true regional planning authorities through state legislation. American metropolitan regions in the 1920s almost all maintained the fragmented political structure that had become typical of the 20th-century metropolis. Land-use zoning, in most cases, remained a patchwork of local ordinances serving local interests; so-called regional plans relied on local cooperation and the power of suggestion to achieve any degree of implementation.[21]

In certain cases, especially in planning regional water supplies, sewerage systems, and highway networks, independent regional commissions were granted powers that extended over many suburban municipalities. Because building these vital utilities demanded regional cooperation, special-function metropolitan district authorities had been successfully established in Boston, New York, Philadelphia, and other cities since the 1890s. Special-function metropolitan authorities were able to achieve important public improvements requiring coordinated planning over large geographic areas. But by providing essential services and improvements independently, these successes also undermined the cause of general regional planning since they removed some of the most powerful reasons for empowering a regional planning commission. In 1928, Los Angeles created a metropolitan water district to build reservoirs and aqueducts for a dozen municipalities, but by that time the innovative county regional planning commission, which would have put water planning into the context of general land-use planning, had been completely frustrated. Aqueducts, flood control, and other improvements were subsequently made; but the plans for a regional park system designed by F. L. Olmsted, Jr., and Harland Bartholomew were largely ignored, as were many suggested restrictions of subdivision layouts and regional land-use zones.[22] The metropolitan regional plan was put forward as an ideal in the 1920s, but regional master plans that integrated municipal plans into a greater whole almost never experienced the popular success and political empowerment that municipal zoning schemes enjoyed.

For other planners in the 1920s, the "regional plan" referred to a regional park and parkway plan. In the 1890s, Charles Eliot's Metropolitan Park Commission had been one of the first regional planning agencies of any kind; it followed on the heels of a regional sewer commission that had been formed for suburban Boston just two years earlier. By the 1920s, many regional park commissions (which were often county agencies) acted in this sense as special-function planning authorities. Although coordinated with reservoir, highway, and sewer construction, county park commissions planned only one dimension of regional development: local parks, regional reservations, and non-commercial parkways. This made these suburban county park commissions, which were among the most productive regional planning entities of the 1920s, the direct heirs of the planning functions now relinquished by most municipal park commissions. County park systems often connected to earlier municipal park systems, extending them into the larger metropolitan area. Regional park planning affected land values and the development of new residential districts in more distant suburbs much as 19th-century municipal park and parkways had influenced suburban patterns closer to the central city. Regional parks and parkways, in fact, often remained at the heart of many of the more comprehensive regional plans assembled during the 1920s. Some of the most salient (and successful) proposals of the New York regional plan outlined extensive systems of automotive parkways, scenic reservations, and other parks throughout the New York metropolitan area. It would have been difficult for the New York regional planners not to make such proposals, since suburban Westchester County was already building a very successful system of automotive parkways and regional parks to the north of the city. The first of these projects, the Bronx River Parkway, was the first fully grade-separated, limited access, public highway in the world when it opened to automobile traffic in 1923. Connecting the suburban Bronx to new, more distant suburbs to the north, the parkway also immediately attracted automotive day trippers who took advantage of the fast and scenic route out of the city. By the end of the decade, the Westchester park commission had developed several parallel parkway projects, along other north-south river corridors of the county that provided natural right-of-ways to scenic reservations and beach parks that were also part of the regional park system.[23]

As the Westchester system expanded, the Long Island division of the New York State park commission began to develop a similar regional system of automotive parkways, scenic reservations, and beach parks that in this case connected eastern portions of metropolitan New York to suburban areas on Long Island. In both Westchester and Long Island, the success of regional parks and parkways depended on the fact that, after a decade-long buying spree, the New York area now experienced the greatest concentration of automobile ownership in the world. Planners such as Robert Moses, the Long Island commissioner, and

Gilmore D. Clarke, the landscape architect who designed parkways for Westchester, realized that their park systems affected not only patterns of recreation, but patterns of urban expansion. Their regional park systems opened the woods of Westchester and the beaches of Long Island to millions of grateful people who had purchased cars and now had someplace to drive them; and since the same people took advantage of automotive parkways as commuter routes, large areas were opened to new suburban development. Suburban land near new parkways rapidly accrued value, and tax assessments soared to many times their former levels (a fact emphatically reported by suburban park commissions). In the best tradition of American landscape architecture, regional park development paid for itself: increased tax revenues quickly met and exceeded the costs of acquiring and developing suburban park systems. Regional planning of this type, firmly rooted in the formal and economic precedents of municipal park and parkway planning, could not be ignored by the planners assembling the New York regional plan in the 1920s; in the course of the 1930s, the regional plan's recommendations for noncommercial automotive routes and regional parks successfully guided extensive public works development.

Still other "regional planners" in the 1920s suggested more far-reaching, even visionary schemes that extended from the metropolitan to the continental scale. This extension of landscape architectural theory had already been suggested by Henry Hubbard and Theodora Kimball in their 1917 textbook. In the bifurcated theoretical framework they describe in *An Introduction to the Study of Landscape Design*, landscape parks of all types, including regional reservations and national parks, demanded development defined by a "naturalistic," as opposed to a "formal" approach. National parks and other scenic reservations therefore remained in the realm of Fairsted School landscape architecture, a school that epitomized a conservative, essentially Reptonian, landscape architectural practice. But if the Fairsted School represented a conservative design philosophy in the 1920s, it also contained a Progressive set of aspirations for the planned development and use of all kinds of parks, including national parks. Hubbard and Kimball express these aspirations, as well. They describe federal scenic reservations as part of "one great system" that encompassed "state parks, state highways, state parkways . . . and national parks." A national park system could become, if it were properly developed, the ultimate system of scenic reservations: the final park system that would reach beyond the scope and scale of regional scenic reservations as those parks had expanded beyond 19th-century municipal park systems. In the conclusion of their textbook, the authors exhort that "the lands of the nation should be studied as to their various fitness to all the purposes to which land may serve, and then so regulated that each may best serve that purpose, economic or esthetic, to which in the general national scheme it is best fitted." The history of American park and parkway planning, then, would logically culminate in what they describe as "national planning."[24]

In this expansive description of the ultimate context for national park development, Hubbard and Kimball were once again summarizing the work of leading professionals of the day. Nolen, Olmsted, and others were already devising town plans and regional plans that blended increasingly scientific inventory and analysis with continued strong traditions of physical landscape design and scenic preservation. But no one had seized the initiative as ardently as the Boston landscape architect Warren H. Manning, who by 1919 had produced (at his own expense) the initial version of a "national plan." Manning had begun his career working for the elder Olmsted at Fairsted in the 1880s. The son of a prominent Massachusetts nurseryman, Manning had moved from horticulture, to landscape design, to city planning, in a progression that mirrored that of the profession itself. After opening his own practice in Boston in 1896, he was one of the founders both of the American Park and Outdoor Art Association and the American Society of Landscape Architects. Working for clients such as the cities of Harrisburg, Pennsylvania (where he formed a lifelong association with J. Horace McFarland), and Billerica, Massachusetts, Manning developed planning techniques based on the compilation of extensive environmental information assembled as a series of maps depicting watersheds, topography, soil types, vegetative cover, and other features.[25]

At about the time Olmsted and McFarland were lobbying for the creation of a national park bureau, Manning began to apply the same comprehensive environmental assessment techniques in "land classification studies" on a national scale. The result was his startling "national plan," which identified regions of the country "most fit" for recreational, industrial, and other uses based on analysis of population and other statistics, topography, natural transportation corridors, concentrations of natural resources, and many other factors. The goals of the plan were audacious: "A National Plan would aim to conserve values, to make prosperity dominant, and to minimize adversity by eliminating wastes and securing the best possible use of all our material, human, and aesthetic resources." Perhaps the most tangible expression of these broad goals was Manning's study for a "national park system," which represented the recreation and scenic preservation components of the overall national plan. Manning's plan linked the existing national parks along a proposed national system of "recreation ways." These noncommercial arteries also connected other future "recreation areas," primarily in mountainous and other scenic areas, to "future urban areas," where urban expansion could be expected and encouraged. Manning's national plan articulated an expansive vision of what a national park system could mean to the future development of the nation as a whole. An expanded national park system, in Manning's plan, formed an armature of preserved scenic areas and protected natural systems around which sustainable development of natural resources and the continued growth of cities could proceed.[26] Although his plan extended contemporary landscape architectural theory and practice to their ultimate scale, planning activities within the federal government in the 1930s would confirm the essential viability of Manning's "national planning" methodology. And of all Manning's proposals, the national system of parks and parkways was the dimension that would come closest to being fully realized in the next decade.

Manning published descriptions of his plan in a number of professional journals in the early 1920s. During this rich period, other "regional planners" also conceived and published national land-use planning schemes. In 1921, the Cambridge planner Benton MacKaye proposed an "Appalachian Trail" running along the ridges of the Appalachian Range from Maine to Georgia. MacKaye, trained as a forester, had worked for the Forest Service and the Department of Labor in Washington. He proposed far more than a hiking trail in 1921. The Appalachian Trail comprised a regional park corridor that would encourage outdoor recreation from New England to the Ohio Valley and all along the Eastern Piedmont: a "super-trail . . . conceived as a backbone on which to build a series of public forests, parks, and open ways."[27] A communitarian idealist, MacKaye had long felt that the future management of natural resources could be combined with the establishment of new communities of homesteaders, miners, and forest workers. His proposals for the recreational uses of the Appalachian Range sought to combine the creation of recreational, agricultural, and even industrial communities with the planned management of forested land. MacKaye hoped that farmers and industrial workers, drawn by sustainable economic opportunities, could establish new communities around the recreational trails and the healthful influences of the extended mountain park. But at the heart of the proposal lay a simple hiking trail, with group camps and other community recreation features, that would be built by volunteers. The Appalachian Trail would not only preserve the mountain scenery, but would make it a meaningful aspect of new patterns of industry, agriculture, and recreation, all rooted in daily experience and appreciation of regional landscapes.[28]

MacKaye, one of the planners and architects who loosely organized as the Regional Planning Association of America, later elaborated this basic proposal into a "philosophy of regional planning." He suggested that corridors of "primeval landscapes" dedicated primarily to recreational purposes could provide frameworks for the expansion of ideal communities and industries in Appalachia and other regions of the country. In his 1928 book, *The New Exploration*, MacKaye suggests a social organization based in the sustainable development of natural resources, and the integration of outdoor recreation into daily patterns of life. He deplores the unplanned growth of cities, or "metropolitanization," as an invasive urban sprawl that destroys the regional character of landscapes and social organizations. This sprawl is described as an organic force, with ebb and flow, susceptible to channelling, damming, and diversion through the construction of "levees," or corridors of land devoted to public recreation. These "open ways" would engender an appreciation for regional beauty and natural resources, and would also "control the metropolitan invasion" and preserve the "indigenous environment" from the "exotic intrusion" of the "metropolitan flow." Properly channelled, this flow would lead to independent "indigenous" communities, not sprawling "metropolitan" suburbs. Such control would also preserve the true urban character of existing cities by limiting their endless expansion and subsequent loss of character. If the great flood of urbanization could be harnessed and dammed, MacKaye felt the "indigenous landscape" of existing "rural, urban, and primeval" landscape uses, patterns, and characteristics would be preserved.[29]

But again, what might be construed as a national park system composed the heart of this expansive vision of planned communities and preserved environments; MacKaye relied on regional and interregional corridor parks (his "levees" or "open ways") to preserve regional landscapes. MacKaye's Appalachian Trail, in fact, was one of several Appalachian national park proposals advocated in the early 1920s. Since 1911, Congress had authorized the purchase of land for the creation of national forests in the East, and by 1920 over two million acres of cutover land had been acquired, mostly in the Appalachians.[30] Since at least 1919, Mather had been interested in creating national parks in the East as well, although (as in the case of the national forests) this would require purchasing vast tracts of privately owned land. In 1924 Mather formed a Southern Appalachian National Park Commission to investigate and recommend areas that expressed in "the highest terms, the particular class or kind of exhibit which they represent," and which would therefore meet national park scenic and scientific standards.[31] As a result of the usual boosting by local park advocates and official prodding from the Park Service, Congress authorized Great Smoky Mountains, Mammoth Cave, and Shenandoah national parks in 1926. The parks were to be established through donations of land, however, which left it to the states and private individuals to actually acquire the property. John D. Rockefeller, Jr., donated five million dollars to the creation of Great Smoky Mountains National Park, in one of his largest gifts to the national park system.[32] It would be hard to imagine a greater contrast, however, from MacKaye's "indigenous landscape" of socialistic agricultural and industrial communities, since the inhabitants of the existing mountain communities within the new parks were bought out and evicted in the 1930s. Although the Park Service maintained some particularly scenic agricultural landscapes in Great Smoky Mountains, generally parkland was allowed to succeed back to a condition that approximated (it was hoped) the presettlement wilderness conditions considered appropriate for national park scenery.

There were, nevertheless, many ways in which the theory and practice of contemporary regional planners of the early 1920s related directly to the master planning process developed by Thomas Vint and his staff in San Francisco. The national park system itself can be seen as an early initiative in national planning. Just as municipal park and parkway systems prefigured more comprehensive city planning, the creation of regional scenic reservations and national parks in the late 19th century had suggested beginnings for planning at a national scale. The activities of the National Park Service after 1917 furthered this national planning project; Mather's Park-to-Park Highway and the expanded national park system constituted an interregional park system that profoundly affected land uses and economic development in the western states, and by 1929 in Appalachia as well. Vint's task of master planning for the national park system was inescapably linked to developments in the contemporary theory of regional planning. Even if planners such as Manning and MacKaye seemed visionary and idealistic in the early 1920s, their work, and that of their regional planning colleagues, would directly influence the development of a new kind of regional planning that was specifically adapted to the needs of the Park Service.

But the theory and techniques of contemporary regional planners were not immediately employed at the Park Service. Once he was established in the San Francisco field headquarters in 1927, Vint had to struggle to implement comprehensive planning procedures for the national parks. If contemporary planners wanted to coordinate land-use regulations, highway networks, and utility planning for a number of municipalities, Vint's general planning process for national parks also attempted to integrate the development of park villages, circulation systems, utilities, and all other aspects of planned development throughout a particular park, which itself made up an entire region. But bringing together various policies and goals for park management into a single, comprehensive plan took time and generated debate. The master planning process above all needed to be a means to reach consensus among groups whose interests did not always coincide. As Vint observed, the master plan was "the counterpart of the city plan; everyone wants to get in the act, [and] the procedure calls for how they get in and out."[33]

The institution of specialized regional planning techniques for park master plans soon encountered difficulties within the Park Service analogous to the opposition regional planning encountered throughout the country in the 1920s. Mather and Albright, for example, had decided to put chief engineer Frank Kittredge in charge of the San Francisco field headquarters. The activities of the combined offices were reported as "engineering accomplishments" and Kittredge was considered the lead professional, in part because his former colleagues at the Bureau of Public Roads administered the vast majority of park construction money. Albright, who had done so much to advance the park road construction program, was at first pleased with the arrangement, and felt that at last the Park Service had "a field office that is doing things, and has the full confidence and cooperation of the superintendents." Writing to Mather during an inspection of the new San Francisco offices in 1927, Albright gushed with admiration for Kittredge, who had "taken hold of our problems" and understood how to handle the Bureau of Public Roads. At the same time Albright seemed honestly perplexed with "some difficulty" he was having "with the landscape boys." Albright complained that Vint was "hard to keep organized," and when "Kittredge and I determined to organize him . . . we got charged with trying to subordinate the landscape division and trying to destroy its identity."[34] Vint had reason for concern; under Albright's influence park road planning clearly threatened to overwhelm the general park planning process, just as arterial highway engineering had begun to dominate metropolitan regional planning in the 1920s. Vint soon articulated his difficulties, directly questioning Albright about whether national park planning should proceed "on a landscape or an engineering basis."

In the meantime, Albright had pressing reasons to reinforce Kittredge's authority within the Park Service. Construction supervision, for example, would need to be more vigorous; the failure to adequately supervise the landscape preservation clauses of the Going-to-the-Sun Road construction contracts could not be repeated. Early in 1927 Albright expressed a number of other concerns regarding Bureau of Public Roads activities in parks, most of which recalled his original misgivings about entering into the interbureau agreement. Albright knew that the Bureau of Public Roads engineers did not always cooperate or communicate with Park Service officials while supervising park road construction. Albright also felt that the roads bureau personnel ran up high overhead costs, made excessive use of contract motor vehicles, and in general were unaccountable while working in the parks. In some cases, such as the Big Oak Flat Road in Yosemite, Albright complained that the engineers had insisted on overly demanding standards; by minimizing grades and straightening curves, they greatly increased cuts and fills (and costs) and prevented the road from conforming more closely to existing topography. Albright wanted the Bureau of Public Roads brought to heel, and "who else is better qualified to do this," he asked Mather, "than F. A. Kittredge, who has been the technical advisor and aid to Dr. Hewes on park plans for several years." By the end of the year, Albright had hired Kittredge away from the Bureau of Public Roads and was drafting a revision of the interbureau memorandum of agreement to give his new chief engineer "definite status" in the cooperative road building arrangements. The revision to the interbureau memorandum was simple enough: the title of "landscape engineer" was to be replaced throughout the document with that of "chief engineer." Other changes clarified and strengthened the role of the new chief engineer in review and approval processes.[35]

Continuing to plead the case for better Park Service control of park road construction, Stephen Mather presented a paper on "Engineering Applied to National Parks" to the American Society of Civil Engineers at their annual conference the next January. Observing that nine million dollars of the projected fifty-one million dollars for road construction had already been spent, Mather insisted that the Park Service and the Bureau of Public Roads had a "splendid working agreement." But he also insisted that certain policies for park roads would be adhered to: "Rigid standards calling for railroad cuts must give way to rolling grades; straight alignments must be sacrificed for graceful curves," and contractors "must be watched to see that they comply" with contract provisions preventing indiscriminate blasting and "sidecasting" of debris down steep slopes.[36] Throughout 1927 and 1928, the interbureau agreement with the Bureau of Public Roads continued to develop, and Mather and Albright felt that Kittredge's enhanced status as "chief engineer" of the Park Service was essential to the successful outcome of the collaborative effort. Thomas Vint therefore had to bide his time, apparently at least somewhat disturbed that park road planning would be pursued independently of the comprehensive plans he had been charged with producing.

Vint was busy, in any case, assembling his staff and clarifying office procedures during what was an extremely busy period for the Park Service. Visitation had continued to grow at an even faster pace, and the immediate reaction was to continue to press for more road appropriations. "Despite excellent progress made under the road budget act," Mather and Albright reported in 1927, "motor travel to the parks has increased so tremendously . . . that it will be difficult to accommodate this heavier traffic unless larger appropriations are made available."[37] Tourists in cars overwhelmed parks wherever improved federal-aid state highways and national forest approach roads to the parks were built. After the All-Year Highway to Yosemite opened in 1926, the annual number of visitors approached 500,000; on one day during Memorial Day Weekend in 1927, the crowd in the valley was estimated at 25,000. Asphalt paving for the valley's roads was completed that summer to handle the dense traffic. Yellowstone, Mount Rainier, and Rocky Mountain all reported over 200,000 visitors that year, a number that Grand Canyon approached by the end of the decade. The total number of motor vehicles entering the parks jumped from 315,000 in 1924 to almost 690,000 in 1929. Although Congress had just doubled the annual road budget authorization for the Park Service, doubled it again to five million dollars for fiscal year 1929.[38] As Vint organized his San Francisco office, keeping up with this progress meant that "the duties of the landscape division were greatly increased . . . giving advice as to the location of roads now under construction so as to least affect the major scenic features of the park," as well as "harmonizing . . . bridges and culverts with the landscape."[39]

Although the landscape division was barely keeping up with the Bureau of Public Roads during Vint's early years as chief landscape architect, he and his designers refined other aspects of their design work for national park development at this time. In 1927 and 1928, for example, Vint's office designed administration buildings for Mount Rainier and Grand Canyon national parks. Vint's Grand Canyon administration building, already described, was one of the finest Park Service Rustic structures yet produced when it opened in 1929. At Mount Rainier, where Ernest Davidson was now assigned as resident landscape architect during the summers, the new administration building was designed as the heart of the Longmire Village administrative area. The simple rectangular plan, with stone veneer on the first story and half-log wood siding above, recalled Myron Hunt's Yosemite administration building. At Mount Rainier, however, the masonry veneer was made up of the massive round boulders typical of glacial outwash; the log siding and porch columns also evoked the building's context on the forested southern slopes of the mountain.[40] When it opened in 1928, the Longmire administration building clearly demonstrated that the Park Service landscape division, among its other responsibilities, would continue to produce the refined architectural designs that it had under Daniel Hull. In 1929, when Horace Albright first saw the Longmire administration building, he described it as "the finest building that we have yet constructed with National Park funds," adding that he knew "Assistant Landscape Architect Davidson [was] entitled to much credit" for the high quality of design and construction in the park generally.[41]

Like many regional planners of the day, however, Thomas Vint was aware that good town planning and architectural design at the local level would be worth little if not done within the context of a sound plan for regional land use. Park villages, administration buildings, roads, and bridges would not "harmonize" with their surroundings unless drawn together in a comprehensive plan that clearly defined the overall goals and desirable limits for park development. Above all, the need to limit the construction of roads (and therefore to preserve "wilderness") catalyzed the comprehensive planning process. In his 1928 address to the American Society of Civil Engineers, Mather had again asserted (as he had for years now) that the parks "would not be gridironed with roads." Albright, in his initial description of the comprehensive plans he wanted drawn up for all the parks, had asked the superintendents to begin by determining "the areas in the parks that are not to be developed at all." Thomas Vint later recounted that "when we first developed the Master Plan, the subject that received the most attention was that of the wilderness area."[42] Although the definition of "wilderness" within what was already a national park would be debated for years, above all the designation implied one condition: that the area would forever remain roadless.

By the late 1920s, the danger of overdeveloping parks with road construction had become very real. As automobiles poured into parks from improved state highways, the public demand for better park roads was intense. Tremendous funds were now available, and the Bureau of Public Roads, although cooperative, still had its own personnel and procedures that were not always easy to control. Maintaining wilderness in national parks became a question of developing firm, comprehensive plans that clearly delineated all aspects of park development (especially road construction) as confluent parts of a unified park design, not as isolated elements of a system-wide road construction "program." As Vint would soon put it in a challenge to Horace Albright, the national parks would either be developed on a "landscape or an engineering basis." Eventually the master plan, as Vint was to define it, elaborated and systematized the basic design policies for how national parks would be developed as 20th-century landscape parks. But Vint's procedures for master planning would not be officially instituted at the Park Service until events had progressed far enough to make the necessity of such comprehensive plans clear. This occurred in the late 1920s, as the "second program" of road construction progressed; and the place where it occurred, above all, was Mount Rainier National Park, a smaller park for which a particularly ambitious motor road system had been planned and was under construction.

The Nisqually (or
Government) Road, Mount
Rainier National Park, as it
appeared in the 1920s.
The photograph is by
Asahel Curtis, an
accomplished
photographer,
conservationist, and
longtime advocate of
Mount Rainier National
Park. When the Seattle-
Tacoma Rainier National
Park Advisory Board was
formed in 1912 by local
boosters and businessmen,
the group chose Curtis as
its chairman.

Mount Rainier was the fifth national park when it was created in 1899. Visible from the inland Columbia Basin as well as Puget Sound, the volcanic peak had awed Native American and European explorer alike. As American settlers arrived in numbers in the 1850s, the mountain assumed great significance for them as well. The difficult crossing of the Cascade Range was first made by the emigrants at Naches Pass, a route that brought them within close proximity of Mount Rainier. Once established in the Washington Territory, the new residents continued to be fascinated by the mountain, which remained a dramatic backdrop for the communities they established. With the arrival of the Northern Pacific Railroad in the 1870s and 1880s, Tacoma and Seattle rapidly grew into major cities. At the same time, logging and mining activities opened easier access to the forests and mountains of the interior. At 14,410 feet, Mount Rainier towered over the surrounding Cascade Range and soon proved an irresistible lure for mountaineers, tourists, and resort entrepreneurs. Drawn by the awesome scenery and beautiful subalpine "parks" to be found on its slopes, the people of Washington soon made Mount Rainier the regional cynosure of outdoor recreation and scenic preservation.[43]

The Carbon River region and Spray Park on the mountain's northwestern slopes drew the first tourists. This rugged region also attracted the attention of Northern Pacific executives, who were always on the lookout for resort destinations along their lines. In the 1870s, a spur line had been built from Tacoma to the lucrative coal deposits northwest of

Mount Rainier; by the 1880s tourists were being guided from the railhead at Wilkeson into the spectacular wilderness of the Carbon River drainage. It was soon apparent, however, that the center of Mount Rainier tourism would gravitate to the mountain's southern slope, in part because of an easier ascent to the summit from the south. Mount Rainier fascinated and enticed early mountaineers as no other summit in the Northwest. Unsuccessful attempts to make the arduous climb had already been made in the 1850s, and in 1870 two groups of climbers reached the summit by variations of the Gibraltar route on the mountain's southern side.[44] In 1883, this route was traced again by a group that included James Longmire, a local homesteader and mountain guide, who had also led the two 1870 expeditions as far as the base of the mountain. Returning from the group's successful ascent of the mountain in 1883, Longmire happened upon the mineral springs on the banks of the Nisqually River that today bear his name.

Longmire knew that the attractions of the mountain would only increase with time, and he hoped that the mineral springs could become the center of a future resort. In 1884 Longmire built the first permanent buildings in what would become the Longmire Village area of Mount Rainier National Park. By the next year he was guiding tourists to his springs and boarding them in a rudimentary hotel. Longmire located a mineral claim on the site of the springs, and with the help of his sons he expanded his operation over the next decade. He had cleared a crude wagon road from Ashford to his hotel, and his sons also extended a pack trail up to a scenic subalpine park they called Paradise. This high plateau featured spectacular views and wildflower displays, and it served as a logical camp for mountaineers bound for the summit. By the time James Longmire died in 1897, the family establishment included a two-story hotel as well as numerous cabins and outbuildings on twenty acres of private land around the mineral springs. The small resorts of Longmire Springs and Paradise had become the centers of early tourism to the region.[45]

By this time, Mount Rainier also concerned scenic preservationists who were anxious to prevent grazing and logging in the high valleys and on the forested slopes of the mountain. Visitors to the southern side of the mountain increased in number, and the wagon road from Tacoma to Ashford began seeing considerable tourist traffic. As the region became more accessible to tourists, advocates for the preservation of the mountain grew in number. But the area was becoming more accessible to miners and loggers as well, and other forms of potential economic development competed with the relatively benign exploitation of tourism. The threat of impending logging activity that would destroy the forests on the slopes of the mountain caused particular concern. John Muir climbed the mountain in 1888 and the famous naturalist, joined by local park advocates from Tacoma and Seattle, soon clamored for some kind of protection for Mount Rainier. After the passage of the Forest Reserve Act in 1891, the Department of the Interior responded by sending an inspector, Cyrus A. Mosier, to investigate the desirability of establishing a forest reserve around the mountain. Mosier made an impassioned and apparently effective plea to create a forest reserve around Mount Rainier in order to preempt logging in the vicinity, which he felt threatened to "tear the frame from this grand painting against the sky."[46] Benjamin Harrison subsequently declared the Pacific Forest Reserve, which encompassed Mount Rainier, in 1893, the same year he declared the Cascade and Sierra forest reserves.

The creation of vast forest reserves may have seemed at first to answer the call for scenic preservation. The grand scenery of Mount Rainier had clearly influenced the decision to create the Pacific Forest Reserve, and the reserve was to remain, like the national parks, under the jurisdiction of the Department of the Interior. But this success in 1893 only encouraged national park advocates to achieve more comprehensive protection for Mount Rainier through national park legislation. The park movement was led, as usual, by politicians, civic boosters, and scenic preservationists who recognized the economic potential (as well as other reasons) for preserving spectacular scenery. In 1893, the Seattle Chamber of Commerce and Senator Watson C. Squire petitioned Congress to establish a national park around the mountain (out of the forest reserve territory) and other groups soon pressed for preservation as well. The Geological Society of America, the Sierra Club, the National Geographic Society, the Appalachian Mountain Club, and the American Association for the Advancement of Science jointly memorialized Congress in 1894 in favor of a national park.[47] Park legislation proved difficult to pass, however, and when it finally succeeded in 1899 the park boundaries had been reduced in order to exclude valuable timber lands. The park act also did not preclude further mining claims, and the Northern Pacific had been bought off through a provision that allowed the railroad to swap less accessible land within the park for far more valuable forested tracts elsewhere. Neither had Congress made a commitment to fund the new park; on the contrary, the Washington delegation had to promise Speaker of the House Joseph Cannon that they would never seek appropriations for the park as long as he remained in Congress.[48]

Progress in developing the park was correspondingly slow. No park administration at all existed until 1902, when Secretary Hitchcock directed the forest supervisor for the state of Washington, Grenville F. Allen, to assume responsibility for the management of the national park. Since Allen would have been in charge of the area if it had remained a forest reserve, this was hardly a step forward. Beginning in 1903, a few rangers were available to patrol particular areas of the park, but they had little hope of consistently enforcing regulations that Allen promulgated that year regarding hunting, fishing, grazing, vandalism, and the operation of businesses within park boundaries. Allen reported about three hundred visitors in 1903, most of whom boarded at the hotel in Longmire Springs and also at an establishment of eight tent cabins in Paradise Park run by another operator through a lease arrangement. A number of mineral claims continued to be entered, although most were not validated by legitimate mining operations. Allen still lacked an adequate survey of park boundaries and an adequate ranger force to enforce regulations.[49]

Interest in the mountain and its surrounding wilderness continued to grow. Congress finally had made an appropriation for the construction of a park road, and a survey for the route had begun in 1903 under the direction of the Army Corps of Engineers. After considering other routes into the park, the engineers decided the new road should follow the wagon road and trail that the Longmires had established between Ashford (just outside the park boundary) up the Nisqually River to Longmire Springs and continuing up to the wildflower meadows of Paradise. The decision permanently reinforced these sites as the primary destinations for most tourists visiting the mountain. The assistant engineer in charge, Eugene V. Ricksecker, started the survey working up from Longmire, since the existing six-mile wagon road from the park boundary to Longmire was considered at least serviceable. From Longmire the survey followed the established trail up to what was then the snout of the Nisqually Glacier, past Narada Falls, to the tent hotel located on the plateau of Paradise Park. Clearing and grading for the new "Government Road" began in 1904; but work soon encountered the difficulties presented by short seasons, rough terrain, and scarce labor.[50] The same summer, the Tacoma and Eastern Railroad opened between Tacoma and Ashford, and the spur line brought over five hundred tourists to Mount Rainier before the end of the season. In addition to the hotels at Longmire and Paradise, seasonal tourist establishments began to appear at the park's southern boundary near Ashford. By the next year, the number of visitors to the park approached one thousand and the Tacoma and Eastern Railroad began construction of its own hotel at Longmire through a lease arrangement with the Department of the Interior. The hotel, later known as the National Park Inn, opened in 1906.[51]

The same year, Allen advised that "upon completion of the Government road it is probable that there will be a desire to take automobiles into the park." Mount Rainier was destined to become a popular destination for the machines, although at this point Allen felt the conveyances represented "a great annoyance" and even "some danger."[52] In the meantime, the construction of the Government Road continued, although with considerable difficulties. The first contractor defaulted in 1906, and construction continued through the direct supervision of hired labor. At this time, Hiram Chittenden, the engineer of the Yellowstone road system, was nominally the senior officer in charge of Mount Rainier road construction. He visited the park that year and described the existing wagon road between Ashford and Longmire as the worst he had ever traveled. Ricksecker subsequently adjusted priorities and improvements were begun on this lower portion of the road. By 1908, construction of the Government Road had reached Nisqually Glacier, making it the first American road to reach a glacier. Over 2,600 people entered the park that year, and 117 permits were issued for automobiles, which were subject to the usual long list of regulations restricting hours of operation and speeds.[53] By 1910, the road was complete as far as

Paradise Valley, although it had not opened to the public that far. Acting Superintendent Allen praised Ricksecker's work locating the route and supervising construction. The engineer had been "particular to see that the road passed all points of interest," while maintaining a four percent maximum grade throughout the twenty-five miles from the park boundary to Paradise. Allen felt that "a very creditable piece of engineering" had resulted in "one of the finest scenic roads in America."[54]

Nevertheless, the road apparently remained rough and poorly drained in places. In 1911, William Howard Taft visited the park and the presidential party was invited to become the first to make the trip all the way to Paradise Valley by motor vehicle. The President's touring car became hopelessly bogged down between the Nisqually Glacier and Paradise, although it did complete the trip with the help of a mule team. The same year, an entrance arch built of "heavy cedar logs" was constructed at the beginning of the Government Road at the park's boundary. Measuring twenty-two feet wide and twenty-four feet high, the massive post and beam span bore the name of the park cut and burned into a three-foot-diameter log hung from the top beam by chains. The massive entrance arch symbolized a turning point in the administration of the park that had occurred by 1911. That year a permanent superintendent, Edward S. Hall, was finally appointed for Mount Rainier; during the next few years budgets increased significantly. Over ten thousand visitors arrived at the park in 1911, and over half of them were in automobiles that took advantage of the new Government Road. Responding to the influx, Superintendent Hall outlined an extensive list of requirements for improved park administration, stressing the need for more trail construction and the necessity of sanitary improvements at Longmire, where two hotels now disposed of sewage and refuse directly into the Nisqually River. A new set of preservation concerns were becoming evident as Mount Rainier became, with Yellowstone and Yosemite, one of the nation's most popular national parks.[55]

As visitation soared, the park's constituency grew stronger. In 1912 a number of civic groups, including commercial clubs and chambers of commerce from both Seattle and Tacoma, jointly formed the Seattle-Tacoma Rainier National Park Advisory Board. The committee represented the continued interest of local boosters and businessmen in plans for Mount Rainier, especially in the planned development of motor roads both to the park and in the park itself. The group chose the photographer and conservationist Asahel Curtis as its chairman. Seattle resident and former Secretary of the Interior Richard Ballinger was also a member of the board, and the group subsequently took up the campaign (which Ballinger had begun the year before) to create a national park bureau within the Department of the Interior. The Rainier National Park Advisory Board was also the group that in 1912 sent Samuel Lancaster to Washington, DC, where the road engineer fruitlessly lobbied for a $100,000 appropriation for the development of roads at Mount Rainier. The board also pressed the Forest Service to improve the three miles of road directly outside the national park that ran through the adjacent national forest. The disastrous condition of this short approach road continued to frustrate park advocates for years.[56]

Approach roads to Mount Rainier concerned a number of good roads groups at this time. The improvement of the entire Mountain Highway, as the route between Tacoma and Ashford became known, had first been urged by James Longmire, who had originally blazed the trail from his homestead on the Yelm Prairie to Mount Rainier. Longmire could not interest Pierce County in the project, however, and in the 1890s he improved portions of the route at his own expense. The pressure to improve the Mountain Highway soon increased because of the efforts of the Washington State Good Roads Association, bicycle enthusiasts, and other groups. By 1909, the State of Washington had taken an active interest in improving roads by assuming maintenance responsibilities from the counties. Three years later portions of the Mountain Highway were being relocated and regraded; in 1913 the route was listed as a "primary state highway," called National Park Highway. By 1917, portions of the route were being paved, and the highway was functioning as a major automotive approach route to Mount Rainier from Puget Sound. That year, Mount Rainier recorded as many visitors as Yosemite and Yellowstone, although the park, at 324 square miles, was a fraction of the size of those older parks.[57]

Plans for a more extensive road system within the park itself had also been proposed in various forms for a number of years. The first topographic map of the park was compiled by assistant engineer Ricksecker and published in Grenville Allen's 1904 annual report. The map, with five hundred-foot contour intervals, showed the Government Road (then under construction) all the way to the summit roughly along the Gibraltar route. Also shown was an extensive "proposed graded trail" encircling Mount Rainier, which was connected to park entrances at the four corners of the park by spur roads. Hiram Chittenden is credited as the first to suggest this "round-the-mountain" road.[58] Like the Grand Loop that Chittenden had recently completed at Yellowstone, the proposed circuit drive for Mount Rainier would have maximized the potential for driving (whether in carriages or in early motor vehicles) and seeing as much of the park as possible from a well-graded road. Eugene Ricksecker apparently was enthusiastic about the plan for a road around the mountain as well, as were many of the members of the Rainier National Park Advisory Board. In 1911, an illustrated tourist guide to Mount Rainier was published, one of the finest guides yet to appear for any national park. The author, John H. Williams, suggested that since the Government Road had been completed to Paradise the year before, the next step "in opening the National Park to public use should be the carrying out of Mr. Ricksecker's fine plan for a road around the Mountain." Williams published Ricksecker's revised map of the park, which showed the assistant engineer's proposed road as a dashed line. The route connected with the Government Road at Christine Falls and worked its way around to access as many of the "great parks" on the mountain's slopes as possible. The route also reached the "snout of each glacier . . . in turn" before returning to the existing road near Mazama Ridge. In 1913, preliminary surveys were made for a complete circuit, which was to circumscribe the mountain in an 80- to 100-mile irregular loop just below the glacier line.[59]

Although the "round-the-mountain" road would never be built as such, trail construction did intensify during these years, partly as a result of surveying and planning for a more elaborate park road system. Local mountaineering groups, especially The Mountaineers (first organized in 1906) also pressed for a comprehensive system of trails connecting the still remote corners of the park. Between 1911 and 1913, members of The Mountaineers hiked around the mountain investigating routes and establishing a series of backcountry camps. Under Superintendent Hall and his successor, Ethan Allen, budgets increased from three thousand dollars in 1911 to an average of almost fifteen thousand dollars annually for 1913 through 1915. Much of these funds were spent improving and enlarging the trail system, and in 1915 the park's new superintendent, DeWitt L. Reaburn, was able to report that 150 miles of park trails completely encircled the mountain. That summer, The Mountaineers organized an outing in which one hundred of their members made the trip around the mountain in twenty-two days. In 1916, just before the Park Service began operations, Reaburn reported that two hundred miles of trails had been completed, including the over ninety-mile Wonderland Trail, which roughly followed the route around the mountain that had been proposed ten years earlier as a road, and which The Mountaineers had blazed as a trail by 1915.[60] Proposals and surveys for automotive routes around the mountain, however, were not forgotten, and would continue to be put forward over the next decade.

The period just before the establishment of the Park Service was a busy one for Mount Rainier, in part because Stephen Mather had arrived at the Department of the Interior. In 1905, Stephen Mather, then still a Chicago businessman, climbed Mount Rainier with a Sierra Club expedition; his experience contributed to a lifelong passion for mountaineering and augmented his personal concern for the fate of the national parks. Mather became close friends with Asahel Curtis, who was also on the 1905 Sierra Club climb. In 1915, Mather and the Rainier National Park Advisory Board held many similar views about the direction park management should take at Mount Rainier. Dissatisfaction with the park's concessioners, for example, was widespread; although the park was beginning to enjoy a constituency as great as any national park, Mount Rainier still had limited overnight accommodations and no outstanding, first-class lodge. The situation among the many park concessioners at Mount Rainier had also grown quite hectic by that time. Superintendent Reaburn issued forty-two special-use permits that year, mostly to individual operators seeking to open small businesses catering to tourists. The same year, the Longmire family sold its tourist establishment to the Longmire Springs Hotel Company, a new group that then began construction of another hotel at Longmire Springs.

After his arrival at the Department of the Interior, Mather acted quickly in the case of Mount Rainier. Taking advantage of his connections in Tacoma and Seattle, he encouraged local park advocates and businessmen to form a publicly held corporation that could become the unified concessioner for the park. Mather also removed restrictions on automobiles, opening the Government Road to automobile traffic all the way to Paradise Valley, greatly increasing the potential for hotel development in that scenic, subalpine area. In 1916, the Rainier National Park Company (a separate organization from the Rainier National Park Advisory Board) was capitalized by the sale of $200,000 of stock to park supporters and other investors. The Department of the Interior arranged to grant the new company an exclusive park concession with the understanding that it would immediately start construction on a large hotel on the plateau of Paradise Park. In 1917, the Paradise Inn was completed according to plans provided by the Tacoma architects, Heath, Grove and Bell. The two-and-a-half-story lodge featured huge, steeply pitched, shingled roofs with a series of intersecting gables. The log frame construction employed Alaskan cedar from a nearby area in the park called the "silver forest," which had been burnt over in the 1880s leaving standing dead trees which had weathered to a silver gray. The stone for the foundation was quarried locally as well. Furnished with handcrafted wooden furniture and wrought-iron details, the luxurious inn was everything that Mather and the Rainier National Park Advisory Board could have wished. Over the next few years, the Rainier National Park Company took over the hotels at Longmire Springs and other businesses to become the park's sole concessioner.[61]

By 1917, the struggle to create the park, strengthen its legislation, and unify its management had largely succeeded. In 1908, for example, the park's legislation had been altered to prevent further mining claims.[62] The Government Road had been completed in 1910, and by 1915 it was open to cars from the park boundary all the way to Paradise. Soon state highway approaches (and the troublesome national forest road outside the park entrance) had been improved as well. The reorganization of park concessions had resulted in better control over private enterprise in the park. And the same year the Paradise Inn opened, the Park Service had been funded, a bureaucratic success which would help secure more generous budgets to patrol Mount Rainier, maintain its trails, and plan further improvements. By 1918, the Government Road (now called the Nisqually Road) had already undergone its first reconstruction, including the addition of "very attractive rustic bridges" over Tahoma and Kautz creeks. Over six thousand automobiles entered the park on the Nisqually Road that year, and Horace Albright felt that "there was every reason to expect automobile traffic will continue to increase by leaps and bounds." Mather felt the "future was bright" for Mount Rainier, where events so far had been "an object lesson that should guide the improvement of many other parks." Indeed, the park's budget was more than doubled in 1918 (to seventy-five thousand dollars), a tangible indication of political as well as popular success.[63]

During his brief tenure with the Park Service, the landscape architect Charles Punchard visited Mount Rainier several times. Although Punchard was able to make only limited observations and recommendations, this was a busy time for the development of both Paradise and Longmire Springs. Punchard felt the acquisition of the Longmire facilities by the Rainier National Park Company "cleared up one of the most unsatisfactory conditions in the park." The landscape architect was especially concerned with the wet meadow around which several mineral springs bubbled, and he hoped that the meadow would now be "improved in such a manner that the village of Longmire Springs will be an attractive one." The next year, the new superintendent, Roger W. Toll, dismantled and burned the "unsightly and utterly useless" Longmire Hotel that had been built in the 1880s. The new hotel, begun in 1915, (called the National Park Inn Annex) was moved across the road, away from the mineral springs and the older National Park Inn (1906).[64] Punchard also recommended that the mineral springs be "walled up or confined in a neat, orderly way, and made more inviting." By 1920, the stone work enclosing the soda and iron springs had been completed by the Rainier National Park Company, presumably according to plans approved by Punchard; these enclosures remain today. That year he also laid out an "industrial group," or utility area, for the village at Longmire, and felt that "further concern" regarding the impact of tourism on the wet meadow and its surrounding mineral springs "had been removed."

More construction was underway in Paradise as well in 1920. A large annex was added to the Paradise Inn, and a power plant for the hotel, a guide house, and an administration building were built nearby. The combined cost of this construction totaled twice that of the original hotel. Campgrounds had also been established near the Nisqually entrance, at Longmire Springs, and at Paradise. Punchard had overseen the installation of rudimentary water and sewer systems at the new campgrounds that served growing numbers of campers who arrived in cars.[65]

In 1921, the first Park Service road construction projects got underway under the guidance of engineer George Goodwin and landscape architect Daniel Hull. Besides Going-to-the-Sun Road, two other projects were begun that year: the Generals Highway in Sequoia National Park and the Carbon River Road at Mount Rainier. The interest in potential tourism to the Carbon River region of Mount Rainier had been rekindled by the completion of a rail spur from Enumclaw to Fairfax, just outside the northwest corner of the park. By 1917, a reconnaissance survey and plans were prepared for the construction of a road from the Fairfax railhead up the Carbon River to the snout of the Carbon Glacier. Because of the rail connection (and a new state highway that was planned to parallel the tracks and extend to the park entrance) the Carbon River Road had the potential of opening another side of Mount Rainier to large numbers of tourists. A hotel was planned for the end of the road that would create a center for tourism near Carbon Glacier comparable to that of Paradise; the proposed hotel on the mountain's northwestern slopes, however, would be twenty to forty miles closer to the cities along Puget Sound.[66] Across the park, another state highway project was about to open up the northeastern slopes of the mountain to tourism as well. In 1916, the state of Washington approved funding to extend the McClellan Pass Highway (which would eventually cross the crest of the Cascades at the Cayuse and Chinook passes) as far as the White River entrance of the national park. Two years earlier a mining company had completed a wagon road that extended up the White River ten miles to the scenic Glacier Basin, at the foot of the massive Emmons Glacier. Once the state highway had progressed far enough, tourists with automobiles were expected to demand permission to use the mining road to reach the Glacier Basin area. In the meantime, more mineral springs had been discovered in the Ohanapecosh region, near the southeast corner of the park, and the Forest Service had already begun to allow concession development there.[67]

By 1919, all four corners of the roughly square national park had demonstrated considerable potential for tourist development. At that time, Mather, George Goodwin, and Superintendent Toll revived plans for a motor road that would encircle the mountain and connect all these points of interest in a single park road system. Goodwin pointed out to Toll that only twenty miles of road across the rugged north side of the mountain would be required to connect the proposed hotel site at Carbon Glacier with Glacier Basin. From the proposed state highway location over Cayuse Pass, less than thirty miles of new road would connect Glacier Basin to the Ohanapecosh region in the southeastern corner, and from there could extend all the way back to the Nisqually Road near Narada Falls by following Stevens Canyon across the mountain's southern slopes. That left only a connection across the west side of the mountain to complete the "round-the-mountain" road Chittenden and Ricksecker had first described. The Carbon River Road could be thought of as the first portion of that west side road, and Goodwin proposed to eventually extend it to Mowich Lake and from there south, all the way back to the Nisqually Road near the park entrance at Ashford. Mather and Albright officially described the entire scheme in 1919 as "an ideal road system of the future."[68] By 1921, the new superintendent, William H. Peters, an engineer by training, had caught the enthusiasm and argued forcefully for the construction of an extensive "highway encircling the Mountain." Sensing it would be "one of the world's most spectacular scenic highways," Peters even drew up a twelve million dollar budget for his plan of "necessary ultimate road development" in the park.[69]

In 1921, Goodwin oversaw the start of work on the Carbon River Road, a modest beginning compared to the big plans and reconnaissance surveys that had been underway. But if national park road construction presented difficulties in general during these early years, the Carbon River Road project soon degenerated into a fiasco. In 1921, contractors graded six miles of the road as far as Ipsut Creek; the next year the project met with delays. By 1923 Goodwin was afraid the contractor would default, although by the next year, two more miles had been graded, extending the road up to Cataract Creek near the snout of Carbon Glacier. That February, however, flooding damaged the new road extensively. Goodwin was required to build expensive and unattractive revetments along a road that had apparently not been well located in the first place. The connecting county road to Fairfax was completed in 1925, and a campground was opened for motorists at Ipsut Creek that summer. But that was as far as the Carbon River Road would ever progress. To this day the road terminates at a campground at Ipsut Creek, about six miles from the park entrance.[70]

Thomas Vint later claimed that at the Carbon River "we were building an impossible thing," and that Goodwin's refusal to acknowledge that fact in 1924 had been the final disagreement that caused Mather to dismiss him.[71] In any case, the experience with the Carbon River Road clearly helped Mather and Albright decide to enlist the assistance of the Bureau of Public Roads. Once the interbureau agreement was in place in 1925, the situation began to improve at Mount Rainier, as it did at Glacier National Park. But there were other forces at work at this time that spurred a broad reconsideration of elaborate road development plans like those Mather and Albright described in 1919. By 1920, a public debate had been initiated at Mount Rainier regarding the extent to which the park should be developed. This debate, which intensified in the course of the 1920s, would help transform Park Service procedures for devising general development plans limiting the extent of road construction in national parks.

Up to this point, Mather, Albright, Goodwin, and superintendents like William Peters had based their assumptions regarding the desirable limits of park development on what was essentially a 19th-century model of landscape park development. The quintessential feature of this model was the carriage drive, which wound around the park in a great loop reaching as many points of interest within the park as possible. Chittenden's Yellowstone road system (although completed in the early 20th century) was the most fully elaborated example of this type among national scenic reservations. The Yellowstone Grand Loop brought tourists to the most famous geothermal and scenic attractions in the park and connected to multiple park entrances all around its circuit by way of spur roads. But the desirability of such a complete road system was predicated on conditions of a bygone era. For Chittenden, the primary means of appreciating park scenery was assumed to be from a horse-drawn vehicle. Extensive roads were therefore planned and built, but as wagon roads they were engineered to less demanding specifications and made less physical impact than motor roads. Early national scenic reservations, like Yellowstone and Yosemite, also tended to be much larger than those set aside later. After the Forest Reserve Act of 1891, extensive national forests were declared that encompassed entire watersheds and mountain ranges. The Forest Service could subsequently argue (with power, logging, and grazing interests) that park designation should be limited to scenic features themselves; there was no reason to give park status to surrounding forests and watersheds, since those areas were often already being "conserved" as national forests. Progressive-era parks like Mount Rainier or Rocky Mountain tended to be smaller as a result. And as smaller parks they would be more thoroughly affected by a "complete" loop road system that left a relatively limited area free from the influence of such development.

Mount Rainier's proximity to urban populations was also bound to make the park a "weekend resort . . . [with] a traffic problem which we do not find in parks more remote from large centers of population," as Daniel Hull observed in 1920.[72] By that time, one thousand cars a day were winding up the Nisqually Road to Paradise Valley on summer weekends, grinding the crushed stone surface of the road into a fine powder that coated everything within two hundred feet of either side of the road. This volume of traffic was another indication of the changing dynamic behind the creation of parks in the early 20th century. Yellowstone and Glacier owed their existence to their location along transcontinental rail lines; Mount Rainier and Rocky Mountain, however, were created largely because they were within day-tripping distance for automotive tourists from Seattle, Tacoma, and Denver. When Chittenden suggested his "round-the-mountain" road for Mount Rainier, he had railroads, livery concessioners, and relatively small numbers of vacationers in mind. The reality would be thousands of private automobiles arriving every weekend, overwhelming narrow roads that had been designed for slower, lighter traffic. Motorists would inevitably demand more heavily engineered roads, requiring grading, excavation, and construction in a wider, far more visible road corridor. For all these reasons, a "complete" loop of motor roads at Mount Rainier would have had a much greater visual and environmental impact than a comparable system of carriage drives. This reality would soon dramatically alter proposed plans for the park.

Auto enthusiasts, chamber of commerce boosters, and Park Service officials were not the only groups concerned with the future development of Mount Rainier. From the beginning of its history as a national park, organized climbing clubs also influenced events there. The expanding interest in outdoor recreation—another hallmark of the early 20th century—powerfully affected the perception of how much and what kind of development would be appropriate for the park. The first notable mountaineering club in the Northwest was the Mazamas, a group that organized in 1894 in Portland. A permanent climbing club was established in Washington in 1906, when The Mountaineers organized in Seattle. Mount Rainier, of course, drew the members of The Mountaineers, and the management of the park was a subject of great concern to them. Like the Rainier National Park Advisory Board, The Mountaineers became an important voice representing an organized segment of the park's constituency. In 1916, The Mountaineers arranged to have the first shelter at Camp Muir erected, honoring the founder of the Sierra Club who had died two years earlier.[73] Other clubs, especially the Mazamas and the Sierra Club, also held "outings" to Mount Rainier, climbed to the summit, and lobbied to improve its funding and management. In 1919, Mather (a lifetime member of the Sierra Club) recognized the "help of the mountaineering clubs," which had "effectively aided in the advancement of the national parks ever since the establishment of this bureau." Mather included a directory of the mountaineering clubs, which he seemed to see as his civilian auxiliary, in the appendix of his annual report that year.[74]

But soon different groups (and different individuals within some of the same groups) began to make it clear that there were conflicting visions of what constituted appropriate development in national parks. In particular, hikers, mountaineers, and the various outdoor organizations they formed soon called into question what Mather and Albright had seen as "progress" at Mount Rainier. These outdoor enthusiasts may have arrived in parks by car, but they wanted to limit the use of automobiles once within park boundaries. After considerable debate and voicing of concerns, in 1922 The Mountaineers printed a broadside, "The Administration of National Parks," which accused the Park Service of managing Mount Rainier primarily for the benefit of the Rainier National Park Company and its paying customers, therefore betraying its obligation to serve the general public. In a rebuttal, the concessioner accused The Mountaineers of blindly opposing any form of development in the park, whether it was of public benefit or not. As the controversy escalated, it soon was revealed that The Mountaineers themselves were hardly of a single mind on the issues raised. The matter was of no small concern to Mather, however, who dreaded internecine strife among his still fragile park coalition. He ordered Roger Toll, who had moved on to become superintendent at Rocky Mountain National Park, to meet with the outdoor club early in 1923.[75] Toll took the opportunity to defend the monopoly granted to the Rainier National Park Company, despite what he admitted were shortcomings in the arrangement. Since 1917, the publicly owned concessioner had invested more money in the park than the federal government had since 1899. So far, he argued, the improvements brought about by the concessioner had justified the monopolistic arrangement. Toll asked the outdoor club to stop indulging in diatribes and produce specific proposals for improving management.[76]

Peace was restored; but The Mountaineers, the Rainier National Park Company, and the Rainier National Park Advisory Board (which usually represented the concessioner's interests) were on a collision course. The Park Service was taking up position squarely in the middle. The controversies becoming apparent at Mount Rainier, however, were hardly limited to a single park by the mid-1920s. At Yosemite, in particular, which was now the most visited park in the system, automotive tourists were flooding in, prompting critics from the Sierra Club and elsewhere to claim that the famous valley had been "spoiled" by crowds, roads, cars, and overnight accommodations. For many long-time national park advocates, the overwhelming popularity of national parks among automotive tourists demanded a fundamental reconsideration of the values and policies that were guiding the management of the parks. Mather's expert manipulation of concessioners had resulted in great improvements in park visitor services. The federal government, on its own, never would have assumed the costs of comparable facilities at this time. But these concessioners now needed to make profits and pay dividends to stockholders; the Park Service therefore was at least partially committed to accommodating their need to expand, attract customers, and promote diverse recreational uses that would encourage longer hotel stays. By mid-decade, the Park Service had won the major battles with power and logging interests; but the task of balancing the financial needs of its concessioners with the preservation of park landscape features and natural systems was just beginning.

These concerns led to the formation of the Yosemite National Park Board of Expert Advisors in 1928. That group, which included Frederick Law Olmsted, Jr., offered critical advice regarding proposed concession expansions, the modernization of the Tioga Road, and other developments that affected the already overcrowded valley.[77] Well-established concessioners, however, and the demands of the ever growing crowds of visitors in the valley, made it difficult to deny park businesses permission to expand. At Mount Rainier, as well, the Rainier National Park Company continued to make proposals to expand and diversify its operations. The concessioner also encouraged the Park Service to make planning decisions that would bring more visitors into the park. A bewildering array of new activities were promoted by the concessioner and approved by the new park superintendent, Owen A. Tomlinson. In 1925, the Rainier National Park Company hired a group of Yakima Indians to camp near the Paradise Inn and entertain tourists. In 1928, the company operated a summer camp for boys, featuring swimming and boating on Reflection Lakes. In 1931, it received permission to build and operate a nine-hole golf course in Paradise Valley, despite the ludicrously short playing season. Golfers played downhill from the Paradise Inn and returned to their starting point by bus.[78] Although all of these experiments were short-lived, winter sports were also encouraged (as they were at Yosemite) and had significant success at Mt. Ranier. Since 1912, The Mountaineers had led "winter outings" to Longmire and Paradise, and Mather felt that "as a winter resort" Mount Rainier had potential that "would make it famous" for snow sports. Already in 1920, the Northwest Ski Club held a tournament at Paradise that drew one thousand spectators. In 1923, a world record ski jump was made off of Alta Vista; by 1924, the road to Longmire was plowed all winter, and a one thousand-foot toboggan run near the village was strung with electric lights. Skiers regularly hiked from Longmire to Paradise, and later plowing was extended to Nisqually Glacier to shorten the walk. By the early 1930s regular downhill races and "winter carnivals" were held on the slopes of Paradise Park, and in 1934, the Olympic skiing trials were held there, although a motorized ski tow (from behind the guide house to the top of Alta Vista) was only built in 1937.[79]

At Paradise, as at Yosemite Valley, Park Service officials needed to allow concession operators to expand and diversify their operations in order to keep the companies, which were providing needed visitor services, financially viable. But this balancing act became increasingly difficult for Park Service officials to perform. By 1928, construction had begun on a second lodge and housekeeping cabin complex at Paradise, the Paradise Lodge, about five hundred feet southwest of the Paradise Inn. Connected by a short spur road to the Paradise parking area, the new lodge opened in 1931.[80] In 1927, the Rainier National Park Company had also started to push for the construction of a "scenic loop" motor road around Paradise. The proposed road would have extended from the Paradise Inn to Alta Vista and Panorama Point and then back via Sluiskin Falls and the Mazama Ridge, making a circuit of the entire valley. The road project eventually received the backing of Tomlinson, Albright, and the Rainier National Park Advisory Board. Others were outraged, however, and claimed that Paradise Valley was in the process of being ruined, as they felt Yosemite Valley already had been.

The controversy regarding the Paradise scenic loop road continued for years and began to call into question basic assumptions regarding the development of national parks. The debate was affected by other plans for road construction at Mount Rainier. In 1924, when Albright secured funds for the first program of park road construction, the park still had very few roads compared to other parks with similar numbers of visitors. Since the Carbon River Road had not turned out to be much of an attraction, the twenty-five-mile Nisqually Road served virtually all the vehicles that poured out of Tacoma and Seattle on summer weekends. Albright's 1924 road program made the reconstruction of Nisqually Road, which had been pulverized by the heavy traffic, a first priority. It also included funds for a survey of a forty-mile West Side Road across the western slopes of the mountain, connecting the Carbon River country to the Nisqually Road near the park's main entrance at Ashford. But the Rainier National Park Advisory Board felt betrayed; they issued their own broadside in 1925 criticizing Congress for not funding a more extensive road program for the park. The state and surrounding counties had spent some $7,500,000 on approach roads to four park entrances at the four corners of the park, but Congress had so far appropriated only $280,000 for roads within the park. The committee wanted larger appropriations so that the "system of roads" at Mount Rainier could be "completed" along the lines of the proposed route around the mountain that the Park Service had repeatedly endorsed.[81]

Once the Bureau of Public Roads assumed control of park road projects in 1925, the pace and efficiency of construction improved. The reconstruction of the Nisqually Road remained a priority, and the location survey for the West Side Road continued, and construction began on its southern end. But the Nisqually Road still terminated at Paradise, and since many of their customers arrived in private cars, the Rainier National Park Company logically felt that a scenic drive around the area would be a strong attraction. H. A. Rhodes, president of the concession company, estimated that the road would be worth fifty thousand dollars annually in increased business at Paradise.[82] In the spring of 1927, Asahel Curtis and the Rainier National Park Advisory Board strongly supported the plan for a loop drive at Paradise, stating that his committee was "deeply interested in . . . the financial success" of the concessioner, who was counted on to provide needed hotel accommodations in the park. Curtis kept plans for a "complete" road system for the park alive as well. That year at the Seattle Chamber of Commerce, he described a five million dollar program of road construction at Mount Rainier. Together with commercial clubs from the Puget Sound region, he continued to call for a road system that would encircle the mountain.[83]

By 1926, however, Park Service officials had begun to back away from such extensive road plans. Owen A. Tomlinson, who became superintendent at Mount Rainier in 1923 and remained for the next eighteen years, had begun drafting an "Outline for Park Development" (as requested by Albright in 1925) and submitted it to Mather in 1926. The following summer, Tomlinson sent the development outline to Thomas Vint at the new landscape division office in San Francisco. Vint and Tomlinson concurred that a road across the rugged north side of the mountain was unnecessary and unwise. In so doing, they effectively set aside the northern slopes of the mountain as a "wilderness area" within the park, and finally began to amend the "round-the-mountain" model that had been guiding plans for the future development of Mount Rainier since at least 1904. The 1926 development outline briefly described a six-year program of prioritized construction projects for the park. First, the superintendent called for the complete reconstruction of the Nisqually Road. Next, he asked for the completion of the forty-mile West Side Road, which would connect the Nisqually Road to the northwestern entrances to the park at Mowich Lake and Carbon River. In the northeastern corner of the park, a fourteen-mile road was proposed to connect the McClellan Pass Highway (which had reached the park boundary in 1923 and was now known as the Naches Pass Highway) to a subalpine plateau above Glacier Basin called Yakima Park. (The Yakima Park Highway project involved the reconstruction of portions of the existing White River mining road.) Tomlinson's plan also called for a road through Stevens Canyon, which would eventually cross the southern slopes of the mountain to connect Paradise and Longmire to the Ohanapecosh region.

The road construction outlined by Tomlinson constituted the most ambitious development program planned for any national park at this time. The development outline, however, treated road construction as only one aspect of the ultimate plan. Improvements to the extensive trail system in the park were carefully described. New buildings were listed and prioritized for the Longmire and Paradise developed areas. Four new developed areas were suggested: Spray Park and Sunset Park (to be reached via the proposed West Side Road), Yakima Park, and the Ohanapecosh Hot Springs area. Utility, sanitation, and fire protection were all addressed, as well, in this preliminary plan for future park needs.[84]

Nowhere in the general plan was there any mention of a scenic drive around Paradise Park. Thomas Vint, in particular, had objected to the proposal, and other Park Service officials seemed to be at least ambivalent about the idea. Albright, responding to the concessioner's request to proceed with plans for its construction, delayed any immediate decision in 1927, stating that the landscape division "was not sure the road ought to be built" and that money for such a road had not been budgeted in any case.[85] But considerable pressure in favor of the road was applied, and with Superintendent Tomlinson's blessing, the Bureau of Public Roads made a preliminary survey for the scenic loop that fall. At that point, a member of The Mountaineers, George Vanderbilt Caesar, published an article in *The Saturday Evening Post*, accusing the Park Service of "excessive road building programs in our national parks." Although he did not mention Mount Rainier by name, he clearly had it in mind: "Why . . . should the Government incur enormous expense," he asked, "to encircle the wilderness with roads?" Noting that "at least one national park in the West [Yosemite] is already spoiled to anyone with taste or appreciation," he feared the same thing seemed "bound to be repeated elsewhere." Mountaineering groups and other outdoor organizations, he continued, were ready to help counter the influence of those who regarded the parks only as "magnets to draw in the maximum tourist trade."[86]

The short article struck a nerve at the Park Service. George Horace Lorimer's magazine had always been one of the bureau's most important supporters, and the apparent shift in editorial orientation was not dismissed lightly. Albright sent the article to the San Francisco field headquarters, and included another letter that Caesar had subsequently sent to Lorimer in which the author (obviously pleased with the effect his article was having) specifically denounced the road plans for Mount Rainier as the most deplorable example of national park overdevelopment. Thomas Vint seemed to enjoy reading the letter and wrote in the margin that he wanted copies made for the entire San Francisco office. He also asked that Albright elicit Caesar's comments specifically on the scenic loop road at Paradise. "Ask him to see Mr. Rhodes," Vint suggested (referring to the president of the Rainier National Park Company) and then ask him for "a little of the help he mentions" in opposing the Paradise road. "As to circling the mountain," the landscape architect continued, "the north slope is programmed by Tomlinson and myself as a wilderness area already."[87]

If Vint felt vindicated, Superintendent Tomlinson and Chief Engineer Frank Kittredge were much more on the defensive. They began drafting suggested responses defending their position and defending "park development" in general. They asked that either Albright or Asahel Curtis submit an article to *The Saturday Evening Post* in response to the criticism. Albright did finally draft a response in which he drew on some of the suggested points made by Tomlinson and Kittredge regarding the limited impact of the roads proposed for Mount Rainier.[88] But in his rebuttal to the criticism he had received (now from a number of sources) Albright chose to reaffirm and restate the primary and essential mandate of the Park Service: the preservation of "wilderness." In the title of his article, "The Everlasting Wilderness," he made it clear that his defense of the "second program" of park road construction underway in 1928 would not emphasize any aspect of the engineering of the roads themselves as much as it would emphasize the planning process that assured that roads did not end up where they should not be. "The present road-building program includes only a few miles of new road in many of the national parks," he clarified, since at Yellowstone and Yosemite, for example, construction concentrated on modernizing older, existing roads for automobile use. Albright saw two groups trying to affect park planning: "Those who want no roads into the parks, and who would keep them unbroken wildernesses reached only by trails . . . and those who are spokesmen for automobile clubs, chambers of commerce and other development organizations, whose appetites for road building are never appeased." The Park Service, Albright assured the magazine's readers, had "attempted to steer a course between these two extremes," making significant scenic features of a given park accessible to motorists, but keeping the vast majority of the park's total area accessible only by trail. And in all cases, "the landscape engineer is the final authority," even if "his recommendations involve long and painstaking planning and more than ordinary construction costs."[89]

This reassuring scenario, however, was being disproved by events at Mount Rainier taking place at the very time Albright's article was being published. The Rainier National Park Company, in its 1928 report, continued to insist that "the completion of a Mountain-encircling road" was only a matter of time and funding. According to the concessioner, any financial problems the company was having were due to "the Government's failure to open up the entire area of the park by the construction of adequate roads."[90] Superintendent Tomlinson, therefore, had to struggle even to retain the limited wilderness designation he and Vint had unofficially made for the north slopes of the mountain. That summer he asked Mather to request that Secretary of the Interior Hubert Work make "a formal declaration . . . designating the areas referred to as permanent 'Wilderness Areas.'" He backed up his request with formal resolutions made by The Mountaineers asking that certain sections of the park be declared wilderness areas and that the anticipated road construction program be curtailed.[91] Despite Vint's repeated condemnations, the Paradise scenic loop seemed to be moving ahead as well. In 1928, the Bureau of Public Roads completed a location survey for the motor road, including alternative routes and two new parking lots at scenic points along the circuit. Superintendent Tomlinson endorsed the project that summer, now using the rationalization that it would allow the elderly and handicapped to see the whole valley.[92] Plans, surveys, and alternate surveys for the road continued until 1931, by which time Albright had succeeded in stalling the project to death. With the new Paradise Lodge opening that year (and business withering as the Depression deepened) the Rainier National Park Company apparently relented and the road was never built. The Skyline Trail today follows much of the proposed route.[93]

In 1928, however, the situation at the Park Service had begun to change rapidly. After Mather was stricken that fall, Albright moved to

Washington to assume the directorship. Albright's tenure was characterized by expansion and reorganization, and one of his particular interests was the "comprehensive" park planning process, which clearly had not yet been fulfilled as a powerful tool for planning (and limiting) park development. By February, Albright had drafted and distributed a memorandum on "General Planning," which he asked Cammerer, Vint, and Kittredge to review. In it, Albright proposed that "park development plans," like the one Tomlinson had drawn up for Mount Rainier, now be required for all parks. In addition to the "general picture" regarding circulation, utility, and communication systems, the new director also asked that "more detailed plans of developed areas" be drawn up and included with the general plan. Albright wanted to see regional land-use zones defined that would make it clear which areas of the park were to be "developed" and which were to remain "wilderness areas." The success of the process, he noted, depended on "the proper collaboration of study and effect on the part of the Park Superintendent, the Landscape Architect, the Chief Engineer, and the Sanitary Engineer." And since "Park Development is primarily a Landscape development, these plans will be coordinated by the Landscape Division."[94]

If Albright saw Vint "coordinating" the general planning process, however, he still wanted Frank Kittredge to remain "chief engineer," responsible for the overall activities of design and construction. And although he expected "the fullest cooperation and coordination of the various divisions" of the office, his tone suggested that he had not been receiving it. In another draft memorandum also distributed for review at this time, Albright attempted to clarify the organizational chart of the San Francisco field headquarters. To better define the respective roles of the civil engineering, landscape architecture, sanitary engineering, and forestry divisions, he described the responsibilities of each. The chief engineer, Frank Kittredge, was in charge of all aspects of road and trail design and construction; the chief engineer also oversaw "clerical personnel and office administration." Vint, as chief of the "landscape division," had a much more diverse set of responsibilities. He was charged with preparing "landscape lay-outs for all development areas, architectural sketches and working plans for buildings, bridges and other structures . . . [and] inspecting construction . . . from the landscape architectural viewpoint." Vint was also to continue to inspect and investigate all road projects. The landscape architect, in fact, was asked to "pass upon and recommend approval" for virtually all work done in any park or monument of the national park system—always, of course, with the "landscape viewpoint" in mind.[95]

Despite what might have seemed an affirmation of the broadest possible planning and review powers, the memorandum provoked a long and thoughtful response from Vint in which he somewhat philosophically questioned Albright's understanding of the role of landscape architecture in the development of national parks. Vint, who never enjoyed writing and was often chided for his failure to keep up with paperwork, drafted an uncharacteristically long and personal statement regarding landscape architecture, national parks, and the need for comprehensive planning.

Vint doubted that national park construction work could ever be neatly divided into categories for determining whether individual projects should be handled by the engineering or landscape divisions. "Above a few distinctive characteristics," he pointed out, "many problems can easily be claimed by both." A possible solution, he risked suggesting, was to "definitely classify it all as either Engineering or Landscape and make a single division." The consolidated office might be headed either by him or by Frank Kittredge; but Vint made it clear that this choice was not a "question of personalities." The decision depended on whether Albright wanted to plan park development "on a Landscape or an Engineering basis." There was no doubt how Vint felt the question should be answered, but he buttressed his opinion with an exegesis on the profession of landscape architecture as it related to national parks. Landscape architecture was still a new profession, he observed, one which attempted to offer "a practical solution to the problem at hand" but also considered "the element of beauty." And the element of beauty could only be attained in park development, Vint asserted, when the "congruity of parts gives harmonious form to the whole." National park plans would not be aesthetically or otherwise successful if the landscape architect did no more than "embellish the work of another," specifically the civil engineer. If the landscape division continued to merely advise on the location surveys and contract specifications that the engineering division and the Bureau of Public Roads already had in hand, the landscape architects "could be little more than a nuisance."[96]

In his analysis of the role of landscape architecture in national parks, Vint was paraphrasing the elder Olmsted's justification of the landscape park as a work of fine art. As Daniel Hull had earlier, Vint drew on Olmsted's description of the landscape park as a "single work of art . . . framed on a single, noble motive." Vint's opinions perhaps had been shaped by his close contact with Frederick Law Olmsted, Jr. By this time, the two landscape architects had worked together to resolve a number of contentious issues, especially at Yosemite Valley.[97] Vint was no doubt aided as well by the publication in 1928 of the first significant volume of the elder Olmsted's writings, edited by F. L. Olmsted, Jr., and Theodora Kimball.[98] But Vint also understood the potential application of Olmstedian theory and practice to the future management of federal scenic reservations: "The first work of the National Park Service is the protection and preservation of these landscapes [national parks]. Its second work is to make these areas accessible to the people that they might be used and enjoyed. What is the work of the Park Service but landscape work? What organization was ever given a nobler landscape problem?" The very essence of the Park Service's mandate from its inception, according to Vint, was essentially a landscape architectural project, typically referred to as "park development." Albright could put the engineers in charge of the project if he saw fit, but that would not alter the essential nature of the task that lay before the Park Service. In any case, Vint indicated that he had been patient over the last two years, and he wanted Albright to take decisive action soon. Vint advised that the engineering and landscape divisions be combined, and he did not hesitate to add that "if this is done, the Landscape should be dominant."[99] With his office now organized and with a new director in Washington, Thomas Vint asked for no less than centralized control of all design and construction activities undertaken by the Park Service.

Frank Kittredge, confident in his close relationship with Albright, seemed genuinely mystified by Vint's sudden vehemence. Kittredge, in fact, had probably precipitated the entire sequence of events by asking Albright to draft a memorandum regarding the organization of the field headquarters that would reaffirm the position of the chief engineer. Now Kittredge just hoped that Albright would "permit the Field Headquarters organization to remain" as it was then organized. In another letter to Arthur Demaray, Kittredge betrayed some anxiety over Vint's sudden "attack." The chief engineer attempted to delay any further action, asking "if it would not be a good plan to let this entire matter of Field Headquarters Memorandum rest until next fall." Kittredge explained to Albright, rather disingenuously, that he was "surprised at the feelings expressed" in Vint's letter. He had felt "that all of us had been cooperating in fine shape and on a 'give and take' basis." Kittredge assured the new director that he had "supported and assisted [Vint] in all his landscape architecture." All his engineers, he continued in the same patronizing tone, were instructed that "landscaping . . . [was] vital to the parks." Nothing the engineer said, however, indicated any understanding of the points Vint was making about the larger issues of how planning should proceed in national parks.[100]

Although Albright does not appear to have taken any immediate or dramatic administrative steps, events at Mount Rainier and elsewhere soon indicated a shift in policy that effectively assured that park development would indeed be planned in the future "on a landscape basis." Mount Rainier was critical at this time, in part simply because of the amount of construction undertaken in the park during the mid-1920s. In 1928, as the Paradise scenic loop controversy continued to build, four other road projects were either being surveyed or were under construction: the West Side Road, connecting the Nisqually entrance to the Carbon River country; the Mowich Lake Road, a spur road leading to Mowich Lake in the northwest corner of the park; the Stevens Canyon Highway, which traversed the southern side of the mountain; and the Yakima Park Highway, the spur road on the east side of the mountain from the new state highway up to Yakima Park. As this ambitious development program proceeded, more controversies emerged. Vint and Ernest Davidson, who was assigned to Mount Rainier, had indeed been making "nuisances" of themselves. For the West Side Road project, for example, Vint had inspected the Bureau of Public Roads location survey in 1925. Accompanied by Asahel Curtis and the locating engineer, C. R. Short, he traveled the route by horseback to assess the impact of the proposed construction. In his report to Superintendent Tomlinson, Vint approved of the southern end of the proposed road but objected forcefully to the location of the northern section of the route. Short had recommended the road pass through the scenic Ipsut Pass, a difficult engineering feat that Vint felt would result in catastrophic (and unnecessary) damage to the area. The road location, he claimed, would destroy "one of the landscape views the Park Service was bringing people into the park to see," replacing it with "an extremely visible example of extravagant road construction."[101] Construction on the south end of the West Side Road soon began, but funds for the disputed north end were diverted. That portion of the project, which would have connected the road to Mowich Lake, was delayed indefinitely in part because of Vint's objections.

Forced into this type of antagonistic role, Vint and Davidson next became embroiled over the proposed Stevens Canyon route. Davidson and C. R. Short made the initial reconnaissance survey in 1926, and several more surveys of alternate routes followed over the next two years. By the fall of 1929, Superintendent Tomlinson, the Bureau of Public Roads, Davidson, and Vint had all agreed on a location for the road that carried it on a "low line" through Stevens Canyon. That October, Frank Kittredge arrived in the park and subsequently demanded a relocation that would put the road on a "high line" along Stevens Ridge, rather than in the canyon itself. The ridge route was longer and considerably more expensive than the canyon route. But Kittredge, and soon Tomlinson and others, anticipated it would be "a more spectacular scenic route" that would "offer more educational value" since it would bring motorists closer to glaciers and other geologic features. It was just as clear, however, that "damage caused by construction would be much more noticeable," and that the higher road would be plagued by rock and snow slides when completed.[102] Ernest Davidson, who had become a strong advocate of landscape preservation in the park, reacted angrily to Kittredge's interference in 1929. The landscape architect held out against the superintendent and the chief engineer and demanded that the "low line" remain the approved location. Vint backed his assistant and wrote to Albright and Arthur Demaray in Washington. Although he did not presume to be a judge of the purported "educational value" of the ridge route, he did feel that "spectacular" engineering that devastated the surrounding landscape would require further justification than Kittredge had provided. He also felt the scenic value of the canyon route had been greatly underestimated, and provided Albright with photographic studies (with road alignments inked in) to prove his point. His main objection, however, addressed his concern for the park resources themselves: "Every time a highway is moved *uphill*," he conjectured, "the effective and usable size of the park is *decreased*." Hikers and others would not make use of an area below a highway on a steep slope, "and that area" of the park, therefore, was "just lost."[103]

The matter was not completely resolved until 1931, when Albright traveled the canyon on horseback and personally inspected the options for the road's location. Afterwards the director unequivocally backed his landscape architects.[104] By that time, however, Vint had already succeeded in making his larger points about landscape planning to the Washington office. Reacting to Kittredge's interference at Mount Rainier in 1929, Arthur Demaray (who had advanced to "Senior Assistant

Director") observed that Kittredge was "apparently determined to have a hand in these questions," an unfortunate circumstance since "Vint [had] a hard enough problem to get the Bureau [of Public Roads] engineers to accept the landscape viewpoint without having opposition on his hands from within our own organization." Demaray noted that Kittredge had engaged in similar interference at Crater Lake and asked that Albright "take some action defining the authority of the landscape and engineering divisions."[105] Other complaints had come in from the field at this time. J. Ross Eakin, then superintendent at Grand Canyon, wrote a personal letter to Albright complaining that "Mr. Kittredge assumes his ideas of landscape are better than those of Mr. Vint's." Summing up the situation, he continued, "I am keen for Kittredge as Chief Engineer and keen for Vint as Chief Landscape Architect. But I am not keen for Kittredge as Chief Landscape Architect, if you get what I mean."[106]

Events soon indicated that Albright did understand the situation. The organizational chart of the San Francisco field headquarters remained essentially unchanged in 1929, but Vint's authority in the planning process was reinforced as "general planning" became the required prerequisite and context for all park construction projects. As the authority of "park development plans" was enhanced, decisions and controversies were addressed at that level and therefore came under Vint's supervision; Kittredge increasingly was left to implement and supervise road and trail construction according to decisions that had been made through the planning process. Soon national parks became paradigms of regional planning technique during a time when circumstances often frustrated the success of regional planning elsewhere in the United States.

In the late 1920s the general plan for Mount Rainier, specifically, became the first and the most completely developed example of what soon became known as the Park Service "master planning" process. There were a number of reasons why the plan for this park assumed particular significance. The "development outline" for Mount Rainier was the most ambitious being planned for a national park at the time. During the mid-1920s, Mount Rainier was just entering the most intense period of its development; many other national parks already had major lodges and other facilities planned or built by that time. At Mount Rainier, dedicated and diverse groups of local park advocates (from The Mountaineers to the Rainier National Park Advisory Board) had assured that every decision and policy was examined and debated. The controversies surrounding the Paradise scenic loop and the Stevens Canyon Highway, in particular, had forced Albright to reconsider Park Service planning policies and procedures. Similar controversies of course had erupted in other parks, but at Mount Rainier the debate revolved around the conception of the park plan as a whole. The "round-the-mountain" route represented a compelling, but anachronistic, model for that plan. Its eventual rejection required not only the revision of a specific road or other project, but a broad reassessment of the goals of a national park master plan. If similar controversies regarding preservation versus use arose elsewhere in the

park system at this time, at Mount Rainier the debate assumed a diagrammatic clarity that lent itself to the production of a model master plan.

Mount Rainier also benefited from a dedicated and capable superintendent, Owen A. Tomlinson, who remained at the park throughout this period, turning down promotions in order to do so. And Vint's first and perhaps most trusted assistant, Ernest Davidson, also remained assigned to Mount Rainier during these years. In general, Mount Rainier was fortunate to have a dedicated and talented staff, a fact that Albright repeatedly mentioned in his park inspection reports. Ernest Davidson's influence was a particularly important factor in determining the general planning principals that emerged at the park. In 1940, Vint recognized that Davidson "was most sensitive to natural values" among the Park Service landscape architects, and was "our best man for the type of work that involves large natural areas."[107] When Davidson died unexpectedly in 1944, Vint eulogized him as "my oldest associate in landscape architectural work," one who possessed a "unique sense of the fitness of things man-made, and the necessity of sublimating them to the end of preserving great scenic areas in their natural state."[108]

It was Davidson's contribution to the master planning process at Mount Rainier, above all, that had earned Vint's approbation. But this contribution consisted of far more than Davidson's inspection of road locations and construction. The two landscape architects also worked together on a host of more detailed site development plans and on the design of many individual buildings and structures. All of the "developed areas" of Mount Rainier, in fact, were either designed or redesigned to become part of the master plan package that took shape in the late 1920s. At Longmire Springs, which became known as Longmire Village, Vint's and Davidson's plans called for new development to be moved away from the fragile meadow where the mineral springs themselves were located. After the National Park Inn burned in 1926, the stone enclosures around the springs and the old Elcaine Longmire cabin (1888) were all that remained of the original resort at the site. A nature trail called the "Trail of the Shadows" interpreted the area, stressing its natural beauty as well as its history as a resort.

Longmire Village itself was taking shape on the other side of the Nisqually Road, where the 1928 administration building served as the anchor for a new administrative area. The old administration building (1916) was moved to its present location in 1929 and remodeled as the park museum. The National Park Inn Annex, now called the National Park Inn, had been moved to its present location in 1920 (and so did not burn with the original National Park Inn in 1926). A simple comfort station was built in 1926, and a new service station was built in 1929. Together these buildings helped define the central plaza of the village, which like other park village plazas, provided a well-defined arrival and gathering point. The principal public buildings of the park, with their front doors opening onto the Longmire plaza, projected a strong civic presence on the space. But even the less imposing buildings, especially the service station, were remarkable for the quality of the design and attention to detail and siting. And also like other park village plazas, the plaza at Longmire eventually became a parking lot, since arriving motor vehicles inevitably assembled there. In this case, however, the park road did not terminate at the plaza, but actually moved through it in a wide curve. As they passed through on the Nisqually Road, motorists continuing past Longmire on to Paradise experienced a sweeping view of the Longmire plaza and the facade of the administration building with Eagle Peak (part of the Tatoosh Range) as a backdrop. Even for those who did not stop at Longmire, therefore, the plaza imparted a strong sense of arrival and civic responsibility.

Longmire Village, like other park villages, was carefully zoned into civic, utility, and residential areas. The village plaza defined the center of the civic zone of the village. A utility area was designated nearby, and by 1927, functional sheds and garages began to be built in a simple, rectilinear arrangement that segregated daily maintenance and other activities from the more public areas of the village. The rectangular utility buildings were separated by wide, straight streets with no sidewalks or curbs. Sited along the banks of the Nisqually River, the threat of flooding disqualified the relatively flat utility zone for other uses, and the area was physically and visually separated from other areas of the village by vegetation and by the utility buildings themselves. The area nevertheless retained direct access to the Nisqually Road and to the nearby administration building. The utility area was also convenient to the residential area, which was developed on rising ground to the north. The narrower, winding streets of the residential zone were laid out beginning in 1923, when the first wood frame bungalows were built. Daniel Hull provided the first typical bungalow designs, as well as plans for "duplex" residences of two units, both of which typically featured shingle siding and foundations of local stone. Access to the houses in the residential area generally was from the front (street) side, and no elaborate pedestrian system was proposed for this relatively small subdivision. More residences as well as separate garages were constructed through the 1920s and 1930s.

The residential area was separated from the utility area by the central street of the village, which led from the plaza to a "public auto-camp" on the other side of the Nisqually River. In 1924, a small suspension bridge was built to reach the campground site, which retained a relatively quiet and isolated atmosphere away from the rest of the village. In 1927, a community building was built at the campground to be a center for various meetings and entertainments for both visitors and employees. Designed by Vint and the landscape division, the log post-and-beam, two-story building featured slab siding and a massive, steeply pitched shake roof. The interior space was open, with log posts, beams, and trusses left exposed. Although many community buildings were built for campgrounds and park villages in the 1920s, the Longmire community building is perhaps the finest surviving example of the type.[109] Comfort stations, fireplaces, and the campground loop roads were added to the Longmire campground in the 1930s with the help of CCC labor.

Longmire Village typified Park Service village planning of the 1920s in other ways. The hierarchy of street sections, for example, included at least six distinct types: pedestrian paths; campground loops; narrow streets in the residential area; wider, rectilinear streets in the utility area; a wide main street bisecting the village and leading to the campground; and the Nisqually Road itself, which swept along the edge of the village, separating the mineral springs and wet meadow from the rest of the developed area. As in other park villages, planting and "landscape naturalization," much of it done by CCC labor in the 1930s, stressed native species transplanted from nearby locations and grouped by ecological associations in naturalized masses. And again, planting was used to reinforce the spatial organization of the site plan, never to obscure the definition of spaces or the facades of public buildings. The Park Service Rustic facade of the administration building, for example, was left mostly clear to project its strong presence on both pedestrians and motorists passing through the plaza. Site construction details and site furniture in the village, like the architecture of the administration building, responded to the regional context in the choice of materials. Round river boulders set as curbs along walkways and around planted areas created a characteristic image. And like other park village plans, the plan for Longmire responded to the topography, views, and vegetation of the site, and preserved and exploited these characteristics to the greatest degree possible. As Hull had done for Grand Canyon, Vint and Davidson consolidated and expanded an existing resort site at Longmire by providing a town plan that embodied the ideals of contemporary professional practice.

Longmire Village, like other developed areas in the park, has retained remarkable integrity.[110] A recent rehabilitation of the village landscape and of the National Park Inn, however, resulted in a significant alteration of the historic plan. All parking for the village was relocated from the village plaza to an expanded parking lot on the other side of the National Park Inn, and the back of the hotel now serves as its front entrance. The major public space of the village has therefore been relocated from what was the central village plaza to the service side of the National Park Inn, which is where cars now arrive and park. This new arrival point lacks the dramatic views of Eagle Peak and Mount Rainier that originally gave the old plaza its powerful and unique character. Visitors now arrive at what was designed as a parking lot, not a civic plaza; they are greeted by the backs of the Longmire buildings, the fronts of which line the old plaza. The facade of Vint's administration building, which imbued the old plaza with a strong civic presence, does not have a similar relationship to the new parking area, an unimposing space at best. Although Longmire Village retains its physical integrity, this alteration to its circulation and site plan compromises the original experience of the place. The old Longmire plaza remains a strong space today, but it has been denied the role it once had as a central arrival and gathering place. Now emptied of cars, it has been heavily planted in a strategy of "revegetation" (as at Yosemite Village) which will eventually erase any perception of the space.

Longmire was the largest developed area in the park, but perhaps the most significant park village at Mount Rainier was being planned for the opposite side of the park. Since 1923, when progress on the Naches Pass State Highway had reached the park's northeastern corner, Superintendent Tomlinson had advocated the construction of a sixteen-mile spur road (in part a reconstruction of the White River mining road) to enable motorists to reach a particularly scenic subalpine plateau on the rugged northeastern slopes of the mountain. Called Yakima Park, the plateau was a relatively large, flat area at an elevation of 6,400 feet. With stunning views of the massive glaciers on Mount Rainier's northern side, Tomlinson and others felt Yakima Park was one of the most impressive and interesting areas in the park. The existing mining road, combined with the access of the new state highway, also made Yakima Park potentially more easily accessible than other subalpine parks considered for development. Tomlinson hoped that the new facilities at Yakima Park could become as great an attraction as those at Paradise Valley, and so ease the overcrowding there and at Longmire. The Bureau of Public Roads surveyed the new Yakima Park Highway in 1926 and construction began the next year. By 1928, Vint, Davidson, and Merel Sager were all working to assure that road construction did as little damage as possible to its immediate surroundings. That summer, Stephen Mather visited Yakima Park during his last tour of the national parks. Accompanied by H. A. Rhodes, Superintendent Tomlinson, and Thomas Vint, Mather inspected what they all hoped would be an ideal new park village planned completely by the Park Service at a location that had no previous history of resort development.[111]

After visiting Mount Rainier early in the summer of 1929 (his first visit as director), Horace Albright was enthusiastic about the prospects for the development of Yakima Park. "I regard Yakima Park as a sensation," he wrote to Tomlinson, adding that he now favored pushing ahead the construction of the Stevens Canyon Highway (that would connect the Nisqually Road to the eastern regions of the park) over completing the disputed northern portion of the West Side Road. His reasons for this shift in policy were determined, again, by an evolving diagram for the overall development of the park. The new director had formed "definite, but not yet conclusive ideas" of how the new village at Yakima Park would contribute to a revised plan for the park as a whole. Albright envisioned a loop tour that would begin from Seattle or Tacoma and arrive at Paradise Valley via the old Mountain Highway and the Nisqually Road. From there the loop would continue east along the proposed Stevens Canyon Highway eventually connecting to the new Naches Pass State Highway on the east side of the park. At that point, tourists could make a side trip to Yakima Park via the Yakima Park Highway. After descending from that higher elevation, they could then exit the park at its northeastern corner and return to the Puget Sound area on the state road, which would take them back on a northern route through Enumclaw.

This new circulation diagram for the park made the completion of the West Side Road unnecessary and perhaps (like the proposed road across the north side of the park before it) undesirable; the new scenic loop described a much larger circle that passed through the park only on the southern and eastern slopes of the mountain. This new model for more limited automotive access within the park made the construction of the Stevens Canyon Highway a much higher priority than the completion of the West Side Road. It also implied that two of the proposed four new developed areas in the park, at Spray Park and Sunset Park, would never be built, since they would have been made accessible only by the completion of the West Side Road. "I could not get enthusiastic about the plans for Spray Park," the director confessed in 1929, although he was now "quite enthusiastic about building a connection between Paradise Valley and Yakima Park."[112] With the completion of the West Side Road no longer a priority and the future of two new developed areas in question, Albright had further modified the "round-the-mountain" model, and again curtailed the total amount of development considered appropriate for the park. The revised scenic loop he described (the loop many park visitors travel today) suggested that the west side of the mountain, like the north side, would remain "wilderness."[113]

By 1929, Superintendent Tomlinson emphasized the urgency of completing visitor services, trails, and other facilities for Yakima Park before the fragile area was opened to the motoring public. The unprecedented opportunity to plan every aspect of a new park village stimulated park managers and planners; but the potential damage to an extraordinary scenic area was all the more apparent since Yakima Park at that point remained relatively undisturbed. The landscape architects and the park superintendent all knew that fragile volcanic soils and subalpine vegetation would quickly be destroyed unless human and automobile traffic were carefully controlled. In 1929, following a directive from

Albright to complete plans for Yakima Park that year, Davidson labored intensively over the design for the park village.[114] The landscape architect eventually produced at least six alternative plans for review by Vint, Tomlinson, and H. A. Rhodes. Vint later acknowledged that Davidson spent "a great deal of energy learning the ground" and gave "a great deal of study to the problems involved" in what was the first chance the landscape division had been given to design every aspect of a major developed area.[115]

The new park village needed to accommodate the concessioner's plans for a new lodge and cabin complex similar to the Paradise Lodge that was also being planned at this time. An extensive auto campground, trails, parking, and an administration building would all be required. Sewers, water, and electricity needed to be provided for the large crowds anticipated once the Yakima Park Highway was completed. Sites for the future construction of a large new hotel were also considered, although once the Depression struck, the concessioner would not be in a position to finance such a project. Thomas Vint had hoped to keep both auto camping and the concessioner's lodge and cabin complex discreetly sited at either end of the plateau, leaving the "park proper" (the large, central meadow) free of construction. It was soon clear, however, that Rhodes wanted room for an eventual complement of six hundred tourist cabins, which would have to be grouped around the central lodge in order to be convenient to dining and other facilities. Only the "park proper" offered a site for such an extensive and consolidated grouping. The concessioner was willing, however, to site the complex on the northern side of the park, away from the edge of the plateau overlooking the White River Valley, an arrangement that would leave the views from the park towards the mountain (to the southwest) unimpaired. Davidson also argued that Shadow Lake, just west of the park itself, be designated a "sacred area," precluding any kind of development for that small and fragile feature of the subalpine landscape.[116] A second lake, Frozen Lake, was tapped as the water source for the village. During one of their site inspections, Tomlinson and Davidson sited the main automobile campground on high ground to the west of the lodge and cabin complex. At Albright's insistence, they had selected a campground that would have views at least as dramatic as those enjoyed by visitors staying in the concessioner's cabins. The location they chose was more sheltered than the plateau below it, and had originally been considered as a future hotel location because of the views it offered. It was also close enough to the lodge complex to make use of the centralized services there.[117]

Planning continued through the summer and fall of 1929, as Vint, Tomlinson, and Rhodes reviewed and discussed Davidson's sketches of alternative plans. In addition, sanitary engineer Harry B. Hommon, from the Public Health Service, Paul H. Sceva, the assistant manager of the Rainier National Park Company, and many others also made site visits with Davidson to discuss the implications of various plan options.[118] By the fall, Albright instructed Vint to draw up "a complete set of development plans for Yakima Park" for his approval. The plans were to show all aspects of the proposed work, whether that work was to be carried out by the Park Service or the concessioner. The plans were also to include "all types of necessary development," including utilities. Tomlinson was instructed to prepare a supplementary budget estimate for completing the necessary work to have the area open for the 1931 season.[119] Davidson drew up a site plan at one inch to two hundred feet, with twenty-five-foot contour intervals. (Topographic information, as usual, was supplied by the Park Service engineering division.) The plan showed the Yakima Park Highway terminated by a large plaza, which inevitably became a parking lot, with the concessioner's lodge and Park Service administration building again facing directly onto this central arrival point. The buildings were located on the west and north sides of the central plaza, where they would not block the views. Vint noted that up to three thousand cars were expected to arrive at Yakima Park on peak weekends, and that spur roads should be developed to take some of the traffic west of the "park proper." A short road therefore led to a second campground and picnic area above Shadow Lake, relieving the pressure on the Yakima village plaza. Another spur road led to a powerhouse and concessioner utility area, also well out of the "park proper" to the west. A site above the concessioner's utility area was reserved for a potential hotel development.[120]

In the design of the Yakima Park administration building, Davidson departed from the precedents of the Yosemite and Longmire administration buildings. Davidson combed through 19th-century photographs at the Tacoma Historical Museum searching for an example of a "log blockhouse" of the type erected by "pioneers . . . of the locality." The landscape architect sketched an administration building based on his research, and A. Paul Brown drafted the final plans that winter in San Francisco. The result was the Yakima Park stockade group, a complex of three buildings and a small utility area built between 1930 and 1943. The group consisted of two "blockhouses," which housed rangers and offices, and a separate park museum building between them. The log post and beam structures were all two stories high, with the second story projecting slightly. The walls were of chinked white pine logs laid horizontally with saddle notches at the corners. A log stockade around the back of the group eventually screened the Park Service utility area from view. With low, hipped roofs and modest stone foundations, the effect created by the group of three buildings differed substantially from earlier Park Service Rustic structures at Mount Rainier and elsewhere. Davidson's effort to create "local or historical interest" that would make the building "suited to its landscape environment," however, recalled the kind of design research that the Nussbaums put into the Pueblo architecture of the Mesa Verde administrative buildings, and was entirely consistent with the overall theory of Park Service Rustic architecture.[121]

One wing of the concessioner's lodge for Yakima Park, Sunrise Lodge, was completed in 1931. It served as a cafeteria and support building for over two hundred tourist cabins marshaled in straight rows on a flat area immediately behind it. Since the cabins were removed during World

War II, Sunrise Lodge has served only day-tripping motorists; the Rainier National Park Company was never again in a position to finish the lodge, and it has remained a fragment of the original tourist accommodations at the site. Just east of the lodge, Davidson designed a service station (along the lines of the Longmire service station), which was also completed in 1931.[122]

The plans for Yakima Park were quickly finalized in 1929, and soon became part of the overall, master plan for the park. Several conditions that had previously irritated park planners were noticeably absent from this process. Working directly with the superintendent, the concessioner, and the engineering division, Vint and Davidson presented plans, made revisions, and in general controlled the entire procedure (although the final decisions of course were not theirs). Vint and Davidson expressed strong reservations about the village plan as it was delineated early in 1930, but they had received cooperation from everyone involved and felt they reached successful compromise arrangements. Perhaps for the first time, the landscape division had managed to address the conflicting concerns and interests of all parties, and produce a plan, which if it completely satisfied none, avoided the piecemeal developments and resulting controversies that had plagued Paradise and other favorite destinations in the national park system. As Davidson put it, "purely from a landscape viewpoint, the whole development might be classed as a failure since the area is far less attractive than it was before." But in the end, "the plan was adopted, followed, and to date [1933] has proven satisfactorily workable with a smaller amount of landscape damage to natural conditions than such development usually involves."[123] Thomas Vint was disappointed because he had not been able to keep the central area of the plateau free from development. The size of the Sunrise Lodge complex was "of such large scale" that it could not "be submerged sufficiently to preserve the original beauty of the park." Nevertheless, the chief landscape architect felt the plan "more nearly [fit] the requirements of all better than any plan yet proposed," and that was "all that [could] be expected of any plan."[124] If their concern for the delicate soils and fragile vegetation still haunted the planners, they appeared comforted by the fact that a sound precedent for landscape planning had been set.

Yakima Park opened as planned in 1931. The completion of the state highway over Chinook Pass the next year opened Mount Rainier to visitors from Yakima, Spokane, and eastern Washington, and the number of visitors to Yakima Park grew proportionally. The park's boundaries were also extended east in 1931 (to the crest of the Cascades) adding 34,000 acres to the park and making Chinook Pass the new park entrance from the east. The portion of the Naches Pass State Highway running through the national park and adjacent national forests was rededicated as the Mather Memorial Parkway in a ceremony at Tipsoo Lake in 1932. Elsewhere in the park, Vint and Davidson were busy laying out and designing new entrance stations, the new Paradise Lodge, and various other small developed areas at scenic points all along the park road system. All of this activity was being drawn together, however, in a manner that indicated Vint's desire to see every aspect of a park's development "give harmonious form to the whole." Already by 1930, the "general development plans" being drawn up for parks consisted of two complementary parts, drawn at design and planning scales respectively. The first part included a series of design development "studies" for every developed area in a given park, drawn at scales from one inch to twenty feet to one inch to two hundred feet. The second part consisted mainly of a topographic map of the entire park (supplied by the U.S. Geographical Survey) showing how the developed areas were linked by existing and proposed roads.[125]

During the years of Horace Albright's directorship between 1929 and 1933, the landscape division continued to grow in number and the general planning process continued to gain stature. By 1931, the San Francisco office had grown to fourteen landscape architects, and four more now worked in an eastern field office under landscape architect Charles Peterson. About half of the staff spent the construction season assigned to a specific park or parks.[126] That summer, Albright met with Thomas Vint and Frank Kittredge at the San Francisco field headquarters; there the director permanently settled the question of whether planning would proceed on "a landscape or an engineering basis." Since then, Albright insisted, there had been "the most perfect harmony in the San Francisco Office."[127] By the end of the year, the landscape division "embarked upon the largest scale of future planning yet undertaken." In 1932, Albright reported that Vint and his landscape architects had made "important progress . . . in the preparation of a master plan for each national park . . . [to] assure each park of a well worked out and properly coordinated plan of development." Albright noted that the engineering division had supplied "basic data" for the plans, but that the landscape division "exercised an increasing influence" on the location and design of roads, and on the design and review of all proposed park development.[128]

Both the term "master plan," and the policy that required its implementation, were officially promulgated at the superintendents' conference held in the spring of 1932 at Hot Springs, Arkansas. The Hot Springs conference was the first national conference held in almost three years, and the first since Mather's death. At the conference, Albright described the history so far of the "comprehensive planning program" that he had initiated in 1925 at the Mesa Verde conference. Although the plans he had received since then were "worthwhile," he felt the planning they represented had not been "comprehensive." The situation in 1932 demanded a revitalized planning initiative. A year earlier, Congress had passed the Employment Stabilization Act in response to the worsening Depression. The act required all government bureaus to prepare six-year plans for needed construction work, so that the information would be available in the event that an emergency public works spending program were enacted. More important even than this legal mandate, for Albright, was the Park Service's "own need for planning our activities." And planning, the director made clear to the officials gathered at Hot Springs, was a "function of architecture and landscape architecture primarily," although "engineering must be relied on for technical information." Therefore "the plans in the National Park Service should be coordinated with the Landscape Department; the origination of the plans for the national parks . . . should be its primary function."[129]

Albright had instructed Vint to bring along the Mount Rainier master plan (and other park master plans) to Hot Springs as examples of exactly what he meant. Vint felt the Mount Rainier plan, at that time, was "practically in a form that we can call it a complete plan," making it the first complete master plan for a national park. For the purposes of the conference, Vint had taken Tomlinson's 1931 "park development outline" and bound it together with plans and maps drawn up by his division. The development outline was the superintendent's prioritized list of what work remained to be carried out in the park. It took the form of an inventory of "existing facilities" and "proposed facilities" for each developed area in the park, and included observations on policies and goals for the development of the park as a whole.[130] From that point on, the textual "development outlines" and Vint's planning and design "studies" were combined to create what Albright officially designated at Hot Springs as "master plans" for every national park.[131]

By this time, Vint had considerably elaborated his planning procedure in other ways. The Mount Rainier plan (dated 1931) he presented at Hot Springs included a number of prints made from a photostat enlargement of a tracing of the U.S. Geological Survey map of the park. On each print of the map, one aspect of the park's complete development was delineated. One map showed the park's road system, another showed the trail system, and another showed the "fire control system" (basically a system of fire roads). Each was delineated as an independent circulation network; together they described an integrated system that met the total circulation needs of the park. This planning method was as old as the landscape park itself; Olmsted and Vaux had designed independent, overlaid systems of carriage, bridle, and pedestrian trails at Central Park. Another map in Vint's master plan showed the locations and relationship of all the "developed areas" at Mount Rainier, each of which received its own "design study" at a more detailed scale. "The sheets form a volume," Vint explained, "that will give an outline for the whole park development." Six copies of the "volume" were produced to be distributed to Washington, DC, the park, and the San Francisco field headquarters; the copies sent out were rendered with pastels and colored pencils.[132]

Other maps in Vint's 1931 master plans reflected more recent influences in landscape architecture and planning. If successful regional planning continued to be the exception rather than the rule for American metropolitan areas, it nevertheless attained ideal expression through the planned development of national parks. Since Vint's master plans encompassed entire parks, they represented regional plans that incorporated a number of individual municipal plans (developed areas) together with plans for regional transportation, utilities, sewage, and other systems. Regional land-use zones could also be enforced as part of the park master plan. As part of Vint's 1931 master plan for Mount Rainier, the entire park was zoned into "wilderness," "research," "sacred," and "developed" areas. This typology of land-use zones had been elaborated through a heated debate over the implications of declaring a "wilderness area" in what was already a national park. Since 1926, Vint and Tomlinson had attempted to designate certain portions of Mount Rainier as wilderness to justify the curtailment of planned road development. The master plan strengthened this tactic; with a regional zoning plan in place that designated wilderness as a land use, road construction or other uses that constituted essentially a zoning variance could be rejected on that basis.

The meaning of the word "wilderness" in the context of Park Service master planning, however, was itself in flux. When Vint and Tomlinson used the term in 1926, they indicated that the region would remain roadless. The Forest Service had recently begun to designate wilderness areas with essentially the same definition. When other groups used the term, however, they often hoped for a total elimination of any sign of human presence, including the construction of trails, fire roads, or back-country ranger cabins. The minimum size and necessary extent of wilderness areas was also debated. In 1935 groups such as the Sierra Club and The Mountaineers were joined by the Wilderness Society, led by Robert Marshall, which pressed for the adoption of strict regulations for areas within national forests and parks to be designated as wilderness. In 1930, Marshall had observed that opening the country's few remaining wilderness areas to automobiles in order to allow more people to enjoy them was "as irrational as contending that because more people enjoy bathing than art exhibits . . . we should change our picture galleries into swimming pools."[133] Within the Park Service as well, scientists and educators argued that certain portions of every park should remain absolutely undisturbed—even by backcountry hikers—to retain an area where scientists could find "things in a normal, natural condition for study." At the 1932 Hot Springs conference, Harold C. Bryant, the assistant director for research and education, felt that "most of us subscribe to the idea of setting aside a few specially fine biological units just to save for the future." But this definition of wilderness would mean that only certain limited areas of a park could be so designated; obviously existing trail systems already precluded most of Mount Rainier, for example, from being eligible. Horace Albright, who often repeated that over ninety percent of every national park would remain "everlasting wilderness," could not abide a definition of that word that would completely exclude human beings. Therefore another land-use category was advanced, the "research area," which implied a complete restriction of all human activities and access. Still another land-use category was needed, however, for smaller areas that often were accessible by car, but nevertheless needed total protection from any form of development. "Sacred areas" were defined as usually limited zones around major attractions (such as Old Faithful) that precluded any construction or even access. "Wilderness," therefore, as defined by

Albright and Vint, was simply "the rest of the park": areas that were not accessible by car but that did allow trails, fire roads, and backcountry use.[134]

If all three designations suggested types of wilderness, the "research areas" suggested, as Bryant put it, "sanctuaries within sanctuaries."[135] This idea would remain controversial throughout the 1930s. The 1931 Mount Rainier master plan designated the rugged north slopes of the mountain as a "research area," and other master plans similarly indicated that the most remote and rugged regions of parks would be reserved for scientific purposes. There is little indication of how much practical effect this had on everyday park management, but superintendents, including Tomlinson, were soon on record resisting "research" designations that limited their ability to fight fires or extend trail systems into areas of their parks. In 1936, for example, Tomlinson objected to the research area designation for the northern slopes of Mount Rainier on the basis that it implied that the rest of the park was "open to unlimited development." This was untrue and the superintendent knew it; the assertion indicated, however, that by that time the research area designation had lost much of its official backing.[136]

In 1938, Vint attempted to clarify his use of wilderness land-use zoning in park master plans. The landscape architect (now "chief of planning" at the Park Service) noted that some definitions of wilderness permitted no use, or even access, by human beings. If parks were merely wilderness, by this definition, Vint observed that his job would be considerably simplified: "The development plan could be limited to the construction of an effective barrier around the boundary. The administration would not need to go beyond an adequate control to prevent trespass." Although he felt that "the growth of a protective attitude toward wilderness values" had resulted in tremendous support for national parks (particularly since 1929), his mandate "included the words 'for the benefit and enjoyment of the people.'" The definition of "wilderness" had been debated since 1932 at the Hot Springs conference, he continued, but he felt the issue needed to be readdressed. "Rather than approach the problem from the angle of setting aside wilderness areas within the national parks," he suggested, "we must approach it from the other direction—that is we must restrict the limits of developed areas and apply the protection that would be given to the wilderness area to *all* the area within the boundaries of the park that is not a developed area."[137] Whether this is seen as the triumph or the defeat of "wilderness" designation within national parks, it essentially describes how the word has been used in the context of park planning since that point.[138]

As a planning document, the master plan was not the direct basis for any construction activity. Even the more detailed (one inch to twenty feet) plan drawings for developed areas, such as Longmire or Paradise, only served as the guidelines for the production of detailed construction

Mount Rainier National Park Historic District

Left: *The fate of Paradise Park, the most famous and accessible of Mount Rainier's subalpine parks, was of particular concern for preservationists who feared the area would become as heavily developed as the floor of Yosemite Valley. A "scenic loop" motor road, which was to encircle the entire area, was stridently opposed in the late 1920s.*

Below: *The Longmire administration building (1928), Mount Rainier National Park. Designed by landscape architects Thomas Vint and Ernest Davidson, the building helped define the administrative core of Longmire Village, one of the many park villages designed by the Park Service landscape division during the 1920s.*

Above: Stephen Mather, right, looks over plans for the development of Yakima Park (the meadow seen to the far right) in 1928. His 1928 tour of the parks was Mather's last before suffering a stroke that left him disabled. H. A. Rhodes, the president of the Rainier National Park Company, is seated in the foreground, and Superintendent Tomlinson is in the center. Photograph by Asahel Curtis, National Archives, Record Group 79.

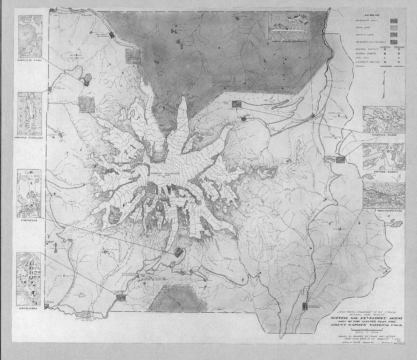

Left: The "special and developed areas" sheet of the 1940 master plan for Mount Rainier National Park. The comprehensive plan for Mount Rainier was the first of its type to be fully elaborated in the late 1920s. On this sheet, individual developed areas are depicted in plan vignettes in the margins. Color coding indicates land-use zones, from dark green "research areas," such as the large area on the north slopes of the mountain, to the red "developed areas" along the road corridor, which included park villages and entrance stations. The vast majority of the park was coded in light green, indicating "wilderness areas." National Archives, Cartographic Division.

Left: The Longmire Village campground in the 1930s. The boulders restricted automobile access to specific parking spurs along the campground loop road, an arrangement known as the "Meinecke System" after the plant pathologist Emilio P. Meinecke, who popularized the idea. National Archives, Record Group 79.

Below: A view of the East Side Highway (Route 123) in Mount Rainier National Park. Road construction at Mount Rainier, as in other national parks, employed construction standards and details meant to minimize impacts on natural systems and scenery. In this view, for example, a necessary road cut was reduced by extending an enlarged shelf of fill to carry the roadway. The retaining wall and guardwall made necessary by this solution were constructed in rusticated ashlar masonry of native granite, further integrating the road into its setting. Despite such "landscape engineering," the construction of roads remained the most controversial of all aspects of park development. Photograph by Jet Lowe, courtesy Historic American Engineering Record.

documents after projects had been funded. The design and planning process Vint described at Hot Springs in 1932, however, became the basis for the design and planning activities of the Park Service for decades to come. To some degree, it remains the basis of landscape architectural planning for national parks to this day.

The Mount Rainier master plan, for many reasons, was the prototype that guided the plans drawn up for other parks in the 1930s. Throughout this period, the Mount Rainier plan remained the most fully developed example of the master planning process.[139] A unique set of circumstances came together at Mount Rainier in the late 1920s. The extensive program of development for the park, the dedication of a talented staff, and the controversies of preservation versus use contributed to the actualization of the master planning process. Mount Rainier became the showcase for how the Park Service landscape division could produce master plans that would preserve parks while addressing the needs of all the park's users and constituencies.

Today the road system, trail system, and developed areas of Mount Rainier retain extraordinary integrity to the period during which the master plan for the park was initiated and developed. Through the largesse of the New Deal, much of the ambitious program of park development at Mount Rainier was completed in the 1930s. CCC labor again was employed in "landscape naturalization" and "roadside improvement" in developed areas all over the park. Up to six CCC camps were active in the park, and two resident landscape architects assisted Ernest Davidson in planning and directing the recruits' work.[140] Trailside structures, park entrances, and new utility lines were built by the CCC. Campgrounds were expanded and new minor developed areas were constructed. The stockade group at Yakima Park, the utility, residential, and camping areas at Longmire, and many other park facilities were all completed through New Deal programs. The park road system—now abbreviated from the original "round-the-mountain" model—was almost completely finished, although portions of the Stevens Canyon Highway would only be completed after World War II. The final decision not to pursue the completion of the West Side Road in 1935 left that long spur road as a permanent monument to the evolving sense of how much development was appropriate for a 20th-century landscape park.

As a whole, the developed areas, road system, and historic trails of Mount Rainier constitute a more complete and uncompromised picture of Park Service master planning of the 1920s and 1930s than is available in any other national park. In addition, Mount Rainier is where that historic park planning process was first fully elaborated. The integrity of the park's developed areas, combined with the historic significance of the planning process they represent, has led to the designation of a comprehensive historic district that includes all the historic developed areas in the park.

The implementation of the master planning process, and the scientific methods of park management that it implied, were perhaps the greatest achievements of Horace Albright's short but important tenure as director of the Park Service. Among the many changes that swept through Washington in 1933 was the appointment of Harold L. Ickes as secretary of the interior. "The old curmudgeon" became the most effective secretary in history, and his administration saw unprecedented growth and expansion for the Park Service and the national park system. Horace Albright, however, personified an earlier era of Progressive bureaucracy; never sanguine about the Roosevelt administration, he had not been reassured by the abrasive Ickes that he belonged in the new order of things. Still only forty-three years old, Albright left the federal government in the summer of 1933 to take a position in private industry. He was replaced by Arno Cammerer, who for the rest of the decade would administer the parks during a period of enormous change.

In 1933, Thomas Vint moved to Washington, DC, and continued to assume increased responsibilities for park planning as the Park Service expanded. The master planning process he had initiated had only begun to reach its full potential. As the New Deal got underway, the landscape division would expand to many times its former size, and the Park Service would take on the most ambitious and advanced national recreational planning that has ever been undertaken in the United States. No federal bureau, in the end, offered more important planning expertise for New Deal activities than the Park Service. Before the end of the decade, the diagrams of Warren Manning and Benton MacKaye would become reality. "National planning," as Hubbard and Kimball had described it in 1917, would be undertaken by numerous departments of the federal government. Thomas Vint and the other landscape architects employed with the Park Service would be called upon to guide the unprecedented expansion of national parks and parkways, and also to plan new state park systems all across the country. The greatest period of American park development was about to begin.

The National Park Service and National Recreational Planning

Chapter 6

The national economic restructuring that forever changed American life in the early 1930s also permanently reconfigured the profession of landscape architecture in the United States. The "country place" practice, which had grown precipitously since the 1890s, contracted severely as the Great Depression worsened. The owners of great estates from Long Island to Lake Michigan to Pasadena, if not ruined outright by the collapse of financial markets, at least became circumspect in plans for their residences. At the same time, the frenzy of subdivision and resort development that had employed scores of planners and landscape architects in the 1920s abated near the end of the decade. The period following World War I had generally been good to the many landscape architects who specialized in the design of opulent estates or lucrative subdivisions, but dependence on these activities took a terrible toll after 1929. During the bleak years of the Hoover administration, few professions withered more completely. By 1933, unemployment among American landscape architects probably approached 90 percent.[1]

Other businesses and professional groups caught in the relentless economic stagnation of the early 1930s may have experienced equally dire circumstances; but landscape architecture remained a small profession, and the consequences of economic depression threatened its very existence. Competition from nonprofessional "landscape services" organized by commercial nurseries, for example, previously could be ignored. Now the cheaper nursery services, working at a more modest scale and usually dispensing with professional designers, seemed destined to inherit what was left of the residential landscape design business. Municipalities and developers, similarly seeking to reduce costs, could also replace "town planners" with civil engineers who could produce reliable (and often much cheaper) plans for subdivisions, street improvements, and even parks. And since 1909, many prominent landscape architects and their students had begun to identify themselves as "city planners," further weakening the professional organization and identity that had really only been firmly established since the 1890s.[2] To address the situation, landscape architects needed to radically reorient their profession (much as had been done at the beginning of the century) and exploit new opportunities. As Albert D. Taylor, the managing editor of *Landscape Architecture* magazine, put it in 1933, "New occasions teach new duties."[3]

The new duties Taylor had in mind, of course, were those demanded by the New Deal, Franklin Delano Roosevelt's collection of emergency relief, public construction, and resource conservation programs initiated that spring. Perhaps recalling their experiences during World War I, officials of the American Society of Landscape Architects had been preparing for a total mobilization of their profession at least since the 1932 election. Henry Hubbard, as president of the society, lobbied to maximize the role of landscape architects in proposed New Deal programs. Earle S. Draper, who headed the group's committee on legislation, moved to Washington that fall to examine new legislation and report back on employment opportunities. By the time Roosevelt was inaugurated, Hubbard anticipated that a new era had begun. In his annual address to his membership in April 1933, he envisioned the great promise the Roosevelt administration held after years of crippling economic conditions. "If we now identify ourselves with those things that are going to be important in the future," he wrote, "we shall grow with them and find ample opportunity for service. . . . Since, therefore, our ship is about to sail, it behooves us to get aboard, and since there will be rough weather we would better learn the ropes and serve as able seamen, rather than call ourselves passengers and run the risk of turning out to be Jonahs, with no guarantee of any convenient whale!"[4]

Salvation was on the minds of Hubbard and many other landscape architects, who seized upon the New Deal in the spring of 1933 with tremendous and productive enthusiasm. Widespread unemployment was not unique to landscape architects; but the nature of their professional training made them peculiarly suited to the varied needs of New Deal programs. As the scope of the emergency spending became evident, Hubbard outlined the enormous responsibility he felt his colleagues should assume. "There is need, and bitter need, at this moment for all the knowledge that we have. . . . The country is going to get too many towns in the wrong place, subdivisions in the wrong place, roads, trees, and people in the wrong place, if *we* do not do the job that we have spent many years in learning how to do."[5] The dramatic recruitment of landscape architects as participants and organizers of New Deal programs was fueled by a sense of urgency on both sides: the New Deal needed landscape architects as badly as they needed new opportunities for practice. New Deal conservation programs, for example, threatened to do catastrophic, irreparable harm in national parks and forests if they proceeded without adequate planning and supervision.

One of the first pieces of New Deal legislation passed by the new Congress funded the Civilian Conservation Corps (CCC). Within two months of Roosevelt's inauguration, the Department of Labor and the U.S. Army had mobilized multitudes of formerly unemployed youths to undertake soil, forest, and water conservation projects on public lands all over the country. The CCC, over 300,000-strong by 1935, needed things to do, whether planners and supervisors had prepared plans for productive activities or not. The Park Service and the Forest Service, as the "technical agencies" in charge of planning and supervising most CCC projects, immediately hired as many landscape architects and foresters as they could find. In the fall of 1933, Taylor reported that sixty percent of the landscape architects looking for work through emergency relief programs had been picked up by the CCC, or more correctly by the various state, county, and federal agencies cooperating with the CCC and planning its activities. Within a year, virtually every landscape architect available for work (which often required relocating to a state park or regional office) had been hired, directly or indirectly, through New Deal spending. In the fall of 1934, Taylor reported that "practically every landscape architect who is not otherwise employed in private practice . . . is now employed in Government work. The proportion of the heretofore unemployed membership approximates ninety percent."[6]

Civilian Conservation Corps enrollees in Glacier National Park. The exuberant youths heralded unprecedented opportunities to expand and develop American parks at every level. They also threatened to do irreparable harm if their activities were not adequately planned and supervised. National Archives, Record Group 79.

In a matter of months, what Taylor characterized as "unlimited opportunity for landscape architects" took American landscape architecture from near dormancy into the most active period in its history. But very few professionals worked for private clients any longer. The New Deal retrieved but inevitably altered the profession. A considerable number of positions within various government agencies eventually were made permanent. The National Park Service, for example, became the largest single employer of landscape architects in 1933 and it remains so today. Many of the older "country place" generation retired during these years. Many others died, including O. C. Simonds, Charles Platt, James Greenleaf, Ferrucio Vitale, and others. But the vast majority of the several hundred of members of the American Society of Landscape Architects went to work for the federal government or for local agencies funded through federal programs. They took positions as technical advisors to the CCC, as junior landscape architects planning state park and other developments, as foremen supervising work in the field, and as executives in Washington, DC. Hubbard and Taylor, as editors of *Landscape Architecture* magazine, encouraged the trend and advised members "as to definite procedure in applying for positions . . . for either National Park or State Park work," areas in which proliferating CCC camps generated an insatiable demand for qualified designers and construction supervisors. The Park Service, in particular, endeavored to have one qualified landscape architect in every CCC camp operating in a national or state park—and there were over three hundred such camps operating by the spring of 1934.[7] Noting that the New Deal "brought the entire profession of landscape architecture into a relatively new field of action," Albert Taylor asserted that no other profession had a "greater demand for its services . . . in connection with the Government's emergency expenditures."[8] The demand extended from recent graduates to even to the most established professionals. Earle Draper, a town planner who had worked with John Nolen designing Kingsport, Tennessee, was appointed director of land planning and housing for the Tennessee Valley Authority; Hubbard and Taylor both served as high-ranking technical advisors for a number of federal and state agencies; Warren Manning served as a consultant for Massachusetts state park development; Charles W. Eliot II (Charles Eliot's nephew) was named executive officer of the new National Planning Board; Norman Newton, Phillip H. Elwood, Daniel Hull, and others served as regional inspectors for the CCC.[9] American landscape architects quickly incorporated themselves into the heart of New Deal planning and construction activities at every level.

It should be noted, however, that despite the fact that many women had successfully entered the profession of landscape architecture by 1933, almost none went to work as Park Service planners. While women professionals were accepted as estate and garden designers, they rarely made the transition to park planning and design, a fact which must have greatly set back women in the profession of landscape architecture at this time. The Park Service bias against women planners was an unfortunate aspect of the Fairsted School legacy; women had never been welcome as apprentices at Fairsted, and the Harvard Graduate School of Design did not accept women until the 1940s. If the New Deal rescued the profession of landscape architecture, not all members, regardless of their professional accomplishments, were allowed to exploit the potential of public practice.[10]

Albert Taylor, a former estate designer based in Cleveland, also revealed a deep ambivalence many established landscape architects felt about the "condition of socialism" into which the profession was drifting. "Social currents," he observed ominously, were "carrying us through an uncharted sea under most abnormal conditions." Public employment, he felt, threatened to reduce independent professionals to the status of civil servants. It would be "much better," he warned, "that the kind of contract between the landscape architect and government agency . . . be such as to assist him in reestablishing his normal office activities." Park agencies, however, tended to hire professionals outright rather than pay higher costs for consultant services. More and more private offices were closing as professionals took permanent positions within government bureaucracies. Uncertainties about when and how private practice would resume were widespread, and a growing number of professionals recognized that permanent changes, for better or for worse, were taking place. Nevertheless, Taylor recommended early in 1934 that the profession "reconcile itself to the acceptance of the socialistic trend. . . . Those who feel that it is not necessary to adapt ourselves to the changed conditions of the present are still *living in the past*."[11] Taylor's sentiments were seconded by Hubbard, who that year admitted, "We may or may not like the great changes which have come over our so-called civilization, but we certainly cannot return to the good old times. The way out of our present wilderness lies ahead and not behind."[12] Years of hardship tempered any misgivings; New Deal activities absorbed hundreds of unemployed professionals almost immediately.

One reason for this successful integration—and for the successful implementation of the New Deal in general—was that there had been many advance indications of the directions that massive public works and work relief programs might take. Since the days of Central Park (and earlier in Europe), park projects had been valued as an efficient means for the relief of unemployed industrial workers. Park work could quickly employ large numbers of people with mixed backgrounds and limited skills. The tools and materials required were less elaborate and expensive than for other categories of public works. During the Hoover administration, conservation initiatives and park development projects were widely anticipated as desirable categories for work relief activities (should Congress ever enact such measures). By 1932, the Forest Service, in cooperation with state and county governments, already operated dozens of work camps for the unemployed in forests in California and Washington. Several governors, including Gifford Pinchot of Pennsylvania and Franklin Roosevelt of New York, had implemented reforestation and other conservation projects paid for with work relief funds. Other governors planned similar efforts to put thousands of people to work planting trees, checking erosion, and building fire roads and fire breaks in state and national forests.[13] Hoover himself was a dedicated conservationist, and strongly supported the conservation orientation of proposed relief programs. It was the Employment Stabilization Act of 1931 that had prompted Horace Albright to ask Thomas Vint to undertake national park master planning systematically for every park and monument. Hoover's creation of the Reconstruction Finance Corporation in 1932, and the broadening of its powers through the Emergency Relief Act later that year, helped finance many early conservation and work relief experiments.[14]

If conservation and work relief plans failed to achieve significant momentum before 1933, they did indicate the kinds of activities that might be undertaken in the near future. And if some landscape architects were willing to wait for the economic "pendulum to swing" and restore their private clientele, others quickly pursued these new opportunities in park design and conservation planning. For this group, experience in "country place" estate design would be of little help. In 1932, Richard Schermerhorn, Jr., noted that "the cry for public parks has spread across the country . . . [and] who is better suited to design parks . . . than the landscape architect?" In the meantime, he felt, "Schools should not fill their students' minds too full of the spirit of design of 'the ducal palace grounds,' merely to have them later discover that the only available job is in a commercial nursery."[15] These were radical words from Schermerhorn, an accomplished "country place" figure and a fellow of the American Society of Landscape Architects. Other reports and articles published in *Landscape Architecture* magazine presaged changes to come. Landscape architect Herbert J. Kellaway described a public park project in Winchester, Massachusetts, that employed hundreds of laborers and showed how "alert communities" could "create public values in hard times." Kellaway had been employed by the town in the 1920s to plan improvements for the Aberjona River, but the plans were shelved because of their cost. "Little did anyone think," he wrote in 1932, ". . . that these would be the basis of progressive improvements in such times as the present." Operating with limited work relief funds provided by private charity and the town government, Kellaway oversaw the dredging of ponds, construction of playgrounds, and stabilization of riverbanks. Similar stories came in from all over the country. Cities from Los Angeles to Evansville, Indiana, were discovering that they could "meet unemployment problems in a constructive way" by implementing park development plans that had often been drawn up years earlier, but which had never been implemented because of their cost.[16]

In all of these activities, the education and experience of many landscape architects had done little to prepare them. Studies of the "ducal palace grounds," although skillfully put to use in many so-called "Beaux-Arts" municipal park designs in the 1930s, would be of limited use in the majority of New Deal conservation and work relief efforts. Large-scale park planning, river improvements, scenic reservation development, park road and parkway design all recalled an older tradition of public park planning that had been de-emphasized since the beginning of the century. Many landscape architects now needed to expand their practice beyond residential design, in what amounted to a return to the Olmstedian roots of their profession. As Albert Taylor observed, "We have suddenly discovered that government work, confined as it now is to planning highways, parks, recreation areas, and other public lands, requires a kind of training which some of the older— and certainly many of the younger—members of the profession have not had."[17] The relative importance of the Fairsted School had diminished steadily since Charles Eliot's death; but in the New Deal it would find its apotheosis.

If many were unprepared, one group of landscape architects had brought 20th-century landscape park planning and design to new levels of maturity in the late 1920s. By 1933, Thomas Vint and his atelier of Park Service landscape architects were in a unique position to guide their fellow professionals on what many considered their perilous voyage into public employment. In 1933, Vint's office in San Francisco still consisted of only sixteen professionals, most of whom alternated between months spent in the central office during the winter and field assignments during the construction season. Besides Ernest Davidson, other landscape architects working for Vint included Merel Sager (Crater

Lake, Lassen Volcanic, Sequoia), John Wosky (Yosemite), Harry Langley (Grand Canyon and Southern Utah), and Kenneth McCarter (Yellowstone and Grand Teton). Vint was assisted in the San Francisco office by William G. Carnes, another Berkeley graduate who soon was acting as his office manager. The office's architects and engineers, including A. Paul Brown and Herbert A. Kreinkemp, also generally remained in San Francisco and produced most of the contract documents as projects moved from design development to construction.[18] Since 1927, this closely knit group had been growing in number and refining its procedures. The division's authority within the Park Service had been steadily enhanced as Horace Albright and other officials came to recognize the usefulness and efficiency of the master planning process. The compilation of master plans would prove to be a particularly significant activity in the early 1930s. Besides safeguarding parks from excessive or poorly coordinated road construction and other development, the plans also detailed a six-year program of prioritized construction activity. Updated annually, by 1933 the master plans completed or underway represented a considerable reservoir of schematic and partially developed designs that could be quickly converted into construction projects if the opportunity arose. After Albright's resignation in the summer of 1933, his successor, Arno Cammerer, remarked on what seemed his predecessor's most salient achievement since 1929: "Extension of the landscape architectural activities and development of the six-year master plans for all national parks received special attention from [Albright]. . . . Had not this advance planning been done, the National Park Service would have been unable to take part so quickly and competently in the emergency conservation and public-works program."[19]

Park construction, as well as planning, had continued unabated during the Hoover administration. Despite the Depression, park concessioners such as the Rainier National Park Company expanded with new tourist cabin groups, which were more affordable than centralized hotels and generally better suited to auto tourists. Vint reviewed many proposed expansions of concessioner facilities, and many official buildings also went up during these years. Vint's office produced some of its finest architectural designs between 1927 and 1933, including the Longmire administration building and the second administration building at Grand Canyon. In 1931-1932, an entire administrative village was built in the Munson Valley area of Crater Lake, including residences, a utility area, and an administration building. Merel Sager was the chief designer, and Ernest Davidson also was involved. The ensemble was the most comprehensive single building program of its type yet attempted by the landscape division, and one of the most beautiful. In almost all of the western parks, entrance stations, comfort stations, administration buildings, and park residences of particular distinction were designed and built by the San Francisco office during what became a rich period for Park Service Rustic architecture.[20]

Many government bureaus took large budget cuts during the Hoover administration, but the Park Service was an exception. Compared to most of the rest of the economy, the Park Service boomed during the early years of the Depression. Besides the fact that Herbert Hoover certainly approved of the bureau's activities under Horace Albright, there were more compelling reasons to continue to invest in park development during hard times. The numbers of park visitors, for example, continued to grow (less consistently) throughout this period. Between 1928 and 1931, the total number of automobile permits issued rose from about 2,500,000 to over three million. The number of permits dropped beginning in 1932, but by 1934, the year Franklin Roosevelt declared the "national-park year," the numbers began to climb once again. In 1937 over 500,000 permits were issued to park visitors. National parks, perhaps a more affordable vacation destination for many, attracted more and more visitors, a remarkable fact considering that so many other areas of the economy had effectively come to a standstill.[21] At a time when so many American institutions and ideologies had failed or been called into question, the national parks assumed new significance and popularity as settings for public life and as embodiments of permanent national values. As Franklin Roosevelt and his advisors planned an unprecedented era of activist government, they continued to turn to park projects of all types not only as a means to employ thousands of laborers, but also to create public landscapes that extolled certain social values. The Park Service was in a unique position among government bureaus; if the profession of landscape architecture was to play an important role in New Deal planning and construction programs, Park Service landscape architects in particular had pioneered precisely the kind of public practice that would now be in demand.

Roosevelt's actions in 1933 indicated great confidence in the Park Service and great expectations for its future activities. Early that summer, Roosevelt responded to Albright's request that the historic battlefields and other historic sites under the jurisdiction of the War Department be transferred to the Park Service. Albright had long felt that the addition of historical parks in the East (along with the new Appalachian parks) would "bring a much larger constituency and much broader base," permanently establishing the Park Service "as a truly national entity."[22] When Albright reviewed the proposed reorganization, however, he was stunned by the extent of his bureau's new responsibilities. In two executive orders that summer, Roosevelt transferred all the War Department's battlefield parks and national monuments. He also transferred all the national monuments that the Forest Service still administered, and made the parks and public buildings of Washington, DC, the Park Service's responsibility as well. In a matter of weeks the Park Service had gained dozens of major additions to the park system, including the Statue of Liberty, Gettysburg, the Washington Monument, and the Lincoln Memorial. The Park Service assumed the role, as Albright had hoped it would, of the nation's park agency, with many different kinds of parks in all parts of the country. Historian Barry Mackintosh suggests that the 1933 reorganization, which became effective August 10, was "arguably the most significant event in the evolution of the National Park System."[23] From the first months of Roosevelt's administration, new concepts of what national parks could be and what they could mean to the public unfolded rapidly.

The Park Service evolved quickly beginning in 1933 in order to meet the expanded demands made on it. No program would have a greater impact on Park Service organization than the CCC, the peacetime army mobilized to combat the decay of both human and natural resources in the United States. Within days of his arrival at the White House, Roosevelt instructed his new secretary of the interior, Harold L. Ickes, to coordinate an advisory committee that would draft legislation to create the CCC. Ickes named Albright to represent the Department of the Interior; Albright in turn brought Thomas Vint, Frank Kittredge, and his chief forester, John D. Coffman, to Washington to help determine what the new army of youths could accomplish in the national parks.[24] The CCC legislation was introduced on March 21 and was signed into law ten days later, making it one of the earliest New Deal programs to get underway. The Department of Labor screened and selected recruits; the War Department transported, fed, clothed, and housed the volunteers, organizing them into camps of up to two hundred apiece. The Forest Service provided technical and planning assistance for the hundreds of erosion control, fire suppression, and afforestation projects planned for national and state forests all over the country. For its part in the "emergency conservation work," the Park Service was asked to plan, design, and give other technical assistance for all the park and recreational developments undertaken by the CCC outside of national forests. This of course included the work contemplated for the national parks themselves, but it also entailed the planning and design of hundreds of state, county, and even large municipal parks in almost every state and territory. Over seventy percent of the CCC work subsequently supervised by the Park Service was done in the over 560 non-federal park areas the bureau helped plan and develop during the 1930s. To accomplish this, the Park Service cooperated and provided direct technical assistance to state park and other planning agencies in forty-seven states, twenty-six counties, and sixty-nine cities.[25]

The implications of engaging in national recreational planning, in addition to the reorganization of 1933, transformed the Park Service. Until then, the bureau had remained relatively small, dedicated to the preservation and management of about two dozen parks almost all located in the eleven western states. By the end of the summer of 1933, however, the Park Service had acquired responsibility for over fifty new historical parks and monuments. It also operated seventy CCC camps in national parks and helped supervise 105 camps in non-federal (mostly state) parks in thirty-five states. By the end of the next summer, there were 102 national park camps and 268 state park camps in forty states.[26] As the Park Service grew precipitously, portions of its operations were regionalized. Four "districts" were created by Albright in May 1933 to handle the administrative burden of cooperating with scores of state and local governments in the development of new parks. Dividing the country geographically from east to west, "district officers" set up their regional administrations in Washington, Indianapolis, Denver, and San Francisco. By 1935, as the number of CCC camps continued to grow, the number of districts (renamed "regions" that year) had expanded to eight. That year the Park Service, in cooperation with individual state park authorities, was responsible for planning, design, and construction in 475 state park CCC camps.[27] Other divisions of the Park Service (those not involved with state park activities) were not yet regionalized, but discussions were already underway regarding the desirability of unifying the national and state park CCC programs, a change which implied such a reorganization of the entire bureau.

Bureaucratic growth and regionalization were necessitated by a huge expansion of staff and responsibilities. Before the spring of 1933, the Park Service had about 700 permanent and 373 temporary employees. Of these, fewer than 150 worked in the Washington office or in the eastern and western field headquarters.[28] By 1935, over thirteen thousand people were employed with the Park Service, and at the peak of New Deal activities the number was closer to fourteen thousand. This number was inflated by employees who maintained the public buildings of the nation's capital (one of the many responsibilities transferred to the Park Service in the 1933 reorganization); but even when this function was divested to another agency in 1939, permanent Park Service personnel still numbered over 7,300. The Park Service "branch of plans and design," as Thomas Vint's division was now known, went from sixteen design and engineering professionals in 1933 to 120 in 1935. In 1936 the total rose to 220, but that number still did not include professionals working in the national park CCC camps as supervisors and foremen, or the hundreds of professionals working in the Park Service's state park CCC program.[29] Annual appropriations for the Park Service rose steadily as well, from about ten million dollars in 1933 to over twenty-five million dollars in 1939 (before returning to ten million dollars in 1941).[30] Work relief programs also directly funded Park Service construction projects far beyond what regular appropriations would have allowed. By 1940, the Public Works Administration (PWA), the Civil Works Administration (CWA), the Works Progress Administration (WPA), and the CCC had funneled $218 million into national park construction projects, an amount well over one and a half times that of all regular appropriations during the same period. By that time, the number of "units" in the national park system had grown over seven years from sixty-three (a total of 14,701,000 acres), to 161 (a total of 21,550,783 acres), including parks, monuments, military and historical parks, memorials, and other areas.[31]

The enormous expansion and diversification of Park Service activities quickly gave the bureau what the historian Donald C. Swain calls "the earmarks of a New Deal agency."[32] But of course the Park Service was not an invention of the New Deal; to some degree, in fact, the reverse was true. The programs, plans, and technical expertise that Mather and Albright had assembled since 1917 had made the bureau a unique national authority on outdoor recreational planning by 1933. And planning for recreational uses of public lands assumed greater significance during the Roosevelt administration than it had ever before in the United States, and possibly ever has since.

The outdoor recreation movement had been flourishing since before World War I; the creation of the Park Service, as well as numerous state and local park commissions, was evidence of the growing influence of mostly middle class tourists, mostly in automobiles, getting "back to nature" in the early 20th century. The "astonishing increase in motor travel" to national parks had shaped the activities of the Park Service from its inception. As Mather, Albright, Hull, and Vint refined park planning procedures during the 1920s, the popularity of outdoor recreation continued to broaden and expand. In 1921, Mather helped organize a National Conference on Parks in Des Moines, bringing together dozens of prominent park advocates from all over the country. Mather was motivated in part by the desire to protect the standards and integrity of the national park system, since by encouraging the creation of regional and state parks he hoped to avoid substandard properties from being forced on the Park Service. But far more ambitious goals for state park planning were being expressed by other park advocates at the national conference. The group officially proclaimed that outdoor recreation was a basic human need, and that the national parks were often too far from centers of population to meet that need consistently. Municipal parks were more accessible, but insufficient to provide the desired experience of "the great outdoors." A complete, nationwide park system needed to include a full typology of parks, including what J. Horace McFarland described as "broad areas that will give opportunity to enjoy the great outdoors as well as to preserve and make available the characteristic scenery of any particular state." Speaking at the second National Conference on State Parks held in 1922 at the Bear Mountain Inn, McFarland declared, "No American family should have to travel a thousand miles or more to reach a great open space." What was needed was a fully developed, national system of parks, including national parks certainly, but also including far more numerous state and county scenic reservations, which if less spectacular than national parks, were far more accessible to urban populations.[33]

A growing number of park advocates in the early 1920s were calling for coordinated, national outdoor recreational planning that would assure that a full range of recreational opportunities—from neighborhood playgrounds to national parks—would be available. The rapidly organizing state park movement brought together many different park promoters who advocated the coordinated expansion of different park systems. In 1924, Calvin Coolidge recognized this trend by convening the National Conference on Outdoor Recreation, which assembled twenty-eight national organizations and scores of local groups to discuss how, in Coolidge's words, "to expand and conserve throughout the country our recreational opportunities."[34] The conference resulted in the creation of a cooperative association of national, state, and local groups working together to coordinate "national policy" on recreational planning for all categories of public lands. But the creation of such policy remained far beyond the mandate of any federal bureau.

Mather's encouragement of state park planning, like the formation of the National Conference on Outdoor Recreation, relied on the spirit of cooperation for effectiveness and on private charity for most funding. Individual planners, such as Benton MacKaye or Warren Manning, who advocated their own national recreational plans in the early 1920s, did so largely at their own expense. By 1933, no truly coordinated policy for national recreational planning yet existed. Individual state and federal land management agencies pursued park plans independently, without the benefits or drawbacks of a centralized planning authority.

By the late 1920s, however, several states had produced individual statewide recreation plans that later influenced the course of New Deal national planning. In New York, the head of the Palisades Interstate Park Commission, George W. Perkins, initiated a park plan for the entire state, which was published by the New York State Association in 1922. From Niagara Falls to Bear Mountain, many independent but loosely federated park commissions administered the state's numerous scenic and historic sites. The 1922 plan, drafted by the secretary of the New York Association, Robert Moses, called for the creation of a Council of State Parks that would coordinate park commission activities and lobby for a unified bond authorization to finance park improvements statewide. In 1927 the council was reorganized as a division of the state Conservation Commission. By 1929 a wide variety of scenic areas, beach parks, automotive parkways, historic houses, and battlefields had been brought together in what was the nation's largest and most diverse state park system.[35]

In other states as well, what had been scattered collections of scenic reservations and historic sites were consolidated and enlarged as state park systems. Many of these park systems, such as the Forest Preserve Districts around Chicago or the Westchester County parks outside New York, included areas that served large crowds of urbanites looking for picnic groves, swimming pools, and hiking trails within day-tripping distance. But no state park plan proved more significant than the *State Park Survey of California* completed by Frederick Law Olmsted, Jr., in 1929. Like New York, California already had impressive state parks, most of which had been established to preserve groves of coast redwoods. In 1927, the California State Legislature established a state park commission and authorized it to undertake a comprehensive survey to determine the "ultimate development of a comprehensive, state park system" as a means of "conserving and utilizing the scenic and recreational resources of the state."[36] The commission immediately hired Olmsted, already well known in the state for his advocacy of national and state parks and as the planner of Palos Verdes Estates (1923), the town where he also built a home for his family in 1927. Olmsted, in turn, consulted with several California landscape architects over the next two years, including Daniel Hull, who had only recently ended his relationship with the Park Service and remained in private practice in Los Angeles.

Olmsted's California survey demonstrated a standard procedure for planning a diverse park and recreation system over a large and geographically varied area. He began by regionalizing the project into twelve districts and enlisting a committee of residents in each district to serve as an advisory group. He then determined criteria for the development of the "comprehensive system" he had been charged with planning. In what became an influential summary of state park goals, he specified that each park should be "sufficiently distinctive and notable" to attract visitors from all parts of the state, not just the local area. The parks should also be geographically distributed in order to preserve characteristic forests, beaches, mountains, and generally a "wide and representative variety of [landscape] types for the state as a whole." These types included "areas of special interest, historic, scientific, and otherwise," including desert parks and historical parks, which were not yet represented in the state park system. A state map, divided into zones according to vegetative associations, illustrated the diversity and distribution of the new parks recommended by the survey. The plan became a procedural blueprint for scientific and comprehensive state park planning, as well as the basis for the development of California's exceptional state park system.[37]

Examples of state park planning, especially in New York and California, prefigured later events in Washington. After the executive reorganization of 1933, the national park system included a greater variety of park types, such as scenic areas, historic sites, and battlefields, all of which were to be managed as a unified park system. The national park system had grown to represent and preserve landscapes in many regions of the country, just as McFarland and Olmsted had suggested a well-planned state park system should exemplify the characteristic landscapes of a state. But the diversification and expansion of the national park system had only begun. By 1941, several new categories of national parks had been created, including national parkways, national recreation areas, and national seashores. The Park Service had also completed the first true national survey of existing park and recreational facilities; and if few states had developed state park systems in 1933, soon almost every state and territory at least initiated a comprehensive park plan (along the lines of Olmsted's California survey) under the guidance of Park Service planners.

The growth and diversification of Park Service activities was a function of the increased emphasis that New Deal activities placed on recreational planning generally in the management of public lands. The "conservation of recreational resources" (opportunities for outdoor recreation) was described as vital to the future well-being of the nation, just as the conservation of natural resources had been characterized a generation earlier. The Park Service therefore acquired a symbolic role in the New Deal not unlike that played by the Forest Service during the previous Roosevelt's administration. This change in emphasis reflected the continued growth of the economic and social impact of outdoor recreation in the United States. Since the Park Service had positioned itself as a unique authority on planning for outdoor recreation among federal bureaus, its ship, as Henry Hubbard observed, was set to sail in 1933.

The Forest Service had also pursued recreational planning, but in a desultory manner, motivated in part by a desire to prevent further expansion of the national park system. When the forest reserves began to be declared in the 1890s, many local park advocates continued to press for the creation of national parks in scenic areas, even after they had been included within forest reserves. At Mount Rainier, Crater Lake, and Rocky Mountain, for example, park legislation was pursued in order to prevent logging, grazing, and other uses that national forest designations had not precluded. And there was another reason for local boosters to continue to lobby for national park status: once Congress passed park legislation, appropriations for the construction of park roads and other facilities presumably would be forthcoming. If the Forest Service wished to prevent further loss of its territory, it needed to initiate its own park developments in areas where local civic clubs and auto tourists were campaigning for park legislation. These pressures led the Forest Service to begin to designate and develop recreational areas in places already popular with tourists, like Mount Hood in Oregon or the San Isabel National Forest in Colorado. As mentioned earlier, Frank Waugh and Arthur Carhart had both been hired to provide recreational plans for several national forests; but Waugh's services were intermittent, and Carhart left in 1922, disappointed that the Forest Service was unwilling to seriously pursue park development. Since that time, the Forest Service had relied on its rangers to make rudimentary improvements at campgrounds and other public areas. Neither Congress nor the Forest Service considered recreational planning one of that bureau's chief mandates during the 1920s.[38]

It was not immediately clear in the spring of 1933, however, that New Deal programs (particularly the CCC) would emphasize recreational planning to the degree they eventually did. The CCC "tree army," after all, concentrated mainly on forestry and soil conservation activities, and the majority of CCC camps were assigned to national and state forests where the Forest Service oversaw them. The CCC "boys" were in their late teens and early 20s and generally had few skills and little work experience. It was expected that, even in national parks, they would be occupied mostly in constructing fire roads, fighting forest fires, reforesting cutover land, and stabilizing eroded slopes. At the Park Service, Albright at first placed his chief forester, John Coffman, in charge of national and state park CCC activities, anticipating that forestry projects would be the main work of the CCC in the parks.[39]

Once the CCC camps were operational, however, it was soon evident that the enrollees would be able to successfully undertake demanding construction and park development projects in addition to their forestry activities. Trepidation regarding the quality of masonry and wood construction the young men would be capable of soon was assuaged, and the Park Service began to employ CCC labor in more ambitious park projects. There were a number of reasons why the CCC program was so successful. A group of "local experienced men," for example, were hired at each camp and provided vital guidance and training while laboring with the recruits. The construction projects, like the camps themselves, were also extremely well supervised. The silver lining of the Depression was soon revealed: the unemployed condition of thousands of professionals, scientists, and educators made them available and eager to participate in the CCC and other New Deal programs. Landscape architects, in particular, were hired to work in state and national park CCC camps, but many other unemployed professionals were hired as supervisors and foremen. In a CCC camp in Keosauqua, Iowa, landscape architect Kenneth F. Jones worked as a "landscape foreman," supervising work crews of about twenty boys apiece. Each crew, he reported, had a "working foreman" with professional training: a landscape architect, an architect, a civil engineer, an agricultural engineer, a forester, a forest pathologist, and an entomologist.[40] Higher up in the organization, a network of regional inspectors, including many well-known landscape architects and architects, relentlessly enforced uniform high standards for design and construction in national and state parks. Under these circumstances, difficult and complex construction could be successfully undertaken by the CCC. If the CCC program was originally intended to reclaim a generation of unemployed youths by employing them in forestry activities, the great potential of using their labor to build national, state, and local parks became clear within the first months of the program. The political rewards of building new parks for hundreds of local communities also obviously exceeded those of less functional forestry projects.[41] As Herbert Evison later observed, "From the moment it was realized that the CCC could legitimately be utilized to perform Emergency Conservation Work on State parks, the State park

A CCC crew at work burying a utility line in Grand Canyon Village. The role of "local experienced men," or "LEMs," was crucial to the success of the CCC. Working alongside inexperienced recruits, these older laborers and craftsmen raised the standards and expectations of the program immeasurably. National Archives, Record Group 79.

situation underwent, for good or evil, the most radical change in its seventy-year history."[42]

Another reason for the success of CCC camps in the case of national parks was the master plans that Thomas Vint and his colleagues had already developed for virtually every national park and monument by 1933. The plans outlined many useful and carefully designed improvements that were waiting to be implemented. In the fall of 1933, Vint relocated from San Francisco to Washington, and his title was changed from "chief landscape architect" to "chief architect."[43] By 1934, the landscape architecture division had been renamed the "branch of plans and design." In the rapidly growing San Francisco office, Vint's assistant William Carnes took over as head of the "western division" of the branch of plans and design; the "eastern division," which remained under Charles Peterson, moved to Washington and also took on dozens of new employees.[44] As Vint's design division grew to many times its former size, the procedures and policies he had instituted remained in effect. Experienced Park Service landscape architects, such as Ernest Davidson, Merel Sager, John Wosky, Kenneth McCarter, Harry Langley, Herbert Krellenkamp, and Howard Baker, were ready to supervise scores of fresh recruits, many of whom were well qualified but had no experience in park planning. In 1933, Vint assigned each of these veterans responsibility for a "district" (a cluster of national parks), assuring that in every area of the park system new design staff would be supervised by someone he had personally trained in San Francisco.[45]

The CCC was not the only New Deal program that began pouring money into the national parks in 1933. That year Roosevelt asked Secretary of the Interior Ickes to administer the Public Works Administration (PWA) in addition to his other duties. As public works administrator, Ickes needed to find worthwhile projects that were well planned and ready to go to construction immediately. The Park Service, thanks to Albright and Vint, had many such plans, and by 1935 the bureau was enjoying what were officially described as the "thrills of Aladdin" as the PWA "brought about the magical materialization almost overnight of important recreational and educational objectives, long projected, but delayed for lack of appropriations."[46] In its first year, the PWA, guided by the master plans, funded over 150 projects in national parks. Vint's new branch of plans and designs was hard pressed during this time just keeping up with the demand for working drawings so that projects could go to construction as quickly as possible. The organization of his division offices greatly accelerated the process; schematic design, design development, working drawings, contract specifications, and construction supervision were all done in house, speeding the many reviews and approvals necessary for such projects.[47] In the past, Mather and Albright had looked to private capital (concessioners) to finance major park buildings; after 1933, the federal government would be expected to assume the cost of most new facilities.

Much of the best known national park architecture of the 1930s was funded by the PWA. At Grand Canyon Village, the program funded the post office (on the plaza), a new community building, and many of the Park Service bungalows in the residential areas. At Mount Rainier, the Yakima Park stockade fence, backcountry cabins and fire towers, and assorted residential bungalows and comfort stations were built through PWA allotments. Road projects were also funded by the program, including improvements to Going-to-the-Sun Road. In the East, the PWA initiated the massive Appalachian parkway project that would later be called the Blue Ridge Parkway.[48] But the PWA mostly financed architectural construction in the parks, and although in the past most of the Park Service design staff had been trained as landscape architects and engineers, scores of architects were now quickly hired to manage building projects. The change in Vint's title to "chief architect" in 1933 was probably intended to emphasize that he remained in charge of all the bureau's design work; it also reflected the influence that the PWA program was having by funding the construction of so many buildings in national parks.

Established master planning procedures continued to guide the park planners of Vint's branch of plans and design as the CCC and the PWA invested unprecedented labor and capital in the national park system. In state park design, as well, Park Service landscape architects adapted Vint's master planning process to guide state and local park developments. In this case, Park Service planners created state park master plans that mimicked the larger national park master plans in their basic format. There were differences in the state plans, of course, besides their scale. Scenic preservation remained a major goal for state parks as it was for national parks; but state park design, done in cooperation with local park authorities, incorporated a wider and more varied range of recreational uses within a smaller area. If the basic procedures of national park master planning were easily adapted to state parks, different policies determined how much and what type of landscape development would be deemed appropriate in the state reservations. State park design was also administered separately within the Park Service. While chief forester John Coffman remained in overall charge of Park Service CCC programs, state park CCC "planning and cooperation" was supervised out of the "branch of lands" at the Park Service. Vint's new branch of plans and design remained primarily concerned with work related to federal properties; the branch of lands, located in a parallel position on the Park Service organizational chart, took responsibility for all state and local park planning. In 1934, the branch was renamed the "branch of recreational land planning," and in 1936 it became the "branch of recreation, land planning, and state cooperation," indicating the growth and development of its activities.[49] After 1934 it was usually referred to simply as the "branch of planning." The assistant director in charge of the branch was a young landscape architect named Conrad L. Wirth, who had joined the Washington office in 1931.

Wirth was the son of the famous Minneapolis park superintendent, Theodore Wirth, and through his father he enjoyed many contacts with prominent figures in the American park movement. He graduated from Frank Waugh's landscape program at the University of Massachusetts, and later went into business with a partner in New Orleans. When the Gulf Coast real estate market collapsed in 1927, the landscape architect was thrown out of work. Frederick Law Olmsted, Jr., subsequently arranged for him to be hired by the National Capital Park and Planning Commission, where Wirth was in charge of investigating and reporting on potential additions to the Washington park system. Three years later, when the position of assistant director in charge of land planning opened up at the Washington office of the Park Service, Horace Albright asked Wirth to transfer and take over similar planning responsibilities for the national park system.[50]

Wirth's position as the chief land planner at the Park Service made him a logical choice to organize state park planning efforts in 1933. At that time, many states did not yet have state park systems or even a single state park. In order to capitalize on federal work relief programs (especially the CCC), the first requirement for many states was to draft a recreational land use plan to guide the acquisition of new parkland. Wirth's experience investigating and reporting on potential national park areas would serve him well while he assisted in planning the expansion of dozens of state park systems after 1933. Managing CCC state park planning nationwide was a daunting organizational task, and Wirth also proved to be a capable administrator. He quickly established official relationships with local governments that made it possible for the Park Service to "cooperate"—that is, provide extensive planning and design assistance—without suggesting that local authorities were being bypassed or overruled by a federal bureau. This was a massive and sometimes delicate bureaucratic feat, which Wirth performed with great aplomb over the next eight years.

Herbert Evison, the executive secretary of the National Conference on State Parks, was enlisted to assist Wirth, and together they administered CCC state park planning through the district offices established in 1933. The "district officers" of this shadow park service included leading figures from the state park movement. Lawrence Merriam, the California forester, headed the western district office in San Francisco. Paul V. Brown, an important figure in Indiana state parks, led a midwestern district in Indianapolis. John M. Hoffman, who had been commissioner of Pennsylvania state parks, ran the eastern district in Washington. Perhaps most significantly for the subsequent history of Park Service design, Herbert Maier, the architect of the Yellowstone trailside museums, was hired as the district officer for the Rocky Mountain district in Denver.[51] They were an impressive group, and with the resources of the Park Service and CCC behind them, they were prepared to implement state park plans that a few years earlier would have seemed visionary.

Over the next several years the CCC was acclaimed as an unqualified success of the New Deal. New state parks all over the country were particularly convincing evidence of the value and permanence of the work being done by the CCC boys. The state parks were designed by scores of planners and landscape architects who, whether supervised by state park departments ("local park authorities") or directly by the Park Service district offices, were paid through federal funds and met standards for their work imposed by Conrad Wirth and his associates.[52] Wirth insisted that the arrangement was "an extension of the understandings that were developed in 1921 when the National Conference on State Parks was organized," based on a purely voluntary "exchange of ideas"; but the desirability of CCC state park camps and funding gave the Park Service far greater leverage with local governments than Wirth acknowledged. Local park authorities submitted applications for the assignment of CCC camps based on state recreational land-use plans—usually part of an overall state plan—that identified desirable state park areas based on a statewide survey of land suitabilities and characteristics. The Park Service district offices reviewed the applications, supervised park planning, and assigned the camps. State park departments (where they existed) hired professionals to prepare park plans, procured all supplies and materials, and generally were in direct control of their park projects. Of course they did all this with the federal money disbursed to them as part of the CCC program, and the Park Service oversaw and supervised every aspect of park planning and development. Wirth's state park CCC program hired regional inspectors (just as the national park CCC program did) who were usually professional designers or engineers of some standing. Very early in the state park program, when Wirth felt that "the planning and development operation was not up to standard" in many states, he reminded his inspectors (and indirectly state park officials) that failure to meet design and construction standards would result in the loss of CCC state park camps. It was an effective if indirect threat, and Wirth reported receiving excellent cooperation from both his regional inspectors and local park authorities once the point was made.[53]

As chief of state park planning and cooperation at the Park Service, Wirth instituted far-reaching policies in 1933 and 1934. At the fifteenth annual National Conference on State Parks, held at Skyland, Virginia, in 1935, Wirth summarized his planning procedures. He felt that state parks (and for that matter all parks) should be considered in two categories: those set aside for "conservation," and those set aside "primarily for recreation." The two types, he added, might be joined or separated, and "one might even completely surround the other, forming a multiple-use area." But Wirth also warned his planners that they should "always bear in mind the distinction" between conservation and recreational areas, and "forever seek a means of separating these two types." Inappropriate or poorly sited recreational development would simply degrade conservation areas, he explained, something which too often occurred because of public and official pressure to maximize recreational facilities. In either category, proposed state parks were also required to meet certain standards that would distinguish them from county or municipal parks. For the conservation category, proposed state reservations should contain "the outstanding natural scenic areas of the state." The plants, wildlife, and geologic features of the area also should "attract State-wide recognition." Areas suitable for recreational development, on the other hand, were often more difficult to select since they did not possess the obvious scenic features that qualified an area in the conservation category. To know where state recreational developments were needed, extensive statistical and demographic information needed to be compiled for surrounding populations. Topographic and vegetative surveys would be critical as well, since selecting recreational areas required imagination to visualize how perhaps barren or degraded land, which otherwise might be overlooked, "could be transformed to serve good recreational purposes" near cities and towns in need of such areas.[54]

The task of national recreational planning described by Wirth was huge; equally tremendous resources, however, had been made available. Herbert Evison estimated that in 1934, seven hundred landscape architects, architects, and engineers working for various local park authorities (but paid through CCC funds) were engaged in state park planning. This total did not include the 220 professionals employed by Vint's branch of plans and design by 1936, or those working as supervisors and foremen in national park CCC camps. Thomas Vint's assistant, William Carnes, later recalled that of the one thousand or more design and engineering professionals directly or indirectly supervised by the Park Service during the mid-1930s, about four hundred were landscape architects—a figure that suggests more members of the profession were working for the Park Service at the time than were not.[55] By 1934, five states that previously had no state parks (Mississippi, New Mexico, Oklahoma, Virginia, and South Carolina) acquired between one and six; twenty other states acquired new parks and added to existing ones. By 1935, 600,000 acres of state parkland had been added to the national total. That summer ninety thousand CCC boys were at work building state parks in 475 camps, and the CCC was either already developing or planned to develop one half of the total of over three and a half million acres of state parkland in the country.[56] By the end of the year the CCC reported building a total of 4,800 miles of roads, as well as 899 swimming areas, almost two thousand road and trail bridges, and over one hundred overlook shelters in state parks in forty-four states.[57]

States with established state park systems, such as New York, Indiana, Iowa, and California, had been in a position to capitalize immediately on the opportunity. Others may have had more difficulties organizing their programs, but by 1935 had "rapidly fallen into line" according to CCC director Robert Fechner. Certain states, especially in the Southeast and the Midwest, were particularly well positioned to exploit the CCC state park program. If New York and California already had extensive state park systems in 1933, states like Tennessee, Texas, Kentucky, Missouri, and Oklahoma had few developed scenic reservations at that point. Over the previous decade, however, these states (and many others) had either created state park commissions or were otherwise planning to significantly expand their state park systems. In addition, many of these states had powerful congressmen and senators who were long-time state park advocates, and who were now were vitally interested in delivering this new form of federal largesse to their constituencies. For states with few developed parks but many park proposals in 1933, the timing of the New Deal proved felicitous. For the duration of the CCC program, they could expect that any approved park sites they owned or acquired would be developed at federal expense by the CCC. In many cases the CCC developed entire state park systems on land rapidly acquired for the purpose by state officials, who were also able to take advantage of Depression-era land prices.

For all the parks developed by the CCC, the Park Service oversaw the production of master plans, reviewed planning decisions, and inspected park construction. Conrad Wirth's Washington office was directly involved with design reviews, as were the regional office staff and regional inspectors. The state park master plans were miniature versions of national park master plans, and as such they graphically illustrated the degree to which Wirth was building on the landscape architectural practice developed by Thomas Vint. Like the national park plans, the state park master plans typically were composed of a series of maps and more detailed drawings which together showed the full extent and character of all development for a park. Certain areas, especially of larger state parks, were intended to remain undeveloped "conservation" areas, like Vint's "wilderness" zones. Roads, fire roads, and trails would be kept to a minimum, but would allow access to the most important scenic and other features of interest in the park. Developed areas in the park, drawn at more detailed scales, were designated as overnight campgrounds, day use areas, and for other specialized uses. Among significant differences between the state park and national park master plans was the relative proportion of developed areas in each. More activities were considered appropriate for state parks. Swimming, boating, and fishing were among the most popular outdoor recreations, and so the creation of at least one lake was often the centerpiece of state park plans, whereas dam construction for these purposes would have been anathemized in a national park plan.

If swimming pools, ball fields, and other recreational facilities figured prominently in state park plans, however, recreational areas were often juxtaposed significant tracts of woodland developed only with hiking and bridle trails. As in national park plans, development was concentrated in limited areas, typically along a road corridor; the two types of parkland Wirth described were kept as separate as possible. "Although extensive recreational developments have been undertaken," Director Fechner reported in 1935, "the basic purpose underlying the [CCC state park] program has been the conservation of the valuable natural resources that properly selected state parks contain." Further indicating the influence of Park Service landscape architects on CCC activities, Fechner observed that the "highly valuable resource" that most state parks contained in particular was "scenic beauty," and that "if the developed areas are so arranged that use of the park will be concentrated and the majority of its acreage left untouched . . . this scenic beauty and the area's wildlife may go unmolested."[58]

Conrad Wirth's catholic approach to park planning—embracing both scenic preservation and the development of new kinds of recreational areas—articulated an expansion in landscape architectural practice that was needed as much in national park planning as in the planning of state parks. The national park system was assimilating many new and diverse properties, and the comprehensive approach described by Wirth for the design of state park systems was easily adapted as a conceptual model for managing the expanded national system. The criteria and categories for the selection of state parks, for example, needed only to be defined in terms of national significance (rather than statewide significance) to be adapted to the purposes of national park planning. The demographic, geographic, and other scientific data collected for state park plans could also be used to plan national parks where and if appropriate. By 1935, the planning for new kinds of national parks around western reservoirs or along "national seashores" represented both new kinds of park landscapes and new kinds of recreational activities that were being incorporated into the national park system. These new influences originated in the experience of Conrad Wirth and the Park Service landscape architects engaged in recreational planning at the state level.

Within the first two years of the CCC program, Wirth's state park organization influenced the operations of the Park Service as a whole, and the entire project of national recreational planning began to coalesce in the aggregate activities of the Park Service and the over 140 state, county, and municipal authorities with which it eventually cooperated. As the state park CCC program grew, it became desirable to combine all Park Service CCC planning efforts rather than continue with parallel organizations to administer state park and national park CCC projects. Considering the size and scope of the state park operations, Director Cammerer decided in 1936 that Conrad Wirth should assume the administration of both state and national park CCC work, taking over Chief Forester John Coffman's responsibilities. All CCC planning (for national as well as state parks) would then be administered out of the CCC regional offices Wirth had set up.[59] One implication of this consolidation was to effectively regionalize most of the Park Service; seventy percent of the bureau's personnel—the portion involved in CCC related work—were brought under the supervision of the regional offices by this action. Another result was the consolidation of the vital system of regional inspectors that reviewed CCC work in the field. In the past the national park CCC inspectors, who reported directly to Washington, tended to be old-line Park Service personnel with whom the park superintendents were comfortable. The inspectors that replaced them reported to the regional offices, and they were generally newcomers to the Park Service, paid out of emergency appropriations. The superintendents resented the change; the new CCC inspectors represented an incursion of Wirth's shadow park service into the management of the national parks themselves.[60]

The superintendents also knew that while Cammerer was consolidating the CCC programs, he was also proposing a complete regionalization plan that would further consolidate Wirth's New Deal recreational planning organization with the rest of the Park Service. Four new Park Service regional offices were proposed to replace and absorb the CCC regional offices; all Park Service operations were to be brought together in a consolidated, but regionalized, administration. Cammerer was careful to point out that the new regional directors would be Park Service veterans, not state park planners. The complete regionalization of the Park Service, however, had been debated since at least 1934 and still inspired bitter opposition from both inside and outside the bureau. Many park superintendents, used to dealing directly with the Washington office, objected to an additional level of management between them and the director. Other concerns about regionalization called into question the expanded mandate the Park Service had assumed since 1933. The New Deal invested great amounts of labor and capital into the development of the national park system, inevitably intensifying opposition to any further construction of roads or other facilities in the national parks. As the debate over what defined "wilderness" grew more divisive, many voices warned of an unexpected but potent threat to the parks: the Park Service itself. Robert Sterling Yard at the National Parks Association, Robert Marshall at the Wilderness Society, and Arthur Newton Pack at the American Nature Association, among others, became increasingly concerned by the mid-1930s about what they characterized as the "problem" of outdoor recreation in national parks. These groups felt planning for recreational uses of land was contrary to the true mandate of the Park Service: preserving the integrity of "primeval wilderness." In practice this meant reducing the number of people and automobiles in parks, not accommodating them further. In 1936, Yard's National Parks Association and a coalition of other groups suggested designating the older, larger parks as a "National Primeval Park System," since they felt "the original system" had been "lost sight of among innumerable recreational activities, local, regional and national, assigned to the National Park Service."[61] By 1938, Arthur Newton Pack's *Nature Magazine* regularly printed articles asking "What is Happening to Our National Parks?" and decrying "practical idealists" who compromised the integrity of parks when politically expedient, and who were "proudest of the statistics showing . . . the increased horde of visitors."[62]

For these critics, the full regionalization of the Park Service that was being debated in 1936 signaled the unwelcome substantiation of a larger and more diverse national park system. Where Albright and later Cammerer had seen increased strength in the typological and geographical variety of the park system, purists saw only degradation of national park standards, a development they feared would bring increased "recreational" activities into the great western scenic reservations. And for many of these activists, public recreation could no longer be considered a legitimate program for national parks (at least not in the "primeval" parks). The National Parks Association, for example, described "education" and "inspiration" as the higher uses for national parks; recreation (which implied "entertainment" or "diversion") they felt should be relegated to other places, preferably state or local parks.[63] For these critics, the consolidation of state park and national park planning brought about in the Park Service through its participation in the CCC program promised to be the undoing of the Park Service and of the national parks themselves.

But what "primeval park" advocates perhaps failed to appreciate was that the New Deal was transforming the federal government itself. The Park Service, at the center of so much New Deal activity, had rapidly assumed new and expanded responsibilities in direct response to the social and environmental policies of the Roosevelt administration. The New Deal had remade the Park Service into an instrument of "national planning"; the Park Service, in turn, articulated defining policies for that national plan. The integration of national and local recreational planning and the increased emphasis on the recreational uses of land in general were not distractions for Park Service planners, but unique opportunities to realize the full potential of park planning in the United States. And "recreation," for a landscape architect like Conrad Wirth, was defined in the broadest sense to include the appreciation of landscape scenery and the enjoyment of the most remote backcountry area. Planning for the recreational uses of national parks, therefore, did not imply a threat to the integrity of "primeval" parks, but on the contrary offered a means of preserving "wilderness" by defining its place within a hierarchy of different recreational land uses.

The substantial role of Park Service officials in New Deal "national planning" had begun during the Hundred Days of 1933. When Secretary of the Interior Ickes assumed the administration of the PWA, he knew that the plans for public works prepared in advance by groups like the Park Service would only go so far. To guide massive public works spending efficiently, some form of national planning authority was needed to coordinate the projects proposed by federal, state, and local organizations. Ickes therefore organized the National Planning Board within the PWA. Chaired by Frederic A. Delano, then president of the American Civic Association, the new group found an energetic executive director in landscape architect Charles W. Eliot II, who transferred from the National Capital Park and Planning Commission. The national board, which changed its name several times over the next ten years, immediately encouraged states to initiate coordinated state plans, including the plans for expanded state park systems that became the basis for state park CCC work. Although the National Planning Board could no more than suggest such cooperation from state governments, it was understood that future work relief spending might be influenced by such plans, and within one year thirty-five states had initiated state planning efforts. By 1936 every state except Delaware had at least begun a state plan.[64]

From its beginning, the National Planning Board relied on the Park Service as the best available source for information and advice on the recreational needs and trends of the nation. In 1934 the board, now renamed the National Resources Board, asked the Park Service to begin a comprehensive national study of "national and state parks and related recreational activities." To undertake the study, a "recreation board" was set up within the Park Service, headed by Herbert Evison and George M. Wright, chief of the wildlife division.[65] The report was presented that fall, but in the words of one of the planners, "It was evident, from our first considerations, that the requisite information was not available. The time allotted . . . was all too brief."[66] The only definitive conclusion in 1934 was that a more comprehensive national survey of recreational resources was indeed needed, and that year Secretary Ickes began pressing Congress for legislation that would allow the Park Service to undertake such a project. In June 1936, Congress passed the Park, Parkway and Recreational-Area Study Act, which validated and extended the role the Park Service had already assumed as the nation's recreational planning agency. The law authorized the Park Service to undertake a truly comprehensive national survey of all types of recreational areas, and to use that information to assemble a plan that would coordinate the activities of federal land agencies and local park authorities to meet the future recreational needs of the country. The bill also contained provisions which allowed the Park Service to fund the planning activities of local park authorities, and which gave consent for two or more states to cooperate in completing regional surveys of recreational resources.[67]

The 1936 Park, Parkway and Recreational-Area Study Act marked the high point of the CCC's promise, and therefore of the Park Service's role as a national recreational planning authority.[68] Once the bill became law, Arno Cammerer appointed Conrad Wirth as chairman of a special Park Service "recreation committee," and Wirth also replaced Secretary Ickes as the Interior representative on the CCC advisory council. Wirth's renamed "branch of recreation, land planning, and state cooperation" compiled the ambitious plan, and CCC emergency conservation work appropriations paid for it. The National Resources Board, now called the National Resources Committee, provided assistance and advice.[69] In January 1937, the Park Service recreation committee distributed a procedural manual instructing state and local governments on what the national recreational survey was intended to be and how they could help assemble the needed information. The committee described the "problem of recreational land use" in the United States: although there had been stunning growth in state park systems since 1933, much of it had, "of necessity been based on inadequate planning," resulting sometimes in "unhealthy growth" and "ill-suited and unneeded development of available lands." Wirth suggested that each state conduct a comprehensive survey of "existing park, parkway, and recreational facilities," and of "potential areas . . . for acquisition and development." These surveys could then be compiled by the Park

Service and become the basis of a "comprehensive report on a Nation-wide basis."[70]

Wirth and his committee provided blank forms in their 1937 manual to be used by local park authorities to conduct their surveys. On the forms, classes of recreational areas were divided according to categories suggested by the Natural Resources Committee: "primitive," or the most remote and expansive areas; "modified," essentially primitive areas that might be partially accessible by fire roads or trails; "developed," primarily road corridors and recreational areas; and "scientific," or areas of particular biological or geological significance that were not expansive enough to be in the primitive class. The analogy to Thomas Vint's master plan land-use zones (research, wilderness, developed, and sacred zones) was exact. The forms also asked local planners to survey recreational facilities of all types, including camps, picnic areas, and lodges, and to identify properties by categories of use. The categories of recreational use suggested—aesthetic, social, physical, or creative—indicated the broadest possible sense of "recreation" as any "constructive use of leisure time," from arts and crafts to mountaineering. The other data needed for the Park Service to make its comprehensive report were also described: "physiographical and geological data," including topographic and geologic maps; "climatic data"; "economic data," including land values, tax rates, transportation networks, and average incomes; "biological data" on regional flora and fauna; "historical and archeological data"; and "social data," or statistics on population trends and characteristics.[71] There was no precedent for a study of this type or scope; the forms and procedures outlined by Wirth and the other recreation committee members drew on many sources (notably the practice of landscape planning developed by Thomas Vint), but they delineated a new function for the federal government.

States responded quickly to the call to organize recreational planning efforts. In 1938, forty-three states arranged to participate in the study, and seven states completed tentative final reports. By 1941, when the Park Service published the completed study, thirty-four states had contributed finished surveys which were condensed and published as an index of national recreational resources. The final report, titled *A Study of the Park and Recreation Problem of the United States*, summarized the philosophy of New Deal recreational planning. As Secretary Ickes wrote in its forward, "The proper use of leisure time is a fundamental problem of modern society. . . . Outdoor recreation answers this need." The secretary described the fundamental goal of the Park Service planning activities: "To establish the basis for coordinated, correlated recreation land planning among all the agencies—Federal, state, and local—having responsibility for park and recreational developments."[72]

And so for the Park Service, the preservation of pristine conditions in western national parks could not be considered antithetical to planning and developing state parks and other recreational areas, as critics suggested. Both were aspects of the coordinated effort to meet the ever expanding demand for recreational uses of land; each effort, if different in emphasis, reinforced and assured the success of the other. Rather than compromising its commitment to preserve the western parks, the Park Service sought to expand both national and regional park systems with parks that would offer better recreational opportunities, and therefore spare the "primeval" parks from overcrowding and inappropriate activities.

The physical results of unified, national recreational planning soon appeared. A plethora of new parks—and new kinds of parks—were planned and developed to meet outdoor recreational needs at every level. The national park system acquired some of its most extensive "wilderness" parks during the 1930s, including Everglades and Olympic national parks. At the same time, the bureau created new categories of parks that were unlike earlier scenic reservations. The typological expansion had already begun under Horace Albright with the creation of new historical parks at Yorktown (Virginia) and Morristown (New Jersey); the 1933 transfer of national military, battlefield, and historic sites accelerated the process. Conrad Wirth's planners, however, backed by the CCC, forty-seven state park departments, and other New Deal agencies and programs, introduced whole new categories of national and state parks. In 1934, the Federal Emergency Relief Administration (FERA) committed twenty-five million dollars to the acquisition of "submarginal" farm land, some of which was to be developed by the Park Service for recreational purposes. In 1937 there were a total of forty-six of these projects, described generically as "recreational demonstration areas" (RDAs). Some of the RDAs were expansions of existing national parks and some became new national parks; others were demonstration "waysides," or highway rest stop developments. Thirty-four of the RDAs, however, were designed specifically (although not exclusively) to accommodate "group camp" organizations that operated summer camps for children. Although federally owned at first, these RDAs were intended to be a new kind of state park, featuring secluded clusters of cabins, recreation buildings, and dining halls meant for the exclusive use of non-profit summer camps. Usually located within fifty to one hundred miles of a major city, the RDAs provided organizations like the YMCA and the Girl Scouts with new parks that included (in addition to camp buildings) swimming areas, trails, ball fields, and lakes. By 1941, Conrad Wirth's branch of planning had acquired over 200,000 acres to develop RDAs. Beginning in 1942, all but two of the group camp parks were eventually given to their respective state park departments.[73]

Other new opportunities in recreational land development resulted from collaborations between the Park Service and another bureau within the Department of the Interior, the Bureau of Reclamation. By 1925, over 2,300,000 acres of western land were being irrigated through Bureau of Reclamation projects, and in 1928, Congress authorized the Boulder Canyon Project (Hoover Dam), the bureau's most ambitious undertaking up to that time. Also in 1928, Commissioner of Reclamation Elwood Mead published a short treatise titled *Federal Irrigation Reservoirs as Pleasure Resorts*. Among the other useful products of western reclamation projects, Mead was acutely aware of their social and economic importance as centers of recreation for growing towns and cities in the West.[74] In 1934 the Bureau of Reclamation was assigned nine CCC camps, under the condition that the Park Service would provide technical assistance and supervision for any recreational developments done by the CCC on Bureau of Reclamation land.[75] The agreement implied that the Park Service would be developing new parks that were not predicated on preserving existing landscape features, but on exploiting recreational opportunities associated with massive dam construction. In 1936 the Park Service assumed responsibility for the land around the new reservoir behind Hoover Dam, which was slowly filling at the time. The reservoir, soon named for Elwood Mead, eventually had 550 miles of shoreline offering extensive opportunities for every kind of water-related activity. The first national park of its type, the area was later designated the Lake Mead National Recreation Area and now covers 1,500,000 acres.[76]

In the East, a "national parkway" project connected two new national parks and opened up opportunities for outdoor recreation in the Appalachian Mountains. Proposals for an eastern "park-to-park highway" had been put forward even before Congress authorized Shenandoah, Great Smoky Mountains, and Mammoth Cave national parks in 1926. Like its western counterpart, such an interpark route initially was conceived simply as an improved system of state highways that would link national parks and divert the "flow of tourist gold" into hard pressed mountain communities. The potential of New Deal spending, however, transformed the proposed Appalachian road. In 1933, planning began for a 469-mile "national parkway" between Shenandoah and Great Smoky Mountains.[77] The term parkway, originally coined by Olmsted and Vaux in the late 1860s, implied that an entire corridor of parkland would be acquired for the project, and that the roadway built in the corridor would be restricted to non-commercial traffic. The term also implied that the roadway would be of the most advanced design. Since the 1920s, modern automotive parkways had achieved tremendous success as elements of regional park systems. The Westchester County (New York) parkways, for example, featured automotive roadways with grade crossings eliminated and access to the roadway limited to specific entrance and exit points. The principal landscape architect of the Blue Ridge Parkway, Stanley W. Abbott, had been an assistant to Gilmore D. Clarke, the landscape architect of the Westchester parkway system. And so the eastern "park-to-park highway" promised to be much more than simply a highway linking national parks. A technically sophisticated, limited access, non-commercial roadway, the parkway also became what Stanley Abbott described in 1939 as "an element of recreational planning . . . [and] the fusion of two American national parks into one huge recreational system."[78] Construction on the Blue Ridge Parkway began in 1935 and was advanced by PWA, WPA, and CCC funds and labor.

By 1941, the Park Service had built or was planning at least four distinct new kinds of national parks: recreational demonstration areas, national recreation areas, national parkways, and national seashores. This diversification was enabled and symbolized by the full regionalization of the Park Service that was implemented in the summer of 1937. Four new regions were established under new regional directors who administered all Park Service activity (not just the CCC work funded through emergency appropriations). In the East, Carl P. Russell was named director of a region that extended from Maine to Mississippi (Region I). Russell, who had many years of experience as a park naturalist and an administrator with the Park Service, was headquartered in Richmond. Thomas J. Allen, who headed the Midwest region (Region II) in Omaha, had begun his career with the Park Service as a ranger during the Mather era and had been superintendent of several parks. In the West (Region IV), chief engineer Frank Kittredge, still in San Francisco, took on a new assignment as a regional director. Cammerer wanted to avoid the appearance that the CCC organization had grown to engulf the old-line Park Service, and in all three cases he had chosen regional directors with longtime Park Service experience, not experience with Wirth's branch of planning. Wirth's CCC regional officers now became "associate regional directors" under the new appointees in their respective regions.[79]

The exception was in the Southwest (Region III), where the architect Herbert Maier, who had been the CCC regional officer in the area since 1933, was kept on in the new organization as an "acting regional director." Maier's headquarters, at first located in Denver, had been moved to Oklahoma City and was now relocated to Santa Fe. Maier had already exerted an important influence on national park architecture through his designs for trailside museums and nature shrines at Grand Canyon and Yellowstone. As a CCC regional officer, Maier helped determine the character and quality of state park architecture not only in the Southwest, but also in other regions where park architects emulated the work Maier administered in Region III. It was appropriate that Maier, who was doing so much to standardize and improve park architecture in both state and national parks, would be the only CCC regional officer to remain at least as an acting Park Service regional director.

Cammerer made it clear that the new regional directors were "the director's representatives in the field" and were "responsible for both regular and emergency programs in the regions." The superintendents were now to report to the regional directors exactly as they had reported to Cammerer, and the national and state CCC programs were brought together with regular Park Service activities in the regionalized arrangement.[80] But if the newly appointed regional directors represented the old Park Service, the bureaucratic reorganization itself still signaled the great institutional changes effected by the New Deal. Cammerer's position as director in the new organization was unlike that of Mather or Albright. For that matter, Harold Ickes was unlike any secretary of the interior who had preceded him. The overlapping appointments held by Ickes, as secretary of the interior and as administrator of the PWA, gave him great power not only to plan public works, but to disburse federal funds to realize them. A new relationship between the federal government and local governments was being forged, one based on the direct effects of federal spending on local economies. Since few forms of economic stimulus were more popular or effective than park development, the Park Service immediately became a major vehicle for emergency relief spending. The bureau, more than ever before, became a conduit of substantial federal aid to local economies. This forever changed the political constituencies and economic dynamic that had until then supported national park development. Mather and Albright had been quintessential boosters, cooperating with scores of local chambers of commerce and arranging limited monopolies for park concessioners. Arno Cammerer worked exclusively within the federal bureaucracy, and in fact rarely left Washington. Cammerer also established a very different persona as Park Service director. Quiet and self-effacing, Cammerer had been the ideal assistant director in the 1920s, keeping the bureau running smoothly in Washington while Mather and Albright barnstormed across the country. As director under Ickes, Cammerer continued this understated style, patiently bearing the abuses of the self-important secretary, while Ickes himself became the more public representative of the national park system. Considering the political importance of the economic subsidies now dispensed through the Park Service, it also followed that Ickes took a direct interest in the daily operations and policies of the bureau to a far greater degree than any of his predecessors.

If the roles of the secretary of the interior and the director of the Park Service had changed, so too had the duties of the chief landscape architect. Thomas Vint remained in charge of all design and planning activities at the Park Service throughout this period and beyond; his skills and influence in national park architectural design and planning never were contested. But Vint never assumed the role of chief "recreational planner," nor did the old landscape division assume responsibility for planning and design outside the national park system. Those functions had been left to Conrad Wirth and his branch of planning, and Wirth built up his own enormous staff through emergency spending appropriations and CCC funds. The arrangement apparently worked very well, in part because Wirth structured his branch's activities largely on the theory and practice of park planning Vint had established. Vint and Wirth also remained comfortably separated on the organizational chart. Vint remained the chief planner of the agency, but his landscape division planned only for the national park system itself (including national park CCC activities and the PWA program). Wirth's responsibilities mostly involved non-federal lands, especially state parks. Wirth was also a different kind of Park Service landscape architect. It was the younger man's administrative ability as a planner, not his skills as a designer, that aided him most in the monumental tasks of organizing the CCC state park program and compiling the national recreational survey. The position of chief landscape architect of the Park Service would never again be as simple as it had been for Daniel Hull or Thomas Vint. Vint's dislike of paperwork, for example, hardly made him an exemplary New Dealer; and as the Park Service grew, its planning activities needed to be coordinated not only with various New Deal federal agencies, but with scores of state and local governments as well.

The profession of landscape architecture was itself transformed following its recruitment into public service in 1933. If the Park Service and its cooperating local park authorities were at the heart of this mobilization, they were by no means the only government organizations employing landscape architects. Other federal agencies, including the Tennessee Valley Authority and the Resettlement Administration (later the Farm Security Administration), employed town planners and farm planners. The Forest Service, after resisting recreational planning for a decade, hired Albert Taylor in 1935 to survey national forest recreational facilities and plan for their improvement. Many municipal park departments hired landscape architects and planners and expanded their municipal park systems through the emergency spending programs of the New Deal. If the planning and management of private estates continued at some level through the 1930s and afterwards, those activities would never again resume their positions as the mainstays of American landscape architectural practice. The future of the profession, as the landscape architect P. H. Elwood put it in 1936, depended on becoming "more social- and economic-minded." Only then would the profession have successfully "emerged from what has often been called a luxury to a national necessity."[81]

Of all contributions made by professional landscape architects to the manifold social and economic experiments of the New Deal, perhaps no physical expressions more completely captured the aspirations, innovations, and characteristic spirit of the era to a greater degree than the hundreds of state and local parks built by the CCC and designed by the Park Service in cooperation with local park authorities. This field of park design—state park and recreational planning—was not so much expanded by the New Deal as created by it. To this day, many states owe the origins of their state park systems and the majority of facilities in them to the labor of CCC enrollees and the landscape design and planning of Park Service professionals. National recreational planning at this scale consummated the long and mutually influential relationship between the Park Service and American landscape architecture. The state parks produced through this partnership remain today among the most potent symbols of New Deal idealism.

As Conrad Wirth and the Park Service branch of planning undertook state park planning and design in 1933, no challenge loomed more ominously than that of assuring consistently high standards in the selection and development of state parks. In a rapidly organized program of breathtaking scope, political patronage and simple incompetence threatened to undermine the quality of state park projects. Thomas Vint and his seasoned landscape division, overwhelmed with the simultaneous expansion of the national park system, were in no position to assist overseeing the vast state park planning initiative as well. Wirth, at age thirty-four, assumed a great responsibility. His response was to institute an almost military chain of command, culminating in the branch of planning in Washington headed by himself and Herbert Evison. No work proceeded in the field until plans had been submitted to regional officers, and in turn were passed on to Washington for detailed, individual review. This level of centralized supervision and control permeated every aspect of the state park CCC effort. Wirth was building on the organizational precedent, once again, of Thomas Vint's San Francisco landscape division. Vint had also insisted on direct, centralized review of planning and design; standardized procedures and policies had been the essence of his success with the national parks in the 1920s and early 1930s. But Wirth extended this arrangement to cover not one park system, but forty-seven state park systems, divided into four geographic regions, which together required the careful review of hundreds of park master plans.

Early in the summer of 1933, Wirth began issuing "State Park Bulletins" that included instructions for the district officers appointed that May. In the first bulletin, he instructed his officers to submit comprehensive weekly reports, covering all aspects of their work, including details on the progress of all construction activities. The district officers in turn relied on their district inspectors, who ceaselessly roamed from one construction site to the next making detailed reports illustrated with photographs. In his first weekly report to Wirth that July, Herbert Maier, the district officer for Region III, included photographs and descriptions of "the progress of conservation projects and of the contacts made by the district officer and his inspectors" up to that point. But Maier also indicated he planned to report on "the administrative problems of the various parks, their park policies, the scenic and scientific calibre of each area, historical values, relation to nearby urban centers, etc."[82] All aspects of park selection, planning, development, and to some degree management were overseen by the Park Service district officers, their inspectors, and by Conrad Wirth and his staff in Washington.

But assuring consistent policies and standards nationwide required more than vigilance and organization. Almost all of the hundreds of planners engaged in state park work needed some sort of introduction to Park Service landscape architectural planning. The atelier system Vint had instituted to train new personnel in San Francisco was out of the question. Wirth realized that he immediately needed some kind of textbook, or at least an architectural patternbook, that could be distributed to the district offices and local park authorities. In 1933 he turned to Frank Waugh's daughter, Dorothy Waugh, who was a landscape architect and accomplished illustrator with a particular interest in national park work. Waugh, apparently the only female landscape architect to find work with the Park Service at this time, collected plans and elevations of park structures from a wide range of state and local park commissions and illustrated them in a standard format for reproduction and distribution to Park Service planners and architects in 1934.[83]

Ketch of A PARK

A GENERAL DEVELOPMENT PLAN IN PERSPECTIVE
SHOWING PRINCIPAL FEATURES THAT ARE NORMALLY DESIRABLE
AND AN AGREEABLE RELATIONSHIP OF MAJOR USE AREAS

A "sketch of a park," published by Conrad Wirth's branch of planning in 1941. This bird's-eye view of a prototypical state park plan captured the essence of the state park planning policies encouraged by the Park Service during the New Deal. The single entrance to the park eliminated potential through traffic, and the park road system accessed principal points of interest with the minimum amount of roadway. The creation of a lake was usually necessary to provide for swimming, boating, and fishing.

Wirth also exploited the fact that one of his district officers, Herbert Maier, was perhaps the most accomplished park architect of the day. By 1934, Maier had assembled his own patternbook, consisting largely of photographs of the park museum buildings he had designed for Bear Mountain, Yosemite, Grand Canyon, and Yellowstone. Maier also included views of some of the early state park projects being completed in his region, such as Wintersmith Metropolitan Park and Turner Falls State Park (Oklahoma) and Boulder Mountain State Park (Colorado). The architect also included photographs of Trail Ridge Road in Rocky Mountain National Park, showing details of crenelated guardwall construction and properly graded roadsides and swales. Examples of trailside shelters, footbridges, culverts, museums, and amphitheaters were all featured. A campground laid out according to the "Meinecke system" was shown, demonstrating how both logs and boulders could be used in auto campgrounds to define specific parking bays for cars and prevent widespread compaction of soils and destruction of understory vegetation.[84] Maier's remarks and observations on park architecture, site planning, and road design, together with the photographs of actual construction, turned out to be a powerful tool for quickly introducing new state park planners to the basics of Park Service landscape architectural design.

The commentary Maier wrote for the handbooks also set a tone and vocabulary for discussing state park design. Commenting on his Norris Geyser Basin museum at Yellowstone, he advised that the "heavy scale" was suitable only in "mountainous areas where forests abound." In less mountainous areas, the same type of construction should be "lighter in scale," and presumably employ smaller logs and boulders and less exaggerated proportions. But every effort needed to be made to "steer clear of the 'twig' type of architecture which flourishes under the name of 'rustic.'" Again and again Maier explained—usually using his own work as examples—that "the use of native materials, such as rocks, logs, and shakes causes the building to blend with, and become part of, its surroundings." Warm brown and driftwood gray were preferred stain colors, with window frames and other details painted in lighter tones. The desired effect of building and surrounding site work was described repeatedly as "natural" and "harmonious." In "wilderness areas," all building was to avoid "sharp right angles and rigid straight lines," whether the construction was a dam spillway, a guardwall, or a trailside museum. Maier of course had been an important figure in national park architecture since the 1920s; his architectural style had been tailored to the programmatic and aesthetic requirements of national park interpretation and planning. Maier's influence was now spread throughout Wirth's CCC state park program, and the verbal and formal vocabulary of "rustic" architecture that "blended" with its surroundings became standard for state park planning.[85]

Early in 1935, Maier's position as an unofficial chief architect for the state park effort was made clear at a conference Wirth organized in Washington that assembled state park officials from all over the country. Although Wirth's branch of plans had already funneled fifteen million dollars into state parks during the previous two years, this was the first time the local park authorities had been assembled as a group. The Park Service had to avoid the appearance of dictating park planning decisions to local governments, and Wirth's careful tone reassured the group that by "cooperation" with state park departments, the Park Service meant exactly that. "We are going to try to give you our ideas," he confessed, but more importantly, "we want to know what you know; we want to absorb as much information as we can from the field; and in order to perfect our organization, we want to work out our procedures and cut down some of them." On the subject of "Park Structures," Herbert Maier addressed the group not as a regional officer, but as a national authority on park development. The architect had learned well through his years of experience with Hull, Vint, and other Park Service officials. He noted that developing scenic areas as state parks in order to "conserve" them at first appeared to be an "anomaly," since park development could never "'improve' the picture" presented by outstanding scenery. "But on further investigation," he continued, "such areas are, on account of their superior natural make-up, subjected to trespassing by vacationists, squatters, picnickers and hikers . . . as a result of which a continuous fire hazard exists, sanitation considerations are sometimes unhealthful, and the uncontrolled use of the areas is unfavorable to wildlife conservation." Preserving scenic areas as parks, he observed, required the introduction of "a moderate number of roads, trails, picnic units and various concession buildings . . . in order that the original purpose of the area could be attained by controlling the circulation and activity of the visitors." Herbert Evison made the same point at the conference, observing that earlier in the 1920s, "in certain States, one of the surest ways of destroying a piece of natural landscape was to make a State park out of it," thereby encouraging increased numbers of visitors without planning for their accommodation. "There was the mistaken idea," he concluded, "that a State park was a natural area and needed no development."[86]

Herbert Maier also took the opportunity offered by the 1935 conference to further describe and promulgate his design guidelines for park architecture. Most of his descriptions and examples came directly out of the photographic handbooks he had developed to assure consistent design in his region. "In the treatment of exteriors," he repeated to the assembled state park officials, "the proper use of indigenous native materials is perhaps the happiest means of blending the structure with its surroundings, and this is what has largely resulted in the popular use of what is known as rustic architecture." Maier also noted that an extensive research project was underway in the Park Service to identify and document the "close to one hundred types of indigenous frontier construction" that were supposed to exist. The "tools of the frontiersman consisted usually only of an ax, a pick and a shovel, and a pair of hands," the architect suggested, "and this absence of precision tools resulted in a freehand architecture with an absence of rigidly straight lines. . . . We find that construction which is primitive in character blends most readily with primitive surroundings and is thereby less outstanding and has an intriguing craftsmanlike appearance."[87]

Maier's comments at the 1935 state park conference were the most thorough explication of "rustic" park architecture yet made. Maier had also already begun an important collaborative effort with another architect, Albert H. Good, who had moved from Ohio to Washington to assist in the state park CCC effort. Good was chosen essentially to replace Dorothy Waugh and assemble a comprehensive portfolio more along the lines of Maier's handbooks. Good was a talented draftsman, and had already designed the buildings for Virginia Kendall Metropolitan Park in Ohio.[88] The architect also had a gift for vivid, if overwrought, prose, and he and Maier collaborated on an "apologia" for park structures they submitted to Harlean James, the executive secretary of the American Planning and Civic Association (as the American Civic Association was now known), who published it that year. The ideas were primarily those Maier had already expressed; the belletristic excess can be attributed to Good. "Lamentable is the fact," the authors began, "that during the six days given over to Creation, picnic tables and outdoor fireplaces, footbridges and many other of man's requirements, even in natural surroundings, were negligently and entirely overlooked. . . . Man, confronted with this no less than awesome task of assuming to supply these odds and ends undone when the whistle blew on Creation, may well conclude, pending achievements of greater skill and finesse, that only the most persistent demands for a facility shall trap him into playing the jester in Nature's unspoiled places." Maier and Good advised, as American landscape park designers had since the 1850s, that buildings be designed as subordinate elements in perceived landscape scenes, and that necessary facilities be kept to a minimum: "Since the primary purpose of setting aside these areas is to conserve them as nearly as possible in their natural state, every structure, no matter how necessary, can only be regarded as an intruder."[89]

Good also drew plans, elevations, and sections to go with the photographs to produce an expanded portfolio of park architecture published later in 1935 as *Park Structures and Facilities*. Dorothy Waugh's involvement in the project had not ended, however, since she was part of the committee that selected the examples to be included in the 1935 volume. The other members of the committee were Thomas Vint, Herbert Maier, engineer Oliver G. Taylor, Midwestern Regional Director Paul Brown, and landscape architect Norman Newton. The project was paid for with state park CCC funds and so was overseen by Conrad Wirth. The volume included the "apologia" for park structures, further edited by Good. The publication made enormous progress towards the standardization of park architecture, not only in state and national parks, but in some municipal parks as well. The examples chosen by the committee (like those chosen by Waugh earlier for her "Portfolio") included county, state, and national park structures, often all on the same page. All the examples came from what Good described ambiguously as "natural parks," which he distinguished from "naturalistic or formalized city parks." Structures from municipal and other local parks could be included, however, if "their expression would be equally at home in a completely natural environment."[90]

Maier and Good reinforced, in their own way, the appropriateness of naturalistic construction details in large parks and scenic reservations. If contemporary architectural styles (such as California Arts and Crafts and bungalow architecture) influenced the architects in specific designs, the choice of those stylistic precedents was determined by premises of American landscape park design and planning that had been established at least since the 1880s. Since that time, necessary construction in large scenic reservations had preferably been both minimized and of "rustic" inspiration. Good's distinction between "natural" and "city" parks reiterated Hubbard and Kimball's bifurcation of "naturalistic" and "formal" design, and of course the former continued to be the appropriate treatment for national and state parks. Good's other recommendations for suitably "rustic" architectural design were directly drawn from the planning policies of Hull and Vint. Good advised, for example: "Every structural undertaking in a natural park is only part of a whole. The individual building or facility must bow before the broad park plan, which . . . determines the size, character, location and use of each and every structure. . . . The structures necessary in a park are naturally less obtrusive if they are reasonably unified by a use of one style of architecture."[91]

Good also described specific architectural features and qualities, such as "native" materials, muted colors, and low silhouettes, that created "the desirable and appropriately rugged, handcrafted character of park structures." By 1935, architectural construction for "natural" parks (which could be any large park, whether under national, state, or local jurisdiction) quickly moved towards a common standard of "rustic" construction. That standard was set by hundreds of Park Service designers, and Good's catalog of their work further consolidated their planning and design activities nationwide. But Park Service Rustic architecture, which Good later described simply as a style that "achieves sympathy with natural surroundings and with the past," adapted constantly to its landscape context; if rigorously maintained in every state park the Park Service planned, the style nevertheless yielded a great diversity of individual structures. In 1935, Good warned against using his publication as a patternbook. "If an existing structure is so admired that it persuades duplication," he explained, "careful analysis will inevitably demonstrate that admiration springs from a nice perfection of the subject within one circumstantial pattern. As that pattern changes so must the structure change."[92] Park Service architects attempted to conform to regional traditions and regional landscape character in each case. Huge boulders and logs were only appropriate to landscapes of rugged terrain clothed in ancient forests; traditional adobe construction appeared in desert parks, while milled lumber and more conventional outlines were typical in the East. Native American and "pioneer" construction techniques (real or imagined) provided inspiration everywhere, as they had for Ernest Davidson at Mount Rainier. The Park Service Rustic architecture Good documented, in other words, might be described simply as landscape park architecture. Its designers sought to accomplish what park architects since the days of Lancelot Brown had always attempted to achieve: structures that could be appreciated as "harmonious" elements of perceived landscape compositions. The basic strategy for achieving this harmony had not changed. Pseudo-vernacular construction techniques, roughly worked materials that appeared to be drawn from local forests and quarries, and quasi-historical references to peasant or pioneer cultures were conventions of the artistic genres of landscape that had been assimilated into the practice of picturesque landscape design in the 18th century. "Rustic" park architecture, even in the 20th century, remained in essence picturesque architecture.

The impressive scope of Park Service planning under Conrad Wirth increased further after the Park, Parkway and Recreational-Area Study Act was passed. As part of the federal government, the Park Service had been theoretically restrained from becoming too directly involved in determining individual state park plans. As Herbert Evison put it, "the relationship between the States and the Service had been entirely unofficial."[93] The 1936 act validated the "cooperation" between both levels of government and legitimized the Park Service's official role as a state park planner. The act also justified greater resources to complete the national recreational plan. One of many results from this increased activity was an expanded portfolio of park structures and facilities, which was published in three volumes in 1938. Albert Good still served as editor and compiler, but the new work, *Park and Recreation Structures,* attempted to provide a more comprehensive introduction to Park Service architecture and planning. The first two volumes (introduced again by another version of the "apologia" for park structures) were based on the categories and examples of the 1935 *Park Structures and Facilities* catalog. The first volume, entitled "Administration and Basic Service Facilities," included an expanded number of illustrations of park entrance structures, administration buildings, maintenance facilities, fire lookouts, trail and vehicular bridges, culverts, drinking fountains, and comfort stations. The second volume, "Recreational and Cultural Facilities," featured picnic tables and fireplaces, refectories and concession buildings, trailside shelters, dams and bathhouses, museum and nature shrines, outdoor amphitheaters, and examples of "historical preservations." Good again embellished his dimensioned drawings and collected photographs with memorable commentary. Texas state parks, in the heart of Herbert Maier's Region III, took some good-natured ribbing. Good described a somewhat whimsical administration building at Longhorn Cavern as "an extraordinary creation for a park setting, doubtless transported here by Magic Carpet." At Palmetto State Park, a particularly rugged refectory with a palmetto thatched roof was "no uninspired rehash of a forerunning park building . . . but probably commemorative of some circuitous route between the Congo and the Emerald Isle that must have once passed through Texas." In other comments, Good reiterated the basic requirements of Park Service Rustic architecture. The museum building at Lake Guernsey State Park in Wyoming, for example, adhered to "many of the principles proclaimed for a widely appropriate park architecture—low structure, predominantly horizontal lines and coursing of masonry, and the featuring of few openings by the contrasts of plain, sweeping surfaces." The aggregate effect of the museum's low, rugged outline, rusticated masonry, and heavy shake roofs, Good suggested, was "that intangible factor— personality."[94]

The principles of appropriately "rustic" architectural design, however, were more easily illustrated and distributed than those of Park Service landscape architectural planning. Although *Park and Recreation Structures* served as an invaluable textbook for state (and national) park planners, Conrad Wirth could not rely on such a portfolio to explain Thomas Vint's master planning process or its adaptation to state park design. In the third volume of *Park and Recreation Structures*, however, Good did attempt to illustrate some examples of sound site planning. The volume was titled "Overnight and Organized Camp Facilities" and included examples of park furniture, cabins, lodges, community buildings, and camp administrative facilities. It also illustrated at least some park campground and group camp layouts, subjects that had not been covered in earlier publications. Good's suggestions for automotive campgrounds were limited to suggestions for converting regular campground loops (the "Meinecke system") to more elaborate layouts for the convenience of vehicles towing trailers. A number of campground layouts were illustrated that either simplified or eliminated the task of backing a trailer into the campground spurs along a campground road.[95]

Of more interest, perhaps, was a new category of facility design, the "organized camp," or group camp, which was the principal feature of the "recreational demonstration areas" being built all over the country. These summer camps, according to Good, constituted "a collective recreational use," to be supervised by "some character building, educational, welfare, or other organization." The group camps illustrated by Good consisted of a number of cabin groups clustered around a central dining hall and administrative area. As tentative as these suggested plans were, they were the only drawings in any of his work that showed topography, vegetative cover, or other landscape features. But as he observed, group camp design demanded that the architect provide site plans as well as suggestions for typical cabins. "The number and size of the camp buildings and the relationship between them *are* the camp lay-out," he explained, "and any discussion of the buildings individually is difficult without some preliminary consideration of them as a whole."[96]

Albert Good's few sketches of group camp site plans, however, did not even begin to instruct state park planners in the basic procedures of Park Service master planning. Good's publications cataloged, as their titles made clear, exemplary park structures. The Park Service landscape architects and planners designing state parks received their education in overall park planning through the direct supervision and review of their plans by Wirth and his regional representatives. As Herbert Evison described the arrangements, the "first requirement for any park work undertaken," was "a general development plan." The general plans received preliminary approval from the regional directors, who with their roving inspectors "mostly ran the show." Washington exercised considerable direct authority as well, since "major policies" as well as all budgets and construction contracts were "valid only when approved in Washington." Personnel appointments (with minor exceptions) were also made at the Department of the Interior.[97]

In a 1934 article published in *City Planning* (a magazine founded and edited by Henry Hubbard and Theodora Kimball), Evison made it clear which precedents in state park planning he and Wirth considered in their formulation of "major policies." Evison wrote that "the best approach to the subject" of state park planning began "clear back in the Nineties with Charles Eliot's study that resulted in the creation of the Boston Metropolitan Park system." He also cited John Nolen's 1908 Wisconsin state park survey, Connecticut's 1914 state park initiative, and the New York park plan published in 1922. Olmsted's 1929 California state park survey, however, "quickly outmoded" these earlier efforts, and was "one of the classics of state park literature." Evison reprinted Olmsted's definitions and criteria for standards and selection of state parks, and he described the history of the California study as an ideal state park planning process. He also cited the more recent 1933 Iowa Twenty-five Year Conservation Plan, by Jacob L. Crane, Jr., and George

Wheeler Olcott, as an influence on the state park program he and Wirth were shaping. In his summary, Evison suggested that state park planning should "contemplate the inclusion" of a broad range of park types: "highways," or "scenic routes of parkway character"; "highway parks," or roadside rest areas; "state parks," or "the choicest obtainable examples of natural landscape . . . with which may be joined a reasonably wide variety of recreational use"; "state monuments," of outstanding historical or scientific interest; "state recreation grounds," which were "of value almost solely for active recreation, chiefly . . . fronting on water"; "state trails," mostly easements on private property; "public forests and game preserves," where recreation would be a subordinate use; "game farms and fish hatcheries"; and "public shooting grounds." Evison noted that such a system of public lands could be "satisfactorily determined only after an exhaustive and intelligent search for all areas of possible value in any of the classifications," a study that demanded coordination between municipal, county, and state governments and all their agencies. Adjoining state governments (and evidently the federal government) would need to be involved as well.[98]

Evison, who continued at this point as the executive secretary of the National Conference on State Parks while he helped Conrad Wirth run the state park CCC program, outlined an ideal state park planning process that assumed all types of state lands could be considered essentially as types of "parks." The policies that he and Wirth described suggested that planning for scenic preservation and various types of recreational land use could ultimately unite the management of all the public lands in a given state. This proposition was buttressed by extensive "park use studies" that demonstrated the need for state parks by investigating who used parks, what they did in them, and how far they had traveled to get to them. Park visitors were surveyed at hundreds of parks to determine income level and age, occupations, and recreational needs. The conclusions suggested that as essential as state parks had become, outdoor recreation promised to assume still more significant dimensions in American life in the future.[99] The wheel had indeed turned since the first decade of the century, when Gifford Pinchot suggested that national parks could be better managed as "forests" (that is through the principles of scientific forestry and land reclamation) than as scenic reservations. By the 1930s, Secretary Ickes's ill-fated campaign to transfer the Forest Service to the Department of the Interior indicated that at least some in Washington now envisioned that all federal lands—including national forests—should be categorized and managed as different kinds of public parks, a change in emphasis that would have recognized the economic and social ascendancy of outdoor recreation over other forms of land use. Ickes's proposed reorganization would have unified the management of federal lands according to a typology of public reservations similar to that already elaborated by Wirth and Evison for individual state park systems.

In addition to setting broad planning policies for state park plans, the Park Service also made very specific demands regarding master plans for individual parks. Isabelle F. Story, who had been in charge of public information for the Park Service since the Mather era, in 1933 wrote a brochure explaining the role of the Park Service in the CCC program. In her explanation of "what the landscape architects and engineers do," Story observed that "the landscape process begins with selecting locations which do not tear up the landscape or obtrude into important views. . . . When a general scheme of development has been arrived at, a so-called 'master plan' is prepared by the landscape architects on which is charted an outline of all future construction work. Using this master plan as a guide, designs are then worked out for the individual items, such as roads, buildings, parking areas, bridges, trails, and numerous miscellaneous projects." Story quoted an anonymous landscape architect who suggested that "the reverse of the famous principle of the ostrich generally is followed . . . roads, trails, and buildings all should provide a maximum of scenic view, at the same time being as inconspicuous as possible themselves."[100] The process was essentially the same for state parks. In one of his state park program brochures, Wirth explained his priorities for state park development: "The object is first to conserve and protect the entire area . . . then to develop only necessary facilities for the enjoyment of each park feature without interfering with the use of other features. The cardinal principle governing all of this is that park areas are to be kept as natural as possible." Of course in state parks, "those whose fancy calls for more active recreation" were more liberally provided for. "The CCC has provided artificial lakes . . . [with] beaches, bathhouses, and docks for boating. All state parks have their picnic groves which have been equipped with tables and benches, fireplaces, and water and sanitary facilities. Usually a picnic area has a shelter for retreat from sudden showers. Nearby are parking areas . . . [and] in many regions, state parks offer thrilling winter sports." In addition roads, guard rails, retaining walls, and bridges were built, stream and erosion control projects were undertaken, and public forests were aggressively managed through insect and fire control as well as reforestation.[101]

The master plans that described all of the work for individual state parks were prepared in the field by resident landscape architects, architects, and engineers, working with local park managers. Once the Park Service regional inspector and the local park authority agreed on a general outline for a particular park, the plan was sent to the regional director for review. The landscape architects and other technical staff in the regional office assured that the master plans "solved planning problems on the basis of general information and planning methods and practices which have been developed in the regional office and which . . . conform to National Park Service policies and standards." Once the regional director and the local park authority were in agreement on a master plan, it was sent to Washington for further review and final approval.[102]

Exemplary master plans were distributed to the states and regions, not in Good's architectural catalogs, but in Wirth's *Yearbooks* of "park and recreation progress," separate annual reports on the activities of the branch of planning that Wirth began publishing in 1938.[103] The typical

State Park Historic Districts

During the New Deal, the National Park Service collaborated with many "local park authorities" to plan, design, and supervise construction in over 560 non-federal park areas in forty-seven states. Working primarily with Civilian Conservation Corps (CCC) labor, Park Service landscape architects helped create many extraordinary state parks that to this day form the core of many state park systems. The following state parks were designed by the Park Service in cooperation with various state park departments, and each epitomizes the high artistic standards maintained during this period. Each example is a particularly significant and well preserved result of the historically unique collaboration of the Park Service, New Deal relief agencies, and local park authorities between 1933 and 1942.

Bastrop State Park, Texas

Above: *In 1923, Texas had only five small state parks; by 1942 the state boasted a system of thirty-one parks developed by the CCC and visited by over 1.7 million people annually. Such a transformation was not uncommon during the New Deal. Bastrop State Park, located among the "Lost Pines" of Bastrop County thirty miles east of Austin, was an early showcase of the quality and permanence of Park Service design and CCC construction. This photograph, taken in 1934, shows a footbridge in the new park. National Archives, Record Group 79.*

Below: *Buildings like the Bastrop State Park Refectory (1935-1938) made it clear that CCC boys, when properly supervised, were capable of completing complex construction projects to the highest standards. At Bastrop, in fact, local labor organizers temporarily shut down construction on this building, which they felt should have been built by trade union members.*

Bastrop State Park featured a complement of stone tourist cabins, designed by architect Arthur Fehr, which were some of the finest examples of Park Service Rustic style architecture in any state park of the period. The cabins also show the influence of Herbert Maier, the architect of the Yellowstone trailside museums, who as a Park Service regional director in the 1930s oversaw the development of Bastrop and many other state parks in the Southwest and Midwest.

Lake Guernsey State Park, Wyoming

Located in Platte County north of Cheyenne, Lake Guernsey State Park was an early collaboration between the Park Service, the Bureau of Reclamation, and the CCC. The reservoir at Guernsey was a major component of the North Platte River Project, which the Bureau of Reclamation began in 1903. First filled in 1927, Lake Guernsey was selected in 1934 as one of the first federal reservoirs to be developed by the Park Service (with CCC labor) for recreational purposes. This type of development later resulted in some of the most massive and popular developments the Park Service ever attempted, such as Lake Mead National Recreation Area, as well as scores of state and local park developments around reservoirs. Courtesy Wyoming Department of Commerce, State Parks & Historic Sites.

Above: The park museum (1934-1939) at Lake Guernsey State Park was designed by architect Roland G. Pray and is among the finest state park buildings of the period. The museum survives with near perfect integrity, complete with original interpretive displays designed by John Ewer and the Park Service Berkeley museum staff. Battered walls, randomly laid masonry of native stone, massive timber trusses, and gabled roofs covered with hand-split shakes all characterized Park Service Rustic architecture. Courtesy Wyoming Department of Commerce, State Parks & Historic Sites.

Below: A view, circa 1935, of CCC camp Wyoming BR-9, Company 844, Lake Guernsey State Park. The camp layout, typical of hundreds built, mimicked the cantonment plans familiar to the U.S. Army officers who were responsible for the establishment and daily operation of CCC camps. The construction of barracks, garages, sanitary systems, water lines, and other camp infrastructure were the first tasks of the rapidly assembled companies. National Archives, Record Group 79.

St. Croix State Park, Minnesota

Left: *Located along the scenic St. Croix and Kettle rivers in Pine County, Minnesota, the thirty thousand-acre St. Croix Recreational Demonstration Area (RDA) was the largest project of its type. Now known as St. Croix State Park, the site was one of forty-six RDAs, projects in which federal funds were used to acquire "submarginal" agricultural lands and develop them for recreational use.*

Below: *The park lodge (1938) at St. Croix State Park typified one of the ways in which "rustic" park architecture was adapted to different regions. The rusticated ashlar masonry and buttressed walls, for example, were more refined than the exaggerated masonry techniques preferred in Rocky Mountain parks; the stone, however, was still locally quarried, the exposed trusses were peeled logs, and the massive gabled roofs were covered in hand-split shakes.*

Most RDAs, which were acquired with federal funds, were intended to be turned over to state park departments. Most also featured "group camp" facilities designed specifically for non-profit organizations, such as the YMCA and the Girl Scouts, that sponsored summer camps for children. This "unit lodge" at St. Croix was the heart of a cluster, or "unit," of campers' cabins (some of which are visible in the background). Three or four units, judiciously spaced, made up a group camp.

Mendocino Woodlands, California

Below: Mendocino Woodlands was one of only two RDAs developed west of the Rockies. The park was sited in a second growth redwood forest about nine miles from the Mendocino County coastline, along the banks of the Little North Fork of the Big River. The park features three group camps and an administrative area, all sited along the river canyon.

Most of the cabins at Mendocino Woodlands were built of old growth redwood and remain in excellent condition. Although designed by the Park Service in cooperation with the California State Park Commission, Mendocino Woodlands was not built by the CCC. The park represents one of the most significant contributions of WPA "transient camps" to the RDA program. The "transient camps" were adult work camps that employed men drawn from local relief roles.

Pine Mountain State Park, Georgia

Below: Pine Mountain State Park, now known as FDR State Park (Western Half), is located in Harris County, thirty miles north of Columbus. The resort of Warm Springs—and Franklin Roosevelt's Little White House—are adjacent to the park, and Roosevelt himself boosted Pine Mountain as a potential state park. The state acquired the land for Pine Mountain State Park in 1934, and the CCC completed the Pine Mountain Tavern (seen here) on top of Pine Mountain in 1935.

Above: *The elegant bathhouse and swimming pool at Pine Mountain were completed by the CCC in about 1940. On one of his many visits to the park, Roosevelt remarked that the pool, then under construction, had a shape that reminded him of the Liberty Bell; the name was immediately adopted. The CCC enrollees at work at Pine Mountain State Park enjoyed frequent unofficial inspections by the man they recognized as the "father of the CCC."*

Below: *Roosevelt loved to picnic on Pine Mountain while in Warm Springs, and the Pine Mountain Parkway was built by the CCC along a route first suggested by FDR himself. This view from the parkway shows the extent to which the area became a cynosure of New Deal activity in Georgia. The lake below (Lake Franklin) was one of two built for the new fifteen hundred-acre Pine Mountain State Park and adjacent three thousand-acre RDA. The settlement of Pine Mountain Valley, a thirteen thousand-acre Resettlement Administration "agricultural and industrial community," is visible in the distance, just beyond the park's boundaries.*

state park master plans illustrated Wirth's basic premise that "conservation" and "recreation" were not incompatible, as long as they were carefully accommodated in each case; even "natural" state parks could support a variety of recreational uses if the master plan successfully and efficiently separated and accommodated those uses. Olmsted and Vaux had expressed a similar conviction in the 1860s. For the 19th-century landscape architects, landscape park design could conserve the "rural character required in a park," and still provide for the "assemblage and movement of great crowds," as long as "the driving room, riding room, walking room, skating, sailing and playing room" were "not only liberally designed," but "studied and adapted to the natural circumstances of the site with the greatest care." As quoted earlier, they felt "success in realizing either [purpose] must be limited," but "by a careful adjustment of parts, and by accommodating the means necessary to the effecting of one purpose to those necessary to the effecting of the other, both may be accomplished."[104] The process of landscape park planning that Wirth advocated for state parks seventy years later could not have been more precisely described.

The most comprehensive planning guideline that Wirth published did not appear until 1941. *A Study of the Park and Recreation Problem of the United States*, the final report of the Park, Parkway and Recreational-Area Study, summarized the goals and achievements of Wirth's branch of planning. The report began with a broad summary of demographic and other trends that demonstrated that the interest in outdoor recreation had not yet begun to peak. Leisure time would continue to increase; the population as a whole would continue to grow older; the distribution of income would continue to flatten. Above all, as a result of fundamental human needs, the recreational use of public lands would continue to escalate as it had since the beginning of the century. A sense of urgency and historic opportunity permeated the 1941 report. "The introduction of an industrial economy has brought about many . . . changes in man's environment and living habits," the authors suggested, forcing him "to seek recreation by vicarious means, as exemplified by attendance at motion-picture shows, football games, etc., rather than by means through which he is an active participant." These "inadequacies in his present way of life may be . . . offset through adequate provision of compensating forms of recreation." Recreation included all "constructive uses of leisure time," including (roughly in order of popularity) touring and sightseeing, picnicking, water sports, hunting and fishing, hiking and climbing, winter sports, nature studies, music and drama, arts and crafts, history and archeology, and camping. What unified these diverse activities was their setting. "Tastes in natural scenery have infinite variety" and were "not governed by extent of leisure or limitation of pocketbook." From "far-away wildernesses" to "the nearby pastoral landscape," many different "types of settings [were] necessary to gratify the desires and needs of our population for outdoor recreation." Conrad Wirth and his branch of planning were describing a great deal more than state park systems: "This country can afford to preserve its irreplaceable objects of outstanding worth—the giant redwoods, Independence Hall, the trackless wilderness of the Olympic Peninsula, and the wonders of the Yellowstone. . . . We must have unspoiled scenic areas, retain irreplaceable natural scenes, preserve the character of the superlative. Parks, forests, wildlife areas, large resort sections, all have cultural, financial, and social values to this generation, and are a heritage we can and should pass on to future generations. Needed are both the area for constant day-by-day use and the spot to be visited once in a lifetime."[105]

The 1941 report included an instructive summary of recreational land planning policies and procedures. Many of these suggestions had already been printed in Wirth's Yearbooks. The typology of park types that Evison described in 1934 was simplified slightly, and presented again as an official terminology for the various components of a fully developed park system. Standard criteria for state park selection and development were also discussed, stressing the value of advance surveys and study. "A gift of land is no gift at all," the authors cautioned, ". . . if development or operation and maintenance entail unduly high costs." Of primary concern for the planners were the feasibility of road construction (both approaches and park roads) and the availability of nearby quarries and lumber, since "native" materials were necessary for Park Service Rustic construction. The suitability of the site for dam construction was another vital factor, since a lake was the prerequisite of so many of the most popular outdoor activities. Acknowledging that every park master plan was "an individual problem in planning," the authors ventured nevertheless to suggest certain guidelines for park master plans. An adequate supply of water for drinking and recreation, for example, and provisions for the safe disposal of sewage were required aspects of every state park plan. A central, well-separated maintenance and administration area, and a certain complement of park roads were also necessitated by the demands of normal park use. Entrances to a park typically were to be kept to a minimum (preferably one or two) since "a multiplicity of entrances means also a multiplicity of road mileage to build and maintain." Picnic areas and campgrounds should be well defined to avoid spreading their impact over too large an area; they should not, however, be crowded, denying visitors the kind of experience they had come to enjoy. Above all, the "genuine natural charm and beauty" of the site should not be compromised: "It is not necessary to construct a road to every beauty spot in the park . . . [and] every development, whatever its character or purpose, should be subordinated" to the preservation of scenery.

In their 1941 report, Conrad Wirth and his planners documented the degree to which the planning of state parks could be guided by many of the basic principles of national park town planning and master planning that Thomas Vint developed during the previous decade. In other ways, however, the ideal state park plan expressed its own set of civic ideals, which were as peculiar to the New Deal as the national park master plan had been to the 1920s. The provision of recreational facilities, for example, took on great importance in state park design. Noting that, except in the "rarest instances," man does not "live long on bread and scenery alone" while visiting state parks, Wirth instructed planners to provide "a fairly diverse choice of other means of passing the time enjoyably." Three considerations governed the suitability of proposed ball fields, swimming pools, or other recreational facilities. First they must not "involve destruction or serious modification of or encroachment upon significant or rare scenic, historic, or scientific features." Second, all proposed development should "supplement, and be subordinate to the primary purpose . . . of the area," which was the preservation of scenery and other resources. Third, all such facilities must be easily maintained.

Wirth's 1941 recommendations for state park planners concluded with "three basic requirements" for the overall process: reconnaissance, determination of "the logical and economical relationship" between various elements of the park system, and "modification of the natural environment only when it is certain that values resulting will fully balance the losses." The "master plan" remained "the first key to ultimate success in operation and utilization of any area . . . [and] at the same time, safeguarding natural or historic features." Wirth reproduced an aerial perspective of a "park"—an idealized and prototypical "general development plan" for a state park—illustrating all of the "principal features that are normally desirable, and an agreeable relationship of major use areas" (see page 281). At the center of the plan (which was inspired by scores of state parks that had already been built) was a large lake created by impounding a stream running through the area. The site was defined, typically, by a wide valley together with its forested slopes and a number of surrounding high points or other features of scenic or scientific interest. Group camps and other facilities were evenly distributed around the lakeshore. From a single, controlled entrance, the park road system led to the main features and facilities in the park, terminating in cul-de-sacs at the farthest points. A well-separated administrative area was sited near the entrance, and a day use area, located well away from the group camps, also was easily accessible to the main entrance. The majority of the park, and many of its most scenic points, could be accessed only by foot and bridle trails. The simple diagram for a state park master plan captured the essence of Wirth's CCC state park master planning policies.[106] The plan also showed a clear lineage. If the ideal state park plan descended from the national park master plan, in other ways, such as its accommodation of increased recreational activities and crowds, it exhibited traits of classic municipal landscape park design.

Once the New Deal gained momentum after 1933, the Park Service CCC state park program seized the initiative of the American park movement. By 1939, Wirth reported that his program had encouraged state governments to acquire over one million acres of new parkland since 1933.[107] In their 1941 report on parks, parkways, and recreational areas, Wirth's branch of planning at the Park Service envisioned both the modern national park system as we know it today, and a framework for unified national recreational planning intended to transform their cooperative planning initiative from an "emergency" program to a permanent function of the federal government and make the CCC a permanent institution in the process. Not only the scale of the undertaking, but also the intent and character of the planning and design work made the CCC state parks unique physical records of the New Deal. "We must realize that in park work we are dealing with conservation in its broadest meaning," Wirth wrote. "Our job concerns not only conservation of natural resources, but conservation of human resources . . . and in the conservation of the human wealth recreation plays a major part."[108]

At a time when many critics questioned the appropriateness of providing for any outdoor recreation in national parks, state park planning became the more active field for landscape architects; and it was the Park Service model for ideal state park design—more than the model of the national park master plan—that embodied the New Deal goal of "human resource conservation." The consistent emphasis on the needs of people—as well as the mandate to preserve places of scenic and scientific importance— recurred constantly in the planning literature of the CCC program, connecting it as much to the rhetoric of Frederick Law Olmsted as to that of Stephen Mather. "The power of scenery to affect men" and increase happiness had become the power of "outdoor recreation" to "conserve the human wealth." In either case, landscape park design and scenic preservation were advanced by professional planners as the means to create a physical context for modern society that would allow the "public" to lead more fulfilled lives.

Hundreds of state parks designed between 1933 and 1942 (the years the CCC program remained active) continue to serve the people of virtually every state and territory of the United States. It was a truism of the day that the New Deal advanced the state park movement by fifty years. That may have been true; but over the sixty years since then, state park departments, so many of them created in the wake of New Deal spending, have been hard pressed even to maintain their park systems. In many cases pressures to expand recreational and other facilities, as Wirth feared, have compromised the preservation of scenery and natural resources. State legislatures in recent decades have come to see their Depression-era parks not as scenic reservations, but as under-developed resort sites, which when further developed with golf courses, conference centers, or other facilities can yield enhanced returns and even turn a profit. The fundamental aspirations originally advanced for state parks are lost in the bargain. Goals such as scenic preservation require a balanced development plan and a limit on recreational facilities in parks. Private resorts, intended to produce direct profits, rarely achieve such a balance. In the past, state park systems served as general economic catalysts by encouraging regional tourism and attracting tourists from other regions and states. Once state parks have sacrificed their unique regional scenery for the sake of a few extra golf courses and conference centers, however, they cannot continue to provide that general economic stimulus to a region. Theme parks and golf courses, after all, can be found anywhere.

The historically unique collaboration of the Park Service, local park agencies, and New Deal relief agencies left an unmatched legacy of preserved scenic areas and increased opportunities for outdoor recreation. The nation has greatly dissipated that endowment by failing to provide adequate budgets for public park maintenance and expansion. This unfortunate observation is confirmed by the overcrowding of outdoor recreational areas—many of them state parks built so long ago by the CCC—in almost every region of the country. The fact that these parks have lasted this long is a testament to the quality of their design and construction; the fact that they have had to serve this long, and that in many areas they remain the principal facilities for outdoor recreation, indicates the faltering progress of the American park movement since World War II.

The Blue Ridge Parkway

Conclusion

"There is nothing so American as our national parks," Franklin Roosevelt exclaimed while seeing Glacier National Park for the first time in 1934. The "fundamental idea" behind them, he suggested, was "that the country belongs to the people; that what it is and what it is in the process of making is for the enrichment of the lives of all of us. Thus the parks stand as the outward symbol of this great human principle."[1]

No American since Frederick Law Olmsted better realized the fundamental responsibility of democratic government to preserve areas of profound scenic beauty and to make them available to all citizens as public parks. As Olmsted wrote in 1865 regarding the preservation of Yosemite Valley, this "political duty of grave importance" involved the obligation on the part of a representative government to assure that the experience of great outdoor spaces—assumed to be a prerequisite of human happiness—would not be monopolized by the few and therefore denied to the many. And for Roosevelt as well as Olmsted, the landscape park continued to symbolize national unity and imperishable common values during a time of national crisis and social dissension. Many considered the Great Depression to be the most severe test of the Republic since the Civil War. From the outset of the New Deal, Roosevelt encouraged the development of parks of all types—national, state, and municipal—as powerful expressions of public art, rich in the deepest senses of national identity and shared purpose.

The massive park developments of the New Deal were complemented by other aspects of what once was called land "improvement." Every biographer of Roosevelt has commented on the personal conviction and attention that the president brought to his programs to conserve the nation's forests and soils. Most would agree with Eleanor Roosevelt when she observed that "the Hudson River Valley was in my husband's blood," and that his deeply felt responsibilities as a steward of the nation's agricultural and forested lands resulted from his early experience as manager of the family estate in Hyde Park.[2] Soil conservation, dam construction, reforestation, and planned relocations of rural populations were all New Deal initiatives that, with the landscape park, had been aspects of modern landscape planning since the 18th century. Roosevelt, like a benevolent landlord overseeing a national estate, became the ultimate client of land improvement and scenic preservation; after 1933, the president was in a position to attempt to "improve" entire regions of the country.

If Roosevelt's experience as an estate owner helped shape his conservation policies, it perhaps followed that the New Deal found its most characteristic artistic expression in great works of landscape art, specifically in state and national park developments. Just as Roosevelt rescued American capitalism by offering businessmen and financiers alternatives to more radical reforms, he also used the New Deal to further the modernization of the American landscape at a time when "progress," in this sense, seemed to have halted. In both cases, the federal programs of the 1930s rebuffed more European, socialistic influences by reasserting traditional (if altered) social values and landscape aesthetics. If in the realm of economics Roosevelt offered a kind of socialism that maintained the sanctity of private property, the New Deal produced landscapes that were quintessentially "modern," while remaining firmly rooted in picturesque theory and Fairsted School aesthetics.

This helps explain how many landscape architects, who in the 1920s had been conservative "country place" designers, were enlisted with such enthusiasm into what they often considered socialistic New Deal programs. The New Deal offered more than just employment to the unemployed. A generation of professionals also discovered that New Deal landscape architecture—defined above all by the work of the National Park Service—constituted a powerful response to the challenges they felt were presented by contemporary European Modernist design. By the late 1920s, architectural Modernism had begun to inspire some American designers, while inciting defensive responses from others. The debate intensified as the economic collapse of the early 1930s brought an end to the "country place" era, leaving uncertainty about the shape of things to come. In the early 1930s, resistance among established American landscape architects to transatlantic Modernism signified a reluctance to accept the permanence of the conditions that had beset both their profession and society as a whole.

At the 1932 conference of the American Society of Landscape Architects, for example, the ongoing economic catastrophe went largely unmentioned; the papers presented mostly were concerned with the debate over whether or not landscape architecture should "go modern." Member after member warned against obeying Modernist dictums to "cut off the past by deprecating the work that has already been accomplished." Willing to accept that the profession may have descended into a "state of semi-stagnant eclecticism" in recent years, there was still little question, according to one participant, that the theory and practice of landscape architecture as elucidated by the elder Olmsted and his successors was "fundamentally modern in spirit" and therefore could continue to be relevant to contemporary society.

The assembled practitioners may have been unemployed in 1932, but in general they were very aware of the historical origins of their professional tradition and believed in its future. Many of the conferees bridled at the suggestion that European architectural Modernism

The Blue Ridge Parkway, like contemporary automotive parkways in Westchester County and elsewhere, was based on the most advanced highway engineering of the day. Automotive parkways of the 1920s and 1930s were clearly works of "modern" art and technology in this sense. But the non-commercial parkways also featured bridges veneered in rusticated stone, winding alignments, massed plantings of shrubs and trees, and a concern for preserving and revealing regional landscape scenery. They were, in other words, products of traditional Fairsted School landscape planning, as well as modern engineering.

represented the only effective response to the social and economic conditions of the times. The landscape architect Ralph E. Griswold pointed to "the explosion of Romanticism [that] created a new conception of landscape design distinct from its parent Arts—a conception modern in itself." Achievements in modern landscape design since then, he continued, had included comprehensive city and regional planning, the design of new campuses, industrial complexes, and residential subdivisions, all of which were "modern functions of our art." New automotive parkways in Westchester County (New York) and Washington, DC, were also "distinctly modern artistic achievements." Norman Newton insisted that the qualities ascribed to Modernist design—"simplification of treatment, directness of plan, and careful adaptation of various units to the functions which they must perform"— had been the subject of careful study by generations of American garden designers. Newton concluded that "the landscape architect must devote his energies to the application of changeless principles to our changing modes of living; the question of `modern' or `not modern' will take care of itself."[3]

By defending the established profession of landscape architecture as already "modern," the 1932 conferees affirmed their faith that the economic emergency would pass, and that professional practice would someday resume a recognizable form that could be served by existing theoretical frameworks. But by simply maintaining that professional landscape planning had indeed been a product of the "modern" historical era (a function, in other words, of capitalism, industrial technologies, and picturesque aesthetics), landscape historians such as Griswold and Newton evaded the challenge presented by Modernist design movements in the 1930s. New economic and social conditions demanded new residential and civic design. When a viable market for private landscape design services finally began to reemerge around 1937, it did so under entirely changed circumstances. New clients tended to own smaller suburban properties, and garden designers needed to exploit cheaper and more easily standardized materials and plans. Commercial corporations began to relocate their headquarters into distant suburbs, and so became the new "country place" clients, replacing the affluent suburban estate owners who would never again be as numerous. As International Style became the desired postwar architectural idiom both of corporate America and of many suburban homebuilders, the debate over what made landscape design "modern" quickly faded into obscurity; in both small residential gardens and large corporate parks, landscape architects sought to provide a consistent and appropriate context for the Modernist-inspired architecture that often preceded their own involvement in both types of projects.

The eventual transcendence of Modernist planning and architectural design in the United States after World War II was foretold by the demise of the Harvard School of Landscape Architecture. In the early 1930s, the school was reorganized as a department in the new Graduate School of Design under the direction of Walter Hudnut. In 1937 Hudnut brought the architect Walter Gropius to Harvard as the chairman of the architecture department of the new graduate school. Gropius, the designer and administrator of the Dessau Bauhaus and a leading figure of European Modernism, greatly influenced the curriculum and student body of the Graduate School of Design. Two years later Gropius was joined by an English landscape architect, Christopher Tunnard, who was the leading figure in a small but growing movement of landscape designers who were attempting to define site planning and garden design that would complement the formalist aesthetics of Modernist architecture. Tunnard had gained prominence through the publication of a series of articles brought together in his 1938 book, *Gardens in the Modern Landscape*, and through a small number of built landscapes. Drawing examples from Adolf Loos, Le Corbusier, Mies van der Rohe, and his own collaborations with Serge Chermayeff, Tunnard bewailed the fact that "gardens had remained aloof" from contemporary trends in architecture and the fine arts. Garden design, he felt, was clearly "in need of the invigorating modern spirit."[4]

After arriving at Harvard, Tunnard continued to assert that "modern landscape design is inseparable from the spirit, technique, and development of modern architecture." Attempting to further revise American landscape architectural theory as it then was understood, he explicitly denounced Hubbard and Kimball's bifurcated model of "formal" and "naturalistic." "Conventional methods of axial composition or of naturalistic arrangement of plant material," Tunnard claimed, "just haven't the right approach to the modern garden." He denounced the former as "design cliches . . . fatal to the uninhibited garden maker"; the latter he describes as "the dying breath of the romantic age, long since broken down and already discarded by the sister art of architecture."[5]

By the end of the decade, a generation of students at Harvard, some of whom would become the most active professionals of the postwar era, had responded to these invigorating influences. Proclaiming their confidence that new "modern" landscape architecture could be based on Modernist architectural principles, students such as James Rose and Garrett Eckbo designed gardens that employed overlay plan organizations, asymmetric compositions, and new materials and design motifs that evoked contemporary architectural design and fine arts. Biomorphic forms, bold patterns, abstract sculpture, and specimen plants used for their "sculptural" habits characterized their landscape design.[6] In postwar America, European Modernist architecture, like the Italian villas and palazzi chosen by a previous generation of Americans, came to embody personal affluence, cosmopolitan politics, and "international" culture. Just as Charles Platt had demonstrated the vitality of Renaissance architectural prototypes in the design of new residential landscapes for American industrialists, a new group of American landscape designers proved that design principles and motifs drawn from Modernist architecture could again transform the practice of landscape architecture and continue its viability for new groups of clients.

But if a fundamental reorientation of American landscape design had begun in the 1930s, the full implication of these changes only became evident when the private economy restarted in earnest after World War II. In the meantime, architectural Modernism played only a limited role in the landscape architecture of the New Deal. Divorced from the vicissitudes of the marketplace, the National Park Service, in particular, offered a refuge for traditional, Fairsted School landscape planning and design at a time when the private sector, responding to irresistible economic forces, began to move in very different directions.

Certain New Deal agencies, in particular Rexford Tugwell's Resettlement Administration (later the Farm Security Administration), sponsored landscape design and community planning that perhaps reflected Modernist influences, but these efforts remained limited experiments compared to the massive developments undertaken by the Park Service after 1933. Under Thomas Vint and Conrad Wirth, landscape park planning continued along orthodox lines that furthered the techniques of landscape park planning established by the Olmsteds and Charles Eliot. Contemporary European design movements had little influence on Daniel Hull, Vint, or Wirth; the picturesque facades of Park Service Rustic buildings, for example, hardly stripped away ornament or denied historical associations. The 20th-century landscape park remained a bastion of picturesque aesthetics and Reptonian landscape theory. Park village planning, park master planning, and every aspect of national and state park development undertaken by the Park Service continued to be predicated on the perceived economic and social benefits of preserving certain places by developing them as parks, opening them to the public, and thus transforming land into landscape.

For most of this generation of national park planners, therefore, the word "Modern" (when spelled with a capital "M") was an anathema. Proponents of the "Modern" had dismissed landscape park planning, after all, as "the dying breath of the romantic age," and many established landscape architects in the United States reciprocated this contempt. At the same time, landscape architects involved in regional and town planning, automotive parkway design, and public park development recognized that they were responding to contemporary social, economic, and technological trends as much as anyone; they resented being considered somehow un-modern, or obsolete. In the 1920s, landscape architects like Gilmore Clarke, the designer of the Westchester parkways, had employed rigid-frame concrete construction, spiral transition road alignments, high-speed interchanges, and other highly sophisticated technologies in the design of regional automotive parkways. In New York during the 1930s, Clarke, working for Park Commissioner Robert Moses, oversaw the design of the world's first true regional arterial road system, which connected regional parkways in Westchester and Long Island with new municipal automotive parkways in the city itself. Massive park and playground development accompanied the road construction in New York, creating the first park and automotive parkway system of its type. Clarke's parkways exploited the latest automotive and construction technology, and the new parks of the system were designed to meet the recreational needs of the largest metropolitan area in the country.

But if Clarke's automotive parkways were technically sophisticated, they also continued to feature curvilinear alignments, bridges with rusticated stone veneers, wide roadsides planted with shrubs and trees, and associated recreational areas that preserved regional scenery. As parkways, they also continued to be strictly non-commercial; and since they were not designed for truck traffic, the roadways could be narrower, bridges could be lower, and curves could be tighter, all of which meant automotive parkways could conform to the surrounding topography and landscape to a greater degree that regular highways. Parkways could also be integrated with recreational areas far more successfully than busier commercial roads could be. The municipal parks developed in New York in association with the new parkways also continued to employ historical references in architectural design and detailing. And whether "formal" or "naturalistic" in inspiration, the site plans for the new parks clearly derived from well established traditions of American landscape architecture.

Regional and municipal park and parkway planning of this type, in other words, clearly continued traditional landscape planning practices, and yet also responded to the most contemporary social trends and technological possibilities. Although their practice remained firmly rooted in Fairsted School landscape planning, it was difficult for landscape architects like Gilmore Clarke to see what was less than "modern" about their work.

One landscape architectural project of the 1930s, in particular, demonstrated the degree to which Fairsted School landscape architecture was capable of embracing technological and social change in the 1930s. The 469-mile Blue Ridge Parkway, the construction of which began in 1935, simply dwarfed any work of park planning that had ever been attempted. Although ideas for a great Appalachian Ridge road had been circulating since before Benton MacKaye's day, the "eastern park-to-park highway" was boosted aggressively in the early 1930s and became a reality through the New Deal. The most ambitious project of its type ever completed, the Blue Ridge project offered Conrad Wirth's planners the opportunity to combine state parks, national parks, Recreational Demonstration Areas, and (by implication) national forests, into a unified strategy for exploiting the recreational potential of mountain scenery across Virginia and North Carolina. More than a road, the parkway was planned as the physical core of an inter-regional plan for the entire Appalachian Range. As mountain farms and cutover forests were abandoned by impoverished inhabitants, the Blue Ridge Parkway was the means of planning and enabling coordinated outdoor recreational land uses as the basis of new regional economies. No other Park Service project of the period more fully embodied the ultimate ambitions of national recreational planning. But the promise of a system of national parkways (which Warren Manning had seen so clearly fifteen years earlier) would never be fulfilled in the postwar era.

If the New Deal marked a dynamic high point in the historic partnership between the Park Service and the profession of landscape architecture, it also ended the most productive era of landscape park development in the United States. The rise of the International Style and the restructuring of private sector practice around corporate clients changed the profession of landscape architecture profoundly following World War II. Modernist landscape architecture produced its own masterpieces over the next decades, but its usefulness in national park design and management would never be significant. Other changes reflected the political climate of the postwar period. Concepts like national recreational planning suddenly seemed radical, and if the Park Service continued to employ large numbers of landscape architects, the bureau's program of comprehensive recreational planning ended by the 1960s.

Since then, the history of national parks and of landscape architecture seem to have diverged. The preservation and development of national parks in the early 20th century expressed ideal civic arrangements, centered around a public experience of landscape beauty. Visitors were vital to the success of landscape preservation; without people there were no parks, only wild regions of the public domain, easily subject to other forms of exploitation. By the 1960s, however, under the pressures of brutal overcrowding in some national parks, a wider range of park managers and planners came to identify the public as the enemy of preservation. Parks no longer needed to be "opened up for the convenience and comfort of tourists," therefore, as much as protected from the environmental impacts of their attentions. The idea of national parks as public places and ideal civic expressions shifted to a scientific model of parks as assemblages of environmental systems and ecological communities. Humans had no legitimate place in such a model, since they could only further degrade the environmental purity that presumably preceded their appearance. Park Service landscape architects, many of whom were leading this shift, therefore rejected Olmstedian theory and turned to environmental sciences to replace landscape aesthetics in new planning and design processes.

Today it is accurate to say that much of the national park system does not only contain certain historic resources (such as buildings), but is itself historic. The system's planning and development represent the goals and aspirations of certain portions of early 20th-century American society just as surely as many municipal park systems embody related civic visions of the 19th century. This awareness of the cultural and historical significance of large "natural" parks (in addition to their obvious biological significance) indicates that conceptual models of national parks continue to evolve, as they always have. The preservation of the national park system as unique cultural infrastructure, for example, is beginning to be considered alongside the mandate to preserve (as best we can) undisturbed ecological communities and environmental systems.

Landscape architecture and the National Park Service have indeed grown more distant in the last three decades. Park development and landscape preservation today are often characterized as mortally antagonistic, not mutually enabling. The symbiosis that took both the Park Service and landscape architecture to their highest points in the 1930s has been reduced to a historical interest. But today both state parks and national parks face unprecedented threats. Many state governments see their state parks as underdeveloped resorts. Strapped for cash, legislators look to new conference centers, ski resorts, and golf courses, not only to cover the cost of park administration, but to turn a profit. National parks potentially face an almost opposite, but related fate. As existing facilities become more and more crowded, the parks will cease to be public in any meaningful sense, since only those who make reservations far in advance will have access. And federal budget cutters and environmentalists alike have recently agreed that raising park entrance fees would serve both their interests, in one case by exploiting the profit-making potential of parks and in the other by further restricting public access.

The national and state park historic districts described in this study can perhaps serve to remind both parties of the significance of what Park Service landscape architects achieved in the 1920s and 1930s: the creation of a middle ground between excesses of commercialism and of exclusivity. In an era of increasingly strident extremes, the historical partnership of landscape architecture and the National Park Service may yet serve as a viable precedent for preserving scenic landscapes by planning for limited recreational uses of public lands.

Endnotes

Introduction

(pp. 1-10)

¹Visitor statistics from Department of the Interior, National Park Service, *A Study of the Park and Recreation Problem of the United States* (Washington, DC: Government Printing Office, 1941), 52; Department of the Interior, National Park Service, *National Parks for the 21st Century: The Vail Agenda* (Post Mills, Vermont: Chelsea Green Publishing Company, n.d.), 67.

²Department of the Interior, *Proceedings of the National Park Conference Held at Yellowstone National Park, September 11 and 12, 1911* (Washington, DC: Government Printing Office, 1911), 3.

³Platt National Park and the Hot Springs Reservation accounted for an estimated 145,000 of the total number of visitors. The third and fourth most visited parks were Yellowstone (23,054) and Yosemite (12,530). Congress appropriated $819,181.67 between 1907 and 1913 for national parks, and an additional $326,809.48 was raised through automobile and concession fees. Department of the Interior, *Reports of the Department of the Interior for the Fiscal Year Ending June 30, 1913* (Washington, DC: Government Printing Office, 1914), 114-116.

⁴Hillory A. Tolson, *Laws Relating to the National Park Service and the National Parks and Monuments* (Washington, DC: Government Printing Office, 1933), 32-33.

⁵Yosemite Valley had been a state park until 1906. Department of the Interior, *Report of the Superintendent of National Parks to the Secretary of the Interior for the Fiscal Year Ended June 30, 1916* (Washington, DC: Government Printing Office, 1917), 15.

⁶Donald C. Swain, "The Passage of the National Park Service Act of 1916," *Wisconsin Magazine of History* 50, no. 1 (September 1966): 5.

⁷Samuel P. Hays, *Conservation and the Gospel of Efficiency: The Progressive Conservation Movement, 1890-1920* (New York: Athenaeum, 1979), 27-48, 196.

⁸The landscape architect Mark Daniels, among others, fully expressed this set of aspirations for national parks by 1914. Department of the Interior, *1915 Annual Reports*, 843-852.

⁹Quoted in Alfred Runte, *National Parks: The American Experience*, Second Edition, Revised (Lincoln: University of Nebraska Press, 1987), 92.

¹⁰Department of the Interior, *1910 Annual Reports*, 57-58.

¹¹Daniels was paraphrasing an earlier comment by Secretary Lane in the first portion of this observation. Department of the Interior, *1915 Annual Reports*, 843, 849.

¹²Department of the Interior, National Park Service, *Report of the Director of the National Park Service to the Secretary of the Interior for the Fiscal Year Ended June 30, 1918* (Washington, DC: Government Printing Office, 1918), 10.

¹³Department of the Interior, National Park Service, *1917 Annual Report*, 18, 22.

¹⁴Several American parks have already been made National Historic Landmarks, including the Boston Common and the Boston Public Garden, Central Park in New York, Fairmount Park in Philadelphia, the Niagara Reservation and the Adirondack Park in New York State, and the Palisades Interstate Park in New York and New Jersey. Most of these parks were made landmarks in the historical "theme" of Natural Resource Conservation. See Charles W. Snell, *Conservation of Natural Resources: National Survey of Historic Sites and Buildings*, unpublished report (Washington, DC: Department of the Interior, Main Interior Library, 1963).

"The Power of Scenery": Picturesque Theory and Landscape Design in National Parks

[1]The text of the act passed by the New York State Legislature is reprinted in Frederick Law Olmsted, Jr., and Theodora Kimball, eds., *Forty Years of Landscape Architecture: Central Park* [1928] (Cambridge: The MIT Press, 1973), 539.

[2]Tolson, *Laws*, 64, 26.

[3]Alfred Runte, for example, sees Americans, suffering from the "embarrassment of a dearth of recognized cultural achievements," embracing "the wonderlands of the West as replacements for man-made marks of achievement." Runte, *National Parks*, 11-12. Roderick Nash also sees cultural nationalism as one of the motives for the American appreciation of wilderness: "The nation's short history, weak traditions, and minor literary and artistic accomplishments seemed negligible . . . [but] wilderness had no counterpart in the Old World." Roderick Nash, *Wilderness and the American Mind*, Third Edition (New Haven: Yale University Press, 1982), 67.

[4]Christopher Hussey, *The Picturesque: Studies in a Point of View* (London: G.P. Putnam's Sons, 1927), 2-4, 64.

[5]One of the most important early American guidebooks was Theodore Dwight, Jr.'s *The Northern Traveller* (1825). For discussions of 19th-century travel American literature, see Hans Huth, *Nature and the American: Three Centuries of Changing Attitudes*, New Edition (Lincoln: University of Nebraska Press, 1990), 71-86; John F. Sears, *Sacred Places: American Tourist Attractions in the Nineteenth Century* (New York: Oxford University Press, 1989), 49-86; Dona Brown, *Inventing New England: Regional Tourism in the Nineteenth Century* (Washington, DC: Smithsonian Institution Press, 1995), 28-31.

[6]A number of historians have written on the peculiarly American appreciation of "sublime" landscape spectacles, from Niagara Falls to Yosemite Valley. This aesthetic category encompassed the grander scale and proportion of such scenes, and also appealed to a developing American Transcendentalism that Emerson, above all, identified with the awe and mystery of natural phenomena. See Elizabeth McKinsey, *Niagara Falls: Icon of the American Sublime* (New York: Cambridge University Press, 1985); Walter L. Creese, "Yosemite National Park," in *The Crowning of the American Landscape: Eight Great Spaces and their Buildings* (Princeton: Princeton University Press, 1985).

[7]William Gilpin, *Three Essays* [1792] (Westmead, Farnborough, Hants.: Gregg International Publishers, 1972), 50.

[8]James Flexner observes that Cole emerged from a "vernacular mode" of landscape sketching and engraving that had already been developed in England, especially by watercolorists. As a more competent landscapist, Cole employed compositional rules that recalled the scenes of 17th-century painters, especially Claude Lorraine and Salvator Rosa, as they had been interpreted by British artists in the 18th century. James Thomas Flexner, *That Wilder Image: The Painting of America's Native School from Thomas Cole to Winslow Homer* [1962] (New York: Dover Publications, 1970), 3-18. Barbara Novak describes the "psychic and philosophical investment" that American painters placed in the "Claudian mode" of pictorial composition. Barbara Novak, *Nature and Culture: American Landscape Painting, 1825-1875* (New York: Oxford University Press, 1980), 227-228.

[9]The diverse influences on British landscape gardening in the mid-18th century have been the subject of intensive study in recent years. John Dixon Hunt describes the influence of Italian Renaissance culture in the formulation of early Georgian landscape gardens, which juxtaposed the more architectonic "garden" and the wooded "grove." John Dixon Hunt, *Garden and Grove: The Italian Renaissance Garden in the English Imagination, 1600-1750* (Princeton: Princeton University Press, 1986), 181-222. For an introduction to some of the themes and debates of recent scholarship, see John Dixon Hunt and Peter Willis, eds., *The Genius of the Place: The English Landscape Garden, 1620-1820* (Cambridge: The MIT Press, 1988).

[10]Or as Ann Bermingham puts it: "Because the landscape garden was contiguous with the enclosed landscape, the antithesis between the instrumental and noninstrumental (aesthetic) use of land was pronounced, finally coming to shape the aesthetics of garden composition itself." Ann Bermingham, *Landscape and Ideology: The English Rustic Tradition, 1740-1860* (Berkeley: University of California Press, 1986), 10-

11. For an explanation of commercial considerations in the management of private parkland, see Tom Williamson, "The Landscape Park: Economics, Art, and Ideology," *Journal of Garden History* 13, nos. 1/2 (Spring/Summer 1993): 49-55.

[11]Humphry Repton produced several textbooks which were the first to systematically present the theory and practice of picturesque landscape design, beginning with *Sketches and Hints on Landscape Gardening* (1795). "Landscape gardening" for Repton referred to the "united powers of the landscape painter and the practical gardener." Humphry Repton, *The Art of Landscape Gardening*, John Nolen, ed. (Boston: Houghton Mifflin Company, 1907), 3.

[12]The Massachusetts Horticultural Society financed the project through the sale of stock in future grave plots. See Blanche Linden-Ward, *Silent City on a Hill: Landscapes of Memory and Boston's Mount Auburn Cemetery* (Columbus: Ohio State University Press, 1989).

[13]David Schuyler describes rural cemeteries as examples of "didactic landscapes" (in opposition to "naturalistic parks") and notes the limitations for public recreation inherent in cemetery design. David Schuyler, *The New Urban Landscape: The Redefinition of City Form in Nineteenth-Century America* (Baltimore: The Johns Hopkins University Press, 1986), 37-56.

[14]Schuyler, *The New Urban Landscape*, 77-100; Roy Rosenzweig and Elizabeth Blackmar, *The Park and the People: A History of Central Park* (Ithaca: Cornell University Press, 1992), 15-58.

[15]Olmsted and Kimball, eds., *Forty Years of Landscape Architecture,* 18-29.

[16]Victoria Post Ranney, ed., *The California Frontier, Volume V of the Papers of Frederick Law Olmsted* (Baltimore: The Johns Hopkins University Press, 1992), 385. The "public" referred to here was constituted primarily from the urban middle classes, who in Europe and the United States made up the principal constituencies for "public" parks. This remains true today, although the American park's public has grown more diverse as new groups have entered the middle classes and have subsequently confirmed their status by demonstrating what Humphry Repton described in 1812 as "the taste to appreciate the beauties of nature."

[17]The story of the design competition and the political complexities involved have been thoroughly documented. See Olmsted and Kimball, eds., *Forty Years of Landscape Architecture*, 41-50; Rosenzweig and Blackmar, *The Park and the People*, 95-120.

[18]Olmsted, and Kimball, eds., *Forty Years of Landscape Architecture*, 45. For the textual description that accompanied the "Greensward" plan, see Charles E. Beveridge and David Schuyler, eds., *Creating Central Park, Volume III of the Papers of Frederick Law Olmsted* (Baltimore: The Johns Hopkins University Press, 1983), 119-175.

[19]Used in its technical, aesthetic sense, "picturesque" referred to a rougher, more rugged landscape, in contrast to the "beautiful," or pastoral, landscape of smooth meadows and sheets of water. Brown's parks, in this sense, were by definition "beautiful." Olmsted, who was well versed in British landscape aesthetics, specifically advocated the "beautiful" for Central Park (as indicated by the name of the plan, "Greensward") because he considered it appropriate to the purpose of providing a calming influence in contrast to the jarring realities of city streets. In this case pastoral scenes also were considered more suitable to the "genius of the place," that is the park site's pre-existing character; but in the locations where "picturesque" effects were appropriate and feasible (such as in the Ramble, an area where a rockier, more precipitous topography prevailed) they were employed.

[20]Pope urged that in park design, "Let Nature never be forgot . . . Consult the Genius of the place in all; That tells the waters or to rise, or fall." Alexander Pope, "Epistle to Lord Burlington," (1731) in *The Oxford Book of Garden Verse*, John Dixon Hunt, ed. (Oxford: Oxford University Press, 1993), 88.

[21]Olmsted described the sense of community he hoped groups could achieve in park settings as "communitiveness." Laura Wood Roper, *FLO: A Biography of Frederick Law Olmsted* (Baltimore: The John Hopkins University Press, 1973), 253.

[22]Frederick Law Olmsted and Calvert Vaux, "Preliminary Report for Laying Out a Park in Brooklyn, New York: Being a Consideration of Circumstances of Site and Other Conditions Affecting the Design of Public Pleasure Grounds," [1866] in Albert Fein, ed., *Landscape Into Cityscape: Frederick Law Olmsted's Plans for a Greater New York City* (New York: Van Nostrand Reinhold Company, 1967), 98-102.

[23]Quoted in Schuyler, *The New Urban Landscape*, 96.

[24]Schuyler, *The New Urban Landscape*, 195. Schuyler goes on to point out that "Olmsted's vision of the naturalistic city may have been appropriate at an earlier time, but to Progressive reformers it must have seemed as naive as Richard Morris Hunt had predicted" (184-185).

[25]Olmsted considered Uvedale Price's *An Essay on the Picturesque* (1794) and William Gilpin's works (which he read as a young man) to be "the most educative books on park-making in our language or in any language." Beveridge and Schuyler, eds., *Creating Central Park*, 40. He also described Price and Gilpin as "books of the last century . . . which I esteem so much more than any published since, as stimulating the exercise of judgement in matters of my art, that I put them into the hands of my pupils as soon as they come into our office, saying, 'You are to read these seriously, as a student of Law would read Blackstone.'" Quoted in Charles E. Beveridge, "Frederick Law Olmsted's Theory on Landscape Design," *Nineteenth Century* 3, No. 2 (Summer 1977): 38-43. Later, Olmsted added the works of Repton, Loudon, and John Ruskin to a list of recommended reading for landscape architectural training. See David Schuyler and Jane Turner Censer, eds., *The Years of Olmsted, Vaux & Company, 1865-1874, Volume VI of the Papers of Frederick Law Olmsted* (Baltimore: The Johns Hopkins University Press, 1992), 468-470.

[26]A State Senate special committee investigating the park came to the same conclusion the next year. Olmsted and Kimball, eds., *Forty Years of Landscape Architecture*, 173-174.

[27]Fein, ed., *Landscape Into Cityscape*, 158-159.

[28]The parkway, through its design in section and its legal status, could therefore provide some of what would later be perceived as the benefits of zoning. Although historians have emphasized the role of rail and other forms of mass transportation in the development of 19th-century metropolitan areas, parkway design, at the forefront of highway engineering at the time, represented another developing transportation technology with great influence on 19th-century urban form. William H. Wilson's examination of Kansas City's park and parkway system demonstrates that the influence of improved roadways was felt long before the use of automobiles became widespread. William H. Wilson, *The City Beautiful Movement* (Baltimore: The Johns Hopkins University Press, 1989), 99-125. Clay McShane has written on the influence of improved pavements and other aspects of municipal engineering in transforming city streets. Clay McShane, "Transforming the Use of Urban Space: A Look at the Revolution in Street Pavements, 1888-1924," *Journal of Urban History* 5, no. 3 (May 1979).

[29]The picturesque subdivision, like the picturesque cemetery, had appeared in the antebellum decades as a form of speculative development. See Norman T. Newton, *Design on the Land: The Development of Landscape Architecture* (Cambridge, The Belknap Press of Harvard University, 1971), 464-478; Kenneth Jackson, *The Crabgrass Frontier: The Suburbanization of the United States* (New York: Oxford University Press, 1985), 73-86.

[30]Olmsted and Kimball, eds., *Forty Years of Landscape Architecture*, 46. In the northern, less disturbed portion of park site, Olmsted and Vaux felt it was "desirable to interfere with [the existing landscape] . . . as little as possible." Beveridge and Schuyler, eds., *Creating Central Park*, 119.

[31]A particularly scenic area of farmland in West Roxbury became Boston's Franklin Park in the 1880s. J. C. Olmsted planned the Seattle park system, which exploits the lakes, topography, and mountain views in that city, in the first decade of the 20th century.

[32]Henry Vincent Hubbard and Theodora Kimball, *An Introduction to the Study of Landscape Design* [1917] (New York: The Macmillan Company, 1929), 58.

[33]The authorship of a "national park idea" has been claimed for numerous individuals, including Thomas Jefferson, George Catlin, and Frederick Law Olmsted. See (respectively): Roper, *FLO*, 286; Hiram Martin Chittenden, *The Yellowstone National Park: Historical and Descriptive* [1895], New Edition, Revised (Saint Paul: J. E. Haynes, 1924), 73-74; Huth, *Nature and the American*, 149. Cornelius Hedges, a member of the 1870 Washburn-Doane expedition to Yellowstone, was said to have suggested to the other members of that expedition that the Yellowstone region be made a national park. The Park Service traditionally has perpetuated this famous story as the origin of the "national park idea."

[34]Ranney, ed., *The California Frontier*, 500. The open meadows and clumps of trees in the valley made it easily understood within the formal vocabulary of the landscape park. This appearance was probably the result of periodic burning by the Ahwahneechees, who managed the oak woodlands for acorn mast and other products. Alfred Runte, *Yosemite: The Embattled Wilderness* (Lincoln: University of Nebraska Press, 1990), 9.

[35]Anne Farrar Hyde makes clear the limitations of American picturesque aesthetics in the context of far western landscapes. She asserts that vast deserts and arid basin and range country "would require an entirely new aesthetic language to describe them," a language which only developed in the 20th century. She also acknowledges, however, that views of Yosemite Valley and the American tourist sites "were not so different that they could not be described in familiar aesthetic terms," and that "educated Americans . . . wanted to find English parks, Swiss Alps, and Italian vistas; and in parts of the Far West, they found them." Anne Farrar Hyde, *An American Vision: Far Western Landscape and National Culture, 1820-1920* (New York: New York University Press, 1990), 23, 50-52.

[36]For the text of Raymond's letter and the details of the legislation, see Hans Huth, "Yosemite: The Story of an Idea," *The Sierra Club Bulletin* 33, no. 3 (March 1948): 47-78.

[37]The alliance of transportation and other tourist related interests with the cause of scenic preservation has been described by the historian Alfred Runte as a "pragmatic alliance"which had great implications for the history of the national park system. Alfred Runte, "Pragmatic Alliance: Western Railroads and the National Parks," *National Park and Conservation Association Magazine* 48 (April 1974): 14-21.

[38]Laura Wood Roper could find no evidence of Olmsted's direct involvement in the initiation of Yosemite legislation. She points out, however, that "the demand for rural parks in cities and the interest in natural scenery were both growing stronger. . . . It was not remarkable that the two trends should combine to precipitate the idea that regions of unusual beauty should be set aside as public parks." Olmsted himself, she notes, "attributed the concept [of setting aside Yosemite] . . . to 'the workings of the national genius.'" Roper, *FLO*, 282-283, 285, 287.

[39]Quoted in Huth, "Yosemite," 69.

[40]For the text of the letters sent to Thomas Hill, Carleton Watkins, and Virgil Williams, see Huth, "Yosemite," 70.

[41]For the complete text of the Yosemite report, see Ranney, ed., *The California Frontier*, 488-516.

[42]See Olmsted and Kimball, eds., *Forty Years of Landscape Architecture*, 45-46.

[43]Runte, *Yosemite*, 28-44.

[44]For a thorough history of the exploration of the Yellowstone region and the creation of the park, see Aubrey L. Haines, *The Yellowstone Story*, 2 vols. (Boulder: The Yellowstone Library and Museum Association in cooperation with Colorado Associated University Press, 1977), vol. 1, 84-173.

[45]Haines, *The Yellowstone Story*, vol. 1, 154-155, 164-165; Louis C. Cramton, *Early History of Yellowstone National Park and Its Relation to National Park Policies* (Washington, DC: Government Printing Office, 1932), 24-28.

[46]Tolson, *Laws*, 26-27.

[47]Haines, *The Yellowstone Story*, vol. 2, 54-60, 80, 242; John Ise, *Our National Park Policy: A Critical History* (Baltimore: The Johns Hopkins University Press, 1961), 26-29, 45-49.

[48]Chittenden left the park in 1893 and returned in 1899. In 1895, he published the most important early history of Yellowstone: Hiram Martin Chittenden, *The Yellowstone National Park: Historical and Descriptive* [1895], New and Enlarged Edition, Entirely Revised (Saint Paul: J. E. Haynes, 1927).

[49]Chittenden, *Yellowstone National Park*, 238.

[50]Mary Shivers Culpin, *The History of the Construction of the Road System in Yellowstone National Park, 1872-1966: Historic Resource Study, Volume I* (Denver: Government Printing Office, 1994), 25-68; Haines, *The Yellowstone Story*, vol. 2, 209-255.

[51]Chittenden, *Yellowstone National Park*, 237-238, 240.

[52]Chittenden, *Yellowstone National Park*, 248-249.

[53]Quoted in Culpin, *Construction of the Road System in Yellowstone*, 27.

[54]The Yellowstone bridge was constructed of steel and concrete and spanned 120 feet, compared to the sixty-foot span of the cast-iron Bow Bridge; but the two arches share the same attenuated, gently bowed proportions and both featured solid ornamental railings with medallion apertures. Chittenden, who was from New York State and attended West Point, may or may not have ever visited Central Park. The park aesthetic he embraced, however, was pervasive by the end of the 19th century.

[55]Cynthia Zaitzevsky, *Frederick Law Olmsted and the Boston Park System* (Cambridge: The Belknap Press of Harvard University, 1982), 96-101.

[56]"Sand gardens" opened in Boston as early as 1885 were playgrounds for small children, inspired by contemporary examples in Berlin. See Richard F. Knapp and Charles E. Hartsoe, *Play For America: The National Recreation Association, 1906-1965* (Arlington, Virginia: National Recreation and Park Association, 1979), 19-39; Allen F. Davis, "Playgrounds, Housing, and City Planning," in Donald A. Krueckeberg, ed., *Introduction to City Planning History in the United States* (New Brunswick, New Jersey: Rutgers University Center for Urban Policy Research, 1983), 73-87.

[57]Jacob Riis, *Report of the Committee on Small Parks* (New York: the Martin B. Brown Company, 1897), 1-2.

[58]Davis, "Playgrounds, Housing, and City Planning," 75-76.

[59]Others perhaps dreaded the incursion of mostly Catholic and Jewish children into mostly Protestant neighborhoods. For a thorough analysis of ethnic rivalries as they related to competing visions of park use and management, see Rosenzweig and Blackmar, *Central Park*, 307-339.

[60]Rosenzweig and Blackmar, *Central Park*, 392-393, 412-413. According to these authors, "The nineteenth-century conception of parks as landscape art now took second place in the minds of many New Yorkers to their value as places for play."

[61]Newton, *Design on the Land*, 623-626; Knapp and Hartsoe, *Play for America*, 28.

[62]Joseph Lee, "Play as Landscape," *Charities and the Commons* 16, no. 4 (July 1906): 427-432. In 1910, Lee became president of the Playground Association (later the National Recreation Association).

[63]David Schuyler describes "a different conception of what the city should be" at the end of the 19th century, and suggests "the most immediate manifestation of this conception of civic culture and city design was the transformation of the great urban parks created before and after the Civil War." Schuyler, *The New Urban Landscape*, 184-185.

[64]The famous "Court of Honor" of the 1893 World's Columbian Exposition in Chicago inspired many of these municipal plans. Civic centers, or portions of them, survive in dozens of American cities. See Werner Hegeman and Elbert Peets, *The American Vitruvius: An Architect's Handbook of Civic Art* [1922] (Princeton: Princeton Architectural Press, 1988), 133-150; Mel Scott, *American City Planning Since 1890* (Berkeley: University of California Press, 1969), 47-109; Wilson, *The City Beautiful Movement* , 168-192, 234-253.

[65]Ray F. Weirick, "The Park and Parkway System of Kansas City, Mo.," *The American City* 3, no. 5 (November 1910): 211-218.

[66]Flexner suggests that although "Whistler and La Farge inaugurated this new movement a few years before the outbreak of the Civil War . . . it was that conflict and its aggressive industrial aftermath that made flight from native inspiration the dominant artistic trend." Flexner, *That Wilder Image*, 256, 258-290.

[67]Charles A. Platt, *Italian Gardens* [1894], reprint, with an overview by Keith N. Morgan (Portland, Oregon: Sagapress/Timber Press, 1993), 97.

[68]Newton describes "a period of increased activity in the design of large residential properties in the country," which were "not truly 'country estates'" but were better described as "country places." Newton, *Design on the Land*, 427.

[69]Newton, *Design on the Land*, 285-292.

[70]Sarah Lewis Pattee, "Landscape Architecture in American Colleges," *Landscape Architecture* 14, no. 3 (April 1924): 171-177.

[71]By 1911, the principal administrator of the Harvard program, James Sturgis Pray, recognized that the design problems solved were of two types: "private residences," and "public recreation areas and the larger problems of city-planning." He also felt that basic architectural training was "the greatest saving of time" in preparing for a graduate degree

in landscape architecture. James Sturgis Pray, "The Department of Landscape Architecture in Harvard University," *Landscape Architecture* 1, no. 2 (January 1911): 53-70.

[72]Jackson, *The Crabgrass Frontier*, 138-156.

[73]William Cullen Bryant, ed., *Picturesque America; or, The Land We Live In*, 2 vols. [1874], Centennial Edition (Seacaucus, New Jersey: Lyle Stuart, Inc., 1974).

[74]Quoted in Huth, *Nature and the American*, 172.

[75]Olmsted had a lifelong interest in the falls, which he had first visited as a child in the 1830s. In 1869 he met at the falls with the architect H. H. Richardson and Buffalo park advocate William Dorsheimer to discuss the creation of a park. The campaign to preserve the falls, however, really began in 1878, after Lord Dufferin, the Governor General of Canada, called for international cooperation in their management. Roper, *FLO*, 378-380.

[76]Alfred Runte, "Beyond the Spectacular: The Niagara Falls Preservation Campaign," *The New-York Historical Society Quarterly* 57, no. 1 (January 1973): 30-50; Roper, *FLO*, 381, 395.

[77]Commonwealth of Massachusetts, Metropolitan Park Commission, *A History and Description of the Boston Metropolitan Parks* (Boston: Commonwealth of Massachusetts, Wright & Potter Printing Co., 1900), 10.

[78]Since 1981, Fairsted has been managed by the National Park Service as the Frederick Law Olmsted National Historic Site.

[79]James Sturgis Pray, "John Charles Olmsted," *Landscape Architecture* 12, no. 3 (April 1922): 129-135.

[80]Zaitzevsky, *Olmsted and the Boston Park System*, 81, 127-130.

[81]Zaitzevsky, *Olmsted and the Boston Park System*, 162-183; James F. O'Gorman, *H. H. Richardson: Architectural Forms for an American Society* (Chicago: The University of Chicago Press, 1987), 91-111; Linda Flint McClelland, *Presenting Nature: The Historic Landscape Design of the National Park Service, 1916 to 1942* (Washington, DC: Government Printing Office, 1993), 22-25, 42.

[82]The Playstead Shelter, designed by Frederick Law Olmsted and J. C. Olmsted for Franklin Park, epitomizes this architecture. A massively proportioned Shingle building with heavy, projecting eaves, it sat on a foundation of large boulders and provided a viewing terrace overlooking the Playstead. Zaitzevsky, *Olmsted and the Boston Park System*, 176-177.

[83]Charles W. Eliot, *Charles Eliot, Landscape Architect: A Lover of Nature and of His Kind Who Trained Himself for a New Profession, Practised It Happily, and Through It Wrought Much Good* (Boston: Houghton Mifflin, 1902).

[84]Eliot, *Charles Eliot*, 37, 39-40.

[85]The influence of Humphry Repton on Eliot's conception of professional practice was profound. During Eliot's travels in Europe in 1886, he spent half of his time in Great Britain visiting landscape parks. On the Continent, he was most impressed by the park at Muskau, designed in the 1830s by another ardent admirer of Repton, Prince Hermann von Puckler-Muskau. When J. C. Olmsted, Eliot and other Boston area professionals began to meet as a group informally in the 1880s, they named their society the "Repton Club." Newton, *Design on the Land*, 386; Keith N. Morgan, *Held in Trust: Charles Eliot's Vision for the New England Landscape*, National Association of Olmsted Parks Workbook Series, Volume I (Bethesda, Maryland: National Association of Olmsted Parks, 1991), 2-3.

[86]Frederick Law Olmsted, "A Letter Relating to Professional Practice from F. L. Olmsted, Sr., to Charles Eliot (1886)," *Landscape Architecture* 11, no. 4 (July 1921): 189-190.

[87]Alfred Rehder, "Charles Sprague Sargent," *Journal of the Arnold Arboretum* 8, no. 2 (April 1927): 69-87.

[88]Eliot, *Charles Eliot*, 318-319.

[89]Commonwealth of Massachusetts, Metropolitan Park Commission, *Boston Metropolitan Parks*, 31.

[90]Commonwealth of Massachusetts, Metropolitan Park Commission, *Boston Metropolitan Parks*, 26.

[91]Playgrounds and squares were also considered, but their acquisition and development were to be the responsibility of local town governments. For the text of Eliot's 1893 report to the Metropolitan Park Commission, see Eliot, *Charles Eliot*, 384-415.

[92]Eliot, *Charles Eliot*, 385.

[93]This rhetoric had first been put forward for American parks by A. J. Downing, who as early as 1851 recommended that a park have "space enough to have the broad reaches of park and pleasure-grounds, with a real feeling of the breadth and beauty of green fields, the perfume and freshness of nature." Andrew Jackson Downing, "The New-York Park," in Andrew Jackson Downing, *Rural Essays* (New York: George F. Putnam and Company, 1853), 147-153.

[94]American Scenic and Historic Preservation Society, *Fourth Annual Report of the Trustees of Scenic and Historical Places and Objects in the State of New York* (Albany: Wynkoop Hallenbeck Crawford Co., 1899), 6-7.

[95]American Scenic and Historic Preservation Society, *Fifth Annual Report* (1900), 28-29.

[96]In New Jersey, the Federation of Women's Clubs successfully lobbied the State Legislature; in New York, Governor Theodore Roosevelt favored the legislation. Palisades Interstate Park Commission, *Palisades Interstate Park, 1900-1960* (Bear Mountain, New York: Palisades Interstate Park Commission, 1960), 18-20.

[97]The Adirondack Park, also in New York State, was initially set aside in 1885, although it was only after the constitutional convention of 1894 that the park received adequate legal protection to prevent wholesale timber theft and other abuses.

[98]Roy W. Meyer, *Everybody's Country Estate: A History of Minnesota's State Parks* (St. Paul: Minnesota Historical Society Press, 1991), 5-8, 17-19.

[99]Joseph H. Engbeck, Jr., *State Parks of California from 1864 to the Present* (Portland, Oregon: Graphic Arts Center Publishing Co., 1980), 29-33, 41-43.

[100]Newton, *Design on the Land*, 562. Newton points out that only New York, Indiana, Wisconsin, Connecticut, and California had state park "systems" with varied sites managed according to consistent policies. It should also be noted that historic preservation played as important a role as scenic preservation in the creation of early state parks. Several states and the federal government acquired battlefield sites in the 19th century, although these historic sites tended to be smaller than scenic parks. See Raymond H. Torrey, *State Parks and the Recreational Uses of State Forests in the United States* (Washington, DC: The National Conference on State Parks, 1926), 20-22.

[101]See Frederick W. Kelsey, *The First County Park System: A Complete History of the Inception and Development of the Essex County Parks of New Jersey* (New York: J. S. Ogilvie Publishing Company, 1905).

[102]Robert E. Grese, *Jens Jensen: Maker of Natural Parks and Gardens* (Baltimore: The Johns Hopkins University Press, 1992), 64-67.

[103]John Barstow Morrill, "Forest Preserve District of Cook County, Illinois: An Outer Park and Reservation System for Chicago," *Landscape Architecture* 38, no. 4 (July 1948): 139-144. By 1948, thirty-seven thousand acres of suburban reservations had been set aside by Cook County.

[104]Ann Moss, *National Register of Historic Places Nomination for the Denver Mountain Parks System,*1988. National Register nominations are available at the National Register of Historic Places, National Park Service, 800 North Capitol Street, Washington, DC.

[105]The report was published posthumously. Charles Eliot, *Vegetation and Scenery in the Metropolitan Reservations of Boston* (Boston: Lamson, Wolffe and Company, 1898), 7.

[106]Eliot, *Vegetation and Scenery*, 7-8.

[107]Eliot, *Vegetation and Scenery*, 23. The watercolor sketches Eliot provided (by Arthur A. Shurtleff) featured movable flaps, or slides, to represent the proposed removal of trees, clearing of notches, and other effects. This conscious allusion to Repton's "redbook" presentations again indicated the degree to which Eliot admired and imitated Reptonian theory and practice. In his call for selective thinning of forests both to improve views and to speed the recovery of cutover stands, Eliot agreed with the elder Olmsted, who advocated "the use of the axe" in such cases. To justify his position, Olmsted cited Brown and Repton, in addition to 19th-century scientific foresters, such as

Bernhard E. Fernow and Charles Sprague Sargent. Frederick Law Olmsted, "The Use of the Axe," [1889] *Landscape Architecture* 3, no. 4 (July 1913): 145-152.

[108]In 1893 Eliot had returned to Fairsted as a partner, and the firm (now known as Olmsted, Olmsted & Eliot) was hired by the Metropolitan Park Commission. As a result, the same landscape architects worked on both the municipal and the metropolitan park systems.

[109]At Lake Itasca, the Douglas Lodge opened in 1905. The Bear Mountain Inn, another massive log building, opened in 1915.

[110]Palisades Interstate Park Commission, *Palisades Interstate Park*, 31.

[111]American Park and Outdoor Art Association, *Second Report of the American Park and Outdoor Art Association, Minneapolis, 1898* (Boston: Rockwell and Churchill Press, 1898), 5.

[112]In an 1888 article in *Garden and Forest*, Charles Eliot decried the "universal abuse of the word park," in which "the strict meaning of the word is completely lost." He suggested the term "country park" to describe "those public lands which the word park alone ought by rights to describe," that is "lands intended and appropriated for the recreation of the people by means of their rural, sylvan, and natural scenery and character." Eliot, *Charles Eliot*, 305. The "Country Park" was the name F. L. Olmsted had given the largest, pastoral portion of Franklin Park in Boston in the 1880s. J. C. Olmsted preferred the term "large park" to describe much the same thing.

[113]For the full text of the address, see [American] Park and Outdoor Art Association, *First Report, 1897*, 11-19.

[114]Richard Hofstadter observes that the United States itself was "born in the country and moved to the city" during this period. Hofstadter also describes a "new middle class of technicians and salaried professionals, clerical workers, salespeople, and public-service personnel that multiplied along with the great corporations and the specialized skills of corporate society" who were among Americans enjoying increased leisure time at the turn of the century. After 1900 the trend was reinforced by state legislatures that passed laws affecting child labor, hours of work, minimum wages, and pensions. Richard Hofstadter, *The Age of Reform* (New York: Knopf, 1955), 23, 218, 242-243.

[115]Foster Rhea Dulles, *A History of Recreation: America Learns to Play* Second Edition (New York: Appleton-Century-Crofts, 1965), 182-199, 201-210.

[116]Palisades Interstate Park had over one million visitors annually by 1913, a number which swelled to two million after the Bear Mountain Inn opened in 1915. Palisades Interstate Park Commission, *Palisades Interstate Park*, 9.

[117]Revere Beach, one of Eliot's metropolitan reservations, was the first example of a designed, public beach park accommodating large crowds of swimmers.

[118]This was up from about eight thousand in 1900. John B. Rae, *The Road and Car in American Life* (Cambridge: The MIT Press, 1971), 50; James J. Flink, *The Automobile Age* (Cambridge: The MIT Press, 1988), 37-39.

[119]Warren James Belasco describes how early automotive "gypsies" enjoyed the challenges and adventures of outdoor auto camping over the restricting luxuries of the monopolistic railroad and hotel establishments. Warren James Belasco, *Americans on the Road: From Autocamp to Motel, 1910-1945* (Cambridge: The MIT Press, 1979), 7-69.

"Conserve the Scenery": The National Park as 20th-Century Landscape Park

[1]By withdrawing such land from all future claims, the proclamation of a national monument implied that the area would remain under federal administration indefinitely. Tolson, *Laws*, 296.

[2]Robert W. Righter, "National Monuments to National Parks: The Use of the Antiquities Act of 1906," *Western Historical Quarterly* 20, no. 3 (August 1989): 281-301.

[3]Monuments not designated later as parks remained under the supervision of whatever department originally had jurisdiction, which in these cases was the Department of Agriculture. For the chronology of national park legislation, see Barry Mackintosh, *The National Parks: Shaping the System* (Washington, DC: Government Printing Office, 1991).

[4]Alfred Runte points out that advocates of national park legislation in the 19th and early 20th centuries consistently stressed to legislators that proposed parks contained only "worthless lands," that is lands unfit for agricultural settlement or even mineral or timber extraction. Runte, *National Parks*, 48-64. Richard W. Sellars asserts that the "rhetorical ploy" of describing the lands as worthless did not alter their tremendous economic value—for resort development or as reservoir sites, for example. He rebuts the notion that competing economic uses would have disqualified scenic areas from becoming national parks, and feels that the creation of national parks did not depend on establishing their economic worthlessness, as much as on recognizing the ascendancy of their other, noncommercial values. Richard W. Sellars, "National Parks: Worthless Lands or Competing Land Uses?" *Journal of Forest History* 27, no. 3 (July 1983): 130-134.

[5]The population of eleven western states and territories in 1890 was 4,309,000; California, with a population of 1,213,000, was the only western state with over half a million residents. New York State, in comparison, had over six million residents in 1890, and the national population was just under sixty-three million. Of three hundred cities of over eleven thousand people in 1890, fifteen were in the eleven western states and territories. Department of Commerce, Bureau of the Census, *Historical Statistics of the United States* (White Plains, New York: Kraus International Publications, 1989), 8, 22; *The World Bureau of Information Almanac 1891* (New York: Copyright Press Publishing Co., 1891), 244.

[6]Lary M. Dilsaver and William C. Tweed, *Challenge of the Big Trees: A Resource History of Sequoia and Kings Canyon National Parks* (Three Rivers, California: Sequoia Natural History Association, 1990), 62-69.

[7]Dilsaver and Tweed, *Challenge of the Big Trees*, 73. Alfred Runte, in his recent history of Yosemite National Park, also agrees that despite the growing public awareness of the beauty of the High Sierra, "motivation sufficient to induce Congress to seriously consider park expansion awaited sources other than preservation interests, most notably the Southern Pacific Railroad and irrigationists in the San Joaquin Valley." Runte, *Yosemite*, 45. Richard J. Orsi points out that the Southern Pacific, like other large railroad companies, had long identified its interests with those of tourism and scenic preservation, as well as protecting watersheds for irrigation. Richard J. Orsi, "'Wilderness Saint' and 'Robber Baron': The Anomalous Partnership of John Muir and the Southern Pacific Company for the Preservation of Yosemite National Park," *The Pacific Historian* 29, nos. 2&3 (Summer/Fall 1985): 137-156.

[8]Harlan D. Unrau, *Administrative History of Crater Lake National Park, Oregon* (Denver: Government Printing Office, 1988), 27-38; 61-69.

[9]Arthur D. Martinson, "Mount Rainier Park: The First Years," *Forest History* 10, no. 3 (October 1966): 26-33.

[10]Michael P. Cohen, *The History of the Sierra Club, 1892-1970* (San Francisco: Sierra Club Books, 1988), 9.

[11]Hays, *Conservation and the Gospel of Efficiency*, 27.

[12]Rehder, "Charles Sprague Sargent," 70-72.

[13]The Adirondack Park legislation is excerpted chronologically in Alfred L. Donaldson, *A History of the Adirondacks* [1921] (Port Washington, Long Island: Ira J. Friedman, Inc., 1963), 175-189.

[14]Harold K. Steen, *The U.S. Forest Service: A History* [1976] (Seattle: The University of Washington Press, 1991), 26-27; Michael Williams, *Americans & Their Forests: A Historical Geography* (New York: Cambridge University Press, 1989), 403-415.

[15]Mary S. Culpin, "Yellowstone and Its Borders: A Significant Influence Toward the Creation of the First Forest Reserve," in Harold K. Steen, ed., *The Origins of the National Forests* (Durham, North Carolina: The Forest History Society, 1992), 276-283.

[16]Dilsaver and Tweed, *Challenge of the Big Trees*, 83-85.

[17]Williams, *Americans & Their Forests*, 307; Gerald W. Williams, "John Waldo and William G. Steel: Forest Reserve Advocates for the Cascade Region of Oregon," in Steen, ed., *The Origins of the National Forests*, 314-332.

[18]Quoted in James Muhn, "Early Administration of the Forest Reserve Act: Interior Department and General Land Office Policies, 1891-1897," in Steen, ed., *The Origins of the National Forests*, 259-275.

[19]Muhn, "Early Administration of the Forest Reserve Act," 262-263.

[20]Steen, *The U.S. Forest Service*, 58.

[21]Hays makes it clear that irrigationists had been primary sponsors of forest reserve creation and had attempted to prevent logging and grazing in forests when a perceived threat to watersheds existed. The need for water conservation subsequently helped shape forestry policy, and the collaboration of Newell and Pinchot exemplified the "common attitude toward resource development then emerging in the federal government." Hays, *Conservation and the Gospel of Efficiency*, 6-28.

[22]Hays, *Conservation and the Gospel of Efficiency*, 35-48. John Ise notes that the persistent failure of Pinchot and other American foresters to embrace scenic preservation may have been a byproduct of their continental educations in forest science. Ise, *National Park Policy*, 189.

[23]Ise, *National Park Policy*, 120-121; Arthur D. Martinson, "Mountain in the Sky: A History of Mount Rainier National Park" (Ph.D. diss., Washington State University, 1966), 45-54.

[24]Unrau, *Administrative History of Crater Lake*, 27-38. Separate legislation in 1908 and 1916 closed Mount Rainier and Crater Lake to mining claims. The boundaries of both parks were enlarged in the early 1930s. Tolson, *Laws*, 101-117.

[25]John Ise states that Glacier National Park "was not really a national park, in the proper sense of the word, but sort of a hybrid national forest with a few park features, and it was administered as such." Ise, *National Park Policy*, 175. The creation of substandard parks by local congressional delegations also emerged as a problem during these years. In 1903, for example, Congress authorized Sully's Hill National Park, North Dakota, despite the fact that it was little more than a modest prairie game preserve.

[26]Laura Soullière Harrison, *Architecture in the Parks: A National Historic Landmark Theme Study* (Washington, DC: Government Printing Office, 1986), 91.

[27]Many of the hotels built during this period remain the finest accommodations available in the national parks. All of these examples, among others, including the Wawona Hotel (1876) in Yosemite and the Paradise Inn (1916) in Mount Rainier, were made National Historic Landmarks for their architectural significance in 1987. Harrison, *Architecture in the Parks*, 1-19, 61-76, 87-122, 135-172. For further information on western resort architecture, see Hyde, *An American Vision*, 244-295.

[28]Department of the Interior, *1915 Annual Reports*, 855; James W. Sheire, *Glacier National Park: Historic Resource Study* (Washington, DC: Government Printing Office, 1970), 193-201.

[29]Ise, *National Park Policy*, 43-45.

[30]Tolson, *Laws*, 2-3.

[31]Dilsaver and Tweed, *Challenge of the Big Trees*, 95-96, 135-136.

[32]Peter J. Blodgett, "Visiting the Realm of Wonder: Yosemite and the Business of Tourism, 1855-1916," in Richard J. Orsi, Alfred Runte, and Marlene Smith-Barzini, eds., *Yosemite and Sequoia: A Century of National Parks* (Berkeley: University of California Press, 1990), 33-48.

[33]Department of the Interior, *1915 Annual Reports*, 41-42, 860-867; Department of Commerce, Bureau of the Census, *Historical Statistics*, Part 1, 396.

[34]Department of the Interior, *1907 Annual Reports*, 55-56.

[35]Robert M. Utley and Barry Mackintosh, *The Department of Everything Else: Highlights of Interior History* (Washington, DC: Department of the Interior, 1989), 14, 18-24.

[36]Hays, *Conservation and the Gospel of Efficiency*, 196-198; Ise, *National Park Policy*, 188-191.

[37]This according to J. Horace McFarland's often quoted claims. See The American Civic Association, *National Parks*, pamphlet series 11, no. 6 (Washington, DC: The American Civic Association, 1912), 28-29. For a more detailed description of the administrative situation, see Horace M. Albright and Robert Cahn, *The Birth of the National Park Service: The Founding Years, 1913-33*, (Salt Lake City: Howe Brothers, 1985), 32-33.

[38]This was especially true after 1899, when professional landscape designers established their own group, the American Society of Landscape Architects.

[39]Frederic A. Delano, "What the American Civic Association Is," in *American Civic Annual* (Washington, DC: The American Civic Association, 1929), v-viii. According to Delano, the American Civic Association was dedicated to the "dual purpose of

preservation of outdoor beauty with the attendant promotion of landscape art and the civic improvement of towns and cities."

[40]The American Civic Association, *Seventh Annual Convention*, pamphlet (Washington, DC: The American Civic Association, 1912), 5-6.

[41]Ernest Morrison, *J. Horace McFarland: A Thorn for Beauty* (Harrisburg: Pennsylvania Historical and Museum Commission, 1995), 68-92.

[42]J. Horace McFarland, "Niagara Falls—A National Asset," in *American Civic Annual* (Washington, DC: The American Civic Association, 1929), 26-30. McFarland pointed out that if the two million visitors to the New York side of the falls spent only twenty-five dollars apiece, the total annual revenue would be double that produced by hydroelectric development.

[43]George Kunz, the president of the American Scenic and Historic Preservation Society, also attended the conference.

[44]Most of McFarland's address is reprinted in Morrison, *J. Horace McFarland*, 123-137.

[45]Elmo R. Richardson, "The Struggle for the Valley: California's Hetch-Hetchy Controversy, 1905-1913," *California Historical Society Quarterly* 38, no. 3 (September 1959): 249-258.

[46]Ise, *National Park Policy*, 89-91; Gifford Pinchot, *Breaking New Ground* [1947] (Washington, DC: Island Press, 1974), 442-451.

[47]For one of many contemporary examples of this reasoning, see Allen Chamberlain, "Scenery as a National Asset," *The Outlook* 95, no. 4 (May 28, 1910): 157-169.

[48]McFarland reported the amount to be $350 million and later $500 million. The American Civic Association, *National Parks*, 28.

[49]Department of the Interior, *1910 Annual Reports*, 55-58.

[50]Morrison, *J. Horace McFarland*, 175.

[51]Olmsted became the senior partner of Olmsted Brothers when his brother John Charles died in 1920 after a long illness. He remained professionally active until 1950.

[52]In a letter to Olmsted, Pinchot claimed that McFarland, in particular, was unable to distinguish between policies appropriate for Eastern, municipal parks, and those suited to the vast public lands of the West. Morrison, *J. Horace McFarland*, 184.

[53]Olmsted and Nolen defined six "important types of public grounds": "Streets, boulevards and parkways; City squares, commons and public gardens; Playgrounds [in three categories based on age]; Small or neighborhood parks; Large parks; Great outlying reservations." Frederick Law Olmsted, Jr., and John Nolen, "The Normal Requirements of American Towns and Cities in Respect to Public Open Spaces," *Charities and the Commons* 16, no. 14 (July 7, 1906): 411-426.

[54]Central Park, for example, was located in central Manhattan in part because land for a future reservoir, which was subsequently built within the park, had already been acquired. Druid Hill Park (Baltimore), Fairmount Park (Philadelphia), and Prospect Park (Brooklyn), are just some of the examples of municipal parks that successfully incorporated the acquisition, protection, or impounding of drinking water.

[55]Frederick Law Olmsted, Jr., *The Relation of Reservoirs to Parks* (Boston: The American Park and Outdoor Art Association, 1899), Paper 32.

[56]The article was reprinted in *Landscape Architecture* 4, no. 2 (January 1914): 37-46.

[57]The 1865 "Preliminary Report upon the Yosemite and Big Tree Grove" by the elder Olmsted is often supposed to have been completely lost until 1952, when his biographer Laura Wood Roper pieced together portions of the report and published it in something like its original form (*Landscape Architecture* 43, no. 1, 13-25). Most of the texts Roper pieced together, however, had always been accessible to F. L. Olmsted, Jr., and he quotes from them extensively in his 1913 analysis of the Hetch-Hetchy controversy.

[58]Department of the Interior, *Proceedings of the National Parks Conference Held at the Yellowstone National Park, 1911* (Washington, DC: Government Printing Office, 1912), 4-5. Canada had created its own national park service in 1911. Better managed Canadian parks drew large numbers of American tourists to the Canadian Rockies, much to Hill's dismay, since those tourists rode the Canadian Pacific Railroad, not Hill's Great Northern, to get there. William C. Everhart, *The National Park Service* (New York: Praeger Publishers, 1972), 208-210.

[59]Department of the Interior, *Proceedings of the National Park Conference Held at Yellowstone*, 3, 6-7.

[60]Olmsted did not attend the conference but did draft a letter, which McFarland had read into the record, supporting the creation of a national park bureau. The letter suggested that a "permanent independent 'board of overseers'" be established to "discuss questions of general policy with the executive officer," in other words the director of the proposed bureau. "This is the theory of unpaid park commissions all over the country, and it is a sound theory," he concluded. Olmsted would later serve as chairman of the Yosemite National Park Board of Expert Advisors, organized in 1928 along these lines. Department of the Interior, *Proceedings of the National Parks Conference Held at Yellowstone*, 20-21.

[61]The American Civic Association, *Seventh Annual Convention*, 2.

[62]The American Civic Association, *National Parks*, 16-18.

[63]The American Civic Association, *National Parks*, 27-28. Like many of his fellow Progressives, McFarland worried that the tremendous influx of Southern and Eastern European immigrants in the late 19th and early 20th centuries had eroded national identity and patriotism. Besides being sound investments in public "healthful efficiency," McFarland and others often portrayed parks, and the appreciation of American scenic beauty generally, as a sure means of promoting sincere patriotism and unified national spirit.

[64]A resolution suggested by Richard B. Watrous, secretary of the American Civic Association (he attended the Yosemite conference in McFarland's place) specified that the proposed bureau be known as the National Park Service, stressing the counterpoint to the U.S. Forest Service. Department of the Interior, *Proceedings of the National Park Conference Held at the Yosemite National Park, October 14, 15, and 16, 1912* (Washington, DC: Government Printing Office, 1913), 96.

[65]Fry's principal concern was that when automobiles startled horses on narrow mountain roads, tragedy could result. Most of the objections raised to admitting motor vehicles stressed the need of safety and road engineering improvements. Department of the Interior, *Proceedings of the National Park Conference Held at Yosemite*, 33, 61, 117-119, 139.

[66]Department of the Interior, *1913 Annual Reports*, 88, 704, 723-724.

[67]Early restrictions on automobiles could be Byzantine, running on for six pages for some parks. The goal, however, was simply to restrict motor traffic to certain directions, during stated hours, in order to avoid the risk of startling teams of horses on narrow roads. Department of the Interior, *1913 Annual Reports*, 87-88, 746-750.

[68]Department of the Interior, *1914 Annual Reports*, 26-27, 88-89.

[69]Department of the Interior, *1914 Annual Reports*, 88. The arrival of Secretary Lane and Professor Miller in Washington in 1913 ushered in an era of national park management shaped by Berkeley alumni. Besides Lane and Miller, the University of California at Berkeley also graduated Stephen Mather, Horace Albright, Mark Daniels, Thomas Vint, Professor Joseph Grinnell, Dr. Harold Bryant, and other influential figures in national park history. Richard West Sellars, "The University of California—Present at the Creation," *Courier: Newsmagazine of the National Park Service* 35, no. 2 (February 1990): 3.

[70]Albright and Cahn, *Birth of the National Park Service*, 1-4, 9-10.

[71]Robert Shankland, *Steve Mather of the National Parks* (New York: Alfred A. Knopf, 1954), 61-64, 83.

[72]Department of the Interior, *1915 Annual Reports*, 843-852.

[73]Albright and Cahn, *Birth of the National Park Service*, 9.

[74]Department of the Interior, *Proceedings of the National Park Conference Held at Berkeley, California, 1915* (Washington, DC: Government Printing Office, 1915), 15-20.

[75]Department of the Interior, *1915 Annual Reports*, 849-850.

[76]Department of the Interior, *1915 Annual Reports*, 843-867. It is interesting to note, however, that Daniels went on to work on some of the most famous town plans of the day, including Bel-Air and Miramar Estates, in California. He later served as the president of the San Francisco Art Commission. "Biographical Notes on the Life of Mark Roy Daniels," Mather Collection, Entry 135, RG 79, National Archives, Washington, DC.

[77]Shankland, *Steve Mather*, 84-85.

[78]Department of the Interior, *Annual Report of the Superintendent of National Parks to the Secretary of the Interior for the Fiscal Year Ended June 30, 1916* (Washington, DC: Government Printing Office, 1916), 4-5, 14-15.

[79]Stephen T. Mather, *Progress in the Development of Our National Parks* (Washington, DC: Government Printing Office, 1916), 4. The idea for such a portfolio had been discussed since at least 1912.

[80]Polly Welts Kaufman, *National Parks and the Woman's Voice: A History* (Albuquerque: University of New Mexico Press, 1996), 32-36. Speaking at the Berkeley national park conference in 1915, Sherman also pointed to local women's clubs that were actively lobbying for national park legislation in Colorado, Arizona, New Mexico, and Utah. Department of the Interior, *Proceedings of the National Park Conference Held at Berkeley*, 141.

[81]See, for example, Stephen T. Mather, "The National Parks on a Business Basis," *The American Review of Reviews* (April 1915): 428-431. Shankland reports that 1,050 magazine articles on national parks appeared between 1917 and 1919, after Mather's public relations efforts had been institutionalized. Shankland, *Steve Mather*, 95.

[82]Richard B. Watrous, "The Proposed National Park Service," *Landscape Architecture* 6, no. 3 (April 1916): 101-105.

[83]American Society of Landscape Architects, "Resolutions," *Landscape Architecture* 6, no. 3 (April 1916): 111-112.

[84]Frederick Law Olmsted, Jr., "The Distinction Between National Parks and National Forests," *Landscape Architecture* 6, no. 3 (April 1916): 114-115.

[85]Swain, "The Passage of the National Park Service Act of 1916"; Shankland, *Steve Mather*, 100-113; Albright and Cahn, *Birth of the National Park Service*, 34-43. Perhaps the most fascinating lobbying technique employed in the legislative campaign was the "Mather Mountain Party" of 1915, in which Mather and Albright led a party of influential journalists and legislators on a memorable trek through the High Sierra, forever cementing their national park enthusiasms. Horace Marden Albright and Marian Albright Schenk, *The Mather Mountain Party of 1915* (Three Rivers, California: Sequoia Natural History Association, 1990).

[86]Tolson, *Laws*, 9-10. The bill was drafted during a series of meetings in which Representative William Kent (California), Robert Sterling Yard, J. Horace McFarland, Frederick Law Olmsted, Jr., Robert B. Marshall, and Horace M. Albright, among others, participated. Albright and McFarland both credited Olmsted with drafting this paragraph of the bill. Albright and Cahn, *Birth of the National Park Service*, 35-36; J. Horace McFarland, "The Economic Destiny of the National Parks," in Department of the Interior, *Proceedings of the National Park Conference Held in the Auditorium of the New National Museum, 1917* (Washington, DC: Government Printing Office, 1917), 104-111.

[87]In his Yosemite report of 1865, the elder Olmsted specifically prioritized management concerns for the valley. "The duty of preservation is the first," he stated, because "for the millions who are hereafter to benefit" careful preservation was a necessary consideration. "Next to this [duty]," he continued, "is that of aiding to make this appropriation of Congress [the Yosemite Grant] available as soon and as generally as may be economically practicable to those whom it is designed to benefit." Ranney, ed., *The California Frontier*, 508. Since these statements clearly inspired the younger Olmsted in his composition of key portions of the Park Service Act, there should be no question that landscape preservation was intended as the primary mandate of the 1916 legislation.

[88]Department of the Interior, *Proceedings of the National Park Conference Held in the New National Museum*, 4-5, 45-49, 173-184.

[89]Mather had experienced an earlier breakdown in 1903, and suffered another episode in 1922. Shankland, *Steve Mather*, 109-113, 163-164; Albright and Cahn, *Birth of the National Park Service*, 51.

[90]Although grazing was allowed in most of the parks during the war, Albright managed to limit its impact and end the practice with the armistice. Donald C. Swain, *Wilderness Defender: Horace M. Albright and Conservation* (Chicago: University of Chicago Press, 1970), 61-75.

[91]Albright and Cahn, *Birth of the National Park Service*, 53-67.

[92]Albright always favored N. P. Langford's 1905 account of the 1870 Yellowstone campfire discussion as the origin of "the National Park Idea." He put this anecdote

forward with great effect in 1917; it was largely unquestioned within the Park Service for the next sixty years. Department of the Interior, National Park Service, *Report of the Director of the National Park Service to the Secretary of the Interior for the Fiscal Year Ended June 30, 1917* (Washington, DC: Government Printing Office, 1917), 3-4, appendices.

[93]Department of the Interior, National Park Service, *1917 Annual Report*, 9-10, 17-19, 97-98. Most of these policies and activities had been initiated by Mather in 1915-16. See Stephen T. Mather, *Progress in the Development of the National Parks* (Washington, DC: Government Printing Office, 1916).

[94]Albright later referred to the policy statement as "one of the best things I ever did." Swain, *Wilderness Defender*, 89-90; Albright and Cahn, *Birth of the National Park Service*, 68-69.

[95]These policies were restated by Secretary Herbert Work in a second letter in 1925. For the text of the letters, see Department of the Interior, National Park Service, *Compilation of the Administrative Policies for the National Parks and National Monuments of Scientific Importance* (Washington, DC: Government Printing Office, 1970), 68-71, 72-75.

[96]Olmsted also revised park, parkway, and civic center plans within the city. Olmsted's work culminated in a 1920 report that recommended a metropolitan system of over forty-one thousand acres, although less than fourteen thousand had been acquired by 1941. Wilson, *The City Beautiful Movement*, 84-85; Moss, *National Register Nomination for Denver Mountain Parks*, E8-E11.

[97]C. W. Buchholtz, *Rocky Mountain National Park: A History* (Boulder: Colorado Associated University Press, 1983), 117-123.

[98]Buchholtz, *Rocky Mountain National Park*, 136.

[99]Shankland, *Steve Mather*, 62-63, 78-79, 148.

[100]Wilson, *The City Beautiful Movement*, 147-167; Gene Allen Nadeau, *Highway to Paradise: A Pictorial History of the Roadway to Mount Rainier* (Puyallup, Washington: Valley Press, 1983), 63-70.

[101]Martinson, "Mount Rainier National Park: First Years," 26-33.

[102]Quoted in Ronald J. Fahl, "S. C. Lancaster and the Columbia River Highway: Engineer as Conservationist," *Oregon Historical Quarterly* 74, no. 2 (June 1973): 114.

[103]Samuel Christopher Lancaster, *The Columbia: America's Great Highway Through the Cascade Mountains to the Sea* [1915], Third Edition (Portland: J.K. Gill Company, 1926); Fahl, "S. C. Lancaster and the Columbia River Highway," 126.

[104]Department of the Interior, National Park Service, *1917 Annual Report*, 189-191.

[105]See James J. Flink, *The Automobile Age* (Cambridge: The MIT Press, 1988), 178-180.

[106]The epithets were contemporary park ranger slang, according to Albright. Horace M. Albright and Frank J. Taylor, *Oh Ranger!* [1928] (Golden, Colorado: Outbooks, 1986), 17.

[107]Stephen T. Mather, "The Ideals and Policy of the National Park Service Particularly in Relation to Yosemite National Park," in Ansel F. Hall, ed., *Handbook of Yosemite National Park* (New York: G.P. Putnam's Sons, 1921), 77-86.

[108]Department of the Interior, National Park Service, *1920 Annual Report*, 37-44; Department of the Interior, National Park Service, *1921 Annual Report*, 24-26. Grand Canyon and Zion national parks were established in 1919, tranferring jurisdiction from the Forest Service to the Park Service.

[109]Entrance fees for automobiles originally were exorbitant: ten dollars to enter Yellowstone in 1916, for example. The fees were lowered as traffic volume (and protests against the high fees) increased. After 1918, revenues from auto entrance fees began reverting to the general treasury and were no longer available to the parks that collected them. In compensation, Congress began raising appropriations for the parks, and park expenditures from that point were not linked to the direct revenues produced by parks. Mather, *Progress in the Development of National Parks*, 6, 9; Department of the Interior, National Park Service, *1918 Annual Report*, 26. Although this would indicate a withdrawal from the rhetorical assertion that parks would pay for themselves, in another sense the parks were already more than self sufficient. The economic activity and tax receipts generated by domestic tourism dwarfed the costs of developing and maintaining

national parks. Considering their catalyzing effect on domestic tourism, national parks not only have supported themselves in this sense, but like highways, they place among the most lucrative investments that the federal government has ever made.

[110]Russ Olsen, *Administrative History: Organizational Structures of the National Park Service, 1917-1985* (Denver: Department of the Interior, National Park Service, 1985), 33-35.

[111]Albright and Cahn, *Birth of the National Park Service*, 93.

[112]Arno Cammerer to Frederick Law Olmsted, Jr., September 11, 1922, Personal Papers of Arno B. Cammerer, Entry 18, RG 79, National Archives. Norman Newton also credits Cammerer with first suggesting a landscape engineering division for the Park Service. Newton, *Design on the Land*, 532.

[113]Henry V. Hubbard, "Charles Pierpont Punchard, Jr.," *Landscape Architecture* 11, no. 2 (January 1921); Linda Flint McClelland, "Punchard, Charles Pierpont, Jr.," in Charles A. Birnbaum and Julie K. Fix, eds., *Pioneers of Landscape Design II: An Annotated Bibliography* (Washington, DC: Government Printing Office, 1995), 122-125.

[114]Congress created the seven-member Commission of Fine Arts in 1910. From 1910 to 1918, Olmsted served on the commission, which was often asked to review national park development proposals. Sue A. Kohler, *The Commission of Fine Arts: A Brief History, 1910-1990* (Washington, DC: The Commission of Fine Arts, 1990), 4-5.

[115]Department of the Interior, National Park Service, *1919 Annual Report*, 23-25, 42. Later in 1919 Mather made landscape engineering a separate division in the Park Service with Goodwin remaining in charge of a civil engineering division.

[116]Department of the Interior, National Park Service, *1919 Annual Report*, 25-27. See McClelland, *Presenting Nature*, 81-93.

[117]Department of the Interior, National Park Service, *1919 Annual Report*, 260-267.

[118]Department of the Interior, National Park Service, *1920 Annual Report*, 331-339.

[119]Charles P. Punchard, Jr., "Landscape Design in the National Park Service," *Landscape Architecture* 10, no. 3 (April 1920): 142-145.

[120]This frank assessment was made in response to a private inquiry by F. L. Olmsted, Jr. In more public statements, such as in the *Annual Reports*, Punchard's achievements were more positively assessed. Arno Cammerer to Frederick Law Olmsted, Jr., September 11, 1922, Personal Papers of Arno B. Cammerer, Entry 18, RG 79, National Archives.

[121]Department of the Interior, National Park Service, *1920 Annual Report*, 93.

[122]Despite an increase between 1916 and 1921 from 356,097 to 1,007,336 visitors and an increase in estimated total needs from $280,850 to $2,488,004, the budget for the parks only increased from $252,746 to $1,402,200. Department of the Interior, National Park Service, *1921 Annual Report*, 14.

[123]Department of the Interior, National Park Service, *1920 Annual Report*, 21-22; Donald C. Swain, *Federal Conservation Policy, 1921-1933*, (Berkeley: University of California Press, 1963),128-129.

[124]Department of the Interior, National Park Service, *1920 Annual Report*, 21-32.

[125]Tolson, *Laws*, 4.

[126]Infamous primarily because in 1922 Secretary Fall leased the Teapot Dome naval oil reserves to private interests in exchange for cash, bonds, and interest-free loans; he was later convicted of felonies in connection with the scandal and served time in federal prison. Swain, *Federal Conservation Policy*, 66-69.

[127]Swain describes Mather's campaign of "'impromptu' dinners for cabinet officers, influential senators, and 'a few others'" that enlisted the "political elite of Washington" as well as the "Eastern press" and led to the defeat of Fall's schemes for Yellowstone. Support for the Park Service's position came from McFarland's American Civic Association, the American Association for the Advancement of Science, and from a newer group, the National Parks Association (later the National Parks and Conservation Association) founded by Robert Sterling Yard in 1919. Swain, *Federal Conservation Policy*, 128-130.

[128]Charles P. Punchard, "Hands Off the National Parks," *Landscape Architecture* 11, no. 2 (January 1921): 53-57.

[1]Carl Rust Parker, Bremer W. Pond, and Theodora Kimball, eds., *Transactions of the American Society of Landscape Architects, 1909-1921* (Amsterdam, New York: The Recorder Press, 1922), 18.

[2]The degrees were mostly Bachelor of Science, although Smith offered a Bachelor of Arts and Harvard had already created its Masters in Landscape Architecture. Six other schools offered "special certificates" in the subject. Five of the programs were for women only. Pattee, "Landscape Architecture in American Colleges," 172-173.

[3]Department of the Interior, National Park Service, *1919 Annual Report*, 27-28; idem, *1921 Annual Report*, 277.

[4]Kohler, *Commission of Fine Arts*, 211.

[5]Newton, *Design on the Land*, 219. Although written many years later, the quotation expresses an attitude common earlier in the century. In his book Newton also reveals his long allegiance to Charles Platt and his preference for the study of Renaissance villas over examples of the "English Landscape Gardening School."

[6]William Robinson, *The Wild Garden* [1870] (Portland, Oregon: Sagapress/Timber Press, 1994), 1-16, 48, 100, 146.

[7]M. G. Van Rensselaer, *Art Out-of-Doors: Hints on Good Taste in Gardening* (New York: Charles Scribner's Sons, 1907), 157-158, 161. Van Rensselaer was a founding member of the American Park and Outdoor Art Association. A large portion of her discussion of garden styles in 1893 revolves around the relative virtues and definitions of "naturalistic" and "architectonic" ideals in landscape design.

[8]Frank A. Waugh, *The Natural Style in Landscape Gardening* (Boston: Richard G. Badger, 1917), 12. Hubbard and Kimball, in their textbook, also expected landscape architects to be fluent in both approaches. Henry V. Hubbard and Theodora Kimball, *An Introduction to the Study of Landscape Design* [1917] Revised Edition, (New York: The Macmillan Company, 1929), 247-274.

[9]Grese, *Jens Jensen*, 2-7, 63-64.

[10]Miller was best known as the author of *What England Can Teach Us About Gardening* (1911). Although a follower of William Robinson, in the "Prairie Spirit" he advocated a rigorous proscription of exotic species that was the antithesis of the Robinsonian wild garden. For Miller's complete text, see Christopher Vernon, "Wilhelm Miller and *The Prairie Spirit in Landscape Gardening*," in Therese O'Malley and Marc Treib, eds., *Regional Garden Design in the United States*, Dumbarton Oaks Colloquium on the History of Landscape Architecture, XV (Washington, DC: Dumbarton Oaks Research Library and Collection, 1995).

[11]Grese, *Jens Jensen*, 46, 52, 94-103.

[12]See J. Ronald Engle, "Social Democracy, the Roots of Ecology, and the Preservation of the Indiana Dunes," *Forest History* 28, no.1 (January 1984): 4-13.

[13]Donald Worster, *Nature's Economy: A History of Ecological Ideas*, Second Edition, (New York: Cambridge University Press, 1994), 198-204.

[14]Frederick R. Steiner, "Frank Albert Waugh," in William H.Tishler, ed. *American Landscape Architecture: Designers and Places* (Washington, DC: Preservation Press, 1989), 100-103.

[15]Waugh, *The Natural Style*, 20.

[16]Waugh, *The Natural Style*, 17-18, 24-25.

[17]Waugh, *The Natural Style*, 52.

[18]First quotation in Gert Groening and Joachim Wolschke-Buhlman, "Changes in the Philosophy of Garden Architecture in the 20th Century and Their Impact on the Social and Spatial Environment," *Journal of Garden History* 9, no. 2 (1989): 53-70. Second quotation in idem, "Notes on the Mania for Native Plants in Germany," *Landscape Journal* 11, no. 2 (Fall 1992): 116-126. See Anna Bramwell, *Ecology in the 20th Century: A History* (New Haven: Yale University Press, 1989), 177-208.

[19]Restrictions on the introduction of non-native plants in national parks probably resulted more from the enhanced role of ecological sciences in park management than from the influence of contemporary garden design. See Richard West Sellars, "The Rise

and Decline of Ecological Attitudes in National Park Management, 1929-1940: Part I," *The George Wright Forum* 10, no. 1 (1993): 55-78.

[20]Frank A. Waugh, *Landscape Engineering in the National Forests* (Washington, DC: Government Printing Office, 1918), 4-5; idem, *Recreation Uses on the National Forests* (Washington, DC: Government Printing Office, 1918), 26-27.

[21]Earl E. Bachman, *Recreation Facilities: A Personal History of Their Development in the National Forests of California* (San Francisco: Department of Agriculture, 1967), 1-5; Robert W. Cermak, "In the Beginning: The National Forest Recreation Plan," *Parks & Recreation* 9, no. 11 (November 1974): 20-24; William C. Tweed, *Recreation Site Planning and Improvement in National Forests, 1891-1942* (Washington, DC: Government Printing Office, 1980), 8-13.

[22]Both quotations in Arthur H. Carhart, "Landscape Architecture and the 152 National Forests," *Landscape Architecture* 11, no. 2 (January 1921): 57-62. Carhart resigned from the Forest Service in 1922.

[23]Tweed, *Recreation Site Planning and Improvement in National Forests*, 11. Tweed points out that Stephen Mather, who was fighting for appropriations for Park Service development plans at the time, did not support the initiation of Carhart's efforts at the Forest Service and publicly challenged the whole idea of a Forest Service recreation program.

[24]Ossian Cole Simonds, *Landscape Gardening* (New York: The McMillan Company, 1920), 329. Like Waugh, Simonds preferred the term "landscape-gardening" to "landscape architecture" because he wished to distinguish his work from the more architectonic garden styles being employed by so many of his colleagues.

[25]Henry V. Hubbard and Theodora Kimball, *An Introduction to the Study of Landscape Design* [1917] Revised Edition (New York: The Macmillan Company, 1929).

[26]Bradford Williams, "Henry Vincent Hubbard: An Official Minute on His Life and Work," *Landscape Architecture* 38, no. 2 (January 1948): 47-50.

[27]A selection from Repton's writings edited by the landscape architect John Nolen was published in the United States in 1907. Humphry Repton, *The Art of Landscape Gardening*, John Nolen, ed. (Boston: Houghton Mifflin Company, 1907). Compare Repton's "Affinity Betwixt Painting and Gardening," selected by Nolen for inclusion in that edition (53-57), to Hubbard and Kimball's "Composition in Landscape and in Painting," in *An Introduction to the Study of Landscape Design* (88-90).

[28]Hubbard and Kimball, *An Introduction to the Study of Landscape Design*, 296-318.

[29]The central, pastoral portion of Franklin Park is called "The Country Park," which probably explains Hubbard and Kimball's use of the term for this type of park development. Kimball was also an important link to Olmsted's written work, since she was an early editor of his papers. F. L. Olmsted, Jr., had been editing his father's papers since at least 1912, and Kimball was collaborating with him by 1920.

[30]Hubbard and Kimball, *An Introduction to the Study of Landscape Design*, 189-90, 314, 319, 321.

[31]Olmsted felt that city planning involved three distinct divisions, roughly corresponding to the contributions of the engineer, landscape architect, and lawyer: first, "the means of circulation . . . and all means of transportation and communication"; second, "the distribution and treatment of the spaces devoted to all other public purposes"; and third, "the remaining or private lands and the character of the development thereon, in so far as it is practicable for the community to control or influence such development." Frederick Law Olmsted, Jr., *City Planning* (Washington, DC: American Civic Association, 1910), 6.

[32]U.S. Congress. Senate. Committee of the District of Columbia. *The Improvement of the Park System of the District of Columbia*. 57th Congress, 1st Sess. Washington: Government Printing Office, 1902.

[33]Cass Gilbert and Frederick Law Olmsted, Jr., *Report of the New Haven Civic Improvement Commission, December 1910* (New Haven: Tuttle, Morehouse & Taylor Company, n.d.); Frederick Law Olmsted, Jr., *Pittsburgh: Main Thoroughfares and the Down Town District* (Pittsburgh: Pittsburgh Civic Commission, 1911); Arnold W. Brunner, Frederick Law Olmsted, Jr., and Bion J. Arnold, *A City Plan for Rochester* (Rochester: Civic Improvement Committee, 1911).

[34]George E. Kessler, *A City Plan for Dallas* (Dallas: Dallas Park Board, 1911).

[35]Scott, *American City Planning*, 110-116.

[36]John L. Hancock, "Planners in the Changing American City, 1900-1940," *Journal of the American Institute of Planners* 33, no. 5 (September 1967): 290-303.

[37]Scott, *American City Planning*, 163.

[38]Department of the Interior, *1910 Annual Reports*, 57.

[39]Department of the Interior, *1915 Annual Reports*, 849.

[40]Department of the Interior, *Proceedings of the National Park Conference Held at Berkeley, California, 1915* (Washington, DC: Government Printing Office, 1915), 18-19.

[41]Department of the Interior, *1913 Annual Reports*, 723-24, 731.

[42]Stephen Mather's initial impulse to involve himself directly in national park affairs resulted from his dismay with conditions at Yosemite and Sequoia as he found them in 1914. Shankland, *Steve Mather*, v-vi; Horace M. Albright, "How the National Park Service Came into Being—A Reminiscence,"in *American Civic Annual* (Washington, DC: The American Civic Association, 1929), 9-12.

[43]Department of the Interior, *1914 Annual Reports*, 88.

[44]Mark Daniels, "Preliminary Plans and Tentative Studies of Architectural Character for the New Village, Yosemite National Park," n.d., Yosemite National Park Research Library.

[45]Department of the Interior, *Proceedings of the Berkeley Conference, 1915*, 20.

[46]Department of the Interior, *1915 Annual Reports*, 849-850.

[47]Linda Wedel Greene, *Yosemite: The Park and Its Resources*, Historic Resource Study, 3 vols. (Denver: Department of the Interior, National Park Service, 1987), vol. 1, 446-450.

[48]John Hancock, "John Nolen: The Background of a Pioneer Planner," in Donald A. Krueckeberg, ed., *The American Planner: Biographies and Recollections* (New York: Methuen, 1983), 37-57.

[49]John Nolen, *Replanning Small Cities* (New York: B. W. Huebsch, 1912), 3.

[50]Raymond Unwin, *Town Planning in Practice: An Introduction to the Art of Designing Cities and Suburbs* (London: T. Fisher Unwin, 1909).

[51]Department of Labor, Bureau of Industrial Housing and Transportation, *Report of the United States Housing Corporation*, 2 vols. (Washington, DC: Government Printing Office, 1919), vol. 1, 185-187, vol. 2, 15-18. Plans of the projects are reproduced in the second volume of the report.

[52]Department of Labor, Bureau of Industrial Housing and Transportation, *Report of the United States Housing Corporation*, vol. 2, 497-504.

[53]Department of Labor, Bureau of Industrial Housing and Transportation, *Report of the United States Housing Corporation, December 3, 1918* (Washington, DC: Government Printing Office, 1919), 74.

[54]University of Illinois, *Notes for a Study in City Planning in Champaign-Urbana by the 1913 and 1914 Classes in Civic Design* (Chicago: R.R. Donnelly and Sons, 1915).

[55]"Daniel Ray Hull," Mather Collection, Entry 135, RG 79, National Archives, Washington, DC.

[56]McClelland, *Presenting Nature*, 113. According to Park Service reports, Hull was living in Milwaukee at the time he was hired in July 1920. He probably had relocated earlier that year. Department of the Interior, National Park Service, *1920 Annual Report*, 93. See Carol Roland, "Hull, Daniel Ray," in Birnbaum and Fix, eds., *Pioneers of American Landscape Design II*, 79-83.

[57]James Sturgis Pray, "Planning the Cantonments," *Landscape Architecture* 8, no. 1 (October 1917): 1-17. In recognition of Olmsted's contributions to planning the war effort, the American Society of Landscape Architects struck a bronze medal, the Olmsted Medal, and presented it to him at the end of 1918.

[58]Greene, *Yosemite*, vol. 2, 580-581.

[59]Department of the Interior, National Park Service, *1919 Annual Report*, 26-27, 331-332.

[60]Mather himself financed the rangers' club, an indication of still inadequate congressional appropriations. The building was made a National Historic Landmark for its architectural significance in 1987. Harrison, *Architecture in the Parks*, 199-210.

[61]Department of the Interior, National Park Service, *1921 Annual Report*, 14-16, 22-23.

[62]Department of the Interior, National Park Service, *1921 Annual Report*, 274-275. The landscape engineering branch of the Park Service remained headquartered in Yosemite Valley until 1923. Olsen, *Organizational Structures of the National Park Service*, 34-35.

[63]Department of the Interior, National Park Service, *1922 Annual Report*, 157.

[64]Department of the Interior, National Park Service, *1924 Annual Report*, 151-152.

[65]Joyce Zaitlin, *Gilbert Stanley Underwood: His Rustic, Art Deco, and Federal Architecture* (Malibu: Pangloss Press, 1989), 6-14.

[66]Underwood's post office was eventually built, but the architect complained that the contractor—working only from sketches and not from construction plans—had "taken liberties . . . and completely ruined the building." Underwood described the result as "a sad failure." Gilbert Stanley Underwood to Arno Cammerer, September 15, 1925, Papers of Arno B. Cammerer, Entry 18, RG 79, National Archives, Washington, DC.

[67]David Gebhard, ed., *Myron Hunt, 1868-1952: The Search for a Regional Architecture,* ex. cat. (Santa Monica: Baxter Art Gallery, California Institute of Technology, 1984), 112-113.

[68]The contemporary work of Greene and Greene and especially Bernard Maybeck were among the strongest influences on early Park Service Rustic architecture. Several histories of Park Service Rustic have recently been completed: Tweed et al., *Rustic Architecture*; Harrison, *Architecture in the Parks*; Zaitlin, *Gilbert Stanley Underwood*, 17-28; McClelland, *Presenting Nature*, 50-68; Edward Mills, *Rustic Building Programs in Canada's National Parks, 1887-1950* (National Historic Sites Directorate, Parks Canada, 1994).

[69]Department of the Interior, National Park Service, *1923 Annual Report*, 52-53; 184.

[70]Land and Community Associates, *Yosemite Valley: Cultural Landscape Report, 2* vols. (Denver: Department of the Interior, National Park Service, 1994), vol. 1, fig. V-2.

[71]Land and Community Associates, *Yosemite Valley*, vol. 1, 2*99-2*116; Greene, *Yosemite*, vol. 2, 580-591. The Native American community in Yosemite Valley was eventually relocated to a new site as well. See Mark Spence, "Dispossessing the Wilderness: Yosemite Indians and the National Park Ideal, 1864-1930," *Pacific Historical Review* 65 (February 1996): 27-59.

[72]Department of the Interior, National Park Service, *1922 Annual Report*, 157; Tweed, et al., *Rustic Architecture*, 37.

[73]Department of the Interior, National Park Service, *1923 Annual Report*, 71. The six buildings at the core of the Mesa Verde administrative village, built mostly between 1921 and 1928, were incorporated in a National Historic Landmark District for their architectural significance in 1987. Harrison, *Architecture in the Parks*, 211-228.

[74]The Forest Service retained jurisdiction over national monuments created out of existing national forests until 1933, when Roosevelt transferred management of all the national monuments to the Park Service. The Forest Service had managed the Grand Canyon as a national forest since 1893, and as a national monument since 1908. Mackintosh, *The National Parks*, 24.

[75]Margaret M. Verkamp, *History of Grand Canyon National Park* [1940] (Flagstaff: Grand Canyon Pioneers Society, 1993), 22-23.

[76]Hal Rothman, *America's National Monuments: The Politics of Preservation* (University Press of Kansas by arrangement with the University of Illinois, 1989), 64-68.

[77]Verkamp, *History of Grand Canyon*, 23-26, 39.

[78]Henry Graves, "Memorandum on Conditions at the Grand Canyon National Monument and Suggestions for Improving Them," November 23, 1914, Grand Canyon, General Files, Entry 749A, RG 48, National Archives, Washington, DC.

[79]Verkamp, *History of Grand Canyon*, 40; Rothman, *America's National Monuments*, 97. George Horace Lorimer, in particular, published a series of articles in the *Saturday Evening Post* in 1916 (with titles such as "Ballyhooing in the Temple") in support of legislation to make the Grand Canyon a national park. In 1916 the number of visitors to the canyon returned to about one third of the 1915 total.

[80]W. R. Matoon, "A Working Plan for Grand Canyon National Monument," 1909, manuscript #17460, pp. 61, 85-87, 105. Grand Canyon Museum Collection, Grand Canyon National Park.

[81]W. R. Matoon, "A Townsite Plan for Grand Canyon National Monument," 1910, manuscript #17460. Grand Canyon Museum Collection, Grand Canyon National Park.

[82]Many of the railroad's facilities were constructed within the acreage granted as part of its right-of-way. Michael P. Scott, *National Register of Historic Places Nomination for the Grand Canyon Village Historic District*, 1995. National Register nominations are available at the National Register of Historic Places, National Park Service, 800 North Capitol Street, Washington, DC.

[83]Don P. Johnston and Aldo Leopold, "Grand Canyon Uses Working Plan," 1916, manuscript #18555, Grand Canyon Museum Collection, Grand Canyon National Park, no page numbers.

[84]Don P. Johnston and Aldo Leopold, "Grand Canyon Working Plan," 1917, manuscript #28343, Grand Canyon Museum Collection, Grand Canyon National Park, no page numbers.

[85]The cabin group was never built at Indian Gardens, although Colter's Phantom Ranch, a similar cabin group on the floor of the canyon, was built in 1922.

[86]Frank A. Waugh, *A Plan for the Development of the Village of Grand Canyon* (Washington, DC: Government Printing Office, 1918), 8-11. The grand canyon depot was made a National Historic Landmark for its architectural significance in 1987. Harrison, *Architecture in the Parks*, 123-133.

[87]Such development on the rim of the canyon did not accord with the "rim zone" restrictions suggested by Johnston and Leopold. Waugh, *Grand Canyon Plan*, 14-16.

[88]Stephen Mather to Charles Punchard, September 3, 1919, Grand Canyon, Central Files, Entry 6, RG 79, National Archives, Washington, DC.

[89]George Goodwin to Stephen Mather, August 17, 1919, Grand Canyon, General Files, Entry 749A, RG 48, National Archives, Washington, DC.

[90]Department of the Interior, National Park Service, *1919 Annual Report*, 96.

[91]Department of the Interior, National Park Service, *1919 Annual Report*, 96-98. Mather makes no mention of Waugh's village plan, which was not implemented. Punchard dismissed Waugh's plan lightly, and wrote to Goodwin that he was "sure that the Forest Service plan [could be] improved upon." Charles Punchard to George Goodwin, September 3, 1919, Grand Canyon, Central Files, Entry 6, RG 79, National Archives, Washington, DC.

[92]Charles Punchard to Stephen Mather, July 28, 1920, Grand Canyon, Central Files, Entry 6, RG 79, National Archives, Washington, DC.

[93]Department of the Interior, National Park Service, *1921 Annual Report*, 57.

[94]Stephen Mather to Ford Harvey, March 15, 1920, Grand Canyon, Central Files, Entry 6, RG 79, National Archives, Washington, DC.

[95]Arno Cammerer to DeWitt Reaburn, October 12, 1921, Grand Canyon, Central Files, Entry 6, RG 79, National Archives, Washington, DC.

[96]Department of the Interior, National Park Service, *1921 Annual Report*, 102.

[97]Assistant Director Cammerer (acting for Director Mather) approved sketches for the "tentative layout" of the village in 1921. Arno Cammerer to Daniel Hull, March 17, 1921, Grand Canyon, Central Files, Entry 6, RG 79, National Archives, Washington, DC. Only one print of Hull's early sketches for Grand Canyon Village has so far been recovered; signed by Hull and dated July 18, 1922, it is drawn (like the 1917 survey) at one inch to one hundred feet with five-foot contour intervals. "Grand Canyon National Park, Tentative General Plan," Central File, Entry 6, RG 79, National Archives, Washington, DC. Official correspondence contains numerous references to earlier sketch plans, however, which were distributed to Mather and others for approval in 1921, and which must have shown more or less the same arrangement as this 1922 sketch.

[98]A portion of this road already existed at the time of the 1917 survey, and was used to access horse and mule pastures that covered the sites of the proposed subdivisions.

[99]Numerous items of correspondence make it clear that Hull designed buildings as well as landscape plans as part of his work. A letter from Cammerer in 1921, for example, specifically states that Hull designed the administration building and other buildings at Grand Canyon. Arno Cammerer to Daniel Hull, March 17, 1921, Grand Canyon, Central Files, Entry 6, RG 79, National Archives, Washington, DC. In 1921 Hull also designed a more modest administration building for Sequoia and a log cabin

entrance station for Rocky Mountain at this time. Tweed, et al., *Rustic Architecture*, 31-32.

[100]A new wing was added to the first administration building when it was converted into the superintendent's residence in 1931. In the early 1980s the interior was remodeled to serve as an office annex for the Fred Harvey Company. Billy Garret, "Adaptive Reuse: The Superintendent's Residence at Grand Canyon National Park," *Cultural Resource Management 7*, no. 4 (December 1984), 6-7.

[101]Colter's architecture, however, emphasized anthropological allusions and elaborate masonry effects that were more suited to resort architecture than to official buildings. Hull also would have been familiar with Colter's plans for tourist cabins at Indian Gardens that had been inserted in the 1918 Forest Service Working Plan. Four of Colter's south rim buildings (including her 1931 Desert Watchtower) were made National Historic Landmarks for their architectural significance in 1987. Harrison, *Architecture in the Parks*, 99-121.

[102]The cottage locations were approved by Superintendent Reaburn and Director Mather. Daniel Hull to DeWitt Reaburn, May 28, 1921, Grand Canyon, Central Files, Entry 6, RG 79, National Archives, Washington, DC. The Santa Fe cottages were designed by the railroad's architect, William H. Mohr. For the dates of construction and other details for all the buildings in the Grand Canyon Village historic district, see Scott, "Grand Canyon National Register Nomination."

[103]Cameron had a long history on the south rim. He had built and operated a hotel at the site of the Bright Angel Lodge, and for many years he charged a toll for the use of the Bright Angel Trail. See Douglas Hillman Strong, "The Man Who 'Owned' Grand Canyon," *The American West* 6, no. 5 (September 1969): 33-54; Albright and Cahn, *Birth of the National Park Service*, 169-186.

[104]Arno Cammerer to Daniel Hull, April 7, 1922, Grand Canyon, Central Files, Entry 6, RG 79, National Archives, Washington, DC. Anderson, a principal of the Chicago firm of Graham, Anderson, Probst & White, had trained in Paris and was an accomplished master of early 20th-century neoclassism. He is best known as the architect of Union Station (1902) in Washington, DC, and as Daniel Burnham's assistant in planning the Philippine summer capital of Baguio (1903). It would be difficult to suggest two projects, however, more antithetical to the design and planning efforts underway within the Park Service in the 1920s.

[105]Arno Cammerer to Daniel Hull, July 26, 1922, Grand Canyon, Central Files, Entry 6, RG 79, National Archives, Washington, DC.

[106]William Crosby to Daniel Hull, December 10, 1922, Grand Canyon, Central Files, Entry 6, RG 79, National Archives, Washington, DC.

[107]Arno Cammerer to Ford Harvey, January 4, 1923, Grand Canyon, Central Files, Entry 6, RG 79, National Archives, Washington, DC.

[108]Stephen Mather to Daniel Hull, December 18, 1923, Grand Canyon, Central Files, Entry 6, RG 79, National Archives, Washington, DC. Hull had finally met that August with "the architect employed by the operator" at Grand Canyon. He reported that "various schemes" were being considered. Department of the Interior, National Park Service, *1923 Annual Report*, 57, 189.

[109]William Crosby to Daniel Hull, November 13, 1923, Grand Canyon, Central Files, Entry 6, RG 79, National Archives, Washington, DC.

[110]Cammerer quoted Mather directly in his own letter to the Grand Canyon superintendent. Arno Cammerer to J. Ross Eakin, January 8, 1924, Grand Canyon, Central Files, Entry 6, RG 79, National Archives, Washington, DC.

[111]Drawing NP.GC/46, Technical Information Center, Denver Service Center, National Park Service, Denver. The plan was drawn at one inch to one hundred feet without the contour lines of earlier sketches. Tree masses were rendered in this presentation drawing.

[112]Department of the Interior, National Park Service, *1924 Annual Report*, 39-40.

[113]The powerhouse was made a National Historic Landmark for its architectural significance in 1987. Harrison, *Architecture in the Parks*, 257-267.

[114]Scott, "Grand Canyon National Register Nomination," 7-18.

[115]The second administration building was made a National Historic Landmark for its architectural significance in 1987. Harrison, *Architecture in the Parks*, 301-309.

Chapter 3
(pp. 133-135)

[116]Arizona, New Mexico, and Wyoming were subsequently represented as well. Each camp consisted of up to two hundred recruits. "Narrative Reports Concerning ECW (CCC) Projects in National Park Service Areas, 1933-35," Arizona, Entry 42, RG 79, National Archives, Washington, DC.

[117]Harry Langley, "Report to Chief Landscape Architect," September 8, 1932, Grand Canyon, Entry 7, RG 79, National Archives, Washington, DC.

[118]Scott, "Grand Canyon National Register Nomination," 19-21.

[119]Among the assistant and resident Park Service landscape architects making reports to the chief landscape architect (through Superintendent Tillotson) during this period were Harry Langley, Thomas E. Carpenter, and Alfred C. Kuehl. "Reports to the Chief Landscape Architect Through Superintendent," Grand Canyon, Central Files, Entry 7, RG 79, National Archives, Washington, DC.

[120]"Narrative Reports Concerning ECW (CCC) Projects in National Park Service Areas, 1933-35," Arizona, Entry 42, RG 79, National Archives, Washington, DC.

[121]McClelland, *Presenting Nature*, 149-161, 221. McClelland discusses important, if ephemeral, examples of "natural gardens" cultivated as interpretative displays in national parks in the 1920s and 1930s, including the Yosemite Nature Garden.

[122]Ernest Davidson and Merel Sager were particularly active in the Pacific Northwest, and the administrative village and rim village areas of Crater Lake National Park retain original ornamental planting designs of particular significance from this era. Cathy A. Gilbert and Gretchen A. Luxenberg, *The Rustic Landscape of Rim Village, 1927-1941* (Seattle: Department of the Interior, National Park Service, 1990).

[123]Scott, "Grand Canyon National Register Nomination," 7-18.

[124]Land and Community Associates, *Yosemite Valley*, vol. 1, 2*114-2*116.

Chapter 4
(pp. 139-143)

The Going-to-the-Sun Road Historic District: "Landscape Engineering" and Changing Roles of Park Service Professionals

[1]Horace Albright to Arno Cammerer, December 18, 1926, Papers of Arno B. Cammerer, Entry 18, RG 79, National Archives, Washington, DC.

[2]Angus M. Woodbury, "A History of Southern Utah and Its National Parks," *Utah State Historical Society* 12, nos. 3-4 (July-October 1944, revised and reprinted, 1950): 195-198.

[3]Rothman, *America's National Monuments*, 98-101.

[4]The Forest Service obliged with a similar arrangement for Bryce Canyon. The Utah Parks Company also established a bus station in Cedar City and eventually bought out competing livery and tourist camp concerns that had started up since 1910. Woodbury, "History of Southern Utah," 203-204.

[5]Quoted in Zaitlin, *Gilbert Stanley Underwood*, 32. Zaitlin suggests that Hull's influence secured the Union Pacific work for Underwood.

[6]Department of the Interior, National Park Service, *1924 Annual Report*, 62.

[7]The Zion Lodge was rebuilt in the late 1960s following a devastating fire. The original cabin group remains, although the site work has been significantly altered with the addition of concrete sidewalks and other incompatible construction details. Bryce Canyon Lodge, which retains only its fifteen "deluxe" cabins out of its originally much larger complement, was made a National Historic Landmark for its architectural significance in 1987. Harrison, *Architecture in the Parks*, 229-242.

[8]Both the Ahwahnee and the Grand Canyon Lodge were made National Historic Landmarks for their architectural significance in 1987. Harrison, *Architecture in the Parks*, 243-256, 285-299.

[9]"Herbert Maier," Mather Collection, Entry 135, RG 79, National Archives, Washington, DC.

[10]Harold C. Bryant and Wallace W. Atwood, *Research and Education in the National Parks* (Washington, DC: Government Printing Office, 1936), 48-50; C. Frank Brockman, "Park Naturalists and the Evolution of National Park Service Interpretation Through World War II," *Journal of Forest History* 22, no. 1 (January 1978): 24-43.

333 Wilderness by Design

[11]Maier complied with the request for chapter heading illustrations of park scenes. See Ansel F. Hall, ed., *Handbook of Yosemite National Park* (New York: Knickerbocker Press, 1921).

[12]Ralph H. Lewis, *Museum Curatorship in the National Park Service, 1904-1982* (Washington, DC: Department of the Interior, National Park Service, 1993), 7-8, 31-34.

[13]The roughly contemporary Mesa Verde museum was built in the Pueblo style and was also paid for by the Laura Spelman Rockefeller Memorial. John D. Rockefeller, Jr.'s interest in Mesa Verde had initiated the involvement of that charitable foundation in park museum construction. The Mesa Verde museum, which is part of the Mesa Verde National Historic Landmark District, was remodeled and expanded in the 1930s. Harrison, *Architecture in the Parks*, 214-215.

[14]Lewis, *Museum Curatorship*, 38.

[15]Herbert Maier to Thomas Vint, July 28, 1927, Records of the Field Headquarters in San Francisco, Entry 29, RG 79, National Archives, Washington, DC.

[16]Lewis, *Museum Curatorship*, 39.

[17]Lewis, *Museum Curatorship*, 38-39, 48.

[18]The Old Faithful museum was demolished and replaced by the existing visitor center in 1971. The three remaining trailside museums at Yellowstone were made National Historic Landmarks for their architectural significance in 1987. Harrison, *Architecture in the Parks*, 311-330.

[19]The original site development around the Old Faithful, Norris, and Madison museums has been significantly altered. At Fishing Bridge, however, Maier's original amphitheater and naturalist's residence, as well as the slightly later parking lot, have been retained and together are a unique example of trailside museum site planning of the period.

[20]The Obsidian Cliff Nature Shrine (1931) at Yellowstone was the first (and remains the best) example of such a roadside display. In this case the adjacent road, parking area, and planted island are also well preserved.

[21]In 1925 Mather described a "great flow of tourist gold . . . adding new life to communities unprogressive for years. It is a particularly dependable annual source of income for many western States." Department of the Interior, National Park Service, *1925 Annual Report*, 1.

[22]Mather, "Ideals and Policies of the National Park Service," 80-81.

[23]Department of the Interior, National Park Service, *1921 Annual Report*, 11, 23-25.

[24]Bruce E. Seely, *Building the American Highway System: Engineers as Policy Makers* (Philadelphia: Temple University Press, 1987), 46-59.

[25]This was a healthy ten percent of the total federal-aid spending. W. Stull Holt, *The Bureau of Public Roads: Its History, Activities and Organization*, Institute for Government Research, Service Monograph No. 26 (Baltimore: The Johns Hopkins University Press, 1923), 30-36; William A. Proctor, "Problems Involved in the Planning and Development of Through-Traffic Highways" (Master's Thesis, Leland Stanford Junior University, 1939), 767.

[26]Goodwin's "temporary office" in Portland was closed in 1920, and the engineer was transferred to serve as acting superintendent at Glacier. Department of the Interior, National Park Service, *1920 Annual Report*, 90-93.

[27]Mather, "Ideals and Policy of the National Park Service," 81.

[28]Department of the Interior, National Park Service, *1923 Annual Report*, 9-10.

[29]"George Estyn Goodwin," Mather Collection, National Archives, Entry 135, RG 79, National Archives, Washington, DC; Albright and Cahn, *Birth of the National Park Service*, 103-4.

[30]Department of the Interior, National Park Service, *1921 Annual Report*, 54.

[31]Department of the Interior, National Park Service, *1922 Annual Report*, 156.

[32]Department of the Interior, National Park Service, *1922 Annual Report*, 20.

[33]Albright made sure that the committee members, including park advocates Louis C. Cramton (Michigan) and Carl Hayden (Arizona), experienced miserable park road conditions firsthand. Shankland, *Steve Mather*, 154-156.

[34]One such pocket size notebook from 1924-1925 is conserved in the National Park Service History Collection, Harpers Ferry Center, Harpers Ferry, West Virginia.

[35]Congress, House of Representatives, Committee on the Public Lands, *Construction of Roads, etc. in National Parks and Monuments: Hearings Before the Committee on the Public Lands*, 68th Cong., 1st sess., February 7, 8, 12, and 14, 1924, 3-6.

[36]Committee on the Public Lands, *Construction of Roads, etc. in National Parks and Monuments*, 27.

[37]Department of the Interior, National Park Service, *1924 Annual Report*, 11-12.

[38]Eliot, *Vegetation and Scenery*, 7.

[39]Chittenden, *Yellowstone National Park*, 237.

[40]Department of the Interior, National Park Service, *1923 Annual Report*, 48-49.

[41]Culpin, *Construction of the Road System in Yellowstone*, 120-121.

[42]William D. Reiley and Roxanne S. Brouse, *Historic Resource Study for the Carriage Road System, Acadia National Park, Mount Desert Island, Maine* (Boston: Department of the Interior, National Park Service, 1989), 43-51.

[43]Albright and Cahn, *Birth of the National Park Service*, 162-163; Department of the Interior, National Park Service, *1925 Annual Report*, 8.

[44]Chittenden, *Yellowstone National Park*, 248-249.

[45]Department of the Interior, National Park Service, *1921 Annual Report*, 56.

[46]Department of the Interior, National Park Service, *1922 Annual Report*, 21.

[47]Department of the Interior, National Park Service, *1925 Annual Report*, 18.

[48]Quoted in Culpin, *Construction of the Road System in Yellowstone*, 122-124.

[49]Culpin, *Construction of the Road System in Yellowstone*, 123-124.

[50]Arthur Demaray to Stephen Mather, November 12, 1924, Glacier National Park, Central Files, Entry 6, RG 79, National Archives, Washington, DC. Demaray, who had joined the Park Service as a draftsman in 1917, was in the process of assuming the responsibilities of "assistant in operations and public relations." Olsen, *Organizational Structures of the National Park Service*, 35.

[51]R. B. Marshall, "Report on the Glacier National Park in Montana" [1910], Glacier National Park, Central Files, Entry 6, RG 79, National Archives, Washington, DC.

[52]Mather, *Progress in the Development of the National Parks*, 35.

[53]P. N. Bernard to Franklin Lane, November 4, 1914, Glacier National Park, Central Files, Entry 6, RG 79, National Archives, Washington, DC.

[54]Henry Myers to Franklin Lane, September 25, 1914, Glacier National Park, Entry 6, Central Files, RG 79, National Archives, Washington, DC.

[55]"House Joint Memorial No. 10," April 1, 1915, Glacier National Park, Central Files, Entry 6, RG 79, National Archives, Washington, DC.

[56]Sheire, *Glacier National Park*, 195-197.

[57]The Many Glacier Hotel, the Sperry and Granite Park Chalets, and the Two Medicine Chalet (now the Two Medicine Store) were all made National Historic Landmarks for their architectural significance in 1987. Harrison, *Architecture in the Parks*, 135-158.

[58]Kathryn Steen, "Going-to-the-Sun Road" (Historic American Engineering Record No. MT-67, 1992), 6-7. The Historic American Engineering Record recorded the Going-to-the-Sun Road in 1990-91. These records are available through the Library of Congress.

[59]Shankland suggests that Walsh, along with the disgruntled Robert B. Marshall, were among the causes of Mather's nervous breakdown in 1917. See Shankland, *Steve Mather*, 109, 122-23; Albright and Cahn, *Birth of the National Park Service*, 46-49; Ise, *Our National Park Policy*, 180.

[60]Department of the Interior, *Proceedings of the Berkeley Conference*, 24-33.

[61]Department of the Interior, National Park Service, *1917 Annual Report*, 19-20.

[62]Department of the Interior, National Park Service, *1922 Annual Report*, 18.

[63]Department of the Interior, National Park Service, *1919 Annual Report*, 20-22.

[64]Shankland, *Steve Mather*, 62-63, 78-79, 148.

[65]Mather, *Progress in the Development of the National Parks*, 30; Department of the Interior, National Park Service, *1921 Annual Report*, 281.

[66]Department of the Interior, National Park Service, *1917 Annual Report*, 43.

[67]Department of the Interior, National Park Service, *1919 Annual Report*, 23.

[68]The Glacier Hotel (later renamed the Lake McDonald Lodge) was built in 1913-1914 on the site of an 1890s hotel establishment. Like Louis Hill's contemporary lodges, the wooden lodge is Alpine in inspiration. It was acquired by the Park Service in 1930, and it was made a National Historic Landmark for its architectural significance in 1987. Harrison, *Architecture in the Parks*, 159-171.

[69]Department of the Interior, National Park Service, *1918 Annual Report*, 68-69.

[70]Steen, "Going-to-the-Sun Road," 9-10.

[71]George Goodwin to A. J. Breitenstein, August 17, 1921, Glacier National Park, Central Files, Entry 6, RG 79, National Archives, Washington, DC.

[72]Herbert Evison, Interview with Thomas Vint, 1960, p. 12. Transcript in Thomas C. Vint Collection, Papers of Charles E. Peterson.

[73]W. W. Crosby and George Goodwin, *Highway Location and Surveying* (Chicago: Gilette Publishing Company, 1928), 182-83.

[74]George Goodwin to A. J. Breitenstein, August 17, 1921, Glacier National Park, Central Files, Entry 6, RG 79, National Archives, Washington, DC.

[75]Department of the Interior, National Park Service, *1920 Annual Report*, 90.

[76]George E. Goodwin, Glacier National Park, Annual Report, Glacier National Park, General Records of the Engineering Division, Entry 22, RG 79, National Archives, Washington, DC; Department of the Interior, National Park Service, *1920 Annual Report*, 121.

[77]Department of the Interior, National Park Service, *1921 Annual Report*, 54-55, 286. Work also began on the Carbon River Road in Mount Rainier and the Middle Fork Road in Sequoia.

[78]J. M. Hyde, "That Fairy Highway Through Glacier National Park, Cut Bank Pioneer Press," April 29, 1921, Glacier National Park, Central Files, Entry 6, RG 79, National Archives, Washington, DC.

[79]George Goodwin to A. J. Breitenstein, August 17, 1921, Glacier National Park, Central Files, Entry 6, RG 79, National Archives, Washington, DC.

[80]J. Ross Eakin to Stephen Mather, October 6, 1921; J. Ross Eakin to Stephen Mather, October 25, 1921, Glacier National Park, Central Files, Entry 6, RG 79, National Archives, Washington, DC. Numerous endorsements of the Transmountain Highway subsequently arrived from chambers of commerce in Kalispell, Missoula, and elsewhere, as well as from local newspapers.

[81]George Goodwin to Stephen Mather, March 27, 1922, Glacier National Park, Central Files, Entry 6, RG 79, National Archives, Washington, DC.

[82]Department of the Interior, National Park Service, *1923 Annual Report*, 10, 41.

[83]Department of the Interior, National Park Service, *1925 Annual Report*, 17. Two out of three of Goodwin's assistants in Portland had in fact resigned for higher paying jobs in 1923.

[84]Daniel Hull to Stephen Mather, November 20, 1923, Glacier National Park, Central Files, Entry 6, RG 79, National Archives, Washington, DC.

[85]Department of the Interior, National Park Service, *1924 Annual Report*, 152.

[86]Evison, Interview with Thomas Vint, 1960, p. 12-13.

[87]Thomas C. Vint, Personnel Information Sheet, United States Civil Service Commission, July 1, 1940, Thomas C. Vint Collection, Papers of Charles E. Peterson.

[88]Evison, Interview with Thomas Vint, 1960, p. 13-14.

[89]Shankland, *Steve Mather*, 157-58.

[90]Evison, Interview with Thomas Vint, 1960, p. 13-14.

[91]Frank A. Kittredge, "Trans-Mountain Highway, Glacier National Park, Report to National Park Service," February 5, 1925, p. 3, Glacier National Park, Central Files, Entry 6, RG 79, National Archives, Washington, DC.

[92]Frank A. Kittredge, "The Survey of the Going-to-the-Sun Highway, 1924," 1952, p. 87, Glacier National Park Archives.

[93]"Frank A. Kittredge," Mather Collection, National Archives, Entry 135, National Archives, RG 79, Washington, DC.

[94]Evison, Interview with Thomas Vint, 1960, p. 14.

[95]Frank A. Kittredge, "Trans-Mountain Highway, Glacier National Park, Report to National Park Service," February 5, 1925, p. 8, Glacier National Park, Central Files, Entry 6, RG 79, National Archives, Washington, DC; Frank A. Kittredge, "The Survey of the Going-to-the-Sun Highway, 1924," 1952, p. 88, Glacier National Park Archives.

[96]Frank A. Kittredge, "Trans-Mountain Highway, Glacier National Park, Report to National Park Service," February 5, 1925, p.1-3, 9-10, 22. Glacier National Park, Central Files, Entry 6, RG 79, National Archives, Washington, DC.

[97]Charles Kraebel to Stephen Mather, October 8, 1924, Glacier National Park, Central Files, Entry 6, RG 79, National Archives, Washington, DC.

[98]Thomas C. Vint, "Memorandum to D. R. Hull . . . Re: Report by Highway Engineer Frank A. Kittredge," Glacier National Park, Central Files, Entry 6, RG 79, National Archives, Washington, DC.

[99]Steen, "Going-to-the-Sun Road," 19-20; Evison, Interview with Thomas Vint, 1960, p. 14.

[100]W. G. Peters, "Construction Progress Report (1925) on Transmountain Highway, Glacier National Park," 1925, Contracts and Proposals and Specifications, Entry 25, RG 79, National Archives, Washington, DC.

[101]Evison, Interview with Thomas Vint, 1960, p. 14; Albright and Cahn, *Birth of the National Park Service*, 194; Shankland, *Steve Mather*, 157; Steen, "Going-to-the-Sun Road," 24.

[102]Department of the Interior, National Park Service, *1926 Annual Report*, 155.

[103]"Minutes of the Eighth National Park Conference Held in Mesa Verde National Park, Colorado, October 1 to 5, 1925, Inclusive," unpublished minutes, National Park Service History Collection, Harpers Ferry Center, Harpers Ferry, West Virginia, 1-2.

[104]G. F. Reynolds, "The Park Superintendents' Tour," *Yosemite Nature Notes* 4, no. 20 (November 1925): 105.

[105]"Minutes of the Eighth National Park Conference Held in Mesa Verde National Park," p. 23-25.

[106]"Minutes of the Ninth National Park Conference Held in Washington, DC, November, 1926," unpublished minutes, National Park Service History Collection, Harpers Ferry Center, Harpers Ferry, West Virginia, 96.

[107]Department of the Interior, National Park Service, *1926 Annual Report*, 15.

[108]"Memorandum of Agreement Between the National Park Service and the Bureau of Public Roads Relating to the Survey, Construction, and Improvement of Roads and Trails in the National Parks and National Monuments," January 18, 1926, Papers of Horace M. Albright, Entry 17, RG 79, National Archives, Washington, DC.

[109]Steen, "Going-to-the-Sun Road," 25-26.

[110]Department of the Interior, National Park Service, *1928 Annual Report*, 176.

[111]Department of the Interior, National Park Service, *1926 Annual Report*, 15.

[112]"Minutes of the Ninth National Park Conference Held in Washington," 97.

[113]Department of the Interior, National Park Service, *1927 Annual Report*, 133.

[114]"Minutes of the Eighth National Park Conference Held in Mesa Verde National Park," p. 29, 107.

[115]"Minutes of the Ninth National Park Conference Held in Washington," 98.

[116]Department of the Interior, National Park Service, *1925 Annual Report*, 135.

[117]E. K. Burlew and J. F. Gartland, Office of Chief Inspector, "Memorandum for the Secretary: Daniel R. Hull, Landscape Engineer, National Park Service," October 2, 1926, Papers of Arno Cammerer, Entry 18, RG 79, National Archives, Washington, DC.

[118]Arno Cammerer to Stephen Mather, October 6, 1926; Arno Cammerer to Stephen Mather, telegram, October 6, 1926, Papers of Arno B. Cammerer, Entry 18, RG 79, National Archives, Washington, DC.

[119]Horace Albright to Arno Cammerer, December 18, 1926, Papers of Arno B. Cammerer, Entry 18, RG 79, National Archives, Washington DC.

[120]Arno Cammerer to Horace Albright, December 24, 1926; Horace Albright to Arno Cammerer, July 15, 1927, Papers of Arno B. Cammerer, Entry 18, RG 79, National Archives, Washington, DC.

[121]Arno Cammerer to Stephen Mather, July 25, 1927, Papers of Arno B.Cammerer, Entry 18, RG 79, National Archives, Washington, DC.

Chapter 4

(pp. 179-186)

[122]W. G. Peters, "Final Construction Report on Transmountain Highway, Westside Project #287," October 20, 1928, p. 20, Glacier National Park Archives.

[123]Horace Albright to Daniel Hull, January 18, 1932, Papers of Horace M. Albright, Entry 17, RG 79, National Archives, Washington, DC.

[124]Dilsaver and Tweed, *Challenge of the Big Trees*, 126-133.

[125]Quoted in McClelland, *Presenting Nature*, 133-134. See Runte, *Yosemite*, 154-159.

[126]Steen, "Going-to-the-Sun Road," 27-30.

[127]A. V. Emery, "Final Report of the Location Survey of the Transmountain Highway, East Side (1929-30)," Road Survey Reports, 1920-1926, Entry 26, RG 79, National Archives, Washington, DC; A. V. Emery, "Final Construction Report (1931-32), Transmountain Highway, East Side," Glacier National Park Archives.

[128]"Going-to-the-Sun Highway Dedication, Glacier National Park, July 15, 1933," program brochure; E. T. Scoyen, "Press Release," re: Glacier ceremonies, Glacier National Park Archives.

[129]Horace M. Albright, "Memorandum for the Secretary," re: Glacier ceremonies, July 17, 1933, Glacier National Park, General File, RG 48, National Archives, Washington, DC.

[130]Steen, "Going-to-the-Sun Road," 31-36.

[131]Christie Amos and Alan S. Newell, *National Register of Historic Places Nomination for the Going-to-the-Sun Road Historic District*, 1983. National Register nominations are available at the National Register of Historic Places, National Park Service, 800 North Capitol Street, Washington, DC. The American Society of Civil Engineers designates National Historic Civil Engineering Landmarks.

Chapter 5

(pp. 190-194)

The Mount Rainier National Park Historic District: Regional Planning and National Park Service "Master Planning"

[1]Thomas C. Vint, Personnel Information Sheet, United States Civil Service Commission, July 1, 1940, Thomas C. Vint Collection, Papers of Charles E. Peterson; William G. Carnes, "Tom Vint," *National Park Service Courier* (August 1980). See McClelland, "Vint, Thomas Chalmers," in Birnbaum and Fix, eds., *Pioneers of American Landscape Design II*, 148-153.

[2]Hull's first wife also became seriously ill at about this time, which was another reason why he was unwilling to relocate from Los Angeles for an extended period. Daniel Hull to Horace Albright, January 4, 1932, Papers of Horace M. Albright, Entry 17, RG 79, National Archives, Washington, DC.

[3]Arno Cammerer to Horace Albright, December 24, 1926, Papers of Arno B. Cammerer, Entry 18, RG 79, National Archives, Washington, DC.

[4]Horace Albright to Daniel Hull, April 24, 1925, Thomas Vint Collection, Papers of Charles E. Peterson. Paul Kiessig, Vint's predecessor as Hull's assistant, had been fired because of his antagonistic relationships with superintendents. Cammerer felt that Kiessig, although "an excellent designer," was "lacking in tact." Arno Cammerer to Frederick Law Olmsted, Jr., September 11, 1922, Papers of Arno B. Cammerer, Entry 18, RG 79, National Archives, Washington, DC.

[5]Frederick Law Olmsted to Alfred Geiffert, February 7, 1930, Thomas C. Vint Collection, Papers of Charles E. Peterson.

[6]Interview with Charles E. Peterson by the author, August 25, 1995.

[7]Tweed, et al., *Rustic Architecture*, 49-51. In 1976, William Tweed and Laura Harrison were able to interview John Wosky, Merel Sager, and William Carnes for their important study on Park Service Rustic architecture.

[8]McClelland quotes from the civil service job description and examination questions extensively in *Presenting Nature*, 117.

[9]Tweed et al., *Rustic Architecture*, 50; Charles E. Peterson, letter to the author, June 6, 1996.

[10]McClelland, *Presenting Nature*, 117.

[11]Department of the Interior, National Park Service, *1929 Annual Report*, 163-165.

[12]Thomas Vint, "National Park Service Master Plans," *Planning and Civic Comment* (April-June 1946); Department of the Interior, National Park Service, *1930 Annual Report*, 186.

[13]Frederick Law Olmsted, Jr., "The Town-Planning Movement in America." *Housing and Town Planning* 51, no. 1 (January 1914): 172-181.

[14]See Flavel Shurtleff and Frederick Law Olmsted, Jr., *Carrying Out the City Plan* (New York: Survey Associates, 1914); John Nolen, *City Planning* (New York: D. Appleton and Company, 1916).

[15]Scott, *American City Planning*, 152-163; Richard F. Babcock, *The Zoning Game: Municipal Practices and Policies* (Madison: University of Wisconsin Press, 1966), 3-6.

[16]Frederick Law Olmsted, Jr., and Alfred Bettman, an attorney, were among the drafters of the 1927 legislation. Theodora Kimball Hubbard and Henry Vincent Hubbard, *Our Cities To-Day and To-Morrow: A Survey of Planning and Zoning in the United States* (Cambridge: Harvard University Press, 1929), 162-163; Edward M. Bassett, *The Master Plan* (New York: The Russell Sage Foundation, 1938), 82-90.

[17]Bassett, *The Master Plan*, 86.

[18]Scott, *American City Planning*, 152, 196.

[19]Vint, "National Park Service Master Plans."

[20]Exceptions to this situation included, for example, the private entrepreneurs operating through mineral claims on the south rim of the Grand Canyon and the private property owners on Lake McDonald.

[21]Hubbard and Hubbard, *Our Cities*, 46-64; Blake McKelvey, *The Emergence of Metropolitan America: 1915-1966* (New Brunswick, New Jersey: Rutgers University Press, 1968), 55-63; Scott, *American City Planning*, 213-242.

[22]John Nolen, "Regional Planning," in *City Planning*, Second Edition (New York: D. Appleton and Company, 1929), 472-494; Scott, *American City Planning*, 209.

[23]Jay Downer and James Owen, "Public Parks in Westchester County" in Alvah P. French, ed., *History of Westchester County* (New York: Lewis Historical Publishing Company, 1925), 1-15.

[24]Hubbard and Kimball, *Introduction to the Study of Landscape Design*, 322-323.

[25]"Warren Manning, Landscape Designer," *Landscape Architecture* 28, no. 3 (April, 1938): 148-149; Lance M. Neckar, "Developing Landscape Architecture for the Twentieth Century: The Career of Warren H. Manning," *Landscape Journal* 8, no. 2 (Fall 1989): 79-91. Neckar sees Manning's plan for Harrisburg as "a foretaste of modern environmentally-based planning."

[26]Warren H. Manning, "A National Plan Study Brief," *Landscape Architecture* 13, no. 4 (July 1923): 3.

[27]Benton MacKaye, *The New Exploration: A Philosophy of Regional Planning* [1928] (Urbana-Champaign, Illinois: The Appalachian Trail Conference with the University of Illinois Press, 1990), xxiii.

[28]Benton MacKaye, "The Appalachian Trail: A Project in Regional Planning," *Journal of the American Institute of Architects* 9, no. 10 (October 1921): 325-330.

[29]MacKaye, *The New Exploration*, 56-64, 74, 168-188.

[30]Steen, *The U.S. Forest Service*, 128.

[31]Department of the Interior, National Park Service, *1923 Annual Report*, 14; Ise, *Our National Park Policy*, 252.

[32]Mackintosh, *The National Parks*, 21.

[33]Evison, Interview with Thomas Vint, p. 10.

[34]Horace Albright to Stephen Mather, n.d. [1927], Papers of Horace M. Albright, Entry 17, RG 79, National Archives, Washington, DC.

[35]Albright's files include a copy of the interbureau memorandum of agreement with proposed changes to the text written in by Frank Kittredge. An official revision apparently was not signed at this time, however, since later correspondence continues to refer to the original memorandum dated January, 1926. Horace Albright to L. I. Hewes, January 26, 1928; Horace Albright to Stephen Mather, n.d. [1927], Papers of Horace M. Albright, Entry 17, RG 79, National Archives, Washington, DC.

[36]Albright provided Mather with much of this text. Stephen T. Mather, "Engineering Applied to National Parks," *Proceedings of the American Society of Civil Engineers* 4 (December 1928): 2673-84.

[37]Department of the Interior, National Park Service, *1927 Annual Report*, 133-137.

[38]Department of the Interior, National Park Service, *1928 Annual Report*, 173; idem, *1929 Annual Report*, 50.

[39]Department of the Interior, National Park Service, *1927 Annual Report*, 134.

[40]The Longmire administration building was made a National Historic Landmark for its architectural significance in 1987. Harrison, *Architecture in the Parks*, 269-283.

[41]Horace Albright to Owen Tomlinson, July 18, 1929, Mount Rainier National Park, Central Classified Files, Entry 7, RG 79, National Archives, Washington, DC.

[42]"Minutes of the Eighth National Park Conference Held in Mesa Verde National Park," p. 29; Thomas Vint, "Development of National Parks for Conservation," *American Civic and Planning Annual*, 1938, (Washington, DC: American Planning and Civic Association, 1938), 69-71.

[43]C. Frank Brockman, *The Story of Mount Rainier National Park* [1940] Second Revision (Longmire, Washington: Mount Rainier National Park Natural History Association, 1952), 22-26.

[44]Aubrey L. Haines, *Mountain Fever: Historic Conquests of Rainier* (Portland: Oregon Historical Society, 1962), 29-57, 207. Haines suggests that one of three expeditions in the 1850s reached the summit, but the 1870 expeditions seem to have been the first to make verifiable ascents.

[45]Erwin N. Thompson, *Mount Rainier National Park Historic Resource Study* (Denver: Department of the Interior, National Park Service, 1981), 60-61, 77-78; Martinson, "Mountain in the Sky," 28-31.

[46]Quoted in Martinson, "Mountain in the Sky," 46.

[47]The memorialization is reprinted in Caroline Leona Tolbert, *History of Mount Rainier National Park* (Seattle: Lowman & Hanford Co., 1933), 11-16.

[48]Ise, *Our National Park Policy*, 112-123; Martinson, "Mountain in the Sky," 49-54.

[49]Department of the Interior, *Reports of the Secretary of the Interior, 1903* (Washington, DC: Department of the Interior, 1903), 162-163.

[50]Richard H. Quin, "Nisqually Road (Government Road), Mount Rainier National Park" (Historic American Engineering Record No. WA-119, 1992), 2-9. The Historic American Engineering Record performed extensive documentation and research on the roads and bridges of Mount Rainier National Park in 1992. These records are available through the Library of Congress.

[51]Department of the Interior, *1904 Report of the Acting Superintendent of the Mount Rainier National Park to the Secretary of the Interior* (Washington, DC: Department of the Interior, 1904), 7; Department of the Interior, *1906 Report of the Acting Superintendent of Mount Rainier*, 5; Shankland, *Steve Mather*, 9.

[52]Department of the Interior, *1906 Report of the Acting Superintendent of Mount Rainier*, 7.

[53]Department of the Interior, *1908 Report of the Acting Superintendent of Mount Rainier*, 8-12, 15-16; Quin, "Nisqually Road," 9-11.

[54]Department of the Interior, *1910 Report of the Acting Superintendent of Mount Rainier*, 7.

[55]Department of the Interior, *Report of the Superintendent of Mount Rainier National Park*, 6-10, 12; Quin, "Nisqually Road," 13-14.

[56]Martinson, "Mount Rainier National Park: First Years," 29-32.

[57]Department of the Interior, National Park Service, *1917 Annual Report*, 100.

[58]Department of the Interior, *1904 Report of the Acting Superintendent of Mount Rainier*, 9; Richard H. Quin, "Mount Rainier National Park Roads and Bridges" (Historic American Engineering Record No. WA-35, 1992), 16; Thompson, *Mount Rainier*, 202. Although the road to the summit is occasionally mentioned in later years, the superintendent's annual report for 1907 shows the planned extension of the Government Road reaching only as far as Panorama Point.

[59]John H. Williams, *The Mountain That Was "God"* (Tacoma: John H. Williams, 1911), 63; Quin, "Mount Rainier Roads and Bridges," 18.

[60]Department of the Interior, National Park Service, *1917 Annual Report*, 214; Tolbert, *History of Mount Rainier*, 45-47. A firsthand account of the 1915 outing of The Mountaineers is reprinted in Dee Molenaar, *The Challenge of Rainier* [1971] (Seattle: The Mountaineers, 1987), 197-223.

[61]Martinson, "Mountain in the Sky," 83, 91-94; Harrison, *Architecture in the Parks*, 185-198. The Paradise Inn was made a National Historic Landmark for its architectural significance in 1987.

[62]Tolson, *Laws*, 107-108.

[63]Department of the Interior, National Park Service, *1917 Annual Report*, 52, 214; idem, *1918 Annual Report*, 58, 60.

[64]After the National Park Inn burned in 1926, the Annex, which today is the only hotel remaining at Longmire, took the name of the National Park Inn.

[65]Department of the Interior, National Park Service, *1919 Annual Report*, 265; idem, *1920 Annual Report*, 130, 336; Thompson, *Mount Rainier*, 69-70.

[66]Department of the Interior, National Park Service, *1917 Annual Report*, 50-51; idem, *1919 Annual Report*, 80-81.

[67]Quin, "Roads and Bridges of Mount Rainier," 18-20; Thompson, "Mount Rainier," 204-211.

[68]Department of the Interior, National Park Service, *1919 Annual Report*, 81-82; Thompson, *Mount Rainier*, 202-204.

[69]Quoted in Quin, "Mount Rainier Roads and Bridges," 22-24.

[70]Richard H. Quin, "Carbon River Road" (Historic American Buildings Survey Record No. WA-120, 1992), 2-5.

[71]Evison, Interview with Thomas Vint, 1960, p. 14.

[72]Daniel Hull to Stephen Mather, memorandum, October 29, 1920, Mount Rainier National Park, Central Files, Entry 6, RG 79, National Archives, Washington, DC.

[73]The simple stone hut was designed by a member of the club, Carl F. Gould. The Park Service added a second shelter at the site, designed by Superintendent Peters, in 1921. Copies of Peters's drawings for 1921 hut are in the National Archives. William Peters to Daniel Hull, May 14, 1921, Mount Rainier, Central Files, Entry 6, National Archives, Washington, DC.

[74]Besides the clubs mentioned, Mather recognized the Appalachian Mountain Club, the Colorado Mountain Club, the Prairie Club, and the Associated Mountaineering Clubs of North America. Department of the Interior, National Park Service, *1919 Annual Report*, 33-34.

[75]Superintendent Peters had left the Park Service in 1923 leaving only an acting superintendent at Mount Rainier at this point. There were other reasons to ask Toll to come back to Mount Rainier to intercede. A Denver native and an ardent mountaineer himself, Toll had published a guide to mountaineering in Rocky Mountain National Park in 1919, and he had strong relationships with the Northwest mountaineering groups.

[76]Martinson, "Mountain in the Sky," 95-96; Department of the Interior, National Park Service, *1922 Annual Report*, 55.

[77]Runte, *Yosemite*, 154.

[78]This was the first golf course in a national park, since the Wawona golf course was not made part of Yosemite National Park until 1932. Albright drew the line at mini-golf, however, denying the concessioner permission for a "Tom Thumb Golf Course." Horace Albright, "Memorandum to Messrs. Cammerer and Demaray," July 24, 1930, Mount Rainier National Park, Central Classified Files, Entry 7, RG 79, National Archives, Washington, DC.

[79]Interest in skiing in the valley soon ended, however, when larger and more accessible skiing resorts opened elsewhere after World War II. Winter resort activities had never resulted in significant profits for the park concessioner in any case. Department of the Interior, National Park Service, *1922 Annual Report*, 26-27; idem, *1924 Annual Report*, 45-46; Thompson, *Mount Rainier*, 84-85; Martinson, "Montain in the Sky," 105-108; Tolbert, *History of Mount Rainier*, 50.

[80]Thompson, *Mount Rainier*, 83, 91. The development of the Paradise Lodge, which primarily provided food and other services for associated housekeeping cabins around it, was hampered by the Depression. The lodge was destroyed in 1965 and replaced by a new visitor center and parking lot on the same site.

Chapter 5

(pp. 222-227)

[81]Rainier National Park Advisory Board, "A Message to Congress," June, 1925, Papers of Horace M. Albright, Entry 17, RG 79, National Archives, Washington, DC.

[82]H. A. Rhodes to Stephen Mather, May 18, 1927, Mount Rainier National Park, Central Classified Files, Entry 7, RG 79, National Archives, Washington, DC.

[83]Curtis added that "the majority of members" of the Rainier National Park Advisory Board were not stockholders in the Rainier National Park Company, although apparently a strong minority were. Asahel Curtis to Stephen Mather, May 17, 1927, Mount Rainier National Park, Central Classified Files, Entry 7, RG 79, National Archives, Washington, DC.

[84]"1926 Outline of Park Development" sent by Owen Tomlinson to Thomas Vint, August 19, 1927, Mount Rainier National Park, Classified Files, Entry 29, RG 79, National Archives, Washington, DC. For an extended description of Tomlinson's 1926 development outline, see McClelland, *Presenting Nature*, 174-177.

[85]Horace Albright to H. A. Rhodes, July 31, 1927, Mount Rainier National Park, Central Classified Files, Entry 7, RG 79, National Archives, Washington, DC.

[86]George Vanderbilt Caesar, "National or City Parks?" *The Saturday Evening Post* (October 22, 1927).

[87]Horace Albright to Frank Kittredge, December 15, 1927, Mount Rainier National Park, Central Files, Entry 29, RG 79, National Archives, Washington, DC. Vint's comments to Albright were handwritten in the margins of the returned letter.

[88]Albright's files include drafts for suggested responses which were collected and sent to him by Superintendent Tomlinson. Frank Kittredge to Owen Tomlinson, December 20, 1927; Owen Tomlinson to Horace Albright, January 3, 1928, Mount Rainier National Park, Central Classified Files, Entry 29, RG 79, National Archives, Washington, DC.

[89]Horace M. Albright, "The Everlasting Wilderness," *The Saturday Evening Post* (September 29, 1928).

[90]"Rainier National Park Company, President's Report, 1928," Mount Rainier National Park, Central Classified Files, Entry 29, RG 79, National Archives, Washington, DC.

[91]Tomlinson was not in sympathy with all the mountaineering club's resolutions, however, since he felt that the park's rugged topography and dense forests made proposed roads less of an impact on surrounding regions than The Mountaineers anticipated. Owen Tomlinson to Stephen Mather, June 11, 1928, Mount Rainier National Park, Central Classified Files, Entry 7, RG 79, National Archives, Washington, DC.

[92]Owen Tomlinson to Stephen Mather, July 20, 1928, Papers of Horace M. Albright, Entry 17, RG 79, National Archives, Washington, DC; R. N. Kellogg, "Report of the Reconnaissance and Location Surveys, Paradise Scenic Route," 1928, Contracts, Proposals, and Specifications, Entry 26, RG 79, National Archives, Washington, DC.

[93]Quin, "Nisqually Road," 24-26.

[94]Horace Albright, "General Planning," draft memorandum, February, 1929, Papers of Horace M. Albright, Entry 17, RG 79, National Archives, Washington, DC.

[95]Horace Albright, "Office Order, Re: Field Headquarters, National Park Service," n.d. [before May, 1929], Papers of Horace M. Albright, Entry 17, RG 79, National Archives, Washington, DC.

[96]The draft of Vint's letter to Albright, written in longhand, was thirteen pages long. A copy is in the Thomas C. Vint Collection, Papers of Charles E. Peterson. Albright received a virtually unchanged typed version when he arrived in San Francisco that spring. Thomas Vint to Horace Albright, May 22, 1929, Papers of Horace M. Albright, Entry 17, RG 79, National Archives, Washington, DC.

[97]A proposal for a scenic tramway to Glacier Point at Yosemite inspired a particularly long and thoughtful response from Vint in 1930. In his recommendation against the cable car, he closely followed some of the arguments Olmsted had made on the same subject. Similar controversies arose in reference to proposals for tramways at Mount Rainier and Mount Hood at this time as well. Thomas Vint to Horace Albright, November 21, 1930, Thomas C. Vint Collection, Papers of Charles E. Peterson. See Runte, *Yosemite*, 157; Tweed, *Recreation Site Planning and Improvement in National Forests*, 14.

[98]Frederick Law Olmsted, Jr., and Theodora Kimball, *Forty Years of Landscape Architecture: Central Park* [1928] (Cambridge, The MIT Press, 1973).

[99]Thomas Vint to Horace Albright, May 22, 1929, Papers of Horace M. Albright, Entry 17, RG 79, National Archives, Washington, DC.

[100]Frank Kittredge to Horace Albright, May 23, 1929; Frank Kittredge to Arthur Demaray, May 23, 1929; Frank Kittredge to Horace Albright, May 25, 1929, Papers of Horace M. Albright, Entry 17, RG 79, National Archives, Washington, DC.

[101]Quoted in Richard H. Quin, "West Side Road" (Historic American Engineering Record No. WA-122, 1992), 4.

[102]Owen Tomlinson to Horace Albright, November 2, 1929, Mount Rainier National Park, Central Classified Files, Entry 7, RG 79, National Archives, Washington, DC.

[103]Thomas Vint to Horace Albright, December 21, 1929, Mount Rainier National Park, Central Classified Files, Entry 7, RG 79, National Archives, Washington, DC.

[104]Richard H. Quin, "Stevens Canyon Highway" (Historic American Engineering Record No. WA-123, 1992), 3-5.

[105]Arthur Demaray to Horace Albright, memorandum, November 5, 1929, Mount Rainier National Park, Central Classified Files, Entry 7, RG 79, National Archives, Washington, DC.

[106]J. Ross Eakin to Horace Albright, November 12, 1929, Mount Rainier National Park, Central Classified Files, Entry 7, RG 79, National Archives, Washington, DC.

[107]Thomas Vint to Newton Drury, July 6, 1940, Thomas C. Vint Collection, Papers of Charles E. Peterson.

[108]Thomas Vint to Harlean James, August 28, 1944, Mount Rainier National Park, Central Classified Files, Entry 7, RG 79, National Archives, Washington, DC.

[109]The Longmire community building, the Longmire administration building, and the Longmire service station were made National Historic Landmarks for their architectural significance in 1987. Harrison, *Architecture in the Parks*, 269-283.

[110]See Stephanie Toothman, *National Register of Historic Places Nomination for Mount Rainier National Park*, 1987. National Register nominations are available at the National Register of Historic Places, National Park Service, 800 North Capitol Street, Washington, DC.

[111]Richard H. Quin, "Yakima Park Highway (White River Road)" (Historic American Engineering Record No. WA-126, 1992), 4-6. The history of the development of Yakima Park is presented as a case study in McClelland, *Presenting Nature*, 185-192.

[112]Horace Albright to Owen Tomlinson, July 18, 1929, Mount Rainier National Park, Central Classified Files, Entry 7, RG 79, National Archives, Washington, DC.

[113]By 1935, Ernest Davidson had convinced Vint and the new superintendent, Preston Macy, that the West Side Road should never be completed. Although the road had been considered somewhat superfluous since 1929, the official decision to abandon the project altogether indicated a turning point in attitudes towards park development. Quin, "West Side Road," 8-9.

[114]Owen Tomlinson, "Matters Decided by Director Albright During his Inspection," memorandum, July 18, 1929, Mount Rainier National Park, Central Classified Files, Entry 7, RG 79, National Archives, Washington, DC.

[115]Thomas Vint to Owen Tomlinson, October 22, 1929, Mount Rainier National Park, Central Classified Files, Entry 7, RG 79, National Archives, Washington, DC.

[116]Ernest Davidson to Thomas Vint, July 16, 1929, Mount Rainier National Park, Central Classified Files, Entry 7, RG 79, National Archives, Washington, DC.

[117]Owen Tomlinson to Horace Albright, August 1, 1929, Mount Rainier National Park, Central Classified Files, Entry 7, RG 79, National Archives, Washington, DC.

[118]Department of the Interior, National Park Service, *1929 Annual Report*, 113.

[119]Horace Albright, "Mount Rainier National Park Matters," memorandum, October 1, 1929, Mount Rainier National Park, Central Classified Files, Entry 7, RG 79, National Archives, Washington, DC.

[120]Drawing number NP-R3019-D, Mount Rainier National Park, Cartographic Division, National Archives, Washington, DC; Thomas Vint to Owen Tomlinson, October 22, 1929, Mount Rainier National Park, Central Classified Files, Entry 7, RG 79, National Archives, Washington, DC.

[121] Quoted in Harrison, *Architecture in the Parks*, 335. Many of Davidson's observations on the development of Yakima Park were summarized in a 1933 report to Thomas Vint, which is excerpted in McClelland, *Presenting Nature*, 185-192. The Yakima Park stockade group was made a National Historic Landmark for its architectural significance in 1987.

[122] Thompson, *Mount Rainier*, 94-99.

[123] Harrison, *Architecture in the Parks*, 336; McClelland, *Presenting Nature*, 189.

[124] Thomas Vint to Owen Tomlinson, October 22, 1929, Mount Rainier National Park, Central Classified Files, Entry 7, RG 79, National Archives, Washington, DC.

[125] Department of the Interior, National Park Service, *1931 Annual Report*, 66; idem, *1932 Annual Report*, 54.

[126] Department of the Interior, National Park Service, *1930 Annual Report*, 186; idem, *1931 Annual Report*, 129.

[127] "Minutes of the Twelfth Conference of National Park Executives Held at Hot Springs National Park, April 3-8, 1932," unpublished minutes, National Park Service History Collection, Harpers Ferry Center, Harpers Ferry, West Virginia, 93.

[128] Department of the Interior, National Park Service, *1932 Annual Report*, 27.

[129] "Minutes of the Twelfth Conference of National Park Executives," 92-93.

[130] The text was printed on long narrow sheets (eight and a half by twenty-four inches) that could be easily bound with the drawing sheets (typically twenty-four by thirty-six inches). "Minutes of the Twelfth Conference of National Park Executives," 96; "Mount Rainier National Park Development Outline, and Six-Year Advance Program," Mount Rainier National Park, Central Classified Files, Entry 7, RG 79, National Archives, Washington, DC.

[131] Conrad Wirth, who joined the Park Service as a landscape architect in 1931 and went on to become director in 1951, also recalled that "the master plan had its origin at Mount Rainier in the late 1920s." Retelling events as described to him by Superintendent Tomlinson, Wirth writes in his memoirs that Horace Albright asked Vint to draw up "master plans" for all the parks based on the plans that had been drawn up for Mount Rainier at that time. "The master plan concept," Wirth observes, "was one of Tom Vint's finest contributions to the National Park System." Conrad L. Wirth, *Parks, Politics, and the People* (Norman, Oklahoma: University of Oklahoma Press, 1980), 59-60, 62.

[132] "Minutes of the Twelfth Conference of National Park Executives," 96. The National Archives Cartographic Division in Washington, DC, conserves master plans dating between 1931 and 1941 for over one hundred national parks, monuments, battlefields and historic sites.

[133] Quotation from Robert Marshall's 1930 article "The Problem of Wilderness" *Scientific Monthly* 30 (1930). The article is excerpted in Roderick Nash, ed., *The American Environment: Readings in the History of Conservation* (Reading, Massachusetts: Addison-Wesley Publishing Company, 1968), 121-126. Robert Marshall was a natural scientist, Forest Service planner, and private wilderness advocate. Robert B. Marshall was the great geographer who served as "general superintendent" of national parks in 1915-16.

[134] "Minutes of the Twelfth Conference of National Park Executives," 97-99. All three designations had been used and defined in various ways over the previous three years. At Hot Springs, Vint settled on the definitions described here.

[135] "Minutes of the Twelfth Conference of National Park Executives," 98.

[136] Lowell Sumner to Victor Cahalane, December 1, 1936, Mount Rainier National Park, Central Classified Files, Entry 7, RG 79, National Archives, Washington, DC.

[137] Thomas C. Vint, "Wilderness Areas: Development of National Parks for Conservation," in *American Planning and Civic Annual*, Harlean James, ed. (Washington, DC: American Planning and Civic Association, 1938), 69-71.

[138] The rise and decline of interest in the "research area" between 1929 and 1940 corresponds to what historian Richard West Sellars describes in his article "The Rise and Decline of Ecological Attitudes in National Park Management."

[139] When Professor Norman Newton of the Harvard Graduate School of Design requested a Park Service master plan for the Department of Landscape Architecture's records in 1940, he was sent a plan for Mount Rainier, which Herbert Evison described as "more inclusive" than other plans. Newton replied that the plan indeed covered "the

possibilities of progressive indication . . . as thoroughly as any Master Plan I can recall." Herbert Evison to Norman Newton, December 12, 1940; Norman Newton to Herbert Evison, December 17, 1940, Mount Rainier National Park, Central Classified Files, Entry 7, RG 79, National Archives, Washington, DC.

[140]Beginning in 1934, Davidson was assisted by landscape architects Russel L. McCown and Halsey A. Davidson. With engineers C. E. Drysdale, R. D. Waterhouse, and Henry J. Cremer, these professionals were "detached technicians," directly supervised by Superintendent Tomlinson. Together they oversaw all CCC acivitities in the park. "Final Reports, ECW Activities," Mount Rainier National Park, Narrative Reports Concerning ECW (CCC) Projects in National Park Service Areas, Entry 42, RG 79, National Archives, Washington, DC. See McClelland, *Presenting Nature*, 206-210.

The National Park Service and National Recreational Planning

[1]Albert D. Taylor, a trustee of the American Society of Landscape Architects, estimated that ninety percent of the organization's membership had found employment through various government spending programs by the fall of 1934. This figure suggests that the vast majority of landscape architects had previously been either unemployed or underemployed. Albert D. Taylor, "Notes on Federal Activity Relating to Landscape Architecture," *Landscape Architecture* 25, no. 1 (October 1934): 41.

[2]In 1929, Harvard established a separate School of City Planning, under the leadership of Henry Hubbard, replacing the Master of Landscape Architecture in City Planning degree it had offered since 1923. Scott, *American City Planning*, 265-267.

[3]Albert D. Taylor, "Landscape Architecture To-Day: Is the Profession Keeping Abreast of the Changes in Social and Economic Life?" *Landscape Architecture* 23, no. 2 (January 1933): 85-96. Besides competition from nonprofessionals, other trends cited by Taylor included the breaking up of larger estates, the reduction of maintenance budgets for those that remained, and the lower average incomes of typical clients.

[4]Henry V. Hubbard, "ASLA Notes," *Landscape Architecture* 23, no. 3 (April 1933): 201-202.

[5]Henry V. Hubbard, "ASLA Notes," *Landscape Architecture* 24, no. 3 (April 1934): 163.

[6]Albert D. Taylor, "Notes on Federal Activity Relating to Landscape Architecture," *Landscape Architecture* 25, no. 1 (October 1934): 41. The membership of the American Society of Landscape Architects numbered only 284 in 1933, although not all professionals (especially recent graduates) were members. As demand exceeded supply, there were soon complaints of "unqualified" professionals calling themselves landscape architects. See Phoebe Cutler, *The Public Landscape of the New Deal* (New Haven: Yale University Press, 1985), 83-89.

[7]Arno Cammerer's August 1933 directive to this effect was reprinted in *Landscape Architecture* 24, no. 1 (October 1933): 49.

[8]Albert D. Taylor, "Public Works and the Profession of Landscape Architecture," *Landscape Architecture* 24, no. 3 (April 1934): 135-141.

[9]Henry V. Hubbard, "ASLA Notes," *Landscape Architecture* 24, no. 1 (October 1933): 42-48.

[10]Although Dorothy Waugh went to work in the Washington office in 1933, it was not until 1957 that the next woman landscape architect, Laura Wilson, was hired as a full-time employee by the Park Service. In other fields, including park management and interpretation, women had begun to take on roles of greater importance in the Park Service during the New Deal. Kaufman, *National Parks and the Woman's Voice*, 172-175.

[11]Taylor, "Public Works and the Profession of Landscape Architecture," 136, 141.

[12]Henry V. Hubbard, "ASLA Notes," *Landscape Architecture* 24, no. 3 (April 1934): 163.

[13]John C. Paige, *The Civilian Conservation Corps and the National Park Service, 1933-1942: An Administrative History* (Denver: Department of the Interior, National Park Service, 1985), 2-4; John A. Salmond, *The Civilian Conservation Corps: A New Deal Case Study* (Durham, North Carolina: Duke University Press, 1967), 4-8. Salmond also indicates that the German Labor Service, which put unemployed young men to work on forestry projects beginning in 1931, may have been a useful model for the CCC.

[14]Paige, *The CCC and the National Park Service*, 6; Salmond, *The Civilian Conservation Corps*, 8-10.

[15]Richard Schermerhorn, Jr., "Landscape Architecture—Its Future," *Landscape Architecture* 22, no. 4 (July 1932): 286-287.

[16]Quotations from Herbert J. Kellaway, et al., "Park Improvement and Unemployment Relief," *Landscape Architecture* 22, no. 4 (July 1932): 304-310.

[17]Taylor, "Public Works and Landscape Architecture," 136-137.

[18]Thomas C. Vint and Edward A. Nickel, eds., *Report on the Building Program from Allotments of the Public Works Administration, Western Division, 1933-1937*, (Washington, DC: Department of the Interior, Main Interior Library, 1937), 8; Tweed et al., *Rustic Architecture*, 50-51, 114-115.

[19]Department of the Interior, *Annual Report of the Department of the Interior, 1933* (Washington, DC: Government Printing Office, 1933), 153. Beginning in 1933, National Park Service *Annual Reports* were reduced in length and integrated with reports from the other bureaus of the Department of the Interior.

[20]Tweed, et al., describe many of the "uncommon number of first-rate structures" completed in national parks during the Hoover years. *Rustic Architecture*, 55-68.

[21]Department of the Interior, *1932 Annual Report*, 89; idem, *1934 Annual Report*, 164-65; idem, *1935 Annual Report*, 219; idem, *1937 Annual Report*, 73. Promotions for the "national-park year" in 1934 included a commemorative series of postage stamps.

[22]Albright and Cahn, *The Birth of the National Park Service*, 286, 298.

[23]Mackintosh, *The National Parks*, 24.

[24]Albright and Cahn, *The Birth of the National Park Service*, 289-290.

[25]Conrad L. Wirth, *The Civilian Conservation Corps Program of the United States Department of the Interior* (Washington, DC: Department of the Interior, National Park Service, 1944), 27-29; Department of the Interior, National Park Service, *The CCC and Its Contribution to a Nation-Wide State Park Recreational Program*, pamphlet (Washington, DC: Department of the Interior, National Park Service, n.d. [ca. 1940]), 16.

[26]Department of the Interior, *1933 Annual Report*, 155-158; idem, *1934 Annual Report*, 168-169.

[27]Conrad L. Wirth, *Parks, Politics, and the People* (Norman, Oklahoma: University of Oklahoma Press, 1980), 127, 130-131.

[28]Harlan D. Unrau and G. Frank Williss, *Administrative History: Expansion of the National Park Service in the 1930s* (Denver: Government Printing Office, 1983), 236-238. Unrau and Williss point out that there is some confusion over the exact number of Park Service employees in 1933, but they feel these figures best indicate pre-New Deal staffing levels.

[29]James F. Kieley, *A Brief History of the National Park Service*, unpublished report (Washington, DC: Department of the Interior, Main Interior Library, 1940), 23.

[30]More than half of all Park Service employees were being paid out of emergency appropriations, however, and not out of these annual budgets. Department of the Interior, *1940 Annual Report*, 203; idem, *1941 Annual Report*, 319.

[31]Shankland, *Steve Mather*, 303; Department of the Interior, *1941 Annual Report*, 203.

[32]Donald C. Swain, "The National Park Service and the New Deal, 1933-1940," *Pacific Historical Review* 51, no. 3 (August 1972): 312-332.

[33]All of these different park types, according to McFarland, would ideally be connected by "interstate parkways." National Conference on State Parks, *Proceedings of the Second National Conference on State Parks at Bear Mountain Inn*, 3, 56-58.

[34]National Conference on Outdoor Recreation, *Proceedings of the National Conference on Outdoor Recreation Held in the Auditorium of the New National Museum, Washington, DC* (Washington, DC: Government Printing Office, 1924), 2.

[35]The 1922 state park report led to Moses's appointment as Long Island state park commissioner in 1924. New York State Association, *A State Plan for New York* (New York State Association, 1922); New York State Council of Parks, *First Annual Report* (New York State Conservation Commission, 1925); Robert Caro, *The Power Broker: Robert Moses and the Fall of New York* [1974] (New York: Vintage Books, 1975), 166-171.

[36]Frederick Law Olmsted, Jr., *Report of State Park Survey of California* (Sacramento: California State Printing Office, 1929), 3.

[37]Olmsted, *State Park Survey*, 9, 39-53; Engbeck, *State Parks of California*, 47-56; Newton, *Design on the Land*, 572-575.

[38]Bachman, *Recreation Facilities*, 1-5; Tweed, *Recreation Site Planning and Improvement in National Forests*, 5-15.

[39]Several thorough summaries of Park Service CCC activities have been published by the Park Service. See Paige, *The CCC and the National Park Service*; Unrau and Williss, *Expansion of the National Park Service in the 1930s*; McClelland, *Presenting Nature*, 195-268.

[40]Kenneth F. Jones, "Emergency Conservation Work," *Landscape Architecture* 24, no. 2 (January 1934): 29-30. Jones later became a regional inspector for the Midwest (Region VI).

[41]Tweed, et al., *Rustic Architecture*, 88-89; Newton, *Design on the Land*, 576-585; Wirth, *Parks, Politics, and the People*, 114. Wirth tells of being personally instructed by Franklin Roosevelt in the fall of 1933 to undertake more ambitious state park development projects with CCC labor.

[42]Herbert Evison, "Recent Progress in State Parks," in *American Planning and Civic Annual*, Harlean James, ed. (Washington, DC: American Civic and Planning Association, 1935), 164-166.

[43]In 1938, Vint's title changed again to "chief of planning." Thomas C. Vint, Personnel Information Sheet, United States Civil Service Commission, July 1, 1940. Thomas C. Vint Collection, Papers of Charles E. Peterson.

[44]Thomas C. Vint and J. R. Thrower, eds., *Report on the Building Program from Allotments of the Public Works Administration, Eastern Division, 1933-1937*, (Washington, DC: National Park Service, 1937), 1; Unrau and Williss, *Expansion of the National Park Service in the 1930s*, 249.

[45]Charles Peterson had of course been in charge of the "eastern division" since 1931. Olsen, *Organizational Structures of the National Park Service*, 51.

[46]Official memorandum quoted in Unrau and Williss, *The Expansion of the National Park Service in the 1930s*, 97.

[47]Vint and Nickel, eds., *Report on the Building Program of the PWA, Western Division*, 10-11. At times, "so heavy was the pressure of work," Vint reported, it became necessary to hire consultants; but in general the Park Service clearly preferred to hire professionals outright and pay them through emergency appropriations. Department of the Interior, *1934 Annual Report*, 195.

[48]Thomas Vint oversaw the compilation of photographic reports of PWA construction completed by both his eastern and western divisions. See Vint and Nickel, eds., *Report on the Building Program of the PWA, Western Division*; Vint and Thrower, eds., *Report on the Building Program of the PWA, Eastern Division*. For summaries of PWA building activities in national parks, see Tweed, et al., *Rustic Architecture*, 76-91; McClelland, *Presenting Nature*, 196-200.

[49]Olsen, *Organizational Structures of the National Park Service*, 53.

[50]Wirth, *Parks, Politics, and the People*, 11-15, 32.

[51]Wirth, *Parks, Politics, and the People*, 76-78.

[52]According to Herbert Evison, Wirth himself established "central design offices" within state park departments, staffed by landscape architects, engineers, and planners on his CCC payroll. Although they technically were state park employees, they answered directly to Park Service officials who paid them and oversaw their work. Herbert Evison, "Civilian Conservation Corps in the National Park Service," transcribed interview, University of California, Berkeley: Forestry, Parks and Conservation Oral History Collection, No. 14, 1963, p. 41.

[53]Wirth, *Parks, Politics, and the People*, 110-113.

[54]Conrad L. Wirth, "Parks and Their Uses," in *American Planning and Civic Annual*, Harlean James, ed. (Washington, DC: American Civic and Planning Association, 1935), 156-161.

[55]William G. Carnes, "Landscape Architecture in the National Park Service," *Landscape Architecture* 41, no. 4 (July 1951): 145-150. Intense demand created what were sometimes called "instant landscape architects," and at least some of those counted

as landscape architects by Carnes must have been originally trained as engineers or architects.

[56]Herbert Evison, "The Civilian Conservation Corps in State Parks," in *American Civic Annual*, Harlean James, ed. (Washington, DC: The American Civic and Planning Association, 1934), 181-185; Newton, *Design on the Land*, 580; Department of the Interior, *1934 Annual Report*, 168-169.

[57]Emergency Conservation Work, Office of the Director, *Summary Report of the Director of Emergency Conservation Work on the Operations of Emergency Conservation Work For the Period Extending From April 1933, to June 30, 1935* (Washington, DC: Government Printing Office, 1935), 34-35.

[58]Emergency Conservation Work, Office of the Director, *1935 Summary Annual Report*, 34.

[59]In January 1936, the number of CCC state park regions was reduced from eight back to four, in part because of a reduction in the number of CCC camps. Paige, *The CCC and the National Park Service*, 48-51.

[60]Wirth, *Parks, Politics, and the People*, 118-119; Unrau and Williss, *Expansion of the National Park Service in the 1930s*, 252.

[61]Unrau and Williss, *Expansion of the National Park Service in the 1930s*, 267-269.

[62]Henry Baldwin Ward, "What is Happening to Our National Parks? A Frank Discussion of the Threats Against the Integrity of These Great Public Reservations," *Nature Magazine* (December 1938), 611-615; Arthur Newton Pack, "Practical Idealism in Our National Parks," *Nature Magazine* (February 1939), 97-98.

[63]Quoted in John C. Miles, *Guardians of the Parks: A History of the National Parks and Conservation Association* (Washington, DC: Taylor & Francis in cooperation with the National Parks and Conservation Association, 1995), 124.

[64]Scott, *American City Planning*, 300-310.

[65]Department of the Interior, *1934 Annual Report*, 171, 183-184; National Resources Board, *A Report on National Planning and Public Works in Relation to Natural Resources* (Washington, DC: Government Printing Office, 1934), 144-147.

[66]Ben H. Thompson, "The Park, Parkway, and Recreational Area Study," in *American Planning and Civic Annual*, Harlean James, ed. (Washington, DC: American Planning and Civic Association, 1937), 210-213.

[67]Department of the Interior, National Park Service, *Procedure for Park, Parkway and Recreational-Area Study* (Washington, DC: Government Printing Office, 1937).

[68]In his memoirs, Wirth claims that the 1936 act "plays a key role in the history of parks in the United States." Wirth, *Parks, Politics, and the People*, 166-172.

[69]Kieley, *A Brief History of the National Park Service*, 37.

[70]Department of the Interior, National Park Service, *Procedure for Park, Parkway and Recreational-Area Study*, 3-5.

[71]Department of the Interior, National Park Service, *Procedure for Park, Parkway and Recreational-Area Study*, 1, 6-8.

[72]Department of the Interior, National Park Service, *A Study of the Park and Recreation Problem of the United States* (Washington, DC: Government Printing Office, 1941), v.

[73]Wirth, *Parks, Politics, and the People*, 176-192; Department of the Interior, National Park Service, *Proceedings of Conference on Camp Planning Held at Camp Edith Macy, Briarcliff Manor, New York, May 20-23, 1936* (Washington, DC: Government Printing Office, 1936), 70-86.

[74]Elwood Mead, *Federal Irrigation Reservoirs as Pleasure Resorts* (Washington, DC: Government Printing Office, 1928).

[75]William E. Warne, *The Bureau of Reclamation* (New York: Praeger Publishers, 1973), 13-14, 27, 64, 256.

[76]The even larger Franklin D. Roosevelt Lake, behind the Grand Coulee Dam completed in 1941, was designated a national recreation area in 1946. Unrau and Williss, *Expansion of the National Park Service in the 1930s*, 153-155; Mackintosh, *The National Parks*, 55-56.

[77]Harley E. Jolley, *The Blue Ridge Parkway* (Knoxville: The University of Tennessee Press, 1969), 13-19.

[78]Stanley W. Abbott, "The Blue Ridge Parkway as an Element of Recreational Planning," *The Regional Review* (published by the National Park Service, Region I, Richmond, Virginia) vol. 3, no. 1 (July 1939): 3-6.

[79]Wirth, *Parks, Politics, and the People*, 128; Unrau and Williss, *Expansion of the Park Service in the 1930s*, 259-265.

[80]Arno B. Cammerer, "Memorandum for the Washington Offices and All Field Offices," re: Regionalization, August 6, 1937, Papers of Arno B. Cammerer, Entry 18, RG 79, National Archives, Washington, DC.

[81]P. H. Elwood, "Some Landscape Architectural Problems in Government Service," *Landscape Architecture* 26, no. 4 (July 1936): 186-191.

[82]Herbert Maier, "Weekly Report, July 1 1933," Reports of District Officers and Inspectors Concerning State Park Emergency Conservation Work, 1933-35, Entry 39, RG 79, National Archives, Washington, DC.

[83]The original artwork for Dorothy Waugh's "Portfolio of Park Structures and Facilities" is conserved at the National Archives (Manuscripts and Illustrations for Publications Concerning Emergency Conservation Work, 1933-38, Entry 43, RG 79, National Archives, Washington, DC). See Wirth, *Parks, Politics, and the People*, 204; McClelland, *Presenting Nature*, 253-255.

[84]Emilio P. Meinecke was a plant pathologist hired by the Park Service in 1926 to assess the damage caused by campers in the Giant Forest of Sequoia National Park. Meinecke's recommendations included restricting camping activity and vehicle access to specific points at regular intervals along a campground road. Meinecke later made reports on campgrounds and their effects on forests for the California Department of Natural Resources and the Forest Service. By the 1930s, the "Meinecke system" referred to any campground layout that restricted automobile access to loop roads and parking bays through the use of logs and boulders as curbs. Emilio P. Meinecke, *A Report on the Effect of Excessive Tourist Travel on the California Redwood Parks* (Sacramento: California State Printing Office, 1928); Dilsaver and Tweed, *Challenge of the Big Trees*, 144-145, 148-149; McClelland, *Presenting Nature*, 161-166.

[85]Herbert Maier, "Inspector's Photographic Handbook," n.d. [1935], Photographs of Engineering Activities, Entry 127, RG 79, National Archives, Washington, DC.

[86]Department of the Interior, National Park Service, "Proceedings of the National Park Service Conference of State Park Authorities in the Auditorium of the Interior Building, Washington, DC, February 25, 1935," bound mimeograph (Washington, DC: Department of the Interior, Main Interior Library), 1, 79, 83.

[87]Department of the Interior, National Park Service, *Proceedings of the National Park Service Conference of State Park Authorities*, 85.

[88]McClelland, *Presenting Nature*, 256-262.

[89]Herbert Maier and Albert H. Good, "Structures in State Parks—An Apologia," in *American Planning and Civic Annual*, Harlean James, ed. (Washington, DC: American Planning and Civic Association, 1935), 171-175.

[90]Albert H. Good, ed., *Park Structures and Facilities* (Washington, DC: Department of the Interior, National Park Service, 1935), 2, 7.

[91]Good, ed., *Park Structures and Facilities*, 6.

[92]Albert H. Good, *Park and Recreation Structures* 3 vols. (Washington, DC: Government Printing Office, 1938), vol. 1, p. 5; Good, ed., *Park Structures and Facilities*, 8. *Park and Recreation Structures* was reprinted by Graybooks (Boulder, Colorado) in 1990.

[93]Evison, "The Civilian Conservation Corps in State Parks," 185.

[94]Good, *Park and Recreation Structures*, 84, 111, 181.

[95]Good, *Park and Recreation Structures*, 5-16. Good indicated that the trend towards bringing longer and more elaborate vehicles into parks was already well underway.

[96]Good, *Park and Recreation Structures*, 109-119.

[97]Evison, "The Civilian Conservation Corps in State Parks," 182-183.

[98]Herbert Evison, "State Park and Recreation Planning," *City Planning* 10, no. 4 (October 1934): 153-163.

[99]In 1938, the most popular state park activity recorded by Park Service planners was swimming, followed by history (listed as an activity), picnicking, and hiking. The

researchers noted that most visitors arrived in automobiles, and that, in general, industrial and agricultural occupations were underrepresented. African Americans in Southern states, restricted to the few parks and areas of parks developed specifically for their use, were statistically absent from the use surveys, a fact noted by the researchers. Recommendations were made to overcome these "deficiencies in service," in part by increasing the number and diversity of parks. Department of the Interior, National Park Service, *Park Use Studies and Demonstrations* (Washington, DC: Government Printing Office, 1941), 4-5.

[100]Isabelle F. Story, *The National Parks and Emergency Conservation* (Washington, DC: Government Printing Office, 1933), 15-16.

[101]Department of the Interior, National Park Service, *The CCC and Its Contribution*, 9-13.

[102]Department of the Interior, National Park Service, *1937 Yearbook: Park and Recreation Progress* (Washington, DC: Government Printing Office, 1938), 1-3.

[103]The *Yearbooks* reported on some national park planning projects as well as on the progress of the Park, Parkway and Recreational-Area Study. The first volume, covering the year 1937, was published in 1938. Department of the Interior, National Park Service, *Yearbook: Park and Recreation Progress* (Washington, DC: Government Printing Office, 1938-42).

[104]Olmsted and Vaux, "Preliminary Report for Laying Out a Park in Brooklyn, New York," [1866] in Fein, ed., *Landscape Into Cityscape*, 98-102.

[105]Department of the Interior, National Park Service, *A Study of the Park and Recreation Problem*, 4, 20-22.

[106]Department of the Interior, National Park Service, *A Study of the Park and Recreation Problem*, 42-48.

[107]Conrad L. Wirth, "Federal Aid for State Parks—The NPS," in *American Planning and Civic Annual*, Harlean James, ed. (Washington, DC: The American Planning and Civic Association, 1939), 168-173.

[108]Conrad L. Wirth, "The National Aspect of Recreation," *1937 Yearbook: Park and Recreation Progress* (Washington, DC: Government Printing Office, 1938), v.

[1]Edgar B. Nixon, ed., *Franklin D. Roosevelt & Conservation*, 2 vols. (Hyde Park: Franklin D. Roosevelt Library, 1957), vol. 1, 322.

[2]Eleanor Roosevelt, *Franklin D. Roosevelt and Hyde Park* (Washington, DC: Government Printing Office, 1949), 1.

[3]All quotations from "Contemporary Trends and Future Possibilities in Landscape Design," *Landscape Architecture* 22, no. 4 (July 1932): 288-303.

[4]Christopher Tunnard, *Gardens in the Modern Landscape* (London: The Architectural Press, 1938), 75.

[5]Christopher Tunnard, "Modern Gardens for Modern Houses," *Landscape Architecture* (January 1942): 57-64.

[6]See Marc Treib, "Axioms for a Modern Landscape Architecture," in Marc Treib, ed., *Modern Landscape Architecture: A Critical Review* (Cambridge: The MIT Press, 1993), 36-67. Treib describes "biomorphic forms" (kidney and similar shapes) as evidence of a "vocabulary [that] accepts the influence of modern art."

Bibliography

Albright, Horace M. "The Everlasting Wilderness." *The Saturday Evening Post* 201, no. 13 (29 September 1928): 28, 63-68.

_____. "How the National Park Service Came Into Being—A Reminiscence." In *American Civic Annual*, Harlean James, ed., Washington, DC: The American Civic Association, 1929.

Albright, Horace M., and Robert Cahn. *The Birth of the National Park Service: The Founding Years, 1913-33*. Salt Lake City: Howe Brothers, 1985.

Albright, Horace Marden, and Marian Albright Schenck. *The Mather Mountain Party of 1915: A Full Account of the Adventures of Stephen T. Mather and His Friends in the High Sierra of California*. Three Rivers, California: Sequoia Natural History Association, 1990.

Albright, Horace M., and Frank J. Taylor. *"Oh Ranger!": A Book About the National Parks* [1928]; reprint, Golden, Colorado: Outbooks, 1986.

American Civic Association. *National Parks*. Pamphlet. Washington, DC: The American Civic Association, Series 11, no. 6, 1912.

Bachman, Earl E. *Recreation Facilities: A Personal History of the Development in the National Forests of California*. San Francisco: Department of Agriculture, 1967.

Bassett, Edward M. *The Master Plan*. New York: Russell Sage Foundation, 1938.

Belasco, James Warren. *Americans on the Road: From Autocamp to Motel, 1910-1945*. Cambridge: The MIT Press, 1979.

Bermingham, Ann. *Landscape and Ideology: The English Rustic Tradition, 1740-1860*. Berkeley: University of California Press, 1986.

Beveridge, Charles E. "Frederick Law Olmsted's Theory on Landscape Design." *Nineteenth Century* 3, no. 2 (June 1977): 38-43.

Beveridge, Charles E., and David Schuyler, eds. *Creating Central Park, 1857-1861. Volume III of the Papers of Frederick Law Olmsted*. Baltimore: The Johns Hopkins University Press, 1983.

Birnbaum, Charles A., and Julie K. Fix, eds. *Pioneers of American Landscape Design II*. Washington, DC: Government Printing Office, 1995.

Blodgett, Peter J. "Visiting the 'Realm of Wonder': Yosemite and the Business of Tourism, 1855-1916." *California History* 69, no. 2 (June 1990): 118-133.

Bramwell, Anna. *Ecology in the 20th Century: A History*. New Haven: Yale University Press, 1989.

Brockman, C. Frank. *The Story of Mount Rainier National Park* [1940]; reprint, Longmire, Washington: Mount Rainier National Park Natural History Association, 1952.

Brown, Dona. *Inventing New England: Regional Tourism in the Nineteenth Century*. Washington, DC: Smithsonian Institution Press, 1995.

Bryant, William Cullen, ed. *Picturesque America; Or, The Land We Live In* [1874]; reprint, Seacaucus, New Jersey: Lyle Stuart, Inc., 1974.

Buchholtz, C. W. *Man in Glacier*. West Glacier, Montana: Glacier Natural History Association, 1976.

_____. *Rocky Mountain National Park: A History*. Boulder: Colorado Associated University Press, 1983.

Cameron, Jenks. *The National Park Service: Its History, Activities and Organization*. Institute for Government Research, Service Monographs of the United States Government, No. 11. New York: D. Appleton and Company, 1922.

Carhart, Arthur H. "Landscape Architecture and the 152 National Forests." *Landscape Architecture* 11, no. 2 (January 1921): 57-62.

Carnes, William G. "Landscape Architecture in the National Park Service." *Landscape Architecture* 41, no. 4 (July 1951): 145-150.

Cermak, Robert W. "In the Beginning: The First National Forest Recreation Plan." *Parks & Recreation* 9, no. 11 (November 1974): 20-33.

Chamberlain, Allen. "Scenery as a National Asset." *The Outlook* 95, no. 4 (28 May 1910): 157-169.

Chittenden, Hiram Martin. *The Yellowstone National Park: Historical and Descriptive* [1895]. Third Revised Edition. Saint Paul: J.E. Haynes, 1927.

Cohen, Michael P. *The History of the Sierra Club, 1892-1970*. San Francisco: Sierra Club Books, 1988.

Commonwealth of Massachusetts, Metropolitan Park Commission. *A History and Description of Boston Metropolitan Parks*. Boston: Wright & Potter Printing Co., 1900.

Cox, Thomas R., Robert S. Maxwell, Phillip Drennon Thomas, and Joseph J. Malone. *This Well Wooded Land: Americans and Their Forests from Colonial Times to the Present*. Lincoln: University of Nebraska Press, 1985.

Cramton, Louis C. *Early History of Yellowstone National Park and Its Relation to National Park Policies*. Washington, DC: U.S. Department of the Interior, National Park Service, 1932.

Creese, Walter L. *The Crowning of the American Landscape: Eight Great Spaces and their Buildings*. Princeton: Princeton University Press, 1985.

Culpin, Mary Shivers. *The History of the Construction of the Road System in Yellowstone National Park, 1872-1966: Historic Resource Study Volume I*. Selections from the Division of Cultural Resources, Rocky Mountain Region, No. 5. Denver: Government Printing Office, 1994.

_____. "Yellowstone and its Borders: A Significant Influence Toward the Creation of the First Forest Reserve." In *The Origins of the National Forests*, 276-283. Harold K. Steen, ed. Durham, North Carolina: Forest History Society, 1992.

Cutler, Phoebe. *The Public Landscape of the New Deal*. New Haven: Yale University Press, 1985.

Delano, Frederic A. "What the American Civic Association Is." In *The American Civic Annual*, Harlean James, ed. Washington, DC: The American Civic Association, 1929.

Diettert, Gerald A. *Grinnell's Glacier: George Bird Grinnell and Glacier National Park*. Missoula, Montana: Mountain Press Publishing Company, 1992.

Dilsaver, Lary M., and Douglas H. Strong. "Sequoia and Kings Canyon National Parks: One Hundred Years of Preservation and Resource Management." *California History* 69, no. 2 (June 1990): 98-117.

Dilsaver, Lary M., and William C. Tweed. *Challenge of the Big Trees: A Resource History of Sequoia and Kings Canyon National Parks*. Three Rivers, California: Sequoia Natural History Association, Inc., 1990.

Doell, Charles E., and Gerald B. Fitzgerald. *A Brief History of Parks and Recreation in the United States*. Chicago: The Athletic Institute, 1954.

Donaldson, Alfred L. *A History of the Adirondacks*. 2 vols. Empire State Historical Publication XII [1921]; reprint, Port Washington, New York: Ira J. Friedman, Inc., 1963.

Dulles, Foster Rhea. *A History of Recreation: America Learns to Play*. Second Edition. New York: Appleton-Century-Crofts, 1965.

Dunlap, Thomas R. "Wildlife, Science, and the National Parks, 1920-1940." *Pacific Historical Review* 59, no. 2 (May 1990): 187-202.

Eliot, Charles W. *Charles Eliot: Landscape Architect*. Boston: Houghton Mifflin, 1902.

Eliot, Charles. *Vegetation and Scenery in the Metropolitan Reservations of Boston*. Boston: Lamson, Wolffe and Company, 1898.

Emergency Conservation Work, Office of the Director. *Annual Reports of the Director of Emergency Conservation for the Fiscal Year Ending June 30, 1936-1940*. 5 vols. Washington, DC: Government Printing Office.

_____. *Summary Report of the Director of Emergency Conservation Work on the Operations of Emergency Conservation Work for the Period Extending from April 1933 to June 1935*. Washington, DC: Government Printing Office, 1935.

Engbeck, Joseph H., Jr. *State Parks of California: 1864 to the Present*. Portland, Oregon: Graphic Arts Center Publishing Co., 1980.

Engle, J. Ronald. "Social Democracy, the Roots of Ecology, and the Preservation of the Indiana Dunes." *Forest History* 28, no. 1 (January 1984): 4-13.

Everhart, William C. *The National Park Service*. Boulder, Colorado: Westview Press, 1983.

Evison, Herbert. "The Civilian Conservation Corps in State Parks." In *American Planning and Civic Annual*, Harlean James, ed. Washington, DC: American Planning and Civic Association, 1934.

_____. "State Park and Recreation Planning." *City Planning* 10, no. 4 (October 1934): 153-163.

Evison, Herbert, ed. *A State Park Anthology*. Washington, DC: National Conference on State Parks, 1930.

Fahl, Ronald J. "S.C. Lancaster and the Columbia River Highway: Engineer as Conservationist." *Oregon Historical Quarterly* 74, no. 2 (June 1973): 101-144.

Fein, Albert, ed. *Landscape Into Cityscape: Frederick Law Olmsted's Plans for a Greater New York City*. New York: Van Nostrand Reinhold Company, 1967.

Flexner, James Thomas. *That Wilder Image: The Paintings of America's Native School from Thomas Cole to Winslow Homer* [1962]; reprint, New York: Dover Publications, Inc., 1970.

Flink, James J. *The Automobile Age*. Cambridge: The MIT Press, 1990.

Foresta, Ronald A. *America's National Parks and Their Keepers*. Washington, DC: Resources for the Future, Inc., 1984.

Gebhard, David. *Myron Hunt, 1868-1952: The Search for Regional Architecture*. ex. cat. Santa Monica: Baxter Art Gallery, California Institute of Technology, 1984.

Gilbert, Cathy A., and Gretchen A. Luxenberg. *The Rustic Landscape of Rim Village, 1927-1941*. Seattle: Department of the Interior, National Park Service, 1990.

Gilpin, William. *Three Essays: On Picturesque Beauty; On Picturesque Travel; and On Sketching the Landscape* [1792]; reprint, Ann Arbor: University Microfilms International, 1982.

Good, Albert H., ed. *Park and Recreation Structures*. 3 vols. Washington, DC: Government Printing Office [1938]; reprint, Boulder: Graybooks, 1990.

_____. *Park Structures and Facilities*. Washington, DC: Department of the Interior, National Park Service, 1935.

Goodwin, George E., and Walter W. Crosby. *Highway Location and Surveying*. Chicago: Gillette Publishing Company, 1928.

Grant, Madison. *Early History of Glacier National Park, Montana*. Washington, DC: Department of the Interior, National Park Service, 1919.

Grattan, Virginia L. *Mary Colter: Builder upon the Red Earth*. 2nd ed. Grand Canyon, Arizona: Grand Canyon Natural History Association, 1992.

Greene, Linda Wedel. *Yosemite: The Park and Its Resources*. 3 vols. Washington, DC: Department of the Interior, National Park Service, 1987.

Grese, Robert E. *Jens Jensen: Maker of Natural Gardens*. Baltimore: The Johns Hopkins University Press, 1992.

Haines, Aubrey L. *Mountain Fever: Historic Conquests of Rainier*. Portland: Oregon Historical Society, 1962.

_____. *The Yellowstone Story*. 2 vols. Boulder: Yellowstone Library and Museum Association in cooperation with Colorado Associated University Press, 1977.

Hall, Ansel F., ed. *Handbook of Yosemite National Park*. New York: G. P. Putnam's Sons, The Knickerbocker Press, 1921.

Harrison, Laura Soullière. *Architecture in the Parks: National Historic Landmark Theme Study*. Washington, DC: Department of the Interior, National Park Service, 1986.

Hays, Samuel P. *Conservation and the Gospel of Efficiency: The Progressive Conservation Movement, 1890-1920*. Cambridge: Harvard University Press [1959]; reprint, New York: Athenaeum, 1979.

Hegemann, Werner, and Elbert Peets. *The American Vitruvius: An Architect's Handbook of Civic Art* [1922]; reprint, New York: Princeton Architectural Press, 1988.

Hofstadter, Richard. *The Age of Reform*. New York: Random House, 1955.

Holt, W. Stull. *The Bureau of Public Roads: Its History, Activities and Organization*. Institute for Government Research, Service Monographs of the United States Government, No. 26. Baltimore: The Johns Hopkins University Press, 1923.

Hubbard, Henry V., and Theodora Kimball. *An Introduction to the Study of Landscape Design* [1917]. Revised Edition. New York: The Macmillan Company, 1929.

Hubbard, Theodora Kimball, and Henry Vincent Hubbard. *Our Cities To-Day and To-Morrow: A Survey of Planning and Zoning Progress in the United States*. Cambridge: Harvard University Press, 1929.

Hughes, J. Donald. *In the House of Stone and Light: A Human History of the Grand Canyon*. Denver: University of Denver in cooperation with Grand Canyon Natural History Association, 1978.

Hunt, John Dixon. *Garden and Grove: The Italian Renaissance Garden in the English Imagination, 1600-1750*. Princeton: Princeton University Press, 1986.

Hunt, John Dixon, and Peter Willis, eds. *The Genius of the Place: The English Landscape Garden, 1620-1820*. Cambridge: The MIT Press, 1988.

Hussey, Christopher. *The Picturesque: Studies in a Point of View*. London: G. P. Putnam's Sons, 1927.

Huth, Hans. *Nature and the American: Three Centuries of Changing Attitudes*. Berkeley: University of California Press [1957]; reprint, Lincoln: University of Nebraska Press, Bison Books, 1990.

_____. "Yosemite: The Story of an Idea." *Sierra Club Bulletin* 33, no. 3 (March 1948): 47-78.

Hyde, Anne Farrar. *An American Vision: Far Western Landscape and National Culture, 1820-1920*. New York: New York University Press, 1990.

Ise, John. *Our National Park Policy: A Critical History*. Baltimore: The Johns Hopkins University Press, 1961.

_____. *The United States Forest Policy*. New Haven: Yale University Press, 1920.

Jackson, Kenneth T. *Crabgrass Frontier: The Suburbanization of the United States*. New York: Oxford University Press, 1985.

Jakle, John A. *The Tourist: Travel in Twentieth-Century North America*. Lincoln: University of Nebraska Press, 1985.

Jolley, Harley E. *The Blue Ridge Parkway*. Knoxville: University of Tennessee Press, 1969.

Kaufman, Polly Welts. *National Parks and the Woman's Voice: A History*. Albuquerque: University of New Mexico Press, 1996.

Kessler, George E. *A City Plan for Dallas*. Dallas: Report of the Park Board, 1911.

Kieley, James F. *A Brief History of the National Park Service*. Unpublished report. Washington, DC: Department of the Interior, Main Interior Library, 1940.

Knapp, Richard F., and Charles E. Hartsoe. *Play for America: The National Recreation Association, 1906-1965*. Arlington, Virginia: National Recreation and Park Association, 1979.

Kohler, Sue A. *The Commission of Fine Arts: A Brief History, 1910-1990*. Washington, DC: The Commission of Fine Arts, 1990.

Krueckeberg, Donald A., ed. *Introduction to Planning History in the United States*. New Brunswick, New Jersey: The Center for Urban Policy Research, Rutgers University, 1983.

Lancaster, Samuel Christopher. *The Columbia: America's Great Highway Through the Cascade Mountains to the Sea* [1915]. Third Edition, Portland: J.K. Gill Company, 1926.

Land and Community Associates. *Yosemite Valley: Cultural Landscape Report*. 2 vols. Denver: Department of the Interior, National Park Service, 1994.

Lee, Joseph. "Play as Landscape." *Charities and the Commons* 16, no. 14 (7 July 1906): 427-432.

Lewis, Ralph H. *Museum Curatorship in the National Park Service, 1904-1982.* Washington, DC: Department of the Interior, National Park Service, 1993.

Linden-Ward, Blanche. *Silent City on a Hill: Landscapes of Memory and Boston's Mount Auburn Cemetery.* Columbus: Ohio State University Press, 1989.

MacKaye, Benton. "An Appalachian Trail: A Project in Regional Planning." *The Journal of the American Institute of Architects* 9, no. 10 (October 1921): 325-330.

_____. *The New Exploration: A Philosophy of Regional Planning* [1928]; reprint, Urbana-Champaign: The University of Illinois Press, 1990.

Mackintosh, Barry. *The National Parks: Shaping the System.* Washington, DC: Government Printing Office, 1991.

_____. *National Park Service Administrative History: A Guide.* Washington, DC: Government Printing Office, 1991.

Maier, Herbert, and Albert H. Good. "Structures in State Parks—An Apologia." In *American Planning and Civic Annual*, Harlean James, ed. Washington, DC: American Planning and Civic Association, 1935.

Manning, Warren H. "A National Plan Study Brief." *Landscape Architecture* 13, no. 4 (July 1923).

Martinson, Arthur D. "Mount Rainier National Park: The First Years." *Forest History* 10, no. 3 (October 1966): 26-33.

_____. "Mountain in the Sky: A History of Mount Rainier National Park." Ph.D. diss., Washington State University, 1966.

Mather, Stephen T. "Engineering Applied to National Parks." *Proceedings of the American Society of Civil Engineers* 4 (December 1928): 2673-2684.

_____. "The Ideals and Policy of the National Park Service Particularly in Relation to Yosemite National Park." In *Handbook of Yosemite National Park.* Hall, Ansel F. ed. New York: G. P. Putnam's Sons, The Knickerbocker Press, 1921.

_____. "The National Parks on a Business Basis." *The American Review of Reviews* (April 1915): 428-431.

_____. *Progress in the Development of National Parks.* Washington, DC: Department of the Interior, 1916.

McClelland, Linda Flint. *Presenting Nature: The Historic Landscape Design of the National Park Service, 1916 to 1942.* Washington, DC: Government Printing Office, 1994.

McKinsey, Elizabeth. *Niagara Falls: Icon of the American Sublime.* New York: Cambridge University Press, 1985.

McShane, Clay. "Transforming the Use of Urban Space: A Look at the Revolution in Street Pavements, 1888-1924." *Journal of Urban History* 5, no. 3 (May 1979): 279-307.

Mead, Elwood. *Federal Irrigation Reservoirs as Pleasure Resorts.* Washington, DC: Government Printing Office, 1928.

Meinecke, E. P. *A Report on the Effect of Excessive Tourist Travel on the California Redwood Parks.* Sacramento: State of California, Department of Natural Resources, Division of Parks, 1928.

Miles, John C. *Guardians of the Parks: A History of the National Parks and Conservation Association.* Washington, DC: National Parks and Conservation Association, 1995.

Mills, Edward. *Rustic Building Programs in Canada's National Parks, 1887-1950.* National Historic Sites Directorate, Parks Canada, 1994.

Molenaar, Dee. *The Challenge of Rainier.* Seattle: The Mountaineers, 1987.

Morgan, Keith N. *Held in Trust: Charles Eliot's Vision for the New England Landscape.* National Association for Olmsted Parks Workbook Series, Volume 1, Biography. Bethesda, Maryland: National Association for Olmsted Parks, 1991.

Morrill, John Barstow. "Forest Preserve District of Cook County, Illinois: An Outer Park and Reservation System for Chicago." *Landscape Architecture* 38, no. 4 (July 1948): 139-144.

Morrison, Ernest. *J. Horace McFarland: A Thorn for Beauty.* Harrisburg: Pennsylvania Historical and Museum Commission, 1995.

Musselman, Lloyd K. *Rocky Mountain National Park: An Administrative History.* Washington, DC: Department of the Interior, National Park Service, 1971.

Nash, Roderick. *Wilderness and the American Mind* [1967]. 3rd ed., New Haven: Yale University Press, 1982.

Nash, Roderick, ed. *The American Environment: Readings in the History of Conservation.* Reading, Massachusetts: Addison-Wesley Publishing Company, 1968.

National Conference on State Parks. *Proceedings of the National Conferences on State Parks, 1922-24.* 4 vols. Washington, DC: National Conference on State Parks.

Neckar, Lance M. "Developing Landscape Architecture for the Twentieth Century: The Career of Warren H. Manning." *Landscape Journal* 8, no. 2 (September 1989): 79-91.

Nelson, Beatrice Ward. *State Recreation: Parks, Forests and Game Preserves.* Washington, DC: National Conference on State Parks, Inc., 1928.

Newton, Norman T. *Design on the Land.* Cambridge: The Belknap Press of Harvard University Press, 1971.

Nixon, Edgar B., ed. *Franklin D. Roosevelt and Conservation, 1911-1945.* 2 vols. Hyde Park, New York: General Services Administration, National Archives and Records Service [1957]; reprint, New York: Arno Press, 1972.

Nolen, John. *New Ideals in the Planning of Cities, Towns, and Villages.* New York: American City Bureau, 1919.

————. *Replanning Small Cities: Six Typical Studies.* New York: B.W. Huebsch, 1912.

————. *State Parks for Wisconsin.* Madison: Wisconsin State Park Board, 1909.

Nolen, John, and Henry V. Hubbard. *Parkways and Land Values.* Harvard City Planning Series XI. Cambridge: Harvard University Press, 1937.

Novak, Barbara. *Nature and Culture: American Landscape Painting, 1825-1875.* New York: Oxford University Press, 1980.

O'Brien, Raymond J. *American Sublime: Landscape and Scenery of the Lower Hudson Valley.* New York: Columbia University Press, 1981.

O'Gorman, James F. *H. H. Richardson: Architectural Forms for an American Society*. Chicago: The University of Chicago Press, 1987.

Olmsted, Frederick Law. "A Letter Regarding Professional Practice from F.L. Olmsted, Sr. to Charles Eliot (1886)." *Landscape Architecture* 11, no. 4 (July 1921): 189-190.

_____. "The Use of the Axe." *Landscape Architecture* 3, no. 4 (July 1913): 145-152.

Olmsted, Frederick Law, Jr. "'Amusements' and Related Artificial Conveniences in the National Forests." *Landscape Architecture* 24, no. 4 (July 1934): 180-185.

_____. "The Basic Principles of City Planning." *The American City* 3, no. 2 (August 1910): 67-72.

_____. *City Planning*. Washington, DC: American Civic Association, 1910.

_____. "The Distinction Between National Parks and National Forests." *Landscape Architecture* 6, no. 3 (April 1916): 114-115.

_____. "Hetch-Hetchy." *Landscape Architecture* 4, no. 2 (January 1914): 37-46.

_____. *Pittsburgh: Main Thoroughfares and the Down Town District, Adopted by the Commission December, 1910*. Publication No. 8. Pittsburgh: Pittsburgh Civic Commission, 1911.

_____. *The Relation of Parks to Reservoirs*. Boston: American Park and Outdoor Art Association, Paper 32, 1899.

_____. *Report of State Park Survey of California*. Sacramento: California State Park Commission, 1929.

Olmsted, Frederick Law, Jr., and Theodora Kimball, eds. *Forty Years of Landscape Architecture: Central Park* [1928]; reprint, Cambridge: The MIT Press, 1973.

Olmsted, Frederick Law, Jr., and John Nolen. "The Normal Requirements of American Towns and Cities in Respect to Public Open Spaces." *Charities and the Commons* 16, no. 14 (7 July 1906): 411-426.

Olsen, Russ. *Administrative History: Organizational Structures of the National Park Service 1917-1985*. Washington, DC: Government Printing Office, 1985.

Orsi, Richard J. "`Wilderness Saint' and `Robber Baron': The Anomalous Partnership of John Muir and the Southern Pacific Company for the Preservation of Yosemite National Park." *The Pacific Historian* 29, nos. 2 & 3 (June 1985): 137-156.

Pack, Anthony Newton. "Practical Idealism in Our Parks." *Nature Magazine* 32, no. 2 (February 1939): 97-98.

Paige, John C. *The Civilian Conservation Corps and the National Park Service, 1933-1942: An Administrative History*. Washington, DC: Department of the Interior, National Park Service, 1985.

Palisades Interstate Park Commission. *Palisades Interstate Park, 1900-1960*. Bear Mountain, New York: Palisades Interstate Park Commission, 1960.

Parker, Carl Rust, Bremer W. Pond, and Theodora Kimball, eds. *Transactions of the American Society of Landscape Architects, 1909-1921*. Amsterdam, New York: The Recorder Press, 1922.

Pattee, Sarah Lewis. "Landscape Architecture in American Colleges." *Landscape Architecture* 14, no. 3 (April 1924): 171-177.

Pavlik, Robert C. "In Harmony with the Landscape: Yosemite's Built Environment, 1913-1940." *California History* 69, no. 2 (June 1990): 182-195.

Pinchot, Gifford. *Breaking New Ground* [1947]; reprint, Washington, DC: Island Press, 1974.

Platt, Charles A. *Italian Gardens*. New York: Harper & Brothers [1894]; reprint, with an overview by Keith N. Morgan, Portland: Sagapress, Inc., 1993.

Pray, James Sturgis. "John Charles Olmsted." *Landscape Architecture* 12, no. 3 (April 1922): 129-135.

Punchard, Charles P., Jr. "'Hands Off the National Parks.'" *Landscape Architecture* 11, no. 2 (January 1921): 53-56.

_____. "Landscape Design in the National Park Service." *Landscape Architecture* 10, no. 3 (April 1920): 142-145.

Rae, John B. *The Road and the Car in American Life*. Cambridge: The MIT Press, 1971.

Ranney, Victoria Post, Gerard J. Rauluk, and Carolyn F. Hoffman, eds. *The California Frontier, 1863-1865*. Volume V of *The Papers of Frederick Law Olmsted*. Baltimore: The Johns Hopkins University Press, 1990.

Rehder, Alfred. "Charles Sprague Sargent." *Journal of the Arnold Arboretum* 8, no. 2 (April 1927): 69-87.

Rehmann, Elsa. "An Ecological Approach." *Landscape Architecture* 23, no. 4 (July 1933): 239, ff.

Repton, Humphry. *The Art of Landscape Gardening*. John Nolen, ed. Boston: Houghton Mifflin Company, 1907.

Richardson, Elmo R. "The Struggle for the Valley: California's Hetch Hetchy Controversy, 1905-1913." *California Historical Society Quarterly* 38, no. 3 (September 1959): 249-258.

Riis, Jacob. *Report of the Committee on Small Parks, City of New York*. New York: The Martin B. Brown Company, 1897.

Robinson, William. *The Wild Garden* [1894]; reprint, Ilkley, Yorkshire: The Scolar Press, 1977.

Roosevelt, Eleanor. *Franklin D. Roosevelt and Hyde Park*. Washington, DC: Government Printing Office, 1949.

Roper, Laura Wood. *FLO: A Biography of Frederick Law Olmsted*. Baltimore: The Johns Hopkins University Press, 1973.

Rosenzweig, Roy, and Elizabeth Blackmar. *The Park and the People: A History of Central Park*. Ithaca: Cornell University Press, 1992.

Rothman, Hal. *America's National Monuments*. Lawrence: University Press of Kansas by arrangement with the University of Illinois Press, 1989.

Runte, Alfred. "Beyond the Spectacular: The Niagara Falls Preservation Campaign." *New-York Historical Society Quarterly* 57, no. 1 (January 1973): 30-50.

_____. *National Parks: The American Experience* [1979]. Second Edition, Revised. Lincoln: University of Nebraska Press, 1987.

_____. "Pragmatic Alliance: Western Railroads and the National Parks." *National Parks and Conservation Association Magazine* 48 (April 1974): 14-21.

_____. *Yosemite: The Embattled Wilderness*. Lincoln: University of Nebraska Press, 1990.

Salmond, John A. *The Civilian Conservation Corps, 1933-1942: A New Deal Case Study*. Durham, North Carolina: Duke University Press, 1967.

Schuyler, David. *The New Urban Landscape: The Redefinition of Urban Form in Nineteenth-Century America*. Baltimore: The Johns Hopkins University Press, 1986.

Schuyler, David, and Jane Turner Censer, eds. *The Years of Olmsted, Vaux & Company. Volume VI of the Papers of Frederick Law Olmsted*. Baltimore: The Johns Hopkins University Press, 1992.

Scott, Mel. *American City Planning Since 1890*. Berkeley: University of California Press, 1969.

Sears, John F. *Sacred Places: American Tourist Attractions in the Nineteenth Century*. New York: Oxford University Press, 1989.

Seely, Bruce E. *Building the American Highway System: Engineers as Policy Makers*. Philadelphia: Temple University Press, 1987.

Sellars, Richard West. "National Parks: Worthless Lands or Competing Land Values?" *Journal of Forest History* 27, no. 3 (July 1983): 130-134.

_____. "The Rise and Decline of Ecological Attitudes in National Park Management, 1929-1940: Part I." *The George Wright Forum* 10, no. 1 (1993): 55-78.

_____. "The University of California—Present at the Creation." *Courier: Newsmagazine of the National Park Service* 35, no. 2 (February 1990): 4.

Shankland, Robert. *Steve Mather of the National Parks*. Second Edition, Revised and Enlarged. New York: Alfred A. Knopf, 1954.

Sheire, James W. *Glacier National Park: Historic Resource Study*. Washington, DC: Government Printing Office, 1970.

Simonds, O. C. *Landscape-Gardening*. New York: The Macmillan Company, 1920.

Southern Appalachian National Park Commission. *Final Report of the Southern Appalachian National Park Commission*. Washington, DC: U.S. Department of the Interior, National Park Service, 1931.

Spence, Mark. "Dispossessing the Wilderness: Yosemite Indians and the National Park Ideal, 1864-1930." *Pacific Historical Review* 65 (February 1996): 27-59.

Steen, Harold K. *The U.S. Forest Service: A History*. Seattle: University of Washington Press, 1991.

Steen, Harold K., ed. *The Origins of the National Forests*. Durham, North Carolina: Forest History Society, 1992.

Story, Isabelle F. *The National Parks and Emergency Conservation*. Washington, DC: Government Printing Office, 1933.

Strong, Douglas Hillman. "The Man Who 'Owned' Grand Canyon." *The American West* 6, no. 5 (September 1969): 33-40.

Swain, Donald C. *Federal Conservation Policy, 1921-1933*. University of California Publications in History, Volume 76. Berkeley: University of California Press, 1963.

_____. "The Founding of the National Park Service: The Implementation of an Idea." *The American West* 6, no. 5 (September 1969): 6-9.

_____. "The National Park Service and the New Deal." *Pacific Historical Review* 41, no. 3 (August 1972): 312-332.

_____. "The Passage of the National Park Service Act of 1916." *Wisconsin Magazine of History* 50, no. 1 (September 1966): 4-17.

_____. *Wilderness Defender: Horace M. Albright and Conservation.* Chicago: University of Chicago Press, 1970.

Thompson, Erwin R. *Mount Rainier National Park, Washington: Historic Resource Study.* 2 vols. Denver: Department of the Interior, National Park Service, 1981.

Tishler, William H., ed. *American Landscape Architecture: Designers and Places.* Washington, DC: The Preservation Press, 1989.

Tolson, Hillory A. *Historic Listing of National Park Service Officials* [1964]. Revised as 75th Anniversary Edition by Harold P. Danz. Denver: Department of the Interior, National Park Service, 1991.

_____. *Laws Relating to the National Park Service, the National Parks and Monuments.* Washington, DC: Department of the Interior, National Park Service, 1933.

Torrey, Raymond H. *State Parks and Recreational Uses of State Forests in the United States.* Washington, DC: National Conference on State Parks, 1926.

Treib, Marc, ed. *Modern Landscape Architecture: A Critical Review.* Cambridge: The MIT Press, 1993.

Tunnard, Christopher. *Gardens in the Modern Landscape* (London: The Architectural Press, 1938.

_____. "Modern Gardens for Modern Houses." *Landscape Architecture* (January 1942): 57-64.

Tweed, William C. *Recreation Site Planning and Improvement in National Forests, 1891-1942.* Washington, DC: Government Printing Office, 1980.

Tweed, William C., Laura E. Soullière, and Henry G. Law. *National Park Service Rustic Architecture: 1916-1942.* Unpublished report. Washington, DC: Department of the Interior, Main Interior Library, 1977.

University of Illinois. *Notes for a Study in City Planning in Champaign-Urbana.* Chicago: R. R. Donnelly and Sons, 1915.

Unwin, Raymond. *Town Planning in Practice: An Introduction to the Art of Designing Cities and Suburbs.* London: T. Fisher Unwin, 1909.

U.S. Department of the Interior. *Annual Reports of the Department of the Interior.* Washington, DC: Government Printing Office.

_____. *Proceedings of the National Park Conference Held at the Yellowstone National Park, September 11 and 12, 1911.* Washington, DC: Government Printing Office, 1912.

_____. *Proceedings of the National Park Conference Held at the Yosemite National Park, October 14, 15, and 16, 1912.* Washington, DC: Government Printing Office, 1913.

_____. *Proceedings of the National Park Conference Held at Berkeley, California, March 11, 12, and 13, 1915.* Washington, DC: Government Printing Office, 1915.

_____. *Report of the General Superintendent and Landscape Engineer of National Parks for the Fiscal Year Ended June 30, 1915.* Washington, DC: Government Printing Office, 1916.

_____. *Report of the Superintendent of National Parks to the Secretary of the Interior for the Fiscal Year Ended June 30, 1916.* Washington, DC: Government Printing Office, 1917.

U.S. Department of the Interior. National Park Service. *The CCC and Its Contribution to a Nation-Wide State Park Recreational Program.* Washington, DC: Government Printing Office, 1937.

_____. *An Invitation to New Play Areas.* Pamphlet. Washington, DC: Department of the Interior, National Park Service, n.d.

_____. *Minutes of the Eighth National Park Conference Held in Mesa Verde National Park, October 1-5, 1925, Inclusive.* Unpublished minutes. Washington DC: National Park Service History Collection, Harpers Ferry Center, Harpers Ferry, West Virginia, 1925.

_____. *Minutes of the Ninth National Park Conference Held in Washington, DC, 1926.* Washington DC: Government Printing Office, 1926.

_____. *Minutes of the Twelfth Conference of National Park Executives Held at Hot Springs National Park, Arkansas, April 3-8, 1932.* Unpublished minutes. Washington DC: National Park Service History Collection, Harpers Ferry Center, Harpers Ferry, West Virginia, 1932.

_____. *Park Use Studies and Demonstrations.* Washington, DC: Government Printing Office, 1941.

_____. *Procedure for Park, Parkway and Recreational Area Study.* Washington, DC: Government Printing Office, 1937.

_____. *Proceedings of the National Parks Conference, Held in the Auditorium of the New National Museum, Washington, D.C., January 2, 3, 4, 5, and 6, 1917.* Washington DC: Government Printing Office, 1917.

_____. *Proceedings of the National Park Service Conference on State Park Authorities.* Unpublished minutes. Washington, DC: Department of the Interior, Main Interior Library, 1935.

_____. *Proceedings of Conference on Camp Planning Held at Camp Edith Macy, Briarcliff, New York, May 20-23, 1936.* Unpublished report. Washington, DC: Department of the Interior, 1936.

_____. *Recreational Demonstration Projects as Illustrated by Chopawamsic, Virginia.* Pamphlet. Washington, DC: Government Printing Office, n.d.

_____. *Reports of the Director of the National Park Service to the Secretary of the Interior for Fiscal Year Ended June 30, 1917-1932.* 16 vols. Washington, DC: Government Printing Office.

_____. *A Study of the Park and Recreation Problem of the United States.* Washington, DC: Government Printing Office, 1941.

_____. *Yearbook: Park and Recreation Progress, 1937-1943.* 5 vols. Washington, DC: Government Printing Office.

U.S. Department of Labor. Bureau of Industrial Housing and Transportation. *Report of the United States Housing Corporation.* 2 vols. Washington, DC: Government Printing Office, 1920.

Van Rensselaer, Mariana Griswold. *Art Out-of-Doors: Hints on Good Taste in Gardening.* New York: Charles Scribner's Sons, 1893.

Verkamp, Margaret M. *History of Grand Canyon National Park* [1940]; reprint, Flagstaff: Grand Canyon Pioneers Society, 1993.

Vint, Thomas C. "Development of National Parks for Conservation." In *American Planning and Civic Annual,* Harlean James, ed. Washington, DC: American Planning and Civic Association, 1938.

_____. "National Park Service Branch of Plans and Design, San Francisco." *Landscape Architecture* 24, no. 1 (October 1933): 31-32.

_____. "National Park Service Master Plans." *Planning and Civic Comment* (April 1946).

Vint, Thomas C., and Edward A. Nickel, eds. *Report on the Building Program from Allotments of the Public Works Administration, 1933-1937, Western Division*. Unpublished report. Washington, DC: Department of the Interior, Main Interior Library, 1937.

Vint, Thomas C., and J. R. Thrower, eds. *Report on the Building Program from Allotments of the Public Works Administration, 1933-1937, Eastern Division*. Unpublished report. Washington, DC: Department of the Interior, Main Interior Library, 1937.

Ward, Henry Baldwin. "What is Happening to Our National Parks?" *Nature Magazine* 31, no. 10 (December 1938): 611-615.

Warne, William E. *The Bureau of Reclamation*. New York: Praeger Publishers, 1973.

Watrous, Richard B. "The Proposed National Park Service." *Landscape Architecture* 6, no. 3 (April 1916): 101-123.

Waugh, Frank A. *Landscape Engineering in the National Forests*. Washington, DC: Government Printing Office, 1918.

_____. *The Natural Style in Landscape Gardening*. Boston: Richard G. Badger, 1917.

_____. *A Plan for the Development of the Village of Grand Canyon, Ariz*. Washington, DC: Government Printing Office, 1918.

_____. *Recreation Uses on the National Forests*. Washington, DC: Government Printing Office, 1918.

Williams, John H. *The Mountain That Was "God"*. Tacoma, Washington: 1910.

Williams, Michael. *Americans & Their Forests: A Historical Geography*. New York: Cambridge University Press, 1989.

Williamson, Tom. "The Landscape Park: Economics, Art, and Ideology." *Journal of Garden History* 13, no. 1/2 (March 1993): 49-55.

Wilson, William H. *The City Beautiful Movement*. Baltimore: The Johns Hopkins University Press, 1989.

Wirth, Conrad L. *The CCC and Its Contribution to a Nation-Wide State Park Recreational Program*. Washington, DC: Department of the Interior, National Park Service, n.d. [ca. 1940].

_____. *Civilian Conservation Corps Program of the United States Department of the Interior, March 1933 to June 30, 1943*. Washington, DC: Government Printing Office, 1944.

_____. "Parks and Their Uses." In *American Planning and Civic Annual*, Harlean James, ed. Washington, DC: American Planning and Civic Association, 1935.

_____. *Parks, Politics, and the People*. Norman, Oklahoma: University of Oklahoma Press, 1980.

Wolschke-Bulmahn, Joachim, and Gert Groening. "Changes in the Philosophy of Garden Architecture in the 20th Century and Their Impact Upon the Social and Spatial Environment." *Journal of Garden History* 9, no. 2 (April 1989): 53-70.

_____. "The Ideology of the Nature Garden: Nationalistic Trends in Garden Design in Germany During the Early Twentieth Century." *Journal of Garden History* 12, no. 1 (January 1992): 73-80.

Woodbury, Angus M. "A History of Southern Utah and Its National Parks." *Utah State Historical Society Quarterly* 12, no. 3-4 (July 1944): 111-224. Revised and Reprinted, 1950.

Worster, Donald. *Nature's Economy: A History of Ecological Ideas* [1977]. Second Edition. New York: Cambridge University Press, 1994.

Yard, Robert Sterling. *Glimpses of Our National Parks*. Washington, DC: Department of the Interior, National Park Service, 1916.

_____. *The National Parks Portfolio* [1916]. 3rd ed. Washington, DC: Department of the Interior, National Park Service, 1921.

Zaitlin, Joyce. *George Stanley Underwood: His Rustic, Art Deco, and Federal Architecture*. Malibu: Pangloss Press, 1989.

Zaitzevsky, Cynthia. *Frederick Law Olmsted and the Boston Park System*. Cambridge: The Belknap Press of Harvard University, 1982.

Index

Niagara Falls, 12, 41, 260, 312 n.6; scenic preservation of, 26, 42, 56, 66, 68, 317 n.75

Nisqually Road, 160, *208*, 217, 222, 235; as Government Road, 211-212, 213, 215, 340 n.58; and Longmire Village, 232, 233; reconstruction of, 174, 222, 223

Noble, John W., 59, 60

Nolen, John, 128; influences on, 195, 328 n.27; on park typology, 69, 322 n.53; planning by, 103-104, 105, 108-109, 110, 124, 252, 287; recreation areas designed by, 102-103

Northern Pacific Railroad, 61, 71, 158, 208-209, 210; and Yellowstone Park, 30, 31, 62

North Platte River Project, *291*

Norton, Charles Eliot, 42

Nôtre, André le, 37

Novak, Barbara, 312 n.8

Nussbaum, Aileen, 115, 124

Nussbaum, Jesse, 115, 124

Nussbaum, Robert L., 132

Olcott, George Wheeler, 287-288

Olmsted, Frederick Law, 58, 201, 314 n.24 n.33; and architectural structures, 36, 38; influence of, 23, 46, 51, 227; and landscape design, 21-22, 313 n.21, 314 n.24, 318 n.107; and Modernism, 304-305, 307; and Niagara Falls, 42, 317 n.75; park designs by, 5, 19-21, *22*, 24, 42-44, 317 n.82; and parkways, 25, 37, 276; and picturesque aesthetics, 102, 313 n.19, 314 n.25; "Preliminary Report upon the Yosemite and Big Tree Grove," 81, 322 n.57; and recreation, 34, 297; and road construction, 32, 184-185; on scenic preservation, 79, 300, 324 n.87; as teacher, 39, 44; on value of parks, 24, 303; writings of, 103, 328 n.29; and Yosemite, 27-30, 70, 315 n.38

Olmsted, Frederick Law, Jr., 109, 195, 266, 307, 322 n.53, 326 n.114; and American Society of Landscape Architects, 39, 95; and Cammerer, 88, 178, 326 n.120; career of, 40, 43, 68-69, 322 n.51; and city planning, 110, 137, 328 n.31, 339 n.16; influence of, 6, 78, 128; and national parks, 5, 79, 81, 322 n.52; and Olmsted Sr.'s writings, 322 n.57, 328 n.29; and Park Service Act, 72, 106, 323 n.60, 324 n.86 n.87; parks designed by, 36, 82, 102-103, 105, 325 n.96; planning by, 103-104, 105, 106, 108, 111, 124, 198, 329 n.57; "The Relation of Reservoirs to Parks," 69; and scenic preservation, 9, 70, 79, 92, 103, 261; *State Park Survey of California*, 260-261, 287; and Vint, 191-192, 227, 342 n.97; and Yosemite, 184, 221

Olmsted, John Charles (J. C.), 43, 68, 97, 103-104, 317 n.85, 322 n.51; and landscape architectural organizations, 39, 50; on large parks, purpose of large parks, 50-51, 319 n.113; park designs by, 34-35, 36, 83, 314 n.31, 317 n.82

Olmsted and Vaux, 26

Olmsted Brothers, 68, 69, 82, 102, 322 n.51

Olmsted, Olmsted & Eliot, 68

Olympic National Park, 55, 275

Oregon, 84

Orsi, Richard J., 320 n.7

Pacific Forest Reserve, 59, 210

Pack, Arthur Newton, 271

painting, landscape, 79, 102, 312 n.8; Barbizon school, 38, 316 n.66; Impressionism, 38; Native school, 38; and picturesque aesthetics, 11-13, 14

Palisades Interstate Park, 46, 47, 319 n.116; Bear Mountain, 47, 49, 52, 260, 281; Bear Mountain Inn, 49, 259, 319 n.109 n.116; Bear Mountain museum, 144; Douglas Lodge, 319 n.109; Lake Itasca, 47, 49, 51, 319 n.109; as National Historic Landmark, 311 n.14

Palisades Interstate Park Commission, 260

Palmetto State Park, 286

Paradise Park, 213; development of, 216, 223, *243*; Paradise Inn, 215, 221, 222, 321 n.27, 341 n.61; Paradise Lodge, 222, 225, 236, 238; Paradise Valley, 160, 212, 215, 219, 234, 235; scenic loop near, 222, 224-225, 228, 230, *243*, 341 n.80; and tourism, 209, 210, 211, 232

Park, Parkway and Recreational-Area Study Act, 8, 273-274, 285, 297-299, 348 n.68, 350 n.103

Parker, Barry, 109, 110

parks, county, 199, 257, 319 n.112

parks, interstate, 46, 47, 318 n.96

parks, landscape, *22*, 52, 92, 102-103, 297, 313 n.1, 319 n.112, 322 n.53; aesthetics of, 23, 44, 259, 284-285; to Great Britain, 14-15; as middle class institutions, 28, 85; theory of, 20, 21-22, 29, 256

parks, municipal: aesthetics of, 51-52, 316 n.63; and city planning, 25, 40; and dams, 69, 322 n.54; and National Park Service, 56, 257; and parkways, 25, 308; purpose of, 50-51, 72, 75; and regional parks, 6, 66, 83; small parks as, 34, 36, 43-44, 322 n.53

parks, national, 319 n.3, 321 n.37; in 1960s, 309-310; benefits of, 72, 145; creation of, 55, 320 n.4; diversification of, 270, 276-277; education of visitors to, 142, 145; employing landscape architects, 251-252; entry fees for, 310, 325 n.109; jurisdiction over, 64-65; and "the National Park Idea," 26, 80, 314 n.33, 324 n.92; purpose of, 75, 78, 79, 271-272, 310; as system, 78, 201; threats to, 218, 310; tourism in, 56, 80, 86-87; utilitarian development in, 58-65. *See also* National Historic Landmarks; *and names of specific national parks*

parks, public, 21, 253, 254, 303, 313 n.16

parks, regional, 6, 44-46

parks, state, 257, 310; and CCC, 265-266, 347 n.41; current condition of, 300-301; emergency conservation work in, 263-264; employing landscape architects, 251-252; planning and developing of, 259, 260-261, 268-269, 279; recreation in, 267-268, 349 n.99; types of, 288, 322 n.53

Park Service, National, 115, 166, 171, 256, 310, 323 n.64; administration of, 47, 76, 77, 180; and Bureau of Public Roads, 156, 168, 204-206; and CCC, 250-251, 257, 262, 289, 299-300; and concessioners, 220-221, 221-222; and dams, 91, 275-276,

Turner Falls State Park, 281
Tweed, William C., 57, 338 n.7

Underhill, Francis T., 111
Underwood, Gilbert Stanley, 57, 67, 141, 192, 193; designs by, 121-122, 141-142, 330 n.66; and Hull, 112-113, 139, 177-179, 190; and Park Service, 139, 145
Union Pacific Railroad, 140, 141, 191
Unwin, Raymond, 109-110, 124, 128; *Town Planning in Practice*, 109
U.S. Geographical Survey, 239, 240
Utah Parks Company, 141, 142, 333 n.4

vandalism, 3, 31, 210
Vandever, William, 56-57
Van Rensselaer, Mariana Griswold, 97, 327 n.7
Vaux, Calvert, 24, 36, 42, 43, 86; and Central Park design, 19, 20-21, *22*; influence of, 23, 51; on landscape design, 18, 21-22; and parkway design, 25, 37, 276; and scenic preservation, 32
Vaux, Downing, 39
Verkamp, Margaret, 116
Vest, George V., 63
villages, 15, 82, 135; and landscape engineering, 89, 179; at Mount Rainier, 232-234, *243, 244*; planning of, 74, *74*, 113-114, 194, 204
Vint, Thomas Chalmers, 179, 284, 342 n.97, 347 n.43; background of, 95, 190-192, 323 n.69; and branch of plans and design, 258, 266; buildings designed by, 128, 145, *131*, 132, *243*; and Bureau of Public Roads, 173-174, 204-205, 228-230; as chief architect, 127, 189, 192-195, 206-207, 264, 265; and colleagues, 139, 142, 173, *231*, 278, 347 n.47; and comprehensive park planning, 204, 231, 347 n.69; at Hot Springs, *192*, 246; influence of, 92, 269, 280, 286, 297; and Kittredge, 169, 170, 228-230; on landscape architecture, 7, 100, 134, 226-228, 307, 342 n.96; and master plans, 180, 196-197, 223-224, 240, 253, 344 n.131; and public works projects, 133, 247, 254-255, 257, 347 n.48; and road construction, 175-176, 177, 218; and Transmountain Highway, 162, 166-168, 170, 171, 186; village planning by, 127-128, 143, 233; and West Side Road, 228-229, 343 n.113; and wilderness areas, 207, 225, 242; and Yakima Park, 231, 236, 238, 344 n.121; zoning by, 241, 274, 344 n.134
Virginia Kendall Metropolitan Park, 283
Vista Rock, 20
Vitale, Ferruccio, 96, 110, 191, 251

Walsh, Thomas J., 158, 335 n.59
War Department, 256, 257. *See also* Cavalry, U.S.
Warm Springs, *295, 296*
Warming, Eugenius: *The Oecology of Plants*, 98-99
Washburn-Doane expedition, 314 n.33
Washington, DC, 160; buildings in, 28, *30*, 30, 256, 258, 332 n.104; features of, 17, 105, 256; lobbying in, 83, 212; Mather in, 73, 83; parks and parkways in, 256, 266, 305; park service employees in, 76, 87, 143,

226, 247, 251, 258, 266; plans for, 68, 88, 105
water, 60, 64, 68, 198. *See also under* conservation
Waterhouse, R. D., 345 n.140
Watkins Glen, 47
Watrous, Richard B., 4, 78, 323 n.64
Waugh, Dorothy, 280, 283, 284, 345 n.10; "Portfolio of Park Structures and Facilities," 349 n.83
Waugh, Frank A., 262, 280, 331 n.87; and design, 97, 107; and ecology, 99, 100; as educator, 95, 134, 266; *The Natural Style in Landscape Gardening*, 99; "Village of Grand Canyon," 118-119
waysides, 275, 288
Weidenman, Jacob, 25
Wellman, W. P., 141
Westchester County, NY, 199, 200, 260, 276, 305, 308
West Parks District, 98
What England Can Teach Us About Gardening (Miller), 327 n.10
White, John R., 184
White Mountains, 12, 41
White River, 217
Whittlesey, Charles, 62
wilderness, 207, 226, 282, 241-242, 271-272, 274-275; at Mount Rainier, 223, 224, 225, 235, *244*
Williams, John H. 213
Wilson, Laura, 345 n.10
Wilson, Woodrow, 73, 74, 79, 91, 140-141
Wintersmith Metropolitan Park, 281
Wirth, Conrad L., 278, 285, 286-287, 307, 309, 344 n.131; and recreation, 268, 273-275, *275*, 348 n.68; and state park architecture, 280-281, 282; and state park planning, 265-266, 267, 279-280, *281*, 288, 347 n.41 n.52; *A Study of the Park and Recreation Problem of the United States*, 297-299; supervision by, 269, 270, 287; *Yearbooks*, 289, 297, 298, 350 n.103
Wirth, Theodore, 266
Wolschke-Buhlman, Joachim, 100
women, 39, 79, 252, 324 n.80, 345 n.10
Work, Hubert, 149, 150, 178, 225, 325 n.95
work relief, 253, 255. *See also* Civilian Conservation Corps (CCC); Public Works Administration (PWA); Works Progesss Administration (WPA)
Works Progress Administration (WPA), 258, 276, *295*
World's Columbian Exposition, 36, 104-105, 316 n.64
World War I, 80, 109-110, 190, 324 n.90, 329 n.57
Wosky, John, 192, 255, 264, 338 n.7
Wright, Frank Lloyd, 98, 190
Wright, George M., 273
Wright, Henry, 128
Wright, Lloyd, 190

Yakima Park (Sunrise Park), 237, 265; development of, 135, 234-238, *244*, 344 n.121; Sunrise Lodge, 237, 238; Yakima Park Highway (Road), 174, 223, 228, 234, 236, 237